Learn C Programming

A beginner's guide to learning C programming the easy and disciplined way

Jeff Szuhay

BIRMINGHAM - MUMBAI

Learn C Programming

Commissioning Editor: Richa Tripathi
Acquisition Editor: Denim Pinto
Content Development Editor: Digvijay Bagul
Senior Editor: Rohit Singh
Technical Editor: Pradeep Sahu
Copy Editor: Safis Editing
Project Coordinator: Deeksha Thakkar
Proofreader: Safis Editing
Indexer: Rekha Nair
Production Designer: Joshua Misquitta

First published: June 2020

Production reference: 1260620

Published by Packt Publishing Ltd.
Livery Place
35 Livery Street
Birmingham
B3 2PB, UK.

ISBN 978-1-78934-991-7

www.packt.com

To Jaimie, my daughter and "inload manager," this book is for you.

Packt.com

Subscribe to our online digital library for full access to over 7,000 books and videos, as well as industry leading tools to help you plan your personal development and advance your career. For more information, please visit our website.

Why subscribe?

- Spend less time learning and more time coding with practical eBooks and Videos from over 4,000 industry professionals

- Improve your learning with Skill Plans built especially for you

- Get a free eBook or video every month

- Fully searchable for easy access to vital information

- Copy and paste, print, and bookmark content

Did you know that Packt offers eBook versions of every book published, with PDF and ePub files available? You can upgrade to the eBook version at www.packt.com and as a print book customer, you are entitled to a discount on the eBook copy. Get in touch with us at customercare@packtpub.com for more details.

At www.packt.com, you can also read a collection of free technical articles, sign up for a range of free newsletters, and receive exclusive discounts and offers on Packt books and eBooks.

Contributors

About the author

Jeff Szuhay is the principal developer at QuarterTil2, which specializes in graphics-rich software chronographs for desktop environments. In his software career of over 35 years, he has engaged in the full range of development activities, from systems analysis and systems performance tuning to application design, and from initial development through full testing and final delivery.

Throughout this time, he has taught about computer applications and programming languages at various educational levels, from elementary school to university level, as well as developing and presenting professional, on-site training.

> *I would like to thank, first of all, my teachers who instructed, cajoled, and inspired me. Notable among these are George Novacky Ph.D. and Alan Rose Ph.D. I would also like to thank the following colleagues who had the courage to help me see where I went awry: Dave Kipp, Tim Snyder, Sam Caruso, Mark Dalrymple, Tony McNamara, Jake Penzell, and Bill Geraci. And lastly, thanks to my wife, Linda, who listened patiently through all of it.*

About the reviewer

B. M. Harwani is the founder of Microchip Computer Education, based in Ajmer, India, which provides computer literacy in programming and web development to learners of all ages. He further helps the community by sharing the knowledge and expertise he's gained over 20 years of teaching by writing books. His recent publications include *jQuery Recipes*, published by Apress, *Introduction to Python Programming and Developing GUI Applications with PyQT*, published by Cengage Learning, *The Android Tablet Developer's Cookbook*, published by Addison-Wesley Professional, *UNIX and Shell Programming*, published by Oxford University Press, and *Qt5 Python GUI Programming Cookbook* and *Practical C Programming*, published by Packt.

Packt is searching for authors like you

If you're interested in becoming an author for Packt, please visit `authors.packtpub.com` and apply today. We have worked with thousands of developers and tech professionals, just like you, to help them share their insight with the global tech community. You can make a general application, apply for a specific hot topic that we are recruiting an author for, or submit your own idea.

Table of Contents

Preface

Learning to program is the process of learning to solve problems with a computer. Your journey in gaining this knowledge will be long and arduous with unexpected twists and turns, yet the rewards of this journey, both small and large, are manyfold. Initial satisfaction comes when you get your program to work and to give the correct results. Satisfaction grows as you are able to solve larger and more complex problems than you ever thought possible.

The beginning of your journey is learning a programming language. This book primarily addresses that beginning: learning a programming language, in this case, C. The first step in learning a programming language is to learn its syntax. This means understanding and memorizing important keywords, punctuation, and the basic building blocks of program structure.

The approach taken in *Learn C Programming* is intended to give you the tools, methods, and practices you need to help you minimize the frustrations you will encounter. Every program provided is a complete, working program using modern C syntax. The expected output for each program is also provided.

Learning to program is especially frustrating because there are so many moving parts. By this, I mean that every aspect of the programming process has changed over time and will continue to change in the future. Computer hardware and operating systems will evolve to meet new uses and challenges. Computer languages will also evolve and change to remove old language deficiencies as well as to adapt to solving new problems. The programming practices and methods used today will change as languages evolve. The kinds of problems that need to be solved will also change as people use computers for different uses. And lastly, you will change. As you use a programming language, it will change the way you think about problems. As problems and solutions change, so does our thinking about what will become possible. This leads to changes in computer language. It's a never-ending cycle.

C has evolved considerably from the language first developed by Denis Ritchie in the early 1970s. It was extremely simple yet powerful enough to develop early versions of the Unix operating system at Bell Labs. Those early versions of C were not for novice programmers. Those versions required advanced knowledge and programming skills in order to make programs robust and stable. Over the years, as C compilers became much more widely available, there have been several efforts to rein in unrestricted and sometimes dangerous language features. The first was ANSI C, codified in 1989. The next major refinement came with C99, codified in 1999; it included significant language additions and clarified many C behaviors. Since then, two additional revisions have been made, C11 and C18, both of which have focused on minor language additions and internal corrections to the language.

C today is much more constrained and complex than the early versions of C. Yet it retains its power, performance, and suitability to a wide range of computing problems. This book strives to present the most current syntax and concepts as specified in C99, C11, and C18. Each program has been compiled and run using the C11 standard. As time goes on, C18 compliance will be much more widespread than today. I would expect, however, that all of these programs will compile and run as intended using the C18 standard.

There will always be more to learn, even without the parts moving. After reading *Learn C Programming*, you will find a particular way to make C work for you. As you gain experience solving problems with C, you will discover new things—features, uses, and limitations—about C that you didn't see before. So, we can say that learning to program is as much about *learning how to learn* as it is about solving problems with programs.

Along the way, you will learn about other programming concepts not directly tied to the C. The general development cycle will not only be discussed but will also be illustrated in the development of a card dealing program. While you may not be interested in cards, pay particular attention to the process of how this program is developed. Throughout, the basic practices of experimentation and validation will be illustrated.

Who this book is for

When this book was conceived, it was intended for two very diverse audiences, the absolute beginning programmer and the experienced programmer who wants to learn C. Each of these audiences has very different needs.

For the beginning programmer, I have written this book as if I were sitting beside you explaining the most important concepts and practices you need to know to become a successful C programmer. I have tried to explain every concept thoroughly and have reinforced each concept with a working program. The beginner should be familiar with the general operation of their computer; no other knowledge is assumed.

For the experienced programmer, I have presented the full range of C syntax as well as common C idioms. You may skim the explanations and focus primarily upon the source code provided.

For both, there are over 80 working programs that demonstrate both the syntax of C as well as the flavor of C programming idioms—things that are common in C but not found in other languages. I have sprinkled in programming practices and techniques that have served me well in my nearly 35 years of experience.

What this book covers

Section 1, *C Fundamentals*, introduces the very basic concepts of C syntax and program structure.

Chapter 1, *Running Hello, World!*, introduces the program development cycle and the tools you'll need for the rest of the book. Those tools are used to create, build, and run your first C program, a "Hello, world!" program. The concepts of commenting code and experimenting with code are also introduced.

Chapter 2, *Understanding Program Structure*, introduces statements and blocks. It also describes function definitions and function declarations, also known as function prototypes. How functions are called and their order of execution is illustrated. Statements, blocks, and functions define the structure of C programs.

Chapter 3, *Working with Basic Data Types*, explores how C represents values in various ways through the use of data types. Each data type has a size and possible range of values that C uses to interpret a value.

Chapter 4, *Using Variables and Assignment*, introduces variables and constants, which are used to contain values. For a variable to receive a value, that value must be assigned to it; several types of assignment are explained.

Chapter 5, *Exploring Operators and Expressions*, introduces and demonstrates operations—ways to manipulate values—on each of the various data types.

Chapter 6, *Exploring Conditional Program Flow*, introduces flow of control statements, which execute one group of statements or another depending upon the result of an expression.

Chapter 7, *Exploring Loops and Iteration*, introduces each of the looping statements. It also describes the proper and improper use of goto. Additional means of controller loop iterations are explained.

Chapter 8, *Creating and Using Enumerations*, explains named constants, enumerations, and how to use them.

Section 2, *Complex Data Types*, extends your understanding of the concepts of basic, or intrinsic, data types to more complex types.

Chapter 9, *Creating and Using Structures*, explores how to represent complex objects with groups of variables, called structures. Operations on structures are explored. How structures are related to object-oriented programming is described.

Chapter 10, *Creating Custom Data Types with typedef*, describes how to rename enum and struct declarations. Compiler options and header files are explored.

Chapter 11, *Working with Arrays*, illustrates how to define, initialize, and access simple arrays. Using loops to traverse arrays is explored. Operating on arrays via functions is demonstrated.

Chapter 12, *Working with Multi-Dimensional Arrays*, extends your understanding of the concept of 1-dimensional arrays to 2, 3, and *n*-dimensional ones. Declaring, initializing, and accessing these multi-dimensional arrays in loops and in functions are demonstrated.

Chapter 13, *Using Pointers*, explores direct and indirect addressing with pointers. Operations with pointers are demonstrated. How to think and talk about pointers is described. Using pointers in functions and using pointers to structures is demonstrated.

Chapter 14, *Understand Arrays and Pointers*, explores the similarities and differences between pointers and arrays.

Chapter 15, *Working with Strings*, introduces the ASCII character set and C strings, which are arrays with two special properties. A program to print the ASCII character set in a table is developed. The C Standard Library string operations are introduced.

Chapter 16, *Creating and Using More Complex Structures*, builds upon the concepts of structures and arrays to explore how to create various combinations of complex structures. Throughout the chapter, each complex structure is demonstrated through the development of a complete card dealing program. This chapter provides the most comprehensive example of the method of stepwise, iterative program development.

Section 3, *Memory Manipulation*, explores how memory is allocated and deallocated in a variety of ways.

Chapter 17, *Understanding Memory Allocation and Lifetime,* introduces the concepts of automatic versus dynamic memory storage classes as well as internal versus external storage classes. The static storage class is demonstrated.

Chapter 18, *Using Dynamic Memory Allocation,* introduces the use of dynamic memory and describes various operations on dynamic memory. A dynamic linked-list program is demonstrated. An overview of other dynamic structures is provided.

Section 4, *Input and Output,* explores a wide variety of topics related to the reading (input) and writing (output) of values.

Chapter 19, *Exploring Formatted Output,* goes into thorough detail about the various format specifiers of printf() for each of the intrinsic data types: signed and unsigned integers, floats and doubles, and strings and characters.

Chapter 20, *Getting Input from the Command Line,* demonstrates how to use the argc and argv parameters of main() to get values from the command line.

Chapter 21, *Exploring Formatted Input,* demonstrates how to read values from an input stream using scanf(). It clarifies how the format specifiers for printf() and scanf(), while similar, are really very different. Internal data conversion and unformatted input and output are also demonstrated.

Chapter 22, *Working with Files,* is a largely conceptual chapter that introduces basic file concepts. It demonstrates how to open and close files from within the program and from the command line.

Chapter 23, *Using File Input and File Output,* demonstrates how to use command-line switches with getopt() to read and write files. The basic program is then expanded to read names from input, sort them via a linked list, and then write them out in sorted order.

Section 5, *Building Blocks for Larger Programs,* details how to create and manage programs that consist of multiple files.

Chapter 24, *Working with Multi-File Programs,* demonstrates how to take the single source file program that was developed in Chapter 16, *Creating and Using More Complex Structures,* and separate it into multiple source files. Each of the source files has functions that are logically grouped by the structures they manipulate. Effective and safe uses for the preprocessor are described.

`Chapter 25`, *Understanding Scope,* defines various components of scope and how they related to single- and multi-file programs. Details of variable scope and function scope are described. The epilogue outlines some useful next steps to take in learning both C and programming.

`Appendix`, provides a number of useful reference guides. These include C keywords, operator precedence, a summary of some useful GCC and CLang options, ASCII characters, using Bstrlib, an overview of Unicode, and an itemization of the C Standard Library.

To get the most out of this book

To use this book, you will need a basic text editor, a terminal or console application, and a compiler. Descriptions of each of these and how to download and use them are provided in `Chapter 1`, *Running Hello, World!.* Here are the technical requirements for this book:

Operating System	Cost	Download URL
Linux/Unix		
Text Editor (choose one)		
Nano	Free	https://www.nano-editor.org/download.php
Vim or vi	<Built-in>	N/A
GEdit	<Built-in>	https://wiki.gnome.org/Apps/Gedit
Emacs	Free	https://www.gnu.org/software/emacs/download.html
Compiler		(Installation based on version of Linux/Unix)
GCC	<Built-in>	https://gcc.gnu.org/install/ (see the notes following this table for certain Linux versions)
Terminal		
Terminal	<Built-in>	N/A
macOS		
Text Editor (choose one)		
Vim or vi	<Built-in>	N/A
emacs	Free	https://www.gnu.org/software/emacs/download.html
Bbedit	Free	https://www.barebones.com/products/bbedit/
Compiler		
Clang	<Built-in>	
Terminal		
terminal.app	<Built-in>	N/A
Windows		
Text Editor (choose one)		
Notepad	<Built-in>	N/A
Notepad++	Free	https://notepad-plus-plus.org/downloads/
emacs	Free	https://www.gnu.org/software/emacs/download.html
Compiler		
Cygwin	Free	http://www.cygwin.com
MinGW	Free	http://mingw-w64.org

	Terminal		
	Console	\<Built-in\>	N/A

To install GCC on certain Linux OSes, follow these steps:

- If you are running an RPM-based Linux, such as RedHat, Fedora, or CentOS, on the command line in Terminal, enter the following:

```
$ sudo yum group install development-tools
```

- If you are running Debian Linux, on the command line in Terminal, enter the following:

```
$ sudo apt-get install build-essential
```

To verify your installation of GCC or Clang for any platform, on the command line in the Terminal, enter the following:

```
$ cc --version
```

Whichever version of this book you are using, digital or hard copy, we advise you to type the code yourself. After you do that, you can access the code via the GitHub repository (link available in the next section). Doing so will help you avoid any potential errors related to the copying and pasting of code.

If you are an absolute beginner, once you have the necessary development tools, you will need to learn how to read a programming book. If you have taken an algebra course or a calculus course in school, then you will need to approach learning from a programming book in a similar fashion:

1. Read through the chapter to get an overview of the concepts being presented.
2. Begin the chapter again, this time typing in each program as you encounter it. Make sure you get the expected output before moving on. If you don't get the expected output, try to figure out what is different in your program from the one given. Learning to program is a lot like learning math—you **must** do the exercises and get the programs to work. You cannot learn to program just by looking at programs; to learn to program, you must program. There is no way around that.
3. Focus upon memorizing keywords and syntax. This will greatly speed up your learning time.

4. Be aware that you will need to sharpen the precision of your thinking. Computer language syntax is extremely precise and you will need to pay extra attention to it. You will also have to think much more precisely and in sometimes excruciating detail about the steps needed to solve a particular problem.
5. Review both the concepts and example programs. Make a note of anything you don't understand.

If you are an experienced programmer who is new to C, I still strongly advise you to first skim the text and examples. Then, enter the programs and get them to work on your system. This will help you to learn C syntax and its idioms more quickly.

I have found that it is important to understand what kind of book you are reading so that you can use it in the most appropriate way. There are several kinds of computer programming books:

- **Conceptual books**, which deal with the underlying ideas and motivation for the topics they present. Kernighan and Ritchie's *The C Programming Language* is one such book.
- **Textbooks** that go through every major area of the language, sometimes in gory detail and usually with a lot of code snippets. Deitel and Deitel's books, as well as *C Programming: A Modern Approach*, by K. N. King, are examples of these. They are often best used in a formal programming course.
- **Reference books**, which describe the specifics of each syntax element. *C: A Reference Manual*, by Harbison and Steele, is one such book.
- **Cookbooks**, which present specific solutions to specific problems in a given language. *Advanced C Programming by Example*, by Perry, *Expert C Programming: Deep Secrets*, by Van Der Linden, and *Algorithms in C*, by Sedgewick, are examples of these.
- **Topical books**, which delve deeply into one or more aspects of a programing language. *Pointers in C*, by Reek, is one example.
- **Practice books**, which deal with how to address programming with C generally. *C Interfaces and Implementations*, by Hanson, and *21st Century C: C Tips from the New School*, by Klemens, are two examples of these.

There are different ways to use these books. For instance, read a conceptual book once, but keep a reference book around and use it often. Try to find cookbooks that offer the kinds of programs you are likely to need and use them as needed.

I think of this book as a combination of a C cookbook, a C reference book, and a C practice book. All of the programs are working examples that can be used to verify how your compiler behaves on your system. Enough of the C language has been included that it may also be used as a *first approximation* reference. Throughout, my intent has been to show good programming practice with C.

I would expect that *Learn C Programming* will not be your last book on C. When you consider other C books, be sure that they pertain to C99 at a minimum; ideally, they should include C11 or C18. Most C code before C99 is definitely old school; more effective programming practices and methods have been developed since before C99.

Download the example code files

You can download the example code files for this book from your account at `www.packt.com`. If you purchased this book elsewhere, you can visit `www.packtpub.com/support` and register to have the files emailed directly to you.

You can download the code files by following these steps:

1. Log in or register at `www.packt.com`.
2. Select the **Support** tab.
3. Click on **Code Downloads**.
4. Enter the name of the book in the **Search** box and follow the onscreen instructions.

Once the file is downloaded, please make sure that you unzip or extract the folder using the latest version of:

- WinRAR/7-Zip for Windows
- Zipeg/iZip/UnRarX for Mac
- 7-Zip/PeaZip for Linux

The code bundle for the book is also hosted on GitHub at `https://github.com/PacktPublishing/Learn-C-Programming`. In case there's an update to the code, it will be updated on the existing GitHub repository.

We also have other code bundles from our rich catalog of books and videos available at `https://github.com/PacktPublishing/`. Check them out!

Download the color images

We also provide a PDF file that has color images of the screenshots/diagrams used in this book. You can download it here: `https://static.packt-cdn.com/downloads/9781789349917_ColorImages.pdf`.

Conventions used

There are a number of text conventions used throughout this book.

`CodeInText`: Indicates code words in text, database table names, folder names, filenames, file extensions, pathnames, dummy URLs, user input, and Twitter handles. Here is an example: "As a hint, this pairing involves the lines `int main()` and `return 0;`"

A block of code is set as follows:

```
#include <stdio.h>

int main()
{
    printf( "Hello, world!\n" );
    return 0;
}
```

When we wish to draw your attention to a particular part of a code block, the relevant lines or items are set in bold:

```
#include <stdio.h>

int main()
{
    printf( "Hello, world!\n" );
    return 0;
}
```

Any command-line input or output is written as follows:

```
$ cc hello6.c
```

Bold: Indicates a new term, an important word, or words that you see onscreen. For example, words in menus or dialog boxes appear in the text like this. Here is an example: "This program is useful because it prints something out to the Terminal, also known as the **console**."

Warnings or important notes appear like this.

 Tips and tricks appear like this.

Get in touch

Feedback from our readers is always welcome.

General feedback: If you have questions about any aspect of this book, mention the book title in the subject of your message and email us at customercare@packtpub.com.

Errata: Although we have taken every care to ensure the accuracy of our content, mistakes do happen. If you have found a mistake in this book, we would be grateful if you would report this to us. Please visit www.packtpub.com/support/errata, selecting your book, clicking on the Errata Submission Form link, and entering the details.

Piracy: If you come across any illegal copies of our works in any form on the Internet, we would be grateful if you would provide us with the location address or website name. Please contact us at copyright@packt.com with a link to the material.

If you are interested in becoming an author: If there is a topic that you have expertise in and you are interested in either writing or contributing to a book, please visit authors.packtpub.com.

Reviews

Please leave a review. Once you have read and used this book, why not leave a review on the site that you purchased it from? Potential readers can then see and use your unbiased opinion to make purchase decisions, we at Packt can understand what you think about our products, and our authors can see your feedback on their book. Thank you!

For more information about Packt, please visit packt.com.

Section 1: C Fundamentals

In this section, we're going to jump into writing simple programs as we explore the fundamentals of not only C but general programming.

This section comprises the following chapters:

Running Hello, World! 1

Computer programming is about learning how to solve problems with a computer – about how to get a computer to do all the tedious work for us. The basic development cycle, or process of writing a computer program, is to determine the steps that are necessary to solve the problem at hand and then tell the computer to perform those steps. Our first problem, as we learn this process, is to learn how to write, build, run, and verify a minimal C program.

The following topics will be covered in this chapter:

- Writing your first C program
- Understanding the program development cycle
- Creating, typing into a text editor, and saving your C program
- Compiling your first C program
- Running your program, verifying its result, and, if necessary, fixing it
- Exploring different commenting styles and using them
- Employing guided chaos, followed by careful observation for deeper learning

Let's get started!

Technical requirements

To complete this chapter and the rest of this book, you will need a running computer that has the following capabilities:

- A basic text editor that is able to save unformatted plain text
- A Terminal window that commands can be entered into via the command line
- A compiler to build your C programs with

Each of these will be explained in more detail as we encounter them in this chapter.

The source code for this chapter can be found at `https://github.com/PacktPublishing/Learn-C-Programming`. However, please make every effort to type the source code in yourself. Even if you find this frustrating at first, you will learn far more and learn far more quickly if you do all the code entry for yourself.

Writing your first C program

We will begin with one of the simplest, most useful programs that can be created in C. This program was first used to introduce C by its creators, Brian W. Kernighan and Dennis M. Ritchie, in their now-classic work, *The C Programming Language*, published in 1978. The program prints a single line of output – the greeting Hello, world! – on the computer screen.

This simple program is important for a number of reasons. First, it gives us a flavor of what a C program is like, but more importantly, it proves that the necessary pieces of the development environment – the **Operating System** (**OS**), text editor, command-line interface, and compiler – are installed and working correctly. Finally, it gives us the first taste of the basic programming development cycle. In the process of learning to program and, later, actually solving real problems with programming, you will repeat this cycle often. It is essential that you become both familiar and comfortable with this cycle.

This program is useful because it prints something out to the Terminal, also known as the **console**, telling us that it actually did something – it displays a message to us. We could write shorter programs in C but they would not be of much use. We would be able to build and run them but would have little evidence that anything actually happened. So, here is your first C program. Throughout this book, and during the entirety of your programming experience, obtaining evidence of what actually happened is essential.

Since Kernighan and Ritchie introduced the *Hello, world!* program over 40 years ago, this simple program has been reused to introduce many programming languages and used in various settings. You can find variations of this program in Java, C++, Objective-C, Python, Ruby, and many others. GitHub, an online source code repository, even introduces their website and its functions with a *Hello World* beginner's guide.

Hello, world!

Without further ado, here is the *Hello, world!* C program. It does no calculations, nor does it accept any input. It only displays a short greeting and then ends, as follows:

```
#include <stdio.h>

int main()
{
    printf( "Hello, world!\n" );
    return 0;
}
```

Some minor details of this program have changed since it was first introduced. What is here will build and run with all C compilers that have been created in the last 20 years.

Before we get into the details of what each part of this program does, see if you can identify which line of the program prints our greeting. You may find the punctuation peculiar; we will explain this in the next chapter. Notice how some punctuation marks come in pairs, while others do not. There are five paired and five unpaired punctuation marks in all. Can you identify them? (We are not counting the punctuation in the message `"Hello, world!"`.)

There is another pairing in this simple program that is not obvious at this time, but one that we will explore further in the next chapter. As a hint, this pairing involves the lines `int main()` and `return 0;`.

Before we jump into creating, compiling, and running this program, we need to get an overview of the whole development process and the tools we'll be using.

Understanding the program development cycle

There are two main types of development environments:

- **Interpreted**: In an interpreted environment such as Python or Ruby, the program can be entered line by line and run at any point. Each line is evaluated and executed as it's entered and the results are immediately returned to the console. Interpreted environments are dynamic because they provide immediate feedback and are useful for the rapid exploration of algorithms and program features. Programs entered here tend to require the interpreting environment to be running as well.
- **Compiled**: In a compiled environment such as C, C++, C#, or Objective-C, programs are entered into one or more files, then compiled all at once, and if no errors are found, the program can be run as a whole. Each of these phases is distinct, with separate programs used for each phase. Compiled programs tend to execute faster since there is a separate, full compilation phase, and can be run independently of the interpreting environment.

As with shampoo, where we are accustomed to *wet hair, lather, rinse, and repeat,* we will do the same with C – we will become familiar with the *edit, compile, run, verify, and repeat* cycle.

Edit

Programs are generated from text files whose filenames use predefined file extensions. These are known as **source files**, or **source code files**. For C, the `.c` file extension indicates a C source code file. An `.h` extension (which is present in our *Hello, world!* program) indicates a C header file. The compiler looks for `.c` and `.h` files as it encounters them and because each has a different purpose, it treats each differently as well. Other languages have their own file extensions; the contents of a source code file should match the language that the compiler expects.

To create and modify C files, you will need a plain text editor. This is a program that allows you to open, modify, and save plain text without any formatting such as font size, font family, font style, and much more. For instance, on Windows, Notepad is a plain text editor while Word is not. The plain text editor should have the following capabilities:

- **File manipulation**: Open a file, edit a file, save the file and any changes that have been made to it, and save the file with another name.

- **The ability to navigate the file**: Move up, down, left, right, to the beginning of the line, end of the line, beginning of the file, end of the file, and so on.
- **Text manipulation**: Insert text, delete text, insert line, delete line, selection, cut, copy, paste, undo/redo, and so on.
- **Search and replace**: Find text, replace text, and so on.

The following capabilities are handy but not essential:

- Automatic indentation
- Syntax coloring for the specific programming language
- Automatic periodic saving

Almost any plain text editor will do. Do not get too caught up in the features of any given text editor. Some are better than others; some are free, while others are costly, and may not immediately be worth the expense (perhaps later, one or more might be worthwhile but not at this time), and none will do 100% of what you might want them to do.

Here are some free plain text editors worth installing on your computer and trying out:

- **Everywhere**: Nano, which runs in a Terminal; a moderate learning curve.
- **Linux/Unix**:
    - **Vim,** or **vi**: Runs in a Terminal; a moderate learning curve. It is on every Linux/Unix system, so it's worth learning how to use its basic features.
    - **gedit**: A powerful general-purpose editor.
    - **Emacs**: An *everything and the kitchen sink* editor; a very large learning curve.
- **Windows**:
    - **Notepad**: Very simple – sometimes too simple for programming – but included in every Windows system.
    - **Notepad++**: A better version of Notepad with many features for programming.
- **macOS only**: BBEdit (free version), which is a full-featured GUI programming text editor.

There are many, many text editors, each with its own strengths and weaknesses. Pick a text editor and get used to it. Over time, as you use it more and more, it will become second nature.

Compile

The compiler is a program that takes input source code files – in our case, .c and .h files – translates the textural source code found there into machine language, and links together all the predefined parts needed to enable the program to run on our specific computer hardware and OS. It generates an *executable* file that consists of machine language.

Machine language is a series of instructions and data that a specific **Central Processing Unit** (**CPU**) knows how to *fetch* from the program execution stream and *execute* on the computer one by one. Each CPU has its own machine language or instruction set. By programming in a common language, such as C, the programmer is shielded from the details of machine language; that knowledge is embodied in the compiler.

Sometimes, assembler language is called **machine language**, but that is not quite accurate since assembler language still contains text and symbols, whereas machine language is only binary numbers. Very few people today have the skills to read machine language directly; at one time, many more programmers were able to do it. Times have changed!

When we compile our programs, we invoke the compiler to process one or more source files. The result of this invocation is either a success and an executable file is generated or it will identify the programming errors it found during compilation. Programming errors can be a simple misspellings of names or omitted punctuation, to more complex syntax errors. Typically, the compiler tries to make sense of any errors it finds; it attempts to provide useful information for the problem it found. Note that *try* and *attempts* are merely goals; in reality, the compiler may spew many lines of error messages that originate from a single error. Furthermore, the compiler will process the entire source code when invoked. You may find many different errors in different parts of the program for each compiler invocation.

A complete, runnable program consists of our compiled source code – the code we write – and predefined compiled routines that come with the OS – code written by the authors of the OS. The predefined program code is sometimes called the **runtime library**. It consists of a set of callable routines that know how to interact in detail with the various parts of the computer. For example, in *Hello, world!*, we don't have to know the detailed instructions to send characters to the computer's screen – we simply call a predefined function, printf();, to do it for us. printf() is part of the C runtime library, as are many other routines, as we will see later. The way in which one v sends text to the console is likely different from any other OS, even if they both run on the same hardware. So, the programmers are shielded not only from the minutia of machine language, but they are also shielded from the varying implementation details of the computer itself.

It follows from this that for each OS, there is a compiler and a runtime library specific to it. A compiler designed for one OS will most likely not work on a different OS. If, by chance, a compiler from one OS just happens to or even appears to run on a different OS, the resulting programs and their executions would be highly unpredictable. Mayhem is likely.

Many C compilers for every OS

You can learn C on many computer platforms. Common compilers in use on Unix and Linux OS are the **GNU Compile Collection** (**GCC***)* or the LLVM compiler project, *clang*. For Windows, GCC is available via the *Cygwin Project* or the *MinGW Project*. You could even learn C using a Raspberry Pi or Arduino, but this is not ideal because of special considerations for these minimal computer systems. It is recommended that you use a desktop computer since many more computer resources (memory, hard drive space, CPU capability, and so on) are available on any such computer that can run a web browser.

A note about IDEs

On many OS, the compiler is installed as a part of an **Integrated Development Environment** (**IDE**) for that OS. An IDE consists of a set of programs needed to create, build, and test programs for that OS. It manages one or more files associated with a program, has its own integrated text editor, can invoke the compiler and present its results, and can execute the compiled program. The programmer typically never leaves this environment while developing. The IDE often streamlines the production of a standalone working program.

There are many such IDEs – Microsoft's Windows-only *Visual Studio*, Microsoft's multi-platform *Visual Studio Code*, Apple's *Xcode* for macOS and other Apple hardware platforms, Eclipse Foundation's *Eclipse*, and Oracle's *Netbeans*, to name a few. Each of these IDEs is able to develop programs in a variety of languages. Nearly all of the programs used in this book were developed using a simple IDE named *CodeRunner* for macOS.

We will not use an IDE for learning C. In fact, at this stage of your learning, it is not advised for several reasons. First, learning and using an IDE can be a daunting learning task in and of itself. This task can and should be put off until you have more experience with each of the individual parts of the program development cycle. IDEs, while they have common functions, are sometimes implemented in vastly different ways with far too many different features to explore. Learn C first; you can learn an IDE for your desired environment later.

Installing a compiler on Linux, macOS, or Windows

Here are the steps to follow to install a C compiler on the major desktop computer environments – Linux, macOS, and Windows. For other platforms, you'll have to do some investigation to find the compiler you need. However, since those platforms want you to use them, they'll likely make those instructions easy to find and follow:

- **Linux**:
    1. If you are running a **Red Hat Package Manager** (**RPM**)-based Linux, such as RedHat, Fedora, or CentOS, enter this command from the command line:

       ```
       $ sudo yum group install development-tools
       ```
    2. If you are running Debian Linux, open a Terminal window and enter this command from the command line:

       ```
       $ sudo apt-get install build-essential
       ```
    3. Verify your installation by entering this command from the command line:

       ```
       $ cc --version
       ```
    4. From the preceding command, you will see that you likely have GCC or clang. Either one is fine. You are now ready to compile C programs on your version of Linux.

- **macOS**:
    1. Open `Terminal.app` and enter the following at the command line:

       ```
       $ cc --version
       ```
    2. If the development tools have not been installed yet, simply invoking the preceding command will guide you through their installation.
    3. Once the installation is complete, close the Terminal window, open a new one, and enter the following:

       ```
       $ cc --version
       ```
    4. You are now ready to compile C programs on your version of macOS.

- **Windows:**
    1. Install either *Cygwin* (`http://www.cygwin.com`) or *MinGW* (`http://mingw-w64.org/`) from their respective websites. Either one will work well. If you choose to install Cygwin, be sure to also install the extra package for the **GNU Compiler Collection** (**GCC**). This will install a number of other required compiler and debugging programs with GCC.

2. Once the installation is complete, open a Command Prompt and enter the following:
   ```
   $ cc --version
   ```
3. You are now ready to compile C programs on your version of Windows.

Compilation is a two-part process – compiling and linking. Compiling involves syntax checking and converting source code into nearly-complete executable code. In the linking phase, the nearly-complete machine code is merged with the runtime library and becomes complete. Typically, when we invoke the compiler, the linker is also invoked. If the compiler phase succeeds (no errors), the linking phase is automatically invoked. Later, we will see that we can get error messages from the compiler either at compile-time – the compiling phase – or at link-time – the linking phase – when all the program's pieces are linked together.

We will learn how to invoke the compiler later when we compile our first program.

Throughout this book, once you have a working program, you will be directed to purposely break it – cause the compilation of your program to fail – so that you can start learning about the correlation of various program errors with compiler errors and so that you will not be afraid of breaking your program. You will simply undo the change and success will be yours once more.

Run

Once compilation has completed successfully, an *executable* file will be generated. This executable file, unless we provide an explicit name for it, will be named `a.out`. The executable file will typically be created in the same directory the compiler was invoked from. For the most part, we will make our current working directory have the same location as the source files.

Running an executable file is performed by invoking it from the command line. When invoked, the executable is loaded into the computer's memory and then becomes the CPU's program execution stream. Once loaded into memory, the CPU begins at the special reserved word known as `main()` and continues until either `return;` or a closing `}` is encountered. The program stops and the executable is then unloaded from memory.

To run an executable, open a Command Prompt (Windows) or Terminal window (Linux and Mac), navigate with `cd` to the directory of the executable file, and simply enter the executable's name (`a.out`, or whatever you've specified).

Note: If you successfully navigate to the same location as the executable and you have verified it exists there but you get an error message from the command interpreter, you likely have a problem with your command interpreter's built-in `PATH` variable. To quickly work around this, enter the `$ ./a.out` command to run it. This instructs the command interpreter to look in the current directory for the file named `a.out`.

As the program runs, any output will be directed to the Terminal or console window. When the program has ended, the command interpreter will present you with a new command prompt.

Verify

At this point in the cycle, you may feel that just getting your program to compile without errors and running it without crashing your computer means you are done. However, you are not. You must verify that what you think your program was supposed to do is what it actually did do. Did your program solve the problem it was intended to? Is the result correct?

So, you have to return to writing your original program and then compare that to the output your program gives. If your intended result matches, your program is correct. You are done.

As we get further into writing more complex programs, we will see that a proper or good program exhibits each of the following qualities:

- **Correct**: The program does what it's supposed to do.
- **Complete**: The program does everything it's supposed to do.
- **Concise**: The program does no more than it's supposed to do and it does so as efficiently as possible.
- **Clear**: The program is easily understandable to those who use it and to those who must maintain it.

For most of this book, we will concern ourselves largely with *correctness, completeness,* and *clarity*. Currently, `hello1.c` is not complete, nor clear, and we will see why shortly.

Repeat

Unlike our shampoo metaphor that we mentioned previously, which was *wet hair, lather, rinse,* and *repeat,* instead of repeating the instructions just once, you will repeat this cycle more than once.

Rarely will you be able to go through the program development cycle with only one iteration of it. Most likely, you will repeat parts of it many more times. You may edit the source code and compile it and find that the compiler failed. You will have to go back to edit the source code and compile it, each time figuring out what was wrong and then fixing it. Once it compiles successfully, you will move on to running and verifying it. If the output is not correct or the program crashes, you will have figure out what went wrong and start editing the source code again.

Does this sound frustrating? It can be – especially when you don't know why something went wrong or you can't figure out what the compiler or computer is saying is wrong.

Many, many years ago, when compilers were simpler and not as forgiving as they are today (actually, compilers are still not forgiving – they've just gotten better at figuring out what we humans may have done wrong with our programs and telling us in better ways!), the very first time I attempted to compile my *Hello, world!* program on a Digital Equipment **Virtual Address Extension** (**VAX**) **Virtual Memory System** (**VMS**) C compiler, the compiler gave me 23 *thousand* error messages. It turns out that I had overlooked a single *;* somewhere. One character. Sheesh!

The point of that story is that you will make mistakes, mostly missing or erroneous punctuation or misspelled variables, and you will get frustrated. Part of learning to program is learning how to deal with your own frustration and how to become a sleuth to track down the picayune errors that will crop up.

Get up and away from the computer. *Take a walk. Have a laugh. Get back to work.* Don't omit the first parts (laughing and walking around a bit).

A note about debugging

As you go through the program development cycle and as you get more familiar with the development language, development tools, and yourself (yes, you are learning about yourself as you program), this will all become second nature to you, as it should. When you make a typing error, or when you get an obviously incorrect result, these are not bugs – they are just mistakes. Bugs are far more subtle.

There is a deeper trap that is very difficult for most beginner programmers to see; that is, their own assumptions about what should happen without evidence of what did happen. Most of the most difficult bugs that I introduced in my own code were those that I assumed the program would work on in a certain way but I did not verify that. When I finally went back to my assumptions and proved them in code, I was able to get beyond my self-imposed bugs.

Can you avoid this trap?

Yes. Throughout this book, we will attempt to mitigate this subtle problem with a method we will use to develop programs. As we proceed, we will use trial and error, guided discovery, and evidence through observation. Sometimes, we will purposefully break our programs to see what happens. We will also try to prove each concept so that the expected behavior matches the actual behavior.

This is not to say that even with such an approach, bugs won't creep in. They will. But with careful attention to your own assumptions, observed behavior, and the collection of evidence you have gathered to prove any assumption, most bugs can be avoided.

Creating, typing, and saving your first C program

Let's begin creating our *Hello, world!* program.

Before we begin creating files, create a directory on your computer where you will save all of the work for this book. Perhaps you will create it in your $HOME directory, or in your Documents folder. My advice is to put it somewhere in a user directory of your choice. Let's go ahead with our program:

1. Open a Command Prompt, Terminal window, or console (depending on your OS).
2. Navigate to $HOME or ./Documents, or wherever you chose to work from, and create a directory for the programs you'll write in this book. Do this with the following command:
   ```
   $ mkdir PacktLearnC
   ```
3. Make that directory your current working directory with the following command:
   ```
   $ cd PacktLearnC
   ```
4. Make a new directory for this chapter with the following command:
   ```
   $ mkdir Chapter1_HelloWorld
   ```

5. Make that directory your current working directory with the following command:
```
$ cd Chapter1_HelloWorld
```

6. Picking the text editor of your choice – any will do – open the text editor either from the command line or from the GUI (depending on both your OS and your preference of which one you wish to use):
    - From the command line, you might enter $ myEditor hello1.c, or just $ myEditor, and later, you will have to save the file as hello1.c in the current working directory.

7. Enter the following program text exactly, all while paying attention to spacing, {} versus () versus "" (these double-quotation marks are the key next to the ; and : keys) versus <>, with particular attention being paid to #, \, ., and ;:

```
#include <stdio.h>

int main()
{
    printf( "Hello, world!\n" );
    return 0;
}
```

8. Save your work and exit the editor.
9. Verify that hello1.c exists by listing the directory and verifying that its file size is not zero.

Congratulations! You have completed your first *editing* phase of the program development cycle.

Compiling your first C program

Having successfully entered and saved your hello1.c file, it is now time to compile it:

1. In a Terminal, command line, or console window (depending on your OS), with the current working directory the same as your hello1.c file, enter $ cc hello1.c.
2. Once this is done and you have a new command-line prompt, verify that you have a file named a.out.

You have completed your first *compiling* phase of the program development cycle.

If the compiler spews out some error messages, try to read what the compiler is telling you and try to understand what error it is telling you to fix. Always focus on the very first error message first; later error messages are usually the result of the very first error. Then, go back to the editing phase and see where your entered program is different than what has been shown here. The two must match exactly. Then, come back to this phase; hopefully, your program will compile successfully (no error messages).

As we progress through this book, we'll add more compiler options to the `cc` command to make our life easier.

Running your first C program

Your `hello1.c` program successfully compiled and you now have an `a.out` file in the same directory. It's time to run it! Let's get started:

1. In a Terminal, command line, or console window (depending on your OS), navigate to the directory that holds `a.out`.
2. At the command prompt, usually indicated by a `$` in the first column, enter `./a.out`.
3. You should see `Hello, world!`.
4. If you see that, we can now verify the output of your program.
5. Note that the command prompt, `$`, is not on the same line as `Hello, world!`. This means you correctly entered `\n` in the output stream. If not, you need to re-edit `hello1.c` and make sure `\n` occurs immediately preceding the second ", recompile it, and rerun `a.out`.
6. If `Hello, world!` is on a line by itself with a command prompt before and after it – woohoo! You did it!

It's always important to remember to *do a little dance, and make a little joy, get down tonight!* when you've successfully completed something. Programming can be very frustrating, so remembering to celebrate even your small successes will make your life a little bit more joyful through all the frustration. Too many programmers forget this incremental and regular step of celebrating with joy!

Writing comments to clarify the program later

A lot about writing good code is writing code in a consistent manner. Consistency makes it somewhat easier for the reader (or you) to comprehend at a later time. Consistency is most often a good thing. However, there may be times where we need to step out of that consistency, and for some good reason, when we write code, that code is particularly twisted or obtuse and difficult to understand. Or, we might write code a certain way that may not be obvious or may not be expected, again for good reason. It is in these circumstances we should comment on our code – not for the compiler, but for ourselves and for others who may be reading our code at a later date, scratching our/their foreheads thinking, "*What? What did I/they intend to do here?*"

Code comments are the way to provide an explanation of why a particular piece of code is written in a certain way. Let's explore some of the different ways we can write code comments in C.

Comments in code, when done correctly, are ignored by the compiler. They are only for human edification. Consider the following code comments:

```c
/* (1) A single-line C-style comment. */

/* (2) A multi-line
   C-style comment. */

/*
 * (3) A very common way to
 * format a multi-line
 * C-Style comment.
 */

/* (4) C-style comments can appear almost anywhere. */

/*(5)*/ printf( /* Say hello. */ "Hello, world!\n" );

/*(6)*/ printf( "Hello, world!\n" ); /* Yay! */

// (7) A C++ style comment (terminated by End-of-Line).

   printf( "Hello, world!\n" ); // (8) Say hello; yay!

//
// (9) A more common way
// of commenting with multi-line
```

```
// C++ style comments
//

// (10) anything can appear after //, even /* ... */ and
// even more // after the first // but they will be
// ignored because they are all in the comment.
```

The comments illustrated in the preceding code are not particularly useful comments, but they show various ways comments in C can be employed.

Comments with tags (1) – (6) are old-style C comments. The rules for these are simple – when a /* is encountered, it is a comment until a */ is subsequently encountered, whether it appears on the same line or several lines later. / * (with a space between them) and * / (with a space between them) are not valid comment indicators.

C comments that have been adopted from C++ are shown with tags (7) through (10). When a // is encountered, it is a comment until an **End Of Line** (**EOL**) is encountered. Therefore, these comments cannot appear anywhere like C comments can. Likewise, / / (with a space between them) is not a valid comment indicator.

C comments are more flexible, while C++ style comments are more obvious. Both styles are useful. We'll use both throughout this book.

Some guidelines on commenting code

One of the best guidelines for commenting in code is the same guideline to follow in life. This is sometimes called the **Goldilocks Principle**, also known as the **Three Bears Principle**, named after the children's fairy tale, *Goldilocks and the Three Bears*. The essence of this guideline is *not too much; not too little; just right*. However, *just right* is subjective, depends on several factors, and will be different for each situation. Your own judgment and experience must be your guide to your *Goldilock's moment*.

These are essential guidelines to follow when commenting your code:

- **Assume the reader already knows the language**: You are not teaching your reader how to code. Do not explain the obvious features of the language. You are explaining the non-obvious aspects of your code.
- **Write in full sentences with proper capitalization and punctuation**: Comments are not code. They are the words you are writing to yourself or to other readers of your code. Your comments will be much less cryptic and more easily understood if you follow this guideline.

- **Comment on unusual uses of the language**: Every language has oddities and idiosyncrasies that may not be used often or may be used in unexpected ways. These should be clarified and highlighted.
- **Try to comment in a way that is resilient to code changes**: Very often, as code changes, comments are not necessarily updated to match. One way to mitigate this is to put comments in *globs* at the beginning of functions or to precede blocks of code rather than them being interspersed within code blocks so that if those change, the comments are still valid. You will see examples of this throughout this book.
- **Comment at a high level**: Describe the intent of the code and the way it attempts to solve a problem. This guideline goes hand in hand with the first guideline we mentioned. The higher the level the comments are describing, the less likely they will need to be changed as the code changes.
- **Convey your intent**: With your comments, strive to convey the intent of the code you are writing, why the code is needed, and what the code is trying to accomplish. What the code is actually doing should come from the code itself.

I am often surprised when I revisit code I wrote 6 months ago. Too often I find that I am scratching my head asking, *why did I do this?* or, *what was I thinking here?* (both cases of too little commenting). I also find that when I change code, I have to delete many comments that are no longer necessary (a case of too much commenting). I rarely find that I have commented too much when I have focused on the intent of the code (what was I trying to do here).

At one point in my career, I came across a programmer whose comments were completely divorced from the code that was there. I concluded that this programmer initially intended their algorithm to work one way, but then modified the code so significantly that the comments no longer matched the actual code at all. When I saw that programmer's name in subsequent code, after careful inspection, I more often than not simply deleted the code comments because I found them to be irrelevant. Please do not do this unless you are absolutely certain you understand the code and that the comments do not match the code.

Learning how to effectively comment on code is a lifelong challenge. I do not suppose you will learn this quickly. You will learn this after years of examining your own code and making your code clearer to yourself, let alone making your code clearer to others. As we work through various C example programs, I intend to demonstrate a variety of useful and resilient commenting techniques.

Adding comments to the Hello, world! program

Now that we have explored the various ways we can comment on code and commenting styles, let's copy `hello1.c` to `hello2.c` and add appropriate comments.

You can either copy `hello1.c` to `hello2.c` with your command interpreter or, in your editor, open `hello1.c` and immediately save it as `hello2.c`. Regardless of how you do this, you should have both `hello1.c` and `hello2.c` in your `Chapter1_HelloWorld` directory.

In your editor, modify `hello2.c` so that it looks as follows:

```
/*
 * hello2.c
 * My first C program with comments.
 * by <your name>
 * created yyyy/mm/dd
 */

#include <stdio.h>

int main()
{
    printf( "Hello, world!\n" );
    return 0;
}

/* eof */
```

Note how the `*` at the beginning of each line providing a comment makes it clear that there are several lines of comments in a group; the group begins with `/*` and eventually ends with `*/`. Compile, run, and verify this program. Be certain you haven't introduced an accidental character here or there, which is always possible and should always be verified.

This is now a *complete* program. We know from the evidence from `hello1.c` that the program is *correct* – it displays our intended message in the way we desire. The first six lines of comments provide minimal information about the program's author and the date it was written. This program's heading information may be simple or it may be more comprehensive. For now, we will keep such heading information simple.

The program itself is so simple that anyone who understands C would know that a simple message is printed. No further commenting is needed here.

Finally, we mark the end of the file with a comment; the only benefit to such a marking is when there are multiple editor windows open and/or programs get very long. This simple demarcation lets humans know we're at the **EOF**. This final EOF indicator is entirely optional and becomes more of a stylistic preference than a practice with rigorous rationale.

I have found that in every programming language I have used, my commenting style has adapted to the clarity or obtuseness of the given language. When I programmed in assembler language at university or later in an early version of *Fortran 4*, I commented on almost every line. But for C++ or Objective-C, I found I comment only sparsely or in *globs* – large sections of comments that explain a concept or programming solution.

Furthermore, even within a given language, when the problem being solved is unusual or I am using a novel approach to its solution, more comments are in order.

In the remainder of this book, depending on the code sample, we'll explore various useful commenting practices that are effective, even when the code is subject to change.

Learning to experiment with code

After we have gotten our basic program to work (woohoo!) we can now turn to learn how to intentionally break it (ouch!) so that we can learn more about what the compiler is trying to tell us. What it is telling us isn't always clear, especially as we are learning.

Once you have mastered the language, there would be little need to do this (yay!). While we are learning the language, however, becoming familiar with the various kinds of compiler error messages is essential and will ultimately save us many hours/weeks of debugging, which may have been prevented early on in the iterative program development cycle. Please do not skip this essential step as you learn C as it will save you many hours/weeks.

So, using the full program development cycle outlined previously, inject the following errors into your source file. When you see the error messages, try to correlate them with what you just did to cause them. After each one, correct the error and recompile it to verify the fix:

- Remove { from `hello2.c`. Save it and compile it. What errors does the compiler give?
- Put { back in its appropriate place and remove }. What errors does the compiler give?

- There are three other paired punctuation marks: `<>`, `()`, which occurs twice, and `""`. What errors does the compiler give when you remove the opening of the pair and the closing of the pair? Put them back after each experiment.
- Remove `;` from either line. What error messages does the compiler give?
- Comment out the line `return 0;` What error messages does the compiler give?
- Change `int main()` to `int MAIN()`. What does the compiler tell you?
- Similarly, change `printf(` to `printout(`. With this error, you should see what linker messages look like.
- Now, comment out `#include <stdio.h>`. You should also see linker errors telling you it can't find the `printf()` function.
- Return `hello2.c` to its original state. Compile, run, and verify the program is both correct and complete.

If you get more than 23 thousand lines of error messages from the compiler, I would really like to know. Please email me with the details of your experiments.

Summary

Whew!

You've learned an enormous amount about the program development cycle and setting up your C development environment in this chapter. Getting *Hello, world!* to compile and run is a far larger accomplishment for beginners than they might imagine. You have a working text editor, a working compiler, and you've begun manipulating programs in a command-line interpreter. You have probably experienced frustration to an extent you've rarely experienced before. I, like many programmers before you, feel your pain. We have all lived that pain. And with luck, I'm here to help take away some of that pain. In the rest of this book, we'll explore ways to optimize this whole experience.

You have begun to learn that programming is about solving problems. While we haven't solved many interesting programming problems yet, you are just beginning your journey from simple programs and problems to far more complex programs and problems. We'll encounter a few of these later.

Furthermore, you are now aware of ways to make your programs clearer to both yourself – especially months after you've written the code – and to others who might later be tasked with modifying your code for new demands.

To be sure, getting a C++, C#, Objective-C, or JavaScript environment up and running would be similar yet subtly different.

In the next chapter, we will go into much more detail about how *Hello, world!* works and then modify it in some interesting ways to learn about statements, blocks, and functions – the building blocks of larger and more interesting programs.

Woohoo! You did it! Isn't programming fun?

2
Understanding Program Structure

A C program, as in most programming languages, consists of a sequence of small, individual pieces of computational work called **statements**, which are formed into larger building blocks called **functions**, which are then compiled into a single program. As we examine these programming elements, we will expand on the `main()` function, which we encountered in the previous chapter.

The following topics will be covered in this chapter:

- Introducing the building blocks of programs – statements and blocks
- Introducing the various kinds of C statements
- Understanding delimiters
- Using whitespace to make your program easier to read for humans
- Introducing functions and their parts
- Learning how a computer reads a C program as it runs
- Creating various kinds of functions with parameters and return values
- Learning how to declare a function for use anywhere in a source file

Let's get started with the chapter!

Technical requirements

Throughout the rest of this book, unless otherwise mentioned, you will continue to use your computer with the following:

- A plaintext editor of your choice
- A console, terminal, or command-line window (depending on your OS)
- A compiler—either the **GNU Compiler Collection** (**GCC**) or **Clang** (clang) for your particular OS

For consistency, it is best if you use the same computer and programming tools for all of the exercises. By doing so, you can focus more closely on the details of C on your computer.

The source code for this chapter can be found at https://github.com/PacktPublishing/Learn-C-Programming. Continue to type in the source code completely yourself and get your version of the programs to run it correctly.

Introducing statements and blocks

Before we begin to explore the details of **statements**, let's return to the various uses of punctuation that we encountered in our *Hello, world!* program. Here is the program for reference; comments have been removed so that we can concentrate on the details of the code itself:

```
#include<stdio.h>
int main()  {
  printf( "Hello, world!\n" );
  return 0;
}
```

At first, I'd like to draw your attention to the paired punctuation—the punctuation that occurs with a beginning mark and a very similar ending mark. Going through it line by line, we see the following pairs—< and >, (and) (which occur twice), { and }, and finally, " and ". We also see some other punctuation that may or not be familiar to you. These are #, ., ;, \, <space>, and <newline>. These are punctuation marks that are significant in the C language.

When we look closely at our `"Hello, world!\n"` greeting, we can see the beginning `"` character and the end `"` character. Everything between them is part of what will be printed to the console. Therefore, there are two punctuation marks that we can basically ignore—`,` and `!`. We can ignore the comma and the exclamation point contained between `"` and `"` because, as we have already seen, these are printed out to the screen as part of our greeting. The characters between `"` and `"` represent a sequence of characters, or a **string**, to be displayed on the console. However, `\` is a punctuation mark that has special significance when part of a string.

Note, on your keyboard, the location of two different punctuation marks—`/`, or forward slash, and `\`, or backward slash (also known as backslash). As you read from left to right, the forward slash *falls forward* while the backslash *falls backward*; hence their names. They have different uses in C. As we have seen with C++-style comments, two `//` characters constitute the beginning of a comment, terminated by the `<newline>` character. We'll come back to `<newline>` in a moment. However, if any other character occurs between `//`, then we do not have a C++-style comment; we have something else. A **digraph** in C is a two-character sequence, which means something more than either of the characters alone. Care must be exercised to ensure the digraph of two `/` characters is preserved; otherwise, the compiler will interpret this as something other than a C++-style comment.

In our greeting string, we can see the `\n` digraph, which represents the `<newline>` character to be output to the console. We must distinguish the `<newline>` character, `\n`, from the `<carriage return>` character, `\r`. We'll learn about many more of these digraphs when we explore output formatting in `Chapter 19`, *Exploring Formatted Output*, and `Chapter 21`, *Exploring Formatted Input*. On some computer systems, to get a new line—advance one line down and return to the beginning of the line—`\n` is used (on Linux, Unix, and macOS). On others, `\r` is used (on some versions of Unix and other OSes). Yet, on others, both `\r\n` are used together (on Windows). These digraphs are intended to reflect the operation of manual typewriters. Manual typewriters have a carriage with a rotating platter and a return lever. When the return lever is manipulated, it first rotates the platter, giving a line feed, or a new line. Then, the lever is forcibly pushed to the left and the carriage is returned to its beginning position—hence, carriage return. Most often, these two actions are combined into one swift and firm movement—new line and carriage return.

Experimenting with statements and blocks

What happens on your system when you replace \n with \r? The most likely result is that it will appear as if no greeting was printed at all. If that is the case, what actually happened is the text printing focus went back to the beginning of the line but the line was not advanced; the console prompt wrote over it, wiping out our greeting. If you want to advance to the next line without returning to the beginning of the line, try the <linefeed> character, or \v.

Digraphs that appear in strings are also called **escape sequences** because they *escape* from the normal meaning of each single character. They all begin with the backslash (\) character. The following table shows the legal C digraphs:

Symbol	Meaning
\a	Alert
\b	Backspace
\f	Form feed (or page advance)
\n	New line
\r	Carriage return
\t	Horizontal tab
\v	Vertical tab
\'	Single quote
\"	Double quote
\?	Question mark
\\	Backslash itself

Even though escape sequences appear as two characters, they are actually a single, non-visible character. Here are some examples:

```
"Hello, world without a new line"
"Hello, world with a new line\n"
"A string with \"quoted text\" inside of it"
"Tabbed\tColumn\tHeadings"
"A line of text that\nspans three lines\nand completes the line\n"
```

To see how this works, create a file called `printingExcapeSequences.c` and edit/type the following program:

```c
#include <stdio.h>

int main( void )   {
  printf( "Hello, world without a new line" );
  printf( "Hello, world with a new line\n" );
  printf( "A string with \"quoted text\" inside of it\n\n" );
  printf( "Tabbed\tColumn\tHeadings\n" );
  printf( "The\tquick\tbrown\n" );
  printf( "fox\tjumps\tover\n" );
  printf( "the\tlazy\tdog.\n\n" );
  printf( "A line of text that\nspans three lines\nand completes the
   line\n\n" );
  return 0;
}
```

This program is a series of `printf()` statements that each writes a string to the console. Note the use of the `<newline>` character, `\n`, that typically appears at the end of a string but can appear anywhere in it or not at all. In the third string, an escape sequence, `\"`, is used to print the " character in the output string. Notice how tabs, `\t`, can be embedded into any string.

When you have typed in this program, save it. Compile and run it in a console window using the following commands:

```
cc printingEscapeSequences.c <return>
a.out<return>
```

You should see the following output:

```
> cc printingEscapeSquences.c
> a.out
Hello, world without a new lineHello, world with a new line
A string with "quoted text" inside of it

Tabbed  Column  Headings
The     quick   brown
fox     jumps   over
the     lazy    dog.

A line of text that
spans three lines
and completes the line

>
```

As you examine the output, see whether you can correlate the `printf()` strings to what you see in the console. Notice what happens when there is no `\n` character in an output string, the quotation marks within an output string, and what `\n\n` looks like. Finally, notice how `\t` can be used to align columns of text.

We use the `printf()` function extensively to output strings to the console. Much later, in `Chapter 24`, *Working with Multi-File Programs*, we will use a variant of `printf()` to output strings to a file for permanent storage.

Understanding delimiters

Delimiters are characters used to separate smaller parts of the program from one another. These smaller parts are called **tokens**. A token is the smallest complete C language element. A token is either a single character or a sequence of characters predefined by the C language, such as `int` or `return`, or a sequence of characters/words defined by us, which we will learn about later. When a token is predefined by C, it cannot be used except in a prescribed way. These tokens are called **keywords**. Four keywords we have already encountered are `include`, `int`, `main`, and `return`. We will encounter many others throughout the course of this chapter.

Again, here is the *Hello, world!* program for reference:

```
#include<stdio.h>
int main()   {
 printf( "Hello, world!\n" );
 return 0;
}
```

There are three types of delimiters that we will explore here:

- **Single delimiters**: ; and <space>
- **Paired, symmetric delimiters**: <>, (), {}, and ""
- **Asymmetric delimiters that begin with one character and end with another**: # and <newline> and // and <newline>

Each of these has a specific use. Most of them have unique and unambiguous uses. That is, when you see them, they can mean one thing and only one thing. Others have slightly different meanings when they appear in different contexts.

In our *Hello, world!* program, there are only two required `<space>` characters that are delimiters. We see a delimiting space here, between `int` and `main()`:

```
int main()
```

We also see a delimiting space here, between `return` and the value being returned—in this case, `0`:

```
return 0;
```

In these cases, the `<space>` character is used to separate one **keyword** or **token** from another. A keyword is a predefined word that has a special meaning. It is reserved because it cannot be used elsewhere for some other meaning or purpose. `int`, `main()`, and `return` are all keywords and tokens. `0` and `;` are tokens; one is a literal value and the other is a delimiter. The compiler identifies and translates tokens into machine language as appropriate. Delimiters, including `<space>`, facilitate interpreting text in the program compilation stream into tokens. Otherwise, when spaces are not needed to separate tokens, they are optional and are considered **whitespace**.

You can see the paired symmetric delimiters from the list of types of delimiters. One always begins a particular sequence and the other always ends it. `<>` is used for a specific type of filename, which tells the compiler how to search for the given file. `()` indicates that the token is associated with a function name; we'll explore this more shortly. `{}` indicates a block that groups one or more statements together into a single unit; we will explore statements later. Finally, `" "` indicates the beginning and end of a sequence of characters, also referred to as a **string**.

Lastly, we'll consider the first line, which begins with # and ends with `<newline>`. This is an asymmetric delimiter pair. This particular line is a **preprocessor** directive. The preprocessor is the very first part of the compiler phase where directives are interpreted. In this case, the file named `stdio.h` is searched and inserted into the program compilation stream, or included, just as if the file had been typed into our program. To direct the compiler to insert it, we only need to specify its filename; the compiler has a predefined set of locations to look for it. The compiler finds it and opens and reads it into the stream. If it cannot find it, an error is reported.

This `#include` mechanism allows a single file to be used instead of manually copying the contents of this file into each and every source file that needs it. If the `stdio.h` file changes, all programs that use it can simply be recompiled to pick up the new changes. Otherwise, any changes to any version of the copied text of `stdio.h` would have to *also* be made in every file that also copied its contents directly. We will encounter many of these files—those that are part of the Standard Library and those we create—as we begin to make our programs more complex and useful.

Now, with our understanding of delimiters, we can remove all the extraneous spaces, tabs, and new lines. We can pare it down to just keywords, tokens, and delimiters. Our program, `hello_nowhitespace.c`, would look like this:

```
#include<stdio.h>
int main(){printf("Hello, world!\n");return 0;}
```

Create a new file called `hello_nowhitespace.c`, type this in, save it, compile it, run it, and verify that its output is as before. Note that we do not remove the space in our string message; that part of the program is intended for humans.

Is this good programming practice? In a word—never.

You might think that a practice like this would somehow save space on your computer's hard drive/SSD; in reality, the space-saving is insignificant, especially when compared to the added human time needed to understand and modify such a program.

It is a basic fact of programming that programs are read many tens of times more often than they are created or modified. In reality, every line of code is read *at least* 20 times over its lifetime. You may find that you re-read your own programs several times before you consider changing them or reusing them. Others will read your programs with or without your knowledge. Therefore, while we pay attention to the rules of the compiler and strive to write *complete* and *correct* programs, we also strive to write *clear* programs for other humans to understand. This not only means using comments effectively but also using *whitespace* effectively.

Understanding whitespace

When a `<space>` or `<newline>` character is not required to delimit a portion of C code, it is considered whitespace. Whitespace can also be `<tab>`, `<carriage return>`, and some other obscure characters. However, the use of tabs in C source files is discouraged since the program listing may look different on someone else's computer or when the source code is printed, thereby diminishing clarity and obfuscating your original intent.

Always use spaces instead of tabs in your source code files.

We write `<newline>` to mean the start of a new line, which has the same effect as hitting *Enter* on your keyboard. `<space>` similarly is the same as hitting the spacebar at the bottom of your keyboard.

There are many opinions by as many programmers on how to effectively use whitespace. Some programmers feel strongly about using two spaces to indent a line while others are vehement about using four spaces. Others don't care one way or the other. In reality, there is no one correct way to do it. As you write more of your own programs and read those of others, you should pay attention to whitespace styles to try to get a sense of what is effective and what you might prefer.

Consistency in code formatting, including whitespace, is more important than you might think. Consistent code helps set the code reader's expectations, making the code easier to read, and hence to comprehend. Inconsistent whitespace formatting can make the code harder to read and, consequently, introduce coding errors and bugs.

Here is an example of inconsistent and inappropriate use of whitespace. It is from our *Hello, world!* program, but with excessive and nonsensical whitespace added:

```
#               include           <stdio.h>

int
main
(
)
{
        printf
        (
                            "Hello, world!\n"

        )
;
        return
             0
                   ;

}
```

Note that this is still a valid C program. It will compile and run and provide the same output as before. The C compiler ignores whitespace.

Because this is an example of bad practice, you do not have to type this in yourself. In the remaining programs in this book, all source code will be presented with both consistent whitespace usage as well as consistent commenting style. You don't have to adopt these stylistic guidelines, but you should pay attention to them and compare them to other styles. Whatever style you choose, apply it consistently in your code.

When you are paid to create or modify programs for another individual or for a company, they may have a set of style guides for you to follow. Strive to follow them. More than likely, however, they will not have a set of style guides; the coding style guidelines will be embodied in their existing repository of programs. Here, again, strive to follow the coding styles in the existing code you are modifying. This consistency makes the programs easier to read and faster to comprehend for later programmers.

Some programming teams employ source code **pretty-printers** where each programmer runs their source code through a special program that reads their source file, reformats it according to preset formatting rules, and writes it out in the new format; the language functionality is unchanged. In this manner, all source code looks the same, regardless of who wrote it, since the style guidelines are enforced through the program's single set of rules. Every programmer can then read the formatted source code as if anyone had written it. They can focus on the code itself and not be distracted by various coding styles.

Here is a table of the delimiters that we have already encountered in our simple program:

Symbol	Symbol Name	Symbol Use
`<space>`	Space	Basic token separator or whitespace
`<newline>`	Newline	Terminating deliminator for preprocessor directives and C++-style comments or whitespace
`;`	Semi-colon	Statement terminator
`//`	Double forward slash	Beginning of a C++-style comment
`#`	Octothorp, or hash	Beginning of a preprocessor directive
`< >`	Angle brackets	Filename delimiters used in preprocessor directive, when used in pairs
`{ }`	Curly brackets, or braces	Block delimiters
`( )`	Rounded brackets, more commonly known as parentheses	Function parameter delimiters. Also used for expression grouping (see `Chapter 5`, *Exploring Operators and Expressions*)
`" "`	Double quotation marks	String delimiters or filename delimiters in preprocessor directives for multiple characters (see `Chapter 15`, *Working With Strings*)

| ' ' | Single quotation marks | Character delimiters for single characters (see Chapter 15, *Working with Strings*) |
| [] | Square brackets | Array notation (see Chapter 11, *Working with Arrays*) |

We will see later that some of these punctuation marks have different meanings when used in different contexts. When their use is not as a delimiter, their alternate meaning will be clear from the context. For instance, < is the less than logical operator and will occur alone when it has that meaning. For completeness, we have included the delimiters to indicate an array, which is square brackets; we will encounter them in later chapters.

We are now ready to explore how these delimiters are used in various types of C statements.

Introducing statements

Statements in C are the basic building blocks of programs; each statement forms a complete unit of computational logic. There are many types of statements and they are made up of a wide variety of elements:

- **Simple statements**: End with ;. return 0; is a simple statement.
- **Block statements**: Begin with { and end with }. They contain and group other statements. Here, we represent them as { ... }, where ... represents one or more statements of any type of valid statement.
- **Complex statements**: On the other hand, these consist of a keyword and one or more block statements. main(){...} is a complex statement; it has the main keyword and other pre-defined elements, including a block statement. Complex statements include functions (which are covered in this chapter), control statements (covered in Chapter 6, *Exploring Conditional Program Flow*), and looping statements (covered in Chapter 7, *Exploring Loops and Iteration*).
- **Compound statements**: These are made up of simple statements and/or complex statements that consist of multiple statements. The body of our program is a compound block statement that consists of two statements—a call to printf(); and a return 0; statement.

In our *Hello, world!* program, the following are the kinds of statements we have already encountered:

- **Preprocessor directive**: This begins with # and ends with <newline>. It isn't really a C statement that performs computation; instead, it is a command to the compiler to process our C file in a specified way. Preprocessor directives do not follow C syntax and formatting but they are included in the language; we can think of them as outside of C syntax. They direct the compiler to do extra, preparatory stuff before the compiler gets down to the actual work of compiling the program.

- **Function statement**: The main() function, which is where our program begins executing, is really a pre-defined name for a more general function statement. By adding statements to main(), we define our program. Every executable C program must have one—and only one—main() function defined. It is a complex statement. We will also define our own function statements—or, more simply stated, our own functions.

- **Function call statement**: This is a simple statement. Just as main() is called by the system to execute, we can call functions that have already been defined or that we are defined in our program. In this case, we call the pre-defined printf() function to do some of the work for us. When we call a function, execution of the current statement of the current function is suspended and the execution jumps into the called function and continues in that function.

- **Return statement**: This is a simple statement that causes execution in the current function to end; execution then returns to the caller. In the main() function, when return is encountered, our program ends and control returns to the system.

- **Block statement**: A block statement is a compound statement that consists of one or more statements enclosed in { }. Block statements are required for function statements and control statements—we will call these **named blocks**—and have a well-defined structure. However, we can also group statements together into **unnamed blocks** to organize multiple statements into related units of computation. Unnamed blocks have a simple structure and can appear anywhere that a statement can appear. We'll explore this in greater depth in Chapter 25, *Understanding Scope*. Until then, our use of scoping rules will be both simple and intuitively obvious.

For completeness, here are the other statement types that we will encounter later:

- **Control statements**: These include `if {} else {}`, `goto`, `break`, and `continue`. The `return` statement is also a control statement. Like a call statement function, these change the order of execution of statements within a function. Each has a well-defined structure. We'll explore these further in `Chapter 6`, *Exploring Conditional Program Flow*.

- **Looping statements**: These include `while()...`, `do()... while`, and `for()....` They are similar to control statements but their primary purpose is to *iterate*; that is, to perform a statement 0 or more times. We'll explore these further in `Chapter 7`, *Exploring Loops and Iteration*.

- **Expression statements**: These are simple statements that evaluate expressions and return some kind of result or value. We'll examine these in `Chapter 5`, *Exploring Operators and Expressions*.

Except for control, looping, and the wide variety of expression statements, we have already encountered the essential C program statements that make up the bulk of our C programs.

We will now explore them further.

Introducing functions

Functions are *callable* segments of program code that perform one or more statements of related computational work. Functions group statements into a cohesive set of instructions that perform a specific, complex task. This may comprise a single statement, only a few statements, or many statements. Functions can also call other functions. Functions, made up of one or more statements, are the next, higher-up, more-complex units of program composition. Statements make functions; functions make programs. Indeed, `main()` is a function made of statements and other functions.

The process of writing programs—or rather, solving a given problem—with a computer program is primarily the task of breaking the problem down into smaller pieces—into functions—and focusing on the work to be done in each smaller piece. When we break a problem down into smaller parts, we can more easily see the essence of the problem. We can focus our attention either on aspects of the larger problem or on the fine details of the subdivided problem pieces.

We may be able to reuse a single problem piece—or function—so that we don't have to copy and paste it throughout the program whenever it is needed again. Anytime a function changes, we change it in only one place. If we discover that a function does not cover all the cases we originally expected, we can either expand its functionality, add a similar function to provide a slightly different solution, or further break the function down into smaller functions.

This approach is preferable to writing one large program without any functions. In many cases, writing monolithic, large programs without functions can and has been done. However, each time, a program like this would require modification; it would have to be understood *in toto*, so that even a small change might require the entire program to be considered. When a problem can be expressed so that we can see its major and minor parts, as implemented in functions, it is most often easier to understand it generally and in its components, making it, therefore, easier to modify.

So, a major part of solving problems in C is breaking the problem into smaller, functional parts and writing functions to resolve each of the smaller problems.

Understanding function definitions

Functions, therefore, are an essential part of any C program. Each function that you will create has the following parts:

- **Function identifier**: This is the name of the function. The name of the function *should* match closely to what it actually does.
- **Function result type** or **return value type**: Functions can return a value to the caller; the caller may ignore the result. If a return value type is specified, the function *must* return a value of that type to the caller.
- **Function block**: A block directly associated with the function name and parameter list where additional statements are added to perform the work of the function.
- **Return statement**: The primary mechanism to return a value of the specified type from the called function to its caller.
- **Function parameter list**: This is an optional list of values that are *passed* into the function, which it may use as a part of its calculation.

Let's examine each of these in turn. The goal is for you to begin to recognize, understand, and be able to create the function statement *pattern* for yourself. We'll use the absolute minimum C program with `main()` as our example function and highlight each essential part.

The function type, function identifier, and function parameter list comprise a **function signature**. In a C program, each function identifier must be unique. In other languages, the complete function signature is considered, but not in C. When a function is called, only its function identifier is considered.

Once a function has been defined with a function identifier, that function identifier cannot be redefined with a different function result type or function parameter list. Each function identifier in C must be unique.

Note that function signatures are not used in C to uniquely identify a function. Therefore, two functions with the same identifier but with different parameter lists or result types will cause a compilation to fail.

Exploring function identifiers

So, main() is a function just like any other function. However, it does have some significant differences—the main function identifier is reserved. The signature for it is also pre-defined in two specific ways. You cannot name any other function in your program main. Your program can never call main itself; main can only be called by the system.

Function identifiers should be descriptive of their purpose. You would expect the function named printGreeting() to print a greeting, as its name implies. Likewise, you would expect a function named printWord() to print a single word. Naming functions to match their purpose is a good programming practice. Naming functions any other way, say Moe(), Larry(), and Curly(), gives no real indication of what they do, even if somehow in your conception these three functions are related; this would be considered very bad programming practice.

Function identifiers are case sensitive. This means main, MAIN, Main, and maiN are all different function names. It is never a good idea to write function names all in uppercase since the *shape* of the word is lost. All uppercase text is extremely difficult to read and should, therefore, be avoided if possible. In fact, every identifier in C is case sensitive. This guideline, therefore, applies to every other C identifier, too.

An exception to using all uppercase names is for names used in preprocessor directives. Here, by convention, preprocessor directive names tend to take all uppercase separated by underscores. This is a historical convention. It is best to avoid all uppercase identifiers in your C code and to leave this convention to the domain of the preprocessor. Separating uppercase/preprocessor names from lowercase/program identifiers makes it clearer to the reader of the program which identifiers are handled by the preprocessor and which are actual C program identifiers.

When two functions have a similar purpose but are slightly different, do not rely on differences in the upper or lowercase of their names to differentiate them. It is far better to make them slightly different in length or use different modifiers in their name. For instance, if we had three functions to change the color of some text to three different shades of green, a poor naming choice would be `makegreen()`, `makeGreen()`, and `makeGREEN()` (where the capitalization here seems to imply the intensity of the color green). A better choice that explicitly conveys their purpose would be `makeLightGreen()`, `makeGreen()`, and `makeDarkGreen()`, respectively.

Two common methods to make function names descriptive yet easy to read are **camel-case** and **underscore-separated**, also known as **snake-case**. Camel-case names have the beginning characters of words within the name capitalized. In underscore-separated names, _ is used between words:

- **All-lowercase**: `makelightgreen()`, `makemediumgreen()`, and `makedarkgreen()`.
- **Camel-case**: `makeLightGreen()`, `makeMediumGreen()`, and `makeDarkGreen()`.
- **Snake-case** (or **underscore-separated**): `make_light_green()`, `make_medium_green()`, and `make_dark_green()`.

As you can see, the all-lowercase names are somewhat difficult to read. However, these are not nearly as difficult to read as all-uppercase names. The other two ways are quite a bit easier to read. Therefore, it is better to use either of the last two.

If you choose one identifier naming convention, stick to it throughout your program. Do not mix different identifier naming schemes as this makes remembering the exact name of function identifiers, as well as other identifiers, much more difficult and error-prone.

Exploring the function block

The function block is where the work of the function happens.

Within the function block are one or more statements. In our *Hello, world!* main function, there are only two statements. In the following program, `main.c`, there is only one—the `return 0;` statement:

```
int main()  {
   return 0;
}
```

While there is no ideal size, large or small, for the number of statements in a function block, typically, functions that are no longer than either the number of lines in a terminal, 25 lines, or a printed page, say 60 lines, are preferable to much longer functions. The **Goldilocks target**—given multiple options, the one Goldilocks in the fairy tale *Goldilocks and the Three Bears* would have chosen—in this case, would be somewhere between 25 and 50 lines. Shorter functions are most often preferred over much longer ones.

In some cases, however, longer functions are warranted. Rarely, if ever, are they considered good programming practice. The objective is to break the problem into meaningful subproblems and solve each one independently of the larger problem. By keeping functions small, the subproblem can be quickly grasped and solved.

Exploring function return values

A function statement can return a value to its caller. It does so from within its function block. The caller is not required to use the returned value and can ignore it. In *Hello, world!*, the printf() function call actually does return a value but we ignore it.

When a function statement is specified with a return type, then it must return a value of that type. Such a specification consists of two parts:

- The return type of the function, given before the name of the function
- The return value, which is of the same type as the return type

In main.c, int—short for integer or whole number—is the type specified that the main() function must return to its caller. Immediately before the closing brace, we find the return 0; statement, which returns the 0 integer value. In most OS system calls (such as Unix, Linux, macOS, and Windows), a return value of 0 by convention typically means no error is encountered.

If the return type of a function is void instead of int or some other type, there is no return value. The return statement is optional. Consider the following two functions:

```
void printComma()  {
  ...
  return;
}

int main()  {
  ...
  return 0;
}
```

We have defined the `printComma()` function with a `void` return type. A `void` return type, in this context, means no return value, or nothing is to be returned. In the function body, there is an explicit `return` statement. However, this return statement is actually optional; it is implied when the closing brace of the function body is encountered and execution returns to the caller. Note that the `printComma()` function has a return type of `void`; therefore, the `return;` statement provides no value in it.

In the following program, `hello2.c`, `return` is expressed explicitly:

```
#include <stdio.h>

void printComma()   {
   printf( ", " );
   return;
}

int main()   {
   printf( "Hello" );
   printComma();
   printf( "world!\n" );
   return 0;
}
```

In the `hello2.c` program, we have a function whose purpose is only to print a comma and space to the console. Type out this program. Compile, run, and verify it. Verification should be familiar now since we are creating the same output. Clearly, by itself this is not a particularly useful function.

Our intent is to focus on moving from a single statement in our original *Hello, world!* program to a program that employs a number of functions to do the same thing. In each case, the output will be the same. In this chapter, focus on the mechanism of the function, not the actual utility of the function just yet. As we expand our knowledge of C, our functions will become more useful and more relevant.

A recent development in C is that `return 0;` is optional. If there is no `return;` or `return 0;` statement, then the value of 0 is assumed to be returned by the function. This, by convention, means everything is executed normally and all is well. With this in mind, the modern, minimal `main()` function now becomes the following:

```
int main()   {
}
```

The previous `main()` function becomes the following:

```
int main()  {
  printf( "Hello" );
  printComma();
  printf( "world!\n" );
}
```

We will follow this convention throughout our programs.

For functions that do return result codes, it is good programming practice to capture them and act on them if an error does occur. We will see how to do this in `Chapter 4`, *Using Variables and Assignment*, and `Chapter 6`, *Exploring Conditional Program Flow*.

Passing in values with function parameters

A function can be values given as input to the function. It can then use them within the function body. When the function is defined, the type and number of parameters that can be *passed in* or received by the functions are specified. When the function is called, the values of the parameters are given. The function call parameters must match the type and number of parameters specified. In other words, the function signature must match both the caller of the function and the called function.

We have already encountered a function that takes a parameter—the `printf( "Hello, world!\n" );` function call. Here, the parameter is a string with the `"Hello, world!\n"` value. It could be almost any string, as long it is delimited by `""`.

Function parameters are specified in the function definition between the (...) delimiters. The ellipsis indicates that there can be zero or more function parameters in the parameter list, separated by commas (a C token we haven't yet encountered). When there are no parameters, the definition looks like (`void`) or, as shorthand, just (). `(void)` and () are equivalent empty parameter lists.

Each parameter consists of two parts: a data type and an identifier. The data type specifies what kind of value is being used—a whole number, a decimal number, a string, and so on. The identifier is the name used to access the value. Multiple parameters are separated by a comma. We will explore data types fully in the next chapter. A value identifier is very similar to a function identifier; where a function name can be called from somewhere, the parameter identifier is the name by which the passed in value can be accessed within the function body. Let's look at what parameter lists look like with zero, one, and two parameters:

```
void printComma( void )   {
  ...
}

void printAGreeting( char* aGreeting )    {
  ...
}

void printSalutation( char* aGreeting , char* who )   {
  ...
}
```

Take as given, for the moment, that the C type of a string passed into a function is `char*`. This will be introduced in `Chapter 3`, *Working With Basic Data Types*. We'll explore this in much greater detail in `Chapter 15`, *Working With Strings*. In each of these function parameters, focus first on each parameter and then on each part of each parameter.

Within the function body, the parameter can not only be accessed but can also be manipulated. Any such manipulations on the parameter value are only valid within the function body. Once the function body ends, the parameter values are discarded.

In the following programs, we can see how to use the parameter values within the function body:

```
#include <stdio.h>

void printComma( void )   {
  printf( ", " );
}

void printWord( char* word )   {
  printf( "%s" , word );
}

int main()   {
  printWord( "Hello" );
  printComma();
```

```
    printWord( "world" );
    printf( "!\n" );
}
```

In the two functions defined, because the return type is void, the return; statement is, therefore, optional and is omitted. In the first function, there are no function parameters, so the parameter list is void. In the second function, the parameter identifier is word. The parameter type is char*, which for now we'll take to mean a string. To use word as a string in the printf() function call, we specify a different kind of escape sequence specific to the %s printf function, called a **format specifier**. This specifier says to take the string value given in the next function parameter—in this case, word—and print it at this location in the string. We will casually introduce format specifiers as we encounter them; they will be examined in exhaustive detail in Chapter 19, *Exploring Formatted Output*.

As before, type in this program, then compile, run, and verify its output. The output should be Hello, world!, as before.

Now, with these two functions, we can use them to build a more general greeting function that takes a greeting and an addressee. We could then call this function with two values, one value for the greeting and the other for who is being greeted. To see how this works, create a new file named hello4.c and enter the following program:

```c
#include <stdio.h>

void printComma()   {
  printf( ", " );
}

void printWord( char* word )   {
  printf( "%s" , word );
}

void printGreeting( char* greeting , char* addressee )   {
 printWord( greeting );
 printComma();
 printWord( addressee );
 printf( "!\n" );
}

int main()   {
 printGreeting( "Hello" , "world" );
 printGreeting( "Good day" , "Your Royal Highness" );
 printGreeting( "Howdy" , "John Q. and Jane P. Doe" );
 printGreeting( "Hey" , "Moe, Larry, and Joe" );
    return 0;
}
```

Again, for now, take as given that the `char*` parameter type specifies that a string is being used; this will be explained later. In `hello4.c`, we have moved the statements from the body of `main` into a newly declared function, `printGreeting`, which takes two parameters of a string type. Now, we have a function that can be called with different values, which we saw in the main body. `printGreeting()` is called four times, each time with two different string parameters. Note how each string parameter is delimited by `""`. Also, note how only one `printf()` function prints `<newline>`. Save this program. Compile it and run it. You should see the following output:

```
[> cc hello4.c
[> a.out
Hello, world!
Good day, Your Royal Highness!
Howdy, John Q. and Jane P. Doe!
Hey, Moe, Larry, and Curly!
>
```

Considering our functions and how they work, we may find that we don't really need `printComma()` and `printWord()`, but we still want to provide a general `printGreeting()` function. We will combine `printComma()` and `printWord()` into a single `printf()` statement with two format specifiers. To do that, copy `hello4.c` into a file named `hello5.c`. Modify `hello5.c` to look as in the following program:

```c
#include <stdio.h>

void printGreeting( char* greeting , char* who )  {
  printf( "%s, %s!\n" , greeting , who );
}

int main()  {
  printGreeting( "Hello" , "world" );
  printGreeting( "Greetings" , "Your Royal Highness" );
  printGreeting( "Howdy" , "John Q. and Jane R. Doe" );
  printGreeting( "Hey" , "Moe, Larry, and Curly" );
  return 0;
}
```

This program is simpler than before; it defines only one function instead of three. Yet, it still provides a general way to print various greetings via function parameters. Save this file. Compile and run it. Your output should be identical to that of `hello4.c`.

On the other hand, we may find that we need to break `printGreeting()` into even smaller functions. So, let's do this. Copy `hello5.c` into a file named `hello6.c` and modify it to appear as follows:

```c
#include <stdio.h>

void printAGreeting( char* greeting )   {
   printf( "%s" , greeting );
}

void printAComma( void )   {
   printf( ", " );
}

void printAnAddressee( char* aName )   {
   printf( "%s" );
}

void printANewLine()   {
   printf( "\n" );
}

void printGreeting( char* aGreeting , char* aName )   {
   printAGreeting( aGreeting );
   printAComma();
   printAnAddressee( aName );
   printANewLine();
}

int main()   {
 printGreeting( "Hi" , "Bub" );
 return 0;
}
```

In `hello6.c`, there are more, smaller functions to print a greeting. The advantage of doing is this is to be able to reuse our functions without having to copy one or more statements. For instance, we could expand our program to not just print a greeting but also print a variety of sentences, a question, a normal sentence, and so on. An approach such as this might be appropriate for a program that processes language and generates text. Compile `hello6.c` and run it. You should see the following output:

```
> cc hello6.c
> a.out
Hi, Bub
>
```

That might seem like a lot of functions just to print two words. However, as you can see, we are able to organize our program in many ways with functions. We can create fewer, possibly larger, or more general functions or decide to use more, possibly smaller, more specific functions. We can break functions into one or more other functions and call them as needed. All of these approaches will depend on the problem to be solved. So, while there are many different ways to organize a program, there is rarely a single way.

You may be wondering why we define our functions with specific numbers of parameters, and yet the `printf()` function can take multiple parameters. This is called a **variadic function**. C provides a mechanism to do this. We will not explore this; we will however touch on it briefly in the appendix with the `stdarg.h` header file.

In our explanations, to differentiate a function from some other program element, we will refer to a function with `name()` (the parentheses after the identifier to indicate it is a function, where `name` is the name of the function).

As a means to express the relationship between functions clearly, consider the following:

- Functions are *called* and have a *caller*, which is the function that called them. `printComma()` is called by `printGreeting()`. `printGreeting()` is the caller of `printComma()`.
- The *called* function, or *caller*, returns to its *caller*. `printComma()` returns to `printGreeting()`. `printGreeting()` returns to `main()`.
- A function *calls* another function, the *caller*, which is the function that is called. `main()` calls `printGreeting()`. `printGreeting()` calls `printAddressee()`.

Order of execution

When a program executes, it first finds `main()` and begins executing statements in the `main()` function block. Whenever a function call statement is encountered, a number of actions occur:

1. If there are function parameters, the actual values found in the function call statement are assigned to the function parameter names.
2. Program execution jumps to that function and begins executing statements in that function block.

3. Execution continues until either a return statement is encountered or the end of the block is encountered (the closing }).
4. Execution jumps back, or returns, to the calling function and resumes from that point.

If, in *step 2*, execution encounters another function call statement, the steps are repeated.

The following diagram illustrates the call/return order of execution when function calls are encountered. This order of execution cannot be violated. Since it is very bad practice to jump from within one function to another, C does not allow this:

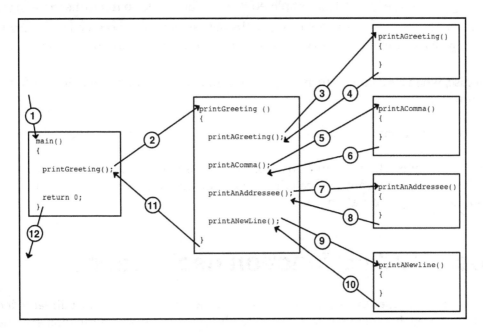

The following are the steps of execution:

1. The program is called by the system and begins execution at main().
2. main() calls printGreeting(). Execution jumps to its function block.
3. printGreeting() calls printAGreeting(). Execution jumps to its function block.
4. printAGreeting() completes its function block and returns back to printGreeting().
5. printGreeting() then calls printAComma(). Execution jumps to its function block.

6. `printAComma()` competes its function block and returns back to `printGreeting()`.

7. `printGreeting()` then calls `printAnAddressee()`. Execution jumps to its function block.

8. `printAnAddressee()` completes its function block and returns back to `printGreeting()`.

9. `printGreeting()` then calls `printANewline()`. Execution jumps to its function block.

10. `printANewline()` completes and returns back to `printGreeting()`.

11. `printGreeting()` has completed its function block, so it returns to `main()`.

12. `main()` must return an integer, so the next statement processed is `return 0;`, which causes `main()` to complete its execution and return to the system.

In each case, when a function returns, it picks up immediately from where it left off in the calling function.

If there were any statements after `return 0;` or a `return;`, they would never be executed.

You may have noticed that all functions that we have used have been defined *before* they were called. What if we wanted to call them in any order? To do that, we need to understand function declarations.

Understanding function declarations

In order for the compiler to recognize a function call when it sees it, it must already know about the function. In other words, it must already have processed the function statement's definition before it can process the call to that function. We have seen this behavior in all of our programs up to this point. In each program, we have defined the function, and then later in our program, we called it.

This behavior is somewhat limiting since we may want to call a function from anywhere in our program. We don't want to get caught up in its relative position in the program and have to reshuffle the definitions of the functions just to make the compiler happy. The compiler is supposed to work for us, not the other way around.

C provides a way to declare a function so that the compiler knows just enough about the function to be able to process a call to the function before it actually processes the function definition. These are called **function declarations**. They declare to the compiler the function name, the return type, and the parameter list only. We saw this earlier as the function signature. Elsewhere, the function definition must exist not only with the same function name, return type, and parameter list, but also to define the function block. In other words, the function signature in a function's declaration must match the function's definition as well as the function when it is called. When function declarations differ from the function definitions, a compiler error occurs. This is a frequent cause of frustration.

Function declarations are also called **function prototypes**. In many ways, using the term function prototypes is less confusing than using the term function declarations; however, using either phrase is fine. We prefer to use function prototypes since that term is less similar to a function definition and so causes less confusion. In the hello7.c program, function prototypes are specified at the beginning of the program, as follows:

```c
#include <stdio.h>

// function prototypes
void   printGreeting(    char* aGreeting , char* aName );
void   printAGreeting(   char* greeting );
void   printAnAddressee( char* aName );
void   printAComma( void );
void   printANewLine();

int main()   {
  printGreeting( "Hi" , "Bub" );
  return 0;
}

void printGreeting( char* aGreeting , char* aName )   {
  printAGreeting( aGreeting );
  printAComma();
  printAnAddressee( aName );
  printANewLine();
}

void printAGreeting( char* greeting )   {
  printf( "%s" , greeting );
}

void printAnAddressee( char* aName )   {
  printf( "%s" );
}
```

```
void printAComma( void )   {
 printf( ", " );
}

void printANewLine()   {
 printf( "\n" );
}
```

In `hello7.c`, we have rearranged the order of the function definitions. In this order, functions are defined in the order that they are called. An ordering such as this is sometimes called **top-down implementation** since the functions that are called first also appear first in the program file. `main()` is called first, so that function definition is at the top. Those that are called later appear later in the file. `printANewLine()` is called last and so shows up as the last function defined in the source file. This approach more closely matches the process of starting with a whole problem and breaking it down into smaller parts. Our previous programs are ordered in a **bottom-up implementation** where we start reading the code from the bottom, as it were. In those programs, `main()` appeared as the last function defined in the source file. It does not matter if you take a top-down or bottom-up approach.

In order for the compiler to be able to process functions in a top-down manner, function prototypes are required. Note that while any function prototype must appear before the function is called, the order they appear in is unimportant.

Before you add the function prototypes, you may want to copy `hello6.c` to `hello7.c` and rearrange the functions instead of typing in the program again. However, either method is fine. Try to compile the program. You may notice that you get the same kind of errors as when we removed the `#include <stdio.h>` line.

Note that the order of execution has not changed. Even though the order of the functions in `hello7.c` has changed in the source file, at execution time each function is called in the same order as in `hello6.c` and the graph of the order of execution, given in the previous section, is also the same.

Once the functions are in the preceding order and `main()` is the first function, add the function prototypes, then compile, run, and verify that the output of `hello7.c` is identical to that of `hello6.c`.

It is good practice to put all the function prototypes together at the beginning of the file. This is not a requirement, however.

Function prototypes do not have to appear in the same order as the function definitions themselves. However, to do so—while tedious—also makes it somewhat easier to find function definitions (`function_C()` is defined after `function_B()` and before `function_D()` and `function_E()`, for instance), especially when there are many function definitions. We can then use the order of the function prototypes as a kind of index of where to find the function definition in our source file.

You can now write programs consisting of the `main()` function and zero or more functions you define. The function definitions can appear in any order and can be called from anywhere within the program.

Summary

In this chapter, we began with a very simple C program and explored C statements. We expanded and changed our program through the use of functions. We saw how to define functions, call them, and declare function prototypes. Lastly, we saw how we can structure our programs using a top-down or bottom-up approach when implementing our program.

Thinking about solving a problem in terms of breaking it down into smaller pieces and solving each of them via functions is an essential skill to be able to solve complex problems in any programming language.

As we explore the remainder of the C syntax, we will demonstrate each feature through functions and further explore how we can change functions to make our programs either more appropriate to our problem or to make it easier to understand how the problem is being solved.

In the next chapter, we will begin to develop an understanding of data types. The data type determines how to interpret a value and what kind of manipulation can be done to that value.

3
Working with Basic Data Types

Everything in a computer is a sequence of binary digits. C's intrinsic data types enable the compiler to tell the computer how to interpret binary sequences of data.

A binary sequence plus a data type results in a meaningful value. The data type not only leads to a meaningful value but it also helps determine what kind of operations on that value make sense. Operations involve manipulating values as well as converting or casting a value from one data type to a related data type.

Once we have explored C's intrinsic data types in this chapter, we can then use them as building blocks for more complex data representations. This chapter, then, is the basis for the more complex data representations we will encounter in `Chapter 8`, *Creating and Using Enumerations*, through `Chapter 16`, *Creating and Using More Complex Structures*.

The following topics will be covered in this chapter:

- Understanding bytes and chunks of data
- Working with whole numbers
- Working with numbers with decimal places
- Using single characters
- Understanding false (or zero) versus true (or anything not exactly zero)
- Understanding how types are implemented on your computer with `sizeof()`
- Understanding casting
- Discovering the minimum and maximum values for each type on your computer

Technical requirements

For the rest of this book, unless otherwise noted, you will continue to use your computer with the following:

- The plain text editor of your choice
- A console, Terminal, or command-line window (depending on your OS)
- The compiler, either GCC or Clang, for your particular OS

For the sake of consistency, it is best if you use the same computer and programming tools. By doing so, you can focus more closely on the details of C on your computer.

The source code for this chapter can be found at `https://github.com/PacktPublishing/Learn-C-Programming`.

Understanding data types

Everything in a computer is a sequence of *binary digits* (or *bits*). A single bit is either off (0) or on (1). Eight bits are strung together to form a *byte*. A byte is the basic data unit. Bytes are treated singly, as pairs called **16-bit words**, as quadruples to form 32-bit words, and as octets to form 64-bit words. These combinations of sizes of bytes are used in the following ways:

- Instructions for the CPU
- Addresses for the locations of all things in the computer
- Data values

The compiler generates binary instructions from our C statements; hence, we don't need to deal with the instructions since we are writing proper C syntax.

We also interact with various parts of the computer via the address of that part. Typically, we don't do this directly. For instance, we've seen how `printf()` knows how to fetch the data from a function call we make and then move it to the part of the computer that spills it out to the console. We are not, nor should we be, concerned with these addresses since from computer to computer and from version to version of our operating system, they may change.

We will deal with the addresses of some, but not all, things in the computer in `Chapter 13`, *Using Pointers*. For the most part, again, the compiler handles these issues for us.

Both instructions and addresses deal with data. Instructions manipulate data and move it around. Addresses are required for the instructions to be able to fetch the data and also to store the data. In between fetching and storing, instructions manipulate it.

Before we get to manipulating data, we need to understand how data is represented and the various considerations for each type of data.

Here is the basic problem. We have a pattern of black and white bits; what does it mean?

To illustrate how a pattern alone may not provide enough information for proper interpretation, let's consider the following sequence. What does **13** mean in this context?

OK, I know what you are thinking. But wait! Look again. Now, what does **13** mean in this context?

Combining both aspects, we can now see the full spectrum of the problem:

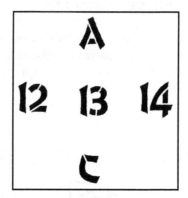

The central picture is just a two-dimensional pattern of black and white pixels. In one context, the central picture makes sense seen as the number 13; in another context, the central picture makes the most sense seen as the letter B. We can only resolve the ambiguity of the pixel pattern from its context with other pixel patterns. How we interpret the patterns of black and white pixels is entirely dependent upon the context in which we view them.

This is very much like the byte sequences the compiler generates, which the CPU processes. Internally, commands, addresses, and data in the computer are nothing more than sequences of 1s and 0s of various sizes. How the computer interprets the patterns of 1s and 0s is entirely dependent upon the context given to them by the computer language and the programmer.

We, as programmers, must provide the guidelines to the compiler, consequently to the CPU, on how to interpret the sequence. We do this in C by explicitly assigning a data type to the data we want to manipulate.

C is a strongly typed language. That is, every value must have a type associated with it. It should be noted that some languages infer the type of a piece of data by how it is used. They will also make assumptions about how to convert one data type into another. These are called **loosely typed languages**. C also does conversions from one type to another, but the rules are fairly specific compared to other programming languages.

In C, as in most programming languages, there are five basic and intrinsic data types. Intrinsic means these types and all operations on them are built into the language.

Five basic types are as follows:

- **Whole numbers**: They can represent a positive-only range of values or a range that includes both positive and negative values.
- **Numbers with fractions**, or **decimal numbers**: These are all the numbers between whole numbers, such as ½, ¾, 0.79, 1.125, and 3.14159 – an approximate value for π, or even 3.141592653589793238462643 – an even more precise but still approximate value for π. Decimal numbers can always include negative values.
- **Characters**: These are the basis of C strings. Some languages have a separate string type. In C, strings are a special case of arrays of characters—not a data type but a special arrangement of contiguous character values.
- **Boolean values**: These can be of any size depending on the preference of the compiler and the machine's preferred whole number size.
- **Addresses**: These are the location of bytes in a computer's memory. C provides for direct addresses of values in memory. Many languages do not allow direct addressing.

Within each of these five types, there are different sizes of types to represent different ranges of values. C has very specific rules about how to convert a given data type into another. Some are valid, others make no sense. We will explore these in `Chapter 4`, *Using Variables and Assignment*.

For now, we need to understand the basic types and the different sizes of values they might represent.

Bytes and chunks of data

The smallest data value in C is a bit. However, bit operations tend to be very expensive and not all that common for most computer problems. We will not go into bit operations in this book. If you find you need to delve deeper into bit operations in C, please check out the annotated bibliography in the appendix for texts that treat this subject more fully.

The basic data value in C is a byte or a sequence of 8 bits. The set of values a byte can represent is 256, or 2^8 values. These values have a range of 0 to 255, or 2^8-1. 0 is a value that must be represented in the set of 256 values; we can't leave that value out. A byte can either represent a positive integer in the range of 0-255, or 2^8-1, or a negative integer in the range of -128-127. In either case, there are only 256 unique combinations of 1s and 0s.

While most humans don't ordinarily count this high, for a computer, this is a very narrow range of values. A byte is the smallest of the chunks of data since each byte in memory can be addressed directly. A byte is also commonly used for alphanumeric characters (like you are now reading) but is not large enough for Unicode characters. ASCII characters and Unicode characters will be explained in great detail in `Chapter 15`, *Working with Strings*.

Chunks, or bytes, increase in multiples of 2 from 1 byte, 2 bytes, 4 bytes, 8 bytes, and 16 bytes. The following table shows how these may be used:

# of bytes	# of bits	Highest integer value	Binary form	Typical uses
1	8	255	$(2^8)-1$	ASCII character
2	16	65,535	$(2^{16})-1$	Integer, small real number, Unicode character, small address space
4	32	4,294,967,295 or over 4.2×10^9	$(2^{32})-1$	Integer, real number, Unicode character, medium address space
8	64	18,446,744,073,709,551,615 or over 1.8×10^{19}	$(2^{64})-1$	Very large integer, large real number, large address space
16	128	over 3.40×10^{38}	$(2^{128})-1$	Very large real number, very large address space

In the history of computing, there have been various byte ranges for basic computation. The very earliest and simplest CPUs used 1-byte integers. These very rapidly developed into 16-bit computers whose address space and largest integer value could be expressed in 2 bytes. As the range of integers increased from 2 to 4 to 8, so too did the range of possible memory addresses and the ranges of floating-point numbers.

As the problems that were addressed by computers further expanded, computers themselves expanded. This resulted in more powerful computers with a 4-byte address range and 4-byte integer values. These machines were prevalent from the 1990s through to the early part of the 21st century.

Today, most desktop computers are 64-bit computing devices that can address incredibly large amounts of memory and model problems that can account for all the atoms in the universe! For problems that require the processing of values that are 128 bytes and higher, very specialized computers have been developed.

You will seldom, if ever, need to consider those astronomically large numbers but they are necessary to solve mind-bendingly large and complex problems. Nonetheless, what you can do with very small chunks and relatively small ranges of values, you can also do with large ones. It is more important for us to learn how different types are represented and used, regardless of their size.

Notice in the preceding table the correlation between the number of bits in a chunk and the exponent in the binary form. Also notice that the number of bytes is a power of 2: 2^0, 2^1, 2^2, 2^3, 2^4. There are no 3-byte, 5-byte, or 7-byte chunks. They are just not needed.

You can also see from the table that the typical use of a chunk is directly related to its size. In C, the machine's preferred whole number size is typically the same size as an address. That is, the machine's natural integer size is the count of the largest number of bytes that the machine can address. This is not a hard rule, but it is a common guideline.

Byte allocations and ranges may vary from machine to machine. Embedded computers, tablets, and phones will likely have different sizes for each type than desktop computers or even supercomputers. We'll create the `sizes_ranges.c` program later in this chapter to confirm and verify the sizes and ranges of integers on your machine. This program will be handy to run whenever you are presented with a new system on which to develop C programs.

Representing whole numbers

The basic whole number type is an integer or just `int`. Integers can either be positive only, called **unsigned**, or they can be negative and positive, called **signed**. As you might expect, the natural use for integers is to count things. You must specify `unsigned` if you know you will not need negative values.

To be explicit, the default type is `unsigned int`, where the keyword `unsigned` is optional.

An unsigned integer has its lowest value of 0 and its highest value when all bits are set to 1. For instance, a single byte value has a possible 256 values but their range is 0 to 255. This is sometimes called the **one-off problem** where the starting value for counting is 0 and not 1, as we were taught when we first learned to count. It is a problem because it takes some time for new programmers to adjust their thinking. Until you are comfortable thinking in this way, the one-off problem will be a common source of confusion and possibly the cause of bugs in your code. We will revisit the need for this kind of thinking when we explore loops (`Chapter 7`, *Exploring Loops and Iteration*) and when we work with arrays (`Chapter 11`, *Working with Arrays*, and `Chapter 12`, *Working with Multi-Dimensional Arrays*) and strings (`Chapter 15`, *Working with Strings*).

Representing positive and negative whole numbers

When negative numbers are needed, that is, whole numbers smaller than 0, we specify them with the `signed` keyword. So, a signed integer would be specified as `signed int`. The natural use for signed integers is when we want to express a direction relative to zero, either larger or smaller. By default, and without any extra specifiers, integers are signed.

A signed integer uses one of the bits to indicate whether the remaining bits represent a positive or negative number. Typically, this is the *most significant bit*; the *least significant bit* is that which represents the value 1. As with positive whole numbers, a signed integer has the same number of values, but the range is shifted so that half of the values are below 0, or, algebraically speaking, to the left of 0. For instance, a single signed byte has 256 possible values but their range is -128 to 127. Remember to count 0 as one of the possible values. Hence the apparent asymmetric range of values (there's that pesky *one-off problem*, again).

Specifying different sizes of integers

Integers can be specified to have various sizes for their data chunk. The smallest chunk is a single byte. This is called a `char`. It is so named for historical reasons. Before Unicode came along, the full set of English characters, uppercase, lowercase, numbers, punctuation, and certain special characters, could be represented with 256 values. In some languages, a byte is actually called a **byte**; unfortunately, not in C.

C99 added more integer types that specify the minimum width of integer values. The basic set of these are of the `int<n>_t` or `uint<n>_t` forms, where `<n>` is either 8, 16, 32, or 64. The values of these types are exactly that number of bits. Such type specifications allow much greater predictability when porting a program from one computer system to a different one with possibly a different CPU and operating system. There are additional integer types to aid portability not listed here:

Type	# of Bytes	Equivalent Types
char	1	signed char
int8_t	1	
unsigned char	1	
uint8_t	1	
short	2	signed short, short int, signed short int

int16_t	2	
uint16_t	2	
int	4 (?)	signed, signed int
unsigned	4 (?)	unsigned int
long	4 (?)	signed long, long int, signed long int
unsigned long	4 (?)	unsigned long int
int32_t	4	
uint32_t	4	
long long	8 (?)	signed long long, signed long long int
int64_t	8	
unsigned long long	8 (?)	unsigned long long int
uint64_t	8	

Notes:

- When `signed` or `unsigned` is specified, the type is guaranteed to be of the specified positive/negative or positive only ranges. When not specified, the default may be signed.
- `short` is guaranteed to be at least 2 bytes but may be longer depending upon the machine.
- `int`, `unsigned`, `long`, and `unsigned long` are guaranteed to be at least 4 bytes but may be longer depending on the machine.
- `long long` and `unsigned long long` are guaranteed to be at least 8 bytes but may be longer depending on the machine.

Do not be too concerned with all of these variations at first. For the most part, you can safely use `int` until you begin developing programs on a wider variety of hardware where portability is a bigger concern.

While `int` types represent whole numbers, this is a relatively small set of numbers unless we can also represent the numbers between whole numbers—numbers with fractions or decimal numbers.

Representing numbers with decimals

Not everything in the world is a whole number. For that, we have numbers with fractions or decimal numbers. Decimal numbers are used most naturally for measuring things.

A real number is of the following form:

$$significand \times 10^{exponent}$$

Here, both the significand and the exponent are signed integers. The size of each depends upon the number of bytes for a given real number type. There are no unsigned components. This provides a very large range of numbers, from positive to negative as well as very small fractional values:

Type	# of Bytes
float	4
double	8
long double	16

Typically, when real numbers are used, either very precise values are desired or the calculations tend to have incredibly large ranges.

For completeness, decimal numbers are just one part of the set of real numbers. Real numbers include all rational numbers, irrational numbers, transcendental numbers, such as π, and integers. Real numbers exist on a number line. These are contrasted with imaginary numbers, sometimes called **complex numbers**. These have an imaginary component, which is $-1^{1/2}$, the square root of -1.

Another use for values is to represent alphabetical characters.

Representing single characters

To specify a single character, use either `char` or `unsigned char`. C was developed in the time before Unicode. The character set they decided upon using was ASCII (short for **American Standard Code for Information Interchange**). All the necessary characters for printing control, device control, and printable characters and punctuation could be represented in 7 bits.

One reason ASCII was chosen was because of its somewhat logical ordering of uppercase and lowercase letters. An uppercase A and lowercase a are different by only 1 bit. This makes it relatively easy to convert from uppercase to lowercase and vice versa. There is an ASCII table provided for your reference in the Appendix; we also develop a program to print a complete ASCII table in Chapter 15, *Working with Strings*.

To summarize ASCII's organization, refer to the following table:

Range	Usage
0..31	Control characters for printing and device communication
32..63	Punctuation and numbers
64..95	Uppercase alphabet plus miscellaneous punctuation
96..127	Lowercase alphabet plus miscellaneous punctuation
128..255	Not used

As Unicode was developed and has become standardized, it used 2-byte or 4-byte encodings for the many character sets of the world's languages. 7-bit ASCII codes were incorporated into the lowest 7 bits for backward compatibility with original ASCII. However, Unicode is not implemented uniformly across all operating systems.

Representing Boolean true/false

A Boolean value is one that evaluates to true or false. On some systems, YES and yes are equivalent to true while NO and no are equivalent to false. For, instance, *Is today Wednesday?* evaluates to true only 1 out of 7 days. The other 6 days, it evaluates to false.

Before C99, there was no explicit type for Boolean. A value of any type that is 0 (exactly zero) is considered as also evaluating to a Boolean false. Any other value than exactly 0 (a bit pattern of only zeros) will evaluate to a Boolean value of true. Real numbers rarely, if ever, evaluate exactly to 0, especially after any kind of operation on them. These data types would therefore almost always evaluate to true and so would be poor choices as a Boolean substitute.

Since C99, a _Bool type has been available, which, when evaluated, will always evaluate to only 0 or 1. When we include the stdbool.h file, we are able to use the bool type as well; this is a bit cleaner than using the cumbersome _Bool type.

As a general rule, it is always more reliable to test for zero-ness, or false, than to rely on the compiler's implementation for interpreting Boolean true values from other types.

Understanding the sizes of data types

As we discussed earlier, the number of bytes that a type uses is directly related to the range of values it can hold. Up to this point, this has all been necessarily theoretical. Let's now write a program to demonstrate what we've been exploring.

The sizeof() operator

The sizeof() operation is a built-in function that takes as its parameter a C data type and returns the number of bytes for that data type. Let's write a program to see how this works.

In the first part, we'll set up the necessary include files, declare function prototypes, and create our main() function. Even though we show this program in two parts, it is really just a single file. The following program, sizes_ranges1.c, shows the first part of our program:

```
#include <stdio.h>
#include <stdint.h>
#include <stdbool.h>

  // function prototypes
void printSizes( void );

int main( void )
{
  printSizes();
}
```

The header file, stdio.h, is included, as are two new header files—stdint.h and stdbool.h. Recall that stdio.h declares, amongst other things, the function prototype for printf(). stdint.h declares the sizes in bytes of each of the intrinsic data types. stdbool.h defines the bool data type and the values true and false. These are part of the C Standard Library. We will encounter several other C Standard Library files but not all of them. All of them are listed with a brief description of their purpose in the Appendix. We will learn a great deal more about header files in Chapter 24, *Working with Multi-File Programs*.

As you can see, we call a function that has been declared, or prototyped, but has not yet been defined. Let's define it in the next section of the program:

```c
// function to print the # of bytes for each of C11's data types
//
void printSizes( void )
{
  printf( "Size of C data types\n\n" );
  printf( "Type                Bytes\n\n" );
  printf( "char                %lu\n" , sizeof( char ) );
  printf( "int8_t              %lu\n" , sizeof( int8_t ) );
  printf( "unsigned char       %lu\n" , sizeof( unsigned char ) );
  printf( "uint8_t             %lu\n" , sizeof( uint8_t ) );
  printf( "short               %lu\n" , sizeof( short ) );
  printf( "int16_t             %lu\n" , sizeof( int16_t ) );
  printf( "uint16t             %lu\n" , sizeof( uint16_t ) );
  printf( "int                 %lu\n" , sizeof( int ) );
  printf( "unsigned            %lu\n" , sizeof( unsigned ) );
  printf( "long                %lu\n" , sizeof( long ) );
  printf( "unsigned long       %lu\n" , sizeof( unsigned long ) );
  printf( "int32_t             %lu\n" , sizeof( int32_t ) );
  printf( "uint32_t            %lu\n" , sizeof( uint32_t ) );
  printf( "long long           %lu\n" , sizeof( long long ) );
  printf( "int64_t             %lu\n" , sizeof( int64_t ) );
  printf( "unsigned long long %lu\n" , sizeof( unsigned long long ) );
  printf( "uint64_t            %lu\n" , sizeof( uint64_t ) );
  printf( "\n" );
  printf( "float               %lu\n" , sizeof( float ) );
  printf( "double              %lu\n" , sizeof( double ) );
  printf( "long double         %lu\n" , sizeof( long double ) );
  printf( "\n" );
  printf( "bool                %lu\n" , sizeof( bool ) );
  printf( "\n" );
}
```

In this program, we need to include the header file, `<stdint.h>`, which defines the fixed-width integer types. If you omit this `include`, you'll get a few errors. Try that—comment out that `include` line and see what happens.

To get the new `bool` definition, we also have to include `<stdbool.h>`. What happens if you omit that file?

The return type of `sizeof()` on my system is `unsigned long`. Therefore, we use the format specifier `%lu` to properly print out a value of that type.

On my system, I get the following output:

```
> cc sizes_ranges1.c -Wall -Werror
> a.out
Size of C data types

Type                      Bytes

char                      1
int8_t                    1
unsigned char             1
uint8_t                   1
short                     2
int16_t                   2
uint16t                   2
int                       4
unsigned                  4
long                      8
unsigned long             8
int32_t                   4
uint32_t                  4
long long                 8
int64_t                   8
unsigned long long        8
uint64_t                  8

float                     4
double                    8
long double               16

bool                      1
_Bool                     1

>
```

On my 64-bit operating system, a pointer is 8 bytes (64 bits). So too, then, are `long` and `unsigned long`.

How do the values reported by your system differ from these?

Ranges of values

Let's extend this program to provide the ranges for each data type. While we could compute these values ourselves, they are defined in two header files—`limits.h` for integer limits and `float.h` for real number limits. To implement this, we add another function prototype, add a call to that function from within `main()`, and then define the function to print out the ranges. In the `printRanges()` function, we use the fixed-width types to avoid variations from system to system.

Let's add another function. In the following code, the additional `include` directives and function prototype are highlighted:

```
#include <stdio.h>
#include <stdint.h>
#include <stdbool.h>
#include <limits.h>
#include <float.h>

 // function prototypes
void printSizes( void );
void printRanges( void );

int main( void )  {
  printSizes();
  printRanges();
}
```

Now, having `printRanges()` prototypes, let's add its definition. The `printSizes()` function is unchanged:

```
void printRanges( void )  {
  printf( "Ranges for integer data types in C\n\n" );
  printf( "int8_t %20d %20d\n" , SCHAR_MIN , SCHAR_MAX );
  printf( "int16_t %20d %20d\n" , SHRT_MIN , SHRT_MAX );
  printf( "int32_t %20d %20d\n" , INT_MIN , INT_MAX );
  printf( "int64_t %20lld %20lld\n" , LLONG_MIN , LLONG_MAX );
  printf( "uint8_t %20d %20d\n" , 0 , UCHAR_MAX );
  printf( "uint16_t %20d %20d\n" , 0 , USHRT_MAX );
  printf( "uint32_t %20d %20u\n" , 0 , UINT_MAX );
  printf( "uint64_t %20d %20llu\n" , 0 , ULLONG_MAX );
  printf( "\n" );
  printf( "Ranges for real number data types in C\n\n" );
  printf( "float %14.7g %14.7g\n" , FLT_MIN , FLT_MAX );
  printf( "double %14.7g %14.7g\n" , DBL_MIN , DBL_MAX );
  printf( "long double %14.7Lg %14.7Lg\n" , LDBL_MIN , LDBL_MAX );
  printf( "\n" );
}
```

Some of the numbers that appear after % in the format specifier string may appear mysterious. These will be explained in exhaustive detail in Chapter 19, *Exploring Formatted Output*. The result of the added function should look like this, in addition to what we had before:

```
Ranges for integer data types in C

int8_t                    -128                        127
int16_t                 -32768                      32767
int32_t            -2147483648                 2147483647
int64_t  -9223372036854775808   9223372036854775807
uint8_t                      0                        255
uint16_t                     0                      65535
uint32_t                     0                 4294967295
uint64_t                     0   18446744073709551615

Ranges for real number data types in C

flaot          1.175494e-38     3.402823e+38
double         2.225074e-308    1.797693e+308
long double    3.362103e-4932   1.189731e+4932

>
```

How do the values from your system compare?

Summary

Again, whew!

There were a lot of details about data types, chunk sizes, and value ranges. The key idea from this chapter is to remember that there are only really four data types—integer, real number, character, and boolean. The fifth type, pointers, is really just a special case of integers.

In the next chapter, we will explore how to use the different types of values when we create and assign values.

4

Using Variables and Assignment

Programs manipulate data values. Whether a program performs a single calculation—such as, say, converting a temperature value from Fahrenheit to Celsius—reads data only to display it, or performs much more complex calculations and interactions, the values a program manipulates must be both accessible and assignable. Accessible means that a value must reside somewhere in computer memory and should be retrievable. Assignable means a value or the result of a calculation must be stored somewhere in computer memory to be later retrieved. Each value has a data type and a named location where it is stored. These can either be variables or constants.

Variables, or non-constant variables, hold values that are the result of calculations or data that will change as the program executes. **Constant variables** are variables that don't change their value once they are given a value. Variables, whether constant or variable, receive their values via **assignment**. Assignment is a simple expression. **Literal values**, or **literals**, are values encoded in the program and can never change.

The following topics will be covered in this chapter:

- Using types to determine the interpretation of values
- Learning some of the pitfalls of the `#define` directive and why constants are preferred
- Writing a program to set various constants in different ways
- Writing a program to use variables and constants (not just set them)
- Understanding four types of assignment

Technical requirements

Continue to use your computer with the following:

- A plaintext editor of your choice
- A console, terminal, or command-line window (depending on your OS)
- A compiler—either GCC or `clang`—for your particular OS

The source code for this chapter can be found at `https://github.com/PacktPublishing/Learn-C-Programming`.

Understanding types and values

Every value in a computer program has an associated type. The type of a value can be inferred by how it is expressed in the program code and how it is coded. Alternatively, the type of a value can be explicitly determined by you, the programmer. A value in C always has a type. So, a value can have either an inferred or *implicit* type or it can have an *explicit* type.

There are also inferred types from literal values. A literal value is a sequence of digits in the program code whose value is implicitly determined by the compiler at compile time, which is when the program is compiled. The value of a literal can never change; it is baked into the program code.

When a value is given an explicit type, the compiler assigns a type to that value. A value of one type can also be converted into another type, either implicitly by how it is used or explicitly with **typecasting**.

So, we should always think of the value/type pair. The type determines not only how the value is interpreted but also what possible valid ranges of values it can have.

If we have a value, then we should always ask *what is its type?* If we have a type, then we should always ask *what values can it have?* and *what value is it now?* This kind of thinking will be critical when we look at looping and arrays.

Introducing variables

A **variable** is a location in memory that holds a value of a specified type that can vary over the life of the variable, identified by its name. When the variable is defined with both a type and an identifier, its life begins. It can hold the same value throughout its life or it can be modified or overwritten with a new value of that type. The variable's life ends—that is, the memory it identifies is deallocated—when the block in which it was declared ends. We'll talk more about variable lifetimes in Chapter 25, *Understanding Scope*.

So, a variable is a memory location with an *identifier* (name) associated with a type that contains a value. The following three components are essential:

- A unique identifier or name
- A type
- A value

The variable should always have some known starting value, even if it is 0; this is called **initialization**. If we don't give the variable an initial value, we can never be sure what value it might have from one run to the next. When function blocks and programs are deallocated, the values occupied by their memory are left behind. It is, therefore, up to us to ensure that we initialize the memory we use for known good values.

A variable is initialized and overwritten by means of an assignment operation, where a value is assigned to the memory location identified by the variable. Once a constant variable is given a value, that value can never change.

Before we explore values and assignment, we need to understand explicit typing when we create and declare variables.

Naming variables

Every variable has an identifier or a name. A variable name is an identifier; function names are identifiers. We will encounter other kinds of identifiers that are used in many different contexts.

An **identifier**, or name, in C is a sequence of capital letters (`A..Z`) and small letters (`a..z`), digits (`0..9`), and the underscore (`_`) character. An identifier may not begin with a digit. Upper and lowercase letters are different from each other, so `achar`, `aChar`, `AChar`, and `ACHAR` would identify different variables. An identifier may not have the same spelling as a C keyword. A list of C keywords can be found in the *Appendix* section of this book.

As with function identifiers, relying on the casing of letters to differentiate variables is not good programming practice. The most essential guideline is that variable names should closely match the kinds of values they hold. Name variables so that their names clearly reflect their purpose—for example, `inch`, `foot`, `yard`, and `mile`.

There are many conventions for naming variables. Two common methods to make variable names descriptive yet easy to read are camel-case and underscore-separated, also known as **snake-case**. Camel-case names have the beginning characters of words within the name capitalized. In underscore-separated names, _ is used between words:

- **All-lowercase**: `inchesperminute`, `feetpersecond`, and `milesperhour`
- **Camel-case**: `inchesPerMinute`, `feetPerSecond`, and `milesPerHour`
- **Snake-case** (or **underscore-separated**): `inches_per_minute`, `feet_per_second`, and `miles_per_hour`

As you can see, all-lowercase names are somewhat difficult to read. However, these are not nearly as difficult to read as all-uppercase names. The other two ways are quite a bit easier to read. Therefore, we prefer to use either of the last two. We will use camel-case identifiers throughout this book.

If you choose one identifier naming convention, stick to it throughout your program. Do not mix different identifier naming schemes as this makes remembering the exact name of a thing, function identifiers, and other identifiers much more difficult and error-prone.

We can now explore explicit types of variables.

Introducing explicit types of variables

The format of a variable declaration is `type identifier;` or `type identifier1, identifiers, ... ;`.

Here, `type` is one of the data types that we encountered earlier and `identifier` is the name of the variable we are declaring. In the first example, a single variable is declared. In the second form, multiple variables are declared, each having the same type, separated by commas. Note that each one is a C statement because it concludes with `;`. Consider the following variable declarations:

```
#include <stdbool.h>    /* So we can use: bool, true, false */

int       aNumber;
long      aBigNumber;
long long aReallyBigNumber;
float     inches;
float     feed;
float     yards;
double    length, width, height;
bool      isItRaining;
```

In each of these declarations, we use spacing to make the type and name of each variable easier to read. Unfortunately, these declarations are not necessarily the best we could use. The values of the variables do not have *any* value yet. However, they are not yet initialized.

Using explicit typing with initialization

A better format for a variable declaration is one where the variable is *initialized* or given a starting value when it is declared, such as `type   identifier1 = value1;`, `type identifier2 = value2;`, or

`type identifier1 = value1 , identifier2 = value2 , ... ;`.

Here, `value` is a literal constant or an already-declared variable. Note that in the second form of variable declaration, each variable must have its own initializing value. These are often accidentally omitted. Therefore, the first form is preferred. Consider the following declarations with initialization:

```
#include <stdbool.h>    /* So we can use: bool, true, false */

int       aNumber           = 10;
long      aBigNumber        = 3211145;
long long aReallyBigNumber  = 425632238789;
```

```
float       inches          = 33.0;
float       feet            = 2.5;
float       yards           = 1780;
double      length = 1 , width = 2 , height = 10;
bool        isItRaining     = false;

int myCounter = 0;
int aDifferentCounter = myCounter;
```

As before, arbitrary spacing is used to vertically align variable names as well as to align their initial values. This is only done for readability. This sort of practice is not required but is generally considered good practice.

Initialization is a form of assignment; we are assigning a starting value to each variable. This is indicated by the = sign.

Note that because the type of the variable is explicit in its declaration, the assigned values—in this case, literal constants—are converted values of that type. So, while the following is correct, it may mislead an already-tired or overworked programmer reading it:

```
double length = 1 , width = 2 , height = 10;
```

Make note here of how a comma (,) is used to separate variable identifiers and the initialization. This declaration is still a single statement since it ends with a semi-colon (;). We will explore this further in Chapter 5, *Exploring Operators and Expressions*.

It is almost always better, although not required, to be explicit. A slightly better version of the preceding would be as follows:

```
double length = 1.0;
double width  = 2.0;
double height = 10.0;
```

Each type, identifier, and initial value is on a single line.

Having examined variables whose values can change, we can now turn our attention to constant variables (yes, that sounds odd to me, as well) and literal constants.

Exploring constants

We use variables to hold values that are computed or can change over their lifetime, such as counters. However, we often have values that we don't ever want to change during their lifetime. These are constants and can be defined in a number of ways for different uses.

Literal constants

Consider the following literal character sequences:

```
      65
      'A'
      8.0
 131072.0
```

Each of these has an internal byte stream of `0000 0000 0100 0001`. However, because of the punctuation surrounding these values, the compiler can infer what types they have from their context:

```
      65 --> int
     'A' --> unsigned char
     8.0 --> float
131072.0 --> double
```

These values are literally typed into our source code and their types are determined by the way in which they are written, or precisely by how punctuation around them specifies the context for their data type.

The internal value for each is constant; it is that same bit pattern. The literal `65` value will always be interpreted as an integer with that value. The literal `'A'` value will always be interpreted as a single character. The literal `8.0` value *may* be interpreted as a float; if it is interpreted as a double, it will have a slightly different internal bit pattern. The literal `131072.0` value also may be interpreted as a float or a double. When it is interpreted as a double, it will also have the same bit pattern as the others.

Here are some examples to expand on each of these explanations:

- **Integer constants**: `65, 1024, -17 , 163758 , 0` , and `-1`
- **Double constants**: `3.5, -0.7 , 1748.3753, 0.0, -0.0000007, 15e4`, and `-58.1e-4`
- **Character constants**: `'A', 'a', '6', '0', '>', '.'`, and `'\n'`

Notice that while the `0` value is present in each case, because they are all typed differently, they will have different internal bitstreams. Integer `0` and double `0.0` are patterns of all zeros. However, the `'0'` character will have a different value, which we will see in `Chapter 15`, *Working with Strings*.

You might also have noticed the strange notation for the 15e4 and -58.1e-4 doubles. These values are expressed in scientific notation, where the first value evaluates to 15×10^4, or 150,000, and the second evaluates to -58.1×10^{-4}, or -0.000581. This is a shorthand notation for values that are either too large or too small to easily express with common decimal notation.

When a constant integer value is too large to fit into the valid ranges of the default type, the type is altered to hold the larger value. Therefore, an int value may become long int or long long int, depending on the value given and the machine architecture. This is implicit typecasting. The compiler does not want to lose any part of a value by stuffing it into a type with a smaller range, so it picks a type that will fit the value.

There is the same issue regarding implicit conversion of floats and doubles—when a literal value is interpreted, the compiler will pick the most appropriate data type depending on both the value and how that literal value is used.

The preceding literal constants are most common and are evaluated using the base-10 or decimal numbering system. In base-10, there are 10 symbols, 0 through 9, to represent 10 values. Every value in a base-10 number system can be represented as a power of 10. The value 2,573 is really 2,000 + 500 + 70 + 3, or, using exponents of base-10, it is $2*10^3 + 5*10^2 + 7*10^1 + 3*10^0$.

Sometimes, we may want to express a constant value in base-8, or *octal*, or base-16, or *hexadecimal*. In C, octal constants begin with the digit 0 and subsequent digits must be in the range of valid octal digits, 0 through 7. Hexadecimal constants begin with ox or 0X (0 followed by the letter x) and the following characters may be the valid hexadecimal digits, 0 through 9 and a through f or A through F.

Without going into greater detail about octal and hexadecimal, here are some examples:

- **Octal integers**: 07, 011, and 036104
- **Unsigned octal**: 07u, 011u, and 036104u
- **Long octal**: 07L, 011L, and 036104L
- **Hexadecimal integers**: 0x4, 0Xaf, 0x106a2, and ox7Ca6d
- **Unsigned hexadecimal**: 0x4u, 0Xafu, 0x106a2u, and ox7Ca6du
- **Long hexadecimal**: 0x4L, 0XafL, 0x106a2L, and ox7Ca6dL

Just remember that base-10, base-8, and base-16 are just different ways to represent values.

Additionally, if you want to guarantee that a decimal number will be a smaller float type than a double, you can follow it with f or F. If you want it to be a much larger long-double, you can follow it with l or L. L is preferred over using l so as not to confuse the number 1 with the letter l. Here are some examples:

- **Float literals**: 0.5f, -12E5f, and 3.45e-5F
- **Double literals**: 0.5, -12E5, and 3.45e-5
- **Long-double literals**: 0.5L, -12E5fL, and 3.45e-5FL

Literal constants are interpreted by the compiler and embedded into our program.

We use these kinds of constants typically when we initialize our variables, as we saw in the previous section, or when we want to perform some known calculation on a variable, such as the following:

```
feet  = inches / 12.0;
yards = feet / 3.0;
```

In these calculations, both denominators are decimal numbers. Therefore, they determine the contexts of the resultant calculation. Regardless of what type inches is, the result will be a decimal number. Then, that result will be implicitly converted into whatever type feet is upon assignment. Likewise, the result of feet / 3.0 will be a decimal number (float or double); upon assignment, that result will be converted into the type of yards.

Defined values

Another way to define constants is to use the #define preprocessor directive. This takes the form of #define symbol text, where symbol is an identifier and text is a literal constant or a previously defined symbol. Symbol names are typically all in uppercase and underscores are used to distinguish them from variable names.

An example would be to define the number of inches in feet or the number of feet in a yard:

```
#define INCHES_PER_FOOT 12
#define FEET_PER_YARD    3

feet  = inches / INCHES_PER_FOOT;
yards = feet / FEET_PER_YARD;
```

When the preprocessing phase of compilation encounters a definition such as this, it carries out a textural substitution. There is no type associated with the symbol and there is no way to verify that the actual use of a symbol matches its intended use. For this reason, the use of these kinds of constants is discouraged. We only included them here for completeness since many older C programs may make extensive use of this mechanism.

Because #define enables textural substitution, there are many other ways it can be and is used. This feature is so powerful that it must be used with extreme caution, if it is used at all. Many of the original reasons for relying on the preprocessor are no longer valid. The proper place for exploration of the preprocessor would be in a much more advanced programming course.

Explicitly typed constants

C provides a safer means of declaring named constants, other than by using the preprocessor. This is done by adding the const keyword to a variable declaration. This sort of declaration must be of the const type identifier = value; form, where type, identifier, and value are the same as in our preceding variable declaration form—except here, the initializing value is not optional. The constant variable loses its ability to change after the statement is evaluated. If we don't give it a value when we declare it, we cannot do so later. Such a declaration without an initializing value is, therefore, useless.

When we declare a constant in this manner, it is named; it has a type and it has a value that does not change. So, our previous example becomes as follows:

```
const float kInchesPerFoot = 12.0;
const float kFeetPerYard   =  3.0;

feet  = inches / kInchesPerFoot;
yards = feet / kFeetPerYard;
```

This is considered safer because the constant's type is known and any incorrect use of this type or invalid conversion from this type to some other type will be flagged by the compiler.

It is an arbitrary convention to begin constant names with the letter k; it is not mandatory to do so. We could also have named these constants inchesPerFootConst and feetPerYardConst, or, simply, inchesPerFoot and feetPerYard. Any attempt to change their values would result in a compiler error.

Naming constant variables

C makes no distinction between a variable identifier and a constant identifier. However, it is often useful to know whether the identifier you are using is a constant.

As with functions and variables, there are several conventions commonly used for naming constants. The following conventions are relatively common to arbitrarily differentiate constants from variables:

- Prefix a constant name with `k` or `k_`—for example, `kInchesPerFoot` or `k_inches_per_foot`.
- Suffix a name with `const` or `_const`—for example, `inchesPerFootConst` or `inches_per_foot_const`.
- Use snake-case with all the capitals—for example, `THIS_IS_A_CONSTANT`. All-uppercase is quite unreadable. This is typically used for the `#define` symbols to show that they are not just a constant—for example, `INCHES_PER_FOOT`.
- None. C does not distinguish between constants—for example, `int inchesPerFoot` versus `const int inchesPerFoot`. It should be obvious that the number of inches per foot does not ever change. Therefore, there is no real need to distinguish its name as a constant.

As with other naming conventions, any convention for constants, if one exists, should be clearly defined and consistently used throughout a program or set of program files. I tend to use either the first or the last conventions in my programs.

Using types and assignment

So, we have variables to hold values of a specified type that we can retrieve and manipulate by their identifiers. What can we do with them? Essentially, believe it or not, we can just copy them from one place to another. Values in variables or constants can only be changed through assignment. When we use them, their value is copied as a part of the evaluation but the value remains unchanged. A variable's value can be used in many ways over its lifetime, but that value will not change except when a new value is copied over it. We will now explore the various ways that variables are copied:

- Explicit assignment using the = operator
- Function parameter assignment

- Function return assignment
- Implicit assignment (this will be covered when we look at expressions in the next chapter)

Let's look at the first three ways of copying the variables in the subsequent sections.

Using explicit assignment, the simplest statement

We have already seen explicit assignment used when we initialized variables and constants. After we have declared a variable, we can change it by using the = assignment operator. An assignment statement is of the form `identifier = value;`, where `identifier` is our already-declared variable and the value can be a constant, another variable, the result of a calculation, or the returned value from a function. We will later see how all of these are expressions are evaluated and provide a result.

Here is an example of assignment statements:

```
feet = 24.75;
```

The `24.75` literal constant is evaluated as a value of float or double type and is assigned to the `feet` variable:

```
feet = yards/3.0 ;
```

The value of `yards` is obtained and then divided by the `3.0` literal constant. The result of the evaluation is assigned to the `feet` variable. The value of `yards` is unchanged:

```
feet = inchesToFeet( inches );
```

The `inchesToFeet()` function is called with the value obtained from the `inches` variable and is executed. Its result (its return value) is assigned to the `feet` variable. The value of `inches` is unchanged.

Assigning values by passing function parameters

When we declare a function prototype that takes parameters, we also declare those parameters as formal parameters. Formal parameters have no value, only a type and, optionally, a name. However, when we call the function, we supply the actual parameters, which are the values that are copied into those placeholder parameters.

Consider the `printDistance()` function declaration and definition in the following program:

```c
#include <stdio.h>

void printDistance( double );

int main( void )
{
   double feet = 5280.0;
   printDistance( feet );
   printf( "feet = %12.3g\n" , feet );
   return 0;
}

   // Given feet, print the distance in feet and yards.
   //
void printDistance( double f )
{
   printf( "The distance in feet is %12.3g\n" , f );
   f = f / 3.0 ;
   printf( "The distance in yards is %12.3g\n" , f );
}
```

In this function, we focus on the assignment that occurs between the function call and the execution of the function (at its definition).

The function prototype says that the function takes a single parameter of the `double` type. The name is not given since it is optional. Even if we did give a name, it is not required to match the parameter name given in the function definition. In the function definition, the parameter is named `f`. For the function, the `f` variable is created as a double with the value given in the function call. It is as if we had assigned the value of the `feet` variable to the `f` function variable. In fact, this is exactly how we do that. We can manipulate `f` because it is assigned a copy of the value of `feet` at the time the function is called. What this example shows is that value of the `f` variable is divided by `3.0` and assigned back to the `f` variable, and then printed to the console. The `f` variable has a lifetime of the block of the function and the changed value in `f` does not change the value in the `feet` variable.

Because we want to use good coding practices that make our intentions clear, rather than obtuse, a better version of this function would be as follows:

```c
   // Given feet, print the distance in feet and yards.
   //
void printDistance( double feet )
{
   double yards = feet / 3.0 ;
```

```
    printf( "The distance in feet is %12.3g\n" , feet );
    printf( "The distance in yards is %12.3g\n" , yards );
}
```

This is clearer because of the following:

- We declare the actual parameter, feet, which tells the reader what exactly is being passed into the function.
- We are explicitly declaring the yards variable and assigning it a value that is the number of feet, or feet, divided by 3.0.

The lifetime of the feet actual parameter and the yards declared variable begins with the start of the function block and ends with the end of the function block.

Assignment by the function return value

A **function** is a statement that can return the result of its execution to its caller. When the function has a data type that is not void, the function is replaced by its returned value, which can then be assigned to a variable of a compatible type.

The returned value may be explicitly assigned to a variable or it may be implicitly used within a statement and discarded at the completion of the statement.

Consider the inchesToFeet() function declaration and definition:

```
#include <stdio.h>

double inchesToFeet( double );

int main( void )
{
  double inches = 1024.0;
  double feet = 0.0;
  feet = inchesToFeet( inches );
  printf( "%12.3g inches is equal to %12.3g feet\n" , inches , feet );
  return 0;
}

  // Given inches, convert this to feet
  //
double inchesToFeet( double someInches)
{
  double someFeet = someInches / 12.0;
  return someFeet;
}
```

In this function, we focus on the assignment that occurs at the `return` statement in the function block and the caller.

In this function, `inches`—known to the function as the `i` variable—is converted via a simple calculation to feet and that value is assigned to the `f` variable in the function. The function returns the value of `f` to the caller. Essentially, the function call is replaced by the value that it returns. That value is then assigned (copied) to the `feet` variable in the `main()` function.

First, we have the following two lines:

```
double feet = 0.0;
feet = inchesToFeet( inches );
```

Those two lines could be replaced with the following single line:

```
double feet = inchesToFeet( inches );
```

This statement both declares `feet` as a double and initializes it via the return value from the function call.

Summary

Variables are the means by which we store values and their associated types. Variables are identified by a given name. Variable declarations allocate memory for the lifetime of the variable. This depends on where the variable is declared. Variables declared within a block, `{` and `}`, only exist while that block is executing. There are variables whose values can change while the program executes, constant variables whose values do not change once they are given a value, and literal values that never change.

Variables are declared with explicit types. However, the type of a value can be implicitly inferred by how it is used. Literal values are constants whose type is inferred both by how they appear and how they are used.

The only way to change the value of a variable is by assigning a value to it. Initialization is the means of giving a variable or constant a value when it is declared. Otherwise, the value of variables can only change through direct assignment, which is assignment as the result of a function return value. Functions receive values via their function parameters when the function is called; these values are copies of the values when called and are discarded when the function returns.

Now, you might be wondering *how do we manipulate variables, not just copy them?* Variables are changed through assigning the resulting value from an evaluation. C has a rich set of operators to perform evaluations; we will explore these in the next chapter.

5
Exploring Operators and Expressions

So far, we have seen how values are stored to and from variables. Simply storing/retrieving values to/from variables, while important, is only a small part of handling values. What is far more important is the ability to manipulate values in useful ways, which corresponds to the ways we manipulate real-world values, such as adding up our restaurant bill or calculating how much further we have to go to get to grandma's house and how much longer that might take.

The kinds of manipulations that are reasonable to perform on one or more values depend entirely on what kinds of values they are, that is, their data types. What makes sense for one data type may not make sense for another. In this chapter, we will explore the myriad ways that values can be manipulated.

The following topics will be covered in this chapter:

- Understanding expressions and operations
- Exploring operations on numbers and understanding the special considerations regarding numbers
- Understanding how to convert values from one type to another—type conversion and casting
- Exploring character operations
- Exploring various ways to compare values
- Writing a program to print out truth tables
- Examining a snippet that performs simple bitwise operations
- Exploring the conditional operator
- Examining the sequence operator
- Exploring compound assignment operators
- Examining multiple assignment statements

- Exploring increment and decrement operators
- Writing a program to illustrate grouping
- Understanding operator precedence and why to avoid relying upon it (there is an easier way)

Technical requirements

As detailed in the *Technical requirements* section of `Chapter 1`, *Running Hello, World!*, continue to use the tools you have chosen.

The source code for this chapter can be found at `https://github.com/PacktPublishing/Learn-C-Programming`.

Expressions and operations

What are expressions? Well, in simple terms, an expression is a way of computing a value. We've seen how to do this with functions and return values. We will now turn to C's basic set of arithmetic operators for addition, subtraction, multiplication, and division, which are common in most programming languages. C adds to this a large number of operations that includes incrementation/decrementation, relational operators, logical operators, and bitwise manipulation. C further extends assignment operations in useful ways. Finally, C includes some unusual operators that are not commonly found in other languages, such as conditional and sequence operators.

The expressions we will explore in this chapter consist of one or more values as variables or constants combined with the help of operators. Expressions can be complete statements; however, just as often, expressions are components of complex statements. Operators work on one or more expressions, where an expression can be simple or complex:

- 5 is a literal expression that evaluates to the value of 5.
- 5 + 8 is an arithmetic expression of two simple expressions (literal constants), which, with the addition operator, evaluates to 13.
- A more complex expression, 5 + 8 - 10, is really two binary arithmetical operations where 5 and 8 are first evaluated to produce an intermediate result, then 10 is subtracted from it.

- 5; is an expression statement that evaluates to 5 and then moves on to the next statement. A more useful version of this would be `aValue = 5;`, which is really two expressions: the evaluation of 5 and then the assignment of that value to the `aValue` variable.

Each value of an expression can be one of the following:

- A literal constant
- A variable or constant variable
- The returned value from a function call

An example expression using all of these would be as follows:

```
5 + aValue + feetToInches( 3.5 )
```

Consider the following statement:

```
aLength = 5 + aValue + feetToInches( 3.5 );
```

The preceding statement is, in reality, five distinct operations in one statement:

- The retrieval of the value from the `aValue` variable
- The function call to `feetToInches()`
- The addition of the literal value 5 with the value of `aValue` giving an intermediate result
- The addition of the function call result to the intermediate result
- The assignment of the intermediate result to the `aLength` variable

An alternative way in which to calculate the same result can involve three simple statements instead of one complex statement, as follows:

```
aLength = 5;
aLength = aLength + aValue;
aLength = aLength + feetToInches( 3.5 );
```

In this way, the different values are evaluated and added to the `aLength` variable. Instead of one assignment, there are three. Instead of a temporary intermediate result, the results of the additions are accumulated explicitly in the `aLength` variable as a result of each statement.

A simple program, `calcLength.c`, that applies each method of using simple and complex expressions, is as follows:

```c
#include <stdio.h>

int feetToInches( double feet )
{
  int inches = feet * 12;
  return inches;
}

int main( void )
{
  int aValue   = 8;
  int aLength  = 0;

  aLength = 5 + aValue + feetToInches( 3.5 );
  printf( "Calculated length = %d\n" , aLength );

  aLength = 5;
  aLength = aLength + aValue;
  aLength = aLength + feetToInches( 3.5 );
  printf( "Calculated length = %d\n" , aLength );
}
```

This program calculates `aLength` from the sum of a literal value, which, in this case, is 5; a variable, `aValue`; and the result of the `feetToInches()` function. It then prints out the result to the Terminal. The program itself is not very useful—we have no idea what we are calculating nor do we know why the values that were chosen are significant. For now, however, let's just focus on the expression of `aLength`. `aLength` is a value calculated by adding three other values together in one complex statement and again with three simple statements.

Now, create the `calcLength.c` file, type in the program, and then save the file. Compile the program and run it. You should see the following output:

```
> cc calcLength.c -o calcLength
> calcLength
Calculated length = 55
Calculated length = 55
>
```

As you can see, the single statement for calculating aLength is far less verbose than using the three statements to do so. However, neither approach is incorrect nor is one method always preferred over the other. When calculations are relatively simple, the first method might be clearer and more appropriate. On the other hand, when calculations become much more complex, the second method might make each step of the computation clearer and more appropriate. Choosing which method to employ can be a challenge as you are trying to find a balance between brevity and clarity. Whenever you have to choose one over the other, always choose clarity.

Introducing operations on numbers

The basic arithmetic operators on numbers are addition (+), subtraction (-), multiplication (*), and division (/). They are binary operations as they work on one pair of expressions at a time. They work largely as you would expect them to for both integers (whole numbers) and real numbers. Division for two real numbers results in a real number. Division for two whole numbers also results in a whole number; any possible fraction part is discarded. There is also the modulo operator (%) that will provide the integer remainder of the division of two integers.

For example, *12.0 / 5.0* (two real numbers) evaluates to *2.5*, whereas *12 / 5* (two integers) evaluates to *2*. If we were working only with integers and we needed the remainder of *12 / 5*, we would use the remainder operator, %. Thus, *12 % 5* evaluates to another integer, *2*.

Many languages have an exponent operator. C does not. To raise an expression to a power, standard C provides the library function, pow(x , y). The prototype for this function is double pow(double x , double y);, which raises the value of x to the power of value y and yields double as its result. To use this function in your program, include the <math.h> header file wherever the prototype is declared.

Let's create a new file, convertTemperature.c, where we will create two useful functions, celsiusToFahrenheit() and fahrenheitToCelsius(), as follows:

```
    // Given a Celsius temperature, convert it to Fahrenheit.
    double celsiusToFahrenheit( double degreesC )
    {
        double degreesF = (degreesC * 9.0 / 5.0 ) + 32.0;
        return degreesF;
    }

    // Given a Fahrenheit temperature, convert it to Celsius.
    double fahrenheitToCelsius( double degreesF )
    {
```

```
    double degreesC = (degreesF - 32 ) * 5.0 / 9.0 ;
    return degreesC;
}
```

Each function takes a `double` value type as an input parameter and returns the converted value as a `double`.

There are a couple of things to take note of regarding these functions.

First, we could have made them single-line functions by combining the two statements in each function body into one, as follows:

```
    return (degreesC * 9.0  / 5.0 ) + 32;
```

Here is another example:

```
    return (degreesF - 32 ) * 5.0 / 9.0;
```

Many programmers would do this. However, as your programming skills advance, this actually becomes a needless practice—it doesn't really save much of anything, and it makes debugging with a debugger (an advanced topic) far more difficult and time-consuming.

Many programmers are further tempted to turn these functions into `#define` macro symbols (another advanced topic), as follows:

```
#define celsiusToFahrenheit( x )   ((x * 9.0  / 5.0 ) + 32)
#define fahrenheitToCelsius( x )   ((x - 32 ) * 5.0 / 9.0)
```

Using macros can be dangerous because we could lose type information or the operations in such a macro might not be appropriate for the type of value given. Furthermore, we would have to be extremely careful about how we craft such preprocessor symbols to avoid unexpected results. For the few characters of typing saved, neither the single-line complex return statement nor the macro definitions are worth the potential hassle.

 There are many temptations of using the preprocessor as much as possible—that is, to overuse the preprocessor. There lies the road to perdition! Instead, if you find yourself being pulled by such temptations for whatever reason, take a look at section *Using preprocessor effectively*, from `Chapter 25`, *Understanding Scope*.

Second, we use the grouping operator, (and), to ensure our calculations are performed in the correct order. For now, just know that anything inside (and) is evaluated first. We will discuss this in more detail later on in this chapter.

We can now finish the program that uses the two functions we created. Add the following to convertTemperature.c before the two function definitions:

```
#include <stdio.h>

double celsiusToFahrenheit( double degreesC );
double fahrenheitToCelsius( double degreesF );

int main( void ) {
  int c = 0;
  int f = 32;
  printf( "%4d Celsius     is %4d Fahrenheit\n" ,
          c , (int)celsiusToFahrenheit( c ) );
  printf( "%4d Fahrenheit is %4d Celsius\n\n"   ,
          f , (int)fahrenheitToCelsius( f ) );
  c = 100;
  f = 212;
  printf( "%4d Celsius     is %4d Fahrenheit\n" ,
          c , (int)celsiusToFahrenheit( c ) );
  printf( "%4d Fahrenheit is %4d Celsius\n\n"   ,
          f , (int)fahrenheitToCelsius( f ) );
  c = f = 50;
  printf( "%4d Celsius     is %4d Fahrenheit\n" ,
          c , (int)celsiusToFahrenheit( c ) );
  printf( "%4d Fahrenheit is %4d Celsius\n\n"   ,
          f , (int)fahrenheitToCelsius( f ) );
  return 0
}

// function definitions here...
```

With all of the parts in place, save the file, compile it, and then run it. You should see the following output:

```
> cc convertTemperature.c -o convertTemperature
> convertTemperature
   0 Celsius     is   32 Fahrenheit
  32 Fahrenheit is    0 Celsius

 100 Celsius     is  212 Fahrenheit
 212 Fahrenheit is  100 Celsius

  50 Celsius     is  122 Fahrenheit
  50 Fahrenheit is   10 Celsius

>
```

Notice how we exercised our functions with known values to verify that they are correct. First, freezing values for each scale were converted to the other scale. Then, boiling values for each scale were converted to the other scale. We then tried a simple middle value to see the results.

You may be wondering how to perform the conversions if we pass values other than doubles into the function. You might even be inclined to create several functions whose only difference is the type of variables. Take a look at the `convertTemperature_NoNo.c` program. Try to compile it for yourself and see what kind of errors you get. You will find that, in C, we cannot overload function names; that is, use the same function name but with different parameter and return types. This is possible with other languages, but not with C.

In C, each function is simply called by its name; nothing else is used to differentiate one function call from another. A function having one name with a given type and two parameters cannot be distinguished from another function of the same name with a different type and no parameter.

We could try to embed the type names into the function names, such as `fahrenheith`**`Dbl`**`ToCelsius`**`Int`**`()` and `celsius`**`Int`**`ToCelsius`**`Dbl`**`()`, but this would be extremely tedious to declare and define for all data types. Additionally, it would be extremely difficult to use in our programs. Compiler errors, due to mistyping the function names and even mistyping the calling parameters, would be highly likely and time-consuming to work through in a large or complicated program. So, how does C deal with this?

Don't fret! We will consider this very topic in the next section, along with a complete program on how to use these functions.

Considering the special issues resulting from operations on numbers

When performing calculations with any numbers, the possible ranges of both the inputs and outputs *must* be considered. For each type of number, there is a limit to both its maximum values and minimum values. These are defined on each system in the C standard library for that system in the header file, `limits.h`.

As the programmer, you must ensure that the results of any arithmetic operation are within the limits of the range for the data type specified, or your program must check for valid inputs thereby preventing invalid outputs. There are three types of invalid outputs that will cause the C runtime to abort— **Not a Number (NaN)**, underflow, and overflow.

Understanding NaN

A NaN result occurs when the result of an operation is an undefined or an unrepresentable number.

Consider this equation: $y = 1 / x$. What is the value of y as x approaches zero from the positive side? It will become an infinitely large positive value. What then is the value of y as x approaches zero from the negative side? It will become an infinitely large negative value. Mathematically, this is called a **discontinuity**, which cannot be resolved. As we approach zero from either direction, the result is a value that will be infinitely different when we approach from one direction or the other (an infinitely large positive value or an infinitely small negative value). Therefore, division by zero is mathematically undefined. In the computer, the result is NaN.

NaNs also occur when the data types are real, but the result of the computation is a complex number, for example, the square root of a negative number or the logarithm of a negative number. NaNs can also occur where discontinuities appear in inverse trigonometric functions.

Understanding underflow NaN

Underflow occurs when the result of an arithmetic operation is smaller than the smallest value that can be represented by the type specified.

For integers, this would mean either a number less than 0 if the integer is `unsigned` or a very large negative number if the integer is `signed` (for instance, -2 is smaller than -1).

For real numbers, this would be a number very, very close to zero (that is, an extremely small fractional part), resulting from the division of an extremely small number by a very large number, or the multiplication of two extremely small numbers.

Understanding overflow NaN

Overflow occurs when the result of an arithmetic operation is greater than the greatest value that can be represented for the type specified.

This would occur with both the addition and multiplication of two extremely large numbers or the division of a very large number by an extremely small number.

Considering precision

When performing calculations with real numbers, we need to be concerned with the exponential difference between two of them. When one exponent is very large (positive) and the other very small (negative), we will likely produce either insignificant results or a NaN. This happens when the calculated result will either represent an insignificant change to the largest exponent value via addition and subtraction—therefore, precision will be lost—or be outside the possible range of values via multiplication and division—therefore, a NaN will result. Adding a very, very small value to a very, very large value may not give any significant change in the resulting value—again, precision in the result will be lost.

It is only when the exponents are relatively close, and the calculated result is within a reasonable range, that we can be sure of the accuracy of our result.

Granted that with 64-bit integer values and up to 128-bit real values, the ranges of values are vast, even beyond ordinary human conception. More often, however, our programs will use data types that do not provide the extreme limits of possible values. In those cases, the results of operations should always be given some consideration.

Exploring type conversion

C provides mechanisms that allow you to convert one type of value into another type of the same value. When there is no loss of precision, in other words, when the conversion of values results in the same value, C operates without complaining. However, when there is a possible loss of precision, or if the resulting value is not identical to the original value, then the C compiler does not provide any such warning.

Understanding implicit type conversion and values

So, what happens when expressions are performed with operands of different types, for example, the multiplication of an `int` with a `float`, or the subtraction of a `double` from a `short`?

To answer that, let's revisit our `sizes_ranges2.c` program from Chapter 3, *Working with Basic Data Types*. There, we saw how different data types took different numbers of bytes; some are 1 byte, some are 2 bytes, some are 4 bytes, and most values are 8 bytes.

When C encounters an expression of mixed types, it first performs an implicit conversion of the smallest data type (in bytes) to match the number of bytes in the largest data type size (in bytes). The conversion occurs such that the value with the narrow range would be converted into the other with a wider range of values.

Consider the following calculation:

```
int     feet  = 11;
double yards = 0.0;
yards = feet / 3;
```

In this calculation, both the `feet` variable and the 3 literal are integer values. The resulting value of the expression is an integer. However, the integer result is implicitly converted into a double upon assignment. The value of `yards` is 3.0, which is clearly incorrect. This error can be corrected by either type casting with `feet` or by using a decimal literal, as follows:

```
yards = (double)feet / 3;
```

```
yards = feet / 3.0;
```

The first statement casts `feet` to a `double` and then performs the division; the result is a `double`. The second statement specifies a decimal literal, which is interpreted as a `double` and performs the division; the result is a `double`. In both statements, because the result is a `double`, there is no conversion needed upon assignment to `yards`; `yards` now has the correct value of 3.66667.

Implicit conversion also occurs when the type of the actual parameter value is different from the defined parameter type.

A simple conversion is when a smaller type is converted into a larger type. This would include short integers being converted into long integers or floats being converted into doubles.

Consider the following function declaration and the statement that calls it:

```
long int add( long int i1 , long int i2 )  {
   return i1 + i2;
}

int main( void )  {
   signed char b1 = 254;
   signed char b2 = 253;
   long int r1;
   r1 = add( b1 , b2 );
   printf( "%d + %d = %ld\n" , b1 , b2 , r1 );
}
```

The add() function has two parameters, which are both long integers of 8 bytes each. Later, add() is called with two variables that are 1 byte each. The single-byte values of 254 and 253 are implicitly converted into the wider long int when they are copied into the function parameters. The result of the addition is 507, which is correct.

Most integers can easily be converted into floats or doubles. In the multiplication of an int (4 bytes) with a float (4 bytes), an implicit conversion will happen—int will be converted into a float. The implicit result of the expression would be a float.

In the subtraction of a double (8 bytes) from a short (2 bytes), two conversions happen on the short— first, it is converted into a long (8 bytes), and then it is converted into a double (8 bytes). The implicit result of the expression would be a double. Depending on what happens next in the compound expression, the implicit result may be further converted. If the next operation involves an explicit type, then the implicit result will be converted into that type, if necessary. Otherwise, it may again be converted into the widest possible implicit type for the next operation.

However, when we assign an implicit or explicit result type to a narrower type in the assignment, a loss of precision is likely. For integers, loss involves the high-order bits (or the bits with the largest binary values). A value of 32,000,000 assigned to a char will always be 255. For real numbers, truncation and rounding occur. Conversion from a double to a float will cause rounding or truncation, depending upon the compiler implementation. Conversion from a float to an int will cause the fractional part of the value to be lost.

Consider the following statements:

```
long int add( long int i1 , long int i2 )  {
   return i1 + i2;
}
```

```
int main ( void )   {
   signed char b1 = 254;
   signed char b2 = 253;
   signed char r1;
   r1 = add( b1 , b2 );
   printf( "%d + %d = %ld\n" , b1 , b2 , r1 );
}
```

The only change in these statements is the type of the r1 variable; it is now a single byte. So, while b1 and b2 are widened to long int, add() returns a long int, but this 8-byte return value must be truncated into a single byte. The value assigned to r1 is incorrect; it becomes 252.

When performing complicated expressions that require a high degree of precision in the result, it is always best to perform the calculations in the widest possible data type, and only at the very end convert the result into a narrower data type.

Let's test this with a simple program. In truncRounding.c, we have two functions: one that takes a double as a parameter and prints it, and the other that takes a long int as a parameter and prints it. The following program illustrates implicit type conversion in which the parameter values are assigned to actual values:

```
#include <stdio.h>

void doubleFunc( double   dbl );
void longintFunc( long int li );

int main( void ) {
   float floatValue   = 58.73;
   short int intValue = 13;
   longintFunc( intValue );
   longintFunc( floatValue ); // possible truncation

   doubleFunc( floatValue );
   doubleFunc( intValue );

   return 0;
}

void doublFunc( double dbl ) {
   printf( "doubleFunc %.2f\n" , dbl );
}

void longintFunc( long int li ) {
   printf( "longintFunc %ld\n" , li );
}
```

We have not yet explored the ways in which `printf()` can format values. For now, simply take for granted that `%.2f` will print a `double` value with 2 decimal places, and that `%ld` will print out a `long int`. This will be explained fully in `Chapter 19`, *Exploring Formatted Output*.

Enter, compile, and run `truncRounding.c`. You should see the following output:

```
> cc truncRounding.c -o truncRounding -std=c11 -Wall -Werror
> truncRounding
longIntFunc    13
longIntFunc    58
doubleFunc 58.73
doubleFunc 13.00
>
```

Notice that no rounding occurs when `58.73` is converted into a `long int`. However, we do lose the fractional part; this is called **truncation**, where the fractional part of the value is cut off. A `short int` is properly converted into a `double` just as a `float` is properly converted into a `double`.

Also, notice that when you compiled and ran `truncRounding.c`, no compiler error nor runtime warning was given when the `float` was converted into a `long int` resulting in the loss of precision.

Using explicit type conversion – casting

If we rely on implicit casting, our results may go awry or we may get unexpected results. To avoid this, we can cause an explicit, yet temporary, type change. We do this by casting. When we explicitly cast a variable to another type, its value is temporarily converted into the desired type and then used. The type of the variable and its value does not change.

Any expression can be prefixed by `(type)` to change its explicit type to the indicated type for the lifetime of the expression. This lifetime is typically a single statement. The explicit type is never changed, nor is the value stored in that explicitly typed variable. An example of this is given in the following program, `casting.c`:

```c
#include <stdio.h>

int main( void ) {
    int numerator    =   33;
    int denominator  =    5;
    double result    =  0.0;
    result = numerator / denominator;
```

```
    printf( "Truncation: %d / %d = %.2g\n" ,
            numerator , denominator , result );
    result = (double) numerator / denominator;
    printf( "No truncation: %.2f / %d = %.2f\n" ,
            (double)numerator , denominator , result );

    result = numerator / (double)denominator;
    printf( "             %d / %.2f = %.2f\n" ,
            numerator , (double)denominator , result );
    return 0;
}
```

Enter, compile, and run `casting` .c. You should see the following output:

```
> cc casting.c -o casting
> casting
Truncation:      33 / 5 = 6
No truncation: 33.00 / 5 = 6.60
               33 / 5.00 = 6.60
>
```

In `casting.c`, we can see, in the first division expression, that there is no casting and no implicit conversion. Therefore, the result is an `int` and the fractional part is truncated. When the `int` result is assigned to a double, the fractional part has already been lost. In the second and third division statements, we guarantee that the operation is done on double values by casting either one of them to `double`. The other value is then implicitly converted to `double`. The result is a `double`, so when it is assigned to a `double`, there is no truncation.

The types of *numerators* and *denominators* are not changed permanently but only within the context of the expression where casting occurs.

Introducing operations on characters

Since characters are internally represented as integers, any of the integer operations can be applied to them too. However, only a couple of operations make sense to apply to characters—the additive operators (that is, addition and subtraction). While multiplying and dividing characters are legal, those operations never produce any practical results:

- `char` - `char` yields `int`.
- `char` + `int` yields `char`.
- `char` - `int` yields `char`.

Remember that a `char` is only one unsigned byte, so any addition or subtraction outside of the range of `0..255` will yield unexpected results due to the truncation of high-order bits.

A common use of the addition and subtraction of characters is the conversion of a given ASCII character to uppercase or lowercase. If the character is uppercase, then simply adding 32 to it will give you its lowercase version. If the character is lowercase, then simply subtracting 32 from it will give you its uppercase version. An example of this is given in the following program, `convertUpperLower.c`:

```c
#include <stdio.h>

int main( void ) {
  char lowerChar = 'b';
  char upperChar = 'M';

  char anUpper = lowerChar - 32;
  char aLower  = upperChar + 32;

  printf( "Lower case '%c' can be changed to upper case '%c'\n" ,
          lowerChar , anUpper );
  printf( "Upper case '%c' can be changed to lower case '%c'\n" ,
          upperChar , aLower );
}
```

Given a lowercase `'b'`, we convert it into uppercase by subtracting 32 from it. Given an uppercase `'M'`, we convert it into lowercase by adding 32 to it. We will explore characters much more thoroughly in Chapter 15, *Working with Strings*.

In your editor, create a new file and enter the `convertUpperLower.c` program. Compile and run it in a Terminal window. You should see the following output:

```
> cc convertUpperLower.c -o convertUpperLower -std=c11 -Wall -Werror
> convertUpperLower
Lower case 'b' can be changed to upper case 'B'
Upper case 'M' can be changed to lower case 'm'
>
```

Another common use of operations on characters is to convert the character of a digit (`'0'` to `'9'`) into its actual numerical value. The value of `'0'` is not 0 but some other value that represents that character. To convert a character digit into its numerical value, we simply subtract the character `'0'` from it. An example of this is given in the following program, `convertDigitToInt.c`:

```c
#include <stdio.h>

int main( void ) {
```

```
    char digit5 = '5';
    char digit8 = '8';

    int sumDigits = digit5 + digit8;
    printf( "digit5 + digit8 = '5' + '8' = %d (oh, dear!)\n" ,
    sumDigits );

    char value5 = digit5 - '0'; // get the numerical value of '5'
    char value8 = digit8 - '0'; // get the numerical value of '8'
    sumDigits = value5 + value8;
    printf( "value5 + value8 = 5 + 8 = %d\n" ,
            sumDigits );
}
```

When we simply add characters together, unexpected results are likely to occur. What we really need to do is to convert each digit character into its corresponding numerical value and then add those values. The results of that addition are what we want.

In your editor, create a new file and enter the `convertDigitToInt.c` program. Compile and run it in a Terminal window. You should see the following output:

```
> cc convertDigitToInt.c -o convertDigitToInt -std=c11 -Wall -Werror
> convertDigitToInt
digit5 + digit8 = '5' + '8' = 109 (oh, dear!)
value5 + value8 = 5 + 8 = 13
>
```

In order to understand the difference between a character and its value, we will explore characters in much greater depth in `Chapter 15`, *Working with Strings*.

Exploring logical and relational operators

Early versions of C did not have explicit boolean (`true`, `false`) data types. To handle boolean values, C implicitly converts any zero value into the boolean `false` value and implicitly converts any nonzero value into the boolean `true` value. This implicit conversion comes in handy very often but must be used with care.

However, when we use `#include <stdbool.h>`, the official `bool` types and `true` and `false` values are available to us. We will explore later how we might choose to define our own boolean values with enumerations (`Chapters 9`, *Creating and Using Structures*) or with custom types (`Chapter 11`, *Working with Arrays*).

There are three boolean operators:

- | |: The binary logical OR operator
- &&: The binary logical AND operator
- !: The unary logical NOT operator

These are logical operators whose results are always boolean `true` (nonzero) or `false` (exactly zero). They are so named in order to differentiate them from bitwise operators whose results involve a different bit pattern, which we shall learn about shortly.

The first two logical operators evaluate the results of two expressions:

```
expressionA operator expressionB
```

When the operator is logical AND &&, if `expressionA` evaluates to `false`, then `expressionB` is not evaluated (it does not need to be). However, when `expressionA` is true, `expressionB` must be evaluated.

When the operator is logical OR | |, if `expressionA` evaluates to `true`, then `expressionB` is not evaluated (it does not need to be). However, when `expressionA` is false, `expressionB` must be evaluated.

The unary logical NOT ! operator is employed, therefore, as `!expressionC`.

It takes the result of `expressionC`, implicitly converting it into a boolean result and evaluating it with its opposite boolean result. Therefore, `!true` becomes `false`, and `!false` becomes `true`.

In the `logical.c` program, three tables are printed to show how the logical operators work. They are known as **truth tables**. The values are printed as either decimal 1 or 0, but they are really boolean values. The first truth table is produced with the `printLogicalAND()` function, as follows:

```c
void printLogicalAND( bool z, bool o )
{
  bool zero_zero = z && z ;
  bool zero_one  = z && o ;
  bool one_zero  = o && z ;
  bool one_one   = o && o ;

  printf( "AND | %1d | %1d\n"      , z , o );
  printf( " %1d | %1d | %1d \n"    , z , zero_zero , zero_one );
  printf( " %1d | %1d | %1d \n\n" , o , zero_one   , one_one );
}
```

The next truth table is produced with the `printLogicalOr()` function, as follows:

```c
void printLogicalOR( bool z, bool o )
{
  bool zero_zero = z || z ;
  bool zero_one  = z || o ;
  bool one_zero  = o || z ;
  bool one_one   = o || o ;

  printf( "OR | %1d | %1d\n"      , z , o );
  printf( " %1d | %1d | %1d \n"   , z , zero_zero , zero_one );
  printf( " %1d | %1d | %1d \n\n" , o , zero_one  , one_one );
}
```

Finally, the `printLogicalNOT()` function prints the NOT truth table, as follows:

```c
void printLogicalNOT( bool z, bool o )
{
  bool not_zero = !z ;
  bool not_one = !o ;
  printf( "NOT \n" );
  printf( " %1d | %1d \n"   , z , not_zero );
  printf( " %1d | %1d \n\n" , o , not_one );
}
```

Create the `logicals.c` file and enter the three truth table functions. Then, add the following program code to complete `logicals.c`:

```c
#include <stdio.h>
#include <stdbool.h>

void printLogicalAND( bool z, bool o );
void printLogicalOR( bool z, bool o );
void printLogicalNOT( bool z, bool o );

int main( void )
{
  bool one = 1;
  bool zero = 0;

  printLogicalAND( zero , one );
  printLogicalOR( zero , one );
  printLogicalNOT( zero , one );
  return 0;
}
```

Save, compile, and run `logicals.c`. You should see the following output:

```
> cc logical.c -o logical
> logical
AND | 0 | 1
  0 | 0 | 0
  1 | 0 | 1


OR  | 0 | 1
  0 | 0 | 1
  1 | 1 | 1

NOT
  0 | 1
  1 | 0

>
```

These are known as truth tables. When you perform the AND, OR, or NOT operations on a value in the top row and a value in the left column, the intersecting cell is the result. So, 1 AND 1 yields 1, 1 OR 0 yields 1, and NOT 0 yields 1.

Not all operations can be simply expressed as strictly boolean values. In these cases, there are the relational operators that produce results that are convenient to regard as true and false. Statements such as if and while, as we shall learn, test those results.

Relational operators involve the comparison of the result of one expression with the result of a second expression. They have the same form as the binary logical operators shown previously. Each of them gives a boolean result. They are as follows:

- **> (greater than operator)**: true if expressionA is greater than expressionB.
- **>= (greater than or equal operator)**: true if expressionA is greater than or equal to expressionB.
- **< (less than operator)**: true if expressionA is less than expressionB.
- **<= (less than or equal operator)**: true if expressionA is less than or equal to expressionB.
- **== (equal operator** (note that this is different from the = assignment operator)): true if expressionA is equal to expressionB.
- **!= (not equal operator)**: true if expressionA is not equal to expressionB.

We will defer exploring these operators in depth until we get to the if, for, and while statements in upcoming chapters.

Bitwise operators

Bitwise operators manipulate bit patterns in useful ways. The bitwise AND &, OR |, and XOR ^ operators compare the two operands bit by bit. The bitwise shifting operators shift all of the bits of the first operand left or right. The bitwise complement changes each bit in a bit pattern to its opposite bit value.

Each bit in a bit field (8, 16, or 32 bits) could be used as if it was a switch, or flag, determining whether some feature or characteristic of the program was *off* (0) or *on* (1). The main drawback of using bit fields in this manner is that the meaning of the bit positions can only be known by reading the source code, assuming that the proper source code is both available and well commented!

Bitwise operations are less valuable today, not only because memory and CPU registers are cheap and plentiful, but because they are now expensive operations computationally. They do, occasionally, find a useful place in some programs, but not often.

The bitwise operators are as follows:

- &: Bitwise AND; for example, 1 if both bits are 1.
- |: Bitwise OR; for example, 1 if either bit is 1.
- ^: Bitwise XOR; for example, 1 if either but not both are 1.
- <<: Bitwise shift left. Each bit is moved over to the left (the larger bit position). It is equivalent to `value * 2`. `0010` becomes `0100`.
- >>: Bitwise shift right. Each bit is moved over to the right (the smaller bit position). It is equivalent to `value / 2`. `0010` becomes `0001`.
- ~: Bitwise complement. Change each bit to its other; for example, 1 to 0, and 0 to 1.

The following is an example of bitwise operators and flags:

```
 /* flag name */  /* bit pattern */
const unsigned char lowercase 1; /* 0000 0001 */
const unsigned char bold 2; /* 0000 0010 */
const unsigned char italic 4; /* 0000 0100 */
const unsigned char underline 8; /* 0000 1000 */

unsigned char flags = 0;

flags = flags | bold; /* switch on bold */
flags = flags & ~italic; /* switch off italic; */
if((flags & underline) == underline) ... /* test for underline bit 1/on? */
if( flags & underline ) ... /* test for underline */
```

Instead of using bitwise fields, custom data types called **enumerations** and more explicit data structures, such as hash tables, are often preferred.

The conditional operator

This is also known as the ternary operator. This operator has three expressions—testExpression, ifTrueExpression, and ifFalseExpression. It looks like this:

testExpression ? ifTrueExpression : ifFalseExpression

In this expression, testExpression is evaluated. If the testExpression result is true, or nonzero, then ifTrueExpression is evaluated and its result becomes the expression result. If the testExpression result is false, or exactly zero, then ifFalseExpression is evaluated and its result becomes the expression result. Either ifTrueExpression is evaluated or ifFalseExpression is evaluated—never both.

This operator is useful in odd places, such as setting switches, building string values, and printing out various messages. In the following example, we'll use it to add pluralization to a word if it makes sense in the text string:

```
printf( "Length = %d meter%c\n" , len, len == 1 ? '' : 's' );
```

Or, we can use it to print out whole words:

```
printf( "Length = %d %s\n" , len, len == 1 ? "foot" : "feet" );
```

The following program uses these statements:

```
#include <stdio.h>

void printLength( double meters );

int main( void ) {
 printLength( 0.0 );
 printLength( 1.0 );
 printLength( 12.0 / 39.67 ); // very nearly 1 foot
 printLength( 2.5 );
}

void printLength( double meters ) {
 double feet = meters * 39.67 / 12.0;
 printf( "Length = %f meter%c\n" ,
        meters,
```

```
            meters == 1.0 ? ' ' : 's' );
   printf( "Length = %f %s\n" ,
           feet,
           0.99995 < feet && feet < 1.00005 ? "foot" : "feet" );
   }
```

In the preceding program, you might be wondering why the statement for determining "foot" or "feet" has become so much more complex. The reason is that the feet variable is a computed value. Furthermore, because of the precision of the double data type, it is extremely unlikely than any computation will be *exactly* 1.0000..., especially when division is involved. Therefore, we need to consider values of feet that are reasonably close to zero but might never be *exactly* zero. For our simple example, four significant digits will suffice.

When you type in the printLength.c program, save it, compile it, and run it, you should see the following output:

```
> cc printLength.c -o printLength -std=c11 -Wall -Werror
> printLength
Length = 0.000000 meters
Length = 0.000000 feet

Length = 1.000000 meter
Length = 3.305833 feet

Length = 0.302496 meters
Length = 1.000000 foot

Length = 2.500000 meters
Length = 8.264583 feet

>
```

Be careful, however, not to overuse the ternary operator for anything other than simple value replacements. In the next chapter, we'll explore how more explicit solutions are commonly used for general conditional executions.

The sequence operator

Sometimes, it makes sense to perform a sequence of expressions as though they were a single statement. This would rarely be used or make sense in a normal statement.

We can string multiple expressions together in sequence using the , operator. Each expression is evaluated from left to right in the order they appear. The value of the entire expression is the resultant value of the rightmost expression.

For instance, consider the following:

```
int x = 0, y = 0, z = 0;   // declare and initialize.
...
...
x = 3 , y = 4 , z = 5;
...
...
x = 4; y = 3; z = 5;
...
...
x = 5;
y = 12;
z = 13;
```

The single line assigning all three variables is perfectly valid. However, in this case, there is little value in doing it. The three variables are either loosely related or not related at all from what we can tell in this snippet.

The next line makes each assignment its own expression and condenses the code from three lines to one. While it is also valid, there is seldom a need for this.

This operator, however, does make sense in the context of iterative statements, such as `while()` ..., `for()` ..., and `do ... while()`. They will be explored in Chapter 7, *Exploring Loops and Iteration*.

Compound assignment operators

As we have already seen, expressions can be combined in many ways to form compound expressions. There are some compound expressions that recur so often that C has a set of operators that make them shorter. In each case, the result is formed by taking the variable on the left of the operator, performing the operation on it with the value of the expression on the right, and assigning it back to the variable on the left.

Compound operations are of the form `variable operator= expression`.

The most common of these is incrementation with an assignment:

```
counter = counter + 1;
```

With the += compound operator, this just becomes the following:

```
counter += 1 ;
```

The full set of compound operators is as follows:

- `+=` assignment with addition to a variable
- `-=` assignment with subtraction to a variable
- `*=` assignment with multiplication to a variable
- `/=` assignment with division (integer or real) to a variable
- `%=` assignment with an integer remaindering to a variable
- `<<=` assignment with bitwise shift left
- `>>=` assignment with bitwise shift right
- `&=` assignment with bitwise AND
- `^=` assignment with bitwise XOR (exclusive OR)
- `|=` assignment with bitwise OR

These operators help to make your computations a bit more condensed and somewhat clearer.

Multiple assignments in a single expression

We have learned how to combine expressions to make compound expressions. We can also do this with assignments. For example, we could initialize variables as follows:

```
int height, width, length;
height = width = length = 0;
```

The expressions are evaluated from right to left, and the final result of the expression is the value of the last assignment. Each variable is assigned a value of 0.

Another way to put multiple assignments in a single statement is to use the , sequence operator. We could write a simple swap statement in one line with three variables, as follows:

```
int first, second, temp;

 // Swap first & second variables.
temp = first, first = second, second = temp;
```

The sequence of three assignments is performed from left to right. This would be equivalent to the following three statements:

```
temp = first;
first = second;
second = temp;
```

Either way is correct. Some might argue that the three assignments are logically associated because of their commonality to being swapped, so the first way is preferred. Ultimately, which method you choose is a matter of taste and appropriateness in the given context. Always choose clarity over obfuscation.

Incremental operators

C provides even shorter shorthand (shortest shorthand?) operators that make the code even smaller and clearer. These are the autoincrement and autodecrement operators.

Writing the `counter = counter + 1;` statement is equivalent to a shorter version, `counter += 1;`, as we have already learned. However, this simple expression happens so often, especially when incrementing or decrementing a counter or index, that there is an even shorter shorthand way to do it. For this, there is the unary increment operator of `counter++;` or `++counter;`.

In each case, the result of the statement is that the value of the counter has been incremented by one.

Here are the unary operators:

- ++ autoincrement by 1, prefix or postfix
- –– autodecrement by 1, prefix or postfix

Postfix versus prefix incrementation

There are subtle differences between *how* that value of the counter is incremented when it is prefixed (++ comes before the expression is evaluated) or postfixed (++ comes after the expression).

In prefix notation, ++ is applied to the result of the expression *before* its value is considered. In postfix notations, the result of the expression is applied to any other evaluation and then the ++ operation is performed.

Here, an example will be useful.

In this example, we set a value and then print that value using both the prefix and postfix notations. Finally, the program shows a more predictable method. That is, perform either method of incrementation as a single statement. The result will always be what we expect:

```c
int main( void )
{
  int aValue = 5;

    // Demonstrate prefix incrementation.
  printf( "Initial: %d\n" , aValue );
  printf( " Prefix: %d\n" , ++aValue );  // Prefix incrementation.
  printf( "  Final: %\n"   , aValue );

  aValue = 5;    // Reset aValue.

    // Demonstrate postfix incrementation.
  printf( "Initial: %d\n" , aValue );
  printf( " Prefix: %d\n" , aValue++ );  // Postfix incrementation.
  printf( "  Final: %\n"   , aValue );

    // A more predictable result: increment in isolation.
  aValue = 5;
  ++aValue;
  printf( "++aValue (alone) == %d\n" , aValue );
  aValue = 5;
  aValue++;
  printf( "aValue++ (alone) == %d\n" , aValue );

  return 0;
}
```

Enter, compile, and run `prefixpostfix.c`. You should see the following output:

```
> cc prefixPostfix.c -o prefixPostfix
> prefixPostfix
Initial: 5
 Prefix: 6
   Final: 6

Initial: 5
Postfix: 5
   Final: 6

++aValue (alone) == 7
aValue++ (alone) == 8
>
```

In the output, you can see how the prefix and postfix notations affect (or not) the value passed to printf(). In prefix autoincrement, the value is first incremented and then passed to printf(). In postfix autoincrement, the value is passed to printf() as is, and after printf() is evaluated, the value is then incremented. Additionally, notice that when these are single, simple statements, both results are identical.

Some C programmers relish jamming together as many expressions and operators as possible. There is really no good reason to do this. I often go cross-eyed when looking at such code. In fact, because of the subtle differences in compilers and the possible confusion about if and when such expressions need to be modified, this practice is discouraged. Therefore, to avoid the possible side effects of the prefix or postfix incrementations, a better practice is to put the incrementation on a line by itself, when possible, and use grouping (we will discuss this in the next section).

Order of operations and grouping

When an expression contains two or more operators, it is essential to know which operation will be performed first, next, and so on. This is known as the **order of evaluation**. Not all operations are evaluated from left to right.

Consider $3 + 4 * 5$. Does this evaluate to 35; $3 + 4 = 7 * 5 = 35$? Or does this evaluate to 23; $4 * 5 = 20 + 3 = 23$?

If, on the other hand, we explicitly group these operations in the manner desired, we remove all doubt. Either $3 + (4 * 5)$ or $(3 + 4) * 5$ is what we actually intend.

C has built-in precedence and associativity of operations that determine how and in what order operations are performed. Precedence determines which operations have a higher priority and are, therefore, performed before those with a lower priority. Associativity refers to how operators of the same precedence are evaluated—from left to right or from right to left.

The following table shows all the operators we have already encountered along with some that we will encounter in later chapters (such as postfix `[]` . `->` and unary `*` `&`). The highest precedence is the postfix group at the top and the lowest precedence is the sequence operator at the bottom:

Group	Operators	Associativity
Postfix	`() [] . ->`	Left to right
Unary	`! ~ ++ -- + - * & (type) sizeof`	Right to left
Multiplicative	`* / %`	Left to right
Additive	`+ -`	Left to right
Shifting	`>> <<`	Left to right
Relational	`< <= > >=`	Left to right
Equality	`== !=`	Left to right
Bitwise AND	`&`	Left to right
Bitwise complement	`^`	Left to right
Bitwise OR	`|`	Left to right
Logical AND	`&&`	Left to right
Logical OR	`||`	Left to right
Conditional	`: ?`	Right to left
Assignment	`= += -+ *= /= %= &= != <<= >>=`	Right to left
Sequence	`,`	Left to right

What is most interesting here is that (1) grouping happens first, and (2) assignment typically happens last in a statement. Well, this is not quite true. Sequencing happens after everything else. Typically, though, sequencing is not often used in a single statement. It can, however, be quite useful as a part of the `for` complex statement, as we shall learn in `Chapter 7`, *Exploring Loops and Iterations*.

While it is important to know precedence and associativity, I would encourage you to be very explicit in your expressions and use grouping to make your intentions clear and unambiguous. As we encounter additional operators in subsequent chapters, we will revisit this operator precedence table.

Summary

Expressions provide a way of computing a value. Expressions are often constructed from constants, variables, or function results combined together by operators.

We have explored C's rich set of operators. We have seen how arithmetic operators (such as addition, subtraction, multiplication, division, and remainder) can apply to different data types—integers, real numbers, and characters. We touched on character operations; we will learn much more about these in `Chapter 15`, *Working with Strings*. We have learned about implicit and explicit type conversions. We learned about C boolean values, created truth tables for logical operators, and learned how relational operations evaluate to boolean values. We have explored C's shorthand operators when used with assignments and explored C's shortest shorthand operators for autoincrement and autodecrement. Finally, we learned about C's operator precedence and how to avoid reliance on it with the grouping operator. Throughout the chapter, we have written programs to demonstrate how these operators work. Expressions and operators are the core building blocks of computational statements. Everything we have learned in this chapter will be an essential part of any programs we create going forward.

In the next two chapters, `Chapter 6`, *Exploring Conditional Program Flow*, and `Chapter 7`, *Exploring Loops and Iterations*, not only will we use these expressions for computations, but we will also learn how expressions are essential parts of other complex C statements (`if()... else...`, `for()...`, `while()...`, and `do...while()`). Our programs can then become more interesting and more useful.

6

Exploring Conditional Program Flow

Not only do the values of variables change when a program runs, but the flow of execution can also change through a program. The order of statement execution can be altered depending upon the results of conditional expressions. In a conditional program flow, there is one mandatory branch and one optional branch. If the condition is met, the first branch, or path, will be taken; if not, the second path will be taken.

We can illustrate such a branching with the following simple example:

> *Is today Saturday?*
> *If so, do the laundry.*
> *Else, go for a walk.*

In this conditional statement, we are instructed to do the laundry if today is Saturday. For the remaining days that are not Saturday, we are instructed to go for a walk.

This is a simple conditional statement; it has a single conditional expression, a single mandatory branch, and a single optional branch. We will explore conditional statements that evaluate multiple conditions. We will also explore conditional statements where multiple branches may be taken.

The following topics will be covered in this chapter:

- Understanding various conditional expressions
- Using `if()`... `else`... to determine whether a value is even or odd
- Using a `switch()`... statement to give a message based on a single letter
- Determining ranges of values using `if()`... `else if()`... `else if()`... `else`...

- Exploring nesting `if()... else...` statements
- Understanding the pitfalls of nesting `if()... else...` statements

Technical requirements

As detailed in the *Technical requirements* section of `Chapter 1`, *Running Hello, World!*, continue to use the tools you have chosen.

The source code for this chapter can be found at `https://github.com/PacktPublishing/Learn-C-Programming`.

Understanding conditional expressions

We have seen how execution progresses from one statement to the next with simple statements. We have also seen how program execution can be diverted or redirected via a function call, after which it returns to the same place. We are now going to see how the flow of execution can change and how statements can be executed or skipped with some of C's complex statements.

Execution flow will be determined by the result of evaluating conditional expressions, which we learned about in the previous chapter. Conditional expressions may be either simple or complex. Complex conditional statements should be clear and unambiguous. If they cannot be made clear and unambiguous, they should be reworked to be less complex. When reworking them results in more awkward code, the complex conditional expression should, however, be thoroughly commented. Careful consideration should be given to the valid inputs and expected results of the conditional expression.

Conditional expressions appear in very specific places within a complex statement. In every case, the conditional expression appears enclosed between `(` and `)` in the complex statement. The result will always be evaluated as `true` or `false`, regardless of the expression's complexity.

Some conditional expressions are given as follows:

```
( bResult == true )
( bResult )                          /* A compact alternative. */

( status != 0 )
( status )                           /* A compact alternative where
status is      */
```

```
                                          /* only ever false when it is 0
      */
      ( count < 3 )
      ( count > 0 && count <= maxCount ) /* Both must be true for overall
      expression */
                                          /* to be true.
      */
```

In each case, the result is one of two possible outcomes. In this manner, we can use the result to perform one pathway, or branch, or the other branch.

Introducing the if()... else... complex statement

`if()... else...` is a complex statement that can have two forms—a simple form where the `if()...` part is present, and a complete form where both the `if()...` and `else...` parts are present.

In the `if()... else...` complex statement, either the `true` path or the `false` path will be executed. The path that is not taken will be ignored. In the simplest `if()...` statement where there is no `false` path, the `true` path is executed only if the conditional expression is true.

The statement has two syntactical forms, as follows:

- The simplest form (no false path), as illustrated in the following code snippet:

```
if( expression )
  statement1

statement3          /* next statement to be executed */
```

- The complete form (both, the `true` path and `false` path), as illustrated in the following code snippet:

```
if( expression )
  statement1
else
  statement2

statement3          /* next statement to be executed */
```

In both the if()... (simple) and if()... else... (complete) statements, expression is evaluated. If the result is true, statement1 is executed. In the complete form, if the expression result is false, statement2 is executed. In either case, the execution continues with the next statement, statement3.

Note that the statements do not indicate whether there is a semicolon or not. This is because statement1 or statement2 may either be simple statements (which are terminated with a ;) or they may be compound statements, enclosed between { and }. In the latter case, each statement with the statement block will be terminated by ;, but not the overall block itself.

A simple use of this statement would be in determining whether an integer value is even or odd. This is a good opportunity to put the % modulo operator into action. A function that does this using the simple form is illustrated in the following code block:

```
bool isEven( int num )  {
   bool isEven = false;   // Initialize with assumption that
                          // it's not false.
   if( (num % 2) == 0 )
      isEven = true;
   return isEven;
}
```

In the preceding function, we first assume the value is not even, and then test it with a simple if statement and return the result. Notice that the if()... branch is a single statement that is only executed if num % 2 is 0. We had to use a relational operator in the condition because when num is even, num % 2 evaluates to 0, which would then be converted to the Boolean false, which would not be the correct result. If the condition is false, the if branch is not executed, and we return the value of isEven.

This function could also be written in a slightly condensed form using multiple return statements instead of the num local variable, as follows:

```
bool isEven ( int num)  {
   if( num % 2 )
      return false;
   return true;
}
```

In the preceding function, we use a very simple conditional that will be nonzero only if num is odd; therefore, we must return false for the function to be correct. This function has two exit points, one that will be executed if the test condition is true, and the second that will be executed when the if branch is not executed. When num is even, the second return statement will never be executed.

The most condensed version of this function would be as follows:

```
bool isEven ( int num)   {
  return !(num % 2 )
}
```

When num is even, num % 2 gives 0 (false), and so we have to apply NOT to return the correct result.

A function that uses the complete form of this complex statement would be as follows:

```
bool isOdd ( int num)   {
  bool isOdd;
  if( num % 2 ) isOdd = true;
  else          isOdd = false;
  return isOdd;
}
```

In the preceding function, isOdd is not initialized. We must, therefore, ensure that whatever value is given as input to the isOdd function is assigned either true or false. As in the preceding examples, each branch of the complex statement is a single statement assigning a value to isOdd.

To explore various uses of this complex statement, let's begin exploring a function that calculates leap years. Understanding of leap years in Western civilization did not appear until the year 1752. In that year, it was then assumed the solar year was 365.25 days, or 356 + 1/4, hence the use of the modulo of 4. So, in our first approximation of calculating leap years, our function would look like this:

```
bool isLeapYear( int year )   {
      // Leap years not part of Gregorian calendar until after 1752.
      // Is year before 1751?
      // Yes: return false.
      // No: "fall through" to next condition.
      //
  if( year < 1751 ) return false;

      // Is year an multiple of 4? (remainder will be 0)
      // Yes: return true.
      // No: "fall through" and return false.
      //
  if( (year % 4) == 0 ) return true;

  return false;
}
```

In this function block, each time we know whether the given year is a leap year or not, we return from the function block with that result using return logic to stop the execution of statements within the function. Note that there are several ways in which we could have written the second conditional expression, some are which are shown in the following code block:

```
if(   (year % 4) == 0 ) ...
if(   (year % 4) < 1 ) ...
if(  !(year % 4)  ) ...
```

Of these, the first way is the most explicit, while the last is the most compact. All are correct.

The remainder of this program looks like this:

```
#include <stdio.h>
#include <stdbool.h>

bool isLeapYear( int );

int main( void )   {
  int year;

  printf( "Determine if a year is a leap year or not.\n\n" );
  printf( "Enter year: ");
  scanf( "%d" , &year );

  // A simple version of printing the result.
  if( isLeapYear( year ) )
    printf( "%d year is a leap year\n" , year );
  else
    printf( "%d year is not a leap year\n" , year );

  // A more C-like version to print the result.
  printf( "%d year is%sa leap year\n" , year , isLeapYear( year ) ? " " : " not " );

  return 0;
}
```

In the main() code block, we use both an if()... else... statement to print out the result and a more idiomatic C-like printf() statement, which uses the ternary (conditional) operator. Either method is fine. In the C-like version, %s represents a string (a sequence of characters enclosed in"..."), to be filled in the output string.

Create a new file named `cle` and add the code. Compile the program and run it. You should see the following output:

```
> cc leapYear1.c
> a.out
Determine if a year is a leap year or not.

Enter year: 2000
2000 year is a leap year
2000 year is a leap year
> a.out
Determine if a year is a leap year or not.

Enter year: 1900
1900 year is a leap year
1900 year is a leap year
>
```

But is this program correct? No, it is not, because of leap centuries. The year 2000 is a leap year but 1900 is not. It turns out that the solar year is slightly less than 365.25 days; it is actually approximately 365.2425 days, or (365 + 1/4 - 1/100 + 1/400). Notice that we'll have to account for 1/100—every 100 years—and 1/400—every 400 years. Our function will have to get a bit more complicated when we revisit it after the next section.

Using a switch()... complex statement

With the `if()... else...` statement, the conditional expression evaluates to only one of two values—`true` or `false`. But what if we had a single result that could have multiple values, with each value requiring a different bit of code execution?

For this, we have the `switch()...` statement. This statement evaluates an expression to a single result and selects a pathway where the result matches the known values that we care about.

The syntax of the `switch()...` statement is as follows:

```
switch( expression )  {
  case constant-1 :     statement-1
  case constant-2 :     statement-2
  ...
  case constant-n :     statement-n
  default :             statement-default
}
```

Here, the expression evaluates to a single result. The next part of the statement is called the **case-statement block**, which contains one or more `case` clauses and an optional `default:` clause. In the case-statement block, the result is compared to each of the constant values in each `case` clause. When they are equal, the code pathway for that `case` clause is evaluated. These are indicated by the `case <value>:` clauses. When none of the specified constants matches the result, the default pathway is executed, as indicated by the `default:` clause.

Even though the `default:` clause is optional, it is always a good idea to have one, even if only to print an error message. By doing so, you can ensure that your `switch()` statement is being used as intended and that you haven't forgotten to account for a changed or a new value being considered in the `switch` statement.

As before, each statement could be a simple statement, or it could be a compound statement.

We could rewrite our leap year calculation to use the `switch` statement as follows:

```
switch( year % 4 )  {
  case 0 :
    return true;
  case 1 :
  case 2 :
  case 3 :
  default :
    return false;
}
```

Notice that for the `case 1`, `case 2`, and `case 3`, there is no statement at all. The evaluation of the result of the expression continues to the next case. It falls through each case evaluation into the default case and returns `false`.

We can simplify this to the only value we really care about, which is 0, as follows:

```
switch( year % 4 )  {
  case 0 :
    return true;
  default :
    return false;
}
```

In the context of the `isLeapYear()` function, the `return` statements exit the `switch()` statement as well as exiting the function block.

However, there are many times where we need to perform some actions for a given pathway and then perform no further case comparisons. The match was found and we are done with the `switch` statement. In such an instance, we don't want to fall through. We need a way to exit the pathway as well as exit the case-statement block. For that, there is the `break` statement.

The `break` statement causes the execution to jump out, and to the end of the statement block, where it is encountered.

To see this in action, we'll write a `calc()` function that takes two values and a single character operator. It will return the result of the operation on the two values, as follows:

```
double calc( double operand1 , double operand2 , char operator )  {
  double result = 0.0;

  printf( "%g %c %g = " , operand1 , operator , operand2 );
  switch( operator )  {
    case '+':
      result = operand1 + operand2;        break;
    case '-':
      result = operand1 - operand2;        break;
    case '*':
      result = operand1 * operand2;        break;
    case '/':
      if( operand2 == 0.0 )  {
        printf( "*** ERROR *** division by %g is undefined.\n" ,
              operand2 );
        return result;
      } else {
        result = operand1 / operand2;
      }
      break;
    case '%':
      // Remaindering: assume operations on integers (cast first).
      result = (int) operand1 % (int) operand2;
      break;
    default:
      printf( "*** ERROR *** unknown operator; operator must be + - * / or
%%\n" );
      return result;
      break;
  }
  /* break brings us to here */
  printf( "%g\n" , result );
  return result;
}
```

In this function, `double` data types are used for each operand so that we can calculate whatever is given to us. Through implicit type conversion, `int` and `float` will be converted to the wider `double` type. We can cast the result to the desired type after we make the function call because it is at the function call where we will know the data types being given to the function.

For each of the five characters-as-operators that we care about, there is a case-clause where we perform the desired operation assigning a result. In the case of `/`, we do a further check to verify that division by zero is not being done.

Experiment—comment out this `if` statement and do the division without the check to see what happens.

In the case of `%`, we cast each of the operands to `int` since `%` is an integer-only operator.

Experiment—remove the casting and add some calls to `calc()` with various real numbers to see what happens.

Also, notice the benefit of having a `default:` clause that handles the case when our `calc` program is called with an invalid operator. This kind of built-in error checking becomes invaluable over the life of a program that may change many times at the hands of many different programmers.

To complete our `calc.c` program, the rest of the program is comprised as follows:

```c
#include <stdio.h>
#include <stdbool.h>

double calc( double operand1, double operand2 , char operator );

int main( void )  {
  calc( 1.0 , 2.0 , '+' );
  calc( 10.0 , 7.0 , '-' );
  calc( 4.0 , 2.3 , '*' );
  calc( 5.0 , 0.0 , '/' );
  calc( 5.0 , 2.0 , '%' );
  calc( 1.0 , 2.0 , '?' );

  return 0;
}
```

In this program, we call `calc()` with all of the valid operators as well as an invalid operator. In the fourth call to `calc()`, we also attempt a division by zero. Save this program, and compile it. You should see the following output:

```
|> cc calc.c
|> a.out
1 + 2 = 3
10 - 7 = 3
4 * 2.3 = 9.2
5 / 0 = *** ERROR *** division by 0 is undefined.
5 % 2 = 1
1 ? 2 = *** ERROR ***  unknown operator; operator must be + - * / or %
>
```

In each case, the correct result is given for both valid operations and for invalid operations. Don't forget to try the experiments mentioned.

The `switch()`... statement is ideal when a single variable is being tested for multiple values. Next, we'll see a more flexible version of the `switch()`... statement.

Introducing multiple if()... statements

The `switch` statement tests a single value. Could we have done this another way? Yes—with the `if()`... `else if()`... `else if()`... `else`... construct. We could have written the `calc()` function using multiple `if()`... `else`... statements, in this way:

```c
double calc( double operand1 , double operand2 , char operator )  {
  double result = 0.0;

  printf( "%g %c %g = " , operand1 , operator , operand2 );
  if( operator == '+' )
    result = operand1 + operand2;
  else if( operator == '-' )
    result = operand1 - operand2;
  else if( operator == '*' )
    result = operand1 * operand2;
  else if( operator ==  '/'
    if( operand2 == 0.0 ) {
      printf( "*** ERROR *** division by %g is undefined.\n" ,
              operand2 );
      return result;
    } else {
      result = operand1 / operand2;
    }
```

```
    else if( operator == '%') {
       // Remaindering: assume operations on integers (cast first).
       result = (int) operand1 % (int) operand2;
    } else {
       printf( "*** ERROR *** unknown operator; operator must be + - * / or
%%\n" );
       return result;
    }
    printf( "%g\n" , result );
    return result;
}
```

This solution, while perfectly fine, introduces a number of concepts that need to be clarified, as follows:

- The first if()... and each else if()... statement correlates directly to each case : clause of the switch()... statement. The final else... clause corresponds to the default: clause of the switch statement.

- In the first three if()... statements, the true path is a single simple statement.

- In the fourth if()... statement, even though there are multiple lines, the if()... else... statement is itself a single complex statement. Therefore, it is also a single statement.
  This if()... statement is slightly different than the other statements; it uses a conditional expression for a different variable, and it occurs in the else if()... branch as a complex statement. This is called a *nested* if()... statement.

- Again, in the last two pathways, each branch has multiple simple statements. To make them into a single statement, we must make them a part of a compound statement by enclosing them in { and }.
  Experiment—remove the { and } from the last two pathways to see what happens.

- You might argue that for this case, the switch()... statement is clearer and thus preferred, or you may not think so.

In this code sample, we are comparing a single value to a set of constants. There are instances where a switch statement is not only unusable but cannot be used. One such instance is when we want to simplify ranges of values into one or more single values. Consider the `describeTemp()` function that, when given a temperature, provides a relevant description of that temperature. This function is illustrated in the following code block:

```
void describeTemp( double degreesF )  {
  char* message;
  if( degreesF > 100.0 ) message = "hot! Stay in the shade.";
  else if( degreesF >= 80.0 ) message = "perfect weather for swimming.";
  else if( degreesF >= 60.0 ) message = "very comfortable.";
  else if( degreesF >= 40.0 ) message = "chilly.";
  else if( degreesF >= 20.0 ) message = "freezing, but good skiing
weather.";
  else message= "way too cold to do much of anything!" ;
  printf( "%g°F is %s\n" , degreesF , message );
}
```

In this function, a temperature is given as a `double` type, representing °F. Based on this value, a series of `if()`… `else`… statements select the appropriate range, and then print a message describing that temperature. The `switch()`… statement could not be used for this.

We could also have written `describeTemp()` using the `&&` logical operator, as follows:

```
void describeTemp( double degreesF )  {
  char* message;
  if( degreesF >= 100.0 )
    message = "hot! Stay in the shade.";
  if( degreesF < 100.0 && degreesF >= 80.0 )
    message = "perfect weather for swimming.";
  if( degreesF <  80.0 && defgredegreesF >= 60.0 )
    message = "very comfortable.";
  if( degreesF <  60.0 && degreesF >= 40.0 )
    message = "chilly.";
  if( degreesF <  40.0  degreesF >= 20.0 )
    message = "freezing, but good skiing weather.";
  if( degreesF < 20.0 )
    message= "way too cold to do much of anything!" ;

  printf( "%g°F is %s\n" , degreesF , message );
}
```

In this version of `describeTemp()`, each `if()`... statement checks for a range of values of `degreesF`. Most of the conditional expressions test an upper limit and a lower limit. Notice that there is no `else()`... clause for any of these. Also, notice that for any given value of `degreesF`, one—and only one—`if()`... statement will be satisfied. It is important that all ranges of possible values are covered by this kind of logic. This is called *fall-through* logic, where executions fall through each `if()`... statement to the very end. We will see further examples of fall-through logic in the next section.

The full program, which also exercises the various temperature ranges, is found in `temp.c`. When you compile and run this program, you see the following output:

```
> cc temp.c
> a.out
100°F is hot! Stay in the shade.
85°F is perfect weather for swimming.
70°F is very comfortable.
55°F is chilly.
40°F is chilly.
25°F is freezing, but good skiing weather.
10°F is way too cold to do much of anything!
-5°F is way too cold to do much of anything!
>
```

We can now return to our `leapYear.c` program and add the proper logic for leap centuries. Copy the `leapYear1.c` program to `leapYear2.c`, which we will modify. We keep some parts from the preceding function, but this time, our logic includes both leap centuries (every 400 years) and non-leap centuries (every 100 years), as follows:

```
   // isLeapYear logic conforms to algorithm given in
   // https://en.wikipedia.org/wiki/Leap_year.
   //
 bool isLeapYear( int year )  {
   bool isLeap = false;

     // Leap years not part of Gregorian calendar until after 1752.

   if( year < 1751 )               // Is is before leap years known.
     isLeap = false;
   else if( (year % 4 ) != 0 )     // Year is not a multiple of 4.
     isLeap = false;
   else if( ( year % 400 ) == 0 )  // Year is a multiple of 400.
     isLeap = true;
   else if( (year % 100) == 0 )    // Year is multiple of 100.
     isLeap = false;
   else
     isLeap = true; // Year is a multiple of 4 (other conditions 400
```

```
                         // years, 100 years) have already been considered.
        return isLeap;
    }
```

This underlying logic we are trying to mimic lends itself naturally to a series
of if()...else... statements. We now handle 100-year and 400-year leap years properly.
Save leapYear2.c, compile it, and run it. You should see the following output:

```
> cc leapYear2.c
> a.out
Determine if a year is a leap year or not.

Enter year: 2000
2000 year is a leap year
> a.out
Determine if a year is a leap year or not.

Enter year: 1900
1900 year is not a leap year
>
```

We are again using a sequence of if()... else if()... else... statements to turn a year
value into a simple Boolean result. However, in this function, instead of returning when the
result is known, we assign that result to a local variable, isLeap, and only return it at the
very end of the function block. This method is sometimes preferable to having multiple
return statements in a function, especially when the function becomes long or contains
particularly complicated logic.

Notice that it correctly determines that 2000 is a leap year and that 1900 is not.

Using nested if()... else... statements

Sometimes, we can make the logic of if()... else... statements clearer by nesting if()...
else... statements within either one or both clauses of the if()... else... statements.

In our isLeap() example, someone new to the intricacies of Gregorian calendar
development and the subtleties of century leap year calculation might have to pause and
wonder a bit about our if/else fall-through logic. Actually, this case is pretty simple; much
more tangled examples of such a logic can be found. Nonetheless, we can make our logic a
bit clearer by nesting an if ... else ... statement within one of the if()... else...
clauses.

Copy `leapYear2.c` to `leapYear3.c`, which we will now modify. Our `isLeap()` function now looks like this:

```
bool isLeapYear( int year )  {
  bool isLeap = false;

    // Leap years not part of Gregorian calendar until after 1752.
    //
  if( year < 1751 )                 // Is is before leap years known?
    isLeap = false;
  else if( (year % 4 ) != 0 )   // Year is not a multiple of 4.
    isLeap = false;
  else {                             // Year is a multiple of 4.
    if( (year % 400 ) == 0 )
      isLeap = true;
    else if( (year % 100 ) == 0 )
      isLeap = false;
    else
      isLeap = true;
  }
  return isLeap;
}
```

Again, we use a local variable, `isLeap`. In the last `else` clause, we know at that point, that year is divisible by four. So, now, we nest another `if()`... `else`... series of statements to account for leap centuries. Again, you might argue that this is clearer than before, or you might not.

Notice, however, that we enclosed—*nested*—the last series of `if()`... `else`... statements in a statement block. This was done not only to make its purpose clearer to other programmers but also to avoid the *dangling else problem*.

The dangling else... problem

When multiple statements are written in `if()`... `else`... statements where a single statement is expected, surprising results may occur. This is sometimes called the **dangling else problem** and is illustrated in the following code snippet:

```
if( x == 0 ) if( y == 0 ) printf( "y equals 0\n" );
else printf( "what does not equal 0\n" );
```

To which if()... does the else... belong—the first one or the second one? To correct this possible ambiguity, it is often best to always use compound statements in if()... and else... clauses to make your intention unambiguous. Many compilers will give an error such as the following: warning: add explicit braces to avoid dangling else [-Wdangling-else].

On the other hand, some do not. The best way to remove doubt is to use brackets to associate the else... clause with the proper if()... clause. The following code snippet will remove both ambiguity and the compiler warning:

```
if( x == 0 )   {
   if( y == 0 ) printf( "y equals 0\n" );
}
else printf( "x does not equal 0\n" );
```

In the usage shown in the preceding code block, the else... clause is now clearly associated with the first if()..., and we see x does not equal 0 in our output.

In the following code block, the else... clause is now clearly associated with the second if()... clause, and we'll see y does not equal 0 in our output. The first if()... statement has no else... clause, as can be seen here:

```
if( x == 0 )   {
   if( y == 0 ) printf( "y equals 0\n" );
   else printf( "y does not equal 0\n" );
}
```

Notice how the if(y == 0) statement is nested within the if(x == 0) statement.

In my own programming experience, whenever I have begun writing an if()... else... statement, *rarely* has each clause been limited to a single statement. Most often, as I add more logic to the if()... else... statement, I have to go back and turn them into compound statements with { and }. As a consequence, I now *always* begin writing each clause as compound statements to avoid having to go back and add them in. Before I begin adding the conditional expression and statements in either of the compound statements, my initial entry looks like this:

```
if( )   {
   // blah blah blahblah
} else {
   // gabba gabba gab gab
}
```

You may find that the `}` `else` `{` line is better when broken into three separate lines. The choice is a matter of personal style. This is illustrated in the following code snippet:

```
if( )  {
   // blah blah blahblah
}
else {
   // gabba gabba gab gab
}
```

In the first code example, the `else`... closing block and the `if()` opening block are combined on one line. In the second code example, each is on a line by itself. The former is a bit more compact, while the latter is less so. Either form is acceptable, and their use will depend upon the length and complexity of the code in the enclosed blocks.

Stylistically, we could also begin each of the `if` blocks with an opening `{` on its own line, as follows:

```
if( )
{
   // blah blah blahblah
} else {
   // gabba gabba gab gab
}
```

Alternatively, we could do this:

```
if( ) {
   // blah, blah blah blah.
}
else
{
   // gabba gabba, gab gab.
}
```

Some people prefer block *openings* on their own line, while others prefer block openings at the end of the conditional statement. Again, either way is correct. Which way is used depends on both personal preference and the necessity of following the conventions of the existing code base; consistency is paramount.

Summary

From this chapter, we learned that we can not only alter program flow with function calls but also execute or omit program statements through the use of conditional statements. The `switch()`... statement operates on a single value, comparing it to the desired set of possible constant values and executing the pathway that matches the constant value. The `if()`... `else`... statement has a much wider variety of forms and uses. `if()`... `else`... statements can be chained into longer sequences to mimic the `switch()`... statement and to provide a richer set of conditions than possible with `switch()`.... `if()`... `else`... statements can also be nested in one or both clauses to either make the purpose of that branch clear or the condition for each pathway less complex.

In these conditional statements, execution remains straightforward, from top to bottom, where only specific parts of the statement are executed. In the next chapter, we'll see how to perform multiple iterations of the same code path, with various forms of looping and the somewhat stigmatized `goto` statement.

7
Exploring Loops and Iteration

Some operations need to be repeated one or more times before their result is completely evaluated. The code to be repeated could be copied the required number of times, but this would be cumbersome. Instead, for this, there are loops—`for` ..., `while` ..., and `do` ... `while` loops. Loops are for statements that must be evaluated multiple times. We will explore C loops. After considering loops, the much-maligned `goto` statement will be considered.

The following topics will be covered in this chapter:

- Understanding brute-force repetition and why it might be bad
- Exploring looping with the `while()`... statement
- Exploring looping with the `for()`... statement
- Exploring looping with the `do` ... `while()` statement
- Understanding when you would use each of these looping statements
- Understanding how loops could be interchanged, if necessary
- Exploring the good, the bad, and the ugly of using `goto`
- Exploring safe alternatives to `goto`—`continue` and `break`
- Understanding the appropriate use of loops that never end

Technical requirements

As detailed in the *Technical requirements* section of `Chapter 1`, *Running Hello, World!*, continue to use the tools you have chosen.

The source code for this chapter can be found at `https://github.com/PacktPublishing/Learn-C-Programming`.

Understanding repetition

Very often, we need to perform a series of statements repeatedly. We might want to perform a calculation on each member of a set of values, or we might want to perform a calculation using all of the members in a set of values. Given a collection of values, we also might want to iterate over the whole collection to find the desired value, to count all the values, to perform some kind of calculation on them, or to manipulate the set in some way—say, to sort it.

There are a number of ways to do this. The simplest, yet most restrictive way is the **brute-force method**. This can be done regardless of the language being used. A more dynamic and flexible method is to iterate or repeatedly loop. C provides three interrelated looping statements—`while()`..., `for( )`..., and `do...while()`. Each of them has a control or continuation expression, and a loop body. The most general form of these is the `while()`... loop. Lastly, there is the archaic `goto label` method of looping. Unlike other languages, there is no `repeat ... until()` statement; such a statement can easily be constructed from any of the others.

Each looping statement consists of the following two basic parts:

- The loop continuation expression
- The body of the loop

When the loop continuation expression evaluates to `true`, the body of the loop is executed. The execution then returns to the continuation expression, evaluates it, and, if `true`, the body of the loop is again executed. This cycle repeats until the continuation expression evaluates to `false`; the loop ends, and the execution commences after the end of the loop body.

There are two general types of continuation expressions used for looping statements, as follows:

- **Counter-controlled looping**, where the number of iterations is dependent upon a count of some kind. The desired number of iterations is known beforehand. The counter may be increasing or decreasing.
- **Condition-** or **sentinel-controlled looping**, where the number of iterations is dependent upon some condition to remain true for the loop to continue. The actual number of iterations is not known. A sentinel is a value that must attain a certain state before the loop completes.

We will explore counter-controlled looping in this chapter and return to sentinel-controlled looping in later chapters when we get input from the console and read input from files.

C also provides some additional looping control mechanisms such as break, which we saw in the switch()... statement in Chapter 6, *Exploring Conditional Program Flow*, and continue. These provide even greater looping control when simple counters or sentinel values aren't enough to meet our needs in special circumstances.

To boost our motivation for iteration and repetition, let's visit a problem that was presented to the young, brilliant mathematician Gauss in the 17th century. When Gauss was in elementary school, to fill time before a recess, the teacher assigned the task of adding numbers 1 to 100 (or some such range). While all the other students were busily performing the tedious task of adding each number one by one (brute-force), young Gauss came up with a simple yet elegant equation to perform the task nearly instantly. His general solution was the following equation:

```
sum(n) = n * (n+1) / 2
```

Here, n is the highest number in a sequence of natural numbers (integers) beginning at 1.

So, throughout this chapter, we will explore the problem presented to the young Gauss—starting with his insightful equation and then moving on to various programmatic solutions—first, using brute-force addition, which Gauss cleverly avoided, then, performing the task using each of the looping constructs C provides, and, finally, looping with the dreaded goto statement.

The following code snippet shows Gauss's equation in a sumNviaGauss() C function:

```c
int sumNviaGauss( int N )   {
  int sum = 0;
  sum = N * ( N+1 ) / 2;
  return sum;
}
```

The input parameter is N. The result is the sum of integer values 1 .. N. This function is a part of the gauss_bruteforce.c program and there are links in that program for delightful explanations of this equation, along with the variations of it, which we need not go into here. The curious reader can download gauss_bruteforce.c and explore the links given there.

Note that the N * (N+1) / 2 equation requires ( ) because * and / have higher precedence than +. () has higher precedence than all the operators here, and thus gives us the desired result.

What is the point of providing this solution here? As C programmers, we have all of these wonderful C statements that we can use to construct complex calculations for solving a complex mathematical problem. However, we must remember that there may be an equation or *algorithm* that exists already that is much simpler and more generalized than anything that we may hope to concoct. For this reason, every programmer should be familiar with the *Numerical Recipes in X* books that provide complex mathematical solutions in the X language, where X is either C, Fortran, or C++, to some of the most demanding and challenging math problems that have vexed mathematicians, scientists, engineers, computer scientists, and operations researchers alike. Ignore such works at your peril!

As an aside, I should mention that some of the most interesting and useful algorithms I've ever encountered as a computer scientist have come from the operations research guys. They seem to be always attempting to solve some really difficult, yet important problems. But that is a topic out of scope for this book.

While young Gauss abhorred the use of brute force to solve the problem he was given, sometimes brute force may be the only way or even the best way, but not often. We examine that next.

Understanding brute-force repetition

In brute-force repetition, a statement or series of statements to be repeated is simply copied over and over the required number of times. This is the most restrictive form of repetition because the number of repeats is hardcoded in and can't be changed at runtime.

There are several other downsides to this type of repetition. First, what if you had to change one or more of the statements that have been copied over and over? Tedious would be the word to describe the work required to either change all of them (error-prone) or to delete, correct, and recopy the lines (also error-prone). Another downside is that it makes the code unnecessarily bulky. Copying 10 lines is one thing, but 100 or 1,000 is another thing altogether.

However, there are also times when copying a single statement multiple times is actually necessary. The situation where this occurs is in an advanced topic involving *loop unrolling*, which we will not cover in this book. If you are still interested after you have finished this chapter, you can perform your own internet search to find out more. It is, as a reminder, an advanced topic related to specialized high-performance situations. You will have many other *fish to fry* before—if ever—you will need to master that topic.

The `sum100viaBruteForce()` function is a brute-force function to perform our desired task, and is shown in the following code block:

```
int sum100bruteForce( void )   {
  int sum = 0;
  sum   = 1;
  sum += 2;
  sum += 3;
  ...
  ...
  sum += 99;
  sum += 100;
  return sum;
}
```

Notice that we do not include every single line of this over-100-line function. It is very tedious and dull. Yet, in fact, it correctly calculates the sum of `1 .. 100`. This function only works for this sequence and no other. You'd need a different brute-force method to calculate `1 .. 10` or `1 .. 50`. Yawn. Even more tedium.

Here is a second version, a bit more general, using some useful C operators—the `sum100viaBruteForce2()` function, illustrated in the following code block:

```
int sum100bruteForce2( void )   {
  int sum = 0;
  int num = 1;

  sum   =   num;
  sum += ++num;
  sum += ++num;
  sum += ++num;
  ...
  ...
  sum += ++num;
  sum += ++num; // 100

  return sum;
}
```

Notice, again, that we do not include every single tedious line of this over-100-line function. While this approach removes the need to actually type in each value from 1 to 100, it is equally tedious. I found that it was actually more difficult to create than the first version (that is, `sum100viaBruteForce()`) because it was hard to keep track of how many `sum += ++num;` lines I had copied. You'll see in the `gauss_bruteforce.c` file that I added comments to help keep things straightfoward and simple.

Each of these functions is over 100 lines long. That's like over 100 miles of dry, dusty, dull road to drive across on a hot, arid, boring day with no rest stops and no ice water. The compiler might not care but those who will later have to read/update your code will.

When you enter these functions yourself, it is acceptable in this case to use copy and paste to help overcome the tedium.

The `main()` function for `gauss_bruteforce.c` is as follows:

```c
#include <stdio.h>
#include <stdbool.h>

int sum100bruteForce( void );
int sum100bruteForce2( void );
int sumNviaGauss( int N );

int main( void )    {
  int n = 100;
  printf( "The sum of 1..100 = %d (via brute force)\n" ,
          sum100bruteForce() );
  printf( "The sum of 1..100 = %d (via brute force2)\n" ,
          sum100bruteForce2() );
  printf( "The sum of 1..%d = %d (via Gaussian insight)\n" ,
          n , sumNviaGauss( n ) );
  return 0;
}
```

Create the `gauss_bruteforce.c` file, then enter the `main()` function and the three sum functions. Compile the program with the `cc gauss_bruteforce.c -o gauss_bruteforce` command. The `-o` command option followed by a name generates an executable file with that name instead of `a.out` (the default executable name that we have been using before now). Run the program. You should see the following output from `gauss_bruteforce`:

```
Learn C : Chapter 7 > cc gauss_bruteforce.c -o gauss_bruteforce
Learn C : Chapter 7 > gauss_bruteforce
The sum of 1..100 = 5050 (via brute force)
The sum of 1..100 = 5050 (via brute force2)
The sum of 1..100 = 5050 (via Gaussian insight)
Learn C : Chapter 7 >
```

In the preceding screenshot, you can see that each of the three methods to calculate the sum of 1..100 gives us the same result.

Thankfully, there are better ways (well, still not as good as Gauss's original solution, but better from a C programming perspective) to solve this problem, and—happily for us—to illustrate looping.

As we examine the various forms of repetitive methods, we will solve Gauss's problem each time. This approach affords a couple of advantages. As you work with loop iteration counters, any starting or stopping errors made in the loop counter condition will result in a different sum; so, by using the same problem that we have already solved, we can verify our code. Also, since we've already solved the problem in two ways, it will not be new, and will even become familiar. Therefore, we can focus more on the variations in the syntax of each looping method.

Introducing the while()... statement

`while()`... statement has the following syntax:

```
while( continuation_expression ) statement_body
```

`continuation_expression` is evaluated. If its result is `true`, `statement_body` is executed and the process repeats. When `continuation_expression` evaluates to `false`, the loop ends; the execution resumes after the `statement_body`. If the `continuation_expression` initially evaluates to `false`, the `statement_body` loop is never executed.

The `statement_body` is—or may be—a single statement, or even the `null` statement (a single ; without an expression), but most often, it is a compound statement. Note that there is no semicolon specified as a part of the `while()`... statement. A semicolon would appear as a part of a single statement in a `statement_body`, or would be absent in the case of the `statement_body` consisting of a { ... } compound statement.

Also note that, within the `statement_body`, there must be some means to change the value(s) used in the `continuation_expression`. If not, the loop will either never execute or it will never terminate once begun. The latter condition is also known as an **infinite loop**. Therefore, in counter-controlled looping, the counter must be changed somewhere in the body of the loop.

Returning to Gauss's problem, we'll use a `while()`... loop in a function that takes N as a parameter, which is the highest value of the sequence to sum, and returns that sum of 1 to N. We need a variable to store the sum that is initialized to 0. We'll also need a counter to keep track of our iterations, also initialized to 0. The counter will have a range of 0 to (N-1). Our loop condition is: is the counter less than N? When the counter reaches the value of N, our loop condition will be `false` (N is not less than N) and our loop will stop. So, in the body of our loop, we accumulate the sum and we increment our counter. When looping has completed, the sum is returned.

The `sumNviaWhile()` function is shown in the `gauss_loops.c` program, as follows:

```
int sumNviaWhile( int N )  {
  int sum = 0;
  int num = 0;
  while( num < N ) // num: 0..99 (100 is not less than 100)  {
    sum += (num+1); // Off-by-one: shift 0..99 to 1..100.
    num++;
  }
  return sum;
}
```

There is a bit of a wrinkle; this wrinkle is known as the *off-by-one problem*. This problem has many forms in other programming languages and not just in C. Notice that our counter starts at 0 and goes to N-1, to give us N iterations. We could start at 1 and check if the counter is less than N+1. Or, we could also start at 0 and test if the counter is less than or equal to N. This second approach would give a correct answer for this problem but would give us N+1 iterations instead of just N iterations. Starting at 0 and going to, say 10, would altogether be 11 iterations.

There is a valid reason we have chosen to start our counter at zero. It has more to do with C array indexes, which we will encounter in `Chapter 11`, *Working with Arrays*. This may seem confusing now, yet zero-based counting/indexing is a very consistent principle in C. Getting accustomed to it now will save many more headaches when working with array indexing and pointer addition later.

To help mitigate any possible confusion with counter ranges, I have found it is always helpful to indicate the expected range of values (that the counter or index will take) in comments. In that way, necessary adjustments, as done previously, can be made to any other calculations that use that counter.

On the other hand, there is another way. (There is always another way in C, as in most programming languages!) In this second way of implementing the `while()` ... loop, instead of counting up, we'll count down. Furthermore, we'll use the N input parameter value as the counter so that in this way, we don't need a separate counting variable. Remember that the function parameters are copied from the caller and also that they become local variables within the function then. We'll use N as a local variable to be our counter. Instead of incrementing our counter, we'll decrement it. The valid range will thus be from N down to 1. In this way, we'll let 0 be the stopping condition because it also evaluates to `false`.

Our `continuation_expression` is simply evaluating whether N is nonzero to continue. We could have also used `while( N > 0 )`, which would be only slightly more explicit, even if redundant. In addition, we get some minor benefits of not having to deal with the off-by-one problem. Then, our counter is also an accurate representation of the value we want to add.

The revised `sumNviaWhile2()` function in the `gauss_loops2.c` program is shown in the following code block:

```
int sumNviaWhile2( int N )  {
  int sum = 0;
  while( N )  {        // N: N down to 1 (stops at 0).
    sum += N;
    N--;
  }
  return sum;
}
```

Is one approach better than the other? Not really. And certainly not in these examples, because our problem is rather simple. When the `statement_body` becomes more complex, one approach may be better in terms of clarity and readability than the other. The point here is to show how thinking about the problem in a slightly different way can make the code clearer sometimes. In this instance, the difference is in how the *count* is performed.

Introducing the for()... statement

The `for()`... statement has the following syntax:

```
for( counter_initialization ; continuation_expression ; counter_increment )
    statement_body
```

The `for()`... statement consists of a three-part control expression and a statement body. The control expression is made up of a `counter_initialization` expression, a `continuation_expression`, and a `counter_increment` expression, where a semicolon separates each part of an expression. Each one has a well-defined purpose. Their positions cannot be interchanged.

Upon executing the `for()`... statement, the `counter_initialization` expression is evaluated. This is performed only once. Then, `continuation_expression` is evaluated. If its result is `true`, the `statement_body` is executed. At the end of `statement_body`, the `counter_increment` expression is evaluated. Then, the process repeats, with the evaluation of `continuation_expression`. When `continuation_expression` evaluates to `false`, the loop ends; the execution resumes after the `statement_body`. If the `continuation_expression` initially evaluates to `false`, the `statement_body` loop is never executed.

The `statement_body` may be a single statement or even a null statement (a single `;` without an expression) but, most often, it is a compound statement. Note that there is no semicolon specified as a part of the `for()`... statement. A semicolon would appear as part of a single statement in the `statement_body` or would be absent in the case of the `statement_body` consisting of the `{ ... }` compound statement.

In the `for()`... statement, all of the control elements are present at the beginning of the loop. This design was intentional so as to keep all of the control elements together. This construct is particularly useful when the `statement_body` is either complex or overly long. There is no possibility of losing track of the control elements since they are all together at the beginning.

The `counter_increment` expression may be any expression that increments, decrements, or otherwise alters the counter. Also, when the counter is both declared and initialized within a `for` loop, it may not be used outside of that `for` loop's `statement_body`, much like the function parameters that are local to the function body. We will explore this concept in greater detail in Chapter 25, *Understanding Scope*.

Returning to Gauss's problem, we'll use a `for()`... loop in a function that takes as a parameter *N*, the highest value of the sequence to sum, and returns that sum of 1 to *N*. We need a variable to store the sum, initialized to 0. The counter we'll need will be both declared and initialized to 0 in the first part of the `for()`... statement. The counter will have the range of 0 to (N-1); when it reaches N, our loop condition *is the counter less than N?* will be `false` (N is not less than N) and our loop will stop. So, in the body of our loop, we need to only accumulate the sum. When looping has completed, the sum is returned.

The `sumNviaFor()` function in the `gauss_loop.c` program is shown in the following code block:

```
int sumNviaFor( int N )  {
  int sum = 0;
  for( int num = 0 ; num < N ; num++ ) { // num: 0..99 (it's a C thing)
    sum += (num+1); // Off-by-one: shift 0..99 to 1..100.
```

```
        }
    return sum;
    }
```

As we saw with the `while()` . . . loop, we have encountered and had to deal with the off-by-one problem. But also, as before, there is a second way to perform this loop. In this second way of implementing the `for()` ... loop, instead of counting up, we'll count down. Again, we'll use the input parameter value (N) as the counter, so we don't need a separate counting variable. Remember that function parameters are copied from the caller, and also that they then become local variables within the function. We'll use N as a local variable to be our counter. Instead of incrementing our counter, we'll decrement it and let 0 be the stopping condition (as well as evaluate it to `false`).

As before, we get the somewhat minor benefit of not having to deal with the off-by-one problem. Then, our counter is also an accurate representation of the value we want to add.

The revised `sumNviaFor2()` function in the `gauss_loop2.c` program is shown as follows:

```
int sumNviaFor2( int N )  {
    int sum = 0;
    for( int i = N ;   // range: 100..1
            i > 0 ;       // stops at 1.
            i--     )  {
        sum += i;        // No off-by-one.
    }
    return sum;
}
```

One final thing to notice in `sumNviaFor2()` is that the parts of the control expression are formatted such that each part is now on its own line. Doing this allows for more complex expressions and comments for each part.

For example, let's assume we want to simultaneously count up and down, using two counters. We can initialize more than one counter in the `counter_initialization` expression by using the `,` sequence operator. We can also increment more than one counter in the `counter_increment` expression, again by using the `,` operator. Our `for()` ... condition might look like this:

```
for( int i = 0 , int j = maxLen ;
        (i < maxLen ) && (j > 0 ) ;
        i++ , j-- )  {
    ...
}
```

However, the indentation should be used to keep the control expression clearly identifiable from the loop body. In this simple example, such code formatting is unnecessary and should only be used where the control expression becomes more complex.

Introducing the do ... while() statement

The do...while() statement has the following syntax:

```
do statement_body while( continuation_expression );
```

The only difference between this statement and the while()_ statement is that, in the do...while() statement, statement_body is executed before continuation_expression is evaluated. If the continuation_expression result is true, the loop repeats. When continuation_expression evaluates to false, the loop ends. Note also the terminating semicolon. If the continuation_expression initially evaluates to false, the statement_body loop is executed once and only once.

Returning again to Gauss's problem, the similarities to the while()_ statement are clear. In fact, for this problem, there is a very little difference between the while()_ and do...while() statements.

The sumNviaDoWhile() function in the gauss_loop.c program can be seen in the following code block:

```
int sumNviaDoWhile( int N )  {
  int sum = 0;
  int num = 0;
  do {
    sum += (num+1);      // Off-by-one: shift 0..99 to 1..100.
    num++;
  } while ( num < N );   // num: 0..99 (100 is not less than 100).
  return sum;
}
```

Notice that, because the statement_body consists of more than one statement, a statement block is required; otherwise, a compiler error would result.

And, as we have already seen before, we can rework this function to use N as our counter and decrement it.

The `sumNviaDoWhile2()` function in the `gauss_loop2.c` program can be seen in the following code block:

```
int sumNviaDoWhile2( int N )  {
  int sum = 0;
  do {
    sum += N;
    N--;
  } while ( N );     // range: N down to 1 (stops at 0).
  return sum;
}
```

Before going any further, it's time to create not one but two programs, `gauss_loop.c`, and `gauss_loop2.c`.

The `main()` function of the `gauss_loop.c` program can be seen in the following code block:

```
#include <stdio.h>
#include <stdbool.h>

int sumNviaFor(     int n );
int sumNviaWhile(   int n );
int sumNviaDoWhile( int n );

int main( void )  {
  int n = 100;
  printf( "The sum of 1..%d = %d (via while() ... loop)\n" ,
            n , sumNviaWhile( n ) );
  printf( "The sum of 1..%d = %d (via for() ... loop)\n"   ,
            n , sumNviaFor( n ) );
  printf( "The sum of 1..%d = %d (via do...while() loop)\n" ,
            n , sumNviaDoWhile( n ) );
  return 0;
}
```

Create the `gauss_loops.c` file, and enter the `main()` function, and the three `sum` function. Compile the program with the `cc gauss_loops.c -o gauss_loops` command. Run the program. You should see the following output from `gauss_loops`:

```
Learn C : Chapter 7 > cc gauss_loops.c -o gauss_loops
Learn C : Chapter 7 > gauss_loops
The sum of 1..100 = 5050 (via while() ... loop)
The sum of 1..100 = 5050 (via for() ... loop)
The sum of 1..100 = 5050 (via do...while() loop)
Learn C : Chapter 7 > 
```

In the preceding screenshot, you can see that each of the three looping methods to calculate the sum of 1..100 gives us the same result as well as the identical result from gauss_bruteforce.

The main body of gauss_loop2.c is as follows:

```
#include <stdio.h>
#include <stdbool.h>

int sumNviaFor2(     int N );
int sumNviaWhile2(   int N );
int sumNviaDoWhile2( int N );

int main( void )  {
  int n = 100;
  printf("The sum of 1..%d = %d (via while() ... loop 2)\n" ,
          n , sumNviaWhile2(n) );
  printf("The sum of 1..%d = %d (via for() ... loop 2)\n" ,
          n , sumNviaFor2(n) );
  printf("The sum of 1..%d = %d (via do...while() loop 2)\n",
          n , sumNviaDoWhile2(n) );
  return 0;
}
```

Create the gauss_loops2.c file, enter the main() function, and the three sum functions. Compile the program with the cc gauss_loops2.c -o gauss_loops2 command. Run the program. You should see the following output:

```
Learn C : Chapter 7 > cc gauss_loops2.c -o gauss_loops2
Learn C : Chapter 7 > gauss_loops2
The sum of 1..100 = 5050 (via while() ... loop 2)
The sum of 1..100 = 5050 (via for() ... loop 2)
The sum of 1..100 = 5050 (via do...while() loop 2)
Learn C : Chapter 7 > 
```

In the preceding screenshot, you can see that each of the alternate three looping methods to calculate the sum of 1..100 gives us the same result as we have seen before.

Understanding loop equivalency

After having typed in both versions of each loop and run them, you may have begun to see some similarities between each of the looping statements. In fact, for counter-controlled looping, each of them is readily interchangeable.

To illustrate, let's examine each counter-controlled loop by comparing each of their essential parts.

The counter-controlled `while()`... loop has the following syntax:

```
counter_initialization;
while( continuation_expression )   {
   statement_body
   counter_increment;
}
```

Notice that both counter initialization and counter increments have been added to the basic syntax of the `while()`... loop and that they are somewhat scattered about.

The counter-controlled `for()`... loop has the following syntax:

```
for( counter_initialization ; continuation_expression ; counter_increment )
   statement_body
```

It would be perfectly logical to assume that the `for()`... loop is really just a special case of the `while()`... loop.

The counter-controlled `do...while()` loop has the following syntax:

```
counter_initialization;
do {
   statement_body
   counter_increment;
} while( continuation_expression );
```

Notice that, as with the `while()`... loop, the counter-control expressions have been added to the basic syntax of the `do...while()` loop and are also somewhat scattered about the loop.

For counter-controlled looping, the `for()`... loop is a natural first choice over the other two. Nonetheless, any of these may be used. However, when we look at sentinel-controlled loops, these equivalencies begin to break down. We will see that the `while()`... loop provides far more general use in many cases, especially when looking for a sentinel value to end continuation.

Understanding unconditional branching – the dos and (mostly) don'ts of goto

The `goto` statement is an immediate and unconditional transfer of program execution to the specified label within a function block. `goto` causes execution to *jump* to the label. In current C, unlike the bad old days, `goto` may not jump out of a function block, and so it may neither jump out of one function into the middle of another nor out of one program into another program (neither were uncommon in those days).

The `goto` statement consists of two parts. First, there must be a label declared either as a standalone statement, as follows—`label_identifier` :—or as a prefix to any other statement, like so: `label_identifier : statement`.

And secondly, there must be the `goto` statement to that `label_identifier`. The syntax for the `goto` statement is as follows:

```
goto label_identifier;
```

The reason for the `goto` statement being shunned comes from the *bad old days* before *structured programming*. The main tenet of structured programming was one entry point, one exit point. We don't hear much about this anymore because, well, programmers have been trained better and languages—starting with C—have become more disciplined, so that `goto` is not really needed. The main aim of the structured programming movement was to counter the spaghetti code of earlier programs, where `goto` ruled because a more disciplined mechanism did not exist, and the use of `goto` in some cases had got completely out of control. Programs jumped from here to there, and to anywhere, and code became extremely difficult to understand or modify (because the `goto` statement made it impossible to know all the possible flows of control). Often, the answer to the question, *How did we end up here?* or *What was the code path that got us to this point?* was not easily discernible, if it was discernible at all. Thanks to C, and subsequent derivative languages of C, the undisciplined use of `goto` was reined in.

The creators of C felt there was occasionally, albeit rarely, a need for `goto`, and so they left it in the language. In C, `goto` is highly constrained in terms of where it can—ahem—go to. Unlike the bad old days, you cannot use `goto` in a label inside another function. You cannot use `goto` out of the current function. You cannot use `goto` in another program, nor can you use `goto` somewhere in the runtime library or into system code. All these things were done and were often done for expediency, only without regard to the long-term maintainability of the code. Mayhem ruled. But no longer, at least with respect to `goto`.

Today, in C, the `goto` statement can only jump to a label within the same function. `goto` is extremely handy in the case of deeply nested `if... else...` statements or deeply nested looping statements when you just need to get out and move on. While this is sometimes necessary, it should be considered rarely necessary. It is also handy at times in high-performance computing. So, for those reasons alone, we consider it here.

Besides, C provides two other extremely useful and disciplined statements that rein in the undisciplined and chaotic use of `goto`, as we will see in the next section.

For the remainder of this section, we'll look at structured uses of `goto` and how to implement the looping statements we've already seen using `goto`. In each case, there is a pair of labels identifying the beginning and end of what in other statements would be the loop block.

In our first example, the end-of-loop label is not needed; it is there for clarity, as shown in the following example of the `sumNviaGoto_Do()` function of the `gauss_goto.c` program:

```
int sumNviaGoto_Do( int N )
{
   int sum = 0;
   int num = 0;
begin_loop:
   sum += (num+1);
   num++;
   if( num < N ) goto begin_loop;     // Go up and repeat: loop!
   // Else fall-through, out of loop.
end_loop:
   return sum;
}
```

In the `sumNviaGoto_Do()` function, we find all the elements of the preceding looping statements. There is the loop block beginning at the `begin_loop:` label. There is the loop block ending at the `end_loop:` label, and, in this example, the body of the loop block is executed exactly once before the loop condition is evaluated. This, then, is the `goto` equivalent of a `do ... while()` loop.

So, you might now be wondering what a `goto`-equivalent `while() ...` loop might look like. Here it is, in the `sumNviaGoto_While()` function of the `gauss_goto.c` program:

```
int sumNviaGoto_While( int N )
{
  int sum = 0;
  int num = 0;
begin_loop:
  if( !(num < N) ) goto end_loop;
```

```
      sum += (num+1);
      num++;
      goto begin_loop;
    end_loop:
      return sum;
    }
```

Notice how the loop condition had to be slightly modified. Also, notice when that loop condition is `true`, we go to the label that is after the `goto begin_loop` statement. This is the only way we get out of the loop, just as in the `while()` ... statement.

Finally, we can implement a `for()` ... loop with `goto`, as shown here in the `sumNviaGoto_For()` function of the `gauss_goto.c` program:

```
int sumNviaGoto_For( int N )
{
   int sum = 0;
   int num = 0;

   int i = 0;                      // Initialize counter.
begin_loop:
   if( !(i < N) ) goto end_loop;   // Loop continuation condition.
   sum += (num+1);
   num++;
   i++;                            // Counter increment.
   goto begin_loop;
end_loop:
   return sum;
}
```

To do this, we had to add a local counter variable, `i`, initialize it to 0, test that its value was not less than N, and, finally, increment it before we unconditionally branch to the top of our loop. You should be able to see how each of these statements corresponds to those in the `for()` ... statement.

In assembler language—a nearly direct translation to machine language—there is no `for()` ... , `while()` ... , or `do ... while()` loops. There is only `goto`. These `goto` looping constructs could very well be translated directly into either assembler language or directly to machine language. But we are programming C, so the point of demonstrating these constructs is to show the equivalence between the various looping mechanisms.

The `main()` function of the `gauss_goto.c` program is given as follows :

```
#include <stdio.h>
#include <stdbool.h>
```

```
int sumNviaGoto_While( int N );
int sumNviaGoto_Do( int N );
int sumNviaGoto_For( int N );

int main( void )
{
  int n = 100;
  printf( "The sum of 1..%d = %d (via do-like goto loop)\n" ,
          n , sumNviaGoto_Do(n) );
  printf( "The sum of 1..%d = %d (via while-like goto loop)\n" ,
          n , sumNviaGoto_While(n) );
  printf( "The sum of 1..%d = %d (via for-like goto loop)\n" ,
          n , sumNviaGoto_For(n) );
  return 0;
}
```

Create the gauss_goto.c file, enter the main() function, and the three sum functions. Compile the program with the cc gauss_goto.c -o gauss_goto command. Run the program. You should see the following output:

```
Learn C : Chapter 7 > cc gauss_goto.c -o gauss_goto
Learn C : Chapter 7 > gauss_goto
The sum of 1..100 = 5050 (via do-like goto loop)
The sum of 1..100 = 5050 (via while-like goto loop)
The sum of 1..100 = 5050 (via for-like goto loop)
Learn C : Chapter 7 > []
```

In the preceding screenshot, you can see that each of the alternate three looping methods to calculate the sum of 1...100 gives us the same result as we have seen before.

So, now, the question before us is: *We can loop with* goto, *but should we?*

The answer is quite resoundingly—No! We don't need to, at all. We use for()... , while()..., or do ... while() instead!

These complex looping statements exist to make our code clearer as well as to obviate the need for goto. Let the compiler generate the goto statement for us. So, for general-purpose computing, goto should rarely be used, if ever. However, in certain high-performance computing situations, goto may be necessary.

Remember, the overuse and/or improper use of goto is a way to perdition! Use goto wisely.

Further controlling loops with break and continue

Rather than relying on `goto` to get out of sticky situations inside of deeply nested statements, the creators of C provided two very controlled goto-like mechanisms. These are `break` and `continue`.

`break` jumps out of and to the end of the enclosing statement block, whereas `continue` is used for looping, which goes immediately to the next iteration of the looping statement, skipping any statements that would otherwise be executed in the loop after the `continue` mechanism.

We have previously encountered the use of `break` in the `switch` statement in the preceding chapter, where `break` caused the execution to resume immediately after the `switch` statement block. `break` can also be used to jump to the end of the enclosing `statement_body` loop.

In the following `isPrime()` function, `break` is used to get out of a loop that determines if the given number is divisible by the counter value; if so, the number is not prime.

The `isPrime()` function of the `primes.c` program can be seen in the following code block:

```
bool isPrime( int num )  {
  if( num < 2 )   return false;
  if( num == 2 )  return true;

  bool isPrime = true;   // Make initial assumption that num is prime.
  for( int i = 2 ; i < num ; i++ )  {
    if( (num % i) == 0 )  {  // We found a divisor of num;
                             // num is not prime.
      isPrime = false;
      break;                 // No need to keep checking; leave the loop.
    }
  }
  return isPrime;
}
```

Here, we are demonstrating `break` in a rather simple example. In this case, you may recall, we could also have simply used `return false` instead, but where's the fun in that? Because `break` is not in a `switch` but is in a loop, `break` takes the execution out of the loop to the very next statement after the closing loop } bracket.

The `continue` statement only works within an enclosing `statement_body`. When encountered, the execution jumps to immediately before the closing loop } bracket, thereby commencing on the next `continuation_expression` loop and possible loop iteration (only if the continuation evaluates to `true`).

Let's say we want to calculate a sum for all prime numbers between 1 and *N* as well as all non-prime numbers in the same range. We can use the `isPrime()` function within a loop. If the candidate number is not prime, do no more processing of this iteration and begin the next one. Our function that adds only prime numbers would look like this `sumPrimes()` function of the `primes.c` program:

```
int   sumPrimes( int num )   {
   int sum = 0;
   for( int i = 1 ; i <   (num+1) ; i++ )   {
     if( !isPrime( i ) ) continue;

     printf( "%d " , i);
     sum += i;
   }
   printf("\n");
   return sum;
}
```

Similarly, a function that adds only non-prime numbers would look like this `sumNonPrimes()` function of the `primes.c` program:

```
int   sumNonPrimes( int num )   {
   int sum = 0;
   for( int i = 1 ; i < (num+1) ; i++ )   {
     if( isPrime( i ) ) continue;

     printf( "%d " , i);
     sum += i;
   }
   printf("\n");
   return sum;
}
```

Care must be exercised when using the `continue` statement to ensure that the loop counter update is performed and not bypassed with the `continue` statement. Such oversight would result in an infinite loop.

The `main()` function of `primes.c`, which illustrates `break` and `continue`, does three things. First, it does a simple validation of our `isPrime()` function using a `for()`... loop. Then, it calls `sumPrimes()` via a `printf()` function, and, finally, it calls `sumNonPrimes()` again via a `printf()` function. If the program logic is correct, the sum of both prime and non-prime numbers should be the same as our preceding summing functions; that is how we will verify the correctness of the program. The `main()` function of the `primes.c` program is given as follows:

```c
#include <stdio.h>
#include <stdbool.h>

bool isPrime( int num );

int    sumPrimes(     int num );
int    sumNonPrimes( int num );

int main( void )   {
  for( int i = 1 ; i < 8 ; i++ )
    printf( "%d => %sprime\n", i , isPrime( i ) ? "" : "not " );
  printf("\n");
  printf( "Sum of prime numbers 1..100       = %d\n" ,
          sumPrimes( 100 ) );
  printf( "Sum of non-prime numbers 1..100 = %d\n" ,
          sumNonPrimes( 100 ) );
  return 0;
}
```

Create and type in the `primes.c` program. Compile, run, and verify its results.

Create the `primes.c` file, enter the `main()` function, the `isprime()` function, and the two `sumPrime` functions. Compile the program with the `cc primes.c -o primes` command. Run the program. You should see the following output:

```
Learn C : Chapter 7 > cc primes.c -o primes
Learn C : Chapter 7 > primes
1 => not prime
2 => prime
3 => prime
4 => not prime
5 => prime
6 => not prime
7 => prime

2 3 5 7 11 13 17 19 23 29 31 37 41 43 47 53 59 61 67 71 73 79 83 89 97
Sum of prime numbers 1..100      = 1060
1 4 6 8 9 10 12 14 15 16 18 20 21 22 24 25 26 27 28 30 32 33 34 35 36 38 39 40 4
2 44 45 46 48 49 50 51 52 54 55 56 57 58 60 62 63 64 65 66 68 69 70 72 74 75 76
77 78 80 81 82 84 85 86 87 88 90 91 92 93 94 95 96 98 99 100
Sum of non-prime numbers 1..100 = 3990
Learn C : Chapter 7 > █
```

In the preceding screenshot, you can see that for each function, we first validate that the isPrime() function properly determines the primeness of one through seven. Not only can you see the sum of prime numbers and non-prime numbers, but you can also see the numbers in each set, for further verification. Note that *1060 + 3990 = 5050* is the expected correct result.

For a complete comparison of break, continue, return, and goto, consider the following code outline:

```
int aFunction( ... ) {
   ...
   for( ... )  {  /* outer loop */
     for( ... )   { /* inner loop */
        ...
        if( ... ) break;          /* Get out of inner loop. */
        ...
        if( ... ) continue;       /* Next iteration of inner loop. */
        ...
        if( ... ) goto ERROR;     /* Get out of ALL loops. */
        ...
        /* Next statement after continue; */
        /* Also next iteration of inner-loop. */
     }
     /* Next statement after break; still in outer-loop. */
     ...
   }
   return 0;  /* normal function exit */

ERROR:       /* Error recovery */
   ...
   return -1; /* abnormal function exit */
}
```

In this outline, there is an inner for() ... loop nested within an outer for() ... loop. break will only go to the end of its immediate enclosing statement_body. In this case, it goes to the end of the inner loop block and executes statements in the outer loop block. continue goes to the point immediately before the end of the enclosing statement_body to repeat the loop iteration. goto ERROR immediately jumps to the ERROR: label at the end of the function body and handles the error condition before returning from the function. In the statement before the ERROR: label, there is a return 0 that returns from the function, thus preventing the execution of the error recovery statements.

Understanding infinite loops

So far, we have considered loops that have an actual end. In most cases, this is both intended and desirable. When loops never end, either unintentionally because we goofed up somewhere or intentionally, they are called an **infinite loop**. There are a few special cases where an infinite loop is actually intentional. The cases are as follows:

- When the user interacts with the program until the user chooses to quit the program
- When there is input with no known end, as in networking where data can come at any time
- Operating system event loop processing. This begins upon boot-up and waits (loops) for events to happen until the system is shut down.

When you start a program that accepts user input—keyboard strokes, mouse movements, and so on, it goes into an infinite loop to process each input. We would then need to use a `break`, `goto`, or `return` statement in the `statement-body` of our infinite loop to end it.

A simplified version using `for()`... might look something like the following:

```
void get_user_input( void )
{
  ...
  for( ; ; )
  {
  ...
  if( ... ) goto exit;
  ...
  if( cmd == 'q' || cmd == 'Q' ) break;
  ...
  }

  exit:
  ... // Do exit stuff, like clean up, then end.
}
```

When `continuation_expression` is null, it is evaluated to `true`. The other parts of the control expression are optional.

The computer's main routine, after it loads all of its program parts, might look something like this:

```
void system_loop( void  )
{
  ...
```

```
while( 1 )
{
   ...
   getNextEvent();
   handleEvent();
   ...
   if( system_shutdown_event ) goto shutdown;
   ...
}
shutdown:
... // Perform orderly shut-down activities, then power off.
}
```

This is an extremely oversimplified version of what actually goes on. However, it shows that somewhere in your computer, an infinite loop is running and processing events.

Summary

We have encountered various repetitious looping techniques, from the ridiculous (brute-force iteration) to the sublime (various loop statements with break, continue, and goto). With functions, conditional expressions, and—now—looping statements, we conclude our journey through C flow-of-control statements. Nearly all of these concepts can be easily translated into other programming languages.

In the bulk of the remainder of the book, we'll broaden our understanding and ability to manipulate data well beyond the simple forms we have so far encountered. In the next chapter, we will explore custom named values called **enumerations**.

8
Creating and Using Enumerations

The real world is complicated—far more complicated than just whole numbers, numbers with fractions, Boolean values, and characters. In order to model it, C provides various mechanisms for custom and complex data types. For the next eight chapters, we are going to explore various ways that our intrinsic data types can be extended and combined to more closely match the real world.

The first of these extensible data types is *enumerated types*. These are groups of values that are related; but, we don't really care about their values—we differentiate each item in the group by its name. The value corresponding to that name is irrelevant to us; the significance lies in its unique name within the group of enumerated items to which it belongs. In truth, however, a unique value for each item in the group can either be specified by us or will be automatically assigned by the compiler. Our program can then choose between them or can select from the group for specific operations. The `switch` statement is particularly handy when dealing with enumerated items, also simply called **enumerations**. The following topics will be covered in this chapter:

- Understanding how enumerations limit values to a specified range
- Declaring various enumerations
- Writing a function to use the enumerations declared
- Using the `switch` statement to select an enumeration to perform actions specific to it

Technical requirements

As detailed in the *Technical requirements* section of `Chapter 1`, *Running Hello, World!*, continue to use the tools you have chosen.

The source code for this chapter can be found at `https://github.com/PacktPublishing/Learn-C-Programming`.

Introducing enumerations

There are times when we want a program or function variable to take only a limited number of values. For convenience, and to make the purpose of each value clear, each value in the set of possible values is given a name. We can think of this set as a grouping of related values.

Let's say we want a variable to represent the suits of a deck of cards. Naturally, we know each suit by its name—spades, hearts, clubs, and diamonds. But C doesn't know about card names or card suits. If we wanted to represent each of these suits with a value, we could pick any value for each, say, 4 for spades, 3 for hearts, 2 for diamonds, and 1 for clubs. Our program, using this simple scheme, might look as follows:

```
int card;
...
card = 3; // Heart.
```

But we would have to do the work of remembering which value corresponds to which suit. This is an error-prone way of solving this problem.

We could, however, improve that solution by either using the preprocessor or by using constants, as follows:

```
#define spade   4
#define heart   3
#define diamond 2
#define club    1

int card = heart;
```

Or, even better, we could do it by using constants for each value, as follows:

```
const int spade   = 4;
const int heart   = 3;
const int diamond = 2;
const int club    = 1;

int card = heart;
```

While each of these values accurately represents the four suits, they are unrelated. The `card` variable could easily be assigned other values that are neither valid nor obvious in terms of what they intend to represent. `card` could be assigned with a value that is not one of the four, and therefore would make no sense.

C provides a way to group values by name so that their interrelationship is clear, and any variable that is specified as having one of these values *can only* have one of these values and no other.

Defining enumerations

The enumeration type allows us to specify a set, or group, of values a variable may have, and only those values. Any assignment of a value outside of that range/group would be a compiler error. The compiler catching such an error rather than it being caught at runtime is preferred since it prevents unexpected program crashes.

The syntax for defining an enumerated type is as follows:

```
enum name { enumeration1, enumeration2, ... , enumerationN };
```

The type consists of the two words, `enum` and `name`. The group of enumerated items is contained within `{` and `}`. Each named item in the group of enumerated items is separated by `,` and the definition is concluded with `;`.

So, the definition of our enumerated type of suit would be as follows:

```
enum suit { spade , heart , diamond , club };
```

Or, we might want to make each item stand on its own, as follows:

```
enum suit {
  spade ,
  heart ,
  diamond ,
  club
};
```

We have created a new data type—`enum suit`. We will see later, in `Chapter 10`, *Creating Custom Data Types with typedef*, that with `typedef`, we can abbreviate this even further.

Any variable of type `enum suit` can take only one of those four possible values. The convenience of this new type is that we no longer have to remember what each numerical value means; the enumerated type tells us that.

When we define an enumerated type as we have done previously, the compiler automatically assigns values to each enumerated item. We could, but don't have to, be completely explicit. Also, we don't have to assign each enumerated item with a value that we might want it to have, as follows:

```
enum suit {
    spade   = 4, // assignments not needed.
    heart   = 3,
    diamond = 2,
    club    = 1
};
```

In Chapter 5, *Exploring Operators and Expressions*, we briefly examined bitwise operators using constants to declare single-bit flags. We can do this more clearly with enumeration. However, when we use enumeration in this manner, we actually *do* care about the value of each enumerated item. An enumerated definition for textStyles would be as follows:

```
/* flag name        binary value */
enum textStyle {
    lowercase      = 0x00000001,
    bold           = 0x00000010,
    italic         = 0x00000100,
    underline      = 0x00001000
}
```

We set each item in the enumeration to be a specific bit for its value, or put another way, a specific bit in its bit field. 0x00000001 is the binary value for 1. Knowing this, we could have alternatively defined enum textStyle as follows:

```
/* flag name binary value */
enum textStyle {
    lowercase = 1,
    bold = 2,
    italic = 4,
    underline = 8,
}
```

You need to be careful when doing this, because the importance of the bit pattern may not be obvious in the second example and an unsuspecting programmer may add an additional item with a clashing bit pattern, such as the following:

```
strikethrough = 5;
```

In our original intended scheme, the added item would be 4 (italic) + 1 (lowercase) and might later give unpredictable results at runtime since tests for italic or lowercase would evaluate to true if strikethrough was intended. To properly add the strikethrough item, it should be defined as a power of 2 so as not to clash with the other enumerated values, as follows:

```
enum textStyle {
    lowercase      =   1,
    bold           =   2,
    italic         =   4,
    underline      =   8,
    strikethrough = 16,
}
```

Using enumerations in this way is possible and sometimes necessary; more often, we only regard the names of enumerated items. By carefully assigning values to each name, we can then combine these textStyles in an integer variable and extract them, as follows:

```
int style       = bold | italic;       // Style has bold and italic
                                        // turned on.
int otherStyle = italic + underline;   // OtherStyle has italic and
                                        // underline turned on.

if( style & bold ) ...                  // bold is on
if( !(otherStyle & bold) )              // bold is off
```

style is an integer that can be assigned enumerated values via bitwise operators or simple arithmetic operators. We can't change the value of bold, italic, or any of the other enumerated items; but, we can use their values to assign them to another variable. Those variables' values can be combined and/or changed.

Using enumerations

We have defined a new type with a specified set of values. To assign values of that type to a variable, we now have to define a variable using our new enumerated type.

Declaring a variable of type enum suit would be done as follows:

```
enum suit card;
...
card = spade;
...
if(      card == club )    ...
else if( card == diamond ) ...
```

```
else if( card == heart )    ...
else if( card == spade )    ...
else
    printf( "Unknown enumerated value\n" );
```

Since `card` is an enumerated type, it cannot take any value other than those specified in the type. To do so would cause a compiler error. You will notice in the preceding code snippet that we check for any enumerated value outside of our known set of values. This is actually not required for a simple `card` suit example; is there a deck of cards with more than 4 suits? I think not. Is it likely then, that our set of enumerations would change? Also not likely. Furthermore, `card` as an enumerated type cannot take any other value.

However, such a practice is recommended when the number of types could expand at some later time. Such a simple check will ensure that the new values are properly handled (or not), but the program behavior will not be unexpected, thereby avoiding a program crash. Note that, while the possible values a variable can take are still limited, we need to consider cases when our program code may not handle all the possible enumerated values. Specifically, new enumerations may have been added, yet the code may not have been updated to handle each one completely.

Imagine if, in the initial version of the program, the `enum shape` enumerated type was the following:

```
enum shape { triangle, rectangle , circle };
```

Later, it may be found that `enum shape` needs to be extended to deal with more shapes, as follows:

```
enum shape { triangle, square, rectangle, trapezoid, pentagon, hexagon,
octagon, circle );
```

All of the existing code that checks for `triangle`, `square`, and `circle` will work as before. However, as we have added new enumerated values, we must also add code to handle each one. It may not be obvious at all whether we remembered to change every place in our program that uses these new types. The unknown type check is a fail-safe plan to help us root out all instances where the handling of new enumerated items may have been missed.

As we saw at the end of the preceding chapter, if our program was large and involved many files, we might even want to perform error processing and exit gracefully, as follows:

```
int shapeFunc( enum shape )
{
  ...
  if(       shape == triangle ) ...
  else if( shape == rectangle ) ...
```

```
    else if( shape == circle ) ...
    else
      goto error:
    }
    ...
    return 0;   // Normal end.

  error:
    ...             // Error: unhandled enumerated type. Clean up, alert user,
  exit.
    return -1; // Some error value.
  }
```

In the preceding code snippet, we may have been pressed for time and have forgotten to handle our new enumerated values—trapezoid, pentagon, hexagon, and octagon. Or as more often happens, we may have failed to have updated code for just one or two of them. By including a check as shown, while we may not completely eliminate unexpected runtime behavior, we can limit the possible negative effects of not handling one of the added enumerated values.

Indeed, we could even make our return type an enumerated type and let the caller handle the error, as follows:

```
enum result_code
{
    noError = 0,
    unHandledEnumeration,
    ...
    unknownError
};
```

Here, noError is specifically assigned the value 0. Any subsequent items are automatically assigned unique values for that enumerated group by the compiler. Then, our function would become as follows:

```
enum result_code shapeFunc( enum shape )   {
  ...
  if( shape == triangle ) ...
  else if( shape == square ) ...
  else if( shape == circle ) ...
  else
    return unHandledEnumeration;
  }
  ...
  return noError;
}
```

The caller of this function should then do a check and handle `result_code`, as follows:

```
enum result_code  result;
enum shape        aShape;
...
result = shapeFunc( aShape );
if( noError != result )
{
    ... // An error condition occurred; do error processing.
}
...
```

A more concise version of the call and error check would be as follows:

```
if( noError != shapeFunc( aShape ) )
{
    ... // An error condition occurred; do error processing.
}
```

In the preceding `if` condition, as it is evaluated, a call is made to `shapeFunc()` and `enum_result` is returned. The enumerated value, which cannot be changed since it is specified elsewhere, is placed first. In this way, we can avoid the somewhat common error of assigning a function result to one element of a conditional expression. Let's explore this a bit further.

In the following snippet, the variable is given first:

```
if( result == noError ) ...  // continue.
```

This could be mistakenly written (or later altered) as follows:

```
if( result = noError ) ...  // continue.
```

In the latter case, `noError` is assigned to the `result` variable. Its value is actually 0 by definition, which would then be interpreted as `false`. The code would behave as if an error condition had occurred, when in fact, no error was encountered.

The preceding code illustrates a defensive coding tactic—in a conditional expression, strive to put the invariant conditional first. In the preceding example, the value of `noError` cannot be changed by definition, whereas `result` can. Therefore, it is safer to put `noError` first in the conditional expression, to avoid any confusion between comparison, ==, and assignment, =, operators.

A more concise version of the call and error check would be as follows:

```
if( noError != shapeFunc( aShape ) )
{
    ... // An error condition occurred; do error processing.
}
```

The returned function value is used immediately. This approach has some advantages and disadvantages. While we avoid the use of the `result` variable, what if, in the error processing code, we want to test for several error conditions and process each differently? This concise method does not allow us to do that. We would have to reintroduce our `result` variable and then use it to check for various values.

The next section will show how we can avoid this possibility even further with enumerated types.

The switch()... statement revisited

The `switch()`... statement is ideally used when we have a single value that can be from a specified set of values only. Doesn't that sound like an enumerated type? It should and, happily, it does.

Using the `switch` statement to evaluate an enumerated type simplifies the intent of our code and helps to prevent some troublesome situations. Here is the `shapeFunc()` function revisited using the `switch()`...   statement:

```
enum_result_code shapeFunc( enum shape aShape)
{
  ...
  switch( aShape )
  {
    case triangle:
      ...
      break;
    case rectangle:
      ...
      break;
    case circle:
      ...
      break;
    default:
      ...          // Error: unhandled enumerated type. Clean up, alert user,
return.
      return unHandledEnumeration;
```

```
            break;
    }
    ...
    return noError; // Normal end.
  }
```

By using the `switch()`... statement, it is clear we are considering only the value of `shape`. Recall that using `if()`...`else`... is more general; other conditions may be introduced into the processing, which would make the intent of processing the value of `shape` less straightforward. The `switch` statement also allows us to remove the need for `goto` and handle the unknown `shape` enumerated type in the `default:` branch of the `switch` statement. Notice that, even though our `default:` branch has a `return` statement, we also add the `break` statement as a matter of safety. As a rule, any `default:` branch should always include a `break` statement because other `case:` branches may occur after the `default:` branch.

Let's put this very function into a working program. In `sides.c`, we define an enumerated list of shapes, and then call `PrintShapeInfo()` to tell us how many sides each shape has. We'll also demonstrate fall-through logic in the `switch` statement.
The `PrintShapeInfo()` function is as follows:

```
void PrintShapeInfo( enum shape aShape)
{
  int nSides = 0;
  switch( aShape )  {
    case triangle:
      nSides = 3;
      break;
    case square:
    case rectangle:
    case trapezoid:
      nSides = 4;
      break;
    case circle:
      printf( "A circle has an infinite number of sides\n" );
      return noError;
      break;
    default:
      printf( "UNKNOWN SHAPE TYPE\n" );
      break;
  }
  printf( "A %s has %d sides\n" , getShapeName( aShape) , nSides );
}
```

The purpose of the function is to determine and print the number of sides of a given shape. Notice that `square`, `rectangle`, and `trapezoid` all have four sides. When one of them is encountered, the logic is the same—assign 4 to the number of sides. For a circle, no number is possible to represent infinity; in that case, we simply print that and return from the function. For all the other cases, we call another function, `getShapeName()`, to return the name of the shape.

Notice that, in this `switch` statement, we have forgotten to handle some of our shapes. The function handles this gracefully. We do not need to return a function result status because we are simply printing out the name and number of sides of a given shape.

The `getShapeName()` function is as follows:

```
const char* GetShapeName( enum shape aShape)   {
  const char * name;
  switch( aShape )   {
    case triangle:  name = nameTriangle;   break;
    case square:    name = nameSquare;     break;
    case rectangle: name = nameRectangle;  break;
    case trapezoid: name = nameTrapezoid;  break;
    case pentagon:  name = namePentagon;   break;
    case hexagon:   name = nameHexagon;    break;
    case octagon:   name = nameOctagon;    break;
    case circle:    name = nameCircle;     break;
    default:        name = nameUnknown;    break;
  }
  return name;
}
```

This function takes a shape enumerated type and returns the name of that shape. Here, we put each branch of the `switch` statement on a single line consisting of `case :`, an assignment, and a `break` statement. But where do these names come from? We will explore strings in `Chapter 15`, *Working with Strings*. For now, let's just take these as given. To use them in our function, we must define them as global constants. We cannot define them in the function itself because they will be destroyed in the function block when the function returns. So, by the time the caller needs those values, they are gone! By making them global constants, they exist for the life of the program and they do not change (they don't need to change). We will explore this concept in greater detail in `Chapter 25`, *Understanding Scope*. The shape names must be defined in our program as follows:

```
#include <stdio.h>

const char* nameTriangle  = "triangle";
const char* nameSquare    = "square";
const char* nameRectangle = "rectangle";
```

```
const char* nameTrapezoid = "trapezoid";
const char* namePentagon  = "pentagon";
const char* nameHexagon   = "hexagon";
const char* nameOctagon   = "octagon";
const char* nameCircle    = "circle";
const char* nameUnknown   = "unknown";

enum shape { triangle, square, rectangle, trapezoid, pentagon, hexagon,
octagon, circle );

void        PrintShapeInfo( enum shape aShape );
const char* GetShapeName(   enum shape aShape );

int main( void )  {
  PrintShapeInfo( triangle );
  PrintShapeInfo( square );
  PrintShapeInfo( rectangle );
  PrintShapeInfo( trapezoid );
  PrintShapeInfo( pentagon );
  PrintShapeInfo( hexagon );
  PrintShapeInfo( octagon );
  PrintShapeInfo( circle );
  return 0;
}
```

Unfortunately, in C, we cannot use an enumerated type to define string values. We define them as constants because we do not want the names to change.

Create the shapes.c file, enter the main function and the two functions, and save your program. Compile and run the program. You should see the following output:

```
> cc shapes.c -o shapes
> shapes
A triangle has 3 sides
A square has 4 sides
A rectangle has 4 sides
A trapezoid has 4 sides
UNKNOWN SHAPE TYPE
UNKNOWN SHAPE TYPE
UNKNOWN SHAPE TYPE
A circle has an infinite number of sides
> []
```

Notice that there are three unknown shape types. Perhaps we forgot to handle them somewhere in our program. Edit the program so that all the shape types are handled. You can find the source code in the GitHub repository for shapes.c and the completed version, shapes2.c, which handles all of the enumerated items.

Summary

An enumerated type is a set of named values. Most of the time, the values are not significant, but items that are in the set itself add meaning to the type. We can use enumerated types to create natural collections or groups of values, as we have seen with card suits and shapes. The `switch` statement is ideally suited to select and process items within an enumerated type.

An enumerated type, unfortunately, doesn't provide everything we might need to model the real world. For instance, in a deck of cards, each card has both a suit and a face value, two different enumerations. To combine them into a single card object that represents reality more closely, we need another custom data type—structures. We will explore these in the next chapter.

Section 2: Complex Data Types

2

The real world is complicated. In order to model it, C provides mechanisms for complex data types. These mechanisms are structures, arrays, and combinations of structures and arrays.

This section comprises the following chapters:

- Chapter 9, *Creating and Using Structures*
- Chapter 10, *Creating Custom Data Types with typedef*
- Chapter 11, *Working with Arrays*
- Chapter 12, *Working with Multi-Dimensional Arrays*
- Chapter 13, *Using Pointers*
- Chapter 14, *Understand Arrays and Pointers*
- Chapter 15, *Working with Strings*
- Chapter 16, *Creating and Using More Complex Structures*

Creating and Using Structures

9

When a number of values all pertain to a single thing, we can keep them organized with structures. A **structure** is a user-defined type. There may be multiple values in a structure and they may be of the same type or different types. A structure, then, is a collection of information representing a complex object.

With structures, not only can we represent complex objects more realistically, but we can also create functions that manipulate the structure in relevant ways. Just like data within a structure is grouped together in a meaningful manner, we can also group functions that manipulate the structure together in meaningful ways.

C is not an **object-oriented programming** (**OOP**) language. However, OOP has been a primary focus of programming languages and programming since the early 1990s. It is extremely likely that after you learn C, you will, at the very least, be exposed to object-oriented programming concepts. Therefore, after we learn about C structures and the operations we can use on them, we will learn how C structures are a logical transition to OOP. Thinking about C in a special manner, then, becomes a stepping stone to learning OOP.

The following topics will be covered in this chapter:

- Understanding how to declare a structure
- Understanding how to initialize the values of various structures
- Writing functions to perform simple operations on a structure
- Modifying a structure to include another sub-structure
- Understanding how C structures and functions are similar to and different from objects in other object-oriented programming languages

Let's get started!

Technical requirements

As detailed in the *Technical requirements* section of `Chapter 1`, *Running Hello, World!*, continue to use the tools you have chosen.

The source code for this chapter can be found at `https://github.com/PacktPublishing/Learn-C-Programming`.

Understanding structures

It would be extremely easy for C programmers if the world were simply made up of objects that were only numbers or names. Imagine if everyone were expressed as only a name or a series of numbers but nothing else. An automobile **Vehicle Identification Number** (**VIN**) precisely describes various attributes of that car and uniquely identifies it. On the other hand, humans are far more complex than automobiles. Perhaps the world would be a very uninteresting place.

For C programs to solve real-world problems, they have to be able to model real-world complex objects. C allows various aspects of real-world objects to be abstracted and modeled via C structures. In the previous chapter, in a very basic way, we explored two such objects – playing cards and two-dimensional shapes. Did we explore every aspect of them? No.

In fact, we barely scratched the surface. For playing cards, we need to be able to describe all 52 cards in a deck uniquely. To do this, we need both the card's suit and its face value. We might also need the card's relative value (spades have a higher value than hearts, an ace might have a high value or low value, and so on). Later, we will learn how to put them in a collection so that we can represent a full deck of 52 cards. For now, we will see how to accurately represent each card individually.

Likewise, with 2-dimensional shapes, we only represented a single, basic aspect of them—the number of corners or sides that they have. Depending on the needs of the model we need to manipulate, we may need to additionally consider the lengths of each side, the angles of each corner, and other aspects of the shape, such as its surface area.

If we were drawing a shape in a field, we would need to be concerned about its x- and y-positions, line thickness, line color, fill color, vertical ordering in relation to other shapes, and possibly other aspects of the shape in the field. Our shape structure might also need to contain other structures representing position and colors. A position would be a structure of two values x and y representing the Cartesian coordinate *(x,y)*. A color would be a structure of four values representing red, green, blue, and transparency levels (this is just one representation of color).

In Chapter 6, *Exploring Conditional Program Flow*, we considered the calculations for a leap year. The year is just one small part of a structure representing a date. Actually, some of the most complex structures are those that accurately represent date and time and then convert between all of Earth's various calendars and time zones.

Lastly, when we consider a structure consisting of multiple aspects, we must also consider the operations we can perform on that structure. This is similar to our basic data types and the operations we perform on those data types. However, because structures are custom to our specific program and problem domain, we must realize that we must also fashion the necessary operations on those structures – how to set and get information within them; how to compare one to another; and what other operations might be possible, such as adding a duration to time or blending two colors. Later, when we have collections of structures, we might want to order them, find a specific structure in a collection of structures, and perform other operations on them.

Declaring structures

The structure type allows us to specify a group of related variables, each representing a facet, or component, of the thing being modeled. There may be just a few components in the modeled thing; more often than not, there are many components. Each component can be of any intrinsic C data type (integer, real, Boolean, char, complex, and so on) or any previously defined custom type. The components in a structure do not have to be of the same type. Therein lies the power of the structure – it allows us to group various aspects of the thing into a single custom data type; in this case, a C structure. We can then use that data type much like we use any other data type.

The syntax for defining a structured type is as follows:

```
struct name  {
    type componentName1;
    type componentName2;
    ... ;
    type componentNameN;
};
```

The type consists of the two words, struct and name. The components of the structure are contained within { and }. Each named component in the structure is separated by a ; and the definition of the structure is concluded with ;. Unlike intrinsic data types, components aren't initialized within a structure when it is defined. Initialization is done when a variable of that structure type is declared.

So, the definition of our enumerated type of card would be as follows:

```
enum Suit {
  club = 1,
  diamond,
  heart,
  spade
};

enum Face {
  one = 1,
  two,
  three,
  four,
  five,
  six,
  seven,
  eight,
  nine,
  ten,
  jack,
  queen,
  king,
  ace
};

struct Card {
  enum Suit  suit;
  int        suitValue;
  enum Face  face;
  int        faceValue;
  bool       isWild;
};

struct Card card;
```

Notice that we must define the enumerations of enum Suit and enum Face before using them in our structure. Also, note that enum Suit and enum Face (custom types) are similarly named but still different from the suit and face variables. Remember that uppercase letters are different from lowercase letters in identifiers/variable names. We are adopting an arbitrary convention here that custom data types begin with an uppercase letter and variables of that type begin with a lowercase letter of the same name.

Our struct Card now has enough information to accurately reflect a playing card's suit and face. We have added integer variables to hold the card's relative suit and face value. We might have chosen to use the values contained within enum Suit and enum Face, but that might cause issues later on, so we have a separate component for each. In some card games, the ace is either high or low. In most card games, the suits have an ordered value, with spades being the highest and clubs being the lowest. For instance, in the card game Blackjack, suit value doesn't matter and aces are the highest value card, whereas in some poker games, suit value does matter and the ace may be high or low. Our struct Card is general enough that it can be used for each of these scenarios.

Finally, we declare a card variable of struct Card, again using the convention that the custom data type name has an uppercase name while an instance of that type has a lowercase name.

The card variable is the overall name for a variable of five components – suit, suitValue, face, faceValue, and isWild. When the card variable is declared, enough space must be allocated to hold all the values of the components within it. If we assume that the enum types are 4 bytes and bool is 1 byte, then the result of sizeof(card) would be 17. So, each time a variable of the struct Card type is declared, 17 bytes would be allocated for it.

Note that, here, we assume that enum types are the same size as int and that a bool is 1 byte. The compiler actually determines the size of each enum type based on the range of values it contains. Therefore, in reality, we cannot always rely on our assumptions. We can verify this, of course, with the following code:

```
printf( "  enum Suit is %lu bytes\n" , sizeof( enum Suit ) );
printf( "  enum Face is %lu bytes\n" , sizeof( enum Face ) );
printf( "        int is %lu bytes\n" , sizeof( int ) );
printf( "       bool is %lu bytes\n" , sizeof( bool ) );
```

Note that we use the type as the parameter of `sizeof()`. To print the result of `size()`, we need to specify `%lu` in `print()`. This will be thoroughly explained in Chapter 19, *Exploring Formatted Output*. We could have also used any declared variable, as follows:

```
printf( "struct Card is %lu bytes\n" , sizeof( struct Card ) );
printf( "        card is %lu bytes\n" , sizeof( card ) );
```

Let's verify our assertions about the size of `struct card` with the following code:

```
// add necessary includes

// add definitions for enum Suit, enum Face, and struct Card

int main( void )   {
  struct Card card;

  printf( " enum Suit is %lu bytes\n" , sizeof( enum Suit ) );
  printf( " enum Face is %lu bytes\n" , sizeof( enum Face ) );
  printf( " int is %lu bytes\n" , sizeof( int ) );
  printf( " bool is %lu bytes\n" , sizeof( bool ) );

  printf( "struct Card is %lu bytes\n" , sizeof( struct Card ) );
  printf( " card is %lu bytes\n" , sizeof( card ) );

  return 0;
}
```

Create the `card.c` file and enter the preceding code, adding the necessary header file(s) and `enum` and `struct` definitions. Save the file, compile it, and run it. You might see the following output:

```
> cc card.c -o card
> card
  enum Suit is 4 bytes
  enum Face is 4 bytes
        int is 4 bytes
       bool is 1 bytes
struct Card is 20 bytes
       card is 20 bytes
> 
```

We calculated that struct Card would be 17 bytes, but our test program shows that it is 20 bytes. What's going on?

It turns out that something else is going on behind the scenes. That something is called **structure alignment**, where a given structure is padded with enough space so that it contains an even multiple of the size of its largest component. In the case of struct Card, it is padded with 3 bytes so that it will occupy an even multiple of 4, with 4 bytes being the largest size of any component in struct Card.

Let's try two different tests. First, add another bool variable to struct Card. Run the program again. Notice that the structure takes the same number of bytes, 20. The 1-byte bool reduced the amount of padding needed, but the structure is still 20 bytes. Now, add a double variable to struct Card and run the program. Notice that the size of struct Card is now 32, or an even multiple of eight, which is the size of a double.

Padding within a structure can occur at the end or even in between components. Holes may appear between two consecutive components or after the last component. For the most part, we don't need to and shouldn't concern ourselves with how padding occurs within a structure.

However, because of the padding that's used to align structures, we cannot compare two structures as whole entities for comparison. If padding is present in the structure, the contents of that padding may be undefined, depending on how it is initialized. Therefore, even if two structures have identical component values, the values in the padding are highly unlikely to be equal.

Instead, if an equality test is required, a function must be written to compare two structures component by component. We'll look at this in more detail later in the *Performing operations on structures – functions* section.

Initializing structures and accessing structure elements

Once a structure is defined, we can declare variables of that type. The variables of that structure type must be initialized before use. C gives us a number of ways to do this, depending on the needs of the situation.

Given the definition of `struct Card`, we can initialize a variable of that type in one of three ways:

- **At the time of declaration**: The first way of initializing a structure variable is at declaration time, as follows:

    ```
    struct Card c1 = { heart , (int) heart , king, (int)king , false };
    ```

  The structure component values are enclosed between { and }, separated by commas. The order is significant. `c1` is a card of the `heart` suit with `suitValue` of the `heart` enumeration and `face` of `king` with `faceValue` of the `king` enumeration, which is not a wildcard. In this form of initialization, we must be careful to get the order exactly correct within the definition of `struct Card`.

  If we wanted a completely zero initial state, we could initialize all bytes in the structure with the following code:

    ```
    struct Card card3 = {0};   // Entire structure is zero-d.
    ```

  Zeroing the structure in this manner can only be done at the same time the variable is declared.

- **After declaration, the entire structure, in toto**: The second way of initializing a structure variable is by assigning it the values of another structure variable *in toto*, or a complete and whole copy. This can be done as follows:

    ```
    struct Card card2 = card1;
    ```

  As `card2` is being declared, every component of `card1` is assigned to the corresponding component of `card2`. Care must be taken that these structures are of the same type, otherwise unpredictable results/assignments may occur. This is because it is a bitwise assignment that assumes all of the components of each structure are identically positioned (with padding) with the structure type.

- **After declaration, component by component**: Lastly, a structure variable can be assigned explicitly, component by component. When doing this, it is a good idea to first nullify, or zero, the entire structure at its definition. Each component is accessed using . notation, which specifies a given component of the structure. This initialization would look as follows:

```
struct Card card3 = {0}; // Entire structure is zero-d.
card3.suit = spade;
card3.suitValue = (int) spade;
card3.face = ace;
card3.faceValue = (int)ace;
card3.isWile = true;
```

In this way, each component is accessed directly. The components do not have to be assigned in the same order that they are defined in the structure, but it is a good practice to do so. This type of initialization is done via component initialization. While tedious, it is often the most error-free approach since the structure can change; as long as the component names are the same, the code will not fail. When using this approach, it is also a good idea to initialize to some default state, which can either be all zeros or a default value.

You might need to create a default structure constant that is assigned to any structure variable of that type when declared, as follows:

```
const struct Card defaultCard = { club , (int)club , two , (int)two , false
};

struct Card c4 = defaultCard;
c4.suit = ... /* some other suit */
...
```

Clearly, for our card example, having a `defaultCard` does not make sense. In other scenarios, especially when the structure type is complex with many components, a default structure constant can provide highly consistent program behavior since all structure variables will begin in a known state of either zeroed values or otherwise valid values.

Performing operations on structures – functions

Except for assignment, there are no intrinsic operations for structures. To perform any operation on a single structure or with two structures, a function must be written to perform the desired operation.

For example, earlier, we mentioned a function that can be used to compare two structures for equality. This must be done component by component, as follows:

```
bool isEqual( struct Card c1 , struct Card c2 )   {
   if( c1.suit != c2.suit ) return false;
   if( c1.face != c2.face ) return false;
   return true;
}
```

Notice that we did not compare every component of struct Card in this function. We'd only have to do that for absolute comparison and when we need to compare each and every component of both structures. This just isn't necessary for our card example.

Does it make sense to perform any or all mathematic operations on two structures? In general, no, but this answer is completely dependent on the nature of the structures we are using.

For the card game *Blackjack*, we need to add up the face values of our hand. First, we'd have to set up our faceValue with the proper values for Blackjack. Then, we need to create an operation to add faceValue for two cards. We could do this in a couple of ways. The first way would be to simply add the faceValue of each card, accessing that component directly, as follows:

```
int handValue = card1.faceValue + card2.faceValue;
if( handValue > 21 ) {
   // you lose
} else {
   // decide if you want another card
}
```

Alternatively, we could write a function that adds two cards, as follows:

```
int sumCards( struct Card c1 , struct Card c2 )   {
   int faceValue = c1.faceFalue + c2.faceValue;
   return faceValue;
}
```

Then, we can get the sum of two cards with the following code:

```
int cardsValue = sumCards( card1 , card2 );
if( cardsValue > 21 ) ...
```

Given these two approaches, is one preferred over the other? It really depends on a number of factors. First, if we need to add the `faceValue` of cards in just one or possibly two places in our program, the former approach is acceptable. If, however, we must add `faceValue` in many places, it is better to consolidate that operation into a single function. Any changes or enhancements that must be made to the operation can then be made in a single place – the one function. All calls to that function would remain unchanged.

For example, what if aces could have either a high value – say, 14 – or a low value – say, 1. If we used the former approach, we'd have to be certain our ace `faceValue` was properly set before performing the addition. If the ace value could change or be either value, depending on the situation, then we'd have to add code to take that into consideration in every place that we added `faceValues`. In the latter approach, we would have to take the ace's value into account in only one place: the `add` function.

Notice in the preceding function that the `faceValue` variable is different than both `c1.faceValue` and `c2.faceValue`. You might think that these variable names conflict because they have the same identifier name, but they don't. `faceValue` is a local variable to the `sumCards()` function, while `c1.faceValue` is a component of `c1` and `c2.faceValue` is a component of `c2`. Each of them is actually a different location in memory capable of holding different values.

Now, let's put these concepts into a simplified yet working program.

Copy the `card.c` file to `card2.c`. Add the `isEqual()` and `sumCards()` functions to it, along with their function prototypes. Delete the body of `main()` and replace it with the following:

```
int main( void )   {
  struct Card card1 = { heart , (int) heart , king, (int)king , false };
  struct Card card2 = card1; // card 2 is now identical to card 1

  struct Card card3 = {0};
  card3.suit = spade;
  card3.suitValue = (int)spade;
  card3.face = ace;
  card3.faceValue = (int)ace;
  card3.isWild = true;

  bool cardsEqual = isEqual( card1 , card2 );
  printf( "card1 is%s equal to card2\n" , cardsEqual? "" : " not" );

  cardsEqual = isEqual( card2 , card3 );
  printf( "card2 is%s equal to card3\n" , cardsEqual? "" : " not" );
```

```
printf( "The combined faceValue of card2(%d) + card3(%d) is %d" ,
card2.faceValue ,
card3.faceValue ,
sumCards( card2 , card3 ) );
return 0;
}
```

Save your work. Compile and run `cards2.c`. You should see the following output:

```
> cc card2.c -o card2
> card2
card1 is equal to card2
card2 is not equal to card3
The combined faceValue of card2(13) + card3(14) is 27
> 
```

After initializing three cards with `enum` and `int` values, we then use the function we wrote to compare two structures for equality. We also use the `sumCards()` function to add up the face value of two cards. Note that while we can copy one structure to another with the = operator, for any other types of comparisons or operations on structures, we need to create and call our own functions.

So far, we have created a structure that is composed of intrinsic types (`int`), as well as custom types (`enum`). We can also compose a structure out of other structures.

Structures of structures

A structure can contain components of any type, even other structures.

Let's say we want to represent a hand of five cards. We'll define a structure that contains five `struct Cards`, as follows:

```
struct Hand {
   int cardsDealt;
   struct Card c1;
   struct Card c2;
   struct Card c3;
   struct Card c4;
   struct Card c5;
}
```

We could have just as easily written this as follows:

```
struct Hand {
   int cardsDealt;
   struct Card c1, c2, c3, c4, c5;
};
```

Both definitions are functionally identical. Do you see how this is similar to how variables of the same type were declared in Chapter 4, *Using Variables and Assignment*? As you work with C more and more, you will begin to see patterns being used repeatedly throughout the language. These repeated patterns make the language concise, consistent (for the most part), and easier to understand.

As we shall see in Chapter 16, *Creating and Using More Complex Structures*, there is a somewhat more appropriate way to express our hand of cards; that is, by using a structure that contains an array of cards.

In the struct Hand structure, we use a counter, cardsDealt, to store how many cards are currently in our hand.

Given the structure definition we have seen, each component would be accessed as before:

```
struct Hand h = {0};
```

In the preceding code, struct Hand h is initialized to 0 for all its components and subcomponents.

Then, we can access each of the card components directly, as follows:

```
h.c1.suit      = spade;
h.c1.suitValue = (int) spade;
h.c1.face      = two;
h.c1.faceValue = (int) two;
h.c1.isWild    = false;
h.cardsDealt++;
```

The preceding code is equivalent to adding a card to our hand. Writing these lines out is tedious. A common way to do this without things getting cumbersome is to use the following code:

```
struct Card c1 = { spade   , (int)spade   ,
                   ten   , (int)ten   , false };
struct Card c2 = { heart   , (int)heart   ,
                   queen , (int)queen , false };
struct Card c3 = { diamond , (int)diamond ,
                   five  , (int)ten   , false };
struct Card c4 = { club    , (int)club    ,
```

```
                                ace    , (int)ace   , false };
         struct Card c5 = { heart   , (int)heart   ,
                                jack   , (int)jack  , false };
         struct Card c6 = { club    , (int)club    ,
                                two    , (int)two   , false };
```

While somewhat tedious, it is less tedious than the preceding method and enables us to see the patterns of the values that have been assigned to each card.

Initializing structures with functions

Another way to initialize our hand is with a function. When given a card as an input parameter to an `addCard()` function, we need to make sure we put it in the correct place in our hand. The function is as follows:

```
struct Hand addCard( struct Hand oldHand , struct Card card )  {
   struct Hand newHand = oldHand;
   switch( newHand.cardsDealt )  {
     case 0:
       newHand.c1 = card;  newHand.cardsDealt++;  break;
     case 1:
       newHand.c2 = card;  newHand.cardsDealt++;  break;
     case 2:
       hewHand.c3 = card;  newHand.cardsDealt++;  break;
     case 3:
       hewHand.c4 = card;  newHand.cardsDealt++;  break;
     case 4:
       hewHand.c5 = card;  newHand.cardsDealt++;  break;
     default:
       // Hand is full, what to do now?
       // ERROR --> Ignore new card.
       newHand = oldHand;
       break;
   }
   return newHand;
}
```

In the preceding function, addCard(), oldHand, and card are inputs to the function. Remember that variables, including structures, are passed by copy (a copy of them is made). Therefore, we have to give the function our struct Hand in its current, or old, state, add a card to it, and then return the updated or new version of it back to the caller, again via a copy. The call to this function would, therefore, look as follows:

```
struct Card aCard;
struct Hand myHand;
...
aCard   = getCard( ... );
myHand = addCard( myHand , aCard );
...
```

We have not defined getCard() yet and will defer that until Chapter 16, *Creating And Using More Complex Structures*.

In this function, rather than copy each struct Card subcomponent of hand, we simply assign one struct Card *in* toto to the hand's appropriate card component.

Also in this function, we pass in a copy of our current hand, create a new hand based on the current hand, modify it, and then return the modified version. This is not necessarily the best way to perform this operation, but it is a common function pattern, that is, copy in the structure, modify a copy of it in the function, and then overwrite the original with the modified structure. In Chapter 13, *Using Pointers*, we will look at an alternate way of doing this that avoids all of the structure copying.

Notice that, in the function, we have not considered what to do if the hand is already full. Do we expect our function to handle it or perhaps handle it with another function, discardCard(), before calling addCard()? The code snippet to do that would look as follows:

```
...
card = getCard();
if( myHand.cardsDealt >= 5 )  {  // should never be greater than 5
  myHand = discardCard( myHand, ... );
}
myHand = addCard( myHand, card );
...
```

To keep things simple, for now, we will assume that more than 5 cards is a programming mistake and that our addCard() function handles the card presented to it by simply ignoring it.

Printing a structure of structures – reusing functions

Let's create a function to print the contents of the hand. This function will use a function that we will create to print the structures it contains. In this way, the minimum amount of code is used since printing an individual card exists in only one function. The following function takes our `struct Hand` as an input parameter, determines which card we are dealing with, and calls `printCard()` with that card as a parameter, as follows:

```
void printHand( struct Hand h )  {
  for( int i = 1; i < h.cardsDealt+1 ; i++ )  {  // 1..5
    struct Card c;
    switch( i )  {
      case 1: c = h.c1; break;
      case 2: c = h.c2; break;
      case 3: c = h.c3; break;
      case 4: c = h.c4; break;
      case 5: c = h.c5; break;
      default:  return; break;
    }
    printCard( c );
  }
}
```

In the preceding `printHand()` function, we iterate over the number of cards in our hand. At each iteration, we figure out which card we are looking at and copy it to a temporary variable so that all subsequent accesses are to the temporary structure variable. We can then call `printCard()` for each card (shown in the following code), which deals with the `face` and `suit` of the given card, even though it is a copy of a different card at each iteration. Alternatively, we could have written a `printHand()` function, as follows:

```
void printHand2( struct Hand h )  {
  int dealt = h.cardsDealt;
  if( d == 0 ) return;
  printCard( h.c1 );  if( dealt == 1 ) return;
  printCard( h.c2 );  if( dealt == 2 ) return;
  printCard( h.c3 );  if( dealt == 3 ) return;
  printCard( h.c4 );  if( dealt == 4 ) return;
  printCard( h.c5 );  return;
}
```

In the preceding function, we use fall-through logic to print the cards in our hand.

`printHand()` contains two `switch` statements to print an individual card – one to print the face and one to print the suit, as follows:

```
void printCard( struct Card c )  {
  switch( c.face )  {
    case two:    printf( "   2 " ); break;
    case three:  printf( "   3 " ); break;
    case four:   printf( "   4 " ); break;
    case five:   printf( "   5 " ); break;
    case six:    printf( "   6 " ); break;
    case seven:  printf( "   7 " ); break;
    case eight:  printf( "   8 " ); break;
    case nine:   printf( "   9 " ); break;
    case ten:    printf( "  10 " ); break;
    case jack:   printf( " Jack " ); break;
    case queen:  printf( "Queen " ); break;
    case king:   printf( " King " ); break;
    case ace:    printf( "  Ace " ); break;
    default:     printf( "  ??? " ); break;
  }
  switch( c.suit )  {
    case spade:    printf( "of Spades\n");    break;
    case heart:    printf( "of Hearts\n");    break;
    case diamond:  printf( "of Diamonds\n");  break;
    case club:     printf( "of Clubs\n");     break;
    default:       printf( "of ???s\n");      break;
  }
}
```

Let's put these concepts into a simplified yet working program.

Copy `card2.c` to `card3.c` and remove the function prototypes and functions from `card3.c`. Add the `addCard()`, `printHand()`, `printHand2()`, and `printCard()` functions and their prototypes. Then, replace `main()` with the following code:

```
int main( void )  {
  struct Hand h = {0};

  struct Card c1 = { spade   , (int)spade   ,
                     ten   , (int)ten    , false };
  struct Card c2 = { heart   , (int)heart   ,
                     queen , (int)queen , false };
  struct Card c3 = { diamond , (int)diamond ,
                     five  , (int)ten    , false };
  struct Card c4 = { club    , (int)club    ,
                     ace   , (int)ace    , false };
  struct Card c5 = { heart   , (int)heart   ,
```

```
                            jack  , (int)jack  , false };
   struct Card c6 = { club     , (int)club     ,
                            two   , (int)two   , false };

   h = addCard( h , c1 );
   h = addCard( h , c2 );
   h = addCard( h , c3 );
   h = addCard( h , c4 );
   h = addCard( h , c5 );
   h = addCard( h , c6 );
   printHand( h );
   printf("\n");
   printHand2( h );
   return 0;
}
```

Compile `card3.c` and run it. You should see the following output:

```
> cc card3.c -o card3
> card3
      10 of Spades
Queen of Hearts
       5 of Diamonds
   Ace of Clubs
  Jack of Hearts

      10 of Spades
Queen of Hearts
       5 of Diamonds
   Ace of Clubs
  Jack of Hearts
> ▯
```

Here, you can see that both `printHand()` functions match our card initializations.

Lastly, we must mention that a structure may not contain a component that is its own type. For example, a `struct Hand` may not contain a component of `struct Hand`. A structure may contain a pointer reference to a component that is its own type. For example, take a look at the following code:

```
struct Hand {
    int cardCount
    struct Hand myHand;    /* NOT VALID */
};
```

This code is not valid because a structure cannot contain a component that is itself. Now, take a look at the following code:

```
struct Hand {
    int cardCount;
    struct Hand * myHand;    /* OK */
}
```

This is valid because the component is a pointer reference to the same type of structure. The type of myHand is struct Hand *, which *points to* a different variable of the struct Hand type. We will explore this feature in more detail in Chapter 13, *Using Pointers*.

The stepping stone to object-oriented programming

OOP has been defined in many ways. At the core of all object-oriented languages are objects. Objects are both collections of data, much like C structures, and also operations on that data that's specific to that object, similar to C functions that operate on a structure. So, an object contains both its data and the set of operations that can be performed on it. Sometimes, the internals of the object are completely hidden to the outside program and its components are only available through functions with access to them, called **accessors**. This is a more self-contained version of C where functions are somewhat independent of the data or structures they operate on and must be passed the data that they manipulate. In C, a function, or a manipulator of data, is loosely tied, or *coupled*, to the data it manipulates.

In this chapter, we have used a set of data structures and enumerations to represent real-world cards. We also made functions specific to that data, such as addCard(), printCard(), printHand(), and so on, which are meant to manipulate those data structures.

So, data structures and functions that manipulate them become the basis for object-oriented programming. Data and operations being used on that data, when combined into a self-contained cohesive unit, is called a **class**. A data object may be a derivative of a more general classification of objects, much like a square is a derivative of the more general shape classification. In this case, the square class derives certain general properties from the shape class. Such a derivation is called **inheritance** and is also common to all object-oriented programming languages. *Methods*, also called **member functions**, are functions that only operate on the data contained within the class, also called **member data**.

Later, in `Chapter 24`, *Working with Multi-File Programs*, we will see that we can approximate object-oriented thinking in C where a single file would contain a set of data structures and constants, as well as a set of functions that are meaningful for those data structures. Such a single C file data and functions approach would be a stepping stone to how you might make the transition from C, a function-oriented programming language, to an object-oriented programming language.

Summary

In this chapter, we learned about user-defined C structures. This is one of the most powerful ways of representing real-world objects in a cohesive and clear manner. First, we learned how to declare structures of our basic intrinsic types and custom types (`enum`). Then, we explored how to directly access and manipulate the components of C structures. The only simple operation that we can perform on structures in *toto* is the assignment operator.

We also explored how to manipulate structures via functions that access structure components and manipulate either the individual components, the entire structure, or multiple structures at the same time. We then expanded on the concept of what can be in a structure by defining structures of other structures. Finally, we learned that while C is not an object-oriented language, we saw how C structures are the stepping stone to the languages that are object-oriented.

You may have found that, while using `enum`s and `struct`s, having to remember to add those keywords is somewhat cumbersome. In the next chapter, we will learn how to make using `enum`s and `struct`s a bit less cumbersome with the `typedef` type specifier. This will allow us to make the names of our data types more expressive, in a way similar to how we make variable identifiers express their intended purpose.

10
Creating Custom Data Types with typedef

As we saw in the last two chapters, C allows you to define your own types from **enumerations (enums)** and **structures (structs)**. C also allows you to **redefine** types for convenience of naming and to provide clarity about how to use the redefined type. The redefined type becomes a **synonym** for the original type. Being able to create a synonym of one type from another is extremely useful to express the purpose of variables, not only through their names but also through their redefined types. The benefits of this mechanism are numerous.

The following topics will be covered in this chapter:

- Creating custom named types from intrinsic types
- Creating new synonyms from other custom named types
- Simplifying the use of enums
- Simplifying the use of structs
- Exploring some important compiler options
- Using header files for custom types and the `typedef` specifiers

Technical requirements

Continue to use the tools you chose from the *Technical requirements* section of Chapter 1, *Running Hello, World!*.

The source code for this chapter can be found at https://github.com/PacktPublishing/Learn-C-Programming.

Renaming intrinsic types with typedef

We have already looked at some of C's basic **data types**—whole numbers (integers), real numbers (floating point and complex numbers), characters, enumerations, and Boolean values. We called them **intrinsic** data types since they are built into the language and are always available. By referring to these types specifically as data types, we give focus to the content of variables of those types—containers of data that can be manipulated. However, the use of the term **data type** is not strictly accurate. In reality, these types are classified in C as **arithmetic** types. C has other types, some which we have encountered—**function types**, **structure types**, and **void types**—and some of which we have not yet encountered—**array types**, **pointer types**, and **union types**. We will explore **array types** and **pointer types** in greater detail in later chapters.

For all of these types, C provides a way to rename them. This is for convenience only. The underlying type that they are based on is unchanged. We use the `typedef` keyword to create a **synonym** for the base type. In this way, we supply additional context about the intent or purpose of a variable via a renamed type declaration. The syntax for using `typedef` is as follows:

```
typedef aType aNewType;
```

Here, `aType` is an intrinsic or custom type and `aNewType` is now a synonym for `aType`. Anywhere that `aType` is used after this declaration, `aNewType` can be used instead.

Remember, when enums and structs are defined, no memory is allocated. Likewise, the `typedef` specifiers do not allocate any memory. Memory allocation does not happen until we declare a variable of the new type, regardless if it is an enum type, a struct type, or a type that has been defined via `typedef`.

Let's now see how and why this is useful.

Using synonyms

Up to this point, we have relied on the variable's name as the sole provider of the purpose, which is our intended use of that variable. The name tells us (humans) what we expect that variable to contain. The computer doesn't really care since a variable is just a location in memory somewhere that holds some value of the given type.

For instance, we might have three variables to hold measurement values—height, width, and length. We could simply declare them as integers, as follows:

```
int height, width, length;
```

Their use as measurements is fairly obvious, but what are the intended units of measurement? We cannot tell this from the int type. However, by using typedef, we can add more useful context, as follows:

```
typedef int meters;

meters height, width, length;

height = 4;
width  = height * 2;
length = 100;
```

meters has been defined as a synonym of the int type. Anywhere we use these, either as standalone variables or as arguments to functions, they are now known as values of meters and not simply as integers. We have added the context of units of measure via the synonym. We can assign integers to them and we can perform integer operations on them. If we assign real numbers to them, truncation will occur in the type conversion.

There is another benefit to using synonyms for types. That is when we may need to change the underlying base type. When we declare variables using intrinsic or custom types, their type is set to and constrained to that type. In the preceding example (before typedef), all the variables are of the int type. What if, however, we needed to change their type either to long long for a much larger range of whole numbers or to double to add greater fractional accuracy? Without using typedef, we'd have to find every declaration of those variables and functions that use them and change their type to the new type, which is tedious and error-prone. With typedef, we would need to change only one line, as follows:

```
typedef double meters;
```

After making the change in the typedef specifier, any variable of the meters type has an underlying type of double. Using typedef in this way allows us some flexibility to easily modify our program.

Note that creating a synonym with typedef is only done as a matter of convenience. Doing so doesn't limit operations on the newly defined type; any operations that are valid on the underlying type are also valid on the synonym type.

Nevertheless, this is extremely useful and very convenient. For instance, in some situations, such as dealing with data to and from a network connection, is it not only useful but also essential to have a clear understanding of the sizes of the various data types and variables that are being used. One way to provide this clarity is through the use of `typedef`, as follows:

```
typedef          char      byte;    // 7-bits + 1 signed bit
typedef unsigned char      ubyte;   // 8-bits
typedef unsigned short     ushort;  // 16 bits
typedef unsigned long      ulong;   // 32 bits
typedef          long long llong;   // 63 bits + 1 signed bit
typedef unsigned long long ullong;  // 64 bits
```

In a program that uses these redefined types, every time a variable of `ubyte` is declared, we know that we are dealing with 1 byte (8 bits) and that any value is positive only (unsigned). The `ubyte` synonym exactly matches the definition of the computer's byte unit, which is 8 bits. As an added benefit, `ubyte` uses far fewer keystrokes than `unsigned char`.

As stated earlier, anywhere where `unsigned char` would be used, `ubyte` can be used instead. This applies to additional `typedef` specifiers, too. We can redeclare a synonym type to be yet another synonym type, as follows:

```
typedef ubyte Month;
typedef ubyte Day;
typedef ulong Year;

struct Date {
  Month m;
  Day   d;
  Year  y;
};
```

In `struct Date`, each component is itself a `typedef` type based on `ubyte` (which is based on `unsigned char`). We have created a new custom type based on a synonym we have already created. In the preceding example, this makes sense because both `Month` and `Day` will never exceed a value in the range provided by `unsigned char` (0..256). For most practical purposes, `Year` could be represented as `ushort`, but here it is as `ulong`.

Use `typedef` when it makes the intended usage of the variables you declare clearer and avoids ambiguity. You can also use it when you are uncertain about whether the chosen type is the final, correct type. Furthermore, you may develop for yourself a **standard set** of the `typedef` specifiers that you use frequently and consistently in the programs you write. We will see, later in this chapter, that we can put them in a file so that they don't have to be repeatedly edited in our programs.

Simplifying the use of enum types with typedef

Before we examine the use of `typedef` with enums, we must first complete the picture of using enums. Remember that defining a new type does not require memory allocation. Only when we declare variables of a given type is memory allocated to the variables. In the last two chapters, we used enums by first defining them and then separately declaring variables of that type, as follows:

```
    // First define some enumerated types.

  enum Face { one , two , three , ... };
  enum Suit { spade , heart, ... };

    // Then declare variables of those types.

  enum Face f1 , f2;
  enum Suit s1 , s2;
```

In the preceding code fragment, we have defined two types—enum `Face` and enum `Suit`. Later, in separate statements, two variables of each type are declared—f1, f2, s1, and s2.

Another way to achieve the same result is to both define the enumerated type and to declare variables of that type in one statement, as follows:

```
    // Defining an enumeration and declaring variables of
    // that type at same time.

  enum Face { one , two , three , ... }  f1, f2;
  enum Suit { spade , heart , ... }      s1 , s2;
```

In this code fragment, instead of four statements, we only have two. In each statement, a type is defined and then variables of that type are declared. This second method is handy if the enumerated type is only going to be used in a single function or within a single file. Otherwise, its use is somewhat limited and the previous method of two-step definition and declaration is preferred. We will see why when we put our custom type definitions in a header file later in this chapter.

The situation is quite different, however, when `typedef` is thrown into the mix. The syntax for using `typedef` in enumerations has three forms. The first form is a two-part definition where in the first part, the enumeration is defined and in the second part, the `typedef` specifier creates a synonym for it, as follows:

```
enum name { enumeration1, enumeration2, ... , enumerationN };
typedef enum name synonym_name;
```

`enum name` is our custom type. We use that type, just as we did with intrinsic types, to create a new synonym. An example we have seen is as follows:

```
enum Face { one , two , three , ... };
enum Suit { spade, heart , ... };

typedef enum Face Face;
typedef enum Suit Suit;
```

We now have two custom types—enum `Face` and enum `Suit`—and convenient short-form synonyms for them—`Face` and `Suit`. Anywhere that we need, say, to use enum `Suit`, we can now simply use `Suit`.

The second form defines both the enumeration and synonyms for it in one statement, as follows:

```
typedef enum name { enumeration1, enumeration2, ... , enumerationN }
synonym1, synonym2, ...;
```

The custom type is enum `name`, with one or more synonyms in the same statement—synonym1, synonym2 , ... This is very different from what we saw earlier when an enum and variables were declared in the same statement. In this case, there is no allocation of memory and no variables are created. Using this form for `Face` and `Suit` would work as follows:

```
typedef enum Face { one , two , three , ... } Face;
typedef enum Suit { spade , heart , ... }    Suit;
```

In each of the two statements, a custom type is defined and a synonym for it is created. While this is similar to the preceding statement where a custom type is defined and variables of that type are allocated, here, `typedef` makes all the difference.

There is an even shorter form, where `name` is omitted and we only have the synonyms for our **unnamed** or **anonymous** custom type. The following code snippet shows this:

```
typedef enum { one , two , three , ... } Face;
typedef enum { spade , heart , ... }    Suit;
```

We have created two anonymous enums that are now only known as a type by their synonyms—Face and Suit. Regardless of which method we use to create synonyms for enum Face and enum Suit, we can now declare variables using our new synonyms, as follows:

```
Face face;
Suit suit;
```

We have declared two variables—face and suit—using a convention where the custom type identifier has the first letter in its name in uppercase and the variables are all lowercase identifiers.

Of the three ways given to create typedef enums, the last method is most common. Once the synonyms for a custom type are defined, there is rarely a need to use the enum name custom type; this, however, is not a strict rule and all three forms can be used depending on what best fits the situation.

Simplifying the use of struct types with typedef

All of the considerations we explored for enums equally apply to structs. We will go through each of them as they apply to structs.

Before we examine the use of typedef with structs, we must first complete the picture of using structs. In the last chapter, Chapter 9, *Creating and Using Structures*, we used structs by first defining them and then separately declaring variables of that type, as follows:

```
// First define a structured type.

struct Card { Face face; Suit suit; ... };

// Then declare variables of that type.

struct Card c1 , c2 , c3 , c4 , c5;
```

In the preceding code fragment, we have defined one type, struct Card. In a separate statement, five variables of that type are declared—c1, c2, c3, c4, and c5.

Another way to achieve the same result is to both define the structured type and declare variables of that type in one statement, as follows:

```
// Defining an structure and declaring variables of that type
// at the same time

struct Card { Face face; Suit suit; ... } c1 , c2 , c3 , c4 , c5;
```

In this code fragment, instead of two statements, we have only one. In that statement, a type is defined and then variables of that type are declared. This second method is handy if the structured type is only going to be used in a single function or within a single file. Otherwise, its use is somewhat limited and the previous method of two-step definition and declaration is preferred. We will see why when we put our custom type definitions in a header file later in this chapter.

The situation is quite different, however, when typedef is thrown into the mix. The syntax for using typedef in structure definitions has three forms. The first form is a two-part definition, where first the structure is defined and then the typedef specifier creates a synonym for it, as follows:

```
struct name { type component1; type component2; ... ; type componentN };
typedef struct name synonym_name;
```

struct name is our custom type. We use that type, just as we did with intrinsic types, to create a new synonym. An example we have seen is as follows:

```
struct Card { Face face; Suit suit; ... };

typedef struct Card Card;
```

We now have one custom type, struct Card, and a convenient short-form synonym for it, Card. Anywhere that we need, say, to use struct Card, we can now simply use Card.

The second form defines both the structure and synonyms for it in one statement, as follows:

```
typedef struct name {
 type component1;
 type component2;
 ... ;
 type componentN
} synonym1, synonym2, ...;
```

The custom type is `struct name`, with one or more synonyms in the same statement—`synonym1`, `synonym2` , ... This is very different from what we saw earlier when a struct and variables were declared in the same statement. In this case, there is no allocation of memory and no variables are created. Using this form for `Card` is as follows:

```
typedef struct Card { Face face; Suit suit; ... } Card;
```

In this statement, a custom type is defined and a synonym for it is created. While this is similar to the preceding statement, where a custom type is defined and variables of that type are allocated, here, `typedef` makes all the difference.

There is an even shorter form where `name` is omitted and we only have the synonyms for our **unnamed** or **anonymous** custom type. The following code snippet shows this:

```
typedef struct { Face face; Suit suit; ... } Card;
```

We have created an anonymous struct that is now only known as a type by its synonym, `Card`. Regardless of which method we use to create synonyms for `struct Card`, we can now declare variables using our new synonyms, as follows:

```
Card c1 , c2 , c3, c4, c5;
```

We have declared five variables—c1, c2, c3, c4, and c5—using a convention where the custom type identifier begins with an uppercase letter and the variables are all lowercase identifiers.

Of the three ways given to create structs defined via `typedef`, the last method is the most common. Once the synonyms for a custom type are defined, there is rarely a need to use the `struct name` custom type; this, however, is not a strict rule, and all three forms can be used depending on what best fits the situation.

Let's put all of this into use with a working program. Let's alter the `card3.c` program from the last chapter, making use of our knowledge of `typedef`. We'll modify a copy of this program to use enums (defined via `typedef`) and structs. Copy `card3.c` to `card4.c` and make the following changes in `card4.c`:

- Use `typedef` for the enums for `Suit` and `Face`.
- Use `typedef` for the structs for `Card` and `Hand`.
- In the structs that use `enum Suit` and `enum Face`, replace these with their synonyms.

- Replace each occurrence of `struct Card` and `struct Hand` with their synonyms wherever they are found (hint—with other structs, function prototypes, function parameters, and so on).

Save, compile, and run `card4.c`. You should see the following output:

```
> cc card4.c -o card4
> ./card4
   10 of Spades
Queen of Hearts
    5 of Diamonds
  Ace of Clubs
 Jack of Hearts

   10 of Spades
Queen of Hearts
    5 of Diamonds
  Ace of Clubs
 Jack of Hearts
>
```

Finally, compare your edits on your local `card4.c` program to the `card4.c` program provided in the source repository for this chapter. You should have eliminated all but two enum keywords and all but two struct keywords in `card4.c`, and the output should be identical to that of `card3.c` from the preceding chapter.

Other uses of typedef

We began this chapter by discussing C's various types beyond arithmetic types and custom types. It should come as no surprise, then, that `typedef` can apply to more than just the types we have explored in this chapter. `typedef` can be applied to the following types:

- Arrays (explored in the next chapter, Chapter 11, *Working with Arrays*)
- Pointer types (explored in Chapter 13, *Using Pointers*)
- Functions
- Pointers to functions

We mention these here as a matter of completeness only. When we explore pointers, we will touch on using `typedef` on variables of pointer types. However, the use of `typedef` for the other types is somewhat advanced conceptually and beyond the scope of this book.

Some more useful compiler options

Up until now, we have been compiling our programs with just the `-o output_file` option. Your compiler, whether `gcc`, `clang`, or `icc`, probably unbeknownst to you before this point, has a bewildering array of options.

If you are curious, type `cc -help` into your command shell and see what spews out. Tread lightly! If you do this, just understand that you will never need the vast majority of those options. Some of these options are for the compiler only; others are passed on to the linker only. They are there for both very specialized system software configurations and for the compiler and linker writers.

If you are using a Unix or Unix-like system, try `man cc` in the command shell to see a more reasonable list of options and their usage.

The most important of these options, and the one we will use from now on, is `-std=c17` or `-std=c11`. The `-std` switch tells the compiler which version of the C standard to use. Some compilers default to older versions of the C standard, such as C89 or C99, for backward compatibility. Nearly all compilers now support the newest standard, C17. On the rather old system that I am using to write this, C17 is not supported. However, on another updated system I have, `-std=c17` is supported; on that system, I will use that switch.

Another very important compiler switch is `-Wall`. The `-W` switch allows you to enable an individual warning or all warnings that the compiler encounters. Without that switch, the compiler will not report the warnings.

It is also a very good idea to treat all warnings as errors with the `-Werror` switch. Any warning conditions encountered by the compiler will then prevent further processing (the linker will not be invoked) and no executable output file will be created.

There are many reasons why using `-Wall` with `-Werror` is always the best practice. As you encounter more C programs and more books about C, you will find that many rely on and are steeped in older versions of C with slightly different behaviors. Some older behaviors are good, while others are not as good. Newer compilers may or may not continue to allow or support those behaviors; without `-Wall` and `-Werror` the compiler *might* issue warnings when they are encountered. In a worst-case scenario, no error or warning will be given but your program will behave in unexpected ways or will crash. Another reason is that you may be using C in a way that is not quite *according to Hoyle*—that is, not quite as it was intended to be used—and the compiler will provide warnings when that happens. When you get a warning, it is then important to do the following:

1. Understand why the warning was presented (what did you do to cause it?).
2. Fix and remove the cause of the warning.
3. Repeat until there are no errors or warnings.

Compilers are notorious for spewing cryptic warnings. Thankfully, we now have the internet to help us out. When you get an error or warning you don't understand, copy it from your command shell and paste it into the search field of your favorite web browser.

Given these considerations, our standard command line for compilation will be as follows:

```
cc source.c -std=c17 -Wall -Werror -o source
```

Here, `source` is the name of the C program to be compiled. Use `c11` if your system does not support `c17` (or consider upgrading your compiler/system). You will get tired of typing these switches. For now, I want you to do this manually.

Using a header file for custom types and the typedef specifiers

Because we have explored custom types (enums, structs, and the `typedef` specifiers), it is now appropriate to explore how to collect these custom types into our own **header file** and include them in our program.

We have seen the following statements:

```
#include <stdio.h>
#include <stdbool.h>
```

These are predefined header files that provide function prototypes—the `typedef` specifiers, enums, and structs—related to those function prototypes. When a header file is enclosed in < and >, the compiler looks in a predefined list of places for those files. It then opens them and inserts them into the source file just as if they had been copied and pasted into the source file.

We can now create our own header file, say `card.h`, and use it in our program. But where do we put it? We could find the location of the predefined header files and save ours there. That, however, is not a good idea since we may end up writing many, many programs; editing, saving, and updating program files in many locations is tedious and error-prone. Fortunately, there is a solution.

When we enclose a header file in " and ", the compiler first looks in the same directory as the source `.c` file before it starts looking elsewhere for a given file. So, we would create and save our `card.h` file in the same directory location as, say, `card5.c`. We would then direct the compiler to use it as follows:

```
#include "card.h"
```

When you create header files for your programs, they will nearly always reside in the same directory location as the source files. We can then rely on this simple convention of using " and " to locate **local** header files. Local header files are those in the same directory as our source file(s).

We must now consider what belongs in header files and what doesn't belong there.

As a general convention, each C source file has an associated header file. In that file are the function prototypes and any custom types used within the source file that are specific to it. We will explore this simplified use of a header file in this section. Basically, we put anything in a header that does not allocate memory (variables) and does not define functions. Anything that allocates memory or defines functions go into the source file itself.

To be clear, anything that *could* go into a header file doesn't *have to* go into a header file; as we have already seen, it can be put into the source file where it is used. Whether to put something in a header or not is a topic covered in `Chapter 24`, *Working with Multi-File Programs*, and `Chapter 25`, *Understanding Scope*. Complications arise when we use a header file in more than one place. For now, we will use a single header file for our single C source file as a means to declutter the source file.

Let's begin reworking `card4.c` into `card.h` and `card5.c`, which will use `card.h` but will otherwise remain unchanged. Depending on the editor you are using, copying and pasting between files may be easy or difficult. The approach we will take will avoid using the editor's copy and paste abilities. Our approach is as follows:

1. Copy `card4.c` to `card.h`.
2. Copy `card4.c` to `card5.c`.
3. Then, pare down each of those two new files into what we want.

Open `card.h` and remove the `#include` statements, the `main()` function definition, and any other function definitions. You should be left with the following:

```
typedef enum {
   club  = 1 , diamond , heart , spade
} Suit;

typedef enum {
   one = 1, two, three, four, five, six, seven, eight, nine, ten, jack,
queen, king, ace
} Face;

typedef struct {
   Suit  suit;
   int   suitValue;
   Face  face;
   int   faceValue;
   bool  isWild;
} Card;

typedef struct {
   int   cardsDealt;
   Card c1, c2, c3, c4, c5;
} Hand;

Hand addCard(    Hand oldHand , Card card );
void printHand(   Hand h );
void printHand2( Hand h );
void printCard(   Card c );
```

Now, open `card5.c` and delete the `typedef` enums, the `typedef` structs, and the function prototypes. Replace them all with a single line, as follows:

```
#include "card.h"
```

Your `card5.c` file should now look like the following:

```
#include <stdio.h>
#include <stdbool.h>
#include "card.h"

int main( void)  {
  ...
  ...
}

// and all the rest of the function definitions.
...
...
```

What we have done is essentially split `card4.c` into two files—`card.h` and `card5.c`. Compile `card5.c` (with our new switches) and run it. You should see the following output (it should be the same as for `card4.c`):

```
> cc card5.c -o card5 -Wall -Werror -std=c11
> ./card5
    10 of Spades
Queen of Hearts
     5 of Diamonds
   Ace of Clubs
  Jack of Hearts

    10 of Spades
Queen of Hearts
     5 of Diamonds
   Ace of Clubs
  Jack of Hearts
>
```

Stop and consider this file organization—a source file with `main()` and function definitions along with its header file containing enums, structs, the `typedef` specifiers, and function prototypes. This is a core pattern of C source files. For now, this is a simple introduction to creating and using our own header files. Henceforth, you'll see custom header files being created and used. These will be simple header files and will typically consist of only a single header that we create. We will explore more complex header files, as well as multiple header files, in `Chapter 24`, *Working with Multi-File Programs*.

Summary

We have seen how to create alternative names, or synonyms, for intrinsic types and custom types declared with enums and structs. Using `typedef`, we have explored convenient ways to create synonyms for intrinsic types and how the `typedef` specifiers simplify the use of enums and structs. We have also seen how synonyms make your code clearer and provide added context for the intended use of variables of that synonym type.

We have seen how it is somewhat cumbersome to declare and manipulate multiple instances of structured data of the same type, especially when there are many instances of a single structure type, such as a deck of cards.

In the next chapter, we will see how to group, access, and manipulate collections of data types that are identical in type but differ only in values. These are called **arrays**. Arrays help us to further model and manipulate, for instance, a deck of cards consisting of 52 cards.

11
Working with Arrays

We have already seen how a structure is a grouping of one or more components that can each be of different data types. Often, we need a grouping that consists of the same type; this is called an **array**. An array is a collection of multiple occurrences of the same data type grouped together under a single name. Each element of the array is accessed via its basename and an offset of that base. Arrays have many uses, from organizing homogenous data types to providing the basis for strings, or arrays of characters.

Before we can learn about some of the wide uses of arrays, we need to explore the basics of declaring and manipulating arrays.

The following topics will be covered in this chapter:

- Declaring an array of values
- Initializing an array in several ways
- Accessing each element of an array
- Understanding zero-based array indexing
- Assigning and manipulating elements of an array
- Using looping statements to access all elements of an array
- Using array references as function parameters

Technical requirements

Continue to use the tools chosen from the *Technical requirements* section of Chapter 1, *Running Hello, World!*.

The source code for this chapter can be found at https://github.com/PacktPublishing/Learn-C-Programming.

Declaring and initializing arrays

An array is a collection of two or more values, all of which have the same type and share a single common basename. It makes no sense to have an array of just one value; that would simply be a variable. An array definition has the following syntax:

```
dataType arrayIdentifier[ numberOfElements ];
```

Here, `dataType` is any intrinsic or custom type, `arrayIdentifier` is the basename of the array, and `numberOfElements` specifies how many values of `dataType` are in the array. `numberOfElements`, for whatever type and values are given, will be converted into an integer. All the elements of the array are contiguous (or side-by-side) so that the size of the array is the size of each element multiplied by the number of elements in the array.

To declare an integer array of `10` elements, we would use the following statement:

```
int anArray[10];
```

`anArray` is the basename of our array of 10 integers. This declaration creates 10 variables, each accessed via a single name, `anArray`, and an **offset** in the range of `0..9`.

We could also declare the size of the array using a variable, a constant variable, or an expression. In the following code sample, we use a constant, as follows:

```
const int kArraySize = 10;
int anotherArray[ kArraySize ];
```

`kArraySize` is an integer whose value does not change. Here, we use a convention where constant values have `k-` as their prefix. This is convenient because we can use `kArraySize` later when we want to access all the elements of the array. Had we used a variable whose value could later change, we must understand that even if that value changes, the size of the array does not. The array size is fixed at the time of its definition; the array size cannot be changed after the array is defined.

Let's say we wanted to keep track of the air pressure and tread depth for the wheels of various vehicles. If we had a function, `getNumberOfWheels( enum VehicleKind )`, that returned an integer, we might want to declare our arrays for each of the wheels of a given vehicle using that function, as follows:

```
double tireTread[ getNumberOfWheels( tricycle ) ];
double tirePressure[ getNumberOfWheels( tricycle ) ];
```

`getNumberOfWheels( tricycle )` would return 3. So, we would have declared two arrays of three `double` elements—one to hold values for each wheel's `tireTread` property and another to hold values for each wheel's `tirePressure` property. If, on the other hand, we needed to do this for an automobile, our use of the function to declare the arrays might look as follows:

```
double tireTread[ getNumberOfWheels( automobile ) ];
double tirePressure[ getNumberOfWheels( automobile ) ];
```

In the preceding code fragment, `getNumberOfWheels( automobile )` would return 4. So, we would have declared two arrays of four `double` elements—one to hold values for each wheel's `tireTread` property and another to hold values for each wheel's `tirePressure` property.

Note that just as we cannot redefine the same name of a variable in the same function, we cannot use the same array names in the same function, even though they are of different sizes. The preceding declarations would have to occur in different places in our program or would have to have different names if they were in the same function.

Initializing arrays

As with all variables, it is important to initialize array elements to some known value before using them. Just as with structures, as we saw in `Chapter 9`, *Creating and Using Structures*, we can initialize an array in several different ways.

The most basic way to initialize an array is to set all of its values to the same value at the time of definition. We set all the array elements to the same value as follows:

```
int anArray[10] = {0};
double wheelTread[ getNumberOfWheels( tricycle ) ] = { 1.5 };
```

All the values of each array are set to the same value given within { and }. All 10 values of `anArray` are set to 0. All three values of `wheelTread` are set to 1.5. However, we could have set them all to a constant value, a variable, or the result of an expression. We can change the value of each element as needed later.

To set each element to different values during initialization, each element's value can be specified between { and }, separated by commas, as follows:

```
int anArray[10] = { 2 , 4 , 6 , 8 , 10 , 12 , 14 , 16 , 18 , 20 };
```

anArray has set each element to an even number. It would be difficult to do the same with the wheelTread array because of the way it is defined. We might have too many or too few values, depending on the result of getNumberOfWheels(). A mismatch between the number of the elements dynamically assigned and the explicit array size would result in a compiler error.

However, dynamically assigning an array size is possible if we don't first specify the number of elements. However, once the size is set in this manner, it cannot be changed. We can do this and let the number of given values determine the size of the array, as follows:

```
float lengthArray[] = { 1.0 , 2.0 , 3.0 , 4.0 , 3.0 , 2.0 , 1.0 };
```

In this definition, lengthArray contains seven floating-point values. Each of these values can later change, but the size of lengthArray will now always be seven values of the float type. We will see, in Chapter 15, *Working with Strings*, how this feature is essential to defining arrays of characters (strings).

We can then determine the size of the array (if we know its type) with the following program:

```
#include <stdio.h>

int main( void )
{
  int    anArray[10]  = {0};  // Initialize the whole thing to 0.
  int typeSize    = sizeof( int );
  int arraySize   = sizeof( anArray );
  int elementNum = arraySize / typeSize;

  printf( "       sizeof(int) = %2d bytes\n"   , typeSize  );
  printf( "  sizeof(anArray) = %2d bytes\n"   , arraySize  );
  printf( "  anArray[] has %d elements\n\n"   , elementNum );

    // Dynamically allocate array size via initialization.

  float lengthArray[] = { 1.0 , 2.0 , 3.0 , 4.0 , 3.0 , 2.0 , 1.0 };

  int floatSize   = sizeof( float );
  int arraySize   = sizeof( lengthArray );
  int elementNum = arraySize / typeSize;

  printf( "       sizeof(int) = %d bytes\n" , floatSize  );
  printf( "  sizeof(anArray) = %d bytes\n" , arraySize  );
  printf( "anArray has %d elements\n"      , elementNum );
}
```

With your editor, create an `array1.c` file and type in the preceding program. Compile it using the compiler options from the previous chapter and run it. You should see the following output:

```
> cc array1.c -o array1 -Wall -Werror -std=c11
> ./array1
        sizeof(int) =  4 bytes
   sizeof(anArray) = 40 bytes
   anArray[] has 10 elements

        sizeof(float) =  4 bytes
   sizeof(lengthArray) = 28 bytes
     lengthArray[] has 7 elements
>
```

`anArray` has a known size that was specified at its definition initialized to `0`. `lengthArray` has a dynamic size specified by the number of values given at its definition/initialization. By using `sizeof()` at runtime, the actual size of an array can be determined when the program runs.

There is another way to initialize an array—element by element. Before we can do this, we must understand how to access each element. We will do this in the next section and in the *Operations on arrays with loops* section when we use a loop to access all elements of an array.

Accessing array elements

Each element of an array is accessed via its basename and an index into the array. An index is also known as a **subscript**. Each element is accessed using the following form:

```
arrayName[ index ]
```

Here, `index` is a value between `0` and the array size minus `1`. We can access any element of an array using this form. Just as with declaring an array, the index may be a literal value, a variable, the result of a function call, or the result of an expression, as follows:

```
float anArray[10] = {2.0};
int    counter = 9;
float aFloat   = 0.0;

aFloat = anArray[ 9 ];                 // Access last element.
```

```
aFloat = anArray[ counter ];          // Access last element via value
                                      // of counter.
aFloat = anArray[ exp( 3 , 2 )  ];    // Access element at result of
                                      // function.
aFloat = anArray[ (sizeof(anArray)/sizeof(float) - 1 ]; // Access
                                      // last element via expression.
```

Each of these statements accesses the last element of the array and assigns the value of that element to the aFloat variable. Notice how the index is evaluated in several ways using a literal, a variable, a function result, and an expression. All of them evaluate to 9, the index of the last element of the array.

Now, it may seem odd that even though we declared an array of 10 elements, the index of the last element is not 10, but 9. To fully understand array indexing, it is critical to understand that the index is really an offset of the basename. We will henceforth use the term **array offset** whenever an index is intended. The first element of an array, therefore, has an offset of 0.

For example, we can declare an array of 4 integers, as follows:

```
int arr[4] = {0}; // 4 elements
```

Then, we can initialize each element of this array element by element, as follows:

```
arr[0] = 1;  // 0th offset, 1st element
arr[1] = 2;  // 1st offset, 2nd element
arr[2] = 3;  // 2nd offset, 3rd element
arr[3] = 4;  // 3rd offset, 4th element (last one)

arr[4] = 5;  // ERROR! there is no 5th element.
```

First, we can see how we can initialize an array element by element. For an array whose size is 4 elements, the valid range of offsets is 0 .. 3. This is called **zero-based indexing**, where the first element's index is 0. It is also sometimes referred to as the **off-by-one problem**, and it requires careful consideration since it can be a great source of programmer frustration. We originally encountered this in Chapter 7, *Exploring Loops and Iteration*, when examining the for() ... loop. It is not actually a problem; some programmers might even consider it an intended design feature of C. It is really only a problem when we misunderstand it.

However, when we instead think of the index as an offset—the first element has no offset or a 0 offset—confusion is dispelled, and therein lies the difference. We will see in a bit how this off-by-one problem can actually work to our advantage when we loop through the whole array.

Note that it is up to the programmer to ensure that the array index is properly within the range of the array's dimension. The compiler may provide a warning if an array index is out of bounds, but it doesn't always do so.

Let's see when we can rely on the compiler and when we cannot with an example program. Copy `array1.c` into `array2.c`, delete `main()`, and then replace it with the following:

```
int main( void )   {
    int    anArray[10]    = {0}; // Initialize the whole thing to 0.
    int x, y , z;
    x = 11;
    y = 12;
    z = 13;

    anArray[ 11 ] = 7; // Compiler error!
    anArray[ x]   = 0;  // No compiler error, but runtime error!
}
```

Compile `array2.c` and run `array2`. You should see something like the following output:

```
> cc array2.c -o array2 -Wall -Werror -std=c11
array2.c:20:3: error: array index 11 is past the end of the array (which
        contains 10 elements) [-Werror,-Warray-bounds]
    anArray[ 11 ] = 7; // Compiler error!

array2.c:14:3: note: array 'anArray' declared here
    int    anArray[10]   = {0}; // Initialize the whole thing to 0.

1 error generated.
>
```

The compiler sees that `anArray[11]` is out of array bounds and generates an error. Now, comment out the second-to-last line (`anArray[11]...`). Again, compile and run `array2`. You should see something like the following output:

```
> cc array2.c -o array2 -Wall -Werror -std=c11
> ./array2
Abort trap: 6
>
```

Here, `anArray[x]` does not cause a compiler error but does cause a runtime error, which is displayed as `Abort trap 6`. The compiler cannot tell that the value of x holds a value that is out of bounds for the array at compile time. At runtime, however, an abort trap is generated.

This demonstrates that the compiler does not always detect array out-of-bounds errors. Therefore, we cannot rely on the compiler to always do so.

Assigning values to array elements

Once you can identify an element of an array, you can retrieve values from it or assign values to it just as you would with any other variable.

To change the value of an array element, we can similarly use the following access forms to assign a value to it:

```
float anArray[10] = {0.0};
int   counter = 9;
float aFloat  = 2.5;

anArray[ 9 ]                              = aFloat;
anArray[ counter ]                        = getQuarterOf( 10.0 );
anArray[ pow( 3 , 2 ) ]                   = 5.0 / 2.0;
anArray[ (sizeof(anArray)/sizeof(float) - 1 ] = 2.5;
```

Each of these array-assignment statements assigns a value (evaluated in various ways) to the last array element, whose index is evaluated in various ways. In each case, the index is evaluated to 9, the index of the last element of the array. The pow() function raises the first parameter to the power of the second parameter, which in this case is 3^2, or 9. In each case, the value assigned to that array element is 2.5.

To summarize, each element of an array is a variable that we can get values from or assign values to via the array's name and its index.

Operating on arrays with loops

When an array is present, a common operation is to iterate over all of its elements. For this, we typically use the for()... loop. We could also use any of the other looping statements described in Chapter 7, *Exploring Loops and Iteration*. However, because, more often than not, we know the loop's size, it is easier and more reliable to use a counter-controlled for()... loop. When we explore arrays of characters (or strings) in Chapter 15, *Working with Strings*, we will begin our exploration of sentinel controlled-loops.

To iterate over the array, the index counter is initialized to 0 (to match the zeroth offset), the continuation expression specifies that the index counter remains less than the number of elements, and the index counter is incremented at each iteration. The loop is as follows:

```
const int kArraySize = 25;
int anArray[ kArraySize ];

for( int i=0 ; i < kArraySize ; i++ )  {    // i: 0..24 (kArraySize-1)
  anArray[ i ] = i;
}
```

anArray has 25 elements. The offsets range for each element in anArray goes from 0 to 24. In the loop statement, each element of the array is initialized to the value of its own offset. Notice that we've made a note about the expected range of the value of the index counter, i, in that line's comment. For historical reasons that predate C and have more to do with another, older language, **FORTRAN** (now referred to as Fortran), the variable names—i, j, and k—are typically used as index counter variables. So, we often see these used as a common index-counting convention in C.

Notice that the continuation expression, i < kArraySize, is rather concise. Here, the zero-based indices work together with the single less-than operator (<) to enable such compactness. There are other ways that this loop could have been expressed, but none are as compact as this. It is a common C idiom that had valid design rationale when **Central Processor Units** (**CPUs**) were slower and simpler; this rationale is seldom valid today. Yet, it lives on. Indeed, this idiom characterizes the innate terseness of C.

Using functions that operate on arrays

An array is a collection of variables bound together by a common name and an offset. In nearly every respect, we can treat an individual element of an array just as we would any other variable. Even with function parameters, array elements can be passed into them as with regular variables, as follows:

```
#include <math.h>
int anArray[10] = {0};

anArray[3] = 5;
anArray[3] = pow( anArray[3] , 2 );
```

The fourth element of the array is assigned a value of 5. The function declared in math.h, pow(), is called with the value found in the fourth element of the array and is raised to the power of 2 (squared) and assigned back to the fourth element of the array, which now has a value of 25.

We want to create functions that operate on all elements of an array, regardless of their size. But how do we use arrays of unknown sizes as parameters to functions? We *can* do this; arrays of unknown sizes can be passed as arguments to functions. To pass an array of unknown size as a function parameter, we must declare that the function parameter is an array, as follows:

```
int findMin( int size, int anArray[] );
int findMax( int size, int anArray[] );

double findMean(  int size , int anArray[] );
double findStdDev( int size , int anArray[] );
```

C does not store the size of an array. We, as programmers, must keep track of that in order to ensure that we do not access memory beyond the bounds of the array. So, for the function declared previously, we pass the size of the array we are going to provide as one of the parameters. By doing this, the function can operate on a valid array of any size. Next, we provide the type of each element—in this case, int—with the array name—in this case, anArray—and [] to indicate that the anArray identifier is actually an array. The size of the array is not relevant.

We have also provided two other function declarations previously that we will soon explore. In all of these declarations, an array is passed in whose size is unknown, except by the passed-in size value.

Now, it might be assumed that C will copy the entire array into the called function as it does with other variables; however, it does not. Since that is not the case, arrays as parameters might appear to violate the rules of passing function parameters by copy, but they do not. How this mechanism works will become clear in Chapter 14, *Understanding Arrays and Pointers*. For now, we will take as given the fact that the array name is a **named reference** to a **memory location** and that the named reference is being copied into the function. Again, we will see, in Chapter 14, *Understanding Arrays and Pointers,* how the array name (a named reference to a memory location) and an offset from that location can become an individual array element. We would define the two functions given previously as follows:

```
int findMin( int size , int a[] )  {
  int min = a[0];
  for( int i = 0 ; i < size ; i++ )
    if( a[i] < min )  min = a[i];
```

```
    return min;
}

int findMax( int size , int a[] )  {
    int max = a[0];
    for( int i = 0 ; i < size ; i++ )
        if( a[i] > max ) max = a[i];
    return max;
}
```

In both functions, we set the `min` or `max` parameters to be the value of the first element (the zeroth offset element) and then compare every subsequent value to `min` or `max`. When a newly encountered value is greater than or less than the current `min` or `max` values, we update `min` or `max`. You might look at this and see that we are comparing `a[0]` to `min` or `max`, which has already been set to `a[0]`, and think "*that's redundant.*" It is, but it also only requires an extremely small cost of computation. If you choose, you could modify these properties to start the loop from the first offset instead of the zeroth offset.

Finding the minimum and maximum values for an array is sometimes useful. So, too, is finding the mean and standard deviation for a set of values. *Mean* is the average value and is computed by finding the sum of all values and dividing it by the number of values. A loop that iterates over the array is indicated. The standard deviation is a value that shows how far from the mean the overall set of numbers is. A set with a small standard deviation has values that are mostly the same. A set with a large standard deviation has values that are all over the place. We would define those two functions as follows:

```
double findMean( int size , int a[] )
{
    double sum   = 0.0;
    for( int i = 0 ; i < size ; i++ )
        sum += a[i];
    double mean = sum / size;
    return mean;
}

double findStdDev( int size , int a[] )
{
    // Compute variance.
    double mean      = findMean( size , a );
    double sum       = 0.0;
    double variance = 0.0;
    for( int i = 0; i < size ; i++ )
        sum += pow( (a[i] - mean) , 2 );
    variance = sum / size;
    // Compute standard deviation from variance.
    double stdDev = sqrt( variance );
```

```
        return stdDev;
    }
```

There are a few things to take note of in `findMean()` and `findStdDev()`. First, notice that variables are declared as they are needed and are not necessarily all declared at the beginning of the function block. Second, notice that the `pow()` and `sqrt()` functions are math functions declared in `math.h` and are available in the C standard runtime library. We will have to use `#include <math.h>` to be able to compile our program. Lastly, recall that the names of function parameters in function declarations are optional. The names of parameters that are actually used are found in the parameter list of the function definition.

To use these functions, create an `array3.h` file and add the function declarations there. Then, create an `array3.c` file and add the following `main()` portion of the program:

```
// build with:
// cc array3.c -o array3 -lm -Wall -Werror -std=c11

#include <stdio.h>
#include <math.h>
#include "array3.h"
int main( void )
{
  int array1[] = { 3 , 4 , 6 , 8, 13 , 17 , 18 , 19 };
  int array2[] = { 34 , 88 , 32 , 12 , 10 };

  int size = sizeof( array1 ) / sizeof( int );
  printf( "array1: range, mean, & standard deviation\n" );
  printf( "     range = [%d..%d]\n" ,
          findMin( size , array1 ) ,
          findMax( size , array1 ) );
  printf( "      mean = %g\n" ,  findMean( size , array1 ) );
  printf( "   std dev = %g\n\n", findStdDev( size , array1 ) );

  size = sizeof( array2 ) / sizeof( int );
  printf( "array2: range, mean, & standard deviation\n" );
  printf( "     range = [%d..%d]\n" ,
          findMin( size , array2 ) ,
          findMax( size , array2 ) );
  printf( "      mean = %g\n" ,  findMean( size , array2 ) );
  printf( "   std dev = %g\n\n", findStdDev( size , array2 ) );
}
```

In this program, two arrays—`array1` and `array2`—are dynamically defined and initialized. Notice that when the functions that expect an array argument are called, only the array name is given. The details of the array are provided in the function prototype. Then, information about each of them is calculated and printed. Compile and run this program. You should see the following output:

```
> cc array3.c -o array3 -Wall -Werror -std=c11
> array3
array1: range, mean, & standard deviation
     range = [3..19]
      mean = 11
   std dev = 6.12372

array2: range, mean, & standard deviation
     range = [10..88]
      mean = 35.2
   std dev = 28.1879

>
```

In one case, we calculated the range, mean, and standard deviation of an integer array with eight dynamically assigned elements, and in another, we did the same calculations for a dynamically assigned integer array of five elements.

Summary

In this chapter, we learned how arrays are homogenous groupings of data types, unlike structures. We then learned how to declare arrays, as well as how to initialize them in various ways depending on how they were declared. We saw that we don't always have to specify the size of an array if we initialize it with values when it is declared. Once arrays have been declared, their size cannot change. We learned how to access array elements via the element's offset, also known as the index or subscript. We further saw how to manipulate the simplest kind of array—a one-dimensional array—directly via the `for()`... loop, as well as by using arrays as function parameters.

This chapter is a prerequisite to `Chapter 12`, *Working with Multi-Dimensional Arrays*, through `Chapter 16`, *Creating and Using More Complex Structures*, where various aspects of arrays will be explored with greater complexity. In `Chapter 12`, *Working with Multi-Dimensional Arrays*, we will examine how to declare, initialize, and manipulate arrays of two, three, and more dimensions. `Chapter 13`, *Using Pointers*, while not directly about arrays, is essential to understanding the relationship between arrays and pointers, which are explored in `Chapter 14`, *Understanding Arrays and Pointers*, which becomes the basis for `Chapter 15`, *Working with Strings*. In `Chapter 16`, *Creating and Using More Complex Structures*, we will complete our exploration of arrays with various kinds of arrays of structures and structures containing arrays.

12
Working with Multi-Dimensional Arrays

Understanding Chapter 11, *Working with Arrays*, is essential to understanding the concepts presented in this chapter. Please read through and ensure you understand that chapter before reading this one.

In Chapter 11, *Working with Arrays*, we explored a one-dimensional array, where an array is a contiguous group of the same data type accessed via a basename and an index. In this chapter, we will extend the concept of arrays from one dimension to many dimensions. Multi-dimensional arrays occur in a myriad of objects that we deal with in daily life—from a simple checkers board or chessboard, a multiplication table, or the pixels on a screen to more complex three-dimensional objects, such as volumetric spaces. We will see that these are simple extensions of one-dimensional arrays.

The following topics will be covered in this chapter:

- Understanding the basic concepts of arrays
- Declaring and initializing arrays of various dimensions
- Accessing elements of arrays of various dimensions
- Using looping to traverse multi-dimensional arrays
- Using multi-dimensional arrays in functions

Technical requirements

Continue to use the tools you chose from the *Technical requirements* section of Chapter 1, *Running Hello, World!*.

The source code for this chapter can be found at https://github.com/PacktPublishing/Learn-C-Programming.

Going beyond one-dimensional arrays to multi-dimensional arrays

It is common to present a two-dimensional array as an array of a one-dimensional array. Likewise, a three-dimensional array can be thought of as an array of two-dimensional arrays. Furthermore, an N-dimensional array can be thought of as an array of $(N - 1)$-dimensional arrays.

This approach, while mathematically correct, may not provide a useful, working framework for multi-dimensional arrays. Therefore, before we can address the C syntax for declaring, initializing, and accessing multi-dimensional arrays, a proper conceptual framework must be developed. With that firmly understood, we can then delve into C's syntax for multi-dimensional arrays.

Revisiting one-dimensional arrays

An array of one dimension is a block, or contiguous grouping, of a specified data type accessed via a basename; each element is then accessed via an offset of that basename.

A one-dimensional array may be called a **vector** in some domains, while in others it may be referred to as a **linear array**. To review what we covered in the last chapter, we will use a one-dimensional array as the basis for our discussion, as follows:

```
int array1D[5] = { 1 , 2 , 3 , 4 , 5 };
```

Here, `array1D` has five integers, initialized to the values of 1 through 5 for the values at the zeroth through fourth offsets. `array1D` is a block of five integers; they are contiguous (or side-by-side) so that the block takes up 5 * `sizeof(int)` bytes of memory. The array has five elements, with offsets from the base to each element in the range of 0..4. This linear array can be represented vertically, as follows:

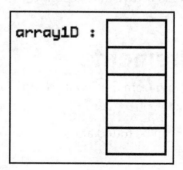

Alternatively, it can be represented horizontally, as follows:

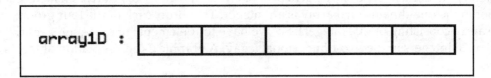

Both of these diagrams represent a one-dimensional array of five elements. In either case, incrementing the array's index provides access to the very next element of the array. This is an essential property of C arrays to keep in mind as we move on to more dimensions.

Of the two graphical representations, the former is more technically accurate with respect to how the computer allocates and accesses the array. We will revisit this representation in Chapter 13, *Using Pointers*, and Chapter 14, *Understanding Arrays and Pointers*. However, for our conceptual framework, the latter is a better representation as a block of linear elements. Looking at array1D in this way will help us make a logical transition to two-dimensional arrays and beyond.

Moving on to two-dimensional arrays

A two-dimensional array can be conceptualized either as an array of arrays (one-dimensional) or as a matrix consisting of rows and columns. For our discussion, we'll consider a two-dimensional array, named array2D, either as an array of four arrays of five one-dimensional elements or as a matrix of four rows and five columns. Both conceptualizations are equivalent.

In terms of the real world, there are many examples of two-dimensional arrays—hotel mail slots, windows on the side of a modern skyscraper, any video display that has a matrix of pixels, the periodic table of elements, a spreadsheet of multiple rows and columns, the selection of snacks in a vending machine, and a baseball innings scoreboard, to name a few. A two-dimensional array in C, therefore, is a useful tool for modeling many real-world matrices or grids.

If we consider `array2D` as an array of arrays, we have an array of four groups of a defined type. Here, the defined type happens to be a one-dimensional array of five elements; each element in the one-dimensional array is an integer. Therefore, each of the four groups has a single array consisting of five integers. So, we have four elements of a five-integer array for a total of 20 integers in the two-dimensional array. A graphical representation of this is as follows:

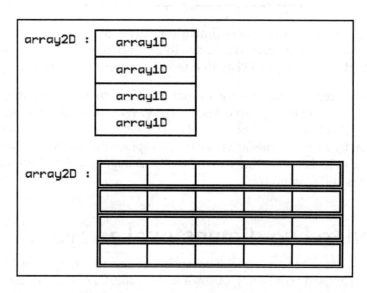

If we consider `array2D` as a matrix, we have a table (or grid) of five columns and four rows. Here, we have 20 integers in our two-dimensional array (five columns by four rows). A graphical representation of this is similar to the previous array of arrays, except that we think of it only in terms of rows and columns. It would look as follows:

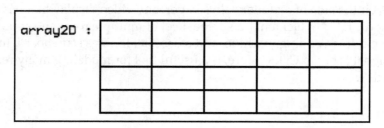

In both cases, `array2D` is a contiguous block of 20 integers, regardless of how we conceptualize it. Note that the basename always takes the leftmost and uppermost location in our block. It is always the very first element in an array.

Having crossed this conceptual chasm from one to two dimensions, we will again apply this concept to three-dimensional arrays.

Moving on to three-dimensional arrays

A three-dimensional array can be conceptualized either as an array of arrays of arrays (two-dimensional arrays of one-dimensional arrays) or as a three-dimensional volume consisting of the *X*, *Y*, and *Z* dimensions, where the *Y* and *X* dimensions are rows and columns, respectively. For our discussion, we'll consider a three-dimensional array, named `array3D`, either as a collection of three arrays, each consisting of 20 two-dimensional arrays, or as a volume of three layers (the *Z* dimension), four rows (the *Y* dimension), and five columns (the *X* dimension). Both conceptualizations are equivalent. **Layers** is an arbitrary name for the arrays in the *Z* dimension.

As you will soon see, the order of array dimensions in C is significant. The natural way to think of three-dimensional space is as an *X*-axis, *Y*-axis, and *Z*-axis. In C, we should think of the higher dimensions first. So, that means the *Z*-axis, the *Y*-axis, and then the *X*-axis. Hold that thought; it will be reflected in C syntax in the next section.

In terms of the real world, there are many examples of three-dimensional arrays—offices in a building with many floors, the three-dimensional space that we live and move around in (useful, for instance, for games), and spatial dimensions for modeling objects, to name just a few. A three-dimensional array in C, therefore, is a useful tool for modeling many real-world volumes and three-dimensional spaces.

When we consider `array3D` as an array of arrays, we have an array of three groups of a defined type. Here, the defined type happens to be a two-dimensional array of four elements; each element in the two-dimensional array is a one-dimensional array of integers. Therefore, each of the three groups has a single array consisting of 20 integers.

So, we have three elements—each of a 20-integer array—for a total of 60 integers in the three-dimensional array. A graphical representation of this is as follows:

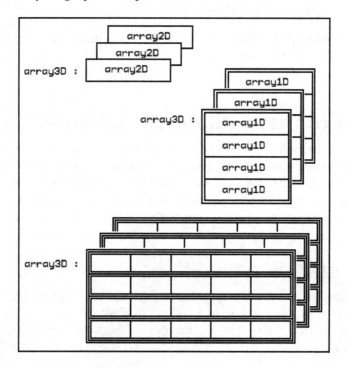

When we consider array3D as a volume, we have a grid of three layers of five columns and four rows. In this case, we have 60 integers in our three-dimensional array (3 layers x 5 columns x 4 rows). A graphical representation of this is similar to the array of arrays, except that we think of it only in terms of layers, rows, and columns. It would look as follows:

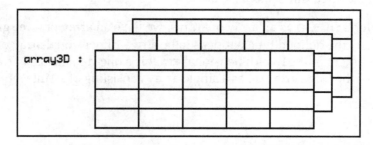

In both cases, array3D is a contiguous block of 60 integers (5 columns x 4 rows x 3 layers), regardless of how we conceptualize it. Note that the basename always takes the leftmost and uppermost location in our block. It is always the very first element in any array.

This ends our visual conceptualization of multi-dimensional arrays; firstly, because graphically representing more than three dimensions is difficult, and secondly, because while we can conceptualize four or more dimensions, for many of us, the visualization of more than three dimensions is difficult. Lastly, just as we have applied the approach of going from one to two to three dimensions, we can likewise extend this same thinking to more dimensions without requiring a graphical representation.

Considering N-dimensional arrays

As we move from three dimensions to four, five, or more, we can continue to conceptualize an array of *N* dimensions either as an array of *(N-1)* dimensions or as a contiguous block of basic elements whose size is the multiplicative result of each dimension. Say we wanted a four-dimensional array that has 7 x 3 x 4 x 5 for each dimension. This four-dimensional array, named array4D, can be conceptualized as an array of seven arrays of array3d or as a block whose size is 420 elements, or 420 = 5 x 4 x 3 x 7

Here, 5 is the number of first-dimension elements, 4 is the number of second-dimension elements, 3 is the number of third-dimension elements, and 7 is the number of fourth-dimension elements.

C, as specified, allows an unlimited number of array dimensions. The actual limit depends on the limits of the compiler used. In general practice, however, it is unwieldy, both in terms of human conceptualization and in terms of machine memory allocation, to have an array greater than, say, three or four dimensions. This does not rule out arrays of a higher number of dimensions, but as we will see in Chapter 16, *Creating and Using More Complex Structures*, we will be able to combine arrays and structures in various ways to make complex collections of data that closely match their real-world representations, as well as provide conceptual clarity and conciseness.

Declaring and initializing multi-dimensional arrays

With a firm, conceptual grasp of multi-dimensional arrays, we can now explore the C syntax for declaring them. As we move from two to more dimensions, we will continue to use array1D, array2D, array3D, and array4D to match the previous section. As each array is declared, pay particular attention to the order in which the array indices appear in each definition. In general, the highest-order dimension appears at the leftmost side and the lowest-order dimension (in our example, array1D) appears in the rightmost position.

Before we begin, we'll define some size constants, as follows:

```
const int size1D = 5;
const int size2D = 4;
const int size3D = 3;
const int size4D = 7;
```

In each of our declarations, we could simply use literal numbers to specify each dimension's size. Instead, we'll use the size1D, size2D, size3D, and size4D constants, not just in this section but for the remainder of this chapter, to firmly fix the relationship of a dimension's position as we declare, initialize, and access multi-dimensional array elements.

Declaring arrays of two dimensions

Just as in declaring a one-dimensional array, [and] are used to specify each dimension. array2D is declared using numeric literals for its two dimensions, as follows:

```
int array2D[4][5];
```

Using the constants that we already defined, we would declare array2D, as follows:

```
int array2D[size2D][size1D];
```

We could also use variables:

```
int rows = 4;
int cols = 5;

int array2D[rows][cols];
```

As with any array declaration using variables, the value of the variables may later change, but the array size is fixed and unchangeable after it is declared.

Initializing arrays of two dimensions

We can initialize array2D at the declaration stage in several ways, as follows:

```
int array2D[4][5] = {0};
```

array2D is initialized with all of its elements set to 0. Note that we cannot use our constant sizes to initialize the array at declaration. Try it and see what error message you get.

To give each element a different value at the declaration stage, we would initialize it as follows:

```
int array2D[size2D][size1D] = { {11 , 12 , 13 , 14 , 15 } ,
                                {21 , 22 , 23 , 24 , 25 } ,
                                {31 , 32 , 33 , 34 , 35 } ,
                                {41 , 42 , 43 , 44 , 45 ) };
```

In this declaration, the first row of elements is given the `11..15` values, and the second row is given the `21..25` values. Notice how the initialization of the array in this manner closely matches our conceptualization of a two-dimensional array earlier in this chapter.

Declaring arrays of three dimensions

Moving on to three dimensions, we would declare `array3D` using numeric literals, as follows:

```
int array3D[3][4][5];
```

Using the constants already defined, we would declare `array3D`, as follows:

```
int array3D[size3D][size2D][size1D];
```

We could also use variables:

```
int x = 5;
int y = 4;
int z = 3

int array3D[z][y][x];
```

Note how the z dimension (the highest order) comes first and the x dimension (the lowest order) comes last in the declaration.

Initializing arrays of three dimensions

We can initialize `array3D` at the declaration stage in several ways, as follows:

```
int array3D[3][4][5] = {0};
```

`array3D` is initialized with all of its elements set to 0. Note that we cannot use our constant sizes to initialize the array at declaration. Try it and see what error message you get.

To give each element a different value at the declaration stage, we would initialize it as follows:

```
int array3D[size3D][size2D][size1D] =
                    { { {111 , 112 , 113 , 114 , 115 },
                        {121 , 122 , 123 , 124 , 125 } },
                      { {211 , 212 , 213 , 214 , 215 },
                        {221 , 222 , 223 , 224 , 225 } },
                      { {311 , 312 , 313 , 314 , 315 },
                        {321 , 322 , 323 , 324 , 325 } } };
```

In this declaration, the first Z layer of elements is given the values 111..115 and 121..125. The second Z layer of elements is given the values 211..215 and 221..225. The third Z layer of values is given the values 311..315 and 321..325. Again, notice how the initialization of the array in this manner closely matches our conceptualization of a three-dimensional array earlier in this chapter.

Declaring and initializing arrays of N dimensions

We can declare array4D as follows:

```
int array4D[size4D][size3D][size2D][size1D];
```

Note how the size4D dimension (the highest order) comes first and the size1D dimension (the lowest order) comes last in the declaration. array4D is declared and all of its elements are initialized to 0. Initializing arrays with many dimensions or large arrays (arrays with a large number of elements in each dimension) at declaration time becomes tedious. Later in this chapter, we'll initialize arrays with loops.

Accessing elements of multi-dimensional arrays

To access an array element using array notation, we must be consistent in using both the dimensions of the array and the valid range of offsets for each dimension.

To access an element of an array, we would use the `[` and `]` notation for each of its offsets in each dimension. Remember that C indices are zero-based. It is better to think of them as offsets from the array base. For example, the column offset for the first element in a one-dimensional array is `[0]`. The row offset for the first row of a two-dimensional array is `[0][x]`. The layer offset for the first layer of a three-dimensional array is `[0][y][x]`. Putting this knowledge to work, let's access the third element of our various arrays, as follows:

```
int third;
first = array1D[2];          // third element.
first = array2D[0][2];       // third element of 1st row.
first = array3D[0][0][2];    // third element of 1st layer and 1st row.
first = array4D[0][0][0][2]; // third element of 1st volume, 1st layer,
                             // and 1st row.
```

Using numeric literals as indices for the last element of each dimension, we can get the last element of each of our arrays, as follows:

```
int last;
last = array1D[4];           // last element.
last = array2D[3][4];        // last element of last row.
last = array3D[2][3][4];     // last element of last layer of last row.
last = array4D[6][2][3][4];  // last element of last volume, last layer,
                             // and last row.
```

Getting the last element is a bit more cumbersome but less error-prone when we know the size of the dimension. Using the constants defined earlier in this chapter, we can get the last element of each array, as follows:

```
int last;
last = array1D[size1D-1];                             // last element.
last = array2D[size2D-1][size1D-1];                   // last element of
                                                      // last row.
last = array3D[size3D-1][size2D-1][size1D-1]; // last element of last
                                                      // layer of last row.
last = array4D[size4D-1][size3D-1][size2D-1][size1D-1];
```

In each case, the last dimension is that dimension's size minus 1; this is consistent with zero-based indexing or zero-based offsets. This method is less error-prone if and when the size of our arrays changes. By using a constant and simple calculation, the last elements always correct themselves for the given dimension size (assuming that the `size` constant is used throughout).

Note that we can both retrieve values from the array elements or assign values to them with array notation. This is to say that anywhere we can have a variable, we can also use an array element using its notation:

```
last = INT_MAX;
array1D[size1D-1] = last;
array2D[size2D-1][size1D-1] = last;
array3D[size3D-1][size2D-1][size1D-1] = last;
array4D[size4D-1][size3D-1][size2D-1][size1D-1] = last;
```

In each case, the very last element of the array is assigned the value of `last`, which is the predefined `INT_MAX` constant.

Manipulating multi-dimensional arrays – loops within loops

There are many ways in which to use loops to access elements within multi-dimensional arrays. The best way, however, is to use nested `for()`… loops. In a nested loop, the outermost loop contains one or more loops within it, nested such that the outer loop completely contains the inner loop. When using nested loops, the outermost loop manipulates the index of the highest-order dimension, while the innermost loop manipulates the index of the lowest-order dimension. We will explore two- and three-dimensional looping. It is then simple to extend the nested loops to as many as are needed for an array with more than three dimensions.

When nesting loops, it is a common convention to use variables named i, j, k, and so on to hold the values of the array offsets, with i being the first-order dimensional offset, j being the second-order dimensional offset, k being the third-order dimensional offset, and so on. This convention is optional. For two-dimensional arrays, row and col might be more descriptive offset variables and for three-dimensional arrays, x, y, and z might be more descriptive. Use whichever best fits the situation and/or appropriately describes what the array represents.

Using nested loops to traverse a two-dimensional array

To traverse a two-dimensional array, we use a loop within a loop. The outer loop controls the row offset and the inner loop controls the column offset. Our nested loop structure is as follows:

```
for( j = 0; j < size2D ; j++ )  {    // j : 0..(size2D-1)
  for( i = 0; i < size1D ; i++ )  {  // i : 0..(size1D-1)
    array2D[j][i] = (10*j) + i ;
  }
}
```

Each element of `array2D` is assigned a value computed from i and j.

Note that for each loop counter variable, we show the range of valid values as a comment. This is only a reminder for us; the goal is to help us keep our offsets within the proper range.

Using nested loops to traverse a three-dimensional array

To traverse a three-dimensional array, we use a two-dimensional loop within a loop. The outer loop controls the layer offset, and the inner loops control the row and column offsets. Our nested loop structure is as follows:

```
for( k = 0 ; k < size3D ; k++ )  {      // k : 0..(size3D-1)
  for( j = 0 ; j < size2D ; j++ )  {    // j : 0..(size2D-1)
    for( i = 0 ; i < size1D ; i++ )  {  // i : 0..(size1D-1)
      array2D[k][j][i] = (k*100) + (j*10) + i ;
    }
  }
}
```

Each element of `array3D` is assigned a value based on the offset values of i, j, and k.

What if we wanted to assign all the values of `array2D` to the last layer of `array3D`? Again, we would use nested loops, as follows:

```
for( j = 0; j < size2D ; j++ )
{
  for( i = 0; i < size1D ; i++ )
```

```
    {
        array3D[(size3D-1)][j][i] = array2D[j][i] + (100*(size3D-1));
    }
}
```

(size3D-1) is the offset of the last layer of the three-dimensional array. This offset doesn't change in the nested loops, whereas the other two offsets do change in the nested loops.

Using multi-dimensional arrays in functions

Now that we can declare, initialize, and access arrays of many dimensions, we are ready to create functions to manipulate them:

1. First, let's create a function to initialize a two-dimensional array and a function to initialize a three-dimensional array, as follows:

```
void initialize2DArray( int row , int col , int array[row][col] )
{
    for( int j = 0 ; j < row ; j++ )  {      // j : 0..(row-1)
        for( int i = 0 ; i < col ; i++ )  {  // i : 0..(col-1)
            array[j][i] = (10*(j+1)) + (i+1);
        }
    }
}

void intialize3DArray( int x , int y , int z , int array[z][y][x]
){
    for( int k = 0 ; k < z ; k++ )  {        // k : 0..(z-1)
        for( int j = 0 ; j < y ; j++ )  {    // j : 0..(y-1)
            for( int i = 0 ; i < x ; i++ )  {// i : 0..(x-1)
                array[k][j][i] = (100*(k+1)) + (10*(j+1)) + (i+1);
            }
        }
    }
}
```

In each function, nested loops are used to iterate over the entire array, initializing each element to a value based on their indices.

2. Next, let's create functions to sum the elements of each array, as follows:

```
int sum2DArray( int row , int col , int array[row][col])  {
    int sum = 0;
    for( int j = 0 ; j < row ; j++ )  {      // j : 0..(row-1)
        for( int i = 0 ; i < col ; i++ )  {  // i : 0..(col-1)
```

```
        sum += array[j][i];
      }
    }
    return sum;
  }

  int sum3DArray( int z , int y , int x , int array[z][y][x] )   {
    int sum = 0;
    for( int k = 0 ; k < z ; k++ )   {              // k : 0..(z-1)
      for( int j = 0 ; j < y ; j++ )   {            // j : 0..(y-1)
        for( int i = 0 ; i < x ; i++ )   {          // i : 0..(x-1)
          sum += array[k][j][i];
        }
      }
    }
    return sum;
  }
```

Each function iterates over the entire two-dimensional or three-dimensional array and totals the values of each element in the array.

3. Next, let's create functions to print the contents of each array, as follows:

```
    void print2DArray( int row , int col , int array[row][col] ) {
      for( int j = 0 ; j < row ; j++ )   {        // j : 0..(row-1)
        for( int i = 0 ; i < col ; i++ )   {      // i : 0..(col-1)
          printf("%4d" , array[j][i]);
        }
        printf("\n");
      }
      printf("\n");
    }

    void print3DArray( int z , int y , int x , int array[z][y][x] ) {
      for( int k = 0 ; k < z ; k++ )   {          // k : 0..(z-1)
        for( int j = 0 ; j < y ; j++ )   {        // j : 0..(y-1)
          for( int i = 0 ; i < x ; i++ )   {      // i : 0..(x-1)
            printf("%4d" , array[k][j][i]);
          }
          printf("\n");
        }
        printf("\n");
      }
    }
```

4. Finally, we create the `main()` function to prove our work, as follows:

```
#include <stdio.h>
#include "arraysND.h"

int main( void )
{
  const int size1D = 5;
  const int size2D = 4;
  const int size3D = 3;

  int array2D[size2D][size1D];
  int array3D[size3D][size2D][size1D];

  int total = 0;
  initialize2DArray(  size2D , size1D , array2D );
  print2DArray(       size2D , size1D , array2D );
  total = sum2DArray( size2D , size1D , array2D );
  printf( "Total for array2D is %d\n\n" , total );
  initialize3DArray(  size3D , size2D , size1D , array3D );
  print3DArray(       size3D , size2D , size1D , array3D );
  total = sum3DArray( size3D , size2D , size1D , array3D );
  printf( "Total for array3D is %d\n\n" , total );
}
```

In this program, we declare some constant sizes and a two-dimensional and three-dimensional array, and then call functions to manipulate them, first to initialize each array, then to print its contents, and finally to compute the sum of all elements in the array.

It is now time, if you have not done so already, to create a program yourself. This program is named `arraysND.c` (for *N*-dimensional arrays). Create a new file in your favorite editor and add `main()` and the functions. Remember to put the function prototypes into `arraysND.h` and save that file. Compile `arrayND.c`. At this point, you may find that any number of typos somehow creep in, so you may have to go through several iterations of editing, saving, and compiling until your compilation succeeds. Then, run the program. You should see the following output:

```
> cc arraysND.c -o arraysND -Wall -Werror -std=c11
> arraysND
  11  12  13  14  15
  21  22  23  24  25
  31  32  33  34  35
  41  42  43  44  45

Total for array2D is 560

 111 112 113 114 115
 121 122 123 124 125
 131 132 133 134 135
 141 142 143 144 145

 211 212 213 214 215
 221 222 223 224 225
 231 232 233 234 235
 241 242 243 244 245

 311 312 313 314 315
 321 322 323 324 325
 331 332 333 334 335
 341 342 343 344 345

Total for array3D is 13680

> ▯
```

As a challenge, if you are up to it, modify the `print2DArray()` and `print3DArray()` functions to also print out the column and row headings or the x, y, and z headings. Printing is fussy; prepare to be at least a little frustrated. I am certain you will have to iterate many times, as well as edit, compile, and run until your output looks something like the following:

```
> cc arraysND.c -o arraysNDpretty -Wall -Werror -std=c11
> arraysNDpretty
       [0] [1] [2] [3] [4]
  [0]   11  12  13  14  15
  [1]   21  22  23  24  25
  [2]   31  32  33  34  35
  [3]   41  42  43  44  45

Total for array2D is 560

  [0]      [0] [1] [2] [3] [4]
       [0] 111 112 113 114 115
       [1] 121 122 123 124 125
       [2] 131 132 133 134 135
       [3] 141 142 143 144 145

  [1]      [0] [1] [2] [3] [4]
       [0] 211 212 213 214 215
       [1] 221 222 223 224 225
       [2] 231 232 233 234 235
       [3] 241 242 243 244 245

  [2]      [0] [1] [2] [3] [4]
       [0] 311 312 313 314 315
       [1] 321 322 323 324 325
       [2] 331 332 333 334 335
       [3] 341 342 343 344 345

Total for array3D is 13680

> ▮
```

While I was creating this output, I had to edit, compile, run, and verify the output about a dozen times until I got all the little tricky bits just the way that I wanted. But persistence pays off.

In case you get frustrated and give up (*please don't give up!*), the source code provided on the GitHub repository provides both a basic print function and a pretty print function for each array. Compare your efforts to the code given, but do so only after you have successfully made your own pretty print functions.

Summary

In this chapter, we have taken the basic idea of a one-dimensional array from Chapter 11, *Working with Arrays*, and extended it to two-dimensional, three-dimensional, and even *N*-dimensional arrays. A conceptual basis for multi-dimensional arrays has been developed. Then, we have seen how to declare, initialize, access, and iterate over multi-dimensional arrays in C's syntax. Emphasis was placed on zero-based array indices (more appropriately known as offsets) and on the somewhat peculiar order in which indices are specified—left to right from the highest-order dimension to the lowest-order dimension. This order, however, lends itself somewhat elegantly to nested looping to iterate over multi-dimensional arrays. This chapter may have seemed long; the intent was to demonstrate how consistently the same concepts can be applied from one-dimensional arrays to *N*-dimensional arrays.

In this chapter, we have not spent too much time delving into what the **base** of an array is. Before we can get a greater understanding of array basenames, we must first visit another essential and unique feature of C—pointers. In Chapter 13, *Using Pointers*, we will explore pointer concepts, basic memory concepts, and elemental pointer arithmetic. Chapter 13, *Using Pointers*, is essential to understanding the chapter that follows, Chapter 14, *Understanding Arrays and Pointers*, where we'll delve further into array basenames and explore some alternate ways to both access and iterate over array elements using pointers.

13
Using Pointers

A pointer is a variable that holds a value that is the location (or memory address) of another value. The pointer type not only identifies the variable identifier as a pointer but also specifies what kind of value will be accessed at the location held by the pointer.

It is essential to learn how to verbally differentiate the address of notation (a pointer value) versus the target of notation (the value found at the address that the pointer points to). In this chapter, we will strive to demystify C pointers.

Learning how to properly use pointers expands both the expressiveness of C programs as well as the range of problems that can be solved.

The following topics will be covered in this chapter:

- Dispelling some myths and addressing some truths about C pointers
- Understanding where values are stored and how they are accessed
- Declaring pointers and naming them appropriately
- Understanding the NULL pointer and void*
- Pointer arithmetic
- Accessing pointers and their targets
- Comparing pointers
- Talking and thinking about pointers correctly
- Using pointers in function parameters
- Accessing structures via pointers

Technical requirements

Continue to use the tools you chose from the *Technical requirements* section of `Chapter 1`, *Running Hello, World!*.

The source code for this chapter can be found at `https://github.com/PacktPublishing/Learn-C-Programming`.

Addressing pointers – the boogeyman of C programming

Before we begin our understanding of declaring, initializing, and using pointers, we must address some common misconceptions and unavoidable truths about C pointers.

C pointers are often considered one of the most troublesome concepts in C, so much so that many modern languages claim to have improved on C by removing pointers altogether. This is unfortunate. In many cases, this limits the language's power and expressiveness. Other languages still have pointers but severely restrict how they may be used.

Pointers in C are one of its most powerful features. With great power comes great responsibility. That responsibility is nothing more than knowing how to correctly and appropriately use the power that is given. This responsibility also involves knowing when not to use that power and to understand its limits.

Untested and unverified programs that incorrectly or haphazardly employ pointers may appear to behave in a random fashion. Programs that once worked reliably but have been modified without understanding or proper testing become unpredictable. The program flow and, consequently, program behavior becomes erratic and difficult to grasp. Improper use of pointers can wreak real havoc. This is often exacerbated by an overly complex and obfuscated syntax, both with and without pointers. Pointers, in and of themselves, are not the cause of these symptoms.

It is my point of view that full knowledge of C pointers greatly enhances a programmer's understanding of how programs and computers work. Furthermore, most—if not all—programming errors that use pointers arise from untested assumptions, improper conceptualization, and poor programming practices. Therefore, avoid those practices. We will focus on proper conceptualization, methods of testing assumptions, and good programming practices.

In the preceding chapters, we emphasized a **test and verify** approach to programming behavior. This is not only a good approach in general but is also especially important when using pointers. This approach, hopefully, is now somewhat ingrained in your thinking about developing programs. With experience—based on practical experiments and proof by example (both of which we covered in earlier chapters)—your knowledge and understanding of pointers is reinforced so that they can be mastered quickly and used safely with confidence.

Why use pointers at all?

If pointers are so problematic, why use them at all? First and foremost, pointers are not the problem; misuse of pointers is the problem.

Nonetheless, there are four main uses for pointers:

- **To overcome the call-by-value restriction in function parameters**: Pointers expand the flexibility of function calls by allowing variable function parameters.
- **As an alternative to array subscripting**: Pointers allow access to array elements without subscripting.
- **To manage C strings**: Pointers allow easy (ahem, *easier*) allocation and manipulation of C strings.
- **For dynamic data structures**: Pointers allow memory to be allocated at runtime for useful dynamic structures, such as linked lists, trees, and dynamically sized arrays.

We will deal with the first point, the mechanics of pointers and variable function parameters, in this chapter. The second point will be explored in Chapter 14, *Understanding Arrays and Pointers*. The third point will be explored in Chapter 15, *Working with Strings*. Lastly, the fourth point will be explored in Chapter 18, *Using Dynamic Memory Allocation*.

Pointers allow our programs to model real-world objects that are **dynamic**—that is, their size or the number of elements is not known when the program is written and their size and number of elements will change as the program runs. One such real-world example is a grocery list. Imagine your list could only ever hold, say, six items; what do you do if you need seven items? Also, what if when you go to the store you remember three more items to add your list?

Because pointers give us an alternative means to access structures, arrays, and function parameters, their use enables our programs to be more flexible. Pointers, then, become another mechanism to access values to choose from to best fit the needs of our program.

Introducing pointers

A **pointer** is a variable whose value is the location (or memory address) of some other variable. This concept is so basic yet so essential to understanding pointers that it bears repeating.

A variable identifies a value stored at a fixed location. It consists of a type and an identifier. Implicit in the definition is its location. This location is fixed and cannot be changed. The value is stored at that location. The location is primarily determined by where a variable is declared in a program. The variable identifier, then, is our assigned name for the location of that value; it is a named location to store a value of a given type. We rarely, if ever, care about the specific value of that location—in fact, we never do. So, we never care about the specific address of a variable. We only care about the name of the location or our variable identifier.

A pointer variable, like any other variable, also identifies a value stored at a fixed location. It also consists of a type and an identifier. The value it holds, however, is the location of another variable or named location. We don't specifically care about the value of the pointer variable itself, except that it contains the location of another variable whose value we *do* care about.

So, while a variable's location cannot change, its contents can. For pointer variables, this means that a pointer's value can be initialized to one named location and then later reassigned to another named location. Two or more pointers can even have the same named location; they can point to the same place.

To highlight the difference between a variable that is named and contains a value and a pointer variable that is also named but whose value is an address, we first need to understand the concepts of the direct addressing of values and the indirect addressing of values.

Understanding direct addressing and indirect addressing

When we use a non-pointer variable, we are, in fact, accessing the value directly through the variable's identifier (its named location). This is called **direct addressing**.

When we use a pointer variable to access a value at its assigned, named location (a variable in a different location), we are accessing that value through the pointer variable. Here, we access the variable indirectly through the pointer. In essence, from the pointer value, we get the address *of* the value we want, then we go to that address to get the actual value.

Before going further, we need to understand some background concepts—memory and memory addressing.

Understanding memory and memory addressing

First, it is essential to understand that everything that runs on a computer is in memory. When we run a program, it is read from the disk, loaded into memory, and becomes the execution stream. When we read from a file on a disk, CD, or flash drive, it is first read into memory and accessed from there, not from its original location (this is an oversimplification since there is a bit more that goes on). All of the functions we call and execute are in memory. All of the variables, structures, and arrays we declare are given their own locations in memory. Finally, all of the parts of the computer that we can read from or write to are accessible through some predefined memory location. How the OS handles all of the system devices, system resources (memory), and the filesystem is beyond the scope of this book.

Second, once we understand that everything is in memory, we must know that each byte of memory is addressable. The memory address is the starting location of a value, a function, or even a device. To a running program, memory is *seen* as a continuous block of bytes, each having their own address from 1 to the largest `unsigned int` value available on that computer. Address 0 has a special meaning, which we will see later in this chapter. An address, then, is the nth byte in the range of all possibly addressable bytes on the computer.

If the computer uses 4 bytes for an `unsigned int` value, then the address space of that computer's memory is from 1 .. 4,294,967,295, just over 4 billion bytes or 4 **Gigabytes** (**GB**). This is known as a 32-bit address space. It may seem like a large number, but most computers today come with at least this much memory, some with 8, 16, or even 64 GB of memory (RAM). Because of this, a 4 GB address space is insufficient and leaves most of the other memory unaddressable, and so inaccessible.

If the computer uses 8 bytes for an `unsigned int` value, then the address space of that computer's memory is from 1 .. 18,446,744,073,709,551,615 bytes, or over 18 quintillion bytes. This is known as a 64-bit address space and holds many orders of magnitude more memory than any computer can hold today or in the foreseeable future.

The actual physical memory (which is physically present on the machine) may be far smaller than the amount of memory that is virtually addressable. A 64-bit computer can address memory over 18 quintillion bytes, but computers of any size rarely have anything even close to that much physical memory. The OS provides mechanisms to map the virtual address space into much smaller physical address space and manage that mapping as needed.

A 64-bit address space provides a very large working address space available to a program. Programs that model sub-atomic reactions, perform finite-element analysis on extremely large structures (such as very long bridges), simulate jet engine performance, or simulate astronomical models of our galaxy require enormous address spaces.

Lucky for us, dealing with the need for such large address spaces is not a problem for us today, nor is it a problem for us tomorrow. We can have a much simpler working concept of an address space while basking in the knowledge that we will not have to worry about the limits of our programs in a 64-bit address space anytime soon.

Managing and accessing memory

C provides ways for a program to allocate, release, and access virtual memory in our physical address space; it is then up to the OS to manage the physical memory. The OS swaps virtual memory in and out of the physical memory as needed. In this way, our program is only concerned with the virtual memory address space.

C also provides some limits as to what memory can be accessed and how it can be manipulated. In Chapter 17, *Understanding Memory Allocation and Lifetime*, and Chapter 18, *Using Dynamic Memory Allocation*, we will explore some of the ways that C gives us limited control of our program's memory. In Chapter 20, *Getting Input From the Command Line*, and Chapter 23, *Using File Input and File Output*, we will explore how C allows us to get data dynamically from the user via the command line, as well as read and write data files. In each of these chapters, we will expand our conceptualization of memory and how it is used by our programs.

C was written before **Graphical User Interfaces** (**GUIs**) were developed; therefore, there is no concept of pixels and colorspaces, audio ports, or network interfaces. To C, these are all just **Input/Output** (**IO**) streams that are tied to a device accessed through memory that we can read from or write to via an intermediary program or library.

Lastly, every time we run our program, the memory addresses within it will likely change. This is why we are concerned with **named locations**. and never specific memory addresses.

So, to summarize, we now know the following:

- Memory is seen as one large contiguous block.
- Everything in a computer is stored somewhere in memory or is accessible via a memory location.

- Every byte in a computer's memory has an address.
- Named locations (variables) are fixed addresses in memory.

Exploring some analogies in the real world

Real-life analogies for pointers are abundant. We'll explore two analogies to help provide some clarity about them.

In our first analogy, John, Mary, Tom, and Sally each own a different thing that they will give to us when we ask them for it. John owns a book, Mary owns a cat, Tom owns a song, and Sally owns a bicycle. If you want, say, a song, you ask Tom. If you want a bicycle, you ask Sally. If we want something, we go *directly* to the owner of it. That is direct addressing.

Now, say we don't know who each of them is or what they own. Instead, there is someone else we know, say, Sophia, who knows each person and what they own. To get something that we want, we have to go to Sophia, who then goes to the proper person, gets what they own, and gives it to us. Now, to get a book, we go to Sophia, who then goes to John to get the book and gives it to us. To get a cat, we again go to Sophia, who then goes to Mary to get the cat and gives it to us. We still don't know anyone but Sophia, but we don't care because we can still get everything indirectly through Sophia. This is indirect addressing.

John, Mary, Tom, and Sally are similar to variables. When we want the things they hold, we go directly to them. Sophia is similar to a pointer variable. We don't know where each thing we want is held, so we go to the pointer, which then goes to where the thing we want is held. We go to the things we want indirectly through the pointer.

Our second analogy involves a mailman and the mailboxes where we receive our mail. In a neighborhood or city, each building has a street name and number, as well as a city, state, or province and a postal code. All of these together uniquely identify a building's address. The building could be a home, a farm, an office, a factory, and so on. In front of or attached to the buildings are mailboxes, each one associated with a specific building. The mailboxes could stand alone or be grouped together. In the mailboxes, envelopes, parcels, magazines, and so on are delivered. Anyone can place something in any mailbox and the addressee (the resident of the building) can remove the content.

We can think of the mailboxes as variable names (fixed locations) and the content placed in those mailboxes as the values we assign to variables. Furthermore, each mailbox has a unique address, comprised of several parts, just as variables have a unique address, comprised of just a single number—its byte address. Just like a mailbox, a value can be assigned to a variable and the value can be accessed from that variable.

If we want to send a parcel to an address, we, in essence, give it to the mailman (a named identifier) to deliver it for us. The mailman travels to the address indicated and places the parcel in the mailbox for that address.

We can think of the mailman as the point that takes an address, travels to it, and takes or leaves a value at that address.

Analogies, however, are rarely perfect. The preceding two analogies, in the end, are not as accurate as we might like. So, let's look at a diagram of memory with some variables and a pointer variable that points to one of the variable's locations:

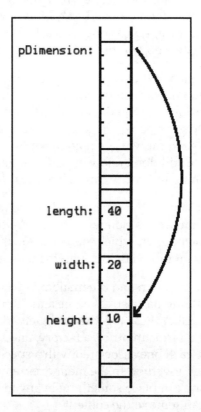

Here, memory is seen as a linear stream of bytes. In this diagram, we are not concerned with the actual byte addresses and so they are not shown. We see three named integer locations (variables)—length, width, and height. Because these are int values, they each take up 4 bytes. We also see a pointer variable, pDimension, which takes up 8 bytes and points *to* the height named location. The value of pDimension is the address of the height named location. We never need to be concerned about the actual value of a pointer. Instead, we should be concerned about the named location it points to.

Note that there are some bytes that are neither named nor used. These are the padding bytes that the compiler uses to align variables of different sizes. We saw this before with structures in `Chapter 9`, *Creating and Using Structures*. While we need to be aware that padding bytes exist, we should also be aware that we cannot predict their presence or absence, nor can we control them. Therefore, we should not be overly concerned about them.

We will come back to this diagram once we have more details about declaring and assigning pointers.

Declaring the pointer type, naming pointers, and assigning addresses

The most basic aspects of pointers are the following:

- We can declare a variable of the pointer type
- We can assign an already-declared named location to it
- We can perform a limited number of operations on pointers

So, while a pointer is a variable and can change, we do not assign values to it willy-nilly. A pointer should only be assigned a value that is an already-declared and named location. This means that a pointer must point to something that already exists in memory.

Because pointers give us values somewhat differently than simple variables, we also need to consider some naming conventions that set them apart from regular variables. These are conventions only and are intended to make the purpose of the variable *as a pointer* clear.

Declaring the pointer type

A pointer is a variable. Therefore, it has a type and an identifying name. It is distinguished as a pointer at declaration with the * notation.

The syntax for a pointer is `type * identifier;`, where `type` is either an intrinsic type or a custom type, * indicates a pointer to the given type, and `identifier` is the name of the pointer variable. The actual type of a pointer variable is not just `type`, but `type*`. This is what distinguishes a direct variable from an indirect variable.

A pointer must have a type for the thing it points to. A pointer type can be any intrinsic type (such as `int`, `long`, `double`, `char`, `byte`, and so on) or any already-defined custom type (such as an array, struct, `typedef`, and so on). The pointer's value (an address) can be any named location (the variable identifier) that has that type. We will see why this is essential when we access the value at the pointer's address.

An example of an integer pointer is the following:

```
int height;
int width;
int length;

int* pDimension;
```

Here, we can see three integer variables—`height`, `width`, and `length`—and a single pointer variable, `pDimension`, which can hold the address of any integer variable. `pDimension` cannot hold the address of a variable of the `float`, `double`, or `char` types (to name just three)—only `int`. The type of `pDimension` is `int*`.

In this code fragment, none of the variables, nor the pointer, has been assigned a value.

Naming pointers

Because pointers hold addresses of values and not the desired values themselves, it is a good idea to differentiate between them by naming the pointers slightly differently than the direct variables. There are several naming conventions that are more or less in widespread use. This includes prefixing or suffixing `ptr` or `p` to the name of the variable identifier. So, our identifiers may appear as follows:

```
int anInteger;

int* ptrAnInteger;   // prefix ptr-
int* pAnInteger;     // prefix p- (shorthand)
int* anIntegerPtr;   // suffix -Ptr
int* anIntegerP;     // suffix -P (shorthand)
```

The general advice is to pick one of these conventions and use it consistently throughout your code. Of the four shown, the p– shorthand prefix is probably the most common and easiest to both type (with your keyboard) and read. This convention will be used for the remainder of this book. So, when we see, say `pDimension`, we know immediately that it is a variable that is a pointer. This will help us to correctly assign and access it.

Assigning pointer values (addresses)

As with all other variables, a pointer has no meaningful value until one is assigned to it. Any variable declaration merely states what value the variable is capable of holding. We must assign a meaningful value to the pointer.

A pointer variable holds the address of another named location. This is the target of the pointer. A pointer points *to* another variable's location. That variable's value is its target. The way to assign an address value to a pointer is to use the & operator and the variable identifier, as follows:

```
int   height;
int* pDimension;

pDimension = &height;
```

This assigns the address of the height named location to the pDimension pointer variable. As we previously mentioned, we don't care about the specific value of &height. But now, we know that pDimension points to the same memory location as height. Another way to express this is that height is the current target of pDimension.

We'll explore how to use this a bit more in the next section.

Operations with pointers

At this point, the only operations that work reasonably with pointers are the following:

- Assignment
- Accessing pointer targets
- Limited pointer arithmetic
- The comparison of pointers

We will explore each of these in turn. As we do, we must also consider the NULL special pointer value (the zeroth address), or null pointer, and the void * special, unspecified pointer type, or void pointer type.

Assigning pointer values

We have just seen how to assign an address to a pointer variable by using another
variable's named location, as follows:

```
int height;
int width;
int length
int* pDimension;

pDimension = &height;
```

A diagram of the memory layout for these declarations is given in the *Accessing pointer
targets* section.

We could later reassign `pDimension`, as follows:

```
pDimension = &width;
```

This assigns the address of `width` to the `pDimension` variable. `width` and `*pDimension`
are now the same memory address. The target of `pDimension` is now `width`.

Each time we assign an address to `pDimension`, it is the address of an already-defined
variable identifier, as follows:

```
pDimension = &height;
  // Do something.
pDimension = &width;
  // Do something else.
pDimension = &length;
  // Do something more.

pDimension = &height;
```

First, we make `height` the target of `pDimension`, then `width`, then `length`. Finally, we set
`height` to again be the target of `pDimension`.

Differentiating between the NULL pointer and void*

A pointer variable should always have an assigned value. Its value should never be unknown. However, there are times when a proper address cannot be assigned or the desired address is currently unknown. For these instances, there is a constant NULL pointer. This value is defined in stddef.h and represents a value of 0. It is defined as follows:

```
#define NULL ((void*)0)
```

Here, (void*) specifies a pointer to the void type. The void type represents no type—a type that is unknown or a non-existent value. You cannot assign a variable to have the void type, but a function can return void (nothing). As we have already seen, functions with the void return type don't return anything.

Understanding the void* type

There are times when the type of a pointer is not known. This occurs primarily in C library functions.

For this reason, the void* pointer type represents a generic, as yet unspecified pointer; in other words, a pointer whose type is not known at declaration. Any pointer type can be assigned to a pointer variable of the void* type. However, before that pointer variable can be accessed, the type of the data being accessed must be specified through the use of a casting operation:

```
void* aPtr = NULL;   // we don't yet know what it points to.
...
aPtr = &height;      // it has the address of height, but no type yet.
...
int h = (int)*aPtr; // with casting, we can now go to that address
                    // and fetch an integer value.
```

In the first statement of the preceding code block, we see how aPtr is declared as a pointer but we don't yet know it's type or what it points to. In the next statement, aPtr is given the address of height, but we still don't know the type of the thing that aPtr points to. You might think that the type could be inferred from the named variable, but C is not that smart; in other words, the compiler does not keep that kind of information about variables around for use at runtime. In the last statement, we provide the (int) type when we use the pointer address to fetch a value at that address by casting aPtr to an int value. Casting tells the compiler exactly how many bytes to fetch and exactly how to interpret those bytes. We will explore these concepts in more detail in the next section.

Coming back to NULL, we see that 0—by default, interpreted as an integer—is cast to the generic pointer type. So, the 0 integer is cast as a pointer to the 0 byte address and is named NULL. There is no value at address 0 ever. So, NULL becomes a useful way to set a pointer to a known value but an inconsequential and unusable target.

We can then assign NULL to any pointer, as follows:

```
int* pDimension = NULL;
...
pDimension = &height;
...
pDimenions = NULL;
```

First, pDimension is both declared as a pointer to an integer and initialized to NULL. Then, pDimension is given the address of height. Finally, pDimension is reset to NULL.

The reason for doing this will become obvious when we explore the comparison of pointer values.

Accessing pointer targets

A pointer must know the type of the value it points to so that it can correctly get the correct number of bytes for that value. Without an associated type, pointer access would not know how many bytes to use when returning a value. For example, an int value is 4 bytes. An integer pointer (8 bytes) would then go to its address and get 4 bytes to return an int value in the correct range.

To access a value indirectly via a pointer variable, we must dereference the pointer. That is to say, we must use the address stored in the pointer variable to go get the value it points to; or, we go to its target. To assign a value to the pointer's target, we use the * operator, as follows:

```
int   height;
...
int* pDimension = &height;
...
height = 10;
...
*pDimension = 15;
```

`height` is assigned a value of `10` directly through that variable identifier. In the next statement, `15` is assigned to the target of `pDimension`. Because `pDimension` points to `height`, `height` now has a value of `15` via `*pDimension`. `height` and `*pDimension` are the same memory location referenced in two different ways.

Note that the `*` operator is used in both the pointer declaration and in pointer dereferencing.

Pointer dereferencing can also be used to access values, as follows:

```
pDimension = &height;
int aMeasure;
...
aMeasure = height;
...
aMeasure = *pDimension;
```

Here, the value at the `height` direct variable and the `pDimension` indirect variable is accessed (retrieved) in two identical ways. In the first way, `aMeasure` is assigned the value directly from `height`. Or, more precisely, the following occurs:

1. `height` evaluates to the value at its fixed location.
2. The value is assigned to `aMeasure`.

In the second way, because `pDimension` points to `height`—in other words, `height` is the target of `pDimension`—the following occurs:

1. `*pDimension` evaluates its target—in this case, `height`.
2. The target (`height`) evaluates to the value of that target.
3. The value is assigned to `aMeasure`.

Let's illustrate direct and indirect access using pointers with a simple program.

In order to print out the addresses and target values that `pDimension` will hold, we have to fiddle a bit with both the `printf()` format specifiers and also use casting, `(unsigned long)`, to coerce `pDimension` into a printable address:

```
#include <stdio.h>
int main( void )
{
    int height = 10;
    int width  = 20;
    int length = 40;
    int* pDimension;
```

```
    printf( "    sizeof(int) = %2lu\n" , sizeof(int) );
    printf( "    sizeof(int*) = %2lu\n" , sizeof(int*) );
    printf( "    [height, width, length] = [%2d,%2d,%2d]\n\n" ,
            height , width , length );
    printf( "    address of pDimension = %#lx\n" ,
            (unsigned long)&pDimension  );

  pDimension = &height;
  printf( "    address of height = %#lx, value at address = %2d\n" ,
          (unsigned long)pDimension , *pDimension );
  pDimension = &width;
  printf( "    address of width  = %#lx, value at address = %2d\n" ,
          (unsigned long)pDimension , *pDimension );
  pDimension = &length;
  printf( "    address of length = %#lx, value at address = %2d\n" ,
          (unsigned long)pDimension , *pDimension );
}
```

Using your program editor, create a new file called `pointers1.c` and type in the preceding program. Pay particular attention to the `printf()` format specifiers. Also, notice how we use casting to coerce the address contained in the `pDimension` variable into a value that `printf()` will output.

In this program, the `%2lu` format specifier prints out two digits of an unsigned long value since that is the type of value that `sizeof()` returns. To print an address in hexadecimal format, we use the `%#lx` format specifier, which prints a long hexadecimal value prepended with `0x` to indicate that it's a hex value. Also, we have to coerce the pointer type of `pDimension` into `unsigned long` with casting; otherwise, `printf()` complains about a type mismatch.

Compile and run this program. You should see something like the following output:

```
> cc pointers1.c -o pointers1 -Wall -Werror -std=c11
> pointers1

Values:

    sizeof(int) =  4
    sizeof(int*) =  8
    [height, width, length] = [10,20,40]

    address of pDimension = 0x7ffee48b3888

Using address of each named variables...

        address of height = 0x7ffee48b389c, value at address = 10
        address of width  = 0x7ffee48b3898, value at address = 20
        address of length = 0x7ffee48b3894, value at address = 40
>
```

Each of the addresses printed is an 8-byte hexadecimal value. When you run this on your system, your addresses will certainly be different. If you look very closely at the addresses of the variables themselves, you may see something a bit unusual. The variables in our program have been defined in one order in our program but have been allocated in a different order in memory by the compiler. A diagram of memory looks something like this:

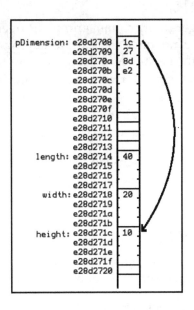

In the preceding diagram, the memory addresses do not match the output given previously because the picture was created at a different time with a different run of the program. Also, the addresses shown are 32-bit hexadecimal values. My computer is a 64-bit computer, so the addresses should include twice as many hex numbers for each address. For brevity, I've omitted the high 32-bit values.

As you study this, pay attention to the *relative* positions of the variables in memory. Your compiler may not order the variables in memory as mine has. Here, even though pDimension was declared last, it appears as the lowest memory address. Likewise, height, which was declared first, appears at a higher memory address. This is an important consideration—we cannot foresee exactly how the compiler will order variables in memory. It is for this reason that we must always use named memory locations (variables). Even though we declare variables in one way, we cannot guarantee the compiler will honor that order.

As an experiment, see what happens when you use %d everywhere in place of %2lu and %#lx when you compile your experiment (copy the program to another file first, and then experiment on the copy).

Pointer arithmetic

Even though pointers are integers, only certain arithmetic operations are possible. Be aware that adding values to pointers is not quite the same as adding values to integers. So, adding 1 to an integer value gives us the next integer value—for example, 9 + 1 = 10. However, adding 1 to a pointer increases the pointer value by the value multiplied by the size of bytes of the pointer's target type. Using the preceding picture, adding 1 to pDimension actually adds 4 to the address of pDimension because 4 equals sizeof(int). So, if pDimension = 0x328d2720, then pDimension + 1 = 0x328d2724.

Pointer arithmetic actually only makes sense in the context of arrays. We will discuss pointer arithmetic in greater detail in Chapter 14, *Understanding Arrays and Pointers*.

Comparing pointers

As we stated earlier, we never concern ourselves about the specific value of a pointer. However, we can carry out comparison operations on pointers for the following:

- Is a pointer equal or not equal to NULL?
- Is a pointer equal to or not equal to a named location?
- Is one pointer equal or not equal to another pointer?

In each case, we can either check for equality (==) or inequality (!=). Because we can never be certain of the variable ordering in memory, it makes no sense whatsoever to test whether one pointer is greater than (>) or less than (<) another pointer.

If we consistently apply the guideline to always assign a value to a pointer, even if that value is NULL, we can then make the following comparisons:

```
if( pDimension == NULL ) printf( "pDimension points to nothing!\n" );

if( pDimension != NULL ) printf( "pDimension points to something!\n" );
```

The first comparison checks whether pDimension points to NULL, which implies it has not yet been given a valid address or that it has been reset to NULL. The second comparison checks whether pDimension has any other value than NULL. Note that this does not necessarily mean pDimension has a valid address; it only means that it is not NULL. If we've been consistent in always initializing or resetting our pointer to NULL, then we can be a bit more certain that pDimension does have a valid address.

Both of the preceding comparisons can be shortened to the following:

```
if( !pDimension ) printf( "pDimension points to nothing!\n" );

if( pDimension ) printf( "pDimension points to something!\n" );
```

If pDimension has a non NULL value alone in a comparison expression, it will evaluate to TRUE. If pDimension has a NULL value in a comparison expression, it will evaluate to FALSE. This is not what we want in the first comparison since NULL will evaluate to 0 or FALSE, so we have to apply the not operator (!) to switch the comparison evaluation to match the condition we want.

Both comparison methods are commonly used. I prefer the more explicit form given in the first example because the intention is very clear. In the second example, ! may be overlooked or even misconstrued.

The comparisons of a pointer to a named location would look as follows:

```
if( pDimension == &height )
  printf( "pDimension points to height.\n" );

if( pDimension != &height )
  printf( "pDimension does not point to height!\n" );
```

The first comparison will evaluate to TRUE if pDimension points exactly to the address of height. If pDimension has any other value, even NULL, it will evaluate to FALSE. The second comparison will evaluate to FALSE if pDimension points exactly to the address of height; otherwise, if pDimension has any other value, even NULL, it will evaluate to TRUE.

The comparisons of one pointer to another would look as follows:

```
int* pDim1 = NULL;
int* pDim2 = NULL;
...
pDim1 = &height;
pDim1 = pDim2;
...
pDim2 = & weight;
```

```
. . .
if( pDim1 == pDim2 )
  printf( "pDim1 points to the same location as pDim2.\n" );
. . .
if( pDim != pDim2 )
  printf( "pDim1 and pDim2 are different locations.\n" );
```

We have now declared two pointers—pDim1 and pDim2—initializing them to NULL. Later on, we make height the target of pDim1. Then, we give pDim2 the same target as pDim1. At this point, both pointers have the same target.

Later, we assign weight as the target of pDim2. The first comparison will succeed if both pDim1 and pDim2 have exactly the same target, or if both are NULL. The second comparison will fail if both pDim1 and pDim2 have exactly the same target, or if both are NULL.

As an aside, when two pointers have the same target—in this case, height—we can assign or access the value of height directly with height by dereferencing pDim1 or by dereferencing pDim2. Each method changes the value at the height named location.

It is one thing to see C pointer syntax in code, but it is quite another to have a clear mental vision of pointer operations in your mind's eye. With explicit verbalization, we can verbally differentiate one pointer operation from another. So, let's explore how we talk about pointer syntax.

Verbalizing pointer operations

In this chapter, we have seen a variety of ways to describe pointers, what they point to, and how they are used. We will now turn our attention to how to verbalize various aspects of pointers. If we can consistently and clearly talk about pointers *to ourselves*, then we'll have a firmer grasp on how they operate and what we're actually doing with them.

 Talking correctly leads to thinking clearly.

The following table shows some actions that we might carry out with pointers, the C syntax for each action (what we see in code), and, lastly, how to mentally verbalize that action:

Action	Syntax	Verbalization
Declare a pointer.	`int* pDim;`	`pDim` is a pointer to an integer.
Assign a named location to a pointer.	`pDim = &height;`	`pDim` has the address of `height`, `pDim` points to `height`, or `height` is the target of `pDim`.
Access the target of a pointer.	`*pDim`	The value dereferenced by `pDim`, the target of `pDim`, the value `pDim` points to, or the value at `pDim`.
Assign a value to the location that the pointer points to.	`*pDim = 10;`	The target of `pDim` is assigned a value of `10` or the value at `pDim` is `10`.
Access the value that the pointer points to.	`width = *pDim;`	`width` is assigned the value of the target of `pDim`, `width` is assigned the value at `pDim`, or `pDim` is dereferenced and assigned to `width`.
Compare pointers for equality.	`if( pDim1 == pDim2 )`	`pDim1` and `pDim2` have the same target or `pDim1` and `pDim2` point to the same address.
Compare pointers for inequality.	`if( pDim1 != pDim2 )`	`pDim1` and `pDim2` have different targets.
Compare targets of pointers.	`if( *pDim1 == *pDim2 )`	The target of `pDim1` is equal to the target of `pDim2`, the dereferenced value of `pDim1` is equal to the dereferenced value of `pDim2`, or the value at `pDim1` equals the value at `pDim2`.

Verbalizing each of these in this manner may take some practice or simply consistent repetition.

So, we have now covered the most basic mechanics of pointers—declaring them, assigning them, accessing them, comparing them, and even talking about them. The examples given have focused on these basic mechanics. You may have already come to the conclusion that you would never need to use pointers in the manner that they have been shown. You would be correct in drawing that conclusion. However, having covered these basic mechanics, we are now ready to put pointers to good use.

For the remainder of this chapter, we'll look at how to use pointers as function parameters and, subsequently, in the function body. After that, we'll expand on pointers to variables to include pointers to structures and then use those in function parameters.

Variable function arguments

As we saw in Chapter 2, *Understanding Program Structure*, function parameters in C are **call-by-value**. In other words, when a function is defined to take parameters, the values the function body receives through them are copies of the values given at the function call. The following code copies the values of two values into function parameters so that the function can use those values in its function body:

```
double RectPerimeter( double h , double w )  {
   h += 10.0;
   w += 10.0;
   return 2*(w + h) ;
}

int main( void )  {
   double height = 15.0;
   double width  = 22.5;
   double perimeter = RectPerimeter( height , width );
}
```

In this simple example, the RectPerimeter() function takes two parameters—h and w—and returns a value that is based on both of them—the perimeter of the rectangle. When RectPerimeter() is called, the h and w function variables are created and the values of height and width are assigned to them so that h has a copy of the value of height and w has a copy of the value of width. In the function body, the values of h and w are modified and then used to calculate the return value. When the function returns, h and w are deallocated (or thrown away), but the values of height and width remain unchanged.

This is how call-by-value works. One advantage of call-by-value is that we can modify the copies of values passed into the function and the original values remain unchanged. One disadvantage of call-by-value is that for parameters that are very large arrays or very large structures, this copying is significantly inefficient and may even cause the program to crash.

But what if we wanted to change the values in the original variables?

We could contrive a structure to hold all three values, as well as copying in and then copying back that structure. This would involve the following code:

```
typedef struct _RectDimensions  {
  double height;
  double width;
  double perimeter;
} RectDimensions;
```

```
RectDimensions RectPerimeter( RectDimensions rd )  {
  rd.height += 10.0;
  rd.width += 10.0;
  rd.perimeter = 2*(rd.height*rd.width);
  return rd ;
}

int main( void )  {
  RectDimensions rd;
  rd.height = 15.0;
  rd.width = 22.5;
  rd = RectPerimeter( rd );
}
```

However, that is quite cumbersome. It is also unnecessary. There is a better way of doing this with pointers, which we will explore in the last section of this chapter, *Using pointers to structures.*

Passing values by reference

If we wanted to change the values of parameters so that they are also changed after the function returns, we can use pointers to do so. We would assign the address of the values we want to modify to pointer variables and then pass the pointer variables into the function. The addresses (which can't change anyway) will be copied into the function body and we can dereference them to get the values we want. This is called **passing by reference**. We would modify our program as follows:

```
double RectPerimeter( double* pH , double *pW )
{
  *pH += 10.0;
  *pW += 10.0;
  return 2*( *pW + *pH ) ;
}

int main( void )
{
  double height = 15.0;
  double width  = 22.5;
  double* pHeight = &height;
  double* pWidth  = &width;
  double perimeter = RectPerimeter( pHeight , pWidth );
}
```

The `RectPerimeter()` function now takes two pointers—pH and pW. When the function is called, pH and pW are created and the values of pHeight and pWidth are assigned to each. pH has the same target as pHeight; pW has the same target as pWidth. To use the desired values, pointers are dereferenced and 10.0 is added to each. Here is an example where the *pH += 10.0; shorthand comes in handy; recall that it is equivalent to *pH = *pH + 10.0;.

When the function call is complete, height now has the value 25.0 and width has the value 32.5. You might want to verify this yourself with a similar program, but one that prints out the values of height and width both before and after the function call in main().

Any function that modifies values that exist outside of its function body is said to have side effects. In this case, these side effects were intended. However, in many cases, side effects may cause unanticipated consequences and so should be employed with careful intention and caution.

Let's return to the earlier program that we looked at in this chapter that dealt with height, width, and length. As you examine it, you might think that the printing part of the program is quite messy, and there might be a way to create a cleaner solution. We can create a function that takes two pointer parameters but does not have any side effects (the pointer targets are not modified in the function body).

Copy the pointers1.c file into pointers2.c and modify it as follows:

1. Add the following two functions (after `#include <stdio.h>` and before `int main()`):

```
void showInfo( int height, int width , int length )  {
    printf( "   sizeof(int)  = %2lu\n" , sizeof(int) );
    printf( "   sizeof(int*) = %2lu\n" , sizeof(int*) );
    printf( "   [height, width, length] = [%2d,%2d,%2d]\n\n" ,
            height , width , length );
}

void showVariable( char* pId , int* pDim )  {
    printf( "      address of %s = %#lx, value at address = %2d\n" ,
            pId,
            (unsigned long)pDim ,
            *pDim );
}
```

2. The body of our `main()` function should now look as follows:

```
int height = 10;
int width  = 20;
int length = 40;
int* pDimension = NULL;
char* pIdentifier = NULL

printf( "\nValues:\n\n");
showInfo( height , width , length );
printf( "   address of pDimension = %#lx\n" ,
        (unsigned long)&pDimension   );
printf( "\nUsing address of each named variables...\n\n");

pIdentifier = "height";
pDimension = &height;
showVariable( pIdentifier , pDimension );
pIdentifier = "width ";
pDimension = &width;
showVariable( pIdentifier , pDimension );
pIdentifier = "length";
pDimension = &length;
showVariable( pIdentifier , pDimension );
```

So, we move the messy bits of `printf()` into `showInfo()` and `showVariable()`. `showInfo()` simply uses call-by-value for each of the variables we want to show. This is what we did before.

The interesting part is making the two parameters to the `showVariable()` pointers—one a pointer to `char` (the target of this will be a string name of the variable's identifier) and the other a pointer to `int` (the target of this will be the value of the variable itself). At each call to `showVariable()`, we provide a pointer to the variable's identifier and a pointer to the variable's location. We will explore the relationship between pointers and strings in `Chapter 15`, *Working with Strings*.

Save, compile, and run this program. Your output should be exactly like that given before:

```
[> cc pointers2.c -o pointers2 -Wall -Werror -std=c11           ]
[> pointers2                                                    ]

Values:

    sizeof(int)  =  4
    sizeof(int*) =  8
    [height, width, length] = [10,20,40]

    address of pDimension = 0x7ffee16b7888

Using address of each named variables...

        address of height = 0x7ffee16b789c, value at address = 10
        address of width  = 0x7ffee16b7898, value at address = 20
        address of height = 0x7ffee16b7894, value at address = 40
 > ▓
```

We can see both the sizes of int and a pointer to int, as well as the values stored at the height, width, and length named locations. Next, we see both the addresses of each variable and, to confirm the correctness of our pointers, we can see the values stored at those addresses. They correctly correlate to the values in our named variables. Note how each address is offset by 4 bytes; this, by no coincidence, is the size of int.

Passing addresses to functions without pointer variables

We can actually go one step further and remove the pointer variables in main() and then pass the desired addresses directly in each function call. We'll still need the pointer variables as function parameters in the function definition, just not in the main() function body.

Copy pointers2.c to pointers3.c and modify only the body of main(), as follows:

```
int height = 10;
int width  = 20;
int length = 40;
printf( "\nValues:\n\n");
showInfo( height , width , length );
printf( "\nUsing address of each named variables...\n\n");
showVariable( "height" , &height );
showVariable( "width " , &width );
showVariable( "length" , &length );
```

---
[284]

The `showInfo()` and `showVariables()` functions do not change. You'll also have to remove the `printf()` statement that prints info about `pDimension`. Save, compile, and run the program. As before, the output should be similar to earlier versions of this program, except we no longer see information about `pDimension` since it now doesn't exist:

```
[> cc pointers3.c -o pointers3 -Wall -Werror -std=c11
[> pointers3

Values:

    sizeof(int)  =  4
    sizeof(int*) =  8
    [height, width, length] = [10,20,40]


Using address of each named variables...

        address of height = 0x7ffee8de789c, value at address = 10
        address of width  = 0x7ffee8de7898, value at address = 20
        address of length = 0x7ffee8de7894, value at address = 40
>
```

You may notice that the variable addresses have changed since we removed `pDimension`. In this case, as you can see, they have not changed.

Pointers to pointers

If we can have a pointer that points to a variable, it should come as no surprise that we have a pointer that points to another pointer, which then points to our desired variable. This is called a **double indirection**. When using a pointer to a pointer to a variable, we must doubly dereference our starting pointer to get to the desired value. Why might we need to do that?

Consider the following snippet in `pointers2.c`:

```
printf( "  address of pDimension = %#lx\n" ,
        (unsigned long)&pDimension  );
```

Now, you might have observed that we didn't move this code snippet into the `showInfo()` function. That is because if we passed `pDimension` into the function as a parameter, a new temporary variable would be created and the value of `pDimension` would be copied into it. We would thus see the address of the function variable, which would be different from the location of `pDimension`. We can move it into `showInfo()`, but we will need to use a bit more trickery with pointers.

To show the value of the pointer itself when we pass it into a function, we have to create a pointer to the pointer. This is a pointer to a pointer to a named location; or, more precisely, it is a pointer variable that points to another pointer variable that points to a variable.

Since this is a somewhat advanced topic, rather than going into more detail, we'll see how this is done with an example. Copy `pointers2.c` into `pointers4.c` and make the following modifications:

1. Change the `showInfo()` function definition. Your modifications to `showInfo()` should look as follows:

```
{
printf( " sizeof(int) = %2lu\n" , sizeof(int) );
printf( " sizeof(int) = %2lu\n" , sizeof(int) );
printf( " [height, width, length] = [%2d,%2d,%2d]\n\n" ,
height , width , length );
printf( " address of pDimension = %#lx\n" ,
(unsigned long)ppDim );
}
```

2. Change how `showInfo()` is called from `main()` function.

3. Remove the `printf()` statement for `pDimension` in `main()` function after the call to `showInfo()`. The modifications to `main()` function should look as follows:

```
int* pDimension = NULL;
int** ppDimension = &pDimension;
char* pIdentifier = NULL;

printf( "\nValues:\n\n");
showInfo( height , width , length , ppDimension );
```

Save, compile, and run `pointers4.c`. Your output should look identical to that of `pointers2.c`:

```
[> cc pointers4.c -o pointers4 -Wall -Werror -std=c11                    ]
[> pointers4                                                             ]

Values:

  sizeof(int)  =  4
  sizeof(int*) =  8
  [height, width, length] = [10,20,40]

  address of pDimension = 0x7ffee4b94888

Using address of each named variables...

      address of height = 0x7ffee4b9489c, value at address = 10
      address of width  = 0x7ffee4b94898, value at address = 20
      address of height = 0x7ffee4b94894, value at address = 40
>  
```

If this makes your head spin, don't worry. It has done the same to many C programmers, just as it did to me. Double indirection is an advanced topic and is only included here for future reference. We will only use double indirection sparingly in upcoming programs, if at all.

Using pointers to structures

Before we finish with pointers, we need to expand the concept of a pointer pointing to a variable of an intrinsic type to that of a pointer pointing to a structure. We can then also expand `typedef` specifiers to structures to include `typedef`-defined pointers to structures.

Recall that a pointer *points to* the first byte of a target data type. We explored pointers to intrinsic types in Chapter 3, *Working with Basic Data Types*. Also, recall that a structure is a named location that holds a collection of named values. The structure as a whole is named, as are each of the member elements of that structure.

Once the structure type is defined, variables may be declared that are of that type. When a variable of any type is declared, the appropriate number of bytes are allocated in memory to store the values of that type. We can then access the member's structure elements directly via the structure variable's name and the . notation.

Declaring a pointer to a structure variable is no different than declaring a pointer to any other variable. The variable must already have been declared (that is, allocated). The pointer address is the first byte allocated to the structure, just as for any other variable.

For this exploration, we'll use a `Date` structure type, representing the numerical day, month, and year. It is defined as follows:

```
typedef struct {
    int day;
    int month;
    int year;
} Date;
```

We can then declare variables of that type, as follows:

```
Date anniversary;
```

We can then assign values to `anniversary`, as follows:

```
anniversary.month = 8;
anniversary.day   = 18;
anniversary.year  = 1990;
```

Now, we can declare a pointer to this structure variable, as follows:

```
Date* pAnniversary = &anniversary;
```

At this point, `pAnniversary` points to the structure variable as a whole, very much like other variables. Unlike intrinsic variables, we are not just interested in the structure as a whole; we are more interested in each of the structure variable's elements.

Accessing structures and their elements via pointers

We access the structure as a whole as we did with intrinsic variables so that `*pAnniversary` and `anniversary` refer to the same memory location.

To access one of the `anniversary` elements via the pointer, we might consider using `*pAnniversary.month`. However, because the `.` operator has higher precedence than the `*` operator, the element reference will fail evaluation and will be inaccessible. We can change the evaluation order with parentheses, as follows:

```
(*pAnniversary).day      <--  anniversary.day;
(*pAnniversary).month    <--  anniversary.month;
(*pAnniversary).year     <--  anniversary.year;
```

Because accessing structure elements via pointers is quite common, an alternative syntax to access structure elements via pointers is available. This is done using the --> operator and appears as follows:

```
pAnniversary->day      <--   (*pAnniversary).day;
pAnniversary->month    <--   (*pAnniversary).month;
pAnniversary->year     <--   (*pAnniversary).year;
```

The alternative syntax uses two fewer characters, a slight improvement. Whether you find one method easier to read than the other, the general advice is to pick one and use it consistently.

Using pointers to structures in functions

Now that we can use an indirect reference (a pointer) to a structure variable as easily as we can with a direct reference (a variable identifier) to a structure variable, we can use the indirect reference in function parameters to avoid the unnecessary copying of structures to temporary function variables. We can use the structure pointer in function parameters, as follows:

```
void printDate( Date* pDate );
```

We declare the pointer to the structure type in the function declaration. We then define the function, accessing each element as follows:

```
void printDate( Date* pDate )  {
    int m, d , y;
    m = pDate->month;
    d = pDate->day;
    y = pDate->year;
    printf( "%4d-%2d-%2d\n" , y , m , d );

// or

    printf( %4d-%2d-%2d\n" , pDate->year , pDate->month , pDate->day );
}
```

In the definition of `printDate()`, we can create local variables and assign the dereferenced pointer values to them, or we can just use the dereferenced pointer values without creating and assigning temporary variables.

We would then call `printDate()`, as follows:

```
Date anniversary = { 18 , 8 , 1990 };
Date* pAnniversary = &anniversary;

printDate( pAnniversary );

// or

printDate( &anniversary );
```

As we saw earlier, we can call `printDate()` using a pointer variable, `pAnniversary`, or by using the `&anniversary` variable reference, without using a pointer variable.

Returning to the `RectDimension` structure shown in an earlier section of this chapter, we can eliminate the need to copy the structure into the function and copy it back as a return value by using a pointer, as follows:

```
typedef struct _RectDimensions  {
  double height;
  double width;
  double perimeter;
} RectDimensions;

void CalculateRectPerimeter( RectDimensions* pRD )  {
   pRD->height += 10.0;
   pRD->width += 10.0;
   pRD->perimeter = 2*(pRD->height * pRD->width);
}

int main( void )  {
   RectDimensions rd;
   rd.height = 15.0;
   rd.width = 22.5;
   CalculateRectPerimeter( &rd );
}
```

In the `main()` function, `rd` is declared (allocated) and given initial values. A pointer to this structure is then passed into the `CalculateRectPerimeter()` function, thereby making a copy of the pointer value, not the structure, to be used in the function body. The pointer value is then used to access and manipulate the structure referenced by the pointer.

Summary

In this chapter, we learned how a pointer is a variable that *points to* or references a value at a named location. To use a pointer, we have learned that we must know, either through definition or through casting, the type of the pointer's target, as well as the address of the target. Pointers should always be initialized to a named location or set to NULL. We have explored the relatively few operations on pointers: assignment, access (dereference), and comparison. We have also extended the idea of pointers to variables to include pointers to structures and their elements. We have also seen how we can use pointers to provide greater flexibility in passing and manipulating function parameters.

This chapter is essential to understanding the next chapter, Chapter 14, *Understanding Arrays and Pointers*, where we will extend our concepts of using pointers to arrays. We will see how to access and traverse arrays with pointers. Remember that an array is also a named location that holds a collection of unnamed values, all of the same type. The array as a whole has an identifier, but each of its elements are unnamed; they are relative to the array's name plus an offset. As we will see, these array concepts dovetail nicely with and extend our existing concepts of pointers.

14
Understanding Arrays and Pointers

C pointers and arrays are closely related; so closely, in fact, that they are often interchangeable! However, this does not mean pointers and arrays are identical. We will explore this relationship and why we might want to use either array notation or pointer notation to access array elements.

Having read two previous chapters, Chapter 11, *Working with Arrays*, and Chapter 13, *Using Pointers*, is essential to understanding the concepts presented here. Please do not skip those chapters before reading this one.

The following topics will be covered in this chapter:

- Reviewing the memory layout of arrays
- Understanding the relationship between array names and pointers
- Using pointers in various ways to access and traverse arrays
- Expanding the use of pointer arithmetic, specifically for array elements
- Creating an array of pointers to arrays and a two-dimensional array to highlight their differences

Technical requirements

Continue to use the tools you chose from the *Technical requirements* section of `Chapter 1`, *Running Hello, World!*.

The source code for this chapter can be found at `https://github.com/PacktPublishing/Learn-C-Programming`.

Understanding array names and pointers

As we have seen, elements of arrays can always be accessed via indices and traversed by means of an integer offset from the zeroth element. Sometimes, however, it is more convenient to access array elements via a pointer equivalent.

Let's begin by declaring an array and two pointers, as follows:

```
const int arraySize = 5;
int       array[5] = { 1 , 2 , 3 , 4 , 5 };
int*      pArray1   = NULL;
int*      pArray2   = NULL;
```

We have declared a contiguous block of `arraySize`, or 5, which are elements that are integers. We don't use `arraySize` in the array declaration because the array cannot be initialized as `array` in this way, even though `arraySize` is a constant. We have also declared two pointers to integers—`pArray1` and `pArray2`. In the memory on my system, this looks something like the following:

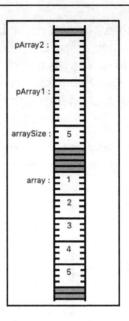

Remember that we can't control the ordering or location of variables, but we do know that arrays are guaranteed to be contiguous blocks of values beginning at the array's name.

The name of the array represents the location or address of its zeroth element. This should sound similar to pointers—in fact, it is. Without [and], the array name is treated just like a pointer. It is better to think of the array name as a special variable location which is the beginning of the array block. Because the array name alone is treated as a pointer, we can do the following:

```
pArray1 = array;
```

The value of pArray1 is now the address of the zeroth element of array[].

We can also be more explicit when we assign the address of the zeroth element, as follows:

```
pArray2 = &array[0];
```

Here, the target of pArray2 is the zeroth element of array[]. To be even more explicit, we could have written this with parentheses, as follows:

```
pArray2 = &(array[0]);
```

Each of these assignments is functionally identical.

Because of precedence rules, parentheses are not needed; the operator precedence of [ ] is higher than & and is, therefore, evaluated first. array[0] evaluates to the specific array element with an offset of 0. Notice how array is treated as a pointer, even though it is a named location, but the array[0] array element is treated as a named location or a variable that happens to be part of an array. Whenever [n] is given with the array name, it is best to think of a specific element within an array.

Now, array, &array[0], pArray1, and pArray2 all point to exactly the same location. In the memory on my system, this looks something like the following:

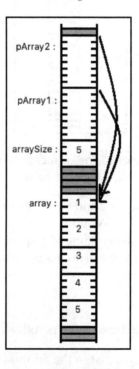

You may notice a bit of asymmetry here. pArray1 and pArray2 are the names of locations of pointer values, whereas array is the name of the beginning location of an integer array. This asymmetry vanishes when we think of the values of the pointer variables and the array name itself as the beginning address of the block of integers. The values of the pointer variables can change, but the address of the array name cannot. This will be clarified in the next section.

Understanding array elements and pointers

Individual elements of an array can be accessed either with array notation or via pointers.

We have already seen how to access the elements of array using array notation—[and]:

```
array[0] = 1;   // first element (zeroth offset)
array[1] = 2;
array[2] = 3;
array[3] = 4;
array[4] = 5;   // fifth element (fourth offset)
```

These statements assign the 1..5 values to each element of our array, just as the single initialization statement did when we declared array[5].

Accessing array elements via pointers

Arithmetic can be performed with addresses. Therefore, we can access the elements of array using a pointer plus an offset, as follows:

```
*(pArray1 + 0) = 1;   // first element (zeroth offset)
*(pArray1 + 1) = 2;   // second element (first offset)
*(pArray1 + 2) = 3;   // third element (second offset)
*(pArray1 + 3) = 4;   // fourth element (third offset)
*(pArray1 + 4) = 5;   // fifth element (fourth offset)
```

Since pArray is a pointer, the * go-to address of notation must be used to access the value at the address of that pointer. In the second through fifth elements, we must first add an offset value and then go to that computed address. Note that we must use (and) to properly calculate the address before assigning the value there. Also, note that *(pArray1 + 0) is identical to the abbreviated version, *pArray1.

You may have already noticed how adding an offset to a base address (pointer) is very similar to using an array name and an index. Now, we can see how array element referencing and pointer element referencing are equivalent, as follows:

```
array[0]        *(pArray1 + 0)
array[1]        *(pArray1 + 1)
array[2]        *(pArray1 + 2)
array[3]        *(pArray1 + 3)
array[4]        *(pArray1 + 4)
```

Notice how `array` is an unchanging address and `pArray` is also an unchanging address. The address of `array` is fixed and cannot be changed. However, even though the value of `pArray` can be changed—it is a variable, after all—in this example, the value of `pArray` is not changed. The address of each element is evaluated as an intermediate value—the unchanged value of `pArray` plus an offset. In the next section, we'll explore other ways of traversing an array by changing the pointer's value directly.

Operations on arrays using pointers

Before this chapter, the only pointer operation we had used with arrays was assignment. Because we can perform simple arithmetic on pointers—addition and subtraction—these operations conveniently lend themselves to array traversal.

Using pointer arithmetic

An integer value in pointer arithmetic represents the element to which the pointer points. When an integer is added to a pointer, the integer is automatically converted into the size of the pointer element in bytes and added to the pointer. This is equivalent to incrementing an array index. Put another way, incrementing a pointer is equivalent to incrementing the index of an array.

Even though pointers are nearly identical to integers—they are positive, whole numbers that can be added, subtracted, and compared—they are treated slightly differently from integers when pointer arithmetic is performed. The following cases illustrate the various results when operations on a pointer and an integer are mixed:

$$pointer + integer \rightarrow pointer$$

$$integer + pointer \rightarrow pointer$$

$$pointer - integer \rightarrow pointer$$

$$pointer - pointer \rightarrow integer$$

When we add 1 to an integer variable, the value of the variable is increased by 1. However, when we add 1 to a pointer variable, the value of the pointer is increased by the `sizeof()` value of the type that the pointer points to. When a pointer points to, say, a `double` value, and we increment the pointer by 1, we are adding 1 * `sizeof(double)`, or 8 bytes, to the pointer value to point to the next `double` value. When a pointer points to a `byte` value and we increment the pointer by 1, we are adding 1 * `sizeof(byte)`, or 1 byte.

We can use pointer arithmetic in one of two ways—either by keeping the pointer value unchanged or by modifying the pointer value as we move through the array. In the first approach, we access the elements of `array` using a pointer plus an offset. We have already seen this in the previous section, as follows:

```
*(pArray1 + 0) = 1;   // first element (zeroth offset)
*(pArray1 + 1) = 2;   // second element (first offset)
*(pArray1 + 2) = 3;   // third element (second offset)
*(pArray1 + 3) = 4;   // fourth element (third offset)
*(pArray1 + 4) = 5;   // fifth element (fourth offset)
```

Throughout these accesses, the value of `pArray1` does not change. Note that we must use (and) to properly calculate the address before accessing the value there. Also, note that `*(pArray1 + 0)` is identical to the abbreviated form, `*pArray1`.

In the second approach, we access the elements of `array` by first incrementing the pointer and then dereferencing the pointer value, as follows:

```
pArray1 = array;

 *pArray1 = 1; // first element (zeroth offset)
pArray +=1; *pArray1 = 2; // second element (first offset)
pArray +=1; *pArray1 = 3; // third element (second offset)
pArray +=1; *pArray1 = 4; // fourth element (third offset)
pArray +=1; *pArray1 = 5; // fifth element (fourth offset)
```

Because the increment of `pArray` is so closely associated with accessing its target, we have placed two statements on the same line, separating them with the end-of-statement `;` character. This method is a bit tedious since we have added four incremental assignment statements.

Using the increment operator

Alternatively, we could modify the pointer value to sequentially access each element of the array using the increment operator. We can, therefore, eliminate the four extra incremental assignment statements and make our code a bit more concise, as follows:

```
*pArray1++ = 1;   // first element  (zeroth offset)
*pArray1++ = 2;   // second element (first offset)
*pArray1++ = 3;   // third element  (second offset)
*pArray1++ = 4;   // fourth element (third offset)
*pArray1   = 5;   // fifth element  (fourth offset)
```

This is a very common C idiom that is used to access and increment the pointer in the same statement. The `*` operator has equal precedence with the unary operator, `++`. When two operators have the same precedence, their order of evaluation is significant. In this case, the order of evaluation is left to right, so `*pArray` is evaluated first and the target of the pointer evaluation is then assigned a value. Because we use the `++` postfix, `pArray` is incremented after the value of `pArray` is used in the statement. In each statement, the pointer reference is accessed and then incremented to point to the next array element. Without the `( )` precedence operations, we rely directly on C's precedence hierarchy.

Let's say we wanted to be a bit more obvious and chose to use the `( )` grouping operator. This grouping operator has higher precedence than both `*` and `++`. What, then, would be the difference between `(*pArray)++` and `*(pArray++)`?

These provide two completely different outcomes. For `(*pArray)++`, `*pArray` is dereferenced and its target is incremented. For `*(pArray++)`, `pArray` is dereferenced, accessing its target, and then `pArray` is incremented.

Let's now see how we'd use these array traversal techniques in loops:

```
#include <stdio.h>
int main( void )   {
   const int arraySize = 5;
   int   array[5] = { 1 , 2 , 3 , 4 , 5 };
   int* pArray1   = array;
   int* pArray2   = &(array[0]);
   printf("Pointer values (addresses) from initial assignments:\n\n");
```

```
    printf( "       address of array = %#lx,      value at array = %d\n" ,
            (unsigned long)array , *array );
    printf( "   address of &array[0] = %#lx, value at array[0] = %d\n" ,
            (unsigned long)&array[0] , array[0] );
    printf( "       address of pArray1 = %#lx,   value at pArray1 = %#lx\n" ,
            (unsigned long)&pArray1 , (unsigned long)pArray1 );
    printf( "       address of pArray2 = %#lx,   value at pArray2 = %#lx\n\n" ,
            (unsigned long)&pArray2 , (unsigned long)pArray2 );
```

In this initial part of our program, we set up our array and create two pointers, both of which point to the first element of the array. Even though the syntax of each statement is slightly different, the end result is identical, as shown by the subsequent printf() statements. The first printf() statement clearly shows how an array name is directly interchangeable with a pointer. The remaining printf() statements show the addresses of each pointer variable and the value contained in each pointer variable.

Throughout the remainder of the program, the array is traversed using three methods:

- Array indexing
- Pointer plus incremented offset
- Pointer incrementation

Pay particular attention to the array indexing and pointer incrementation methods:

```
    printf( "\n(1) Using array notation (index is incremented): \n\n" );
    for( int i = 0; i < arraySize ; i++ )
      printf( "   & (array[%1d]) = %#lx, array[%1d] = %1d, i++\n",
              i , (unsigned long) & (array[i]), i , array[i] );

    printf( "\n(2) Using a pointer addition (offset is incremented): \n\n");
    for( int i = 0 ; i < arraySize; i++  )
       printf( "   pArray2+%1d = %#lx, * (pArray2+%1d) = %1d, i++\n",
               i , (unsigned long) (pArray2+i) , i , * (pArray2+i) );

    printf("\n(3) Using pointer referencing (pointer is incremented):\n\n");
    for( int i = 0 ; i < arraySize ; i++ , pArray1++ )
       printf( "   pArray1 = %#lx, *pArray1 = %1d, pArray1++\n",
               (unsigned long) pArray1 , *pArray1 );
  }
```

This program is formatted for brevity. Looking at it quickly may make you go a bit cross-eyed. The version of this program in the repository is formatted a bit more clearly.

Let's clarify some of the `printf()` format statements. `%1d` is used to print a decimal value constrained to a field of 1. It is critical to note here the subtle appearance of 1 (one) versus l (ell). `%#lx` is used to print a long hexadecimal value preceded by 0x. Additionally, to get the pointer value (an address) to print, it must be cast to `(unsigned long)`. These format options will be more completely explored in `Chapter 19`, *Exploring Formatted Output*. Lastly, because each `for()`... loop contains only one statement—the `printf()` statement—`{ }` is not needed for the `for()`... loop body.

Normally, this program would be formatted with whitespace to make each loop and `printf()` parameters stand out a bit more clearly.

Create a new file called `arrays_pointers.c`. Type in the program and save your work. Build and run the program. You should see the following output in your terminal window:

```
> cc arrays_pointers.c -o arrays_pointers -Wall -Werror -std=c11
> arrays_pointers
Pointer values (addresses) from initial assignments:

        address of array = 0x7ffeeef61930,      value at array = 1
   address of &array[0] = 0x7ffeeef61930, value at array[0] = 1
      address of pArray1 = 0x7ffeeef61910,   value at pArray1 = 0x7ffeeef61930
      address of pArray2 = 0x7ffeeef61908,   value at pArray2 = 0x7ffeeef61930


(1) Array values using array notation (index is incremented):

  &(array[0]) = 0x7ffeeef61930, array[0] = 1, i++
  &(array[1]) = 0x7ffeeef61934, array[1] = 2, i++
  &(array[2]) = 0x7ffeeef61938, array[2] = 3, i++
  &(array[3]) = 0x7ffeeef6193c, array[3] = 4, i++
  &(array[4]) = 0x7ffeeef61940, array[4] = 5, i++

(2) Array values using a pointer addition (offset is incremented):

  pArray2+0 = 0x7ffeeef61930, *(pArray2+0) = 1, i++
  pArray2+1 = 0x7ffeeef61934, *(pArray2+1) = 2, i++
  pArray2+2 = 0x7ffeeef61938, *(pArray2+2) = 3, i++
  pArray2+3 = 0x7ffeeef6193c, *(pArray2+3) = 4, i++
  pArray2+4 = 0x7ffeeef61940, *(pArray2+4) = 5, i++

(3) Array values using pointer referencing (pointer is incremented):

  pArray1 = 0x7ffeeef61930, *pArray1 = 1, pArray1++
  pArray1 = 0x7ffeeef61934, *pArray1 = 2, pArray1++
  pArray1 = 0x7ffeeef61938, *pArray1 = 3, pArray1++
  pArray1 = 0x7ffeeef6193c, *pArray1 = 4, pArray1++
  pArray1 = 0x7ffeeef61940, *pArray1 = 5, pArray1++
>
```

Once you have got the program working, as in the preceding screenshot, you should take some time and experiment further with the program before moving on:

- Try removing the `()` grouping operator in various places. For instance, remove `()` from `(pArray2+i)` in the second loop. What happened to the pointer address? Why?
- Try removing the `(unsigned long)` casting operator in various places.
- See what happens when you place `++` before the pointer or index (prefix incrementation).
- As an added challenge, try traversing the array in reverse order, beginning at the last element of the array, and decrementing the offsets/indices in each of the three methods. As you make these changes, note which method is easier to manipulate. The repository has `syarra_sretniop.c` to show one way that this can be done. However, this is just one example; your version may be very different.

As you perform your experiments, pay attention to which method may be easier to modify, clearer to read, or simpler to execute.

Passing arrays as function pointers revisited

We can now understand how array names and pointers to arrays are passed in function arguments. If arrays were passed by values in a function parameter, the entire array might then be copied into the function body. This is extremely inefficient, especially for very large arrays. However, the array itself is not passed by a value; the reference to it is copied. That reference is then used within the function to access array elements. This reference is actually a pointer value—an address.

So, the array values themselves are not copied, only the address of the zeroth element. C converts the `array` named `location` (without `[]`) to a pointer value, `&array[0]`, and uses that to access `array` from within the function body.

Interchangeability of array names and pointers

The real power of being able to interchange an array name with a pointer is when we use an array name (or a pointer to an array) as a parameter to be passed into a function. In this section, we will explore the four possible ways of using an array in a function parameter:

- Pass an array name in a parameter and then use array notation in the function.
- Pass a pointer to an array in a parameter and then use the pointer in the function.
- Pass an array name in a parameter and use that as a pointer in the function.
- Pass a pointer to an array in a parameter and use array notation in the function.

The third and fourth methods should now come as no surprise to you. In the `arrays_pointers_funcs.c`, program, we'll create the function prototypes for each of the functions, set up a simple array that we want to traverse, print out some information about the array's address, and then call each of the four functions in turn. For each function, the intention is that the output will be identical to the others:

```c
#include <stdio.h>

void traverse1( int size , int  arr[] );
void traverse2( int size , int* pArr );
void traverse3( int size , int  arr[] );
void traverse4( int size , int* pArr );

int main( void )  {
  const int arraySize = 5;
  int array[5] = { 1 , 2 , 3 , 4 , 5 };

  printf("Pointer values (addresses) from initial assignments:\n\n");
  printf( " address of array = %#lx, value at array = %d\n" ,
          (unsigned long)array , *array );
  printf( " address of &array[0] = %#lx, value at array[0] = %d\n" ,
          (unsigned long)&array[0] , array[0] );

  traverse1( arraySize , array );
  traverse2( arraySize , array );
  traverse3( arraySize , array );
  traverse4( arraySize , array );
}
```

This is very similar to what we've already seen in the earlier program used in this chapter. The one thing that might be surprising here is how the functions are all called in the same way. Even though each of the four functions has a parameter that is of either the arr[] or *pArr type, the value that is passed to each is array. You now know that array is both the name of our array and, equivalently, a pointer to the first element of that array (the element with the s zeroth offset).

The first traversal is pretty much what we've seen already. An array name is passed in and array notation is used to print each value in a loop, as follows:

```
void traverse1( int size , int arr[] )  {
   printf("\n(1) Function parameter is array, using array notation:\n\n");
   for( int i = 0; i < size ; i++ )
     printf( "  & (array[%1d]) = %#lx, array[%1d] = %1d, i++\n",
             i , (unsigned long)&(arr[i]), i , arr[i] );
}
```

In the second traversal, a pointer to the first element of the array is passed in. Again, using a loop, the array is traversed using that pointer, as follows:

```
void traverse2( int size , int* pArr )  {
   printf("\n(2) Function parameter is pointer, using pointer :\n\n");
   for( int i = 0 ; i < size ; i++ , pArr++ )
     printf( "  pArr = %#lx, *pArr = %1d, pArr++\n",
             (unsigned long)pArr , *pArr );
}
```

Notice the increment part of the for()... loop; using the , sequence operator, we see that i is incremented, as well as pArr. This is often a useful idiom to keep all incrementation in the **increment expression** of the for()... loop instead of putting the extra increment operation in the for()... loop body.

In the third traversal, an array name is passed in, but because of the interchangeability of arrays and pointers, we traverse the array using pointers. Again, incrementation of the pointer is done in the increment expression of the for()... loop.

```
void traverse3( int size , int arr[] )  {
   printf("\n(3) Function parameter is array, using pointer:\n\n");
   for( int i = 0 ; i < size ; i++ , arr++ )
     printf( "  arr = %#lx, *arr = %1d, arr++\n",
         (unsigned long)arr , *arr );
}
```

Finally, in the fourth traversal, a pointer to the first element of the array is passed in, and because of the interchangeability of pointers and arrays, we traverse the array using array notation with the pointer:

```
void traverse4( int size , int* pArr )  {
  printf("\n(4) Function parameter is pointer, using array notation
:\n\n");
  for( int i = 0; i < size ; i++ )
    printf( "  & (pArr[%1d]) = %#1x, pArr[%1d] = %1d, i++\n",
       i , (unsigned long)&(pArr[i]) , i , pArr[i] );
}
```

Now, in your editor, create a new file called `arrays_pointers_funcs.c`, and type in the five code segments given here. Save, compile, and run your program. You should see the following output:

```
> cc arrays_pointers_funcs.c -o arrays_pointers_funcs -Wall -Werror -std=c11
> arrays_pointers_funcs
Pointer values (addresses) from initial assignments:

        address of array = 0x7ffee276a920,     value at array = 10
  address of &array[0] = 0x7ffee276a920, value at array[0] = 10

(1) Function parameter is an array, using array notation:

    &(array[0]) = 0x7ffee276a920, array[0] = 10, i++
    &(array[1]) = 0x7ffee276a924, array[1] = 20, i++
    &(array[2]) = 0x7ffee276a928, array[2] = 30, i++
    &(array[3]) = 0x7ffee276a92c, array[3] = 40, i++
    &(array[4]) = 0x7ffee276a930, array[4] = 50, i++

(2) Function parameter is a pointer, using pointer:

    pArr = 0x7ffee276a920, *pArr = 10, pArr++
    pArr = 0x7ffee276a924, *pArr = 20, pArr++
    pArr = 0x7ffee276a928, *pArr = 30, pArr++
    pArr = 0x7ffee276a92c, *pArr = 40, pArr++
    pArr = 0x7ffee276a930, *pArr = 50, pArr++

(3) Function parameter is an array, using pointer:

    arr = 0x7ffee276a920, *arr = 10, arr++
    arr = 0x7ffee276a924, *arr = 20, arr++
    arr = 0x7ffee276a928, *arr = 30, arr++
    arr = 0x7ffee276a92c, *arr = 40, arr++
    arr = 0x7ffee276a930, *arr = 50, arr++

(4) Function parameter is a pointer, using array notation :

    &(pArr[0]) = 0x7ffee276a920, pArr[0] = 10, i++
    &(pArr[1]) = 0x7ffee276a924, pArr[1] = 20, i++
    &(pArr[2]) = 0x7ffee276a928, pArr[2] = 30, i++
    &(pArr[3]) = 0x7ffee276a92c, pArr[3] = 40, i++
    &(pArr[4]) = 0x7ffee276a930, pArr[4] = 50, i++
> []
```

It should now be clear to you how array names and pointers are interchangeable. Use array notation or pointer access in whichever manner makes your code clearer and is consistent with the rest of your programs.

Introducing an array of pointers to arrays

Before finishing this chapter, it is worth introducing the concept of an array of pointers to arrays. This may be thought of as an alternate two-dimensional array. Such an array is somewhat different in memory than the standard arrays that we have so far encountered. Even though its memory representation is different, we access this alternate array in exactly the same way as we would a standard two-dimensional array. Therefore, some caution is required when traversing the two kinds of arrays.

We declare a standard two-dimensional array in the following way:

```
int arrayStd[3][5];
```

We have allocated a contiguous and inseparable block of 15 integers, which has three rows of five integers. Our conceptual memory picture of this is a single block referenced via a single name, arrayStd, as follows:

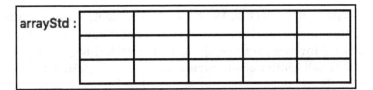

To declare an alternate two-dimensional array using arrays of pointers, we would do the following:

```
int* arrayPtr[3] = {NULL};
...
int array1[5];
int array2[5];
int array3[5];
arrayPtr[0] = array1;
arrayPtr[1] = array2;
arrayPtr[2] = array3;
...
```

We first declare an array of three pointers to integers, `arrayPtr`. As a reminder, when working with pointers, it is always a good practice to initialize them to some known value as soon as possible; in this case, when the array is declared. Later, we declare `array1`, `array2`, and `array3`, each of which holds five integers. We'll call them **sub-arrays** for the purposes of this discussion. Then, we assign the addresses of these arrays to `arrayPtr`. The conceptual memory picture of this group of arrays is as follows:

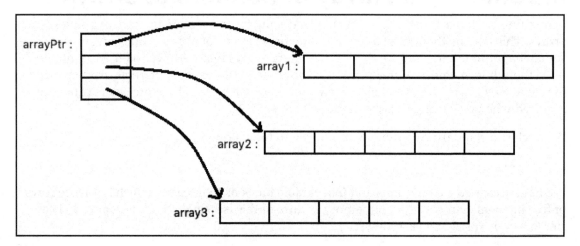

This is a very different memory layout. We have, in fact, created four arrays—one array of three pointers and three arrays of five integers each. Each array is a smaller, contiguous, and inseparable block. However, because these array declarations are separate statements, they are not necessarily all contiguous in memory. Each of the four arrays is a small contiguous block but, taken as a whole, they are not. Furthermore, there is no guarantee that they would all be contiguous, even though they've been declared consecutively.

Notice that there could be a lot of code in between the declaration of `arrayPtr` and the sub-arrays. We have declared these sub-arrays statically; that is, their size and time of declaration are known before the program runs. The other arrays could even be declared in a different function block and at various times. Alternatively, we could declare the sub-arrays dynamically, where their size and time of declaration is only known when the program is running. We will explore static and dynamic memory allocation in Chapter 17, *Understanding Memory Allocation and Lifetime*, and Chapter 18, *Using Dynamic Memory Allocation*.

Using array notation, we would access the third element of the second row or sub-array (remembering the *one-offness* of array offsets) as follows:

```
arrayStd[1][2];
arrayPtr[1][2];
```

Here is where things get interesting. Given that we have two very different in-memory structures, one a single contiguous block and the other four smaller sub-blocks that are scattered, access to any element in either of them is identical using array notation:

```
for( int i=0 ; i<3 ; i++ )
  for( int j=0 ; j<5 ; j++ )
      arrayStd[i][j] = (i*5) + j + 1;
      arrayPtr[i][j] = (i*5) + j + 1;
  }
```

That's great! However, if we use pointer arithmetic to traverse these arrays, we would need to use slightly different approaches. We assign the value of `(i*5) + j + 1` to each array element. This calculation is significant; it shows the calculation the compiler makes to convert index notation into an element's address.

To access the standard array using pointers, we could simply start at the beginning element and iterate through the whole block because it is guaranteed to be contiguous, as follows:

```
int* pInteger = &(array[0][0]);
for( int i=0 ; i<3 ; i++ )
  for( int j=0 ; j<5 ; j++ )
  {
      *pInteger = (i*5) + j + 1;
      pInteger++;
  }
```

Because `array` is a two-dimensional array, we must get the address of the first element of this block; using just the array name will cause a type error. In this iteration, on a standard array using a pointer, `i` is used for each row and `j` is used for each column element. We saw this in `Chapter 12`, *Working with Multi-Dimensional Arrays*.

To access the array of pointers to arrays, we must add an assignment to our iteration using a pointer, as follows:

```
for( int i=0 ; i<3 ; i++ )
{
  int* pInteger = arrayOfPtrs[i];

  for( int j=0 ; j<5 ; j++ )
  {
      *pInteger = (i*5) + j + 1;
      pInteger++;
  }
}
```

Because `array1`, `array2`, and `array3` have been declared in separate statements, we cannot be certain that they are actually adjacent to one another. This means that taken together, they are unlikely to be contiguous across all of them. Therefore, for each sub-array, we have to set the pointer to that beginning element and traverse the sub-array. Take note that this particular pointer traversal relies on the fact that we have declared each sub-array to be the same size.

Let's put this into a working program to verify our understanding. In this program, we'll declare these arrays, assigning them values at the declaration, then traverse each with array notation and with pointers. The goal of the program is to show identical output for each traversal, as follows:

```c
#include <stdio.h>

int main( void)  {
    // Set everything up.
    // Standard 2D array.
  int arrayStd[3][5] = { { 11 , 12 , 13 , 14 , 15 } ,
                         { 21 , 22 , 23 , 24 , 25 } ,
                         { 31 , 32 , 33 , 34 , 35 } };
    // Array of pointers.
  int* arrayPtr[3] = { NULL };
    // Array sizes and pointer for pointer traversal.
  const int rows = 3;
  const int cols = 5;
  int* pInteger;
    // Sub-arrays.
  int array1[5]    = { 11 , 12 , 13 , 14 , 15 };
  int array2[5]    = { 21 , 22 , 23 , 24 , 25 };
  int array3[5]    = { 31 , 32 , 33 , 34 , 35 };
  arrayPtr[0] = array1;
  arrayPtr[1] = array2;
  arrayPtr[2] = array3;
```

Both `arrayStd` and the sub-arrays are initialized upon array declaration. You can see that each row and its corresponding sub-array have the same values. Some other useful constants and a pointer variable are declared. These will be used in the traversals. First, we'll carry out the traversals of the two arrays using array notation. The array notation is the same for both:

```c
    // Do traversals.

  printf( "Print both arrays using array notation, array[i][j].\n\n");

  for( int i = 0 ; i < rows ; i++ )  {
    for( int j = 0 ; j < cols ; j++ )  {
```

```
        printf( " %2d" , arrayStd[i][j]);
    }
    printf( "\n" );
  }
  printf("\n");
  for( int i = 0 ; i < rows ; i++ )  {
    for( int j = 0 ; j < cols ; j++ )  {
        printf( " %2d" , arrayPtr[i][j]);
    }
    printf( "\n" );
  }
  printf("\n");
```

Then, we'll carry out the traversals using the temporary pointer we've already declared:

```
  printf( "Print both arrays using pointers, *pInteger++.\n\n");

  pInteger = &(arrayStd[0][0]);
  for( int i = 0 ; i < rows ; i++ )  {
    for( int j = 0 ; j < cols ; j++ )  {
      printf( " %2d" , *pInteger++);
    }
    printf( "\n" );
  }
  printf("\n");

    // Experiment:
    //  This is here if you comment out "pInteger = arrayPtr[j];",
    //  below.
    //  Otherwise, pInteger is reassigned with that statement
    //  and this one has no effect.
  pInteger = arrayPtr[0];
  for( int i = 0 ; i < rows ; i++ )  {
    pInteger = arrayPtr[i];  // Get the pointer to the
                             // correct sub-array.
    for( int j = 0 ; j < cols ; j++ )  {
      printf( " %2d" , *pInteger++);
    }
    printf( "\n" );
  }
  printf("\n");
}
```

In the traversal for `arrayStd`, the pointer is set to the first element and we use nested loops to iterate through each row and column, incrementing the pointer as we go. In the traversal for `arrayPtr`, note the added assignment that is needed for each row. This is the statement:

```
pInteger = arrayPtr[i];
```

The code snippet has an experiment to prove how `arrayPtr` is not a contiguous block. After you get the program working as intended, then you can perform the experiment to see what happens.

With your editor, create a program named `arrayOfPointers.c` and enter the three code segments given. Save the file, compile it, and run it. You should get the following output:

```
> cc arrayOfPointers.c -o arrayOfPointers -Wall -Werror -std=c11
> arrayOfPointers
Print both arrays using array notation, array[i][j].

  11 12 13 14 15
  21 22 23 24 25
  31 32 33 34 35

  11 12 13 14 15
  21 22 23 24 25
  31 32 33 34 35

Print both arrays using pointers, *pInteger++.

  11 12 13 14 15
  21 22 23 24 25
  31 32 33 34 35

  11 12 13 14 15
  21 22 23 24 25
  31 32 33 34 35

>
```

As you can easily see, each array traversal presents an identical output. Yay! Success.

When you perform the experiment outlined in the last array traversal, you should see something like the following output:

```
> cc arrayOfPointers.c -o arrayOfPointers -Wall -Werror -std=c11
> arrayOfPointers
Print both arrays using array notation, array[i][j].

  11 12 13 14 15
  21 22 23 24 25
  31 32 33 34 35

  11 12 13 14 15
  21 22 23 24 25
  31 32 33 34 35

Print both arrays using pointers, *pInteger++.

  11 12 13 14 15
  21 22 23 24 25
  31 32 33 34 35

  11 12 13 14 15
  32766 379602179   1 -401057600 32766
  -401057632 32766 -401057664 32766 -401057424

>
```

Yay! This was also a success because we can clearly see what happens when pointers go awry. From this, we can conclude that using a pointer to traverse an array of pointers to sub-arrays is definitely not like using a pointer to traverse a two-dimensional array. We get unexpected, odd values in the last two rows because printf() is interpreting the bytes that are not in those two sub-arrays. This also illustrates how we can access values outside of array bounds and that we will get bizarre results when we do—hence, test and verify. You know exactly why this has been emphasized!

However, there are numerous advantages to this alternative array of sub-arrays, especially when each of the *rows* of the sub-arrays is not the same number of elements. Therefore, this is an important concept to master. We will reuse and expand on this concept in Chapter 15, *Working with Strings,* Chapter 18, *Using Dynamic Memory Allocation,* and Chapter 20, *Getting Input from the Command Line.*

Summary

In this chapter, we used the concepts introduced in two earlier chapters, `Chapter 11`, *Working with Arrays*, and `Chapter 13`, *Using Pointers*, to learn how array names and pointers are related and interchangeable.

We have seen various memory layouts of arrays and pointers and used pointers in various ways to access and traverse arrays, both directly and via function parameters. We also have seen how pointer arithmetic pertains to elements of the array and is a bit different to integer arithmetic. We learned about some of the similarities and differences between a two-dimensional array (a contiguous block of elements) and an array of pointers to sub-arrays (a collection of scattered arrays indexed by a single array of pointers). Finally, we looked at a set of simple programs that illustrate as well as prove the concepts we have learned.

Having explored arrays and pointers and their interrelationship, we are now ready to put all of these concepts to good use in the next chapter.

15
Working with Strings

In C, a string is an array with two special properties. First, a string is made up of only characters. Second, the string must conclude with an essential terminating character—the `null` character. While some would say strings are one of C's weakest features, I disagree with that assessment. Because strings build on already-established mechanisms, I believe that they are rather elegant in an unexpected way.

Not all values that we might want to manipulate in a program are numbers. Often, we need to manipulate words, phrases, and sentences; these are built from strings of characters. We have been performing output using simple strings in `printf()` statements. In order to perform the input of strings and numbers, we need to be able to further manipulate strings to convert them into values. In this chapter, the elements and building blocks of C strings will be explored, as well as various ways to use and manipulate C strings.

Chapter 11, *Working with Arrays*, Chapter 13, *Using Pointers*, and Chapter 14, *Understanding Arrays and Pointers*, are essential to understanding the concepts presented here. Please do not skip those chapters, particularly Chapter 14, *Understanding Arrays and Pointers*, before reading this one.

The following topics will be covered in this chapter:

- Characters – the building blocks of strings
- Exploring C strings
- Understanding the strengths and weaknesses of C strings
- Declaring and initializing a string
- Creating and using an array of strings
- Using the standard library for common operations on strings
- Preventing some pitfalls of strings – safer string operations

Throughout this chapter, we will introduce the programming technique of **iterative program development**. We will start with a very simple but small program and repeatedly add capabilities to it until we reach our desired complete result.

Technical requirements

Continue to use the tools you chose from the *Technical requirements* section of `Chapter 1,` *Hello, World!*.

The source code for this chapter can be found at `https://github.com/PacktPublishing/` `Learn-C-Programming`.

Characters – the building blocks of strings

In C, each array element in a string is a **character** from a **character set**. In fact, the C character set, also called **American Standard Code for Information Interchange (ASCII)**, is made up of printable characters—those that appear on the screen—and control characters.

Control characters allow digital devices to communicate, control the flow of data between devices, and control the flow data layout and spacing. The following control characters alter how characters are displayed, providing simple character-positioning functions:

- Horizontal tab (moves the position forward by a number of spaces on the same line)
- Vertical tab (moves the position to the next line but keeps the current horizontal position)
- Carriage return (returns the position to the first column)
- Line feed (advances to the next line)
- Form feed (advances to the next page)
- Backspace (moves back one space)

One special control character is NUL, which has a value of 0. This is known as the **null character**, or `'\0'`. It is this special character value that terminates a properly formed C string. Omitting this character will cause the C string to be formed improperly.

The other control characters have to do with communication between devices. Others serve as data separators for blocks of data from large blocks (files) down to records and, finally, units.

Printable characters are those that appear on the screen or can be printed. These include numerals, upper and lowercase letters, and punctuation marks. Whitespace, or characters that print nothing but alter the position of other characters, consists of the space character and a positioning control character.

The C language requires the following characters:

- **The 52 Latin upper and lowercase letters**: A B C D E F G H I J K L M N O P Q R S T U V W X Y Z and
  a b c d e f g h i j k l m n o p q r s t u v w x y z
- **The 10 digits**: 0 1 2 3 4 5 6 7 8 9
- **Whitespace characters**: SPACE, horizontal tab (HT), vertical tab (VT), form feed (FF), line feed (LF), and carriage return (CR)
- The NUL character
- The bell (BEL), escape (ESC), backspace (BS), and delete (DEL) characters are sometimes called **destructive backspace**.
- **32 graphic characters**: ! # % ^ & * ( ) − + = ~ [ ] " ' and _ | \ ; :
  { } , . < > / ? $ @ `

Any character set is a somewhat arbitrary correlation of values to characters. There have been many different character sets in use since the invention of computers. Many computer system manufacturers had their own character sets; or, if they were not completely unique, they extended standard character sets in non-standard ways. Any of these extended character sets were extended differently than any others and would, therefore, be unique. Before computers, older teleprinters used the first standard digital code invented in 1870. Before teleprinters, the telegraph, invented in 1833, used various non-digital coding systems. Thankfully, there are now only a few character sets in common use today. ASCII, as a subset of **Unicode Transformation Format 8-Bit (UTF-8)**, is one of them.

A character set could be ordered in nearly any fashion. However, it makes sense to order a character set in a manner that makes using and manipulating characters in that set convenient. We will see how this is done with the ASCII character set in the next section.

The char type and ASCII

ASCII was based on older standards and was developed around the same time that C was invented. It consists of 128 character values, which can be represented with a single signed char value. The lowest valid ASCII value is 0 and the highest valid ASCII value is 127 (there's that off-by-one thing again that we first saw in Chapter 7, *Exploring Loops and Iteration*). Each value in this range has a single, specific character meaning.

When we talk specifically about a C character (such as a control character, a digit, an uppercase letter, a lowercase letter, or punctuation), we are really talking about a single byte value that is correlated to a specific position in the character set.

Any `unsigned char` property that has a value greater than `127` or any `signed char` property that has a value that is less than `0` is not a valid ASCII character. It may be some other kind of character, possibly part of a non-standard ASCII extension or a Unicode character, but it is not valid ASCII.

In ASCII, there are four groupings of characters. Each group has 32 characters, with a total of 128 characters in the set. They are grouped as follows:

- **0-31**: Control characters
- **32-63**: Punctuation and numerals
- **64-95**: Uppercase letters and additional punctuation
- **96-127**: Lowercase letters, additional punctuation, and delete (`DEL`)

Observe each of the four column groups in the following ASCII table:

```
                       Table of 7-Bit ASCII and
                    Single-Byte UTF-8 Character Sets

| Control Characters |    Printable Characaters (except DEL)     |
|--------------------|-------------------------------------------|
| SYM Fmt Ch Dec Hex | Ch Dec  Hex | Ch Dec  Hex | Ch Dec  Hex    |
|--------------------|-------------|-------------|----------------|
| NUL  \0 ^@  0   0  |    32 0x20  | @  64 0x40  | `  96 0x60     |
| SOH     ^A  1  0x1 | !  33 0x21  | A  65 0x41  | a  97 0x61     |
| STX     ^B  2  0x2 | "  34 0x22  | B  66 0x42  | b  98 0x62     |
| ETX     ^C  3  0x3 | #  35 0x23  | C  67 0x43  | c  99 0x63     |
| EOT     ^D  4  0x4 | $  36 0x24  | D  68 0x44  | d 100 0x64     |
| ENQ     ^E  5  0x5 | %  37 0x25  | E  69 0x45  | e 101 0x65     |
| ACK     ^F  6  0x6 | &  38 0x26  | F  70 0x46  | f 102 0x66     |
| BEL  \a ^G  7  0x7 | '  39 0x27  | G  71 0x47  | g 103 0x67     |
| BS   \b ^H  8  0x8 | (  40 0x28  | H  72 0x48  | h 104 0x68     |
| HT   \t ^I  9  0x9 | )  41 0x29  | I  73 0x49  | i 105 0x69     |
| LF   \n ^J 10  0xa | *  42 0x2a  | J  74 0x4a  | j 106 0x6a     |
| VT   \v ^K 11  0xb | +  43 0x2b  | K  75 0x4b  | k 107 0x6b     |
| FF   \f ^L 12  0xc | ,  44 0x2c  | L  76 0x4c  | l 108 0x6c     |
| CR   \r ^M 13  0xd | -  45 0x2d  | M  77 0x4d  | m 109 0x6d     |
| SO      ^N 14  0xe | .  46 0x2e  | N  78 0x4e  | n 110 0x6e     |
| SI      ^O 15  0xf | /  47 0x2f  | O  79 0x4f  | o 111 0x6f     |
| DLE     ^P 16 0x10 | 0  48 0x30  | P  80 0x50  | p 112 0x70     |
| DC1     ^Q 17 0x11 | 1  49 0x31  | Q  81 0x51  | q 113 0x71     |
| DC2     ^R 18 0x12 | 2  50 0x32  | R  82 0x52  | r 114 0x72     |
| DC3     ^S 19 0x13 | 3  51 0x33  | S  83 0x53  | s 115 0x73     |
| DC4     ^T 20 0x14 | 4  52 0x34  | T  84 0x54  | t 116 0x74     |
| NAK     ^U 21 0x15 | 5  53 0x35  | U  85 0x55  | u 117 0x75     |
| SYN     ^V 22 0x16 | 6  54 0x36  | V  86 0x56  | v 118 0x76     |
| ETB     ^W 23 0x17 | 7  55 0x37  | W  87 0x57  | w 119 0x77     |
| CAN     ^X 24 0x18 | 8  56 0x38  | X  88 0x58  | x 120 0x78     |
| EM      ^Y 25 0x19 | 9  57 0x39  | Y  89 0x59  | y 121 0x79     |
| SUB     ^Z 26 0x1a | :  58 0x3a  | Z  90 0x5a  | z 122 0x7a     |
| ESC  \e ^[ 27 0x1b | ;  59 0x3b  | [  91 0x5b  | { 123 0x7b     |
| FS      ^\ 28 0x1c | <  60 0x3c  | \  92 0x5c  | | 124 0x7c     |
| GS      ^] 29 0x1d | =  61 0x3d  | ]  93 0x5d  | } 125 0x7d     |
| RS      ^^ 30 0x1e | >  62 0x3e  | ^  94 0x5e  | ~ 126 0x7e     |
| US      ^_ 31 0x1f | ?  63 0x3f  | _  95 0x5f  |DEL 127 0x7f    |
```

We will fully develop a program to output this table later in this chapter. Before we create that program, let's look through the table for a moment.

Group 1 consists of control characters. This group has five columns that show the following:

- Column 1 is the mnemonic symbol for each control key.
- Column 2 shows its `printf()` format sequence, if it has one (some don't).
- Column 3 shows its keyboard equivalent, where ^ represents the *Ctrl* key on the keyboard, which is pressed simultaneously with the given character key.
- Column 4 shows the control key value in decimal form (base-10).
- Column 5 shows the control key value in hexadecimal form (base-16).

> Be careful with control keys! If you attempt to type any of the ASCII control characters into a terminal window, you may get unexpected and/or surprising results. There is no reason to ever use them, except for in programs that communicate with other devices. Please avoid the temptation to do so.

> A terminal window is a program that is designed to work exactly like a hardware terminal device but without the hardware. Terminal devices, which are now nearly extinct, consist of an input device—typically a keyboard—and an output device—typically a CRT screen. A terminal used for both input and output is sometimes called an **I/O device**. These were clunky, heavy pieces of equipment that were connected to a central computer or mainframe. They had no computing capability of their own and served only to input commands and data via the keyboard and echo keyboard entries and the results of commands via the CRT screen.

Note that the decimal and hexadecimal values are shown for each key. As a convention, hexadecimal numbers are preceded by `0x` to indicate that they are not decimal numbers. Hexadecimal numbers are made up of digits `0–9` and `a–f` or `A–F` for a total of 16 hexadecimal digits.

While we have not focused on binary (base-2), octal (base-8), or hexadecimal (base-16) number systems, this might be a good opportunity for you to familiarize yourself with the hexadecimal format. In my experience, you encounter and use hexadecimal far more often than you ever use octal or even binary. Compare the decimal value to its hexadecimal equivalent.

Each group has three columns that show the printable character, the value of the character in decimal form (base-10), and the value of the character in hexadecimal form (base-16):

- Group 2 consists of numerals and punctuation.
- Group 3 consists of all uppercase letters and some punctuation.
- Group 4 consists of all lowercase letters, some punctuation, and the delete (DEL) character.

There are a few things to notice about the organization of this character set, which includes the following:

- All of the control characters but one are in the first 32 values. DEL appears as the very last control character in the character set.
- Printable characters have values from 32 to 126 (groups 2, 3, and 4).
- The uppercase A character differs in value from the lowercase a character by 32, as do all the upper and lowercase characters. This was done to make converting characters between upper and lowercase simple. The bit pattern for any uppercase letter and its lowercase equivalent differs by only a single bit.
- Punctuation is mostly scattered about. While this may appear random, there is some rationale to it, primarily for collating/sorting—certain punctuation marks sort before digits, digits sort before uppercase letters, and lowercase letters sort last.
- Lastly, the entire character set uses only 7 bits of the 8-bit char data type. This is intentional because ASCII dovetails directly into UTF-8 and Unicode. This means that any single-byte character whose value is less than 127 (0 or greater) is an ASCII character. Because of this, if a character (byte value) is outside of that range, we can then test to see whether it is a part of a valid Unicode character.

It should come as no surprise that C requires the ASCII character set to fully represent itself. Of course, C does not need all of the control characters in this character set.

Beyond ASCII – UTF-8 and Unicode

The greatest advantage of 7-bit ASCII is that each character in the character set for English can be represented in a single byte. This makes storing text efficient and compact. The greatest disadvantage of 7-bit ASCII is that it represents a character set that is only suitable for English. ASCII can't properly represent other Romance languages based on the Roman alphabet, such as French, Spanish, German, the Scandinavian languages, or the Eastern European languages. For those, we must consider a more comprehensive character-encoding method—Unicode.

If we catalog all of the characters and ideograms for all of the languages on Earth—past and present—we find that 1,112,064 code points are needed to represent all of them with unique values. The term code point is used here instead of character because not all of the positions in this enormous code set are characters; some are ideograms. To represent a code set (think of a character set but much, much larger), we'll need to use 2-byte and 4-byte values for all of the code points.

Unicode is an industry-standard encoding system that represents all of the world's writing systems and consists of UTF-8 (1 byte), UTF-16 (2 bytes), UTF-32 (4 bytes), and several other encodings. Unicode is also known as a **Universal Coded Character Set** (**UCS**). Out of the enormity of Unicode, UTF-8 is the most widely used encoding. Since 2009, UTF-8 has been the dominant encoding of any kind. UTF-8 is able to use one to four bytes to encode the full 1,112,064 valid code points of Unicode.

The best thing about UTF-8 is that it is completely backward-compatible with 7-bit ASCII. Because of this, UTF-8 is widely used (by around 95% of the World Wide Web, in fact).

When UTF-16 or UTF-32 code sets are used, each and every character in that code set is either 2 bytes or 4 bytes, respectively. Another advantage of UTF-8 is that it provides a mechanism to intermix 1-, 2-, 3-, and 4-byte code points. By doing so, only the bytes that are needed for a code point are used, saving both storage space and memory space.

Covering programming in Unicode, UTF-16, UTF-32, wide characters, or any other encoding is beyond the scope of this book. Before we can master more complex code sets in C, we will focus primarily on the single-byte encoding of UTF-8 (ASCII). Where appropriate, we'll point out where ASCII and Unicode can coexist. For now, our focus will be on ASCII. The `Appendix` is where we will see Unicode provides some introductory strategies and the C standard library routines for dealing with multibyte code sets.

Operations on characters

Even though characters are integer values, there are only a few meaningful things we want to do with or to them. The first two things are declaration and assignment. Let's declare some character variables with the following code:

```
signed char   aChar;
       char   c1 , c2, c3 , c4;
unsigned char  aByte;
```

In C, `char` is the intrinsic data type that is one byte (8 bits). `aChar` is a variable that holds a signed value between −128 and 127 (inclusive). We explicitly use the `signed` keyword, even though it is unnecessary. Next, we declare four single-byte variables, each also having the −128 to 127 range. Variables are assumed to be `signed` unless explicitly specified as `unsigned`. Finally, we declare an `unsigned` single-byte variable, `aByte`, which can hold a value between 0 to 128.

We can also assign values at the declaration, as follows:

```
signed char aChar =  'A';
       char     c1 = 65 ;
       char     c2 = 'a';
       char     c3 = 97 ;
       char     c4 = '7';
unsigned char aByte = 7;
```

These declarations and assignments can be understood as follows:

1. First, `aChar` is declared and initialized with a character set value of A. This is indicated by the ' and ' characters.
2. Next, `c1` is assigned a literal integer value of 65. This value corresponds to the character set value for `'A'`. For reference, see the table provided earlier in this chapter. Using `'A'` is far easier than memorizing all the values of the ASCII table. The C compiler converts the `'A'` character into its character set value, 65.
3. Likewise, `c2` is assigned the `'a'` character value and `c3` is assigned the 97 literal integer value, which happens to correspond to the character set value for `'a'`.
4. Finally, we examine the difference between the `'7'` character (seven) and the 7 integer value. These are very different things in the character set. The character set value for `'7'` is 55 while the literal 7 integer value corresponds to the BEL control character. BEL will make the terminal make a simple beep sound. The point of these two assignments is to highlight the difference between the *character 7* (`'7'`)and the *literal value 7* (7).

To verify this behavior, let's prove it to ourselves. The following program makes the preceding declarations and then calls `showChar()` for each variable:

```
#include <stdio.h>

void showChar( char ch );

int main( void )   {
    signed char aChar = 'A';
           char c1    = 65 ;
```

```
         char c2     = 'a';
         char c3     = 97 ;
         char c4     = '1';
   unsigned char aByte = 1;

   showChar( aChar );
   showChar( c1 );
   showChar( c2 );
   showChar( c3 );
   showChar( c4 );
   showChar( aByte );
}
```

The `main()` function simply declares and initializes six variables. The real work of the program is in the `showChar()` function, which is shown as follows:

```
void showChar( char ch )   {
   printf( "ch = '%c' (%d) [%#x]\n" , ch , ch , ch );
}
```

The `showChar()` function takes `char` as its parameter and then prints out that value in three different forms—`%c` prints the value as a character, `%d` prints the value as a decimal number, and `%x` prints the value as a hexadecimal number. `%x` is modified with # to prepend `0x` to the output hexadecimal number; it now appears in the `printf()` format specifier as `%#x`.

With your chosen editor, create a new file called `showChar.c` and enter the `main()` and `showChar()` functions. Compile and run the program. You should see the following output and you may hear a bell sound:

```
> cc showChar.c -o showChar -Wall -Werror -std=c11
> showChar
ch = 'A' (65) [0x41]
ch = 'A' (65) [0x41]
ch = 'a' (97) [0x61]
ch = 'a' (97) [0x61]
ch = '7' (55) [0x37]
ch = '' (7) [0x7]
>
```

In the output, we see the character, its decimal value, and finally, its hex value.

Let's consider the `showChar()` function for Unicode compatibility. Currently, it takes `char`, or a single byte value, as its input parameter. This function works for ASCII but it won't work for multi-byte Unicode. Fortunately, this can be easily fixed to handle both ASCII and Unicode by changing the type of the input parameter from `char` to `int`, as follows:

```
void showChar( int ch) ...
```

When the input is a single byte (char), the function will coerce it to fill the 4-byte int variable and printf() will then handle it as if it were a single-byte char variable. When the input is a multi-byte Unicode character, it will also be coerced to fill the 4-byte int variable and printf() will also handle it properly.

Getting information about characters

The next thing we might want to do to individual characters has to do with figuring out what kind of character it is. Given a character from an input source, we may want to determine one or more of the following properties of that character:

- Is it a control character?
- Is it whitespace? (that is, does it include SPACE, TAB, LF, CR, VT, or HT?)
- Is it a digit or a letter?
- Is it in uppercase or not?
- Is it even ASCII?

Now, reflecting on the four groups of ASCII characters and how they are laid out, you might consider how you would write functions to test these properties. For instance, to see whether a character is a decimal digit, you could write the following:

```
bool isDigit( int c )  {
  bool bDigit = false;
  if( c >= '0' && c <= '9' )
    bDigit = true;
  return bDigit;
}
```

This function checks to see whether the value of the given character is greater than or equal to the value of the '0' character and whether it is less than or equal to the value of the '9' character. If it is, then this character is one of those digits, and true is returned. Otherwise, it is not in that range and false is returned. As a mental exercise, you might want to think through what the logic might be to check each of the preceding properties.

A function that checks for whitespace might look as follows:

```
bool isWhitespace( int c)  {
  bool bSpace = false;
  switch( c ) {
    case ' ':    // space
    case '\t':   // tab
    case '\n':   // line feed
```

```
      case '\v':    // vertical tab
      case '\f':    // form feed
      case '\r':    // carriage return
        bSpace = true;
        break;
      default:
        bSpace = false;
        break;
    }
    return bSpace;
  }
```

In the `isWhiteSpace()` function, a `switch()`... statement is used. Each `case` variable of the `switch()`... statement compares the given character to one of the whitespace characters. Even though some of the whitespace characters appear as if they are two characters (a backslash (\) and a character), the backslash escapes from the standard character meaning and indicates that the next character is a control character. If we wanted to assign the backslash character, we'd have to do so as follows:

```
  aChar = '\\' ;   // Backslash character
```

Notice how this fallthrough mechanism of `switch()`... works—if any of the cases are true, `bSpace` is set to `true` and then we break out of `switch()`.... Remember that it is a safe practice to always provide a `default:` condition for any `switch()`... statement.

For a final set of operations on characters, we may want to convert an uppercase character into a lowercase one or vice versa. Alternatively, we might want to convert a digit into its internal numerical value. To convert an uppercase letter into a lowercase one, we'd first check to see whether the character is an uppercase letter and if it is, add 32 to it; otherwise, do nothing, as follows:

```
  int toUpper( int c )  {
     if( c >= 'A' && c <= 'Z' ) c += 32;
    return c;
  }
```

To convert a lowercase character into uppercase, we'd likewise check to see whether it is a lowercase character and if so, subtract 32 from it.

To convert the character value of a digit to its numerical value, we add the following function:

```
int digitToInt( int c)   {
   int i = c;
   if( c >= '0' && c <= '9' ) i = c - '0';
   return i;
}
```

In digitToInt(), we first check to see that we have a digit. Then, we subtract the character value of '0' from the given character. The result is the digit's numeric value. Otherwise, the character is not a digit and we simply return the character value that was given.

While it is possible and even tempting to create your own methods/functions to perform these operations, many of them are already provided in the C Standard Library. For these, we look to the ctypes.h, the C standard library header file. There, you will find handy functions to perform character tests and conversions on a given character. The following functions perform simple tests on the given character, c :

```
int   isalnum(int c);     // alphabets or numbers
int   isalpha(int c);     // alphabet only
int   isascii(int c);     // in range of 0..127
int   iscntrl(int c);     // in range 0..31 or 127
int   isdigit(int c);     // number ('0'..'9')
int   islower(int c);     // lower case alphabet
int   isnumber(int c);    // number ('0'..'9')
int   isprint(int c);     // printable character
int   ispunct(int c);     // punctuation
int   isspace(int c);     // space
int   isupper(int c);     // upper case alphabet
```

These functions return 0 for FALSE and non-zero for TRUE. Note that the given character is presented as an int variable because it may be a Unicode 1-, 2-, 3-, or 4-byte code point. int allows the character, whether a single-byte or 4-byte character, to properly hold any of those character values. Therefore, we can expect these functions to work with any UTF-8 or Unicode characters.

Manipulating characters

The following functions alter a given character:

```
int digittoint(int c);   // convert char to its number value
int tolower(int c);      // convert to lower case
int toupper(int c);      // convert to upper case
```

These functions return the changed character, or the original character if the conversion is not necessary or not valid.

There are also other functions available in ctype.h. They have been omitted for simplicity. Some deal with non-ASCII characters; others deal with eclectic groupings of characters. If you are interested in learning more, you can explore ctype.h on your computer system.

We will see some of these functions in action later in this chapter after we introduce strings. However, before we move on to strings, let's take a first pass at creating the ASCII table shown earlier in this chapter. We will write a program that prints a single column of a table of printable characters. The program is surprisingly simple. To start, our approach will be to use a for()... loop to print a single grouping from the ASCII table. The basic loop is as follows:

```
#include <stdio.h>

int main( void )   {
  char c2;
  for( int i = 32 ; i < 64 ; i++ )   {
    c2 = i;
    printf( "%c %3d %#x" , c2 , c2 ,c2 );
    printf( "\n" );
  }
}
```

This loop prints the second group of ASCII characters in the range of 32 to 63—which is punctuation and digits. The printf() statement does three things—first, it prints c2 as a character with the %c format specifier, then it prints c2 as a decimal value with the %d format specifier, and finally, it prints c2 as a hexadecimal, or hex, value with the %x format specifier. # in this format specifier prepends the hex number with 0x; this convention clearly tells us that it is a hex number.

The concept of interpreting a value in different ways, as printf() does in this code statement, should not be new. If you recall from Chapter 3, *Working with Basic Data Types*, any value is simply a series of 0 and 1. The format specifiers embedded in the string parameter to printf() tell the function how to interpret the given values. In this case, we are printing the same value but in three different ways—as a character, as a decimal number, and as a hex number.

Create a file called printASCII.c and open the program. Compile and run the program. You should see the following output:

```
> cc printASCII_temp1.c -o printASCII_temp1 -Wall -Werror -std=c11
> printASCII_temp1
     32 0x20
 !   33 0x21
 "   34 0x22
 #   35 0x23
 $   36 0x24
 %   37 0x25
 &   38 0x26
 '   39 0x27
 (   40 0x28
 )   41 0x29
 *   42 0x2a
 +   43 0x2b
 ,   44 0x2c
 -   45 0x2d
 .   46 0x2e
 /   47 0x2f
 0   48 0x30
 1   49 0x31
 2   50 0x32
 3   51 0x33
 4   52 0x34
 5   53 0x35
 6   54 0x36
 7   55 0x37
 8   56 0x38
 9   57 0x39
 :   58 0x3a
 ;   59 0x3b
 <   60 0x3c
 =   61 0x3d
 >   62 0x3e
 ?   63 0x3f
>
```

We have one column printed. This is our starting point. To get the full ASCII table, we will modify this basic program several times until we get to our finished and complete ASCII table.

In the next iteration of `printASCII.c`, we want to add printing of groups 3 and 4 and add column heading lines to indicate what each column represents:

1. The code for the heading lines look like this:

```
printf( "| Ch Dec  Hex | Ch Dec  Hex | Ch Dec  Hex |\n" );
printf( "|-------------|-------------|-------------|\n" );
```

We use the vertical bar (|) as a visual guide to separate the groups. Each group has a character, its decimal value, and its hex value.

2. Next, we need to add some character variables for each of the groups:

```
char c1 , c2 , c3 , c4;
```

c1 will hold values for group 1 characters, c2 will hold values for group 2 characters, and so on. Note that we've added c1 for the group 1 control characters, even though we will ignore this capability for now.

3. Next, we need to change the `for()` ... loop to go from 0 to 31. By doing this, we can simply add an offset to the character for the proper group, as follows:

```
for( int i = 0 ; i < 32; i++) {
    c1 = i;    // <-- Not used yet (a dummy assignment for now).
    c2 = i+32;
    c3 = i+64;
    c4 = i+96;
```

4. Lastly, the `printf()` statement needs to print the characters for each group on a single line, as follows:

```
printf( "| %c %3d %#x | %c %3d %#x | %c %3d %#x |" ,
        c2 , c2 , c2 ,
        c3 , c3 , c3 ,
        c4 , c4 , c4 );
printf( "\n" );
}
```

This may appear more complex than before, but it's really just the same format sequence repeated three times, with variables to fill each format specifier.

If you made those changes to your version of `printASCII.c`, you will see the following output:

```
> cc printASCII_temp2.c -o printASCII_temp2 -Wall -Werror -std=c11
> printASCII_temp2
| Ch Dec  Hex | Ch Dec  Hex | Ch Dec  Hex |
|-------------|-------------|-------------|
|    32 0x20  | @  64 0x40  | `  96 0x60  |
| !  33 0x21  | A  65 0x41  | a  97 0x61  |
| "  34 0x22  | B  66 0x42  | b  98 0x62  |
| #  35 0x23  | C  67 0x43  | c  99 0x63  |
| $  36 0x24  | D  68 0x44  | d 100 0x64  |
| %  37 0x25  | E  69 0x45  | e 101 0x65  |
| &  38 0x26  | F  70 0x46  | f 102 0x66  |
| '  39 0x27  | G  71 0x47  | g 103 0x67  |
| (  40 0x28  | H  72 0x48  | h 104 0x68  |
| )  41 0x29  | I  73 0x49  | i 105 0x69  |
| *  42 0x2a  | J  74 0x4a  | j 106 0x6a  |
| +  43 0x2b  | K  75 0x4b  | k 107 0x6b  |
| ,  44 0x2c  | L  76 0x4c  | l 108 0x6c  |
| -  45 0x2d  | M  77 0x4d  | m 109 0x6d  |
| .  46 0x2e  | N  78 0x4e  | n 110 0x6e  |
| /  47 0x2f  | O  79 0x4f  | o 111 0x6f  |
| 0  48 0x30  | P  80 0x50  | p 112 0x70  |
| 1  49 0x31  | Q  81 0x51  | q 113 0x71  |
| 2  50 0x32  | R  82 0x52  | r 114 0x72  |
| 3  51 0x33  | S  83 0x53  | s 115 0x73  |
| 4  52 0x34  | T  84 0x54  | t 116 0x74  |
| 5  53 0x35  | U  85 0x55  | u 117 0x75  |
| 6  54 0x36  | V  86 0x56  | v 118 0x76  |
| 7  55 0x37  | W  87 0x57  | w 119 0x77  |
| 8  56 0x38  | X  88 0x58  | x 120 0x78  |
| 9  57 0x39  | Y  89 0x59  | y 121 0x79  |
| :  58 0x3a  | Z  90 0x5a  | z 122 0x7a  |
| ;  59 0x3b  | [  91 0x5b  | { 123 0x7b  |
| <  60 0x3c  | \  92 0x5c  | | 124 0x7c  |
| =  61 0x3d  | ]  93 0x5d  | } 125 0x7d  |
| >  62 0x3e  | ^  94 0x5e  | ~ 126 0x7e  |
| ?  63 0x3f  | _  95 0x5f  |   127 0x7f  |
>
```

Not bad—but wait! There is that pesky DEL character that has a value of 127. How might we deal with that?

The easiest solution is to add an `if()`... statement that checks whether c4 is the DEL character. If not, print the line out as before. If it is, then instead of printing c4 as a character, which actually deletes a character on the terminal, print the "DEL" string instead. The `printf()` format specifiers will need a slight change to reflect this, as follows:

```
printf("| %c %3d %#x | %c %3d %#x |%s %3d %#x |" ,
        c2 , c2 , c2 ,
        c3 , c3 , c3 ,
        "DEL" , c4 , c4 );
```

Now, your `printASCII.c` program should look as follows:

```
#include <stdio.h>

int main( void )  {
  char c1 , c2 , c3 , c4;
  printf("| Ch Dec  Hex | Ch Dec  Hex | Ch Dec  Hex |\n" );
  printf("|-------------|-------------|-------------|\n" );
  for( int i = 0 ; i < 32; i++)
  {
    c1 = i;     // <-- Not used yet (a dummy assignment for now).
    c2 = i+32;
    c3 = i+64;
    c4 = i+96;

    if( c4 == 127 ) {
      printf( "| %c %3d %#x | %c %3d %#x |%s %3d %#x |" ,
              c2 , c2 , c2 ,
              c3 , c3 , c3 ,
              "DEL" , c4 , c4 );
    } else {
      printf( "| %c %3d %#x | %c %3d %#x | %c %3d %#x |" ,
              c2 , c2 , c2 ,
              c3 , c3 , c3 ,
              c4 , c4 , c4 );
    }
    printf( "\n" );
  }
}
```

You might notice that each part of the `if()`... `else`... statement consists of only one statement. Nevertheless, even though the { and } block statements are not necessary since the logic is currently very simple, they are there for if or when this logic is altered and becomes more complicated. Also, notice how the spacing for each line clarifies what is happening.

Edit `printASCII.c` so that it looks like the preceding code. Compile and run it. You should now see the following:

```
[> cc printASCII.c -o printASCII -Wall -Werror -std=c11
[> printASCII
| Ch Dec  Hex | Ch Dec  Hex | Ch Dec  Hex |
|-------------|-------------|-------------|
|    32 0x20  | @  64 0x40  | `   96 0x60  |
| !  33 0x21  | A  65 0x41  | a  97 0x61  |
| "  34 0x22  | B  66 0x42  | b  98 0x62  |
| #  35 0x23  | C  67 0x43  | c  99 0x63  |
| $  36 0x24  | D  68 0x44  | d 100 0x64  |
| %  37 0x25  | E  69 0x45  | e 101 0x65  |
| &  38 0x26  | F  70 0x46  | f 102 0x66  |
| '  39 0x27  | G  71 0x47  | g 103 0x67  |
| (  40 0x28  | H  72 0x48  | h 104 0x68  |
| )  41 0x29  | I  73 0x49  | i 105 0x69  |
| *  42 0x2a  | J  74 0x4a  | j 106 0x6a  |
| +  43 0x2b  | K  75 0x4b  | k 107 0x6b  |
| ,  44 0x2c  | L  76 0x4c  | l 108 0x6c  |
| -  45 0x2d  | M  77 0x4d  | m 109 0x6d  |
| .  46 0x2e  | N  78 0x4e  | n 110 0x6e  |
| /  47 0x2f  | O  79 0x4f  | o 111 0x6f  |
| 0  48 0x30  | P  80 0x50  | p 112 0x70  |
| 1  49 0x31  | Q  81 0x51  | q 113 0x71  |
| 2  50 0x32  | R  82 0x52  | r 114 0x72  |
| 3  51 0x33  | S  83 0x53  | s 115 0x73  |
| 4  52 0x34  | T  84 0x54  | t 116 0x74  |
| 5  53 0x35  | U  85 0x55  | u 117 0x75  |
| 6  54 0x36  | V  86 0x56  | v 118 0x76  |
| 7  55 0x37  | W  87 0x57  | w 119 0x77  |
| 8  56 0x38  | X  88 0x58  | x 120 0x78  |
| 9  57 0x39  | Y  89 0x59  | y 121 0x79  |
| :  58 0x3a  | Z  90 0x5a  | z 122 0x7a  |
| ;  59 0x3b  | [  91 0x5b  | { 123 0x7b  |
| <  60 0x3c  | \  92 0x5c  | | 124 0x7c  |
| =  61 0x3d  | ]  93 0x5d  | } 125 0x7d  |
| >  62 0x3e  | ^  94 0x5e  | ~ 126 0x7e  |
| ?  63 0x3f  | _  95 0x5f  |DEL 127 0x7f |
> 
```

At this point, we have printed out the printable characters and their values and we have dealt with the rather out-of-place "DEL" control character to properly appear in our table. Before we can complete our ASCII table to print control characters without actually sending those control characters to our terminal, we need to learn a bit more about strings.

Remember, printing control characters to a terminal window actually controls that window's behavior as if it were a real terminal device. We don't want to do that without understanding more about why we'd even need to control the device.

Exploring C strings

We have explored individual characters and various operations on them. Dealing with individual characters is useful but more often, we will want to create words and sentences and operate on them. For this, we need a string of characters—or more simply, we need a string.

An array with a terminator

A string is an array of characters with one special property. This special property is that the element after the last character of the C string must itself be a special character—the NUL character. NUL has a value of 0. This character indicates the end of the string.

To implement a string, we extend the concept of an array to be a specially formatted array of characters; an array with an extra terminating NUL character. The terminating character is sometimes called a **sentinel**. This is a character or condition that signals the end of a group of items. The NUL character will be used as a sentinel when we loop through string elements; the sentinel will indicate that we have encountered every element of the string. Because of this, we must be careful to ensure that each string ends with NUL.

Where we use 'x' (single quotes) to indicate a single character, we use "Hello" (double quotes) to indicate a string literal, which is constant and cannot be changed. When double quotes are used to define a string, the null terminator is automatically added to and included in the array of characters. This also means that the string array always has one more element (for NUL) than the number of characters that are in the string. So, the "Hello" string is an array of six elements (five printable characters and the NUL character).

Without the terminating NUL character, we either have just an array of characters or we have an invalid string. In either case, we do *not* have a string. Furthermore, when we try to use standard string operations on an invalid string, mayhem will result. Mayhem also results when we loop through an array like this but the NUL sentinel is not present. For an array to be a string, the NUL terminator must be present.

Strengths of C strings

One of the greatest strengths of C strings is that they are simple, in the sense that they are built upon existing mechanisms—characters, arrays, and pointers. All of the considerations we have for arrays, pointers to arrays, and pointers to array elements also apply to strings. All of the ways we loop through arrays also apply to strings.

Another strength of C strings is that the C standard library comes with a rich set of functions with which to operate on strings. These functions make creating, copying, appending, extracting, comparing, and searching strings relatively easy and consistent.

Weaknesses of C strings

Unfortunately, C strings also have some great weaknesses. The foremost of these is the inconsistent application of the NUL terminator. Sometimes, the NUL terminator is automatically added, but at other times, the responsibility of adding it is left to the programmer. This inconsistency makes creating strings somewhat error-prone so that special attention must be given to correctly forming a valid string with the terminating NUL character.

A minor weakness of C strings is that they are not always efficient. To get the size of a string, for instance, the entire string must be traversed to find its end. In fact, this is how the strlen() function works; it traverses the entire string, counting each character before the first '\0' character it encounters. Often, this traversal may be done multiple times. This performance penalty is not quite as important on fast computing devices, but it remains a concern for slower, simpler computing devices and embedded devices.

For the remainder of this chapter and all the subsequent chapters, we will continue to use C strings so that you gain familiarity with using them. If, after working with C strings for some time, you find them too cumbersome, or you find it too easy to misuse them, causing instability in your programming projects, you may want to consider alternatives to C strings. One alternative is The Better String Library—bstrlib. bstrlib is stable, well-tested, and suitable for any software production environment. bstrlib is described briefly in the Appendix section of this book.

Declaring and initializing a string

There are a number of ways to declare and initialize a string. We will explore the various ways to both declare and initialize strings.

String declarations

We can declare a string in several ways. The first way is to declare a character array with a specified size, as follows:

```
char aString[8];
```

This creates an array of 8 elements, capable of holding seven characters (don't forget the terminating NUL character).

The next way to declare a string is similar to the first method but instead, we don't specify the size of the array, as follows:

```
char anotherString[];
```

This method is not useful unless we initialize anotherString, which we will see in the next section. If you recall from Chapter 14, *Understand Arrays and Pointers*, this declaration looks like a pointer in the form of an array declaration. In fact, without initialization, it is.

The last way to declare a string is to declare a pointer to char, as follows:

```
char * pString;
```

Again, this method not useful until pString is either initialized or actually points a string literal or string array, both of which must have already been declared. The last two methods, both without initialization, are useful as function parameter declarations to refer to a string that has already been declared and initialized.

All of these methods are more useful when the string is both declared and initialized in the same statement.

Initializing strings

When we declare and initialize a string array, there are a few more possibilities that must be understood. We will explore them now:

1. We can declare an empty string—that is, a string with no printable characters—as follows:

   ```
   char  string0[8] = { 0 };
   ```

   string0 is an array of 8 elements, all of which are initialized to NULL, the nul character, or simply 0.

2. Next, we can declare a string and initialize the array with individual characters, as follows:

   ```
   char  string1[8] = { 'h' , 'e' , 'l' , 'l', 'o' , '\0' };
   ```

When doing this, we must remember to add the `nul` character, or `'\0'`. Note that even though the array is declared to have 8 elements, we have only initialized six of them. This method is rather tedious.

3. Thankfully, the creators of C have given us an easier way to initialize a string, as follows:

```
char  string2[8] = "hello";
```

In this declaration, `string2` is declared to have 8 elements and is initialized with the `"hello"` string literal. Each character of the string literal is copied into the corresponding array element, including the terminating `nul` character (`'\0'`). By specifying an array size, we have to make certain that the array declaration is large enough to hold all the characters (plus the `nul` character) of the string literal. If we use an array size that is less than the length of the string literal (plus the `nul` character), a compiler error will occur. This is also tedious.

4. The creators of C didn't stop there. Again, thankfully, they provided an easier way to do this, as follows:

```
char  string3[]  = "hello";
```

In this declaration, by giving `string3` an unspecified size, we are telling the C compiler to allocate exactly the number of characters (plus the `nul` character) that is copied from the string literal, `"hello"`. The `string3` array now has six elements, but we didn't have to count them beforehand.

In each of the preceding array initializations, each element/character of the array can be accessed using the `[]` array notation or pointer traversal. Furthermore, each element/character of the array can be changed. The methods for doing this are identical to those shown in `Chapter 14`, *Understanding Arrays and Pointers*.

Declaring and initializing a character array of an unspecified size with a string literal is very different than declaring a pointer to character and initializing that with the address of that string literal. String literals—like literal numbers, say `593`—are strings, but they cannot be changed.

A pointer to character is declared and initialized with a string literal, as follows:

```
char* string4   = "hello";
```

`string4` is a pointer that points to the first character of the `"hello"` string literal. No characters are copied. `string4` can later be reassigned to point to some other string literal or string array. Furthermore, `"hello"` is a constant. So, while we can traverse this string, accessing each character element, we cannot change any of them.

We can manipulate string elements (characters) in a string array, but not in a string literal, in the same way that we would an array of any other data type. The following program illustrates both initializing strings in various ways and then changing the first character of each string:

```
#include <stdio.h>
#include <ctype.h>

int main( void )
{
  char   string0[8] = { 0 };
  char   string1[8] = { 'h' , 'e' , 'l' , 'l', 'o' , '\0' };
  char   string2[8] = "hello";
  char   string3[] = "hello";
  char*  string4    = "hello";
  printf( "A) 0:\"%s\" 1:\"%s\" 2:\"%s\" 3:\"%s\" 4:\"%s\"\n\n" ,
              string0 , string1 , string2 , string3 , string4 );

  string0[0] = 'H';
  string1[0] = 'H';
  string2[0] = toupper( string2[0]);
  string3[0] = toupper( string3[0]);
//  string4[0] = 'H';   // Can't do this because its a pointer
                        // to a string literal (constant).
  char* string5 = "Hello"; // assign pointer to new string
  printf( "B) 0:\"%s\" 1:\"%s\"  2:\"%s\"  3:\"%s\"  4:\"%s\"\n\n" ,
              string0 , string1 , string2 , string3 , string5 );
}
```

Let's examine each part of this program, as follows:

1. First, the character arrays are declared and initialized. `string0` is a string containing no printable characters or an empty string; it is also an array of 8 elements, as are `string1` and `string2`. These arrays are larger than they need to be. `string3` is an array of exactly the required size for the `"hello"` string, or, 6 elements (6, not 5—don't forget the terminating `nul` character). `string4` is a pointer to a string literal.

2. Next, these strings are printed using a single `printf()` function. To get a double quote mark (") to appear in the output, `\"` is used in the format string before and after each string specifier.

3. Finally, the first letter of each string array is changed to its uppercase letter. The first two strings are changed by assigning `'H'` to that element. The next two strings are changed using the `toupper()` standard library function.

Create the `simpleStrings.c` file and type in the preceding program. Save it, then compile and run it. You should see the following output:

```
> gcc simpleStrings.c -o simpleStrings  -Wall -Werror -std=c11
> simpleStrings
A) 0:""    1:"hello"   2:"hello"   3:"hello"   4:"hello"

B) 0:"H"   1:"Hello"   2:"Hello"   3:"Hello"   4:"Hello"

>
```

You can now use this program for further experimentation. For instance, what happens when you try to change the first letter of `string4`? What happens when you try to initialize `string1` to, say, "`Ladies and gentlemen`" (a string much longer than 8)? You might also try adding a loop by using `strlen()` or by checking for `'\0'` and converting each character of `string2` into uppercase. The `strlen()` function can be used by including `<string.h>`, described in the last section of this chapter. Solutions to these experiments can be found in the source file in the repository.

Passing a string to a function

Just as with arrays and pointers, there are a number of ways to pass a string to a function:

1. The first way is to pass the string explicitly, giving the array size of the string, as follows:

   ```
   Func1( char[8] aStr );
   ```

   This parameter declaration allows a string of up to seven characters, as well as the terminating `nul` character (`'\0'`), to be passed into `Func1()`. The compiler will verify that the array being passed in has exactly 8 char elements. This is useful when we are working with strings of limited size.

2. The next way is to pass the string without specifying the `char` array size, as follows:

   ```
   Func2( char[] aStr );
   Func3( int size, char[] aStr );
   ```

In `Func2()`, only the string name is passed. Here, we are depending on the fact that there is `'\0'`, a `nul` character in `aStr`. To be safer, the size of the string, as well as the string itself, can be passed into the function, as is done in `Func3()`.

3. Lastly, we can pass a pointer to the beginning of the string. The pointer may point to either an array of characters or it may point to a string literal:

```
Func4( char* pStr );
```

4. If in any of the functions you need to ensure that the string is not modified, you can use the `const` qualifier in any of the methods, as follows:

```
Func1_Immutable( const char[8] aStr );
Func2_Immutable( const char[] aStr );
Func3_Immutable(int size, const char[] aStr );
Func4_Immutable( const char* pStr );
```

Each of these function declarations indicates that the string characters passed into the body of function definition cannot be modified.

Empty strings versus null strings

When a string contains no printable characters, it is called an **empty string**. The following declarations are empty strings:

```
char* emptyString1[1] = { '\0' };
char* emptyString2[100] = { 0 };
char* emptyString3[8] = { '\0' , 'h' , 'e' , 'l' , 'l' , 'o' , '\0' } ;
```

The first empty string is a character array of a single element—the `nul` character, or `'\0'`. The second empty string is a character array of 100 elements, all of which are `'\0'`, the `nul` characters. The third empty string is also an empty string; even though it has printable characters, the `nul` character (`'\0'`) in the zeroth element signifies the end of the string, thereby making it empty. After the first `nul` character, `'\0'`, is encountered, it doesn't matter what comes after it; it is still seen as an empty string.

When an array reference or pointer to a string is null (nothing), it is called a **null string**. A null string points to nothing at all. The following declarations are null strings:

```
char  nullString1[];
char* pNullString2 = NULL;
```

The first null string is an uninitialized character array declaration. The second null string is a pointer to the character where the pointer value is NULL. pNullString2 will be a null string until a valid string address is assigned to it.

An empty string and a null string are not the same! One is an array with at least one '\0', the nul character; the other is nothing at all—nothing has been allocated or the null string reference is NULL (points to nothing).

The distinction between an empty string and a null string is particularly important when we create or use functions that expect a valid string (even if it is empty) but are given a null string. Mayhem will occur. To avoid mayhem, when you create string functions, be sure to check for the null string. When you use string functions, either verify a null string could be passed to it or check for the null string before calling the function.

Hello, World! revisited

There is one final way to pass a string into a function, which is to pass a string literal as a function parameter, as follows:

```
Func5( "Passing a string literal" );
```

In this function declaration, the "Passing a string literal" string literal is the string that is passed into Func5() when it is called. Func5() can be declared in any of the following ways:

```
void Func5( char[] aStr );
void Func5( char* aStr );
void Func5( const char[] aStr );
void Func5( const * aStr );
```

The first two declarations take a non-constant array name or pointer parameter, while the last two declarations take a constant array name or pointer parameter. Because the parameter string being passed into Func5() is a string literal, it remains a constant and its elements cannot be changed within the function body.

This is another kind of initialization and it is rather subtle. However, we have already seen this done many times. We first saw it in our very first program, Hello, World!, in Chapter 1, *Running Hello, World!*, with the following statement:

```
printf( "Hello, World!\n" );
```

Let's examine what is happening in this call to `printf()`. In this statement, the `"Hello, World!\n"` string literal, as well as a pointer, is allocated. The pointer points to the first character of this string and is passed into the function body. Within the function body, the string is accessed like any other array (either via a pointer or using array notation). However, in this case, each element of the array is constant—having been created from a string literal—and cannot be changed. When the function returns, both the string literal and the pointer to it are deallocated.

If we want to create a string and use it more than once or alter it before using it again, we would have to declare and initialize it, as follows:

```
char greeting[] = "hello, world!";
```

We could then use it in `printf()`, as follows:

```
printf( "%s\n" , greeting );
```

Then, perhaps, we might change it to all uppercase and print it again, as follows:

```
int i = 0;
while ( greeting[i] != '\0' ) {
  greeting[i] = toupper( greeting[i] );
}
printf( "%s\n" , greeting );
```

In these series of statements, we created a string and used it in multiple `printf()` statements, modifying the string between calls. Create a file called `greet.c` and put the previous statements in the `main()` function block. Remember to include `ctype.h` as well as `stdio.h` so that you can use the `toupper()` function. Compile and run the program. You should see the following output:

```
> cc greet.c -o greet -Wall -Werror -std=c11
> greet
hello, world!
HELLO, WORLD!
>
```

As you can see, first the greeting string of lowercase letters is printed. It is converted into uppercase letters and then printed. Notice how only characters that can be converted into uppercase are actually converted; the comma (,) and exclamation mark (!) remain unchanged.

Also, notice how we could have found the length of the string and used a `for()`... statement. However, because the string has a `sentinel` value, `\0`, which indicates the endpoint, we can more easily use a `while()`... statement.

Creating and using an array of strings

Sometimes, we need to create a table of related string values. This table, in one form or another, is often called a **lookup table**. Once we construct this table, we can then look up string values based on an index into the table. To declare a one-dimensional lookup table for the days of the week, where the array index is equal to the day of the week, we would make the following declaration:

```
char* weekdays[] = {  "Sunday" ,
                      "Monday" ,
                      "Tuesday" ,
                      "Wednesday" ,
                      "Thursday" ,
                      "Friday" ,
                      "Saturday" };
```

Notice that the strings are of different sizes. Also, notice that they are all string literals; this is acceptable because these names won't change. We can then use this table to convert a numerical day of the week to print the day, as follows:

```
int dayOfWeek = 3;
printf( "Today is a %s \n" , weekdays[ dayOfWeek ] );
```

A value of 3 for `dayOfWeek` will print the `"Wednesday"` string.

With a simple lookup table, we can create an array of string literals that represent the mnemonics of control characters to complete our ASCII table. We can create our control character lookup table as follows:

```
char* ctrl[] = { "NUL","SOH","STX","ETX","EOT","ENQ","ACK","BEL",
                 " BS"," HT"," LF"," VT"," FF"," CR"," SO"," SI",
                 "DLE","DC1","DC2","DC3","DC4","NAK","SYN","ETB",
                 "CAN"," EM","SUB","ESC"," FS"," GS"," RS"," US" };
```

Notice that each string literal is the same length; this is so that our table's columns align nicely, even though some mnemonics are two characters and some are three characters.

We are now ready to add the control characters to our ASCII table. Copy the
`printASCII.c` file to `printASCIIwithControl.c` and make the following changes:

1. Add the `ctrl[]` lookup table either before or after the declarations for c1
   through c4.
2. Before the first `printf()` function, add the following:

```
printf("| %s ^%c %3d %#4x ",
        ctrl[i] , c1+64 , c1 , c1 );
```

3. Before the second `print()` function, add the following:

```
printf("| %s ^%c %3d %#4x ",
        ctrl[i] , c1+64 , c1 , c1 );
```

4. The `printf()` statements are getting rather long. You can choose to simplify the
   `printf()` function in the `if()`... `else`... statement.
5. Your program should now look like the following:

```
#include <stdio.h>
int main( void ) {
    char* ctrl[] = {  "NUL","SOH","STX","ETX","EOT","ENQ","ACK","BEL",
                     " BS"," HT"," LF"," VT"," FF"," CR"," SO"," SI",
                     "DLE","DC1","DC2","DC3","DC4","NAK","SYN","ETB",
                     "CAN"," EM","SUB","ESC"," FS"," GS"," RS"," US"
};
    char c1 , c2 , c3 , c4;
    printf( "|-----------------" );
    printf( "|--------------------------------------------|\n" );
    printf( "| SYM Ch Dec  Hex " );
    printf( "| Ch Dec  Hex | Ch Dec  Hex | Ch Dec  Hex |\n" );
    printf( "|-----------------" );
    printf( "|-------------|-------------|-------------|\n" );
    for( int i = 0 ; i < 32; i++)
    {
      c1 = i;
      c2 = i+32;
      c3 = i+64;
      c4 = i+96;
      printf( "| %s ^%c %3d %#4x " ,
              ctrl[i] , c1+64 , c1 , c1 );
      printf( "|   %c %3d %#x " ,
              c2 , c2 , c2 );
      printf( "|   %c %3d %#x " ,
              c3 , c3 , c3 );

      if( c4 != 127 ) {
```

```
      printf( "|  %c %3d %#x \n" ,
             c4 , c4 , c4  );
    } else {
      printf( "|%s %3d %#x |\n" ,
             "DEL" , c4 , c4 );
    }
  }
  c1 = 0x7;
  printf("%c%c%c", c1 , c1 , c1);
}
```

6. Save this program, then build and run it. You should see the following output:

```
> gcc printASCIIwithControl.c -o printASCIIwithControl  -Wall -Werror -std=c11
> printASCIIwithControl
                 Table of 7-Bit ASCII and
              Single-Byte UTF-8 Character Sets

|Control Character|   Printable Characaters (except DEL)   |
|-----------------|---------------------------------------|
| SYM Ch Dec  Hex | Ch Dec  Hex | Ch Dec  Hex | Ch Dec  Hex |
|-----------------|-------------|-------------|-------------|
| NUL ^@   0    0 |    32 0x20 | @ 64 0x40 ||  `  96 0x60 |
| SOH ^A   1  0x1 | ! 33 0x21 | A 65 0x41 || a  97 0x61 |
| STX ^B   2  0x2 | " 34 0x22 | B 66 0x42 || b  98 0x62 |
| ETX ^C   3  0x3 | # 35 0x23 | C 67 0x43 || c  99 0x63 |
| EOT ^D   4  0x4 | $ 36 0x24 | D 68 0x44 || d 100 0x64 |
| ENQ ^E   5  0x5 | % 37 0x25 | E 69 0x45 || e 101 0x65 |
| ACK ^F   6  0x6 | & 38 0x26 | F 70 0x46 || f 102 0x66 |
| BEL ^G   7  0x7 | ' 39 0x27 | G 71 0x47 || g 103 0x67 |
|  BS ^H   8  0x8 | ( 40 0x28 | H 72 0x48 || h 104 0x68 |
|  HT ^I   9  0x9 | ) 41 0x29 | I 73 0x49 || i 105 0x69 |
|  LF ^J  10  0xa | * 42 0x2a | J 74 0x4a || j 106 0x6a |
|  VT ^K  11  0xb | + 43 0x2b | K 75 0x4b || k 107 0x6b |
|  FF ^L  12  0xc | , 44 0x2c | L 76 0x4c || l 108 0x6c |
|  CR ^M  13  0xd | - 45 0x2d | M 77 0x4d || m 109 0x6d |
|  SO ^N  14  0xe | . 46 0x2e | N 78 0x4e || n 110 0x6e |
|  SI ^O  15  0xf | / 47 0x2f | O 79 0x4f || o 111 0x6f |
| DLE ^P  16 0x10 | 0 48 0x30 | P 80 0x50 || p 112 0x70 |
| DC1 ^Q  17 0x11 | 1 49 0x31 | Q 81 0x51 || q 113 0x71 |
| DC2 ^R  18 0x12 | 2 50 0x32 | R 82 0x52 || r 114 0x72 |
| DC3 ^S  19 0x13 | 3 51 0x33 | S 83 0x53 || s 115 0x73 |
| DC4 ^T  20 0x14 | 4 52 0x34 | T 84 0x54 || t 116 0x74 |
| NAK ^U  21 0x15 | 5 53 0x35 | U 85 0x55 || u 117 0x75 |
| SYN ^V  22 0x16 | 6 54 0x36 | V 86 0x56 || v 118 0x76 |
| ETB ^W  23 0x17 | 7 55 0x37 | W 87 0x57 || w 119 0x77 |
| CAN ^X  24 0x18 | 8 56 0x38 | X 88 0x58 || x 120 0x78 |
|  EM ^Y  25 0x19 | 9 57 0x39 | Y 89 0x59 || y 121 0x79 |
| SUB ^Z  26 0x1a | : 58 0x3a | Z 90 0x5a || z 122 0x7a |
| ESC ^[  27 0x1b | ; 59 0x3b | [ 91 0x5b || { 123 0x7b |
|  FS ^\  28 0x1c | < 60 0x3c | \ 92 0x5c || | 124 0x7c |
|  GS ^]  29 0x1d | = 61 0x3d | ] 93 0x5d || } 125 0x7d |
|  RS ^^  30 0x1e | > 62 0x3e | ^ 94 0x5e || ~ 126 0x7e |
|  US ^_  31 0x1f | ? 63 0x3f | _ 95 0x5f ||DEL 127 0x7f |
>
```

You should also hear three system bell tones. We have added to our table a column grouping of ASCII control characters that shows the following:

- The control character mnemonic
- The control character's keyboard equivalent
- The decimal value of the control character
- The hex value of the control character

If you compare this output to the table given at the beginning of this chapter, you may find that we need to add just one more column to our control character group. That column is the printf() format string escape character for printable control characters. Recall that not all control characters are printable since they control other aspects of computer devices. To print this final column, we have to add another lookup table, as follows:

```
char format[] = {   '0',  0  ,  0  ,  0  ,  0 ,   0  ,  0 , 'a' ,
                    'b', 't' , 'n' , 'v' , 'f' , 'r' ,  0 ,  0 ,
                     0 ,  0  ,  0  ,  0  ,  0  ,  0  ,  0 ,  0 ,
                     0 ,  0  ,  0  , 'e' ,  0  ,  0  ,  0 ,  0 };
```

Notice that this is an array of single characters. To print the escape sequence for each control character that is printable, we'll need to build a string with the backslash (\) and that control character's key equivalent, as follows:

```
char fmtStr[] = "   ";
if( format[i] )
{
   fmtStr[1] = '\\';
   fmtStr[2] = format[i];
}
```

This snippet of code should appear within the for() . . . loop just before the first printf() function. At each iteration through the loop, fmtStr is reallocated and initialized to a string of three spaces. If its corresponding lookup table value is not NULL, then we modify fmtStr to have a backslash (\) and the appropriate character.

Then, the first printf() function needs to be modified, as follows:

```
printf( "| %s %s ^%c %3d %#4x " ,
         ctrl[i] , fmtStr , c3 , c1 , c1 );
```

Finally, we have to adjust the table's header lines to match. Copy the `printACIIwithControl.c` file to the file named `printASCIIwithControlAndEscape.c`. Make the following changes:

1. Add the `format[]` lookup table.
2. Add logic to build `fmtStr`.
3. Alter the `printf()` routine to include `fmtStr`.
4. Adjust the heading `printf()` functions to match the added column.

Compile and run `printASCIIwithControlAndEscape.c`. You should see the following output:

```
> gcc printASCIIwithControlAndEscape.c -o printASCIIwithControlAndEscape  -Wall
-Werror -std=c11
> printASCIIwithControlAndEscape
               Table of 7-Bit ASCII and
           Single-Byte UTF-8 Character Sets

| Control Characters |    Printable Characaters (except DEL)    |
|--------------------|------------------------------------------|
| SYM Fmt Ch Dec  Hex | Ch Dec  Hex | Ch Dec  Hex | Ch Dec  Hex |
|--------------------|-------------|-------------|-------------|
| NUL  \0 ^@  0    0 |    32 0x20 | @  64 0x40 ||  `  96 0x60 |
| SOH     ^A  1  0x1 | !  33 0x21 | A  65 0x41 ||  a  97 0x61 |
| STX     ^B  2  0x2 | "  34 0x22 | B  66 0x42 ||  b  98 0x62 |
| ETX     ^C  3  0x3 | #  35 0x23 | C  67 0x43 ||  c  99 0x63 |
| EOT     ^D  4  0x4 | $  36 0x24 | D  68 0x44 ||  d 100 0x64 |
| ENQ     ^E  5  0x5 | %  37 0x25 | E  69 0x45 ||  e 101 0x65 |
| ACK     ^F  6  0x6 | &  38 0x26 | F  70 0x46 ||  f 102 0x66 |
| BEL  \a ^G  7  0x7 | '  39 0x27 | G  71 0x47 ||  g 103 0x67 |
| BS   \b ^H  8  0x8 | (  40 0x28 | H  72 0x48 ||  h 104 0x68 |
| HT   \t ^I  9  0x9 | )  41 0x29 | I  73 0x49 ||  i 105 0x69 |
| LF   \n ^J 10  0xa | *  42 0x2a | J  74 0x4a ||  j 106 0x6a |
| VT   \v ^K 11  0xb | +  43 0x2b | K  75 0x4b ||  k 107 0x6b |
| FF   \f ^L 12  0xc | ,  44 0x2c | L  76 0x4c ||  l 108 0x6c |
| CR   \r ^M 13  0xd | -  45 0x2d | M  77 0x4d ||  m 109 0x6d |
| SO      ^N 14  0xe | .  46 0x2e | N  78 0x4e ||  n 110 0x6e |
| SI      ^O 15  0xf | /  47 0x2f | O  79 0x4f ||  o 111 0x6f |
| DLE     ^P 16 0x10 | 0  48 0x30 | P  80 0x50 ||  p 112 0x70 |
| DC1     ^Q 17 0x11 | 1  49 0x31 | Q  81 0x51 ||  q 113 0x71 |
| DC2     ^R 18 0x12 | 2  50 0x32 | R  82 0x52 ||  r 114 0x72 |
| DC3     ^S 19 0x13 | 3  51 0x33 | S  83 0x53 ||  s 115 0x73 |
| DC4     ^T 20 0x14 | 4  52 0x34 | T  84 0x54 ||  t 116 0x74 |
| NAK     ^U 21 0x15 | 5  53 0x35 | U  85 0x55 ||  u 117 0x75 |
| SYN     ^V 22 0x16 | 6  54 0x36 | V  86 0x56 ||  v 118 0x76 |
| ETB     ^W 23 0x17 | 7  55 0x37 | W  87 0x57 ||  w 119 0x77 |
| CAN     ^X 24 0x18 | 8  56 0x38 | X  88 0x58 ||  x 120 0x78 |
| EM      ^Y 25 0x19 | 9  57 0x39 | Y  89 0x59 ||  y 121 0x79 |
| SUB     ^Z 26 0x1a | :  58 0x3a | Z  90 0x5a ||  z 122 0x7a |
| ESC  \e ^[ 27 0x1b | ;  59 0x3b | [  91 0x5b ||  { 123 0x7b |
| FS      ^\ 28 0x1c | <  60 0x3c | \  92 0x5c ||  | 124 0x7c |
| GS      ^] 29 0x1d | =  61 0x3d | ]  93 0x5d ||  } 125 0x7d |
| RS      ^^ 30 0x1e | >  62 0x3e | ^  94 0x5e ||  ~ 126 0x7e |
| US      ^_ 31 0x1f | ?  63 0x3f | _  95 0x5f ||DEL 127 0x7f |
> ▓
```

You may have to fiddle with your `printf()` statements to get the headings just right. You now have your own table of the ASCII character set, which you can execute as needed.

As an added experiment, you might want to modify `printASCII.c` to print the characters from `128` to `255`. Since these are extended ASCII characters, they are not expected to be identical from one operating system to the next. There is no standard for extended ASCII characters. After you try this yourself, which I urge you to do, you can find the `printExtendedASCII.c` program in the code repository to compare with your version.

Common operations on strings – the standard library

Just as for characters, the C standard library provides some useful operations on strings. These are declared in the `string.h` header file. We will take a brief look at these functions here and then incorporate them into working programs in later chapters to do various interesting things.

Common functions

If you carried out one of the experiments in the earlier sections of this chapter, you will have already encountered the `strlen()` function, which counts the number of characters (excluding the terminating `nul` character) in a given string. The following is a list of some useful functions and what they do:

- **Copy, append, and cut strings**:
    - `strcat()`: Concatenates two strings. This appends a copy of one null-terminated string to the end of a target null-terminated string, then adds a terminating `'\0'` character. The target string must have sufficient space to hold the result.
    - `strcpy()`: Copies one string to another (including the terminating `'\0'` character).
    - `strtok()`: Breaks a string into tokens or sub-strings.
- **Compare strings**:
    - `strcmp()`: Compares two strings. Lexicographically compares two null-terminated strings.

- **Search characters in strings**:
  - `strchr()`: Locates a character in a string. This finds the first occurrence of the desired character in a string.
  - `strrchr()`: Locates a character in a string in reverse. This finds the last occurrence of the desired character in a string.
  - `strpbrk()`: Locates any set of characters in a string.
- **Search for one string in another string**:
  - `strstr()`: Locates a substring in a string.

In these functions, it is imperative that null-terminated strings are supplied. Therefore, some care must be exercised when using these functions to avoid mayhem.

Safer string operations

Sometimes, it is not possible to ensure that a null-terminated array of characters is provided. This is especially common when strings are read from a file, read from the console, or dynamically created in unusual ways. To prevent mayhem, a few string functions have a built-in limiter that only operates on the first N characters of the string array. These are considered safer operations and are described in the following list:

- **Copy and append strings**:
  - `strncat()`: Concatenates two strings. This appends a copy of up to N characters of one null-terminated string to the end of a target null-terminated string, then adds a terminating `'\0'` character. The target string must have sufficient space to hold the result.
  - `strncpy()`: Copies up to N characters of one string to another. Depending on the size of the destination, the destination string may either be filled with the `nul` characters or may not be null-terminated.
- **Compare strings**:
  - `strncmp()`: Compares two strings. Lexicographically, it compares no more than N characters of two null-terminated strings.

To see how these functions operation, create a file called `saferStringOps.c` and enter the following program:

```
#include <stdio.h>
#include <string.h>
#include <ctype.h>
```

```
void myStringNCompare ( char* s1 , char* s2 , int n);

int main ( void )   {
   char salutation[] = "hello";
   char audience[]   = "everybody";
   printf( "%s, %s!\n", salutation , audience );
   int lenSalutation = strlen( salutation );
   int lenAudience   = strlen( audience );
   int lenGreeting1 = lenSalutation+lenAudience+1;
   char greeting1[lenGreeting1];
   strncpy( greeting1 , salutation , lenSalutation );
   strncat( greeting1 , audience    , lenAudience );
   printf( "%s\n" , greeting1 );

   char greeting2[7] = {0};
   strncpy( greeting2 , salutation , 3 );
   strncat( greeting2 , audience    , 3 );
   printf( "%s\n" , greeting2 );
```

In the first part of this program, we are using `strncpy()` and `strncat()` to build strings from other strings. What is significant is that using these functions forces us to consider string lengths, as well as whether the resulting string will be large enough to hold to combined strings.

The remainder of the program is as follows:

```
   myStringNCompare ( greeting1 , greeting2 , 7 );
   myStringNCompare ( greeting1 , greeting2 , 3 );
   char* str1 = "abcde";
   char* str2 = "aeiou";
   char* str3 = "AEIOU";
   myStringNCompare ( str1 , str2 , 3 );
   myStringNCompare ( str2 , str3 , 5 );
}

void myStringNCompare ( char* s1 , char* s2 , int n)
{
   int result = strncmp( s1 , s2 , n );
   char* pResultStr;
   if( result < 0 )        pResultStr = "less than (come before)";
   else if( result > 0 ) pResultStr = "greater than (come after)";
   else                    pResultStr = "equal to";
   printf( "First %d characters of %s are %s %s\n" ,
           n, s1 , pResultStr , s2 );
}
```

In this part of the program, we use `strncmp()` in our own wrapper function, `myStringNCompare()`, to compare the sort order of the various pairs of strings. A wrapper function is a function that performs a desired simple action as well as wraps additional actions around it. In this case, we are adding a `printf()` statement to indicate whether one string is less than, equal to, or greater than another string. Less than means that the first string comes alphabetically before the second string. In each string comparison, we limit the comparison to the first *N* characters of the string. Note also that lowercase letters are greater than (come after) uppercase letters; this implies that care must be taken when comparing strings of mixed cases.

Save, compile, and run the program. You should see the following output:

```
> cc saferStringOps.c -o saferStringOps -Wall -Werror -std=c11
> saferStringOps
hello, everybody!
helloeverybody
heleve
First 7 characters of helloeverybody are greater than (come after) heleve
First 3 characters of helloeverybody are equal to heleve
First 3 characters of abcde are less than (come before) aeiou
First 5 characters of aeiou are greater than (come after) AEIOU
>
```

Notice in these examples how `strncmp()` compares only the first *N* characters of each string and ignores the rest. I would encourage you to further experiment with the copy, concatenation, and comparison operations on various strings of your choosing to get a good feel for how these functions operate.

There are a number of other string functions, but their use is highly specialized. They are as follows:

- `stpcpy()`: Like `strcpy()` but returns a pointer to the terminating `'\0'` character of `dst`.
- `strpncpy()`: Like man but returns a pointer to the terminating `'\0'` character of `dst`.
- `strchr()`: Locates the first occurrence of a character in a string from the left.
- `strrchr()`: Locates the first occurrence of a character in a string from the right.
- `strspn()`: Finds the first character in a string that is not in the given character set.
- `strcspn()`: Finds the first character in a string that is in the given character set.
- `strpbrk()`: Finds the first occurrence in a string of any character in the given character set.

- `strsep()`: Finds the first occurrence in the given character set and replaces it with a `'\0'` character.
- `strstr()`: Finds the first occurrence of a string in another string.
- `strcasestr()`: Like `strstr()` but ignores cases of both strings.
- `strnstr()`: Finds the first occurrence of a string in another string searching no more than *N* characters.
- `strtok()`: Isolates **tokens** in a string. Tokens are separated by any character in the given delimiter character set.
- `strtok_r()`: Similar to `strtok()`.

Further explanation about the use of these functions is beyond the scope of this book. They are listed for completeness only.

Summary

In this chapter, we explored the elements of strings—characters. In particular, we explored the details of ASCII characters and how they are organized by developing a program in several iterations to print out a complete ASCII table. We also explored some simple operations on characters using the C standard library.

From there, we saw how C strings are special arrays made up of characters and a terminating NUL character. The NUL terminating character is something to which we must pay particular attention to when we create and manipulate strings. We explored how strings and string operations are built on other existing C concepts of arrays and pointers. We explored the difference between string literals, which are constant and modifiable strings. We further saw how to pass both of them to functions. All of these string concepts have been employed in the program we've developed to print the full 7-bit ASCII character set table. Finally, we introduced some basic string functions from the C standard library; these will be further explored in later chapters.

Even though characters and strings are built upon existing C concepts, there is quite a bit to absorb in this chapter. I urge you to work through each of the programs and attempt the experiments on them on your own before proceeding to the following chapters.

One of the most important programming skills demonstrated in this chapter is the process of iterative program development. That is, with a rather complex end result in mind, we started by creating a simple program to produce a small but essential part of the result. In the first iteration, we printed just a single column of characters. Each time we revisited that program, we added more functionality until we achieved our desired end result—we printed more columns. Then, we considered the DEL character. Finally, we took two iterations to print control character symbols and their printf() forms.

With the completion of this chapter, we have covered the essentials of C programming syntax. In subsequent chapters, we will explore the various ways that we can use C to solve useful and interesting problems. In each chapter, we will build upon all of the concepts introduced up to this point, as well as introduce the important, yet somewhat abstract, programming concepts that will make our programs robust and reliable.

16
Creating and Using More Complex Structures

In the real world, objects that we may want to model with data types and then manipulate with our program code are often best expressed as collections—sometimes complex collections—of the various data types we have already encountered. We have seen how to make homogenous collections with arrays, where all of the values in the collection are of the same type and size. We have also seen how to make heterogeneous collections with structures, where the various types in the structure are simple intrinsic types, even if they are not all the same type in the real world.

In this chapter, we will explore more complex structures. These include the following:

- Arrays of structures
- Structures consisting of arrays
- Structures consisting of other structures
- Structures consisting of arrays of structures

This may sound bewilderingly complex at first, but it is not. In reality, this is a logical extension of the concepts we have already explored using intrinsic types to create combinations of structures and arrays. We are simply expanding the kinds of data types that we can group into structures and arrays to also include other structures and arrays. We will also explore some new syntax to access elements of these complex structures.

It is my hope that with this exploration, you will see how C establishes simple rules for basic concepts and then uniformly extends them to more complex topics. We have already seen this with how single-dimensional arrays are logically extended to multi-dimensional arrays. We have also seen this with how arrays can be extended to create strings. We will now see this with complex structures.

As we explore these complex structures, we will greatly expand our ability to model real-world objects. As we do that, we will also expand how we think about how to manipulate those complex objects with functions that operate specifically on a given complex structure. Furthermore, we will see how pointers make this manipulation both straightforward and efficient.

The following topics will be covered in this chapter:

- Creating an array of structures
- Accessing structure elements within an array
- Manipulating an array of structures
- Creating a structure consisting of other structures
- Accessing structure elements within the structure
- Manipulating a structure consisting of other structures
- Creating a structure with arrays
- Accessing array elements within a structure
- Manipulating array elements within a structure
- Creating a structure with an array of structures
- Accessing individual structure elements of the array within a structure
- Manipulating a structure with an array of structures

To illustrate these concepts, we will continue our development of the `card4.c` program that we encountered in `Chapter 10`, *Creating Custom Data Types with typedef*. By the end of this chapter, we will have a basic playing card program that will create a deck of cards, shuffle it into a random order, and then deal out four hands of five cards for each hand.

Technical requirements

Continue to use the tools you chose in the *Technical requirements* section of `Chapter 1`, *Running Hello, World!*.

The source code for this chapter can be found at `https://github.com/PacktPublishing/Learn-C-Programming`.

Introducing the need for complex structures

We have explored C's intrinsic types—integers, floats/doubles, Booleans, and characters. We have also explored C's custom types—structures and enumerations. We have seen how a structure is a single instance of a grouping of intrinsic types to represent a set of related characteristics of something. Additionally, we have explored C's collection type—arrays, which are groups containing all of the same type of thing.

Each of the data types we have explored more or less represent real-world objects that we may wish to manipulate. More often, however, real-world things are far more complicated. Therefore, these types alone may not adequately represent the real-world object we want to model and manipulate. So, we need to learn how to combine structures with arrays and arrays of structures to be able to represent a much broader set of real-world things. In doing so, we can model them and then manipulate them with C programs. Complex representations of real-world things are often called **data structures**.

Creating a data structure adds significantly to the meaning and context of each of the values that comprise it. For example, a value that represents a length is not as meaningful alone as a group of values that represents not just the length, but also the width, height, and a set of angles that describes a solid object. With this grouping, each of those values is related in a way that might not be obvious if they were not otherwise grouped together. The data structure becomes a logical representation of the real-world object.

The core concept of programming real-world things involves two levels of abstraction:

- To represent the thing in a minimal but essential manner
- To manipulate the thing or things in meaningful ways for our purposes

We represent the essential characteristics of the thing with data structures. We are unlikely to represent every characteristic of the thing; we represent only the characteristics of the thing we care to manipulate. We also choose a set of manipulations on the thing—its data structure. Not all manipulations are worthwhile or valid. Some manipulations are simple and may only need to be included in a set—that is, is this like other things, or simple equality? (That is, does one thing have identical qualities to another?) Other manipulations can be much more complex depending on the thing being represented and can involve a single thing or multiple things, such as adding two objects together or determining whether one object is greater than another.

As we learn how to create complex data structures, we will explore how to access the various parts of each kind of data structure and then perform manipulations, treating each data structure as a whole, rather than as individual parts.

Revisiting card4.h

We left Chapter 10, *Creating Custom Data Types with typedef*, with the card.h program and card5.c, which split card4.c into a header file and an implementation file. However, instead of going further with multiple-file program development, we will return to card4.c and rework a few things to include the knowledge we've gained since Chapter 10, *Creating Custom Data Types with typedef*. We'll use it to create a series of programs, carddeck.c. carddeck.c will start out simple, but we will continue to modify it until we've added all the complex structures needed. This will remain a single file throughout this chapter. We will see how to logically split up our final carddeck.c program into multiple files and then build it in Chapter 24, *Working with Multi-File Programs*.

Before we begin adding complex structures to our carddeck.c series of programs, we need to rework card4.c to a simpler starting point. So, let's backtrack a little bit. Make a copy of the card4.c file and rename the copy carddeck_0.c. If you have been creating each program file in the same directory, now might be a good time to create a folder for the files we will create in this chapter. You might then have a folder path such as the following:

$HOME/PackT/LearnC/Chapter16

Here, $HOME is the home directory for the username you used to log in to your computer.

Instead of using $HOME, you may be accessing your folders with the tilde (~) symbol, as follows:

~/PackT/LearnC/Chapter16

Both file paths access the same file directory.

You might already have a file organization system with folders named Chapter01 through Chapter15 in your file hierarchy. This sort of organization mirrors the way files are stored in the source code repository. Now, you can move carddeck_0.c from where it was created to ../Chapter16.

carddeck_0.c has a number of structures and functions that we no longer need. Well, not really; we'll add them back later, but they will be different enough that we can delete them for now. Open carddeck_0.c in your editor and remove the struct Hand definition, the function prototypes, all the statements in main(), and all of the function definitions that follow main().

Your file should now consist of two `#include` statements, the enum `Suit` and enum `Face` definitions, a `struct Card` definition, and an empty `main()` function. It should look as follows:

```
#include <stdio.h>
#include <stdbool.h>

typedef enum {
  club = 1,  diamond,  heart,   spade
} Suit;

typedef enum {
  one = 1, two,  three, four, five,   six,   seven,
  eight,   nine, ten,   jack, queen, king, ace
} Face;

typedef struct
{
  Suit suit;
  int  suitValue;
  Face face;
  int  faceValue;
  bool isWild;
} Card;

int main( void )
{
}
```

Save this file and compile it. You shouldn't receive any error or warning messages and the compilation should succeed. Even though the program does nothing, it is still a valid program. We will call this our first **known-good program**. As we add more to this program, we will move in a stepwise fashion from one known-good program to the next known-good version of our program. In this manner, we can build what will become a complex program step by step and limit the level of possible confusion that might occur between steps.

After decades of programming, my personal experience is that it is always easier, faster, and less painful to progress from one known-good program state to the next known-good program state, adding and changing any aspects of your program as needed until you finally arrive at the desired end. The number of changes made and the lines of code added between steps are usually not trivial (often, a dozen or two of lines of code are needed), but are also not so excessive that you have hundreds of lines of new, untested code. If you make too large a step and the compiler fails or the program returns a bad output, the problems are rarely simple to find.

There is seldom a single issue in that huge mass of code changes. Therein lies the challenge—trying to work through a lot of untried, untested code, such that you don't have a good idea of where to start looking for the problems you've unwittingly introduced. So, we will employ a method of making small, stepwise changes throughout this chapter.

Let's add one more set of changes before we move on. Open `carddeck_0.c` and add the following to the `main()` function:

```
int main( void ) {
  Card aCard;

  aCard.suit       = diamond;
  aCard.suitValue  = (int)diamond;
  aCard.face       = seven;
  aCard.faceValue  = (int)diamond;
  aCard.isWile     = true;

  PrintCard( &aCard );
  printf( "\n" );
}
```

This should be familiar from earlier chapters. We declare a `Card` structure and then assign values to each element of the `aCard` variable structure. We also print the values with the `PrintCard()` function. But wait—we need to add that function back in. Notice that when we call the function here, we are using the address of `aCard`, so the function declaration and definition should take a pointer parameter. Add the following function prototype before `main()`:

```
void PrintCard( Card* pCard );
```

After the `main()` function body, add the following function definition:

```
void PrintCard( Card* pCard ) {
  char cardStr[20] = {0};
  CardToString( pCard , cardStr );
  printf( "%18s" , cardStr );
}
```

This function is quite a bit different t0 the `printCard()` function from Chapter 10, *Creating Custom Data Types with typedef.* Instead of copying the structure via the function parameter, here, we are using a pointer to the structure. Only the address of the structure is copied into the function parameter, not the whole structure.

Before, we used multiple `printf()` statements in two `switch()`... statements to print each element of the card. Here, we only use one `printf()` call.

In this version of `PrintCard()`, not only is the name slightly different from before, but we are also declaring a character array into which we'll create a string describing the card. The `CardToString()` function will do that. Then, we'll print the resulting string with `printf()`. The `%18s` format specifier constrains the string output to the 18 characters we actually need to see (rather than 20).

So now, with this approach, we need a function prototype for `CardToString()`. Add the following prototype before `main()`:

```
void CardToString( Card* pCard , char pCardStr[20] );
```

Next, add the following function definition to the end of the file:

```
void CardToString( Card* pCard , char pCardStr[20] )  {
  switch( pCard->face )   {
    case two:   strcpy( pCardStr ,  "    2 " ); break;
    case three: strcpy( pCardStr ,  "    3 " ); break;
    case four:  strcpy( pCardStr ,  "    4 " ); break;
    case five:  strcpy( pCardStr ,  "    5 " ); break;
    case six:   strcpy( pCardStr ,  "    6 " ); break;
    case seven: strcpy( pCardStr ,  "    7 " ); break;
    case eight: strcpy( pCardStr ,  "    8 " ); break;
    case nine:  strcpy( pCardStr ,  "    9 " ); break;
    case ten:   strcpy( pCardStr ,  "   10 " ); break;
    case jack:  strcpy( pCardStr ,  " Jack " ); break;
    case queen: strcpy( pCardStr , "Queen " ); break;
    case king:  strcpy( pCardStr ,  " King " ); break;
    case ace:   strcpy( pCardStr ,  "  Ace " ); break;
    default:    strcpy( pCardStr ,  "  ??? " ); break;
  }
  switch( pCard->suit )   {
    case spade:   strcat( pCardStr , "of Spades  "); break;
    case heart:   strcat( pCardStr , "of Hearts  "); break;
    case diamond: strcat( pCardStr , "of Diamonds"); break;
    case club:    strcat( pCardStr , "of Clubs   "); break;
    default:      strcat( pCardStr , "of ???s    "); break;
  }
}
```

This function looks similar to the `printCard()` function. Instead of using the `printf()` calls, we are calling `strcpy()` in the first `switch()`… statement and `strcat()` in the second `switch()`… statement. We use a character array that is large enough to hold all of our card name characters (don't forget the NULL character at the end). In reality, we need a character array that is only 18 bytes in size, but we rounded it up to 20.

Recall how we access the two structure member elements with the -> notation. We are using a pointer to a Card structure in this function to avoid copying structures into function parameters. When structures are complex and/or very large, the use of pointers can be significantly more efficient for function calls, especially if the function may be called hundreds or thousands of times, for instance, or when we have large arrays of possibly large structures.

Note how we created a character array outside of our call to CardToString(), then filled the character array in CardToString(), and then used the constructed string before exiting PrintCard(). We did this because strcpy() and strcat() do not allocate memory for us; we must do it ourselves. We can't allocate memory in CardToString() because it would be deallocated when we leave the function and then unavailable to the printf() statement, where it is needed. So, we need to allocate the character array in the calling function and fill it in the called function so that we can then use it after we return from the called function. The character array is then deallocated after we have used it when we exit PrintCard(). This is a common C pattern for string creation and usage.

The reasons for making these changes to PrintCard() are as follows:

- First, we get to use some common C string functions in CardToString().
- Second, rather than print a single card on each line, later on, we will print four cards per line.

The preceding printCard() routine had the new line embedded within it; therefore, it did not allow us to do what we now want.

As a checkpoint, you may want to save this file and compile it. Did it compile? No, because we forgot to include the string.h header file that makes strcpy() and strcat() visible to our program. Add the following to the top of your file:

```
#include <string.h>
```

Save, compile, and run the program. You should see the following output:

```
> cc carddeck_0.c -o carddeck_0 -Wall -Werror -std=c11
> carddeck_0
        7 of Diamonds
>
```

There is one final change to this version of `carddeck_0.c` to be made. Currently, we have two operations on a `Card` structure—`PrintCard()` and `CardToString()`. The last one to add is `InitializeCard()`. Change `main()` to the following:

```
int main( void )  {
    Card aCard;
    InitializeCard( &aCard, diamond , seven , true );
    PrintCard( &aCard );
    printf( "\n" );
}
```

Next, after `main()`, add the following function definition:

```
void InitializeCard( Card* pCard, Suit s , Face f , bool w )  {
    pCard->suit      = s;
    pCard->suitValue = (int)s;
    pCard->face      = f;
    pCard->faceValue = (int)f;
    pCard->isWild    = w;
}
```

Notice that we simply moved the statements from `main()` into the `InitializeCard()` function. This change made `main()` both simpler and clearer. Also, the `InitializeCard()` function tells us exactly which values we need in order to populate a `Card` structure properly.

Save, compile, and run the program. You should see the following output (which is the same as before this change):

```
> cc carddeck_0.c -o carddeck_0 -Wall -Werror -std=c11
> carddeck_0
      7 of Diamonds
>
```

To summarize this section, we added three operations to `Card` for the following reasons:

- Each of these routines has specific knowledge of the `Card` structure. Most of the rest of the program doesn't need to know the details and can rely on these operations.
- The caller of these routines needs to know very little about the `Card` structure.
- By focusing the functionality on a single function, we, as programmers, can focus on a smaller set of operations.
- The interaction between the caller and the called function is well-defined.

- By using these operations on a given structure, the behavior is consistent and known.
- If the structure changes, we would need to focus on changes to just the operations on that structure and can ignore large parts of the program. This leads to a more consistent and reliable program operation as the program evolves over time.

These motivations are compelling. As the objects that we model and our programs become more complex, we need to simplify our thinking about solving the larger problem. We can do this by solving a redefined yet smaller set of problems. Here, we are the ones who break down the larger problem into a set of smaller problems. The solution to the larger problem, then, is composed of the set of solutions we made for our smaller problem set. Furthermore, it is easier to modify a small set of routines for changes to a single structure than it is to make these changes in many places over a large program without these routines.

At this point, we have reviewed a wide variety of C concepts that were explored in Chapters 11, *Working with Arrays*, through Chapter 15, *Working with Strings*. We have also introduced some very important new programming concepts. In essence, we have taken card4.c and changed it into a more flexible version that does the same things but can more easily be extended for new functionality. Now would be a good time to review the steps we performed to create carddeck_0.c before we move on to the next section and look at carddeck_1.c, the next iteration of this program:

1. Start with card4.c as a starting point for carddeck_0.c by eliminating a bunch of structures and functions. These will be added back later.
2. Create a function to print a card using a pointer. This function creates a string to be populated by another function and then prints that string.
3. Create a sub-function whose only purpose is to populate the string given to it with a description of the card, returning that string to the calling function.
4. Create a function to initialize a card using a pointer. This function centralizes knowledge of the fields needed to create a card.
5. Rework main() to verify our new functions.

You may notice that except for the new use of pointers in our functions, much of this code is similar to the statements found in card4.c. Pay particular attention to how these have been reworked into more general functions.

If you download the file in the repository, you may notice that the line spacing is different and comments are added. This is done to save space in the text while keeping the program listings valid.

Understanding an array of structures

Before we begin with the next set of changes, make a copy of carddeck_0.c and rename it carddeck_1.c. In this section, we will make changes to carddeck_1.c.

Probably the simplest of the complex structures we will explore in this chapter is an array of structures. Recall that all the elements of an array are of a single type and size. While before, we created arrays of one intrinsic type or another, we will now create an array of one custom type.

Creating an array of structures

In the carddeck_1.c program, we need to model a deck of cards. To do this, we will create an array of the Card structures, as follows:

```
Card deck[52];
```

With this statement, we have created an array of 52 cards.

Note how, in the preceding definition, 52 is a magic number; that is, it is a literal number that has a special meaning. However, there is no context associated with that number unless it is stated in the comments. One problem with magic numbers is that as a program evolves or is applied to different uses, the magic numbers aren't all always updated properly. To avoid this problem, we will define some convenience constants, as follows:

```
enum   {
  kCardsinDeck = 52,
  kCardsinHand =  5,
  kCardsinSuit = 13,
  kNumHands    =  4
}
```

This enum statement declares four constants whose values we defined for each one, these are named literal constants. We would like to have used the following:

```
const int kCardsInDeck = 52;
const int kCardsInHand = 5;
...
```

We cannot use them since we will need them to declare arrays. C sees a const int as a variable even though it is a read-only one. So, when we declare an array with a constant size, C will not permit the use of a const int but will permit the use of a constant.

We can then use this constant, as follows:

```
Card deck[ kCardsInDeck ];
```

This statement declares a deck to have 52 cards, the same as before, but now if, for any reason, we add, say, 2 wildcards to our deck or, say, we want to play a game that uses 104 cards (two decks), we need to simply change our constant value and recompile. The benefit of using this constant will become even more obvious when we create methods to manipulate our deck.

While we're at it, let's create a few more convenience constants pertaining to a card, as follows:

```
const bool kWildCard    = true;
const bool kNotWildCard = false;
```

The last two Boolean constants make it clear whether a card is wild or not and provide more context than just `true` or `false` for the `isWild` property of a card. We can use the `const bool` type here because these will not be used in any array declarations.

To `carddeck_1.c`, add the four constant value definitions before the `main()` function. Next, add the deck array definition to the `main()` function. Save and compile the program. You should not see any errors.

Accessing structure elements within an array

Now that we have an array of 52 cards, how do we access, say, the fourth card?

We can do so with the following declaration:

```
Card aCard = deck[ 3 ];
```

Here, we've declared a new card variable (a structure)—aCard—and assigned (copied) the structure from the fourth element of `deck` to it. We now have two copies of the same structure with each member copied in each. If we make any modifications to `aCard`, they are not made to `deck[3]` because we are operating on a different structure address than that found at `deck[3]`.

To modify the elements of the structure in the fourth array element directly, we use dot (.) notation, as follows:

```
deck[3].suit      = spade;
deck[3].suitValue = (int)spade;
deck[3].face      = five;
```

```
deck[3].faceValue = (int)five;
deck[3].isWild    = kNotWildCard;
```

Because of operator precedence, deck[3] is evaluated first, which gives us a structure. The dot (.) notation is then evaluated, which gives us a specific element within the structure.

Modify main() to initialize a single card, as follows:

```
int main( void ) {
   Card deck[ kCardsInDeck ];

   deck[3].suit      = spade;
   deck[3].suitValue = (int)spade;
   deck[3].face      = five;
   deck[3].faceValue = (int)five;
   deck[3].isWild    = kNotWildCard;
```

Sometimes, it is either convenient or necessary to use a pointer to access the structure elements in the array. We can do so as follows:

```
Card* pCard = &deck[3];
pDeck->suit      = spade;
pDeck->suitValue = (int)spade;
pDeck->face      = five;
pDeck->faceValue = (int)five;
pDeck->isWild    = kNotWildCard;
```

First, a pointer to a Card structure is created and is assigned the address of the fourth element of the deck. Remember that the target of a pointer must first exist before assigning its address to a pointer. In this case, deck[52] has already been created. Again, because of operator precedence, deck[3] is evaluated, which refers to a Card structure; then, & is evaluated to the address of that Card structure. Using the pointer variable with the arrow (->) notation, we then assign a value to each element of the structure.

We are using a pointer to refer to a single structure location, which is deck[3]. No copies of the structure nor any of its members are created.

This is identical to using a pointer to access a single structure. Using pointers to structures gives us the flexibility to modify the structure within a function call, thereby eliminating the need to copy the structure into the function and then copy it back out after it has been modified in the function.

Now, we can modify `main()` to initialize the fourth card and print it out, as follows:

```
int main( void ) {
  Card deck[ kCardsInDeck ];

  Card* pCard = &deck[3];
  pCard->suit = spade;
  pCard->suitValue = (int)spade;
  pCard->face = five;
  pCard->faceValue = (int)five;
  pCard->isWild = kNotWildCard;

  PrintCard( pCard );
  printf( "\n" );
}
```

If you make this modification, save and compile the program. You should see the following output:

```
> cc carddeck_1.c -o carddeck_1 -Wall -Werror -std=c11
> carddeck_1
    5 of Spades
>
```

However, we created the `InitializeCard()` function earlier. Let's use that instead, as follows:

```
int main( void ) {
  Card deck[ kCardsInDeck ];
  Card* pCard = *deck[3];

  InitializeCard( pCard, spade , five , kNotWildCard );
  PrintCard( pCard );
  printf( "\n" );
}
```

As you can now see, the `main()` function not only has fewer lines of code, but it is also much clearer what is happening with each function call. The only oddity here is the final `printf()` function. Remember that `PrintCard()` does not include a new line, so now we have to supply that ourselves.

Save, compile, and run this version of `carddeck_1.c`. You should see the following output:

```
[> cc carddeck_1.c -o carddeck_1 -Wall -Werror -std=c11 ]
[> carddeck_1                                            ]
        5 of Spades
   > ▌
```

At this point, we have an array of cards, which is our deck, and some functions to manipulate individual cards. We can now think about manipulating the entire deck as a whole.

Manipulating an array of structures

Now that we have a deck of cards, what are some operations that we might need to perform on it? Two operations immediately come to mind—first, initializing the deck to the proper suit and face values, and second, printing out the deck of cards.

Let's add the following two function prototypes to the program, as follows:

```
void InitializeDeck( Card* pDeck );
void PrintDeck(      Card* pDeck );
```

In each function, the function takes a pointer to a Card structure, which for now is an array of Card. These will operate on the entire deck, so no other parameters are needed for these functions.

To initialize our deck of cards, we will loop through the array, setting the structure member values. Before we show that, however, consider the patterns of repetition in an ordered card deck. Each suite has 13 cards. Within those 13 cards, the face value goes from two to ace (13). We now have some options for how to loop through the deck:

- We could use one loop with 52 iterations and figure out when the suit and face values change, and then set suit and face as appropriate.
- We could use four loops of 13 iterations each. In each loop, the suit is fixed and the face value is assigned as the loop is iterated.
- We could use one loop, setting the suit and face values for four cards at a time.

The first option sounds like it might involve some tricky calculations. The second option is reasonable but involves more looping structures (more code). So, we will take the third approach. But how can we conveniently assign the face values without the need for the switch()... statement? The answer is to use a temporary lookup table that is set up so that the index of the card matches the lookup table's face value index.

The following function illustrates both the lookup table and the single loop:

```
void InitializeDeck( Card* pDeck )
{
  Face f[] = { two  , three , four , five , six  , seven ,
  eight , nine , ten , jack , queen , king , ace };
  Card* pCard;
  for( int i = 0 ; i < kCardsInSuit ; i++ ) {
  pCard = & (pDeck[ i + (0*kCardsInSuit) ]);
  pCard->suit = spade;
  pCard->suitValue = (int)spade;
  pCard->face = f[ i ];
  pCard->faceValue = (int) f[ i ];

  pCard = & (pDeck[ i + (1*kCardsInSuit) ]);
  pCard->suit = heart;
  pCard->suitValue = (int)heart;
  pCard->face = f[ i ];
  pCard->faceValue = (int) f[ i ];

  pCard = & (pDeck[ i + (2*kCardsInSuit) ]);
  pCard->suit = diamond;
  pCard->suitValue = (int)diamond;
  pCard->face = f[ i ];
  pCard->faceValue = (int) f[ i ];

  pCard = & (pDeck[ i + (3*kCardsInSuit) ]);
  pCard->suit = club;
  pCard->suitValue = (int)club;
  pCard->face = f[ i ];
  pCard->faceValue = (int) f[ i ];
  }
```

To understand the code, we need to do the following:

1. First, we have already seen how arrays and pointers to arrays can be used interchangeably in function parameters. In this function, we use a pointer to the array.
2. Next, we set up the lookup table for the face values. I would prefer to use the kCardsInSuit constant, but C does not permit that when initializing arrays in this manner. So, we leave it out.

3. Finally, we create a loop of `kCardsInSuit` iterations. Within this loop, four cards are configured in each iteration of the loop. To do this, the following five statements are executed for each card:

   1. The address of the card structure is calculated from the loop counter and a multiple of the number of cards in a suit. Note that the spades suit starts at index (`0*kCardsInSuit`); the hearts suit starts at index (`1*kCardsInSuit`); the diamonds suit starts at index (`2 * kCardsInSuit`); and clubs start at index (`3 * kCardsInSuit`). Notice how the pattern of (`<suitNumber> * kCardsInDeck`) is repeated to make the pattern a bit more explicit for all four suits.

   2. `suit` is assigned.

   3. `suitValue` is assigned based on the enumerated `suit` value.

   4. `face` is assigned based on the loop index, which corresponds to the lookup table's indexed value.

   5. `faceValue` is assigned based on the enumerated `face` value.

But hold on just a minute. Aren't we recreating what a function we've already created does? So, instead, let's use that function and see why doing so is far better. Add the following function to `carddeck_1.c`:

```
void InitializeDeck( Card* pDeck )
{
   Face f[] = { two    , three , four , five , six    , seven ,
                eight , nine  , ten  , jack , queen , king   , ace };
   Card* pC;
   for( int i = 0 ; i < kCardsInSuit ; i++ ) {
     pC = &(pDeck[ i + (0*kCardsInSuit) ]);
     InitializeCard( pC , spade , f[i], kNotWildCard );
     pC = &(pDeck[ i + (1*kCardsInSuit) ]);
     InitializeCard( pC , heart , f[i], kNotWildCard );

     pC = &(pDeck[ i + (2*kCardsInSuit) ]);
     InitializeCard( pC , diamond , f[i], kNotWildCard );

     pC = &(pDeck[ i + (3*kCardsInSuit) ]);
     InitializeCard( pC , club , f[i], kNotWildCard );
   }
}
```

As you can see, the overall approach is the same, but instead of five statements for each card in the loop, we only use two statements.

We are still using the lookup table and the suit offsets to get the proper card. In this version, however, knowledge of a `Card` structure remains in the `InitializeCard()` function. Not only does this require quite a bit less typing, but what is happening should also be much clearer to any reader of this function.

If our deck ever changes, we only need to consider `InitializeDeck()` and the routines that manipulate it. We can largely ignore the `Card` manipulation routines. If, on the other hand, our deck remains the same but we need to change the properties of our `Card` structure, we need only consider the `Card` manipulation functions and possibly any changes to the `Card` function calls.

Our final change to `carddeck_1.c` is to add the `PrintDeck()` function. If we merely print one card per line, this routine will be a simple loop of `kCardsInDeck` iterations with a single call to `PrintCard()`. However, to print an ordered, unshuffled deck of cards in as few output lines as possible, we will print four cards per line, 13 lines in total.

As we do that, we'll order the suits to each be in a single column. To do that, our approach will be similar to `InitializeDeck()`, but without the need for a lookup table. Add the following function to `carddeck_1.c`:

```c
void PrintDeck( Card* pDeck ) {
  printf( "%d cards in the deck\n\n" ,
          kCardsInDeck );
  printf( "The ordered deck: \n" );
  for( int i = 0 ; i < kCardsInSuit ; i++ )   {
    int index  = i + (0*kCardsInSuit);
    printf( "(%2d)" , index+1 );
    PrintCard( &(pDeck[ index ] ) );
    index = i + (1*kCardsInSuit);
    printf( "    (%2d)" , index+1 );
    PrintCard( &(pDeck[ index ] ) );

    index = i + (2*kCardsInSuit);
    printf( "    (%2d)" , index+1 );
    PrintCard( &(pDeck[ i + (2*kCardsInSuit) ] ) );

    index = i + (3*kCardsInSuit);
    printf( "    (%2d)" , index+1 );
    PrintCard( &(pDeck[ index ] ) );

    printf( "\n" );
  }
  printf( "\n\n" );
}
```

The first two `printf()` calls provide some information about the deck. Then, we see the same kind of loop as we have in `InitializeDeck()`. For each suit, the following three statements are executed:

1. Compute the index into the `deck` array from the loop index and a `suit` multiplier.
2. Print the number of the card in the deck. Note here the one-off adjustment from a zero-based array index to a natural counting number (that darn *one-off* issue again).
3. Call `PrintCard()` to print the card.

A `<newline>` character is printed after each of the four cards are printed. Finally, two new lines are printed after the loop iterations are complete.

Add this function to the end of `carddeck_1.c`. Save the file, and then compile and run it. You should see the following output:

```
> cc carddeck_1.c -o carddeck_1 -Wall -Werror -std=c11
> carddeck_1
52 cards in the deck

The ordered deck:
( 1)     2 of Spades     (14)     2 of Hearts     (27)     2 of Diamonds     (40)     2 of Clubs
( 2)     3 of Spades     (15)     3 of Hearts     (28)     3 of Diamonds     (41)     3 of Clubs
( 3)     4 of Spades     (16)     4 of Hearts     (29)     4 of Diamonds     (42)     4 of Clubs
( 4)     5 of Spades     (17)     5 of Hearts     (30)     5 of Diamonds     (43)     5 of Clubs
( 5)     6 of Spades     (18)     6 of Hearts     (31)     6 of Diamonds     (44)     6 of Clubs
( 6)     7 of Spades     (19)     7 of Hearts     (32)     7 of Diamonds     (45)     7 of Clubs
( 7)     8 of Spades     (20)     8 of Hearts     (33)     8 of Diamonds     (46)     8 of Clubs
( 8)     9 of Spades     (21)     9 of Hearts     (34)     9 of Diamonds     (47)     9 of Clubs
( 9)    10 of Spades     (22)    10 of Hearts     (35)    10 of Diamonds     (48)    10 of Clubs
(10)  Jack of Spades     (23)  Jack of Hearts     (36)  Jack of Diamonds     (49)  Jack of Clubs
(11) Queen of Spades     (24) Queen of Hearts     (37) Queen of Diamonds     (50) Queen of Clubs
(12)  King of Spades     (25)  King of Hearts     (38)  King of Diamonds     (51)  King of Clubs
(13)   Ace of Spades     (26)   Ace of Hearts     (39)   Ace of Diamonds     (52)   Ace of Clubs


> 
```

The main reason we are printing out the entire deck along with each card's position in the deck array is to verify our deck initialization routine. Each routine proves the validity of the other. When this program was being developed, both routines were developed in tandem so that any errors could be caught and fixed as early as possible.

So, let's quickly review what we did to `carddeck_1.c`:

1. We created a deck of cards from an array of `Card` structures.
2. We added some convenience constants to name and thereby eliminate magic numbers from being sprinkled throughout our program.
3. We created a function to initialize our deck of cards array.
4. We created a function to print our deck of cards.
5. We verified that we have a valid deck of properly initialized cards.

Now that we know that we have a properly initialized deck of cards, we can move on to do more interesting things with it. We are not done with our deck, though; it will become an even more complex structure. Before we get to that, however, let's expand on what we can put into structures.

Using a structure with other structures

In `card4.c` from Chapter 10, *Creating Custom Data Types with typedef*, we saw a structure, `Hand`, that contains another structure, `Card`. However, in that program, we accessed the entire sub-structure. We assigned the `hand.card` sub-structure by copying an entire `Card` structure to it. While this is convenient if we are dealing with complete substructures, we also need to know how to access elements within the sub-structure of a structure.

Here, we are going to look at accessing sub-structure elements within a structure. Before we begin our exploration, copy the `carddeck_1.c` file to `carddeck_2.c`. In `carddeck_2.c`, we'll add the `Hand` structure with sub-structures and operations on `Hand`.

Creating a structure consisting of other structures

We have already seen how to create a `Hand` structure that consists of the `Card` structures, as follows:

```
typedef struct {
  int cardsDealt;
```

```
    Card card1;
    Card card2;
    Card card3;
    Card card4;
    Card card5;
} Hand;
```

Hand is a structure that represents a collection of cards dealt with that hand. In this case, Hand contains five individual instances of a Card structure, each of them named card1 through card5. The cardsDealt member variable allows us to keep track of how many cards are in a hand.

Add the preceding structure definition to carddeck_2.c.

When you consider this structure, you might wonder why an array of Card structures is not used instead. Since an array is a collection of identical times, an array might be more appropriate than five named variables. In reality, using an array is an approach we will take later. For now, we want to explore accessing structures within structures. In the next section, after exploring structures within structures, we will then modify carddeck_2.c to use arrays of structures.

Accessing structure elements within the structure

We declare an instance of a Hand structure as follows:

```
Hand   h1;
```

We can then access its sub-structure member elements and structures, as follows:

```
h1.cardsDealt = 0;
Suit s;
Face f;

h1.card5.suit = club;
h1.card5.face = ace;

s = h1.card5.suit;
f = h1.card5.face;
```

Note that the card5 sub-structure is accessed using dot (.) notation and that the elements of card5 are also accessed using another level of dot (.) notation. In the example given, the member values of card5 are first set to desired values. Then, those values are retrieved from card5 and stored in the s and f variables, respectively.

Using a pointer to the Hand structure, h1, we access each substructure member element, as follows:

```
Hand* pHand = &h1;

pHand->card5.suit = club;
pHand->card5.face = ace.

s = pHand->card5.suit;
f = pHand->card5.face;
```

Note that when accessing the sub-structure elements in this manner, the pointer points to the structure and not the sub-structure. As before, in the example given, the member values of card5 are first set to the desired values. Then, those values are retrieved from card5 and stored in the s and f variables, respectively.

Alternatively, we could use a pointer not to the structure, but directly to the Card sub-structure and access its elements, as follows:

```
Card* pCard = &h1.card5;

pCard->suit = club;
pCard->face = ace.

s = pCard->suit;
f = pCard->face;
```

Here, the pCard pointer points directly to the sub-structure. Note how the pointer to the sub-structure is assigned. The address of the & operator has lower precedence than the dot (.) operator so that h1.card5 is evaluated first and then the address of that Card sub-structure is assigned to the pointer. The card5 elements are then accessed directly via the pointer.

Using this method, we could reuse the Card function, InitializeCard(), as follows:

```
Card* pCard = &h1.card5;

InitializeCard( pCard , club , ace , kNotWildCard );
```

Note that by using a pointer directly to the sub-structure, we can use the functions we've already created to operate on that sub-structure as if it were a standalone structure. Here, card5 is a sub-structure of h1; by using a pointer to the sub-structure, we can call InitializeCard(), regardless of what structure contains it.

Of the two methods given—one using a pointer to the structure containing the sub-structure and the other using a pointer directly to the sub-structure—neither is necessarily better than the other. However, because we have already created functions to manipulate a Card structure, there is some benefit in reusing those methods that operate on a Card structure, rather than the structure that contains them. One advantage of using those methods is that they concentrate the knowledge about the internal members and their inter-relationship in a single location—the InitializeCard() function.

Manipulating a structure consisting of other structures

The operations we want to perform on a Hand structure include the following:

- InitializeHand(): Sets the initial values of a Hand structure to a valid state
- AddCardToHand(): Receives a dealt card from the deck to the hand
- PrintHand(): Prints out the contents of the hand

With our current definition of Hand, we will need a way to determine which card in the hand we want to manipulate. To do this, we need a function:

- GetCardInHand(): Gets a pointer to a specific card within the hand. This method is used by other Hand functions to both set card values within a hand and to retrieve card values.

You can add the following function prototypes to carddeck_2.c:

```
void  InitializeHand( Hand* pHand );
void  AddCardToHand(  Hand* pHand , Card* pCard );
void  PrintHand(      Hand* pHand , char* pHandStr , char* pLeadStr );
Card* GetCardInHand(  Hand* pHand , int   cardIndex );
```

Each of these methods takes a pointer to a `Hand` structure. We can now implement each of these functions. With the current definition of `Hand`, there is not much to initialize, only the number of cards dealt. So, `InitializeHand()` is as follows:

```
void InitializeHand( Hand* pHand ) {
  pHand->cardsDealt = 0;
}
```

The `cardsDealt` structure member is set to 0 to indicate that the given hand is empty. We should initialize the cards to some value, but we don't at this time. The cards will be initialized when a card is added to the hand. With this approach, we have to be extra cautious that we don't access a card in the hand that has not yet been initialized.

The `GetCardInHand()` function is given a pointer to a hand and an index. It then returns a pointer to the desired card, as follows:

```
Card* GetCardInHand(  Hand* pHand , int cardIndex ) {
  Card* pC;
  switch( cardIndex ) {
    case 0:  pC = &(pHand->card1); break;
    case 1:  pC = &(pHand->card2); break;
    case 2:  pC = &(pHand->card3); break;
    case 3:  pC = &(pHand->card4); break;
    case 4:  pC = &(pHand->card5); break;
  }
  return pC;
}
```

In this function, a `switch()`... statement is used to determine from the index which card is desired. Since the `&` and `->` operators have the same precedence, we use `()` to make it clear in the `&(pHand->card1)` expression what type of pointer is being returned. `pHand->card1` gets the `Card` structure and `&` gives the address of that `Card` structure.

Note that this is a zero-based index that works identically to the way we use indices in arrays. This is intentional. Every time we use an index, regardless of its data type (or array or element within a structure), we are using a zero-based index scheme. This is for mental consistency. We don't have to try to remember when and for which data type we have a zero- or one-based index scheme; they are all zero-based.

We can now implement the `AddCardToHand()` function. It takes a pointer to a `Hand` structure and a pointer to a `Card` structure to be added to the hand, as follows:

```
void AddCardToHand( Hand* pHand , Card* pCard ) {
  int numInHand = pHand->cardsDealt;
  if( numInHand == kCardsInHand ) return;
```

```
    Card* pC = GetCardInHand( pHand , numInHand );
    InitializeCard( pC , pCard->suit , pCard->face , pCard->isWild );
    pHand->cardsDealt++;
}
```

The function first checks to see whether the hand is full by accessing the `cardsDealt` member and checking whether it is equal to the `kCardsInHand` constant. If the hand is full, the function returns and nothing more is done; in effect, the card is ignored. If the hand is not full, we use `numInHand` as the index to the card in the hand to be added. We then call `InitializeCard()` with the values from the `Card` pointer passed into the function.

Note that we are copying values from the deck into the hand. In essence, we have two of the same card—one in the deck and another in our hand. This is not a good design; ideally, we'd only want to ever have a single card that would be moved around from deck to hand. We'll soon rectify this condition.

Finally, the `cardsDealt` member variable is incremented to indicate that a card was added to the hand.

For `PrintHand()`, a string is passed to the function that will provide spacing before each card is printed. Like other `Hand` functions, a pointer of the hand to be printed is passed to the function, as follows:

```
void PrintHand( Hand* pHand , char* pHandStr , char* pLeadStr ) {
    printf( "%s%s\n" , pLeadStr , pHandStr );
    for( int i = 0; i < pHand->cardsDealt ; i++ ) {
        Card* pCard = GetCardInHand( pHand , i );
        printf("%s" , pLeadStr );
        PrintCard( pCard );
        printf("\n");
    }
}
```

In this function, a heading line is printed that contains the leading string and the hand-name string. Then, a loop is used to print each `Card` structure that has been dealt with. Within this loop, a pointer to the card is fetched, the leading string is printed, `PrintCard()` is called to print the card, and finally, a new line is printed.

At this point, edit `carddeck_2.c` to include the `Hand` structure, as well as the four functions to manipulate the `Hand` structure. Save the file and compile it. You shouldn't get any compiler errors or warnings. We will make a few more changes to this file before we run the program.

The first change to make is to the `Hand` structure so that it contains pointers to cards, rather than copies of cards. The `Hand` structure is now as follows:

```
typedef struct {
   int cardsDealt;
   Card* pCard1;
   Card* pCard2;
   Card* pCard3;
   Card* pCard4;
   Card* pCard5;
} Hand;
```

Each card in a hand is now a pointer to a card created and initialized in the deck. With this modification, we will now only have one instance of each card; each hand will simply point to the appropriate card in our deck.

Since we have changed the `Hand` structure, we also need to change some aspects of the functions that manipulate a hand. First, we need to do a little more work in `InitializeHand()`, as follows:

```
void InitializeHand( Hand* pHand ) {
   pHand->cardsDealt = 0;
   pCard1 = NULL;
   pCard2 = NULL;
   pCard3 = NULL;
   pCard4 = NULL;
   pCard5 = NULL;
}
```

Each pointer value is initialized to `NULL`. This approach has the added benefit of being able to tell whether a card has been dealt just by checking whether the pointer is `NULL`.

Since we changed the structure member names from card<x> to pCard<x>, we need to make the corresponding name changes in `GetCardInHand()`, as follows:

```
Card** GetCardInHand(  Hand* pHand , int cardIndex ) {
   Card** ppC;
   switch( cardIndex ) {
      case 0:   ppC = &(pHand->pCard1); break;
      case 1:   ppC = &(pHand->pCard2); break;
      case 2:   ppC = &(pHand->pCard3); break;
      case 3:   ppC = &(pHand->pCard4); break;
      case 4:   ppC = &(pHand->pCard5); break;
   }
   return ppC;
}
```

In this function, we don't return the pointer to a card, but rather the address of the variable that contains that pointer. Therefore, we don't need `pCard<x>`, a pointer to one of the cards in the hand; we need the address of that card pointer. We need a pointer to the pointer variable so that we can change that pointer variable. To see why, change the `AddCardToHand()` function, as follows:

```
void AddCardToHand( Hand* pHand , Card* pCard ) {
    int numInHand = pHand->cardsDealt;
    if( numInHand == kCardsInHand ) return;

    Card** ppC = GetCardInHand( pHand , numInHand );
    *ppC = pCard;
    pHand->cardsDealt++;
}
```

In this function, we want the pointer variable in our hand to point to the desired card in the deck. In order to do this, we need the address of the pointer variable. This is double indirection at work.

A conceptually simpler way to achieve the same result would be to write this function as follows:

```
void AddCardToHand( Hand* pHand , Card* pCard ) {
    int numInHand = pHand->cardsDealt;
    if( numInHand == kCardsInHand ) return;

    switch( numInHand ) {
      case 0: pHand->pCard1 = pCard; break;
      case 1: pHand->pCard2 = pCard; break;
      case 2: pHand->pCard3 = pCard; break;
      case 3: pHand->pCard4 = pCard; break;
      case 4: pHand->pCard5 = pCard; break;
      default: break;
    }
    pHand->cardsDealt++;
}
```

In this function, we do not need double indirection. Instead, we manipulate the appropriate pointer element of our `Hand` structure. This requires much more code than that used for double indirection. Remember, the main reason we are using the `GetCardInHand()` function is because of the way the `Hand` structure is currently defined. For this iteration of `carddeck_2.c`, we will use the double indirection method.

The next two changes to be made to `carddeck_2.c` will enable us to verify our current changes by providing some useful output. The first of these changes is to add a new method to our set of `Deck` functions—`DealCardFromDeck()`—as follows:

```
Card* DealCardFromDeck( Card deck[] , int index ) {
  Card* pCard = &deck[ index ];
  return pCard;
}
```

This function takes a `deck` array and an index for the desired card in the deck. Alternatively, we could have declared it as a pointer to `Card`, but we use array notation here instead to indicate the underlying array of our current `deck` representation. The function then returns a pointer to the requested `Card` structure in the given deck at the given index.

Our last change is to put these new methods to use. Modify `main()`, as follows:

```
int main( void ) {
  Card deck[ kCardsInDeck ];
  Card* pDeck = deck;
  InitializeDeck( &deck[0] );
  Hand h1 , h2 , h3 , h4;
  InitializeHand( &h1 );
  InitializeHand( &h2 );
  InitializeHand( &h3 );
  InitializeHand( &h4 );

  for( int i = 0 ; i < kCardsInHand ; i++ ) {
    AddCardToHand( &h1 , DealCardFromDeck( pDeck , i    ) );
    AddCardToHand( &h2 , DealCardFromDeck( pDeck , i+13 ) );
    AddCardToHand( &h3 , DealCardFromDeck( pDeck , i+26 ) );
    AddCardToHand( &h4 , DealCardFromDeck( pDeck , i+39 ) );
  }
  PrintHand( &h1 , "Hand 1:" , "                " );
  PrintHand( &h2 , "Hand 2:" , "    " );
  PrintHand( &h3 , "Hand 3:" , "                        " );
  PrintHand( &h4 , "Hand 4:" , "            " );
}
```

Here, we declare and initialize our `deck` array as before. Then, four `Hand` structures are declared and initialized. Next, using a loop, each hand is dealt cards to fill each one by calling `AddCardToHand()`. Currently, the cards that are being dealt are not randomized. Instead, we use `suit` offsets and the `loop` index to deal with the first five cards of each suit to each hand. We will deal with random card selection in the next iteration of `carddeck.c`. Finally, each hand is printed with calls to `PrintHand()`.

In `carddeck_2.c`, make the changes to the `Hand` structure and the functions that manipulate a hand. Add the function prototype and function definition for `DealCardFromDeck()`. Finally, modify `main()` to create four hands, initialize them, add cards to them, and print them out. Compile and run `carddeck_2.c`. You should see the following output:

```
> cc carddeck_2b.c -o carddeck_2b -Wall -Werror -std=c11
> carddeck_2b
                        Hand 1:
                            2 of Spades
                            3 of Spades
                            4 of Spades
                            5 of Spades
                            6 of Spades
            Hand 2:
                2 of Hearts
                3 of Hearts
                4 of Hearts
                5 of Hearts
                6 of Hearts
                                    Hand 3:
                                        2 of Diamonds
                                        3 of Diamonds
                                        4 of Diamonds
                                        5 of Diamonds
                                        6 of Diamonds
                        Hand 4:
                            2 of Clubs
                            3 of Clubs
                            4 of Clubs
                            5 of Clubs
                            6 of Clubs
>
```

You can now see how the `PrintHand()` function uses the various parameters it takes to print out each hand in a specific place on the console screen. `Hand 1` holds the first five cards from the spades suit, just as the other hands hold the first five cards from each of the other suits.

In this iteration of `carddeck.c`, we have made the following changes:

1. Create a `Hand` structure consisting of `Card` structures.
2. Create functions to initialize a hand, add a card to a hand, print a hand, and get a pointer to a specific card in a hand. In these functions, the cards were manipulated as copies of cards in the deck.
3. Modify the `Hand` structure to use pointers to `Card` structures, rather than copies of `Card` structures.
4. Modify each of the `Hand` functions to use pointers to match the new structure definition.
5. Add the `DealCardFromDeck()` function to get a pointer to `Card` from the deck.
6. Modify `main()` to use the `Hand` structures and each of the `Hand` manipulation functions.

We now have a deck with properly initialized cards and four hands that we can populate with pointers to cards from our deck. The program is becoming more complex as well as more complete. We'll soon have a complete card-dealing program.

Using a structure with arrays

We currently use an array of cards to represent a deck of cards. However, this representation is not sufficient for things we still need to do to a deck of cards. Two operations that are common to a deck of cards are first to shuffle the deck into a random order, and second to properly deal out cards from the randomized deck. We'll need to keep track of how many cards have been dealt and whether the deck is shuffled.

Our model for a deck of cards has just got a bit more complex. A single array representation is no longer sufficient. We will create a new structure, `Deck`, to hold additional information about our deck of cards as well as its shuffled or random state.

Before we begin defining this structure and operations on it, let's consider the randomization (shuffling) of our deck of cards. We could randomize our `deck` array by copying the structures in it from one index to another. However, since we now know about pointers, we can put that knowledge to good use by employing another array to shuffle our deck. This array will consist of pointers to each card in our deck. We will initialize the array so that each pointer points to its ordered deck element; then, we will randomize the order of the pointers in this secondary array. In order to do that, we first need to understand a little about randomness and random number generators on computers.

Understanding randomness and random number generators

A computer is a deterministic machine. This means that when we run a program, we get the same result each time without variance. This consistent behavior is crucial to orderly computation. We depend on consistency regardless of the day of the week, the weather, or any other factor.

However, there are some cases where we need to simulate the random occurrence of events. One obvious example of this is shuffling a deck of cards. It would be of little interest to create a card game program that gives each player exactly the same cards each time they play the game. On the other hand, randomness is pervasive in the real world—the weather, rolling dice, even the fingerprints on our hands, are all unavoidable random events.

To get randomness on an otherwise non-random, deterministic machine, there are two ways to achieve this. The first is via hardware; the best source of this is the static generated by a purposely damaged sound-generating chip. This kind of device is truly random. Also, this device is neither practical nor readily available on common computer systems. The second way is to simulate randomness with a **pseudorandom number generator** (**PRNG**).

A PRNG is an algorithm that generates a very large sequence of numbers. This large sequence is called its **period**, or the **periodicity** of the PRNG. This is the length of the sequence of numbers it can generate before it repeats its sequence. The larger the periodicity, the better the PRNG. Each time we ask the PRNG for a *random* number, it actually gives us the next number in its sequence. Associated with a PRNGs periodicity is a **seed**, or a starting point within its sequence of numbers. A seed is itself some type of varying number that doesn't have to be nearly as random as the PRNG sequence. It could be the number of seconds since 1970, the number of microseconds within the current second, or the position of the disk head over a hard drive platter. The seed is our starting point in the PRNG's sequence of numbers. In fact, if we used the same seed each time, we would always get exactly the same sequence of numbers.

From this, we can surmise that there are two operations on a PRNG that are essential. First, we must initialize the PRNG with a seed, or starting point, and second, we make repeated calls to the PRNG to give us the next random number in its sequence.

Every computer system provides at least one PRNG that is readily available to the programmer. However, PRNGs have been, and are still being, studied extensively because of their importance in simulations of real-world events. There are many classes of PRNGs. Not every PRNG is equally random from one call to the next, nor does every PRNG have the same periodicity. Some PRNGs are simple while others are quite complex. The value a PRNG returns may be an integer between 0 and some maximum value or it may be a floating-point value between 0.0 and 1.0. We can then normalize that value into our desired range of numbers.

On the other hand, not every problem requires the same level of randomness. Very often, for simple games, a simple PRNG is adequate for the task. We will use the relatively simple PRNG supplied in the C standard library by including `stdlib.h` in our program. We can then initialize its PRNG with `srand()` and make subsequent calls to it with the `rand()` function. It is common to initialize `srand()` with the current time by calling `time()`. `time()` returns the number of seconds since 1970 on Unix systems; therefore, this will be a different number each time we run a program that uses it.

We will see how to use these functions in action when we shuffle our deck.

Creating a structure with an array

We will create a structure, Shuffled, which, for now, holds some information about the state of our deck and an array of pointers to Card, which is our shuffled deck. We define Shuffled as follows:

```
typedef struct {
  Card* shuffled[ kCardsInDeck ];
  int numDealt;
  bool bIsShuffled;
} Shuffled;
```

This gives an array of pointers to Card, the number of cards that have been dealt, and a Boolean value to indicate whether the deck has been shuffled.

Accessing array elements within a structure

We have already seen how to access individual elements within a structure with dot (.) notation, or, if we have a pointer to the structure, with the arrow (->) notation. To access an array element with a structure, we would use the same notation for individual elements and simply add array notation ([]), as follows:

```
Shuffled    aShuffled;
Shuffled* pShuffled = &aShuffled;

aShuffled.numDealt     = 0;
aShuffled.bIsShuffled = false;
for( int i = 0 , i < kCardsInDeck; i++ )
  aShuffled.shuffled[i] = NULL;

pShuffled->numDealt    = 0;
pShuffled->bIsShuffled = false;
pShuffled->shuffled[i] = NULL;
```

We have declared a deck structure, aShuffled, and a pointer to a deck structure, pShuffled, initializing it to the address of aDeck. The next three statements access each element of aShuffled using dot (.) notation. The last three statements access each element of pShuffled using arrow (->) notation.

We can now consider operations executed on our Shuffled structure.

Manipulating array elements within a structure

We already have a `Deck` array and two operations in it
`InitializeDeck()` and `PrintDeck()`. We now also have a `Shuffled` structure. We need
to add operations to perform on it, such
as `InitializeShuffled()` and `PrintShuffled()`. To this set of operations, we would
add the `ShuffleDeck()` function. The function prototypes for these would be as follows:

```
void InitializeShuffled( Shuffled* pShuffled , Deck[] pDeck );
void PrintShuffled( Shuffled* pShuffled );
void ShuffleDeck( Shuffled* pShuffled );
```

The `InitializedShuffled()` method is a bit different
from `InitializeDeck()` because the function needs to know about `Deck` when we
initialize our array of pointers. At this point, you might be wondering whether `Deck` and its
operations are somehow very closely related to `Shuffled` and its operations. The fact is,
they are. We will combine both the `Deck` and `Shuffled` data structures as well as these
operations in the final version of the `carddeck.c` program. Before we do this, however,
let's examine the `ShuffleDeck()` function.

To shuffle our deck of cards, we will—for now—assume that `shuffled[]` has been
initialized such that the first element of `shuffled[o]` points to the first element of
`deck[0]`, the second element of `shuffled[1]` points to the second element of `deck[1]`,
and so on, such that `shuffled[]` is in the same order as `deck[]`. We will first initialize our
PRNG and then loop through each element of the array. At each iteration, we will call
`rand()` to get the next random number and normalize that number into a range between 0
and 51 (the number of cards in our deck). This will be a random index in our `shuffled`
array. We'll then swap the pointer at the current index with the pointer at the random
index. This function is as follows:

```
void ShuffleDeck( Shuffled* pDeck ) {
  long randomIndex;
  srand( time() );

  Card* pTempCard;
  for( int thisIndex = 0 ; thisIndex < kCardsInDeck ; thisIndex++ ) {
    randomIndex = rand() % kCardsInDeck; // 0..51
      // swap
    pTmpCard                        = pDeck->shuffled[ thisIndex ];
    pDeck->shuffled[ thisIndex ]    = pDeck->shuffled[ randomIndex ];
    pDeck->shuffled[ randomIndex ]  = pTmpCard;
  }
  pDeck->bIsShuffled  = true;
}
```

First, we declare `randomIndex` and then initialize our PRNG with a call to `time()`. In order to swap two values, we use a third value, `pTempCard`, as a placeholder. Upon each iteration through `shuffled[]`, we get the next random number, use modulo to get a value between `0` and `51`, and then perform the `swap` operation in three statements. Finally, we update the `bIsShuffled` status variable to reflect the fact that we now have a shuffled array of cards.

We can see that accessing an array of simple data types within a structure is very similar to accessing any member element within a structure. We simply add an array notation to the structure's array name as needed.

Copy `carddeck_2.c` into `carddeck3.c`. For the remainder of this chapter, we will modify `carddeck_3.c`. For now, add the `stdlib.h` and `time.h` header files to our program to access `rand()`, `srand()`, and `time()`.

We will modify our `Hand` structure to use an array of pointers to `Card` structures. This will simplify operations on a `Hand` as well as eliminate the need for the `GetCardInHand()` function.

Revisiting the hand structure

In `carddeck_2.c`, we used named member variables for cards in the `Hand` structure. This meant we needed a function to get a pointer to a specific card. While possible, that turned out to be cumbersome. Recall that when all variables are of an identical type and you have a collection of them, an array should immediately come to mind. So, we will rework the definition of our `Hand` structure to use an array of pointers to `Card`, as follows:

```
typedef struct {
  Card* hand[ kCardsInHand ];
  int   cardsDealt;
} Hand;
```

We still have five cards, but they are now contained in an array, and we still have `cardsDealt` to keep track of how many cards are in our hand.

As you will see, this will simplify our `Hand` operations.

Revisiting hand operations

Because we changed this structure definition, we will have to only slightly modify the `Hand` operations. Fortunately, none of the function prototypes will need to change:

1. In `carddeck_3.c`, modify the `InitializeHand()` function, as follows:

```
void InitializeHand( Hand* pHand ) {
  pHand->cardsDealt = 0;
  for( int i = 0; i < kCardsInHand ; i++ )  {
    pHand->hand[i] = NULL;
  }
}
```

We can now use a loop to set each of our `Card` pointers in the `hand[]` array to `NULL`.

2. Next, we can simplify the `AddCardToHand()` function because we no longer need the `GetCardInHand()` method, as follows:

```
void AddCardToHand( Hand* pHand , Card* pCard ) {
  if( pHand->cardsDealt == kCardsInHand ) return;
  pHand->hand[ pHand->cardsDealt ] = pCard;
  pHand->cardsDealt++;
}
```

As before, we first check whether our hand is full. Then, we simply set the pointer value to the given `Card` structure to the appropriate array element. As before, the `cardsDealt` member variable is incremented.

3. Also, the `PrintHand()` function no longer needs to use the `GetCardInHand()` function, as follows:

```
void PrintHand( Hand* pHand , char* pHandStr , char* pLeadStr ) {
  printf( "%s%s\n" , pLeadStr , pHandStr );
  for( int i = 0; i < kCardsInHand ; i++ ) {   // 1..5
    printf("%s" , pLeadStr );
    PrintCard( pHand->hand[i] );
    printf("\n");
  }
}
```

Because the cards in the hand are in an array, we can simply access pointers to them via array notation. Otherwise, this function is identical to its earlier version. `GetCardInHand()` is no longer needed. Both its prototype and definition can be deleted from `carddeck_3.c`.

4. Finally, we will put our collection of four hands into an array of pointers to `Hand`. We can then create a `PrintAllHands()` function, as follows:

```
void PrintAllHands(  Hand* hands[ kNumHands ]  ) {
  PrintHand( hands[0] , "Hand 1:" , "                    " );
  PrintHand( hands[1] , "Hand 2:" , "    " );
  PrintHand( hands[2] , "Hand 3:" , "
" );
  PrintHand( hands[3] , "Hand 4:" , "                    ");
}
```

Each element of the `hands[]` array contains a pointer to a `Hand` structure. We can, therefore, simply use the array and index to call `PrintHand()` for each of our hands. Remember to add the `PrintAllHands()` function prototype to `carddeck_3.c`. Save and compile the program. You should get an identical output to that of `carddeck_2.c` in the previous section.

Using a structure with an array of structures

Because a deck of cards and a shuffled deck of cards are so similar, it makes somewhat more sense to combine them into a single structure, rather than have to declare and manipulate them separately. Our final `Deck` structure will consist of two arrays—one of an ordered set of cards and another of pointers to cards in that deck, which can then be shuffled as needed. We will add additional information to the `Deck` structure to keep track of whether the deck is shuffled and how many cards have been dealt.

As we enhance our `Deck` structure and create/modify operations on the new structure, you should notice how little any of the other structures and methods already created will need to be changed, if at all.

Creating a structure with an array of structures

In earlier versions of `carddeck.c`, we represented a deck of cards with a simple array of structures. Now that we need to shuffle the deck and keep track of other information about the deck, it makes sense to make our `Deck` structure a combination of an array of `Card` structures and an array of pointers to `Card` structures, as well as other information about the deck.

Consider the following definition of a new `Deck` structure:

```
typedef struct {
  Card  ordered[ kCardsInDeck ];
  Card* shuffled[ kCardsInDeck ];
  int   numDealt;
  bool  bIsShuffled;
} Deck;
```

The `ordered` member array will contain the initialized and ordered `Card` structures. Once initialized, the `ordered` array elements will not be modified. Instead of moving cards around in the `ordered` array, we will use another array, `shuffled`, which is a collection of pointers to cards in the `ordered` array. We will rely on the `bIsShuffled` member variable to indicate when the deck has been shuffled.

This new definition collects various types of complex information into a single, somewhat more complex structure. We will see how this makes our program organization and logic more cohesive.

Before we delve into modifying operations on the `Deck` structure, let's explore how to access the various elements and sub-elements within the `Deck` structure.

Accessing individual structure elements of the array within a structure

Accessing structure elements and sub-elements is a matter of layering access from the topmost, or outer structure elements, to the bottommost, or inner sub-structure elements. We have already seen simpler versions of this in the earlier sections of this chapter.

We must, however, be mindful of the data type of the sub-element being accessed. In particular, we must pay attention to whether the member element is a direct intrinsic type or structure or whether it is a pointer to another intrinsic type or structure. Being clear about differentiating member elements and pointer elements determines which notation is required—dot (.) or arrow (->) notation.

Given the preceding definition of `Deck`, consider the following access to each of its various elements and sub-elements:

```
Deck deck;

deck.cardsDealt = 0;
deck.bIsShuffled = false;
deck.shuffled[0] = NULL;
```

```
deck.ordered[3].suit = spade;
deck.ordered[3].face = four;

deck.shuffled[14] = &(deck.ordered[35]);
(deck.shuffled[4])->suit = heart;
(deck.shuffled[14])->face = two;

Suit s = deck.ordered[3].suit;
Face f = deck.ordered[3].face;

s = (deck.shuffled[14])->suit;
f = (deck.shuffled[14])->face;
```

The deck variable is declared as a Deck structure. The next two statements set two
elements of the structure. Next, the zeroth element of the shuffled array is set to NULL.
Then, the sub-elements of the fourth Card structure element are set.

The next statement sets the 14th pointer element of shuffled to the address of the 35th
structure element of the ordered array. The next two statements access, via the pointer
contained in the 14th element of shuffled, the suit and face elements, which are actually
the sub-elements of the 35th array structure in ordered.

The last four statements show how to retrieve sub-element values.

Now, consider how to access the sub-elements of the Deck structure via a pointer to
the Deck structure in the following statements:

```
Deck   anotherDeck
Deck* pDeck = &anotherDeck;

pDeck->cardsDealt = 0;
pDeck->bIsShuffled = false;
pDeck->shuffled[3] = pDeck

pDeck->shuffled[14] = &(deck.ordered[31]);
(pDeck->shuffled[14])->suit = heart;
(pDeck->shuffled[14])->face = two;

Suit s = pDeck->ordered[3].suit;
Face f = pDeck->ordered[3].face;

s = (pDeck->shuffled[14])->suit;
f = (pDeck->shuffled[14])->face;
```

Each of these statements—which are indirect references via a pointer to a Deck structure—has the identical effect of accessing sub-elements as the previous set of direct references to the same sub-elements.

Manipulating a structure with an array of structures

So, a question regarding when to use direct references versus using an indirect reference may come to mind. This is a very pertinent question. Unfortunately, there is no obvious answer or one that must be strictly obeyed.

In general, however, whenever a structure is declared in a function block and its elements are accessed within that function block, direct references typically make the most sense. On the other hand, when structures are declared in one function block and then manipulated by another function block, it is typically best to use indirect references (pointers) to them in the manipulating function called.

With this in mind, we can now redefine the prototypes to the Deck manipulation operations, as follows:

```
void  InitializeDeck(   Deck* pDeck );
void  ShuffleDeck(      Deck* pDeck );
Card* DealCardFromDeck( Deck* pDeck );
void  PrintDeck(        Deck* pDeck );
```

In each case, the Deck structure is not copied into and back out of the functions. Instead, a pointer to the already existing structure variable is passed into each manipulating function.

We will revisit each of these functions in the remainder of this chapter.

Completing carddeck.c

In this section and its sub-sections, we will complete carddeck.c so that it creates a deck of cards using our new Deck structure, shuffle the deck, create four hands, and deal five shuffled cards to each hand. To verify our work, we will print the deck and the hands out at various stages of the program's execution.

Revisiting the deck structure

To `carddeck_3.c`, add the definition for the `Deck` structure, as follows:

```
typedef struct {
  Card  ordered[ kCardsInDeck ];
  Card* shuffled[ kCardsInDeck ];
  int   numDealt;
  bool  bIsShuffled;
} Deck;
```

This is the complex `Deck` structure that we described earlier.

Revisiting deck operations

Since we now have a complex `Deck` structure, we must revisit each of the functions that operate on a deck:

1. The first of these is `InitializeDeck()`. Modify `InitializeDeck()`, as follows:

```
void InitializeDeck( Deck* pDeck ) {
  Face f[] = { two    , three , four , five , six    , seven ,
               eight , nine , ten  , jack , queen , king  , ace };
  Card* pC;
  for( int i = 0 ; i < kCardsInSuit ; i++ )  {
    pC = &(pDeck->ordered[ i + (0*kCardsInSuit) ]);
    InitializeCard( pC , spade , f[i], kNotWildCard );
    pC = &(pDeck->ordered[ i + (1*kCardsInSuit) ]);
    InitializeCard( pC , heart , f[i], kNotWildCard );

    pC = &(pDeck->ordered[ i + (2*kCardsInSuit) ]);
    InitializeCard( pC , diamond , f[i], kNotWildCard );
    pC = &(pDeck->ordered[ i + (3*kCardsInSuit) ]);
    InitializeCard( pC , club , f[i], kNotWildCard );
  }
  for( int i = 0 ; i < kCardsInDeck ; i++ )  {
    pDeck->shuffled[i] = &(pDeck->ordered[i]);
  }
  pDeck->bIsShuffled = false;
  pDeck->numDealt    = 0;
}
```

We use the same lookup array as we did before. We use the same loop that initialized four cards for each iteration through the loop. The only difference in this loop is how we use the card in the ordered array, with `& (pDeck->ordered[ i + (0*kCardsInSuit) ])`.

2. Next, we initialize the `shuffled` array to have pointers to cards in the same order as in `ordered`. The deck is not yet shuffled, but it is initialized. Lastly, we set `bIsShuffled` to `false` and `numDealt` to 0. The deck is now properly initialized.

To shuffle our deck, we are actually only going to change the order of the pointers in `shuffled`. Create the `ShuffleDeck()` function, as follows:

```
void ShuffleDeck( Deck* pDeck ) {
  long randIndex;
  srand( time(NULL) ); // Seed our PRNG using time() function.
                       // Because time() ever increases, we'll get
a
                       // different series each time we run the
                       //  program.

  Card* pTmpCard;

    // Now, walk through the shuffled array, swapping the pointer
    // at a random card index in shuffuled with the pointer at the
    // current card index.

  for( int thisIndex = 0 ; thisIndex < kCardsInDeck ; thisIndex++ )
{
      // get a random index
    randIndex = rand() % kCardsInDeck;  // get next random number
                                        // between 0..52
      // swap card pointers between thisIndex and randIndex
    pTmpCard = pDeck->shuffled[ thisIndex ];
    pDeck->shuffled[ thisIndex ] = pDeck->shuffled[ randIndex ];
    pDeck->shuffled[ randIndex ] = pTmpCard;
  }
  pDeck->bIsShuffled = true;
}
```

In this, the `randIndex` function will be a randomly generated number between 0 and 51. After initializing our PRNG with `srand()`, we loop through all 52 cards. At each iteration, we get the index of a random card pointer and swap that pointer value with the current index of the loop counter. As you will see, this does exactly what we need. Finally, we set `bIsShuffled` to true.

3. Modify `DealCardFromDeck()`, as follows:

```
Card* DealCardFromDeck( Deck* pDeck ) {
  Card* pCard = pDeck->shuffled[ pDeck->numDealt ];
  pDeck->shuffled[ pDeck->numDealt ] = NULL;
  pDeck->numDealt++;
  return pCard;
}
```

In this version of `DealCardFromDeck()`, we use the `numDealt` member variable as the index of the next card pointer to be dealt or returned from the function. Notice that the pointer at that index is set to `NULL` to ensure we don't deal that card again. Next, `numDealt` is incremented to the top of the deck or the next available card. Finally, `pCard`, the pointer to the dealt card, is returned to the caller.

4. Finally, modify the `PrintDeck()` function, as follows:

```
void PrintDeck( Deck* pDeck )   {
  printf( "%d cards in the deck\n" ,   kCardsInDeck );
  printf( "Deck %s shuffled\n", pDeck->bIsShuffled ? "is" : "is
not" );
  printf( "%d cards dealt into %d
hands\n",pDeck->numDealt,kNumHands );

  if( pDeck->bIsShuffled == true ) {           // Deck is shuffled.
    if( pDeck->numDealt > 0 )  {
      printf( "The remaining shuffled deck:\n" );
    } else {
      printf( "The full shuffled deck:\n");
    }
    for( int i=pDeck->numDealt , j=0 ; i < kCardsInDeck ; i++ , j++
) {
      printf( "(%2d)" , i+1 );
      PrintCard( pDeck->shuffled[ i ] );
      if( j == 3  )  {
        printf( "\n" );
        j = -1;
      } else {
        printf( "\t");
      }
    }
  } else {                               // Deck is not
shuffled.
    printf( "The ordered deck: \n" );
    for( int i = 0 ; i < kCardsInSuit ; i++ )  {
      int index  = i + (0*kCardsInSuit);
```

```
                printf( "(%2d)" , index+1 );
                PrintCard( &(pDeck->ordered[ index ] ) );
                index = i + (1*kCardsInSuit);
                printf( "    (%2d)" , index+1 );
                PrintCard( &(pDeck->ordered[ index ] ) );
                index = i + (2*kCardsInSuit);
                printf( "    (%2d)" , index+1 );
                PrintCard( &(pDeck->ordered[ i + (2*kCardsInSuit) ] ) );
                index = i + (3*kCardsInSuit);
                printf( "    (%2d)" , index+1 );
                PrintCard( &(pDeck->ordered[ index ] ) );
                printf( "\n" );
            }
        }
        printf( "\n\n" );
    }
```

The `PrintDeck()` function is now used to print the deck in a few different ways. We have already seen various parts of this function. First, it prints out some information about the current state of the deck. Next, it determines whether the deck is shuffled. If the deck is shuffled, it prints out either the full deck (no cards dealt) or the remaining, undealt portion of the deck. If the deck is not shuffled, it prints out the ordered deck of cards.

Congratulations! You should now be familiar with every syntax element in this rather complex function. You may consider this a complete review of everything you have learned up to this point.

This function will be called several times to verify all parts of our program.

A basic card program

Now that we have all of our new structures and modifications to the functions that operate on them, we are now ready to put everything into play, so to speak. Modify the `main()` function routine in `carddeck_3.c`, as follows:

```
int main( void ) {
    Deck   deck;
    Deck* pDeck = &deck;
    InitializeDeck( pDeck );
    PrintDeck(       pDeck );
    ShuffleDeck( pDeck );
    PrintDeck(    pDeck );
    Hand h1 , h2 , h3 , h4;
    Hand* hands[] = { &h1 , &h2 , &h3 , &h4 };
```

```
for( int i = 0 ; i < kNumHands ; i++ ) {
    InitializeHand( hands[i] );
}

for( int i = 0 ; i < kCardsInHand ; i++ )  {
    for( int j = 0 ; j < kNumHands ; j++ )
    {
        AddCardToHand( hands[j] , DealCardFromDeck( pDeck ) );
    }
}
PrintAllHands( hands );
PrintDeck(    pDeck );
}
```

Does it come as a surprise how few lines of code in `main()` are needed to express all of the work that the program is doing? This was achieved through the use of our manipulation functions. Let's walk through it:

1. First, we declare a deck and a pointer to that deck. Next, the deck is initialized with a call to `InitializeDeck()` and the deck is printed. When you edit, save, compile, and run this program, you should see the first deck print out as follows:

```
> cc carddeck_3.c -o carddeck_3 -Wall -Werror -std=c11
> carddeck_3
52 cards in the deck
Deck is not shuffled
0 cards dealt into 4 hands
The ordered deck:
( 1)     2 of Spades      (14)     2 of Hearts      (27)     2 of Diamonds    (40)     2 of Clubs
( 2)     3 of Spades      (15)     3 of Hearts      (28)     3 of Diamonds    (41)     3 of Clubs
( 3)     4 of Spades      (16)     4 of Hearts      (29)     4 of Diamonds    (42)     4 of Clubs
( 4)     5 of Spades      (17)     5 of Hearts      (30)     5 of Diamonds    (43)     5 of Clubs
( 5)     6 of Spades      (18)     6 of Hearts      (31)     6 of Diamonds    (44)     6 of Clubs
( 6)     7 of Spades      (19)     7 of Hearts      (32)     7 of Diamonds    (45)     7 of Clubs
( 7)     8 of Spades      (20)     8 of Hearts      (33)     8 of Diamonds    (46)     8 of Clubs
( 8)     9 of Spades      (21)     9 of Hearts      (34)     9 of Diamonds    (47)     9 of Clubs
( 9)    10 of Spades      (22)    10 of Hearts      (35)    10 of Diamonds    (48)    10 of Clubs
(10)  Jack of Spades      (23)  Jack of Hearts      (36)  Jack of Diamonds    (49)  Jack of Clubs
(11) Queen of Spades      (24) Queen of Hearts      (37) Queen of Diamonds    (50) Queen of Clubs
(12)  King of Spades      (25)  King of Hearts      (38)  King of Diamonds    (51)  King of Clubs
(13)   Ace of Spades      (26)   Ace of Hearts      (39)   Ace of Diamonds    (52)   Ace of Clubs
```

2. Then, the deck is shuffled with a call to `ShuffleDeck()` and printed again. You should see the second deck print out something like the following:

```
52 cards in the deck
Deck is shuffled
0 cards dealt into 4 hands
The full shuffled deck:
( 1)    Ace of Clubs     ( 2)     3 of Hearts    ( 3)     2 of Spades    ( 4)     4 of Diamonds
( 5)   Jack of Diamonds  ( 6)     3 of Diamonds  ( 7)     7 of Spades    ( 8)  King of Diamonds
( 9) Queen of Hearts     (10)  Jack of Clubs     (11)     3 of Clubs     (12)     4 of Hearts
(13)      6 of Diamonds  (14)    10 of Clubs     (15)     2 of Clubs     (16)     6 of Hearts
(17)   Jack of Spades    (18)     5 of Diamonds  (19)     6 of Clubs     (20)    10 of Spades
(21)   Jack of Hearts    (22)     8 of Diamonds  (23)     9 of Hearts    (24)  King of Spades
(25)      7 of Diamonds  (26)   Ace of Spades    (27)     5 of Clubs     (28)     3 of Spades
(29)      9 of Clubs     (30)     9 of Diamonds  (31)     8 of Spades    (32)  King of Clubs
(33)      5 of Spades    (34)    10 of Hearts    (35)  King of Hearts    (36)     9 of Spades
(37) Queen of Spades     (38)     7 of Clubs     (39)   Ace of Hearts    (40)    10 of Diamonds
(41)      5 of Hearts    (42)     2 of Diamonds  (43)     7 of Hearts    (44)     8 of Clubs
(45)      2 of Hearts    (46) Queen of Clubs     (47)     6 of Spades    (48)     8 of Hearts
(49) Queen of Diamonds   (50)   Ace of Diamonds  (51)     4 of Spades    (52)     4 of Clubs
```

The order of your cards will be different because of our use of a PRNG. Examine the cards closely to be certain that they are all there, that there are no duplicates, and that they are, in fact, shuffled.

3. Next, four hands are declared and then grouped into an array of pointers to each hand. With a simple loop, `InitializeHand()` is called for each of them. Next, a nested loop is used to deal cards to each hand. The `i` index will deal five cards to each hand and the `j` index of the inner loop distributes the card to the proper hand, in turn. Notice how the return value from `DealCardsFromDeck()` is used as the input parameter to `AddCardToHand()`.

4. Finally, all the hands are printed with a call to `PrintAllHands()` and the final call to `PrintDeck()`. You should now see something like the following:

```
                        Hand 1:
                          Ace of Clubs
                         Jack of Diamonds
                        Queen of Hearts
                            6 of Diamonds
                         Jack of Spades
         Hand 2:
             3 of Hearts
             3 of Diamonds
         Jack of Clubs
           10 of Clubs
            5 of Diamonds
                                        Hand 3:
                                          2 of Spades
                                          7 of Spades
                                          3 of Clubs
                                          2 of Clubs
                                          6 of Clubs
               Hand 4:
                   4 of Diamonds
               King of Diamonds
                   4 of Hearts
                   6 of Hearts
                  10 of Spades
52 cards in the deck
Deck is shuffled
20 cards dealt into 4 hands
The remaining shuffled deck:
(21)   Jack of Hearts    (22)     8 of Diamonds  (23)     9 of Hearts    (24)  King of Spades
(25)      7 of Diamonds  (26)   Ace of Spades    (27)     5 of Clubs     (28)     3 of Spades
(29)      9 of Clubs     (30)     9 of Diamonds  (31)     8 of Spades    (32)  King of Clubs
(33)      5 of Spades    (34)    10 of Hearts    (35)  King of Hearts    (36)     9 of Spades
(37) Queen of Spades     (38)     7 of Clubs     (39)   Ace of Hearts    (40)    10 of Diamonds
(41)      5 of Hearts    (42)     2 of Diamonds  (43)     7 of Hearts    (44)     8 of Clubs
(45)      2 of Hearts    (46) Queen of Clubs     (47)     6 of Spades    (48)     8 of Hearts
(49) Queen of Diamonds   (50)   Ace of Diamonds  (51)     4 of Spades    (52)     4 of Clubs

> 
```

Just as in earlier versions of `carddeck.c`, this version consisted of a number of additions and modifications:

1. Modify the `Hand` structure using an array of pointers to `Card`.
2. Modify the `Hand` manipulation functions.
3. Add a new function to print all hands in an array of pointers to hands.
4. Create a complex `Deck` structure.
5. Modify the `Deck` manipulation functions.
6. Use all of our structures and manipulation functions to shuffle a deck and deal to our four hands.

At each stage of the program's development, we went from a known-good state to the next known-good state with relevant output at each stage to verify our program's validity. In this way, we were not only able to build our understanding of complex data structures and operations on them, but we also gained some experience and insight into how program development typically occurs. This approach is also referred to as **stepwise refinement**.

Summary

This chapter not only explored complex structures, but also reviewed nearly all the concepts we've explored in previous chapters.

We learned about various ways to access arrays of structures, sub-structures within structures, and arrays of structures within a structure. Each version of our `carddeck.c` program included a review of what was changed in that version.

We also learned about PRNGs and used a system-supplied PRNG to shuffle our deck of cards.

Throughout this chapter, we developed a complex program using stepwise refinement as we added structures and operations to these structures. More significantly, we got an in-depth view of how a program might change over its development life cycle. When we add or change structures, we also need to add or change the routines that manipulate those structures. This chapter demonstrated the software development process first described in `Chapter 1`, *Running Hello, World!*.

In the next two chapters, we will explore C's various memory allocation mechanisms. `Chapter 17`, *Understanding Memory Allocation and Lifetime*, will provide a review of, and a moderate expansion on, the methods we've used so far. It also prepares us for the following chapter, `Chapter 18`, *Using Dynamic Memory Allocation*. This chapter while conceptually challenging, paves the way for much more interesting and useful programming algorithms.

3
Section 3: Memory Manipulation

Every value or complex data type exists in memory. In this section, we will explore various ways to create and manipulate memory. We'll also explore the life cycle of different kinds of memory structures.

This section comprises the following chapters:

- Chapter 17, *Understanding Memory Allocation and Lifetime*
- Chapter 18, *Using Dynamic Memory Allocation*

17
Understanding Memory Allocation and Lifetime

Every instance of a value—be it a literal, an intrinsic data type, or a complex data type—exists in memory. Here, we will explore various ways in which memory is allocated. The different mechanisms for memory allocation are called **storage classes**. In this chapter, we will review the storage class we've been using thus far, that of *automatic* storage, as well as introduce the *static* storage class. We will also explore the lifetime of each storage class, as well as introduce the scope of a storage class—internal versus external storage.

After exploring automatic and static storage classes, this chapter paves the way for a special and extremely flexible storage class—that of dynamic memory allocation. Dynamic memory allocation is so powerful and flexible that it will be introduced in Chapter 18, *Using Dynamic Memory Allocation*, with the creation and manipulation of a dynamic data structure called a *linked list*.

Each storage class also has a specific scope or visibility to other parts of the program; the scope of both variables and functions will be explored in Chapter 25, *Understanding Scope*.

The following topics will be covered in this chapter:

- Defining storage classes
- Understanding automatic versus dynamic storage classes
- Understanding internal versus external storage classes
- Exploring the static storage class
- Exploring the lifetime of each storage class

Technical requirements

As detailed in the *Technical requirements* section of `Chapter 1`, *Running Hello, World!*, continue to use the tools you have chosen.

The source code for this chapter can be found at `https://github.com/PacktPublishing/ Learn-C-Programming`.

Defining storage classes

C provides a number of storage classes. These fall into the following two general categories:

- **Fixed storage allocation**: Fixed storage allocation means that memory is allocated in the location where it is declared. All fixed storage is named; we have called these variable as identifiers, or just variables. Fixed storage includes both the *automatic* storage class and the *static* storage class. We have been using automatic storage for every variable thus far. When you declare a variable and—optionally—initialize it, you are using automatic storage. We will introduce static storage later in this chapter.
- **Dynamic storage allocation**: Dynamic storage allocation means that memory is allocated upon demand and is only referenced via a pointer. The pointer may be a fixed, named pointer variable, or it may be a part of another dynamic structure.

Two properties of storage classes are their visibility—or scope—within a program or statement block, and their lifetime, or how long that memory exists as the program runs.

Within the general category of fixed storage, there are the following two sub-categories:

- **Internal storage allocation**: Internal storage is storage that is declared within the context of a function block or compound statement; in other words, declared between { and }. Internal storage has both limited scope and a limited lifetime.
- **External storage allocation**: External storage is storage that is declared outside of any function block. It has a much broader scope and lifetime than that of internal memory.

We address each of these categories in turn.

Understanding automatic versus dynamic storage classes

In all the preceding chapters, we have been using a fixed or named storage allocation. That is, whenever we declared a variable or a structure, we gave that memory location a data type and a name. This was fixed in position in our program's main routine and functions. Once that named memory was created, we could access it directly via its name, or indirectly with a pointer to that named location. In this chapter, we will specifically explore the fixed storage classes in greater detail.

Likewise, whenever we declare a literal value—say, 52 or 13—the compiler interprets these values and puts them directly into the code, fixing them in the place where they have been declared. The memory that they occupy is part of the program itself.

In contrast, dynamic storage allocation is unnamed; it can only be accessed via pointers. Dynamic memory allocation will be introduced and explored in the next chapter.

Automatic storage

Automatic storage means that memory is allocated by the compiler at precisely the point when a literal value, variable, array, or structure is declared. A less obvious but well-defined point is when a formal parameter to a function is declared. That memory is automatically deallocated at specific and other well-known points within the program.

In all cases except literal values, when this storage class is allocated, it is given a name—its variable name—along with its data type. Even a pointer to another, already allocated memory location is given a name. When that memory is an element of an array, it is the array name and its offset in the array.

Dynamic storage

In comparison to fixed storage, dynamic storage is a memory that is unnamed but is accessed solely indirectly via pointers. There are special library functions to allocate and deallocate dynamic memory. As we will see in the next chapter, we must take extra care to keep track of the unnamed allocated memory.

Understanding internal versus external storage classes

In the storage class of a fixed or named memory, C has explicit mechanisms to allocate that memory. These correlate to the following four C keywords:

- `auto`
- `static`
- `register`
- `extern`

Note that the `auto` keyword represents the automatic storage class, and the static keyword specifies the `static` storage class. We are currently interested in only the first two of these mechanisms. These keywords precede a variable specification, as follows:

```
<storage class> [const] <data type> <name> [= <initial value>];
```

In this specification, the following applies:

- `<storage class>` is one of the preceding four keywords.
- `[const]` is an optional keyword to indicate whether the named memory can be changed after initialization. If `const` is present, an initial value must be supplied.
- `<data type>` is an intrinsic or custom data type.
- `<name>` is the variable or constant name for the value and data type.
- `[= <initial value>]` is an optional initial value or values to be assigned to the named memory location. If `const` is present, the value in that memory cannot be changed; otherwise, it can be reassigned another value.

When `<storage class>` is omitted, the `auto` keyword is assumed. So, all of our programs up to this point have been using `auto` memory variables by default. Function parameters are also `auto` memory variables and have all the same properties as those we explicitly declare in the body of functions or in compound statements.

The `register` keyword was used in older versions of C to signal to the compiler to store a value in one of the registers of the **central processing unit** (**CPU**) for very quick access to that value. Compilers have become so much more sophisticated that this keyword is ignored, except in some very specialized C compilers.

The `extern` keyword has to do with the scope of external variables declared in other files. We will return to the use of this keyword in Chapter 25, *Understanding Scope*.

Internal or local storage classes

Not only have we been using automatic, fixed storage in all the preceding chapters, we have also been using the sub-class of internal storage. Internal storage is a memory that is allocated either with a compound statement (between { and }) or as a function parameter.

Internal memory includes loop variables that are allocated when the loop is entered and deallocated when the loop is exited or completes.

Internal memory variables are only accessible within the compound statement where they've been declared, and any sub-compound statement declared within that compound statement. Their scope is limited to their enclosing { and }. They are not accessible from any other function or any function that calls them. Therefore, they are often referred to as a local memory because they are strictly local to the code block within which they are declared.

Consider the following function:

```
double doSomething( double aReal, int aNumber ) {
   double d1 = aReal;
   double d2 = 0.0 ;
   int    n1 = aNumber;
   int    n2 = aNumber * 10 ;

   for( int i = 1; i < n1 , i++ ) {
     for( int j = 1; j < n2 ; j++ {
        d1 = i / j;
        d2 + = d1;
     }
   }
   return d2;
```

This function consists of two function parameters and a return value. It also contains within its function body four local variables and two looping variables. This function might be called with the following statement:

```
double aSum = doSomething( 2.25 , 10 );
```

When the function is called, the aReal and aNumber automatic local variables are allocated and assigned (copied) the values of 2.25 and 10, respectively. These variables can then be used throughout the function body. Within the function body, the d1, d2, n1, and n2 variables are automatic local variables. They, too, can be used throughout the function body.

Lastly, we create the loop with the i loop-local variable, where i is only accessible within its loop block. Within that block is another loop with the j loop-local variable, where both j and i, and all other function-local variables, are accessible. Finally, the function returns the value of d2.

In the calling statement, the function assigns the value of the d2 function-local variable to the aSum automatic variable. At the completion of doSomething(), all of the memory allocated by that function is no longer accessible.

External or global storage classes

External storage is memory that is declared outside of any function body, including main(). Such variables can potentially be accessed from any part of the program. These are more often called **global variables** because they are globally accessible from within the file where they are declared.

One advantage of global variables is their ease of accessibility. However, this is also their disadvantage. When a variable can be accessed from anywhere, it becomes increasingly difficult as a program grows in size and complexity to know when that variable changed and what changed it. Global variables should be used sparingly and with great care.

The lifetime of automatic storage

When we consider the various storage classes, not only do we consider when they are created and accessed, but we must also consider when they are deallocated or destroyed. This is their lifetime—from creation to destruction.

Automatic, internal variables are created when the variable is declared either in the body of a compound statement or in a function's formal parameter list. Internal variables are destroyed and no longer accessible when that compound statement or function is exited.

Consider the doSomething() function. The aReal, aNumber, d1, d2, n1, and n2 variables are created when the function is called. All of them are destroyed after the function returns its d2 value. The i loop variable is created when we enter the loop and is destroyed when we exit that outer loop. The j variable is created at each iteration of the outer loop controlled by i and destroyed at the completion of the inner loop controlled by j.

Local variables have a lifetime that is only as long as the compound statement in which they are declared.

Automatic, external variables are created when the program is loaded into memory. They exist for the lifetime of the program. When the program exits (the `main()` function block returns), they are destroyed.

Exploring the static storage class

Sometimes, it is desirable to allocate memory in such a way that it can hold a value beyond the lifetime of automatic memory variables. An example of this might be a routine that could be called from anywhere within a program that returns a continuously increasing value each time it is called, such as a page number or a unique record identifier. Furthermore, we might want to give such a function a starting value and increment the sequence of numbers from that point. We will see how to do each of these.

Neither of these can be achieved easily with automatic storage classes. For this, there is the `static` storage class. As with the `automatic` storage class, it can exist as both internal and external storage.

Internal static storage

When a variable is declared within a function block with the `static` keyword, that variable is accessible only from within that function block when the function is called. The initial value of the static value is assigned at compile time and is not re-evaluated at runtime. Therefore, the value assigned to the static variable must be known at compile time and cannot be an expression or variable.

Consider the following program:

```
#include <stdio.h>

void printHeading( const char* aHeading );

int main( void )  {
  printHeading( "Title Page" );
  printHeading( "Chapter 1 " );
  printHeading( "          " );
  printHeading( "          " );
  printHeading( "Chapter 2 " );
  printHeading( "          " );
  printHeading( "Conclusion" );
}

void printHeading( const char* aHeading )  {
```

```
    static int pageNo = 1;
    printf( "%s \t\t\t Page %d\n" , aHeading , pageNo);
    pageNo++;
}
```

The `printHeading()` function contains the `pageNo` static variable. `pageNo` has `1` as its initial value when the program is started. When `printHeading()` is called, the given heading string is printed along with the current page number value. `pageNo` is then incremented in preparation for the next call to it.

Create a file called `heading.c` and enter the preceding program. Compile and run this program. You should see the following output:

```
> cc heading.c -o heading -Wall -Werror -std=c11
> heading
Title Page           Page 1
Chapter 1            Page 2
                     Page 3
                     Page 4
Chapter 2            Page 5
                     Page 6
Conclusion           Page 7
>
```

The value of the static memory is incremented and preserved even after the function exits.

Now, consider what would happen if the `static` keyword was removed. Do that—remove the `static` keyword. Compile and run the program. You should see the following output:

```
> cc heading.c -o heading -Wall -Werror -std=c11
> heading
Title Page           Page 1
Chapter 1            Page 1
                     Page 1
                     Page 1
Chapter 2            Page 1
                     Page 1
Conclusion           Page 1
>
```

In this case, the automatic variable is initialized each time the function is called, and we never see the incremented value because it is destroyed when the function exits.

External static storage

Because an internal static variable can only be initialized by the compiler, we need another mechanism to safely store a value that we might want to initialize, or seed, ourselves. For this, we can use an external static variable.

External static variables can only be accessible by any other variable or code block, including function blocks, within the file where it is declared. Ideally, then, the code for the external static variable and the function that accesses it should be in a single, separate .c file, as follows:

```
// seriesGenerator.c

static int seriesNumber = 100; // default seed value

void seriesStart( int seed ) {
  seriesNumber = seed;
}

int series( void ) {
  return series++;
}
```

To use these functions, we would need to include a header file with function prototypes for it, as follows:

```
// seriesGenerator.h

void seriesStart( int seed );
int  series( void );
```

We would create the seriesGenerator.c and seriesGenerator.h files with these functions and prototypes. We would also have to add #include <seriesGenerator.h> to any file that calls these functions. We would then compile these files, along with our other source files, into a single executable file. We did this briefly in Chapter 10, *Creating Custom Data Types with typedef*; we will explore this more fully in Chapter 24, *Working with Multi-File Programs*.

This series generator, when compiled into the main program, would be initialized, or seeded, with a call to seriesStart() with some known integer value. After that, each call to series() would generate the next number in the series.

This pattern may seem familiar from the last chapter, Chapter 16, *Creating and Using More Complex Structures*. There, we used srand() to seed our **pseudorandom number generator** (**PRNG**), and then subsequently called rand() to get the next number in the random sequence. You can now more clearly imagine how srand() and rand() would be implemented using static external memory allocation.

The lifetime of static storage

The lifetimes for both internal and external static memory are the same. Static memory is allocated when the program is loaded before any statements are executed. Static memory is only destroyed when the program completes or exits. Therefore, the lifetime of static memory is the same as the lifetime of the program.

Summary

In this chapter, we explored various storage classes, and, how memory is allocated. In particular, we clarified automatic memory allocation, or fixed and named memory—the method we've been using exclusively in all chapters prior to this chapter. In addition to automatic memory allocation, we explored static memory allocation. With both of those approaches, we distinguished between internal memory allocation—variables declared within a compound statement or function parameters—and external memory allocation—variables declared outside of any function. For each of these storage classes (automatic internal, automatic external, static internal, and static external memory allocation), we considered the lifetime of the memory—when that memory is destroyed and no longer accessible.

We are now ready to explore in the next chapter the much more flexible storage class, dynamic memory, which is unnamed and can only be accessed via pointer variables. Dynamic memory techniques will put us at the threshold of very powerful dynamic data structures.

18
Using Dynamic Memory Allocation

Not all data can be allocated statically or automatically. Sometimes, the number of items to be manipulated is not known beforehand; that number can only be known at runtime and may vary from run to run, depending on external inputs (user input, files, and so on). In the preceding chapter, we examined automatic and static memory allocation. We now stand on the threshold of an incredibly powerful feature of C – dynamic memory allocation and manipulation. Once we pass this threshold, many flexible dynamic data manipulations will be available to us. We will briefly introduce many of these data structures and their uses in this chapter.

As mentioned in the preceding chapter, dynamic memory is unnamed, so it can only be manipulated via pointers. Furthermore, dynamic memory has a different lifetime than either automatic or static memory.

The following topics will be covered in this chapter:

- Acquiring an introductory understanding of the power and flexibility of dynamic memory allocation
- Learning how to allocate and release dynamic memory
- Implementing a simple linked list dynamic data structure
- Creating and using a dynamic function pointer
- Becoming aware of various special considerations when using dynamic memory
- Learning about some other important dynamic data structures

Let's get started!

Technical requirements

As detailed in the *Technical requirements* section of `Chapter 1`, *Running Hello, World!,* continue to use the tools you have chosen.

The source code for this chapter can be found at `https://github.com/PacktPublishing/Learn-C-Programming`.

Introducing dynamic memory

Do we always know exactly how many objects we will need to manipulate and allocate memory for in a program? The answer is a resounding *No!*

Not every situation or program can be efficiently addressed using just automatic or static memory. The number of objects may vary widely over the runtime of the program and from one run to another of the same program. The number of objects may depend on inputs from the user (covered in `Chapter 20`, *Getting Input From the Command Line*, and `Chapter 21`, *Exploring Formatted Input*), from one or more existing files (covered in `Chapter 22`, *Working with Files*, and `Chapter 23`, *Using File Input and File Output*), another device, or even from a network connection to a remote server.

Furthermore, some problems cannot be easily solved with simple automatic or static memory. These types of problems include sorting algorithms, efficient searching and lookup of large amounts of data, and many geometric and graph theory optimization techniques. All of these are advanced programming topics. Dynamic memory opens the doors to these fascinating and powerful algorithms.

Before we dive into dynamic memory allocation, let's examine the way C allocates all types of memory in a program's memory space.

A brief tour of C's memory layout

It is now time to gain a cursory understanding of how C organizes memory when a program is loaded and run. This discussion builds upon the *Introduction to pointers* section in `Chapter 13`, *Using Pointers*. Consider the following diagram:

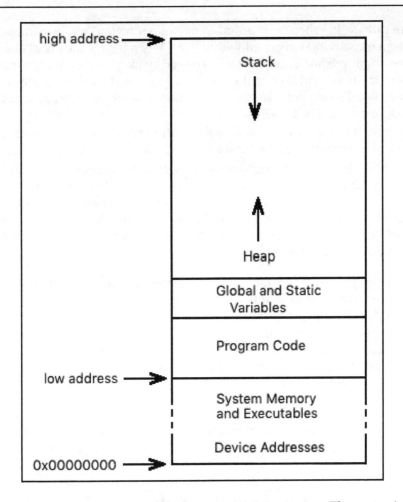

This is a very simple conceptual view of a program's *memory space*. The operating system provides this space to the program when it is loaded to be run. The C runtime then divvies up the memory given to it into segments, each for a specific use. It consists of the following segments:

- **System memory**: This consists of system memory and system programs, as well as the addresses for all of the devices on the computer. This segment is mapped for all running programs so that there is only ever one copy of the system code in the overall system memory space. The system exclusively manages this memory.
- **Program code**: This is where the compiled program is loaded and executed.
- **Global and static memory**: After the program is loaded, global and static variables are allocated and initialized.

- **The call stack**: When your program makes a function call, its parameters, any automatic variables declared within it, and its return value are allocated in this segment or pushed onto the stack. The call stack grows from high memory to lower memory, and then to the heap space, as one function calls another and that function calls yet another. When a function returns, its memory is popped off the stack (deallocated). Think of a stack of plates – you put a plate on top of the stack one after the other; then, you take them off the stack one at a time in the reverse order they were placed on the stack.
- **The heap**: When your program allocates dynamic memory, it is allocated from this segment. Heap space grows from low memory to higher memory, toward the stack space. Most allocations here are done somewhat randomly using the best fit allocation scheme. That is, the lowest available space is allocated, if possible. When that memory is deallocated, it becomes available for other allocations of the same or smaller size.

Each program lives in its own memory space. The system space is common to all programs. After your program has been loaded into this memory space and the global and static variables have been allocated, the system calls the `main()` function and begins execution. When you call a function, execution jumps to the memory address of that function and pushes its parameters, automatic variables, and return values onto the call stack. When the function completes, it pops its memory off the stack and returns execution to the location in the program space where it was called.

All dynamic memory allocations are made from within the heap segment of the program memory space. Now, we will explore the mechanisms we can use to allocate and release dynamic memory.

Allocating and releasing dynamic memory

Dynamic memory is allocated and released (deallocated) only at very explicit points by a program. It doesn't happen automatically; it doesn't happen by accident or by chance. You make this happen when you call specific C Standard Library calls to allocate and release dynamic memory.

Allocating dynamic memory

Memory allocation routines are declared in `stdlib.h` and are a part of the C Runtime Library. There are two very similar allocation routines – `malloc()` and `calloc()` – which are used to allocate a new block of memory from the heap. The main difference between `malloc()` and `calloc()` is that `calloc()` clears the memory block it allocates, whereas `malloc()` only does allocation. There is a third routine, `realloc()`, which is used to resize an existing block of heap memory. These functions have the following prototypes:

```
void* malloc( size_t size );
void* calloc( size_t count , size_t size );

void* realloc( void *ptr , size_t size);
```

Somewhere in `stdlib.h`, `size_t` is defined as follows:

```
type unsigned int size_t;
```

Each of these functions returns a `void*` pointer to a block of memory in the heap space. Recall that `void*` is a pointer type that is of an unknown or generic type; a pointer of the `void*` type must be cast to the required pointer type before you can use that pointer. Notice that `malloc()` takes a single `size` parameter, while `calloc()` takes the `count` and `size` parameters.

If either function cannot find memory in the heap space, the returned pointer will be `NULL`. It is good practice to check whether these routines were successful.

The following code shows how each allocates memory for a single `Card` structure:

```
Card* pCard1 = (Card*)malloc( sizeof( Card );
if( pCard1 == NULL ) ...                       // out of memory error

Card* pCard2 = (Card*)calloc( 1 , sizeof( Card );
if( pCard2 == NULL ) ...                       // out of memory error
```

If we wanted to allocate memory for, say, five cards, we would use the following code:

```
Card* pHand1 = (Card)malloc( 5 * sizeof( Card );
if( pHand1 == NULL ) ... // out of memory error

Card* pHand2 = (Card*)calloc( 5 , sizeof( Card );
if( pHand2 == NULL ) ... // out of memory error
```

In this second example, we are allocating space for five cards contiguously in dynamic memory. This sounds like an array, doesn't it? Well, in fact, it is. Instead of an automatic array declared with Card hand1[5] and Card hand2[5], both of which allocate blocks of memory to hold five cards on the stack, pHand1 and pHand2 both point to contiguous blocks of memory in the heap space.

Recall how array names and pointers to arrays are interchangeable. With these allocations, we can now refer to individual cards in the heap space with pHand1[3] and pHand2[i]. This is simply astounding! We can access arrays in either the stack space or the heap space using array notation or pointer notation. Examples of how to do this are provided in the *Accessing dynamic memory* section.

In both examples, each call to allocate memory using calloc() or malloc() appears to be interchangeable. So, why use one function over the other? Is one of these preferred over the other? Before we can answer that, we need to know that calloc() both allocates memory and initializes it to all zeros, while malloc() simply allocates the memory and leaves initialization up to us. So, the simple answer is to prefer calloc() over malloc().

The realloc() function changes the size of the memory that's pointed to by ptr to the given size, which may be larger or smaller than the original memory allocation. If size is larger, the original contents are copied and the extra space is uninitialized. If size is smaller, the original contents are truncated. If ptr is NULL, realloc() behaves exactly like malloc(). As with malloc() and calloc(), the pointer returned by realloc() must be cast to the required type before it can be used.

Releasing dynamic memory

When we are done with the heap memory we've allocated, we release it with a call to free(). The free() function returns the allocated memory to the available heap pool of memory. This call does not have to occur within the same function where the memory was allocated. The prototype in stdlib.h for free() is as follows:

```
void  free( void* ptr );
```

The pointer that's passed to free() must contain a value that originated from one of the calls to malloc(), calloc(), or realloc(). There is no need to cast the void* pointer argument. If ptr is NULL, free() does nothing.

We would release the memory that was allocated in the previous subsection as follows:

```
free( pCard1 );
free( pCard2 );
free( pHand1 );
free( pHand2 );
```

These four statements release each block of memory we allocated earlier. Allocated dynamic memory can be freed in any order; it does not have to be freed in the same order it was allocated.

Accessing dynamic memory

Once we've allocated dynamic memory, we can access it via the pointer that's returned by the allocation functions, as we would with any other pointer. With each of the previous examples, we could use that dynamic memory as follows:

```
InitializeCard( pCard1 , spade , ace , kNotWild );
InitializeCard( pCard2 , heart , queen , kNotWild );
```

pCard1 and pCard2 are pointers to individual Card structures. Therefore, we can use them just like we used the pointers in carddeck.c using automatic variables.

However, consider the following:

```
pHand1[3].suit = diamond;
pHand1[3].face = two;

for( int i = 0 ; i < kCardsInHand , i++ ) {
    PrintCard( &(pHand[i]) );
}
```

Both pHand1 and pHand2 point to a contiguous block of memory that is equivalent to the size of five Card structures. Using array notation, we set the suit and face structure members of the fourth element via pHand1. The PrintCard() function takes a pointer to a card structure, while pHand2 points to a block of Card structures. Array notation gives us the individual cards in the block; we must then get the address of that card element and pass it PrintCard(). We will see this in action when we rework (yet again!) our cardDeck.c program in Chapter 20, *Getting Input From the Command Line*, and Chapter 24, *Working with Multi-File Programs*.

Rather than using arrays in heap memory, it is far more common to manipulate structures individually, as we shall see when we explore the *linked list* dynamic structure in the next section.

The lifetime of dynamic memory

Heap memory has a lifetime that begins when the memory is allocated. Once allocated, that memory exists until the `free()` function is called to release that memory. Allocating and releasing memory is also called **memory management** within a program.

Alternatively, all memory is deallocated when the program exits, both in terms of fixed memory and dynamic memory. It is generally considered a sloppy practice to ignore memory management for dynamic memory, especially for large, complex programs or for programs that are likely to run for a very long time.

Special considerations for dynamic allocation

Dynamic memory allocation does not come without a cost. In this case, the cost is typically conceptual complexity. This cost also takes the form of added management of heap memory and awareness of the pitfalls of potential memory leaks.

To be honest, I should add that it may take some time to get your head around some of these concepts. For me, some of them took me quite a while to grasp. The best way, I've found, is to take a working program and alter it, see how it behaves, and then understand why it did what it did. Assume nothing. Or, start with a minimal working program that uses the mind-bending feature and then build upon it. Interact with your code; play with it. No matter how you do it, you can't just think about it. You have to twist, poke, prod, and cajole your code until you understand what it is doing. Otherwise, it is just guesswork.

Heap memory management

The amount or degree of heap memory management required in a program is a consideration that depends on the complexity and expected runtime duration of that program.

When heap memory is initialized at the start of a program and remains largely unchanged after it is initialized, little heap management will be required. It may be acceptable to simply let heap memory exist until the program exits. The `free()` function may never be called in such a program.

On the other hand, for programs whose complexity is large, or where heap memory is heavily used, or where the runtime duration is hours, days, months, or even years, heap management is essential. A program that controls, say, a banking system, a fighter jet, or a petroleum refinery might have catastrophic consequences if the heap for that program is not properly managed, causing the program to terminate abnormally. The bank may suddenly show a pile of money in your account or take it all away from you; the fighter jet may lose control while in flight and crash; the petroleum refinery may suddenly react chaotically and explode. The discipline of software engineering exists primarily to make such software systems both maintainable by various levels of programmers and extremely reliable over the long lifespan of such systems.

For some data structures, such as a linked list, which we will explore in depth later in this chapter, memory management is relatively straightforward. However, for others, memory management may not be obvious. Each data structure and algorithm has its own set of memory considerations to be addressed. When we ignore memory management or do not address it fully, we might encounter a common dynamic memory problem known as *memory leaks*.

Memory leaks

One of the main challenges of heap management is to prevent memory leaks. A memory leak is when a block of memory is allocated and the pointer to it is lost so that it cannot be released until the program quits. The following is a simple example of a memory leak:

```
Card* pCard = (Card*)calloc( 1 , sizeof( Card );
...
pCard = (Card*)calloc( 1 , sizeof( Card );   // <-- Leak!
```

In this example, pCard first points to one block of heap memory and then is later assigned to another. The first block of memory is allocated but, without a pointer to it, it cannot be freed. To correct this error, call free() before reassigning pCard.

A more subtle leak is as follows:

```
struct Thing1 {
  int size;
  struct Thing2* pThing2
}

struct Thing1* pThing1 = (struct Thing1*)calloc( 1 , sizeof(Thing1) );
Thing1->pThing2 = (struct Thing2*)calloc( 1 , sizeof(Thing2) );
...
free( pThing1 );   // <-- Leak!
```

In this example, we create the `Thing1` structure, which contains a pointer to another `Thing2` structure. We allocate heap memory for `Thing1`, which is pointed to by `pThing1`. We then allocate heap memory for `Thing2`, which is pointed to by the `pThing2` pointer element of `Thing1`. So far, so good, and we go on our merry way.

Later, we release `pThing1`. Uh oh! What happened to the pointer to `pThing2`? It's gone. That means that whatever `pThing2` pointed to cannot be accessed again. We just leaked the memory of `pThing2`.

The correct way to release all of the memory of `pThing1` is as follows:

```
free( pThing1->pThing2 );
free( pThing1 );
```

First, the `free()` function is called on `pThing1`, which is the pointer element of `pThing2`. Then, and only then, can we release the memory of `pThing1`.

A third, equally subtle leak is as follows:

```
Card* CreateCard( ... ) {
   Card* pCard = (Card*) calloc( 1 , sizeof( Card ) );
   InitializeCard( pCard , ... );
   return pCard;
}
```

In the `CreateCard()` function, memory for `Card` is allocated in the heap space, initialized, and the pointer to it is returned. This is all fine and dandy.

Now, consider how this function might be called, as follows:

```
Card* aCard = CreateCard( ... );
PrintCard( aCard );
aCard = CreateCard( ... );   // <-- Leak!
PrintCard( aCard );
```

This is similar but less obvious than the first memory leak example. Each time the `CreateCard()` function is called, it allocates more heap memory. However, when it is called multiple times, the pointer to the allocated memory may be overwritten as it is in the sequence of `CreateCard()` and `PrintCard()`. The `CreateCard()` function has added the burden on the caller of being responsible for either calling `free()` before reusing `aCard` or to somehow keep track of the various pointer values that are returned, as follows:

```
Card* aCard = CreateCard( ... );
PrintCard( aCard );
free( aCard );
aCard = CreateCard( ... );
```

```
  PrintCard( aCard );
  free( aCard )

  Card* pHand = (Card*)calloc( 5 , sizeof( Card* ) );
  for( int i = 0 ; i<5 ; i++ )
  {
   pHand[i] = CreateCard( ... );
   PrintCard( pHand[i] );
  }
  ...
  for( int i = 0 ; i<5 ; i++ )
   free( pHand[i] );
  free( pHand );
```

In the first group of statements, `free()` is called before `aCard` is assigned a new pointer to the heap memory.

In the second group of statements, an array of five pointers to `Card` is allocated. Note that this is not the same as allocating memory for five `Card`; `CreateCard()` does the allocation for a `Card` one at a time in a loop. Using a loop, five cards are created in the heap space and printed. Later, a loop is used to properly release the `Card` memory allocated in `CreateCard()`, which is pointed to by each element of `pHand`. Finally, `pHand` (a block of five pointers) is released.

Simply being aware of possible memory leaks and what might cause them goes a long way when it comes to recognizing and preventing them from happening in the first place.

We will now explore a general, yet very useful, dynamic structure.

The linked list dynamic data structure

The most basic dynamic data structure is the linked list. A linked list is the basis for other dynamic structures, such as stacks and queues. A stack conforms to the rules that each new element must be added to the front of the list and that each element can only be removed from the front of the list. A queue conforms to the rules that each new element must be added to the back of the list and that each element can only be removed from the front of the list.

We will implement a simple linked list and then test it from within the `main()` function. Later, we will employ this list structure and its routines when we return to our `carddeck.c` program in `Chapter 24`, *Working with Multi-File Programs*.

Create a file called `linklisttester.c`. It is in this single file that we will create our linked list structure, operations, and test code. Before we begin, consider the following diagram of the linked list we will create:

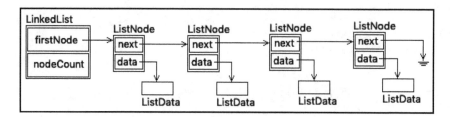

A linked list consists of a header structure that contains information about the list, as well as a link to the first element, or *list node*. Any link that is NULL signifies that it is the last list node in the list. If the head structure has a NULL link, the list is empty. In the preceding diagram, the linked list contains the link list header with four list nodes. Each node contains a pointer to the next list node and a pointer to a data element. We must ensure that each node has a non-NULL data pointer; otherwise, the node is not valid. The data element could be a simple variable or a complex structure.

Linked list structures

It should be no surprise from our diagram of a linked list that we need two structures – a linked list header structure and a list node structure. These are defined as follows:

```
typedef struct _Node ListNode;
typedef struct _Node {
   ListNode*  pNext;
   ListData*  pData;
} ListNode;

typedef struct {
   ListNode*  pFirstNode;
   int        nodeCount;
} LinkedList;
```

First, we define an arbitrary tag, `struct _Node`, as a `ListNode` structure. This is a naming mechanism so that we can use the name `ListNode` in the following structure definition with the members of `struct _Node`. The `struct _Node` tag contains a `ListNode` pointer and a `ListData` pointer, both of which will be known henceforth as simple `ListNode` custom types. We won't need to use `struct _Node` again. Our list will consist of zero or more `ListNode`.

Next, we define a heading for our linked list, `LinkedList`, which consists of a `ListNode` pointer and an `int` element to keep track of the number of elements in our list. Note that we don't need a temporary tag name after `struct`; this structure will only be known as a `LinkedList`.

Note that the data portion of `ListNode` is a pointer to something called `ListData`. We will redefine `ListData` as an `int` element, as follows:

```
typedef int  ListData;
```

We're doing this so that we don't get bogged down in the unnecessary details of `ListData`. Later, when we complete and validate our linked list code, we will change `ListData` for our revised `carddeck.c` program so that it looks as follows:

```
typedef Card ListData;
```

This linked list code will work the same for pointers to `int`, as well as pointers to `Card` or as a pointer to any other structure we want our list to contain. This is the power (or confusion, depending on your perspective) of using `typedef`.

Declaring operations on a linked list

Now that we have the required data structures defined, we can declare operations on those data structures. A data structure is defined by both the data it contains or represents and the operations that can be performed on it. The operations we will need to perform in order to manipulate a general linked list mechanism independently of the specific data contents of the list are as follows:

1. Create a new `LinkedList` header that allocates and properly initializes the header record.
2. Create a new `ListNode` element that allocates and properly initializes the node element. Once created, the node still isn't part of the list.
3. Delete a node. This doesn't involve the list; typically, this will be done after a node is removed from the list.
4. Insert a node either into the front or back of the list.
5. Remove a node either from the front or back of the list and return that node to the caller.
6. Get the node from either the front or back of the list; this only observes the node data – it does not change the list in any way.

7. Determine whether the list is empty.
8. Determine the size of the list.
9. Print the list. This involves traversing the list and printing each node.
10. Print an individual node. This involves printing the `ListData` element of the node. The function to print `ListData` needs to be specific to the type of `ListData`. We will need a way to pass a print function as a parameter to this operation.

These operations lead to the following function prototypes:

```
LinkedList* CreateLinkedList();
bool        IsEmpty(    LinkedList* pList );
int         Size(       LinkedList* pList );
void        InsertNodeToFront(  LinkedList* pList , ListNode* pNode );
void        InsertNodeToBack(   LinkedList* pList , ListNode* pNode );
ListNode*   RemoveNodeFromFront( LinkedList* pList );
ListNode*   RemoveNodeFromBack(  LinkedList* pList );
ListNode*   GetNode(            LinkedList* pList , int pos );
ListNode*   CreateNode( ListData* pData );
void        DeleteNode( ListNode* pNode );
void        PrintList(  LinkedList* pList ,
                        void (*printData)(ListData* pData ) );
void        PrintNode(  ListNode* pNode ,
                        void (*printData)(ListData* pData ) );
void        OutOfStorage( void );
```

As we go through the definitions of each of these operations, you may find it helpful to refer to the diagram of the linked list. Try to identify how each pointer in the list is manipulated in each function.

Here, we will add a `CreateData()` operation. It will be deferred to the final implementation where the specific `ListData` type is known. At that point, we'll also define the `printListData` function.

Notice the `OutOfStorage()` function. We don't know whether we'll ever need this function. We will need it if the `CreateXXX()` function fails to allocate memory. It is generally a good practice to provide some feedback when a program fails, as follows:

```
void OutOfStorage( void ) {
 fprintf( stderr,"### FATAL RUNTIME ERROR ### No Memory Available" );
 exit( EXIT_FAILURE );
}
```

This is a simple function that does the following:

- Prints an error message to a special output stream, stderr.
- Exits the program with a non-zero exit value. The program exits immediately and no further program execution is done. We will learn more about stderr in Chapter 23, *Using File Input and File Output*.

We can now see how each operation is defined.

A new LinkedList header can be created as follows:

```
LinkedList*  CreateLinkedList()  {
   LinkedList* pLL = (LinkedList*) calloc( 1 , sizeof( LinkedList ) );
   if( pLL == NULL) OutOfStorage();
   return pLL;
}
```

The calloc() function is used to allocate memory for the LinkedList header and initialize all the values in the structure to 0; a pointer to that memory is returned unless calloc() fails, in which case OutOfStorage() is called and the program stops. The functions IsEmpty() and Size() are as follows:

```
bool  IsEmpty( LinkedList* pList )  {
   return( pList->nodeCount == 0 );
}
```

and

```
int  Size( LinkedList* pList )  {
   return pList->nodeCount;
}
```

The IsEmpty() utility function returns true if the list is empty and false otherwise.

The Size() utility function simply returns the value of nodeCount. We use a function to get this value rather than access it directly because the structure of LinkedList may need to be changed. This approach encapsulates the size information, regardless of how it might be implemented later.

The next two functions define how a `ListNode` structure can be inserted into the list, as follows:

```
void  InsertNodeToFront( LinkedList* pList , ListNode* pNode )  {
   ListNode* pNext    = pList->pFirstNode;
   pList->pFirstNode = pNode;
   pNode->pNext       = pNext;
   pList->nodeCount++;
}
```

The following is the second function:

```
void InsertNodeToBack( LinkedList* pList , ListNode* pNode )  {
   if( IsEmpty( pList ) )  {
     pList->pFirstNode = pNode;
   } else {
     ListNode* pCurr = pList->pFirstNode ;
     while( pCurr->pNext != NULL )  {
       pCurr = pCurr->pNext;
     }
     pCurr->pNext  = pNode;
   }
   pList->nodeCount++;
}
```

To insert a `ListNode` into the front of the list, we only need to adjust two pointers, `pList->pFirstNode` (saving it before we change it) and the new node's `pNode->pNext` pointer. If the list is empty, `pList->pFirstNode` will be `NULL` anyway, so this code properly handles all cases. Finally, the node count is incremented.

Let's see what inserting a new node at the front of the list looks like. The following diagram illustrates the list when this function is entered:

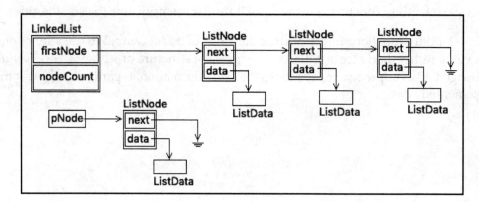

After the two pointers have been adjusted, the list will look as follows:

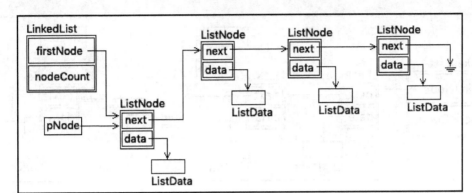

Notice that the pNode pointer is no longer needed since pList->pFirstNode also points to the new node.

To insert a ListNode at the back of the list, we first have to see if the list is empty; if so, we only need to set pList->pFirstNode. Otherwise, we have to traverse the list to the last entry. This is done by first setting a temporary pointer, pCurr, to the first item in the list. When pCurr->pNext is NULL, pCurr is pointing to the last item in the list. We only need to set pCurr->pNext to the new node; its pNext pointer is already NULL. Finally, the node count is incremented.

Now, let's see what inserting a new node at the back of the list looks like. The following diagram illustrates the list when this function is entered:

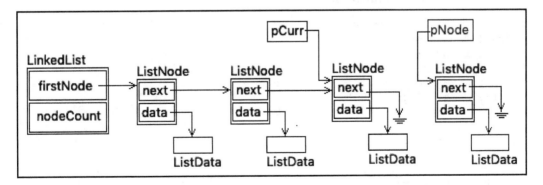

After the `next` final pointer is adjusted, the list will look as follows:

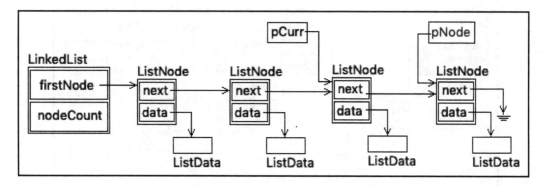

Once `pCurr->next` points to our new node, both the `pCurr` and `pNode` pointers are no longer needed.

Like the insert functions, the next two functions define how a `ListNode` can be removed from the list, as follows:

```
ListNode*  RemoveNodeFromFront( LinkedList* pList )  {
   if( IsEmpty( pList ))  return NULL;
   ListNode* pCurr    = pList->pFirstNode;
   pList->pFirstNode = pList->pFirstNode->pNext;
   pList->nodeCount--;
   return pCurr;
}
```

The following is the second function:

```
ListNode* RemoveNodeFromBack( LinkedList* pList )  {
   if( IsEmpty( pList ) )  {
      return NULL;
   } else {
      ListNode* pCurr = pList->pFirstNode ;
      ListNode* pPrev = NULL;
      while( pCurr->pNext != NULL )  {
         pPrev = pCurr;
         pCurr = pCurr->pNext;
      }
      pPrev->pNext = NULL;
      pList->nodeCount--;
      return pCurr;
   }
}
```

To remove a `ListNode` structure from the front of the list, we need to check whether the list is empty and return `NULL` if it is. Otherwise, we set the node to be returned by `pCurr` to `pList->pFirstNode` and then we set the next node after `pList->pFirstNode`, which is being pointed to by `pList->pFirstNode->pNext`, as the first node. The node count is decremented and returns `pCurr`.

Let's see what deleting a node from the front of the list looks like. The following diagram illustrates the list when this function is entered:

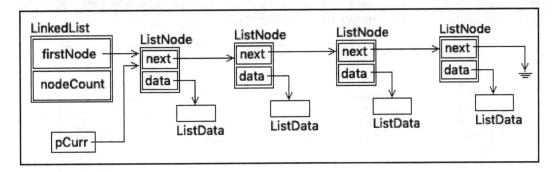

Notice that `pCurr` also points to `pList->pFirstNode`. After the two pointers have been adjusted, the list will look as follows:

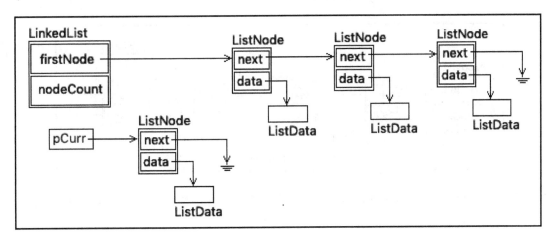

Notice that `pCurr` is the only pointer pointing to the node to be deleted and that the first node in the list pointed to by `pList->pFirstNode` now points to the new first node.

To remove a `ListNode` at the back of the list, we have to see if the list is empty; if so, we return `NULL`. Otherwise, we have to traverse the list to the last entry. This is done by setting a temporary pointer, `pCurr`, to the first item in the list. We need another temporary pointer, `pPrev`, which points to the node before the node we want to remove. Both are adjusted as the list is traversed. When `pCurr->pNext` is `NULL`, `pCurr` is pointing to the last item in the list – the node we want to remove. But we also need to set `pPrev->pNext` to `NULL` to indicate it is the last item in the list. The node count is decremented and `pCurr` is returned.

Now, let's see what deleting a node from the back of the list looks like. The following diagram illustrates the list when this function is entered:

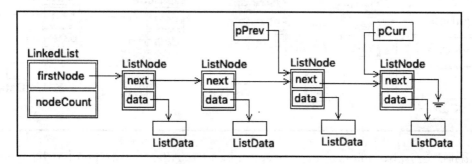

After the final `next` pointer is adjusted, the list will look as follows:

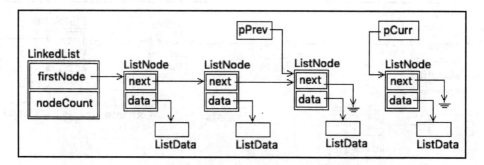

Once `pCurr->next` points to our new node, the `pCurr` and `pNode` pointers are no longer needed.

The `GetNode()` function inspects a node's data without removing it from the list, as follows:

```
ListNode*  GetNode( LinkedList* pList , int pos )  {
   ListNode* pCurr = pList->pFirstNode;
   if( pCurr == NULL )  {
```

```
      return pList->pFirstNode;
    } else if ( pos == 0 )  {
      return pList->pFirstNode;
    } else {
      int i = 0;
      while( pCurr->pNext != NULL )  {
        if( i == pos ) return pCurr;
        i++;
        pCurr = pCurr->pNext;
      }
      return pCurr;
    }
  }
```

Before traversing the list, GetNode() first checks to see whether the list is empty, and then checks to see whether the 0th position (a magic number indicating the front of the list) is requested. If so, the pFirstNode pointer is returned. Otherwise, the list is traversed, adjusting pCurr in order to check for both the end of the list and whether the current node count is the node we are looking for. This will be either a pointer to the node we are requesting or a pointer to the last node that was returned. The list remains unchanged.

The CreateNode() function simply creates a new node structure, as follows:

```
  ListNode*  CreateNode( ListData* pData )  {
    ListNode* pNewNode = (ListNode*) calloc( 1 , sizeof( ListNode ) );
    if( pNewNode == NULL ) OutOfStorage();
    pNewNode->pData = pData;
    return pNewNode;
  }
```

The calloc() function is used to allocate memory for a ListNode and initialize all the values in the structure to 0; a pointer to that memory is returned unless calloc() fails, in which case OutOfStorage() is called and the program stops. Note that the linked list is not involved; this function only creates the node and correctly initializes it with the ListData pointer, which itself needs to have been created before we call this routine.

When items are removed from the list, they are not deleted until DeleteNode() is called, as follows:

```
  void  DeleteNode( ListNode* pNode )  {
    free( pNode->pData );
    free( pNode );
  }
```

Notice that in order to prevent a subtle memory leak, `DeleteNode()` frees both the `ListData` structure (pointed to by `pNode->pData`) and the `ListNode` structure (pointed to by `pNode`).

To print the list, `PrintList()` is called, as follows:

```
void  PrintList( LinkedList* pList ,
                 void (*printData)(ListData* pData ) )   {
  printf( "List has %2d entries: [" , Size( pList ) );
  ListNode* pCurr = pList->pFirstNode;
  while( pCurr != NULL )   {
    PrintNode( pCurr , printData );
    pCurr = pCurr->pNext;
  }
  printf( "]\n" );
}
```

The `PrintList()` function takes two parameters – the first should be familiar to you, while the second deserves some explanation. Recall from our memory layout diagram earlier in this chapter that a function is a named location in memory where program execution jumps to and returns back to the location it was called from. Most of the time, we've simply used the function name. In this case, we don't know the function name because the `ListData` type could change. The `print` function for `ListData` will need to change to reflect its actual type. Therefore, we need to pass a pointer to that function so that we can simply call it by using a pointer to it at some later time.

Pointers to functions

When we declare a pointer to a function, we need more than just the pointer value – we need to specify both the return type of the function and the parameter list of the function being pointed to.

Let's break this apparent syntactical gobbledygook down into understandable parts. It consists of three parts:

- The return type of the function; in this case, `void`.
- The name of the pointer to the function; in this case, `(*printData)`. This indicates that `printData` is the name pointer to a function; the function itself may have a completely different name. Given item 1, we know that the function returns `void`.
- The function we'll implement via this pointer to it has a parameter list; in this case, `(ListData* pData)`.

Given these three parts, compare the function pointer declaration to the function's prototype; in this case, `PrintInt()`:

```
void (*printData)(ListData* pData);   // function pointer
void PrintInt(    ListData* pData);   // function prototype
void PrintInt(    ListData* pData)   { // function definition
   ...
}
```

Notice how, except for the declaration of a function pointer, the other elements of a function call are present – the return type and the function parameter list. A function pointer cannot point to just any function. It must be declared with the same return type and parameter list as the function it will be used to call.

In the function body of `PrintList()`, we do not call the function using the function pointer named `printData`; instead, we pass that pointer value to the function that will call it, that is, `PrintNode()`.

To print the list, we print some information about the list and then iterate through it, updating the temporary pointer, `pCurr`, all while visiting each node in the list. At each iteration, `PrintNode()` is called with the current node pointer and the pointer to the function to print the data.

To print an individual node's data, `PrintNode()` is called, as follows:

```
void PrintNode( ListNode* pNode ,
                void(*printData)( ListData* pData ) )   {
   printData( pNode->pData );
}
```

The parameter list for `PrintNode()` consists of a pointer to a node and the same function pointer specification (you may still call this syntactical gobbledygook). But notice that here, in the function body, the `printData` pointer is used as if it were a function name (it's just a pointer) with the appropriate parameter list. We'll see the definition of `PrintInt()`, the function this will call, very shortly.

Now would be a good time to enter all of the function prototypes, the functions themselves, a dummy `main()` function, and the following `#include` files in `linkedlisttester.c` before going any further:

```
#include <stdio.h>      // for printf() and fprintf()
#include <stdlib.h>     // for calloc() and free()
#include <stdbool.h>    // for bool, true, false
```

Compile the program. You should receive no errors. This will serve as a simple checkpoint. Address any compiler errors. Most likely, they will be typos or omissions of simple things. Do not proceed until you get a clean compile.

More complex operations on a linked list

Our list provides a useful but minimal set of operations. It contains both stack and queue operations so that we can use it for either a stack or a queue, as needed. There are other list operations you might want to try to implement yourself. Some of these might include the following function prototypes:

```
ListNode*  InsertNodeAt( LinkedList* pList , ListNode* pNode );
ListNode*  RemoveNodeAt( LinkedList* pList , ListNode* pNode );
void       SortList     ( LinkedList* pList , eSortOrder order );
void       ConcatenateList( LinkedList* pList1 , LinkedList* pList2 );
```

We will not implement these functions right now. We will, however, implement some of these when we revisit our `carddeck.c` program.

A program to test our linked list structure

OK, so we implemented a linked list in C. Or so we think. We wrote a lot of code that we compiled for errors as we wrote it. However, we can't know for certain until we test it. We need to test it thoroughly and get all the results we expect. The testing and verification part of programming is just as important – sometimes even more important – than just writing code that compiles. Writing and verifying the code you write distinguishes a novice programmer from an expert.

Before we can continue, we need two functions specific to our `ListData` type. The first is as follows:

```
void PrintInt( int* i )   {
  printf( "%2d ", *i );
}
```

The second is as follows:

```
ListData* CreateData( ListData d )   {
  ListData* pD = (ListData*)calloc( 1 , sizeof( ListData ) );
  if( pD == NULL )  OutOfStorage();
  *pD = d;
  return pD;
}
```

The `PrintInt()` function simply prints the integer value passed to it by calling `printf()`. If we were to use a different `ListData` type, we would need to provide an appropriate `PrintData()` routine for it. We'll see how this function is called in `main()` with the `PrintList()` function calls.

The `CreateData()` function calls `calloc()` to allocate memory for a `ListData` structure and initializes all the values in the structure to 0; a pointer to that memory is returned unless `calloc()` fails, in which case `OutOfStorage()` is called and the program stops. This function will be used in our test functions to exercise our linked list.

We can now start with the `main()` function and work backward. The test code in `main()` is as follows:

```
int main( void )  {
   LinkedList* pLL = CreateLinkedList();

   printf( "\nUsing input{ 1  2  3  4 } " );
   PrintList( pLL , PrintInt );
   int data1[] = { 1 , 2 , 3 , 4 };
   for( int i = 0 ; i < 4 ; i++)  {
      TestPrintOperation( pLL , eInsert , data1[i] , eFront );
   }
   TestPrintOperation( pLL , eLook   , 0  , eFront );
   TestPrintOperation( pLL , eDelete , 0  , eBack );

   printf( "\nUsing input{ 31 32 33 }   " );
   PrintList( pLL , PrintInt );
   int data2[] = { 31 , 32 , 33 };
   for( int i = 0 ; i < 3 ; i++)  {
      TestPrintOperation( pLL , eInsert , data2[i] , eBack );
   }
   TestPrintOperation( pLL , eLook   , 0  , eBack );
   int count = pLL->nodeCount;
   for( int i = 0 ; i < count ; i++)  {
      TestPrintOperation( pLL , eDelete, 0 , eFront );
   }
}
```

In `main()`, we are exercising all of the features of our linked list. This test consists of the following operations:

1. Create a new linked list.
2. Print it out, showing that it is empty.
3. Insert four nodes, each into the front of it. Each time a node is inserted, the action is described and the current list is printed.

4. Look at the first node.
5. Delete a node from the back. Each time a node is inserted, the action is described and the current list is printed.
6. Insert three nodes, each into the back of it.
7. Look at the last node.
8. Delete each node from the front of the list until it is empty. Each time a node is deleted, the action is described and the current list is printed.

At each operation, we print some information about what happened and the current state of the list. Most of the test work occurs in the TestPrintOperation(), as follows:

```
void TestPrintOperation( LinkedList* pLL , eAction action ,
                         ListData data    , eWhere   where )  {
switch( action )  {
   case eLook:
     data = TestExamineNode( pLL , where );
     printf( "Get %s node, see [%2d]. " ,
              where==eFront ? "front" : " back" , data );
     break;
   case eInsert:
     printf( "Insert [%2d] to %s.     " , data ,
              where==eFront ? "front" : " back" );
     TestCreateNodeAndInsert( pLL , data , where );
     break;
   case eDelete:
     data = TestRemoveNodeAndFree( pLL , where );
     printf( "Remove [%2d] from %s.    " , data ,
              where==eFront ? "front" : " back" );
     break;
   default:
     printf( "::ERROR:: unknown action\n" );
     break;
   }
   PrintList( pLL , TestPrintInt );
}
```

For testing purposes, some enums are defined, that is, eAction { eLook , eInsert, eDelete } and eWhere {eFront , eBack }, to enable a central test routine, TestPrintOperation(), to be called. For each possible eAction, we use a switch to print information about the action, as well as call one of TestExamineNode(), TestCreateNodeAndInsert(), or TestRemoveNodeAndFree().

Before returning, the current list is printed for inspection. Three action functions are implemented. The first is as follows:

```
void TestCreateNodeAndInsert ( LinkedList* pLL , ListData data ,
                               eWhere where )  {
   ListData* pData = CreateData( data );
   ListNode* pNode = CreateNode( pData );
   switch( where ) {
      case eFront: InsertNodeToFront ( pLL , pNode ); break;
      case eBack:  InsertNodeToBack ( pLL , pNode ); break;
   }
}
```

The second is as follows:

```
ListData TestExamineNode ( LinkedList* pLL , eWhere where )  {
   ListNode * pNode;
   switch( where ) {
      case eFront: pNode = GetNode( pLL , 0 ); break;
      case eBack:  pNode = GetNode( pLL , pLL->nodeCount ); break;
   }
   ListData data = *(pNode->pData);
   return data;
}
```

The third is as follows:

```
ListData TestRemoveNodeAndFree ( LinkedList* pLL , eWhere where )  {
   ListNode * pNode;
   switch( where ) {
      case eFront: pNode = RemoveNodeFromFront ( pLL ); break;
      case eBack:  pNode = RemoveNodeFromBack ( pLL ); break;
   }
   ListData data = *(pNode->pData);
   DeleteNode ( pNode );
   return data;
}
```

Enter each of these test routines after all of the linked list code but before main(). Then, enter the main() routine. Save the file and then compile and run this program. Because there is quite a bit of code, you may have to edit and compile your version several times until you get a clean compile.

When you run the program, you should see the following output:

```
> cc linkedlisttester.c -o linkedlisttester -Wall -Werror -std=c11
> linkedlisttester

Using input{ 1  2  3  4 } List has  0 entries: []
Insert [ 1] to front.    List has  1 entries: [ 1 ]
Insert [ 2] to front.    List has  2 entries: [ 2  1 ]
Insert [ 3] to front.    List has  3 entries: [ 3  2  1 ]
Insert [ 4] to front.    List has  4 entries: [ 4  3  2  1 ]
Get front node, see [ 4]. List has  4 entries: [ 4  3  2  1 ]
Remove [ 1] from  back.   List has  3 entries: [ 4  3  2 ]

Using input{ 31 32 33 }   List has  3 entries: [ 4  3  2 ]
Insert [31] to  back.    List has  4 entries: [ 4  3  2 31 ]
Insert [32] to  back.    List has  5 entries: [ 4  3  2 31 32 ]
Insert [33] to  back.    List has  6 entries: [ 4  3  2 31 32 33 ]
Get  back node, see [33]. List has  6 entries: [ 4  3  2 31 32 33 ]
Remove [ 4] from front.  List has  5 entries: [ 3  2 31 32 33 ]
Remove [ 3] from front.  List has  4 entries: [ 2 31 32 33 ]
Remove [ 2] from front.  List has  3 entries: [31 32 33 ]
Remove [31] from front.  List has  2 entries: [32 33 ]
Remove [32] from front.  List has  1 entries: [33 ]
Remove [33] from front.  List has  0 entries: []
>
```

Notice how each line of the program corresponds to the test outline given previously. Carefully compare the action taken to the impact resulting in the state of the list. When this validation passes, we can feel confident in using this code in other, more useful scenarios. We will employ this list structure and its routines when we return to our carddeck.c program in Chapter 24, *Working with Multi-File Programs*.

You may have noticed that writing test code is nearly as much work as writing the code itself. This is very often the case. Writing concise, complete, and correct test code is hard. From my years of experience, I would argue that writing such test code is as worthwhile as writing the code, for several reasons:

- When your tests fail, you invariably learn something.
- You gain a very high level of confidence that the body of code works as intended.
- You can make changes to the code and verify that the code still works as expected.
- There tends to be much less reworking and debugging with tested code.

Often, as a professional programmer, you may be pushed and cajoled to omit testing. Don't do it, largely for the reasons given here, and to preserve your own sanity.

Other dynamic data structures

In this chapter, we have created a program that implements a singly-linked list where we can add and remove list elements, or list nodes, from the front or back of the list. This is a fairly general, minimal list implementation that leaves out a few other possibly useful operations, such as listConcatenate() to join two lists, listSplit() to break a list into two given criteria, listSort() to order the elements of the list in various ways, and listReverse() to reverse the elements of a list. We may also want to enhance our insert and remove operations so that we can add and remove nodes from anywhere in the list. Because of space limitations, we will not do so here.

The following is a brief, annotated list of other useful, possibly mind-bending, data structures:

- **Doubly-Linked List:** A linked list that contains not only a single pointer to the next list node, but also another pointer that points to the preceding list node. The list may be traversed easily from front to back, as well as from back to front.
- **Stack:** A linked list where each list node is added only to the front of the list (pushed onto the stack). Subsequently, each list node is only removed from the front of the list (popped off the stack). This is also known as a **Last In First Out (LIFO)** list.
- **Queue:** A linked list where each list node is added only to the back of this list (enqueued). Subsequently, each list node is only removed from the front of the list (dequeued). This is also known as a **First In First Out (FIFO)** list.
- **Deque:** A generalized list that combines the properties of both a stack and a queue. Elements can be added or removed from anywhere in the list. Our implementation of a linked list is very close to that of a deque.
- **Priority queue:** A list where each list node also has a given priority. List nodes are added to the list in order of priority and removed from the list according to a priority scheduling scheme.
- **Set:** A collection of unique elements, in no particular order. Sometimes, they are implemented using other dynamic data structures such as trees or hash tables.
- **Map:** A collection of (key, value) pairs where the key is unique and is used to look up a value associated with that key. This can also be called an **associative array, symbol table**, or **dictionary.**

- **Tree:** A tree simulates a hierarchical tree structure, with a single root node from which child nodes form branches. Like branches in a real tree, child nodes can only contain subchildren and cannot be linked to other branches.
- **Graph:** A collection of nodes connected via links. A graph is more of a general form of a tree in that it may have cycles (where a node from one branch may link to the root or a node in another branch).

Studying these data structures and implementing them yourself is beyond the scope of this book. However, such a study would be extremely worthwhile and should be one of the next steps in your journey to becoming an expert C programmer.

Summary

In this chapter, we learned how to allocate, release, and manipulate dynamic memory. We learned about some special considerations to take into account when employing dynamic memory, such as memory management and avoidance of memory leaks. To put our knowledge into practice, we implemented a singly-linked list, which can add and remove list nodes to either the front or back of the list. We learned from this that data structures, as well as performing operations on those data structures, can allow us to create very powerful tools. Consequently, our implementation can be reused for any kind of data wherever needed. In doing so, we have gotten an introduction to the power and flexibility of dynamic data structures.

We also employed another flexible mechanism – pointers to functions – and saw how to pass that pointer to another function, as well as call a function using that pointer. Lastly, we got a brief overview of other important dynamic data structures, such as deques, maps, and trees.

In the next chapter, we will have a chance to catch our breath as we take a deep dive into formatted output and the full range of formatting values that `printf()` provides.

Section 4: Input and Output

So far, all the input in this book has been provided by the program and all the output has been sent in its simplest form to the screen. In this section, we'll expand on the various inputs and outputs, as well as more sophisticated formatting.

This section comprises the following chapters:

19
Exploring Formatted Output

In previous chapters, all the input was provided within each program and all the output was sent in rather simple forms to the console (screen). In this chapter, we will expand on more sophisticated output formatting. However, what if we need a precise layout of numbers and text? We saw in Chapter 15, *Working with Strings*, how to precisely generate a table of ASCII characters. With full knowledge of the possibilities of output formatting, very precise tables of numbers can be created. Furthermore, other kinds of precisely formatted documents can be generated, such as invoices, product price lists, and many others.

The C `printf()` function provides a rich set of formatting options, far beyond what we have used up to this point. We can format numbers—both integers and decimal numbers—characters, and strings in many ways. In this chapter, we will explore, primarily through examples, the various ways in which `printf()` can format values.

The following topics will be covered in this chapter:

- Understanding the general form of the `printf()` format specifier
- Using unsigned integers in different bases
- Considering negative numbers as unsigned integers
- Exploring powers of 2 and 9 in different bases
- Printing pointer values
- Using the signed integer field width, precision, alignment, and zero-filling
- Formatting long-long integers
- Using the floating-point field width, precision, alignment, and zero-filling
- Printing doubles in hexadecimal format
- Printing optimal field width formatting for doubles
- Using the string field width, precision, alignment, and zero-filling
- Exploring sub-string output
- Using single character formatting

Technical requirements

Continue to use the tools you chose in the *Technical requirements* section of `Chapter 1, Running Hello, World!`.

The source code for this chapter can be found at `https://github.com/PacktPublishing/Learn-C-Programming`.

Revisiting printf()

In previous chapters, whenever we printed the output of values to the console, we used relatively simple `printf()` formatting. However, `printf()` provides a very rich set of format specifiers for unsigned integers, pointers, signed integers, floats, doubles, characters, and strings. The examples given in this chapter will not provide an exhaustive example of every possible format specifier, nor of every possible combination of format specifiers. The programs provided are intended to serve as a starting point for your own continued experimentation.

Understanding the general format specifier form

So far, we have seen, for the most part, the simplest format specifier, `%<x>`, or occasionally even `%<n><x>`, where `<x>` is an output conversion type and `<n>` is the field width into which the value is printed. Depending on the value, the formatted output may have added padding or be truncated to fit or even overflow beyond the requested field width. We can expand these simple concepts to the more general form of a format specifier.

The general form of a format specifier begins with the percentage character (`%`) and has the following elements, in order:

- Zero or more **flag** characters:
  - **Left-aligned**: This is the – character. If missing, the value will be right-aligned.
  - The + sign to show a positive or negative value, or a space to only show a – sign.
  - **Zero-padding**: 0.
  - **A variant of formatting**: This is the # character; the variant depends on the conversion type.

- An optional minimum field width denoted by a decimal integer constant
- An optional precision specification denoted by a period (.) and optionally followed by a decimal integer constant
- An optional size modifier expressed as one of the following letters:
    - **Long or long-long**: l, ll, or L.
    - **Short or byte**: h or hh.
    - **Specific type**: j, z, or t.
      We will primarily explore the ll size modifier.
- The conversion operation, which is a single character that may be one of the following:
    - **Unsigned integer**: d, i, o, u, x, or X
    - **Pointers**: n or p
    - **Signed integer**: d or i
    - **Floating-point**: a, A, e, E, f, F, g, or G
    - A character (c) or string (s)
    - The % character itself

If the compiler does not understand a format specifier, the specifier is invalid, or it is inappropriate for the given conversion type, a compiler error will be generated. Not all of the flag characters are appropriate for all of the conversion operations. The conversion operation terminates the format specifier.

Consider the %-#012.4hd format specifier. It is broken up into parts in the following diagram:

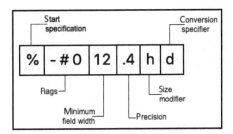

This format specifier will convert a signed integer into a short integer, left-aligning and zero-filling the field of 12 characters using a precision of 4 decimal numbers. In reality, the # flag is inappropriate for the d type conversion. This specifier may be somewhat confusing to you now. However, the example programs we will look at will illustrate the most common and useful combinations of format specifiers.

In all of our example programs, space had to be removed to fit them onto the page. Therefore, if you type in these programs exactly as they are shown, you will not get the same aligned output shown for each program. To do that, I had to repeatedly fiddle with the spacing to make everything align to my rather persnickety satisfaction. Spaces are preserved in the sample programs in the repository.

Also, note that some `printf(" ... " )` strings are longer than the space allotted on this page. When you see this, be aware that the beginning " character and the end " character are on the same line so that your program compiles and runs.

Our first program will deal with unsigned integers.

Using format specifiers for unsigned integers

Unsigned integers include positive integers in several base numbering systems, as well as pointer values. The first example program is `unsignedInt.c`, and it begins as follows:

```
#include <stdio.h>
int main( void )    {
  int smallInt = 12;
  int largeInt = (1024*1024*3)+(1024*2)+512+128+64+32+16+8+4+2+1;
  int negativeInt = -smallInt;
  unsigned anUnsigned = 130;

  // the other code snippets go here.
}
```

This code defines `smallInt`, `largeInt`, `negativeInt`, and `unsigned int` values. These will be used in each snippet that follows. After you type in the program and get it to run, you may want to experiment with different values for each of these variables.

Using unsigned integers in different bases

In the first code snippet, values in various base numbering systems are printed—these are the **octal (base-8)**, **decimal (base-10)**, and **hexadecimal (base-16)** formats. Each of these values is printed in a minimum field width of 12 characters. The numbers are not truncated. If the converted number is longer than the minimum field, it simply spills over the minimum field width:

```
printf ( " Unsigned Printf \n" );
printf ( " Base Base-8 Base-10 Base-16 BASE-16\n" );
printf ( " Name octal unsigned hexadeximal HEXIDECIMAL\n" );
printf ( " Specifier %%12o %%12u %%12x %%12X \n" );
printf ( " [%12o] [%12u] [%12x] [%12X]\n" ,
smallInt , smallInt , smallInt , smallInt );
printf ( " [%12o] [%12u] [%12x] [%12X]\n\n" ,
largeInt , largeInt , largeInt , largeInt );
printf ( " [%12o] [%12u] [%12x] [%12X]\n\n" ,
anUnsigned , anUnsigned , anUnsigned , anUnsigned );
```

For each of these values, a field of 12 is enough such that nothing spills over. You may want to experiment with a smaller minimum field width. Notice how the X conversion type uses uppercase hexadecimal digits.

The following snippet is identical to the previous one except that the # flag is used for the octal and hexadecimal values:

```
printf ( " Specifier %%#o %%#u %%#x %%#X\n");
printf ( " [%#12o] [%12u] [%#12x] [%#12X]\n" ,
smallInt , smallInt , smallInt , smallInt );
printf ( " [%#12o] [%12u] [%#12x] [%#12X]\n" ,
largeInt , largeInt , largeInt , largeInt );
printf ( " [%#12o] [%12u] [%#12x] [%#12X]\n\n" ,
anUnsigned , anUnsigned , anUnsigned , anUnsigned );
```

First, notice how the octal numbers are preceded by 0 and the hexadecimal numbers are preceded by either 0x or 0X. Also, notice that # is not used for the u type conversion since it is a decimal value. Try putting it in and see whether the program compiles; you should get a compiler error.

Considering negative numbers as unsigned integers

We are using the `unsigned` type conversions. This does not mean that we can't convert a negative number. You may be surprised by the output of the following code:

```
printf( " Negative Numbers as Unsigned:\n" );
printf( " -0 [%12o] [%12u] [%12x] [%12X]\n" ,
        -0 , -0 , -0 , -0 );
printf( " -1 [%12o] [%12u] [%12x] [%12X]\n" ,
        -1 , -1 , -1 , -1 );
printf( " -2 [%12o] [%12u] [%12x] [%12X]\n" ,
        -2 , -2 , -2 , -2 );
printf( " -12 [%12o] [%12u] [%12x] [%12X]\n\n" ,
        negativeInt , negativeInt , negativeInt , negativeInt );
```

Negative numbers are treated specially by every computer system; they are converted internally using an algorithm called **two's complement**. Two's complement is a method to avoid the problem of having +0 and −0, which is why the second statement in this code snippet uses −0 as a value to test how it is treated. Unsigned types, by definition, do not have a sign bit; so, we see their internal representation. The takeaway from this is that `printf()` takes a bit pattern found in the given value and formats it to the specified type conversion. It is our responsibility to ensure these conversions make sense and are meaningful.

You may want to change this code to a loop that counts down from 0 to, for example, −16. If you do that, can you see the pattern?

Exploring powers of 2 and 9 in different bases

In the next code snippet, we will examine the formatting for a series of numbers that are powers of 2 in each of the base systems. For comparison, we will repeat the loop, but this time print out powers of 9, as follows:

```
printf( "Powers of 2: 2^0, 2^2, 2^4, 2^6, 2^8 , 2^10\n" );
int k = 1;
for( int i = 0 ; i < 6 ; i++ , k<<=2 )  {
  printf( " [%#12o] [%12u] [%#12x] [%#12X]\n" ,
          k , k , k , k );
}
printf( "\nPowers of 9: 9^1, 9^2, 9^3, 9^4\n" );
printf( " Specifier %%12o %%12u %%12x %%12X \n" );
k = 9;
```

```
for( int i = 0 ; i < 5 ; i++ , k*=9 )  {
  printf( " [%#12o] [%12u] [%#12x] [%#12X]\n" ,
          k , k , k , k );
}
```

Even though we have not explored different base numbering systems, this code is intended to provide a starting point for your own understanding of octal and hexadecimal counting. Of the two numbering systems, pay more attention to hexadecimal as this is much more common today than octal. To do this, you may want to change the first loop to go from 0 to, for example, 32, and then study the pattern of base numbers for each base. Base 9 or powers of 9 have no significance to computer programming and can be considered an idle curiosity.

Printing pointer values

The last bit of code prints out the value of a pointer using two different methods, as follows:

```
printf( "\nPointer Output\n" );
printf( " %%p [%p] pointer\n" , &smallInt );
printf( " %%#lx [%#lx] using hex\n\n" , (unsigned long)&smallInt );
```

The first method uses the p type conversion. Notice that no casting is required. The second method uses the #lx specifier; this must be specified as a long hex value to get the full 64-bit pointer value and not a 32-bit one. Notice the address of smallInt must be cast to an unsigned long variable or a compilation error will result. In this instance, we are coercing the &smallInt pointer type to match the integer type specified by %#lx. Both printed values of &smallInt should match. The p type conversion is certainly simpler and safer.

Enter these code snippets into `unsignedInt.c`. Compile and run the program. You should see something similar to the following output:

```
|> cc unsignedInt.c -o unsignedInt -Wall -Werror -std=c11
|> unsignedInt
 Unsigned Printf
  Base          Base-8          Base-10         Base-16             BASE-16
  Name          octal           unsigned        hexadeximal         HEXIDECIMAL
  Specifier     %12o            %12u            %12x                %12X
         [            14]  [           12]  [            c]  [             C]
         [      14005377]  [      3148543]  [       300aff]  [        300AFF]
         [           202]  [          130]  [           82]  [            82]

  Specifier     %#o             %#u             %#x                 %#X
         [           014]  [           12]  [          0xc]  [           0XC]
         [     014005377]  [      3148543]  [     0x300aff]  [      0X300AFF]
         [          0202]  [          130]  [         0x82]  [          0X82]

  Negative Numbers as Unsigned:
  -0     [             0]  [            0]  [            0]  [             0]
  -1     [   37777777777]  [   4294967295]  [     ffffffff]  [      FFFFFFFF]
  -2     [   37777777776]  [   4294967294]  [     fffffffe]  [      FFFFFFFE]
  -12    [   37777777764]  [   4294967284]  [     fffffff4]  [      FFFFFFF4]

  Powers of 2: 2^0, 2^2, 2^4, 2^6, 2^8 , 2^10
         [            01]  [            1]  [          0x1]  [           0X1]
         [            04]  [            4]  [          0x4]  [           0X4]
         [           020]  [           16]  [         0x10]  [          0X10]
         [          0100]  [           64]  [         0x40]  [          0X40]
         [          0400]  [          256]  [        0x100]  [         0X100]
         [         02000]  [         1024]  [        0x400]  [         0X400]

  Powers of 9: 9^1, 9^2, 9^3, 9^4
  Specifier     %o              %u              %x                  %X
         [           011]  [            9]  [          0x9]  [           0X9]
         [           0121]  [           81]  [         0x51]  [          0X51]
         [          01331]  [          729]  [        0x2d9]  [         0X2D9]
         [         014641]  [         6561]  [       0x19a1]  [        0X19A1]
         [        0163251]  [        59049]  [       0xe6a9]  [        0XE6A9]

  Pointer Output
  %p      [0x7ffeead7b608]    pointer
  %#lx    [0x7ffeead7b608]    using hex

 >
```

Once you have done that, you may want to try some of the experiments mentioned earlier before moving on. You may also want to, if you are persnickety like me, mess around with the spacing between the numbers to match my output. Or, you can simply download the program from the repository after you have successfully run your own program.

In the next section, we will expand the use of a minimum field, precision, and alignment for signed integers. These modifiers also apply to unsigned integers; they just weren't applied here. You may want to also experiment with these modifiers in `unsignedInt.c`, as well as in the next program.

Using format specifiers for signed integers

Signed integers include integers that can have negative as well as positive values. The next example program is `signedInt.c`, and it begins as follows:

```
#include <stdio.h>
int main( void ) {
  int smallInt = 12;
  int largeInt = 0x7fffffff; // int32 max
  int negativeInt = -smallInt;
  unsigned anUnsigned = 130;
  long long int reallyLargeInt = 0x7fffffffffffffff; // int64 max

  // the other code snippets go here.
}
```

The values of `smallInt`, `largeInt`, `negativeInt`, `anUnsigned`, and `reallyLargeInt` will be printed using various field, precision, and alignment modifiers. Notice that `largeInt` is given a hexadecimal value that is the largest positive value a 32-bit integer can hold. Likewise, `reallyLargeInit` is given a hexadecimal value that is the largest positive value a 64-bit integer can hold. What value is printed if the first 7 number in each value is changed to `f`?

Using the signed integer field width, precision, alignment, and zero-filling

Each of these values will be printed using a minimum field of 10 characters, sometimes left-aligned and with different values of precision, as follows:

```
printf( " Signed Printf \n" );
printf( " Name    right left     zero       right left\n" );
printf( "      aligned aligned filled minimum minimum whatever\n" );
printf( " Specifier %%10d %%-10d %%-.10d %%10.3d %%-10.3d %%d\n" );
printf( " [%10d] [%-10d] [%-.10d] [%10.3d] [%-10.3d] [%d]\n" ,
        smallInt, smallInt, smallInt, smallInt, smallInt, smallInt );
printf( " [%10d] [%-10d] [%-.10d] [%10.3d] [%-10.3d] [%d]\n" ,
        largeInt, largeInt, largeInt, largeInt, largeInt, largeInt );
printf( " [%10d] [%-10d] [%-.10d] [%10.3d] [%-10.3d] [%d]\n" ,
        anUnsigned , anUnsigned , anUnsigned ,
        anUnsigned , anUnsigned , anUnsigned );
printf( " [%10d] [%-10d] [%-.10d] [%10.3d] [%-10.3d] [%d]\n\n" ,
        negativeInt , negativeInt , negativeInt ,
        negativeInt , negativeInt , negativeInt );
```

The only difference between each `printf()` call is the variables given to them to convert and print. The column headers have been constructed so that they accurately reflect the format specifier given. Rather than try to explain each statement, we will see how they appear in the output to get an immediate grasp of how the specifiers work. All of these values are converted by their type conversion specifier into 32-bit integers, but what if we want to print a 64-bit integer?

Formatting long-long integers

If we want to print a 64-bit value, we need to use the `ll` length modifier, as follows:

```
printf( " Specifier %%20lld %%-20lld %%-.20lld\n" );
printf( " [%20lld] [%-20lld] [%-.20lld]\n" ,
        reallyLargeInt , reallyLargeInt , reallyLargeInt );
printf( " %%20.3lld %%-20.3lld %%lld\n" );
printf( " [%20.3lld] [%-20.3lld] [%lld]\n\n" ,
        reallyLargeInt , reallyLargeInt , reallyLargeInt );
```

These `printf` statements are the same format specifiers as before, except they are in a minimum field of 20 characters and they use the `lld` type conversion to print a 64-bit value. Also, as before, we will see how these appear in the output and then compare them to the formatted 32-bit values.

Powers of 2 and 9 with different modifiers

In the final code snippet, powers of 2 and 9 are printed, as follows:

```
printf( "Powers of 2: 2^0, 2^2, 2^4, 2^6, 2^8 , 2^10\n" );
int k = 1;
for( int i = 0 ; i < 6 ; i++ , k<<=2 )  {
 printf( " [%6d] [%-6d] [%-.6d] [%6.3d] [%-6.3d] [%d]\n" ,
        k , k , k , k , k , k );
}
printf( "\nPowers of 9: 9^1, 9^2, 9^3, 9^4\n" );
k = 9;
for( int i = 0 ; i < 5 ; i++ , k*=9 )  {
 printf( " [%6d] [%-6d] [%-.6d] [%6.3d] [%-6.3d] [%d]\n" ,
        k , k , k , k , k , k );
}
```

In these printed values, we will pay particular attention to the formatted output—how they are aligned, whether they are zero-filled, and how the precision specifier changes them, if at all.

Enter these code snippets into `signedInt.c`. Compile and run the program. You should see something similar to the following output:

```
> signedInt
 Signed Printf
   Name      right        left        zero       right       left
             aligned      aligned     filled      minimum     minimum     whatever
  Specifier    %10d                   %-10d        %-.10d      %10.3d      %-10.3d      %d
       [          12]    [12        ]  [0000000012]  [        012]  [012      ]  [12]
       [2147483647]    [2147483647]  [2147483647]  [2147483647]  [2147483647]  [2147483647]
       [         130]    [130       ]  [0000000130]  [        130]  [130      ]  [130]
       [         -12]    [-12       ]  [-0000000012]  [       -012]  [-012     ]  [-12]

   Specifier          %20lld                     %-20lld                  %-.20lld
        [ 9223372036854775807]  [9223372036854775807 ]  [09223372036854775807]
                    %20.3lld                   %-20.3lld                    %lld
        [ 9223372036854775807]  [9223372036854775807 ]  [9223372036854775807]

Powers of 2: 2^0, 2^2, 2^4, 2^6, 2^8 , 2^10
       [          1]    [1         ]  [000001]  [      001]  [001      ]  [1]
       [          4]    [4         ]  [000004]  [      004]  [004      ]  [4]
       [         16]    [16        ]  [000016]  [      016]  [016      ]  [16]
       [         64]    [64        ]  [000064]  [      064]  [064      ]  [64]
       [        256]    [256       ]  [000256]  [      256]  [256      ]  [256]
       [       1024]    [1024      ]  [001024]  [     1024]  [1024     ]  [1024]

Powers of 9: 9^1, 9^2, 9^3, 9^4
       [          9]    [9         ]  [000009]  [      009]  [009      ]  [9]
       [         81]    [81        ]  [000081]  [      081]  [081      ]  [81]
       [        729]    [729       ]  [000729]  [      729]  [729      ]  [729]
       [       6561]    [6561      ]  [006561]  [     6561]  [6561     ]  [6561]
       [      59049]    [59049     ]  [059049]  [    59049]  [59049    ]  [59049]
>
```

Pay particular attention to the differences in formatting in each column. Your values will not line up, as in the preceding output. Notice the number alignment when – is used. Notice how zeros are used as fillers when a `.10` or `.3` precision is specified. Notice the field size when nothing is specified (see the last column).

As before, you now have a starting point to experiment with different values for the variables and each of the format specifiers. You may want to do that before moving on to formatting floating-point numbers. With floating-point numbers, we will also use the + flag; this flag applies to signed integers, so you might want to return to `signedInt.c` and experiment with that flag.

Using format specifiers for floats and doubles

Floating-point numbers are floats, doubles, and long doubles that can be expressed in a number of ways mathematically. They can be expressed naturally where there is a whole number part and a fractional part. They can be expressed in scientific notation where there is a coefficient raised to a power of 10, and it takes the 1.234567 x 10^123 form. The decimal point floats such that the coefficient has a whole number part that is between 1 and 10 and the exponent is adjusted accordingly. C provides both of these formats.

The next example program is double.c, and it begins as follows:

```
#include <stdio.h>
int main( void )  {
 double aDouble = 987654321.987654321;

 // the other code snippets go here.
}
```

In this program, only one value is defined. Whenever the value to be converted into float, it is automatically converted to a double value and then formatted. Therefore, there are no float value-specific type conversions. We will explore the various ways that the double values can be formatted.

Using the floating-point field width, precision, alignment, and zero-filling

First, we print aDouble in various ways in its natural form using the f conversion type, as follows:

```
printf( "Use of the %%f, %%e, and %%E format specifiers:\n" );
printf( " Specifier Formatted Value\n" );
printf( " %%f [%f] whatever\n",aDouble );
printf( " %%.3f [%.3f] 3 decimal places\n",aDouble );
printf( " %%.9f [%.8f] 8 decimal places\n",aDouble );
printf( " %%.0f [%.0f] no decimal places\n",aDouble );
printf( " %%#.0f [%#.0f] no decimal places, but decimal point\n",
        aDouble );
printf( " %%15.3f [%15.3f] 3 decimals, 15 wide, left aligned]\n",
        aDouble );
printf( " %%-15.3f[%-15.3f] 3 decimals, 15 wide, right aligned\n",
        aDouble );
```

With no precision specified, the `double` value is formatted to six decimal places (the default). The next three statements print `aDouble` to various precisions; these change how many digits of the fraction are printed. When `.0` is used, no fractional part is printed, not even the decimal point. When `#` is used with `.0`, no decimal digits are printed but the decimal point is. The last two statements use the alignment of `aDouble` in a minimum field of 15 characters.

The next set of statements use the `e` and `E` type conversions to print `aDouble` using scientific notation, as follows:

```
printf( " %%e [%e] using exponential notation\n",aDouble );
printf( " %%E [%E] using EXPONENTIAL notation\n",aDouble );
printf( " %%.3e[%.3e]  exponent with 3 decimal places\n",aDouble );
printf( " %%15.3e [%15.3e] exponent with 3 decimals,15 wide\n",
        aDouble );
printf( " %%015.3e[%015.3e]exponent with 3 decimals,15 wide,0-fill\n",
        aDouble );
printf( " %% 15.3e [% 15.3e] exponent with 3 decimals, 15 wide,
        leave space for sign\n"  , aDouble );
printf( " %%+15.3e [%+15.3e] exponent with 3 decimals, 15 wide,
        show sign\n" , aDouble );
printf( " %%+015.3e [%+015.3e]  exponent with 3 decimals, 15 wide,
        show sign, 0-fill\n" , aDouble );
printf( " %%.0e[%.0e]exponent with no decimals\n"  ,aDouble );
printf( " %%15.0e [%15.0e]  exponent 15 wide, no decimals\n\n",
        aDouble );
```

Each of these statements provides an example of using alignment, minimum field width, precision, zero-filling, and a sign indicator. When the + flag is used, either + or – will always be printed. However, instead of +, a space is used, only the – sign will be printed, and a space will be used for positive values. The explanation of each will be obvious from the output.

Printing doubles in hexadecimal format

The `a` and `A` type specifiers print floating-point numbers such that the coefficient is in hexadecimal format and the exponent is a power of 2, as follows:

```
printf( " %%a [%a] hexadecimal version of double, exponent=2^p\n",
        aDouble );
printf( " %%A [%A] HEXADECIMAL version of double, exponent=2^P\n\n",
        aDouble );
```

These type conversions are a recent addition to C and were added for the internal validation of floating-point values. If you ever find yourself in need of these types of conversion, please email me; I would love to know the circumstance for their use.

Printing optimal field widths for doubles

The g and G type specifiers behave either like the f type conversion or the e and E type conversions, depending on the value to be converted, as follows:

```
printf( "Use of the %%g, and %%G format specifiers:\n" );
printf( " Specifier %%18.12    g%%18.3g" );
printf( "            %%18.3G    %%18g\n" );
double k = aDouble * 1e-15;
for( int i = 0 ; i < 10 ; i++, k *= 1000 )
  printf( " [%18.12g]   [%18.3g]   [%18.3G]   [%18g]\n" ,
          k , k , k , k );
```

The value of k is assigned aDouble multiplied by a very small number, giving a very small number. By using a loop and multiplying k by 1,000, various g or G type conversions are used in each iteration as the value increases. We will see that the g or G type conversions attempt to format the value in the shortest format possible for the given value. This will be clear in the program's output.

Enter these code snippets into double.c. Compile and run the program. You should see something similar to the following output:

```
> cc double.c -o double -Wall -Werror -std=c11
> double
Use of the %f, %e, and %E format specifiers:
 Specifier Formatted Value
 %f         [987654321.987654]      whatever
 %.3f       [987654321.988]         3 decimal places
 %.9f       [987654321.98765433]    8 decimal places
 %.0f       [987654322]             no decimal places
 %#.0f      [987654322.]            no decimal places, but decimal point
 %15.3f     [   987654321.988]      3 decimals, 15 wide, left aligned]
 %-15.3f    [987654321.988   ]      3 decimals, 15 wide, right aligned
 %e         [9.876543e+08]          using exponential notation
 %E         [9.876543E+08]          using EXPONENTIAL notation
 %.3e       [9.877e+08]             exponent with 3 decimal places
 %15.3e     [      9.877e+08]       exponent with 3 decimals, 15 wide
 %015.3e    [0000009.877e+08]       exponent with 3 decimals, 15 wide, 0-fill
 % 15.3e    [      9.877e+08]       exponent with 3 decimals, 15 wide, leave space for sign
 %+15.3e    [     +9.877e+08]       exponent with 3 decimals, 15 wide, show sign
 %+015.3e   [+000009.877e+08]       exponent with 3 decimals, 15 wide, show sign, 0-fill
 %.0e       [1e+09]                 exponent with no decimals
 %15.0e     [          1e+09]       exponent 15 wide, no decimals

 %a         [0x1.d6f3458fe6b75p+29] hexidecimal version of double, exponent=2^p
 %A         [0X1.D6F3458FE6B75P+29] HEXIDECIMAL version of double, exponent=2^P

Use of the %g, and %G format specifiers:
 Specifier          %18.12g               %18.3g              %18.3G               %18g
          [ 9.87654321988e-07]  [       9.88e-07]  [       9.88E-07]  [    9.87654e-07]
          [ 0.000987654321988]  [       0.000988]  [       0.000988]  [    0.000987654]
          [     0.987654321988]  [          0.988]  [          0.988]  [       0.987654]
          [      987.654321988]  [            988]  [            988]  [       987.654]
          [     987654.321988]  [       9.88e+05]  [       9.88E+05]  [        987654]
          [     987654321.988]  [       9.88e+08]  [       9.88E+08]  [    9.87654e+08]
          [      987654321988]  [       9.88e+11]  [       9.88E+11]  [    9.87654e+11]
          [ 9.87654321988e+14]  [       9.88e+14]  [       9.88E+14]  [    9.87654e+14]
          [ 9.87654321988e+17]  [       9.88e+17]  [       9.88E+17]  [    9.87654e+17]
          [ 9.87654321988e+20]  [       9.88e+20]  [       9.88E+20]  [    9.87654e+20]

>
```

For each of the formatted values, pay attention to the number of decimal places printed and whether numerical rounding is taking place. Note the various scientific notation formats. See how the last two formats of .0e truncate the value to all but the most significant digit. I would like to say something meaningful about the output of the a and A type conversions, but I cannot seem to find the words. Finally, notice how the g type specifier changes from scientific notation to natural and back to scientific notation as the magnitude of k increases by 1000. Also, notice that the format that is used not only depends on the value but also the precision specifier. You can see this in the different printed output in each column.

As a final note on floating-point formatting, the internal value of the printed value has not changed. The value of aDouble throughout the program is still 987654321.987654321. It hasn't changed internally one bit (literally); only its external appearance as a printed value has been changed by the format specifiers. Again, printf() is taking a given bit pattern and formatting it in a specified manner.

As before, you now have a starting point to begin your own experimentation with various combinations of format specifiers and values for floating-point numbers.

Whew! That is a rather dizzying array of formats from just a small set of flags, the field width, and precision specifiers. Let's finish with some simple character and string formatting.

Using format specifiers for strings and characters

Our last program is character_string.c, and it begins as follows:

```
#include <stdio.h>
int main( void )   {
   char  aChar = 'C' ;
   char* pStr  = "Learn to program with C" ;
   // the other code snippets go here.
}
```

A character value, aChar, is defined with the C value and a pStr string is defined to point to the start of the "Learn to program with C" string.

Using the string field width, precision, alignment, and zero-filling

When printing a string with the s conversion type, the alignment, minimum field width, and precision modifiers still apply, as follows:

```
printf("String output\n");
printf("Specifier Formatted Value\n");
printf("%%s   [%s] everything\n" ,  pStr);
printf("%%30s [%30s] everything right-aligned, field=30\n",pStr );
printf("%%.10s [%.10s] truncated to first 10 characters\n",pStr );
printf("%%30.10s [%30.10s] first 10 chars right-aligned, fld=30\n",
       pStr);
printf("%%-30.10s [%-30.10s] first 10 chars left-aligned,
       field=30\n\n" , pStr);
printf("%%*.*s [%*.*s] use width & precision in argument list\n\n" ,
       30 , 10 , pStr);
```

The string to be printed must be a valid (null-terminated) string. We have seen each of these modifiers before. Unlike integers, however, truncation may occur, depending on the length of the string and the specified precision. We will see how they appear in the output.

The most interesting format specifier can be found in the last statement, where %*.*s indicates that the minimum field width value will be read from the first argument, which in this case is 30, and the precision value will be read from the second argument, in this case, 10. In this way, the modifiers are not fixed in code but can be supplied as variables at runtime. This notation applies to integers and floating-point numbers; we just saved it for last. For completeness, %*s and %.*s are both valid and both expect the first argument to be either a value for the minimum field width or the precision, respectively.

Exploring the sub-string output

Because the s type conversion is a pointer to a string, we can do a few other pointer arithmetic tricks, as follows:

```
printf("Sub-string output\n");
printf("%%.7s [%.7s] 3rd word (using array offset)\n",&pStr[9]);
printf("%%.12s [%.12s] 3rd and 4th words (using pointer
        arithmetic)\n\n" ,  pStr + 9 );
```

The first string output uses both precision and a pointer offset to print program. The second string output again uses precision but also uses pointer arithmetic to print program with.

Using single character formatting

Finally, we can format a single character with the c type conversion, as follows:

```
printf("Character output\n");
printf("%%c [%c] character\n",aChar);
printf("%%10c [%10c] character right-aligned, field=10\n",aChar);
printf("%%-10c [%-10c] character left-aligned, field=10\n\n",aChar);
```

First, a single character is printed. Then, it is right-aligned in a field of 10. Finally, it is left-aligned in a field of 10.

Enter these code snippets into `character_string.c`. Compile and run the program. You should see something similar to the following output:

```
[> cc character_string.c -o character_string -Wall -Werror -std=c11
[> character_string
String output
 Specifier Formatted Value
 %s        [Learn to program with C]            everything
 %30s      [           Learn to program with C] everything right-aligned, field=30
 %.10s     [Learn to p]                         truncated to first 10 characters
 %30.10s   [                      Learn to p]   only 10 chars right-aligned, field=30
 %-30.10s  [Learn to p                      ]   only 10 chars left-aligned, field=30

 %*.*s     [                      Learn to p]   use width & precision in argument list

Sub-string output
 %.7s      [program]      3rd word (using array offset)
 %.12s     [program with] 3rd and 4th words (using pointer arithmetic)

Character output
 %c        [C]               character
 %10c      [         C]      character right-aligned, field=10
 %-10c     [C         ]      character left-aligned, field=10

> 
```

Notice how the alignment, minimum field width, and precision modifiers behave for strings and characters as they do for integers and doubles.

This completes our exploration of formatted output. With these programs, you can continue with your own exploration.

Summary

In this chapter, we fairly exhaustively explored output formatting for integers—both signed and unsigned—floating-point numbers, characters, and strings. Example programs that demonstrate the most common and useful combinations of print modifiers were also presented. However, not all the possible combinations nor modifiers were demonstrated. These programs can and should be used as starting points for further experimentation for your specific output formatting needs. These programs are also valuable to verify how a particular C runtime performs because there are always minor differences from one implementation of C to the next. This is one place where differences appear most often.

In the next two chapters, we will explore getting simple input from the command line and then getting formatted and unformatted input from the console. We will then expand those topics in subsequent chapters even further for files, including reading various inputs from files and writing various outputs to files. Various inputs and outputs include formatted, unformatted, and even raw data.

Nearly all of the concepts that we learned in this chapter will be useful for `Chapter 21`, *Exploring Formatted Input*, where values are read from the console and converted into the desired type. In the next chapter, we will begin the exploration of simple input, which will direct program flow until the input (user) signals the program to quit.

20
Getting Input from the Command Line

Up to this point, we have not read any input for any of our programs from any source. All program data has been hardcoded in the program itself. In this chapter, we will begin exploring programming input with one of the simplest available methods—inputting from the console's command line.

We will revisit the `main()` function with our added knowledge of function parameters and arrays of strings. We will then explore how to retrieve strings via an argument to the `main()` function.

The following topics will be covered in this chapter:

- Understanding the two forms of `main()`
- Understanding how `argc` and `argv` are related
- Writing a program to retrieve values from `argv` and print them

Technical requirements

Continue to use the tools you chose from the *Technical requirements* section of Chapter 1, *Running Hello, World!*.

The source code for this chapter can be found at `https://github.com/PacktPublishing/Learn-C-Programming`.

Revisiting the main() function

The `main()` function is, as we have seen, the first place our program begins execution. Recall that before execution begins, various kinds of memory are allocated within our program space. Once memory is allocated, the system calls `main()` pretty much as we might call any other function. In this regard, `main()` is a function like any other.

The special features of main()

However, the `main()` function is a special function in C with the following special properties:

- `main()` cannot be called by any other function.
- `main()` is activated as the first function called when the program is invoked to begin execution.
- When we return from the `main()` function, execution stops and the program is terminated.
- There are only two forms of the `main()` function prototype:
  - Has no arguments at all
  - Has exactly two arguments—an `int` value and a `char*` array

We will explore the second form of the `main()` function in this chapter.

The two forms of main()

Up to now, we have been using the first form of `main()`:

```
int main( void ) { ... }
```

The second form of `main()` is as follows:

```
int main( int argc , char* argv[] ) { ... }
```

Here, we have the following:

- `argc` is the short name for the argument count.
- `argv` is the short name for the argument vector.

When our program declares the `main()` function in the second form, the command-line interpreter processes the command line and populates these two variables, passing them into the `main()` function body when the system calls `main()`. We can then access those values through these variable names.

It should be noted that `argc` and `argv` are arbitrary names. You might want to use alternative names in `main()`, as follows:

```
int main( int argumentCount, char* argumentVector[] ) { ... }
```

You could even use the following:

```
int main( int numArgs, char* argStrings[] ) { ... }
```

The names of the variables used in the `main()` function definition are not significant. However, what is significant is that the first parameter is an `int` value (with a name that we choose) and the second parameter is an array of `char*` (also with a name that we choose). `argc` and `argv` are merely common names used in the `main()` function declaration.

You may sometimes alternatively see `main()` declared as follows:

```
int main( int argc, char** argv ) { ... }
```

This form is equivalent to the others because of the interchangeability of pointer notation and array notation. However, I find using array notation clearer in this case, and therefore it is preferred.

We will explore how to use these parameters to retrieve the values from the string vector, or an array of string pointers, `argv`.

Using argc and argv

So, while we could give alternate names for the `argc` and `argv` parameter names, we will use these two names throughout this chapter for consistency.

When we invoke a program, we now see the following:

- Memory is allocated in program space.
- Command-line arguments are processed into function parameters passed into `main()` or ignored if those parameters are absent.
- The execution begins with a call to `main()`.

The first thing to note is that every argument from the command line is broken up into strings. A pointer to the beginning of each string is placed in argv, and argc array is incremented. In many cases, string input is sufficient without any further processing. We will explore converting string input into other values in the next chapter, Chapter 21, *Exploring Formatted Input*.

The program name itself is always placed in argv[0]. Therefore, argc will always be at least 1.

Each argument is separated by whitespace. We can make a single argument of several space-separated words by enclosing the group of words in either single ('...') or double ("...") quotation marks.

A simple use of argc and argv

We can now explore command-line arguments with the following program:

```
#include <stdio.h>
int main(int argc, char *argv[] )   {

  if( argc == 1 )   {
    printf( " No arguments given on command line.\n\n" );
    printf( " usage: %s <argument1> <argument2> ... <argumentN>\n" ,
            argv[0] );
    return 0;
  }
  printf( "argument count = [%d]\n" , argc );
  for( int i = 0 ; i < argc ; i++ )   {
    if( i == 0 )
      printf( "executable = [%s]\n" , argv[i] );
    else
      printf( "argument %d = [%s]\n" , i , argv[i] );
  }
}
```

This program first checks whether any arguments have been passed into main() via argv. If not, it prints a usage message and returns; otherwise, it iterates through argv, printing each argument on a line by itself.

Enter this program into a file called showArgs.c, save it, compile it, and run it with the following invocations:

```
showArgs
showArgs one two three four five six
```

```
showArgs one two,three "four five" six
showArgs "one two three four five six"
showArgs "one two three" 'four five six'
showArgs "one 'two' three" 'four "five" six'
```

You should see the following output:

```
> cc showArgs.c -o showArgs -Wall -Werror -std=c11
> showArgs
 No arguments given on command line.
  usage: showArgs <argument1> <argument2> ... <argumentN>

> showArgs one two three four five six
argument count = [7]
executable = [showArgs]
argument 1 = [one]
argument 2 = [two]
argument 3 = [three]
argument 4 = [four]
argument 5 = [five]
argument 6 = [six]

> showArgs one two,three "four five" six
argument count = [5]
executable = [showArgs]
argument 1 = [one]
argument 2 = [two,three]
argument 3 = [four five]
argument 4 = [six]

> showArgs "one two three four five six"
argument count = [2]
executable = [showArgs]
argument 1 = [one two three four five six]

> showArgs "one two three" 'four five six'
argument count = [3]
executable = [showArgs]
argument 1 = [one two three]
argument 2 = [four five six]

> showArgs "one 'two' three" 'four "five" six'
argument count = [3]
executable = [showArgs]
argument 1 = [one 'two' three]
argument 2 = [four "five" six]

>
```

First, no arguments are given and the usage message is printed. Next, six arguments are given. Notice that because of the one-off issue, `argc` is 7, even though we only entered six arguments. In the remaining argument examples, various placements of a comma and single- and double-quotation mark pairs are tried. Notice that in the last example, `'two'` is part of the first parameter and `"five"` is included in the second parameter. You may want to experiment further with other variations of delimiters and arguments yourself.

Command-line switches and command-line processors

The `showArgs.c` program is an extremely simple command-line argument processor. It merely prints out each command-line argument but otherwise does nothing with any of them. In later chapters, we will see some ways that we might use these arguments.

We have been using command-line switches whenever we compiled our programs. Consider the following command:

```
cc showArgs.c -o showArgs -Wall -Werror -std=c11
```

We have given the `cc` program the following arguments:

- The name of the input file to compile, which is `showArgs.c`.
- A output file specifier, which is `-o`.
- The name of the output file, which is `showArgs`. This represents an argument pair where the specifier and additional information is given in the very next argument. Notice how the specifier is preceded by a hyphen (–).
- The option to provide warnings for all possible types of warnings with `-Wall`. Notice how this is a single parameter is preceded by a hyphen (–) but not with a space separator.
- The option to treat all warnings as errors with `-Werror`. This has a similar format to `-Wall`.
- Finally, the option to use the C-11 standard library with `-std=c11`, where the specifier is `std` and the option is `c11`. Notice how the two parts are separated by an equals sign (=).

This single command exhibits four different types of argument specifier formats—a single argument, an argument pair, two arguments where added options are appended to the specifier, and finally, a specifier using the equals sign (=) to add information to a single argument.

From this, you might begin to imagine how some command-line processors can be quite complicated as they provide a wide set of options for execution. There is no standard command-line processor, nor a standard set of command-line options. Each set of command-line options is specific to the given program that provides those options.

It is beyond the scope of this book to delve deeper into the myriad approaches employed for command-line processing. Some approaches are straightforward, while others are quite complex. Most approaches to command-line processing have evolved over time along with the program of which they are a part. New options and new option formats were often required and added. Old options and option formats are rarely discarded. In many cases, the resulting command-line processor grew to become a tangled web of complex code. Therefore, a high degree of caution is recommended when trying to modify an existing command-line processor.

However, there are two C Standard Library routines—getopt() and getopt_long()—that are intended to simplify command-line option processing. The older getopt() routine, declared in unistd.h, expects single-character options. The newer and preferred getopt_long() routine is declared in getopt.h; it is able to process both single-character options as well as whole-word option specifiers. The following is a very simple program using getopt_long():

```c
#include <stdio.h>
#include <getopt.h>

static struct option long_options[] = {
   {"title",  required_argument, NULL, 't'},
   {"author", required_argument, NULL, 'a'},
   { NULL, 0, NULL, 0}
};
typedef struct _book {
    char* title;
    char* author;
} Book;

int main(int argc, char *argv[]) {
  char ch;
  Book b;
  while( true )  {
    ch = getopt_long( argc , argv , "t:a:" , long_options, NULL )
    if( ch == -1 ) break; // exit the loop
    switch (ch) {
      case 't':   b.title  = optarg;   break;
      case 'a':   b.author = optarg;   break;
      default:
```

```
            printf( "Usage: %s -title 'title' -author 'name'\n" , argv[0] );
            break;
      }
   }
   if( b.title )  printf( "Title is [%s]\n" , b.title );
   if( b.author ) printf( "Author is [%s]\n" , b.author );
   if( optind < argc )  {
      printf( "non-option ARGV-elements: " );
      while( optind < argc )
         printf( "%s ", argv[ optind++ ] );
      printf( "\n" );
   }
}
```

This program first sets up the `long_options` structure, which has two required options—`title` and `author`. Each of these can also be set by their single-character equivalent—`'t'` and `'a'`, respectively. It then declares a book structure to hold the values given on the command line. In the `main()` function, after variables are declared, a loop is entered to process the command-line arguments. Note that it is an infinite loop; the only way we exit this loop is when `getopts_long()` returns –1 when it has no more arguments. We test for that case and then break out of the loop.

In the call to `getopt_long()`, the `"t:a:"` parameter string indicates that each single-letter option has an additional value field associated with it. The value of each argument is found in the `optarg` pointer variable. If an invalid option is encountered, a `Usage:` message is printed. After exiting the `while()`... loop, each argument value is printed. Finally, any remaining command-line arguments are printed.

Then, create this program as `example_getopt_long.c`. Compile and run it. Try invoking it with the following command lines:

```
example_getopts_long -t "There and Back" -a "Bilbo Baggins"
example_getopts_long --author "Jeff Szuhay" --title "Hello, world!"
example_getopts_long -a -t
example_getopts_long -a -b -c
```

You should see the following output:

```
> cc example_getopt_long.c -o example_getopt_long -Wall -Werror -std=c11
> example_getopt_long -t "There and Back" -a "Bilbo Baggins"
Title is [There and Back]
Author is [Bilbo Baggins]
> example_getopt_long --author "Jeff Szuhay" --title "Hello, world!"
example_getopt_long --author "Jeff Szuhay" --title "Hello, world"
Title is [Hello, world]
Author is [Jeff Szuhay]
> example_getopt_long -a -t
Author is [-t]
> example_getopt_long -b -c
example_getopt_long: invalid option -- b

Usage: example_getopt_long -title 'title' -author 'name'

>
```

Note that `getopts_long()` converts the word options into their single-character equivalents. Also, note how several variables have already been declared by `getopts_long()`. These include `optarg`, to hold a pointer to the argument value string, and `optind`, to keep track of which index in the argument list is being processed.

Summary

We have explored the simplest way to provide input to our programs via the command line. We first specified how the `main()` function can receive arguments that contain the count and values of arguments given to the program. We saw how `argc` and `argv` are related and how to access each `argv` string. A simple program to print out arguments given to it was provided for further experimentation. We noted how all arguments are passed into `main()` as strings. Once we access those arguments, we can perform further processing on them to alter the behavior of our program. Finally, a very simple command-line processor was provided to demonstrate the use of the `getopts_long()` C Standard Library function.

In the next chapter, we will explore a more comprehensive way to receive input from the user while a program is running. Just as `printf()` writes formatted data from program variables to the console (screen), the `scanf()` function reads and formats data from the console (keyboard) into program variables.

21
Exploring Formatted Input

Using console command-line arguments to get string input into our running programs is often handy, but not very useful if we want to read lots of values of any data type while our program is running. To do that, we need to explore how to use formatted input. Formatted input is the opposite end of the pipe, so to speak, to formatted output. Just like we can use formatted output with `print()`, various value formats can be easily read to the console by using `scanf()`. Both of these functions do the heavy lifting of converting values into desired output strings or, conversely, converting input character strings into desired values.

To understand input formatting, we will need to first understand the concept of streams. We will then use the technique of experimentation, or more specifically, **trial and observation**, to discover and verify our understanding of how C input streams operate. We will later expand the concept of streams to include files and file processing in Chapter 22, *Working with Files*, and Chapter 23, *Using File Input and File Output.*

As we explore formatted console input, we will also look at a few important side examples to learn about using unformatted input and output, converting unformatted strings into integers or floats, and finally, creating internal strings from values and reading values from an internal string.

The following topics will be covered in this chapter:

- Understanding input and output streams
- Revisiting formatted console output with `printf()`
- Exploring formatted console input with `scanf()`
- Using `scanf()` to read numerical values from the console
- Using `scanf()` to read string and character values from the console
- Controlling the `scanf()` input field width
- Exploring internal data conversion
- Using `sscanf()` and `sprintf()` to convert values into and from strings

- Exploring unformatted input and output
- Getting string input and output from the console using `gets()` and `puts()`
- Converting strings into numbers with `atoi()` and `atof()`
- Creating a sorted list of names with `gets()` and `puts()`

Technical requirements

Continue to use the tools you chose in the *Technical requirements* section of `Chapter 1,` *Running Hello, World!*.

The source code for this chapter can be found at `https://github.com/PacktPublishing/` `Learn-C-Programming`.

Introducing streams

In the simplest terms, a **stream** is a sequence of bytes transferred in one direction from its source to its target. We have already discussed the abstract concept of an execution stream, or the flow of compiled CPU instructions from memory to the CPU. An execution stream is created when we successfully compile our source code files into an executable file. It is initiated when the program is invoked from the command line and flows until the program stops.

In the console, the input stream transfers bytes—in this case, characters—from the keyboard to our program's memory. The console's output stream transfers characters from our program's memory to the screen. A console, therefore, consists of a keyboard source stream for input and a screen destination stream for output. We can think of it simply as a pair of input and output streams, also known as **I/O streams**.

The standard console is enhanced by two additional features:

- First, as the input stream is directed to memory, it is also redirected, or echoed, to the output stream so that we can see each character as we type it. The echoing of characters from the input stream to the output stream is something the Terminal program does for us.
- Second, there is a third stream—the error stream—where output is directed if for some reason the output stream fails. For the console, the output stream and error stream are both directed to the screen by default. The error stream, however, could be redirected to another screen, a file on the hard drive, or to some remote network location.

All streams consist of bytes flowing from one device to another device. We will see, in `Chapter 22`, *Working with Files*, that files are also streams. The flow of a stream is controlled by bytes within the stream itself. As bytes flow from the source to the destination, some bytes are examined by the receiving device and processed, while others are simply passed through. Recall from `Chapter 15`, *Working with Strings*, the column of control characters. These byte sequences cause a stream flow or the device at either end of the stream to alter its behavior. Nearly all of the coordination between devices in a stream is handled by the C runtime library or by the operating system.

Each stream is represented internally by a pointer to a complex data structure called `FILE`, which contains the information needed to control the stream. This includes its current state and associated data buffer. When program execution begins, the C runtime library creates three file streams for us and automatically connects them to our program:

```
#include <stdio.h>

FILE* stdin;            /* standard input: the keyboard     */
FILE* stdout;           /* standard output: the screen      */
FILE* sterr;            /* standard error output: the screen */
```

We rarely have to deal with the internal workings of these stream structures. We can, by means of redirection, connect `stdin`, `stdout`, and `stderr` to files or another device without affecting the contents of our program. We will see that `printf()`, `scanf()`, and other console-oriented I/O functions have corresponding file stream versions that apply to files, as well as to other device streams. These are shown in the following table:

	Output Function		Output Stream	Input Function		Input Stream
Console I/O	`printf()`	⇒	stdout	`scanf()`	⇐	stdin
File Streams	`fprintf()`	⇒	A file	`fscanf()`	⇐	A file
Memory Streams	`sprintf()`	⇒	A string buffer	`scanf()`	⇐	A string buffer

Notice how each output function and input function are similar in name. Also, notice how the input or output streams go either to `stdin` or `stdout` for console I/O, to one or more files for file streams, and to string buffers in memory for memory streams. We will explore console I/O and memory streams in this chapter and file streams in the next chapter.

Notice that there is no entry in the table for the error stream because there is no `stderr` stream function for console I/O or for memory streams. In either of these situations, we must use the `fprintf()` file stream with the `stderr` stream specified, as follows:

```
fprintf( stderr , "Oops! Something went wrong...\n" ) ;
```

In all cases, to send error messages to the console, use the `fprintf()` function with the file stream parameter set to `stderr`. We have already seen a statement like this one in our linked list program in `Chapter 18`, *Using Dynamic Memory Allocation*. If you recall, it appeared in the following function:

```
void OutOfStorage( void ) {
    fprintf( stderr, "### FATAL RUNTIME ERROR ### No Memory Available" );
    exit( EXIT_FAILURE );
}
```

Not every error message indicates that the error is fatal and the program must exit, as in the `OutofStorage()` function. Often, `stderr` is used for less fatal errors, program events and progress logging, and program troubleshooting. Remember that `stderr` is sent by default to the console. This enables file output to be sent to a file, while other non-file-oriented messages can provide immediate console feedback while the program is running.

Whenever we speak of `printf()`, we are also speaking of its related functions—`fprintf()` and `sprintf()`. So, except for the different streams used in each of these functions, what is said for one will apply to all three.

Likewise, whenever we speak of `scanf()`, we are also speaking of its related functions—`fscanf()` and `sscannf()`. So, except for the different streams used in each of these functions, what is said for one will apply to all three.

`sprintf()` and `sscanf()` require some additional considerations, which we will cover when we explore these functions.

Understanding the standard output stream

The standard output stream is a pointer to a complex `FILE` structure named `stdout`. This stream sends all characters to the console screen formatted by the `printf()` function. We can think of this stream as a never-ending flow of characters from our program to the screen. It may not look like that onscreen because of the control characters, which alter how characters appear. These include carriage return (`CR`), new line (`NL`), form feed (`FF`), horizontal tab (`HT`), and vertical tab (`VT`). Other control characters change how the screen appears when we delete or rub out characters. These include backspace (`BS`) and delete (`DEL`). Nevertheless, these characters appear in the stream flow to the console program; the console program either simply prints them or interprets and changes the position of where the next character will be shown on the screen.

One complication to the flow of characters in the stream is that they are typically buffered. That is, they are sent to a memory location—a character array of a fixed size—before being sent to the screen. The buffer coalesces, or groups, output to the screen so that numerous characters are output at once and not one at a time. The buffer is flushed, or sent to the screen, either when the buffer is full, when a new line is encountered in the stream, or when our program exits.

In fact, by default, all the FILE streams are buffered. We can see how this affects the program behavior in the following program:

```
#include <stdio.h>
#include <unistd.h>

int main( void ) {
  printf( "You'll see this immediately.\nNow count to 5 slowly.\n");
  printf( "This will appear after 5 seconds ... ");
  sleep( 5 );
  printf( "when the buffer is finally flushed.\n" );
}
```

In this program, we use the sleep() function declared in the <unistd.h> header file to put the program into an idle state for 5 seconds. This program will demonstrate how the first printf() function is output immediately while the second printf() function is only seen after the sleep() function when the last printf() function with \n is called. To see this in action, create a file called flush.c and enter the preceding program. Compile and run this program. You should see the following output—but pay attention to when you see each line of output:

```
> cc flush.c -o flush -Wall -Werror -std=c11
> flush
You'll see this immediately.
Now count to 5 slowly.
Then, this appears ... when the buffer is finally flushed.
>
```

Given that the sleep() function comes after the second printf() function, you might have expected to see its output before the program slept (or went idle) for 5 seconds. Instead, what actually happened is that without CR, the buffer is not flushed until the very last printf() function. This experiment shows how CR flushes the output buffer immediately, whereas a lack of \n, or CR, as in the second printf() function, prevents that string from being flushed until a CR character is encountered or until the program exits.

If you want to prove that the buffer is flushed when the program exits, remove the very last \n character from the very last printf() call, save the file, then compile and rerun the program. You should see identical behavior.

Understanding the standard input stream

The standard input stream is a pointer to a complex FILE structure named stdin. This stream reads any characters typed from the keyboard to be formatted by the scanf() function.

Like the output stream, by default, the input stream is also buffered. For input, this means that characters are sent to the buffer. The buffer is not flushed until either the buffer is full or until CR is encountered in the input stream. As we enter characters, program control is maintained by the console and is not returned to our program until the buffer is flushed. The processing of the input characters then appears to our program as if they were received one at a time.

In reality, however, it is a bit more complicated than this. The console has two modes of processing—**cooked mode** and **raw mode**.

Cooked mode uses buffered input and is the default mode unless it is explicitly changed. It also means that we can alter our input in the buffer until we type in the CR key. Backspace and delete work as expected in this mode so that we can edit our input in the buffer before the buffer is flushed to our program. The console is managing the buffer in this mode. Even for single character input, we must enter CR for it to leave the buffer and be passed to our program.

In raw mode, each individual character is received by the console, and control is immediately returned to our program to process that single character. The character buffer is a single character only. No input processing is done by the console, so no editing is possible in this mode. We will see how to put the Terminal in raw mode and perform single-character processing after we introduce the scanf() function.

We will later see how these two modes operate in the console.

Revisiting the console output with printf() and fprintf()

The function prototype for `printf()` and `fprintf()` are as follows:

```
int  prinft(              const char* format , ... );
int fprintf( FILE* stream , const char* format , ... );
```

Spaces have been added to emphasize the common parts of each function. We can see the console output with `printf()`, as follows:

```
int myAge = 1;
printf( "Hello, World! I am %d today!\n" , myAge );
```

This is, in fact, a shorthand form of the `fprintf()` function using `stdout` for the file stream parameter, as follows:

```
int myAge = 1;
fprintf( stdout , "Hello, World! I am %d today!\n" , myAge );
```

If you are so inclined, you could replace every `printf( ... )` statement in every program we have seen so far with its equivalent form, `fprintf( stdout , ... )`, and all the programs would execute exactly as before. But please don't bother doing this; we have better things to do!

It is worth emphasizing that the `printf()`, `fprintf()`, and `sprintf()` functions each take values from variables that are in binary form and convert them into a string that is written/copied to the desired output stream. For instance, the `125` value (a number) is formatted with the `%d` format specifier into the `'1'`, `'2'`, and `'5'` characters, and is then inserted into the final output string.

Exploring the console input with scanf()

The function prototypes for `scanf()` and `fscanf()` are as follows:

```
int   scan(              const char* format , ... );
int fscanf( FILE* stream , const char* format , ... );
```

Again, spaces have been added to emphasize the common parts of each function.

For the console input, we can use `scanf()` and `fscanf()` interchangeably. These two function calls are equivalent, as follows:

```
scanf(         "%d" , &anInteger );
fscanf( stdin, "%d" , &anInteger );
```

Whitespace has been added to emphasize where the functions differ. The `scanf(...)` function is shorthand for `fscanf( stdin , ... )` when input is received from the console. One major difference between `scanf()` and `printf()` is that we must pass the address of the variable to be assigned or a pointer to the variable we wish to give a value to the function. Recall that in C, function parameter values are passed by a copy. So, with `printf()`, we only need a copy of the value to the output since `printf()` does not change any values; it only displays them. However, for `scanf()` to be able to change the value of the variable passed into it, we must instead pass the address of that variable.

Apart from that one difference, the format specifiers for `scanf()` are identical, but fewer in number than the format specifiers for `printf()`. We will see, however, that their behavior is a little bit different than for `printf()`.

Similarly to the output functions, the `scanf()`, `fscanf()`, and `sscanf()` input functions each take values from the desired input stream that are in the form of individual characters and convert them into desired binary values. For instance, the `'1'`, `'2'`, and `'5'` characters are received from the input stream, converted into `125` (a number) with the `%d` format specifier, and then assigned/copied to the specified variable. It should be noted that the input stream is not necessarily a valid string because of the lack of the null-terminating character.

We will now explore how to convert characters in the input stream into binary values using various format specifiers.

Reading formatted input with scanf()

In `Chapter 19`, *Exploring Formatted Output*, we exhaustively explored the `printf()` output specifiers using a variety of programs to demonstrate how these specifiers work. We can reuse much of that knowledge for input specifiers.

The input specifiers for `scanf()` are similar in syntax and meaning to the output specifiers of `printf()`, except for a few differences. Therefore, it is best to consider the format string specifiers for `printf()` and `scanf()` as only vaguely similar; do not rely on the documentation for one as a guide for the other.

The following differences should be noted:

- `printf()` accepts precision specification, while `scanf()` does not.
- `printf()` accepts the –, +, <space>, 0, and # flag specifiers, while `scanf()` does not.
  Note that the input strings may have the –, +, and/or # characters and `scanf()` will interpret them as flags; however, these cannot be specified in the format specifier.
- An explicitly specified field width is the minimum for `printf()`; it is the maximum for `scanf()`.
- The [ ] conversion specifier is unique to `scanf()`. It specifies a scan set and is explored in this chapter in the *Using a scan set to limit possible input characters* section.
- `printf()` allows the field width and precision to be specified with the * and arguments; `scanf()` uses * for a completely different purpose—to suppress assignment. For instance, using * allows us to skip over an input value, if needed.

One final difference between `printf()` and `scanf()` is that in the input strings to `scanf()`, whitespace is critical in the process of parsing the input strings into values. We will explore this behavior next.

Reading numerical input with scanf()

To begin our exploration of `scanf()`, we begin by reading an integer and a double from the console. Rather than attempt to explain how `scanf()` interprets the input, I believe it would be far better to first get an intuitive experience of how it works. We begin with the following program:

```
#include <stdio.h>

int main( void )  {
   int     anInteger   = -1;
   double  aDouble     = -1.0;
   printf( "Enter an integer and a decimal number: " );
   scanf( "%d%lf" , &anInteger , &aDouble );
   printf( "1. integer:  %d\n" , anInteger );
   printf( "2.  double:  %lf\n" , aDouble );
}
```

This simple program first initializes values that will be used to store input. If scanf() can't assign values, we will see these default values. We will use two simple numbers for now. However, as we will see, if the user enters these numbers, we will be unable to tell whether they are default values that were not assigned by scanf() or whether the user actually entered these numbers.

The program then prints a prompt for the user to enter an integer and a decimal number. It then reads what is entered using scanf() and tries to assign values to the two variables. The last two statements print the values of the two variables. The essential work of this program takes place in the single scanf() statement. Notice that even though there is no space between %d and %lf, whitespace remains an important consideration for input.

Create a file named read2Numbers.c and enter the preceding program. Compile it and run it. You should run it five times. Each time you run it, use the following input for each run to see how scanf() does its best to interpret what it is given:

```
1234 5678.9012<return>

<return>
        1234<return>
          5678.9012<return>

1234.5678<return>

1234 hello 5678.9012<return>

hello 1234 5678.9012<return>
```

Each test case ends with a final <return> mark. If you run read2Numbers with the preceding input, you should see the following output:

```
[> cc read2Numbers.c -o read2Numbers -Wall -Werror -std=c11
[> read2Numbers
Enter an integer and a decimal number: 1234 5678.9012
1. integer:   1234
2.  double:   5678.901200

[> read2Numbers
Enter an integer and a decimal number:
    1234
          5678.9012
1. integer:   1234
2.  double:   5678.901200

[> read2Numbers
Enter an integer and a decimal number: 1234.5678
1. integer:   1234
2.  double:   0.567800

[> read2Numbers
Enter an integer and a decimal number: 1234 hello 5678.9012
1. integer:   1234
2.  double:   -1.000000

[> read2Numbers
Enter an integer and a decimal number: hello 1234 5678.9012
1. integer:   -1
2.  double:   -1.000000

>
```

In the first test case, an integer and a decimal number are entered, separated by a single space. scanf() easily interprets these values, as expected.

The second test case begins with a <return> mark; scanf() treats it as whitespace, along with the leading whitespace on the next line, ignoring it. It then interprets the integer and again treats all the whitespace up to the decimal number, which it then interprets, as expected. This example emphasizes how repeated, consecutive whitespace is ignored.

In the third test case there appears to only be a decimal number. However, scanf() interprets the digits up to the dot (.) as an integer and then interprets the dot (.) to be the beginning of a decimal number. In this case, there is no whitespace at all and the interpretation of integer digits ends with the decimal point.

The last two test cases show how scanf() interprets, or fails to interpret, integer digits and decimal digits when alphabetic characters—not specified in the format specifier—interrupt the orderly interpretation of digits. In the fourth test case, only the integer is correctly interpreted; for the decimal value, we see its initial value printed. In the fifth case, neither value is interpreted and we see both of the initial values printed. Notice that even though integer digits and decimal digits exist before <return>, they are ignored because the alphabetic characters have interrupted the scanf() attempt to follow the format specifier.

This situation is not ideal since we need to have a better idea about when scanf() reads one or more values and when it doesn't. Fortunately, there is a way to know when the scanf() values have been read. This involves using the return value from scanf()—an integer that reports how many values have been read with scanf(). Copy read2Numbers.c into read2NumbersUsingResult.c and modify it to match the following program (the changes are in bold):

```c
#include <stdio.h>

int main( void ) {
   int   anInteger  = -1;
   double aDouble    = -1.0;
   int   numScanned = 0;

   printf( "Enter an integer and a decimal number: " );
   numScanned = scanf( "%d%lf" , &anInteger , &aDouble );
   printf( "scanf() was able to assign %d values.\n" , numScanned );
   if( numScanned > 0 ) printf( "1. integer: %d\n" , anInteger );
   if( numScanned > 1 ) printf( "2. double: %lf\n" , aDouble );
   printf( "\n" );
}
```

In this program, instead of ignoring the result returned from scanf(), we capture it by assigning it to a variable and then we use that value to determine which input values have been read. If numScanned is 0, no values have been successfully interpreted by scanf(). If numScanned is 1, only the first input value was successfully interpreted and assigned by scanf().

Save this program. Compile and run it five times using the same input used earlier. You should see the following output:

```
> cc read2NumbersUsingResult.c -o read2NumbersUsingResult -Wall -Werror -std=c11
> read2NumbersUsingResult
Enter an integer and a decimal number: 1234 5678.9012
scanf() was able to assign 2 values.
1. integer:   1234
2.  double:   5678.901200

> read2NumbersUsingResult
Enter an integer and a decimal number:
    1234
           5678.9012
scanf() was able to assign 2 values.
1. integer:   1234
2.  double:   5678.901200

> read2NumbersUsingResult
Enter an integer and a decimal number: 1234.5678
scanf() was able to assign 2 values.
1. integer:   1234
2.  double:   0.567800

> read2NumbersUsingResult
Enter an integer and a decimal number: 1234 hello 5678.9012
scanf() was able to assign 1 values.
1. integer:   1234

> read2NumbersUsingResult
Enter an integer and a decimal number: hello 1234 5678.9012
scanf() was able to assign 0 values.

>
```

The results of this input are identical to the earlier program. The first three input cases assign both values, as before. The last two test cases also assign or fail to assign values, as before. However, because the program now has more information from the scanf() function, it can use that information to react to input if needed.

Now that we have seen how to input numbers, we can move on to conversions using scanf() to read strings and characters.

Reading string and character input with scanf()

One way to read a string is to use `scanf()` with the `%s` specifier. We will also see some other ways of doing this later in this chapter. The `%s` specifier assigns a sequence of non-whitespace characters to the given array. As with numbers, leading whitespace is skipped. Recall that whitespace can be `' '`, `'\t'`, `'\n'`, `'\r'`, `'\f'`, or `'\v'`. Conversion stops on the first occurrence of whitespace after one or more instances of non-whitespace or at the maximum field width, if specified. Otherwise, the array to which the input string is assigned must be large enough to hold the string plus the terminating NUL character.

The following program demonstrates this effect:

```c
#include <stdio.h>
const int bufferSize = 80;
int main( void )  {
  char stringBuffer[ bufferSize ];
  printf( "Enter a string: " );
  scanf(  "%s" , stringBuffer );
  printf( "Processed string: [%s]\", stringBuffer );
}
```

The most significant parts of this program are in bold. It first allocates a character array to hold 79 characters (don't forget the NUL character). After providing a prompt to the user, it uses `scanf()` with the `%s` format specifier to read a string into that array. In this case, no maximum field width is given. Note how the array name, the address of the first element of the array, is used as a pointer. Once a string is interpreted and assigned, the last statement prints out the result of the `scanf()` interpretation.

Create a file named `readString.c` and enter the preceding program. Compile and run the program with the following three input test case strings:

```
Anything up to the white space<return>

Every_thing%before;any:white'space\(will%be read into an array.)<return>

        Skipping initial white space.<return>
```

If you run the program three times with this input, you should see the following output:

```
> cc readString.c -o readString -Wall -Werror -std=c11
> readString
Enter a string: Anything up to the white space<return>
Processed string: [Anything]

> readString
Enter a string: Every_thing%before;any:white'space\(will%be read into an array.)
Processed string: [Every_thing%before;any:white'space\(will%be]

> readString
Enter a string:        Skipping initial white space.
Processed string: [Skipping]

>
```

In the first case, all characters up to the first <space> character are read into the array; the rest are ignored. In the second case, any and all characters are read until any whitespace is encountered. The third case shows how the initial whitespace is ignored.

The next program illustrates not only how to read a character but also how to use whitespace between input values. The following program will read a character without whitespace and with whitespace in the format specifier:

```c
#include <stdio.h>
int main( void )  {
   char aChar;
   int  anInt1, anInt2;
   int  numScanned;
   printf( "1st: Enter <integer><char><integer>: " );
   numScanned = scanf(  "%d%c%d" , &anInt1 , &aChar , &anInt2 );
   printf( "Values scanned = %d. Character selected: [%c]\n" ,
           numScanned , aChar );

   printf( "2nd: Enter <integer> <char> <integer>: " );
   numScanned = scanf(  "%d %c%d" , &anInt1 , &aChar , &anInt2 );
   printf( "Values scanned = %d. Character selected: [%c]\n\n" ,
           numScanned , aChar );
}
```

After declaring the variables, this program has two parts. In the first part, it gives an input prompt. It then accepts input for an integer, a character, and another integer. Notice that there are no spaces in the format specifier. Then, it provides some feedback about what it could interpret. In the second part, it does the same as the first part, except there is a single space in the format specifier between the first integer and the character.

We will see how a space in the format specifier changes how the character is or is not interpreted. This will also change how the second integer is or is not interpreted. To see how this works, we'll use the following input:

```
123m    456<return>

123    m456<return>

123   w   456<return>
```

The first input has no whitespace before the character and some whitespace before the second integer; this is to match the first format specifier. The next input has some whitespace before the character and no whitespace before the second integer; again, this is to match the second format specifier. The last input has some whitespace before and after the character; this does not match the first format specifier, so we can see what scanf() tries to do with it.

Create a file called readChar.c. Then, open the preceding program, save it, and compile it. Run the program twice. In the first run, we'll input two lines. In the second run, we'll input just the last line. Notice that we are only using three inputs. The reason for this will become obvious after we input the third line the second time we run the program. Your output should appear as follows:

```
> cc readChar.c -o readChar -Wall -Werror -std=c11
> readChar
1st: Enter <integer><char><integer>: 123m    456
Values scanned = 3. Character selected: [m]
2nd: Enter <integer> <char> <integer>: 123    m456
Values scanned = 3. Character selected: [m]

> readChar
1st: Enter <integer><char><integer>: 123   w   456
Values scanned = 2. Character selected: [ ]
2nd: Enter <integer> <char> <integer>: Values scanned = 0. Character selected: [
  ]

>
```

We can see in the first run that both of the scanf() statements are able to interpret an integer, a character, and another integer. Notice that for integers, the initial whitespace is ignored. However, for a character, the initial whitespace is only ignored if the format specifier has a space before %c.

In the second run with the third input line, two of the three variables are read by the first `scanf()` statement—the `123` integer and the `' '` character, which also happens to be whitespace. `scanf()` then encounters the `'w'` character, which causes the third variable interpretation to fail. But there is still input in the buffer. So, when the next `scanf()` statement encounters what's left in the buffer, it expects a decimal digit but instead finds the `'w'` character and fails completely. The program exits and the buffer, which is still not completely processed, is flushed.

You may have noticed that the third input line will be correctly interpreted by the `"%d %c%d"` format specifier but it causes mayhem when given to the `"%d%c%d"` format specifier. You may want to try additional variations of input with this program.

You may also get the impression that `scanf()` can be finicky, with emphasis on the *icky* part. Be aware that the `scanf()` family of routines is ideally suited to reading input from data files created by other programs; these programs would provide a much higher degree of consistency than most humans can muster.

Using a scan set to limit possible input characters

A scan set is a group of characters that make up a set and are interpreted as valid characters in the input. A scan set is specified in the format string by the `%[` and `]` characters; any characters within the square brackets make up the scan set. The scan set may indicate that either the characters should be included in the input or the characters should be excluded. A circumflex (^) used as the first character indicates negation of the set and indicates all characters except those specified. Consider the following scan sets:

Scan set	Description
`%[aeiouy]`	Any of the specified six characters—a, e, i, o, u, and y—are valid input.
`%[^aeiouy]`	Any characters *except* the specified six characters are valid input.
`%[ \t,]`	A space, horizontal tab, and a comma are valid input.
`%[^,.;: \t]`	Any characters *except* a comma, period, colon, semi-colon, and horizontal tab are valid input.

Input is successfully converted if any inputted characters are in the scan set or if any input characters are not in the negated scan set. Input conversion stops either when the end of file is reached or if the input character is not in the scan set (or in the negated scan set).

Consider the following program:

```
#include <stdio.h>
const int bufferSize = 80;
int main( void )   {
   char stringBuffer[ bufferSize ];
   printf( "Enter only vowels: " );
   numScanned = scanf(   "%[aeiouy]" , stringBuffer );
   printf( "Processed string: [%s]\n\n" , stringBuffer );
}
```

This program specifies that the input string only contains the a, e, i, o, u, and y characters. This program is nearly identical to the readString.c program we created earlier. The only difference is the use of a scan set.

Create a file called readScanSet.c, type it in, and save it, then compile and run it. Run it several times using the following input:

```
aayyeeuuiioo<return>

aeimwouy<return>

a e i o u y<return>
```

You should see the following output:

```
> cc readScanSet.c -o readScanSet -Wall -Werror -std=c11
> readScanSet
Enter only vowels: aaeeiioouuyy
Processed string: [aaeeiioouuyy]

> readScanSet
Enter only vowels: aeimwouy
Processed string: [aei]

> readScanSet
Enter only vowels: a e i o u y
Processed string: [a]

>
```

The first line of the input is all vowels, so all of it is converted into the input string. The second line of the input contains some characters that are not in the scan set; therefore, conversion stops at the first non-vowel character, and only the first three vowels are converted into the input string. The last line of the input contains spaces, which are again characters that are not part of the scan set; conversion stops at the first space and only 'a' is converted into the input string.

Using a scan set is handy if you want to limit what characters can be entered. One example would be to limit the user's response to either y for yes or n for no. This can be accomplished by using the % [YyNn] format specifier.

Controlling the scanf() input field width

Recall how with printf(), we could control the minimum length of the output string. In a similar way, we can control the maximum length of the input string for conversion with a specifier. For example, %3d will accept no more than three digits for conversion into an integer. The following program reads a group of digits, each of which is intended to represent a date—the first four digits for the year, the next two for the month, and the last two for the day:

```
#include <stdio.h>
int main( void )  {
  int year , month , day;
  int numScanned;
  while( printf("Enter mmddyyyy (any other character to quit): "),
         numScanned = scanf( "%2d%2d%4d" , &month , &day , &year ) ,
         numScanned > 0 )
    printf( "%d/%d/%d\n" , month , day , year );
  printf( "\nDone\n" );
}
```

After declaring variables to hold the input values, a while()... loop is used to repeatedly accept eight digits to be converted into a date.

Create a file named readWidth.c, type in the preceding program, save it, and compile it. To see how this behaves, run the program using the following input:

```
01012020<return>
   02   02   2021<return>
12252019<return>
 9302019<return>
12 52020<return>
7/4/2019<return>
```

You should now see the following output:

```
> cc readWidth.c -o readWidth -Wall -Werror -std=c11
> readWidth
Enter mmddyyyy (any other character to quit): 01012020
1/1/2020

Enter mmddyyyy (any other character to quit):    02   02   2021
2/2/2021

Enter mmddyyyy (any other character to quit): 12252019
12/25/2019

Enter mmddyyyy (any other character to quit):   9302019
93/2/19

Enter mmddyyyy (any other character to quit): 12 52020
12/52/20

Enter mmddyyyy (any other character to quit): 7/4/2019
7/52/20

Enter mmddyyyy (any other character to quit):
Done
>
```

The first three test inputs all work as expected. In each case, the month, day, and year are correctly interpreted, which we can see from the printed date. Even the second input line, with spaces before each decimal value, is correctly interpreted. However, things begin to go awry in the fourth and fifth test cases. In these, we have made the incorrect assumption that whitespace is considered part of the maximum field width when it is not. In fact, whitespace is considered separate from the input field width, as these test cases show. In the fourth test input, scanf() skips the whitespace and reads the month as 93, the day as 02, and the year as 019. In the fifth test input, scanf() reads the month as 12, then skips the whitespace to read the day as 52 and the year as 020. Finally, on the last input, scanf() reads the month as 7, but then conversion stops at /. We can see how it assigns only the month and prints out 7/52/20, where the values of the day and year are unchanged from the previous conversion. On the next iteration of the loop, / is interpreted as a non-digit, which caused the loop to fail and the program to exit.

Is there possibly a better solution? Actually, yes, there is. A better solution is to use a single-character input, %c, and to add the non-assignment flag, *. If the non-assignment flag is specified, the input is interpreted but not assigned to any variable. They do not cause the conversion to stop and are, in fact, a required part of the conversion.

The following program illustrates this:

```
#include <stdio.h>
int main( void )  {
   int year , month , day;
   int numScanned;
   while(
       printf("Enter mm*dd*yyyy (any other character to quit): "),
       numScanned = scanf( "%2d%*c%2d%*c%4d" , &month , &day , &year ) ,
       numScanned > 0 )
     printf( "%d.%d.%d\n" , month , day , year );
  printf( "\nDone\n" );
}
```

The only difference between this program and the preceding one, apart from the slight change to the user prompt, is the format specifier:

```
"%2d%*c%2d%*c%4d"
```

Note the %*c specifier between each integer. This specifier tells scanf() to interpret a single character between each integer. This can be any character in the input stream, even whitespace. However, the * flag tells scanf() not to assign that input to any variable. In this way, we can expand on the scanf() function's pattern-matching abilities. However, we have to alter the input to match this new pattern. We will use the following input for this program:

```
01x01x2020<return>
   02   02   2021<return>
12^25^2019<return>
 9!30!2019<return>
12x 5y2020<return>
7/4/2019<return>
x<return>
```

Notice that these are similar to the preceding input, but our new pattern requires us to have at least one character, any character, between each integer. Even a single whitespace character will be considered a valid single character and will be interpreted.

With this new input, let's see how this program behaves. Copy `readWidth.c` into `readDate.c` and make the required modifications to the user prompt, the format specifier, and the `printf()` string. Save, compile, and run the program. You should see the following output:

```
> cc readDate.c -o readDate -Wall -Werror -std=c11
> readDate
Enter mm*dd*yyyy (any other character to quit): 01x01x2020
1.1.2020

Enter mm*dd*yyyy (any other character to quit):    02   02   2021
2.2.2021

Enter mm*dd*yyyy (any other character to quit): 12^25^2019
12.25.2019

Enter mm*dd*yyyy (any other character to quit):   9!30!2019
9.30.2019

Enter mm*dd*yyyy (any other character to quit): 12x 5y2020
12.5.2020

Enter mm*dd*yyyy (any other character to quit): 7/4/2019
7.4.2019

Enter mm*dd*yyyy (any other character to quit):
x

Done
>
```

In each input case, `scanf()` is able to correctly interpret the date values, as well as the non-assigned characters. Notice that any character in this format specifier can be used as an integer delimiter. There can also be additional whitespace in the input without ill effect.

We have now explored all of `scanf()` capabilities. We might correctly conclude that while the use of simple input format specifiers can be somewhat finicky, we can make them less so by setting the field width, scan sets, and non-assignment flags.

We can now explore other ways to perform data conversions to and from strings and values.

Using internal data conversion

It should be fairly obvious that the ability for printf() to convert binary values into strings and of scanf() to convert strings into binary values is very powerful. These facilities are not constrained to console streams, nor are they constrained to file streams. Whenever we need to carry out internal data conversions, we have the same facilities available to us with the related sprintf() and sscanf() functions. Rather than use streams, these functions use strings—arrays of characters—as their initial input and our resultant output.

We have seen how scanf() can be finicky. One way to mitigate irregular or troublesome input is to read that input into a large string buffer and then process that string buffer in various ways with sscanf().

The function prototypes for sprintf() and scanf() are as follows:

```
int sprintf( char* buffer , const char *format , ... );
int sscanf( char* buffer , const char *format , ... );
```

The format specifiers used in these functions are identical to their stream counterparts. Therefore, we do not need to revisit each flag and feature of the format specifiers for sprintf(), nor for those of sscanf().

However, unlike the stream versions, when we use sprintf() and sscanf(), we must be more careful about the sizes of the character buffers.

Using sscanf() and sprintf() to convert values into and from strings

Typically, when using sscanf() to interpret a string buffer into values, the string buffer is already known or has been allocated elsewhere. sscanf() converts the string into the desired values, assigning them to variables. The sizes of these variables are known by their data type.

On the other hand, when using sprintf() to convert values into characters, the final output buffer size required is rarely known. We can either exercise great care to allocate a specific array size or, more commonly, we can simply allocate an array that is reasonably larger than expected, ignoring any unused or even unneeded buffer space.

The following program demonstrates the use of `sscanf()` and `sprintf()`:

```c
#include <stdio.h>
#include <string.h>          // for memset

const int bufferSize = 80;

int main( void )   {
  int       anInteger    = -1;
  double    aDouble      = -1.0;
  int       numScanned   = 0 , numPrinted = 0;
  char sIn[] = "1234 5678.9012";
  char sOut[ bufferSize ];
  memset( sOut , 0 , bufferSize );

  printf("Using sscanf() on [%s]\n" , sIn );
  numScanned = sscanf( sIn , "%d%lf" , &anInteger , &aDouble );
  printf( "sscanf() was able to assign %d values.\n" , numScanned );
  printf( "1. integer:  %d\n" , anInteger );
  printf( "2.  double:  %lf\n\n" , aDouble );
  puts( "Using sprintf() to format values to string buffer:" );
  numPrinted = sprintf( sOut , "integer=[%d] double=[%9.4lf]" ,
              anInteger , aDouble );
  printf( "%d characters in output string \"%s\"\n", numPrinted, sOut );
}
```

Apart from the use of I/O buffers (character arrays), this program is nearly identical to `read2NumbersUsingResult.c`, which we created at the beginning of this chapter. Instead of reading 1234 and 5678.9012 from the input stream, these values are now found in the sIn[] array buffer. Instead of writing to stdout, values are output to the sOut[] array buffer, whose size is a generous 80 characters, or about the length of a standard console line. Remember that sOut[] can hold a string of up to 79 characters, with the 80th character being the required NUL character.

After allocating and initializing variables and buffers, the program uses `sscanf()` to convert the input buffer into two numbers. We use %s to show the contents of the input array.

Finally, the program uses `sprintf()` to convert those values back into a string in the output buffer. Again, we use %s to show the contents of the output buffer. This program introduces the `puts()` function, which is a simplified version of `printf()`. `puts()` simply prints the given string to stdout and is the equivalent of `printf( "%s\n" )`. The input counterpart to `puts()` is `gets()`, which we will encounter a little later in this chapter.

Create a file named `internalFormatting.c`, enter the preceding program, save it, compile it, and run it. You should see the following output:

```
> cc internalFormatting.c -o internalFormatting -Wall -Werror -std=c11
> internalFormatting
Using sscanf() on [1234 5678.9012]
sscanf() was able to assign 2 values.
1. integer:  1234
2.  double:  5678.901200

Using sprintf() to format values to string buffer:
33 characters in output string "integer=[1234] double=[5678.9012]"
>
```

We can see that `sscanf()` was able to convert and correctly assign two values. We can also see that `sprintf()` formatted those values into a string of 33 characters. Note that this count of 33 characters does not include the NUL character.

Converting strings into numbers with atoi() and atod()

Another way to convert strings into values is to use the conversion functions declared in `stdlib.h`—ASCII to integer (`atoi()`) and ASCII to float (`atof()`). These functions take a string buffer as their function parameter and return a value of the relevant type. `atoi()` returns an `int` value while `atof()` returns a `double` value. These functions are based on more general strings to the <type> functions—`strtol()`, `strtoll()`, `strtod()`, `strtof()`, and `strtold()`, where l is a `long` integer value, ll is a `long long` integer value, d is `double`, f is a `float` value, and ld is a `long double` value.

The `ato<type>()` functions assume a single value is given in the input array. The `strto<type>()` functions have additional parameters that allow them to convert either the whole string or a smaller part of a larger string.

We don't always need the specificity or flexibility that the `strto<type>()` functions provide. The following program demonstrates the conversion of strings into an integer and double:

```
#include <stdio.h>
#include <stdlib.h>

int main( void )  {
```

```
    int      anInteger    = -1;
    double   aDouble       = -1.0;
    char sInteger[] = "1234" ;
    char sDouble[]  = "5678.9012";
    printf("As strings: integer=\"%s\" double=\"%s\"\n" ,
    sInteger , sDouble );
    anInteger = atoi( sInteger );
    aDouble   = atof( sDouble );
    printf( "As values: integer=[%d] double=[%lf]\n\n" ,
    anInteger , aDouble );
}
```

This program is very similar to the previous program, but instead of using a single
sscanf() function, it uses atoi() and atof() to convert an integer string and a double
string into their respective values. atoi() and atof() are convenient and simple to use,
but are less flexible than their strto<type>() cousins and sscanf(). If the input data is
irregular or not well-formed, a much more complicated string conversion algorithm may be
devised as needed using all of these functions.

We have now completed our exploration of formatted input with the scanf() family.
However, this chapter would not be complete without a brief exploration of unformatted,
or *raw*, input and output.

Exploring unformatted input and output

Not every string input needs to be converted into some binary value. Often, we simply
need to read or write strings without any additional formatting. There is a family of
unformatted string I/O functions that can be used to read or write entire lines of characters
without any formatting applied. However, these functions require each string to be formed
into lines. A line is loosely defined as a string that is terminated by the <newline>
character. Each of these has a console version as well as a file/stream version. For the
remainder of this chapter, we will briefly explore this family of functions.

Getting the string input and output to/from the console

To read and write a line of text, there are the puts() and gets() console functions and their stream equivalents, fputs() and fgets(), as in the following table:

	Output Function	Output Stream		Input Function	Input Stream	
Console I/O	puts()	⇒ stdout		gets()	⇐	stdin
File Streams	fputs()	⇒ A file/stream		fgets()	⇐	A file/stream

The puts() and fputs() functions write the given string to the output stream or file, adding <newline> to the end of the string.

The gets() and fgets() functions read from the input stream or file until <eof> or <newline> is encountered. The <newline> character, if encountered, is retained. With gets(), no limit for the number of characters to be read can be specified. On the other hand, fgets() must be given the maximum number of characters to be read; it will read up to that limit unless <eof> or <newline> are encountered.

Using the simple input and output of strings with gets() and puts()

The following program demonstrates the use of gets() and puts():

```
#include <stdio.h>

const int bufferSize = 80;

int main( void )  {
  char stringBuffer[ bufferSize ];

  printf( "Enter a string: " );
  gets( stringBuffer );
  puts( "You entered:" );
  puts( stringBuffer );
}
```

This program first declares a string buffer. Next, it provides a user prompt, and then it reads the input into the string buffer with gets(). It then calls puts() twice—once to give a label string and again to write out what the user entered.

You may recall that this program is very similar to readString.c, which we created earlier. Copy the readString.c program into the readString2.c file and modify it to match the preceding program. Save, compile, and run it. You should see something like the following output:

```
> cc readString2.c -o readString2 -Wall -Werror -std=c11
> readstring2
warning: this program uses gets(), which is unsafe.
Enter a string: With charming ease, the quick brown fox jumps over the lazy dog.
You entered:
With charming ease, the quick brown fox jumps over the lazy dog.
>
```

Notice that the C runtime gave a warning about using gets(); we will explain this in the subsequent section. Also, notice that each puts() statement ends with a <newline> character.

You can see that using gets() and puts() make this program somewhat simpler than the original readString.c program, but not by much. While puts() can be used for simple output, gets() must be used with great care, if at all.

Understanding why using gets() could be dangerous

There is a significant difference between gets() and fgets(). The following function prototypes for these two functions highlight their differences:

```
char* gets( char* str );
char* fgets( char* str , int size , FILE* stream );
```

From this, we see that gets() requires no limits on how many characters it reads; therefore, gets() has the potential to read an infinite amount of input. On the other hand, fgets() must be given a maximum number of characters to be read in the size parameter. fgets() will read up to size-1 characters unless EOF or <newline> are encountered.

Because there are no limits on the length of the string to gets(), it has the potential to read beyond the size of the string buffer. If this happens, in a best-case scenario, mayhem will ensue and the program will crash. In a worst-case scenario, malicious input could be devised such that the program does not crash and causes control to extend beyond the program. This is a big security risk, which is why gets() is unsafe.

The solution is to completely replace any gets() function with the fgets() function. We will do this in the following section.

Creating a sorted list of names with fgets() and fputs()

To finish up this chapter, we will create a program that uses fgets() to get a list of names as input, sorts them into an array, and then prints the sorted array using fputs(). Create a file named nameSorter.c and begin by entering the following declarations, function prototypes, and the main() routine:

```
#include <stdio.h>
#include <string.h>
#include <stdbool.h>

const int listMax   = 100;
const int stringMax =  80;

typedef char string [ stringMax ];

void addName(     string* names , string newOne , int* listSize );
void printNames( string* names , int listSize );

void removeNewline( string s ) {
 int len = strlen( s );
 s[ len-1 ] = '\0';
}

int main( void )   {
   string newName;
   string nameList[ listMax ];
   int    numNames = 0;
   while( printf( "Name: %d: ", numNames+1 ),
          fgets( newName , stringMax , stdin ),
          removeNewline( newName ) ,
          strlen( newName ) > 0 )
```

```
        addName ( nameList , newName , &numNames );
    printNames ( nameList , numNames );
}
```

We need the `stdio.h` header file for any I/O functions; we need `string.h` for `strlen()`, `strcmp()`, and `strcpy()` and we need `stdbool.h` for the `bool` type. We then declare some global constants—`listMax` and `stringMax`—to limit the size of the list of names and the length of each name. For convenience, we use `typedef` for an array of the 80 characters to be known in this program as the string. Anywhere that we declare, say, `string aName`, we are really declaring `char aName[stringMax]`. Likewise, when we see `string* names`, this is a synonym for `char* names[stringMax]`—a pointer to a character array of the 80 characters of our program.

In `main()`, we declare a temporary character array, `newName`, and a two-dimensional array of the 100 strings or an array of the 100 names, each consisting of an array of the 80 characters, named `nameList`. The `numNames` variable keeps track of how many names have been entered.

We use a `while()`... loop to repeatedly call `addName()` to add a name to our list. There is a lot of work going on in the `<conditional-expression>` statement of this loop; four statements, actually. The `while()`... loop employs a compound conditional expression that first gives a prompt, then uses `fgets()` for the name, and finally, tests the length of the entered string. If `strlen()` is 0, the `while()`... loop terminates. In the next chapter, we will deal with the unnecessary complexity we have created here.

Finally, the program prints out the list with a call to `printNames()`.

Notice how through the use of a single `typedef` specifier and the two `addName()` and `printNames()` functions, our `main()` routine is both compact yet clear. We can see the overall workings of the program in the eight lines of `main()`. Of course, some of the more interesting parts of the program are in the sub-functions.

Once you have opened the first part of program, save the file but continue to edit it. The central work of the program occurs in the `addName()` function, as follows:

```
void addName ( string* names , string newName , int* pNumEntries )   {
  if( *pNumEntries >= listMax )   {   // List is full.
    puts( "List is full!" );
    return;
  } else {
    int   k    = 0;
    bool found = false;
    while( !found && k < *pNumEntries )
```

```
        found = (strcmp( newName, names[ k++ ] ) < 0);

    if( found )  {
       k-- ;   // newName goes before k.
       for( int j = *pNumEntries ; j > k ; j-- )  {
          strcpy( names[ j ] , names[ j-1 ] );
       }
    }
    strcpy( names[ k ] , newName ); // Insert newName at k-th position.
    (*pNumEntries)++;
  }
  return;
}
```

This function takes as its parameters a pointer to the first element of our array of names, a string that is the newName parameter to be added, and a pointer to numEntries because this value will change within this function.

The first thing to do is to check whether the list of names is full; if so, print a message and return. This is a simple approach; a better one would be to return either a Boolean or some value to indicate success/failure, then act on it in main(). If the list is not full, we then figure out where in the array to insert the new new name with a while()... loop—this will be somewhere in the middle or at the very end of the list. We use the found Boolean variable to determine whether the name needs to be inserted somewhere in the middle of the array. In this case, an insertion at the very beginning of the list is the same as if it were inserted anywhere else in the list, except at the end.

If newName needs to be inserted somewhere in the middle of the list, which is an array, we have a new problem. Array elements are sequential but not dynamic. You can not simply insert an element into the middle of an array, or else you might overwrite an existing value. Therefore, we need to first make room in our array for newName. In other words, we have to open up a free slot in the array for the new element. To open a free slot, we start at the last entry in our array and copy it back one place. So, if the last element is at index 9, we copy it to index 10. This opens a slot in front of that element. We continue copying elements back until we arrive at the desired location in the array. When we are done, we simply copy newName into the opened array entry. If newName needs to be inserted at the very end, we don't need to open up an array element; we just copy newName to the last array element. Before returning to main(), numEntries is incremented.

There are many ways to sort a list of strings. That is one of the main topics of a course on algorithms. For reference, this algorithm is known as a simplified form of an *insertion sort*. That is, as each element is inserted, it is inserted in its proper place within the sorted list. In this way, the list is always in a sorted state.

Once you have entered the `addName()` function, save the file. We are now ready to complete our program with the `printNames()` function:

```
void printNames( string *names , int numEntries )  {
  printf("\nNumber of Entries: %d\n\n" , numEntries );
  for( int i = 0 ; i < numEntries ; i++ )  {
    fputs( names[i] , stdout );
    fputc( '\n' , stdout );
  }
}
```

This function takes as its parameters a pointer to the array of `names` and the number of entries. We are not changing `numEntries`, so we don't need to pass a reference (pointer) to `numEntries`; we can simply pass a copy of the value of `numEntries`. This function prints an informational line and then employs a `for()`... loop to print each name in the array using `fputs()`.

Save the file, compile it, and run it. Enter names that would be entered at the beginning, somewhere in the middle, and at the end of the list as it is running. You should see something like the following output:

```
> cc nameSorter.c -o nameSorter -Wall -Werror -std=c11
> nameSorter
warning: this program uses gets(), which is unsafe.
Name:  1:  Bob
Name:  2:  James
Name:  3:  Adam
Name:  4:  Mary
Name:  5:  Aaron
Name:  6:  Zeke
Name:  7:  Matthew
Name:  8:

Number of Entries: 7

Aaron
Adam
Bob
James
Mary
Matthew
Zeke
>
```

In my sample input, I entered seven names in apparently random order. Some names were inserted at the front of the list, some were inserted at the back of the list, and the rest were inserted somewhere in the middle. When I entered a blank string, the sorted list of names was printed. So, we know our insertion sort is working as expected. You might want to run this several times, each time with names in a different order.

We will revisit the insertion sort in Chapter 23, *Using File Input and File Output*. When we do so, the names will be read from a file, and instead of using an array, we will revisit our dynamic linked list to sort the names. Then, we'll print the sorted list out to a file.

Summary

Just as we thoroughly explored formatted output in an earlier chapter, in this chapter, we nearly exhaustively explored formatted input. We began with a new understanding of I/O streams. We learned how a stream is a flow of bytes from a source to a destination. For the console, the streams are the pre-defined stdin, stdout, and stderr variables. We also learned how nearly all of the input and output functions have multiple forms, depending on which stream is being used.

Once we learned about streams, we then began our exploration of input stream format specifiers. Much of what we learned is borrowed from our exploration of output format specifiers. We wrote simple programs to explore how to input integers, decimal numbers, strings, and characters. We also learned about, through the programs we wrote, scan sets, input field width control, and the non-assignment specifier. All of these expanded our ability to convert various forms of input data streams. After all that we have explored, it should be obvious that while input format specifiers are similar to output format specifiers, they are not identical; they should not be considered interchangeable as each has its own set of unique functionality.

Before closing out this chapter, we explored various methods of internal formatted data conversion. These involved sscanf(), ssprint(), atoi(), and atof(). Finally, we explored unformatted I/O with fputs() and fgets(). These were demonstrated with the nameSorter.c insertion sort program, which we will revisit in a later chapter.

In the next chapter, we will expand our knowledge of file streams. We will see how they are similar to stdin, stdout, and stderr, but we will also see why we need to learn how to create, open, read, write, and perform other manipulations that are unique to files.

22
Working with Files

We have seen how to get data to and from the console via output and input streams. The next step in our exploration of input and output streams is to be able to access a persistent storage mechanism, one where we can save our data, exit the program, and then use it later. Data stored persistently, from one invocation of a program to the next, is saved in a file via standard file operations. Persistently stored data—that is, files—not only exists from one program invocation to the next but also remains in existence after the computer is turned off and then restarted.

In persistent storage, files are the basic entity of storage. In this chapter, we will present the essential properties of files and some basic manipulations that can be performed on them. We will also consider some of the functions that are unique to file manipulations. We will touch briefly on the function of the filesystem, the part of the operating system that manages the organization of files on persistent media.

In this chapter, we are going to explore the very basics of file manipulation in our own C program. In the next chapter, we will perform more interesting and useful file **Input/Output** (**I/O**) operations. This chapter should be considered a prerequisite for `Chapter 23`, *Using File Input and File Output*.

The following topics will be covered in this chapter:

- Expanding our knowledge of streams
- Understanding the properties of the `FILE` streams
- Introducing opening and closing streams
- Understanding various operations on each type of stream
- Differentiating between operations on text and binary files
- Introducing filesystem concepts
- Understanding file paths
- Understanding filenames
- Performing basic open/close operations on files

Technical requirements

Continue to use the tools you chose from the *Technical requirements* section of `Chapter 1`, *Running Hello, World!*.

The source code for this chapter can be found at `https://github.com/PacktPublishing/Learn-C-Programming`.

Understanding basic file concepts

Up to this point, data inputs and outputs have moved into and out of our C programs via streams through `scanf()`, `printf()`, or other related I/O functions. However, most data exists on computers in files. Files represent persistent data storage in that they exist between invocations of any programs and exist even when the computer is turned off.

Any file will have been created because a program captured input from the user and saved it to a storage medium. The files could've been modified by yet another program and then saved, they could have been copied by any number of programs, or they could have been created from other files by yet another program. Ultimately, nothing happens to a file unless a program does something to it.

Revisiting file streams

A stream is the means of transferring data, specifically bytes, between any device and a program. Streams are device-oriented. Devices, as we have seen, include a keyboard and screen. These are associated with the `stdin` and `stdout` predefined streams. A file is an abstract data storage device. Other devices include hard disks, **Solid-State Drives (SSDs)**, **printers**, **Compact Discs (CDs)**, **Digital Video Discs (DVD)**, and **magnetic tape devices**.

For the movement of data—that is, a stream—to exist, there needs to be a connection from one device to the program to be opened for the data transfer to take place. When we run a C program, the connections to `stdin`, `stdout`, and `stderr` have already been made by the C runtime library for us. For any other kind of stream, we must explicitly make that connection and open a stream.

C supports two types of streams—a **text** stream and a **binary** stream. A text stream consists of lines of bytes, primarily printable characters in the range of 32 to 128; these are readable to humans. The added constraint is that each line of bytes should end with `'\n'`.

Text streams are sometimes called **sequential access streams** because each line of text can vary in length, so it would be nearly impossible to position the file at the beginning of any one line with a simple offset. The file must be read sequentially from beginning to end to be properly interpreted.

A binary stream is byte-oriented (using the full 8 bits) and is only intelligible to other programs. We have been using both of these stream types from the very beginning of this book. We generated text streams with `scanf()`, `printf()`, and other related functions. Binary streams were used when we created executable files and ran them on the console.

A binary stream can either be a collection of binary data, such as an executable file, or it can be a collection of fixed-length records or blocks of data, in which case it is sometimes called a **random access stream**. A random access stream is very much like an array of structures, where an offset to the beginning of any structure can be a simple calculation of the x record number and the size of record. The retrieval of individual records is done directly and, therefore, relatively quickly (compared to sequential access files). Random access files are common in transaction-oriented processing systems, such as banking systems, airline reservations systems, or point-of-sale systems.

So, while there are various types of files, files and streams are closely related. Through the creation of a stream, data moves to and from a file and is persistently stored for later use.

Understanding the properties of the FILE streams

We encountered the `FILE` structure in `Chapter 21`, *Exploring Formatted Input*. This structure consists of information needed to control a stream. It holds the following:

- **A current position indicator**: This is relevant if the device has a beginning and an end, such as a file.
- **An End-of-File (EOF) indicator**: To show whether we are at the end of the file or not.
- **An error indicator**: To show whether an error occurred.
- **A data buffer**: When in buffer mode, data is temporarily stored here.
- **A buffer state**: Indicates what kind of buffering is in use.
- **I/O mode**: Indicates whether this is an input, output, or update stream. An update stream performs both input and output; it requires advanced file manipulations to use properly.

- **Binary or text mode**: Is the stream a text stream or a binary stream?
- **An I/O device identifier**: A platform-specific identifier of an associated I/O device.

We never access these fields directly. Instead, each field, if accessible, has an associated file function. For instance, to check the EOF, call the `feof()` function; to check for any error conditions, call the `ferror()` function; and to clear any error condition, call the `clearerr()` function.

Some of these properties are set when the stream is opened and others are updated as the stream is manipulated.

A file stream, declared as a `FILE*` variable, is also known as a **file descriptor**.

Opening and closing a file

To create a stream, a filename, described in the following section, and an I/O mode must be specified.

There are three general I/O modes that are specified with character strings, as follows:

- `r`: Opens an existing file for reading. It fails if the filename does not exist.
- `w`: Opens a file for writing. If the file exists, existing data is lost; otherwise, the file is created.
- `a`: Opens a file for appending. If the file exists, writing commences at the end of the file; otherwise, the file is created.

These are all one-way modes. That is, a file opened for reading with `r` can only be read; it cannot be updated. Two-way modes exist by appending + to each of the preceding modes—for example, `r+`, `w+`, and `a+`. When files are opened for reading and writing, care must be exercised to re-position the current file position so as not to inadvertently overwrite existing data. We will look at the file reposition functions in the next section.

To open a binary stream, `b` can be appended either after the first character or at the end of the string. The following are the possible binary access modes:

- **One-way modes**: `rb`, `wb`, and `ab`
- **Two-way modes**: `r+b`, `w+b`, `a+b`, `rb+`, `wb+`, and `ab+`

Note that some systems ignore the `b` specifier; in these cases, it is provided for backward compatibility.

A stream can be manipulated with the following functions:

- `fopen()`: Using an absolute or relative filename and mode, this creates/opens a stream.
- `freopen()`: This closes the given stream and re-opens it using the new filename.
- `fclose()`: This closes a stream.
- `fflush()`: For output or update streams, this flushes any content in the buffer to the file/device.

> Note: `fflush()` is only intended for the output stream buffer. It would be handy to have a C standard library function to also clear the input stream buffer. Some systems offer the non-standard `fpurge()` function, which discards anything still in the stream buffer. Other systems allow non-standard behavior for `fflush()` to also flush the input stream buffer. Your system may offer yet another non-standard method to flush the input buffer.

`fopen()` will fail if the user does not have permission to read or write the file. It will also fail if a file opened for reading (only) does not exist.

It is a good idea to always close files before exiting the program.

It is also good practice to flush the buffers of output files before closing them. This will be demonstrated in the example programs later in this chapter.

Understanding file operations for each type of stream

Because there are two types of file streams, text streams, and binary streams, there are also different sets of functions to manipulate them.

We have already seen most of the functions that are useful for text streams. They are as follows:

- `fprintf()`: Writes formatted text to the output stream
- `fscanf()`: Reads and interprets formatted text from the input stream
- `fputs()`: Writes an unformatted line to the output stream
- `fgets()`: Reads an unformatted line from the input stream

There are also some single-character functions that we have come across:

- `fgetc()`: Reads a single character from the input stream
- `fputc()`: Writes a single character to the output stream
- `ungetc()`: Puts a single character back into the input stream

These single-character functions are particularly handy when processing the input of one character at a time. Numbers or words can be assembled into strings. If a whitespace or delimiter character is encountered, it can either be processed or pushed back into the input stream for additional processing.

There are a set of functions intended specifically for record- or block-oriented file manipulations. These are as follows:

- `fread()`: Reads a block of data of a specified size from a file
- `fwrite()`: Writes a block of data of a specified size to a file
- `ftell()` or `fgetpos()`: Gets the current file position
- `fseek()` or `fsetpos()`: Moves the current file position to a specified position

In block-oriented file processing, whole records are read at once. These are typically read into a structure. They may also be read into a buffer and then parsed for their individual parts.

Finally, there are some common file stream functions, as follows:

- `rewind()`: Moves the current position to the beginning of the file
- `remove()`: Deletes a file
- `rename()`: Renames a file

With these functions, we can create programs to manipulate files in any number of ways.

C doesn't impose a structure on the content of a file. That is left up to the program and the type of data that is to be preserved in the file. These functions enable a wide variety of ways to create, modify, and delete not only the content of files but also the files themselves.

Before we can put these functions into action, we need to introduce the filesystem and how it fits in with the C standard library.

Introducing the filesystem essentials

A filesystem is a component of an operating system that controls how files are stored and retrieved. The filesystem typically provides a naming and organization scheme to enable the easy identification of a file. We can think of a file as a logical group of data stored as a single unit. A filesystem provides the ability to manage an extremely large number of files of a wide range of sizes, from very small to extremely large.

There are many different kinds of filesystems. Some are specific to a given operating system while others offer a standard interface and appear identical across multiple operating systems. Nonetheless, the underlying mechanisms of a filesystem are meant to guarantee various degrees of speed, flexibility, security, size, and reliable storage.

The filesystem is meant to shield both the operating system and programs that run on it from the underlying physical details of the associated storage medium. There is a wide variety of mediums such as hard drives, SSDs, magnetic tapes, and optical discs. The filesystem can provide access to local data storage devices—devices connected directly to the computer—as well as remote storage devices—devices connected to another computer accessible over a network connection.

Introducing the filesystem

We can think of the filesystem as the interface between the actual storage medium and our program. Despite the underlying complexity and details of any filesystem, its interface is quite simple. C provides a standard set of file manipulation functions that hide the underlying complexities of any filesystem. These complexities are encapsulated in each implementation of the C standard library. From the perspective of a C program, once we can identify a file by name and, optionally, by its location, very little else is of concern to the program.

So, the main aspects of filesystems that we need to care about are how files are named and their location. As much as I would like to say that there is only one way to name and locate files, I cannot say that. Not all filesystems have the same file organization or naming schemes. We will examine filenames briefly.

Each file has two aspects to its name—its location or file path and its filename.

Understanding a file path

A file path can be either an absolute file path or a relative file path. In an **absolute file path**, the base of the file hierarchy is specified, along with the name of each directory and subdirectory to the final directory where the filename exists. The base of the file hierarchy is also called the *root* of the file hierarchy *tree*. In a **relative file path**, only the portions of the path relative to the current program location are required.

The structure of an absolute file path varies from one filesystem to another. It may have a generic root or it may begin with the name of the device where the file hierarchy exists. For instance, on Unix and Linux systems, all files exist somewhere in the file hierarchy with the root beginning with /. On Windows, the root of a file hierarchy typically begins with a device identifier, such as D:.

Thankfully, there are many common features that we can rely upon. Once the base of the file hierarchy, or the root, is identified, various parts of the way the location of the file is specified are common.

Not all files live at the root. There can be many directories at the root, and each directory itself may have numerous sub-directories. Traversing this hierarchy to the desired file is called the **path**. Each layer in the hierarchy can be separated by a forward slash (/) in C, even though this may not be the case in the native filesystem. Also, the current working directory, regardless of its path, is identified by a dot (.). Furthermore, if the current directory has a dot (.), then the parent of this directory—or whatever the layer is when we go up one level in the hierarchy—can be specified by two dots (..).

Default path attributes apply if none are given. For instance, if there is no path, the current directory location is the default path.

In our example programs, we will assume that the data files are in the same directory as the executable program. This is a simplified assumption. Very often, paths to data files are stored in a file with the .init or .config extension, which is read and processed when the program starts.

Understanding a filename

A filename identifies a unique file within a directory. Each filename is typically unique within a directory. We think of this directory as the location where the file exists. A directory name is part of the file path.

A filename can take many forms, depending on the filesystem. In Windows, Unix, and Linux filesystems, a filename consists of one or more alphabetic characters with an optional extension. A file extension consists of one or more characters with a separating dot (.) between it and the name. The combination of the name and extension must be unique within a directory. We have already seen this with our source files that have a .c extension, our header files that have a .h extension, and our executable files, which, by convention, have no extension.

With these concepts in mind, we are now ready to begin manipulating files in C.

Opening files for reading and writing

We can now create a program to open a file for reading and another file for writing. This is where our file I/O exploration will begin and will continue through the remaining chapters of this book. The following program is our starting point:

```c
#include <stdio.h>
#include <stdlib.h>      // for exit()
#include <string.h>      // for strerror()
#include <sys/errno.h>   // for errno

int main( void ) {
  FILE* inputFile;
  FILE* outputFile;
  char inputFilename[] = "./input.data";
  char outputFilename[] = "./output.data";
  inputFile = fopen( inputFilename , "r" );
  if( NULL == inputFile )  {
    fprintf( stderr, "input file: %s: %s\n",
             inputFilename , strerror( errno ) );
    exit( 1 );
  }

  outputFile = fopen( outputFilename , "w" );
  if( NULL == outputFile )  {
    fprintf( stderr, "input file: %s: %s\n",
             outputFilename , strerror( errno ) );
    exit( 1 );
  }
  fprintf( stderr,"\"%s\" opened for reading.\n",inputFilename );
  fprintf( stderr,"\"%s\" opened for writing.\n",outputFilename );
  fprintf( stderr,"Do work here.\n" );

  fprintf( stderr , "Closing files.\n" );
```

```
    fclose(  inputFile );
    fflush( outputFile );
    fclose( outputFile );
}
```

In this program, we are not only introducing minimal file operations, but we are also introducing a very basic system-error reporting mechanism. With this mechanism, we do not need to reinvent the error message; we let the system report its own error message. To do that, we need to include `string.h` and `sys/errno.h`. If we can't open our files for any reason, we need to exit, so we also need to include `stdlib.h`.

We are not (yet) using any inputs from the command line, so the parameters to `main()` are ignored by setting them to `void`. We then declare input and an output file descriptor for each file we will open.

The next two lines set the file path (`"./"`) and filenames (`"input.data"` and `"output.data"`) for the files we will soon try to open. For now, we will hardcode these names. In later versions of this program, we'll get a bit more practical with the user input of filenames.

Now, we are ready for the real work of this program. First, we call `fopen()` to open `inputFilename` for reading; if this succeeds, the file descriptor is set. If the file descriptor is `NULL`, we print an error message to `stderr` and exit. Note that we are using `fprintf()` with `stderr` to provide feedback to the user. This is good practice, one that we will continue for the remainder of this book.

If a C standard library function fails, it typically sets the value of a system-global variable named `errno`. In this case, when `fopen()` fails, the `fprintf()` function uses the `strerror(errno)` function to convert `errno` into a human-readable string. These are defined in the `<sys/errno.h>` file. It is worthwhile to find that file on your system, open it, and peruse the errors defined there. However, don't try to understand everything you see there all at once. So, what we are showing here is a very handy way to display known system errors to the user. This is an extremely useful programming pattern to incorporate into your own programs.

If the first `fopen()` group succeeds, we move on to the next `fopen()` group. This is similar to the first group, except we are opening a file for writing. This will usually succeed, but we need to also be able to handle a situation where it might not.

The next three `fprintf()` statements provide the simple status of the program. These are not really necessary because most often, we can assume the success of system function calls and only need to check and report when they fail.

Finally, the program closes the input file, flushes the output file (even though we haven't done anything yet), and closes the output file.

Create a file named `open_close_string.c`. Type in the preceding program, save it, compile it, and run it. You should see the following output:

```
> cc open_close_string.c -o open_close_string -Wall -Werror -std=c11
> open_close_string
input file: ./input.data: No such file or directory
>
```

Oh, darn! Our input file needs to exist before we can open it. Alright—in your console window, you can create an empty file with the `touch input.data` Unix command, or with your editor, create a file named `input.data` in the same directory as `open_close_string.c` and save it (it doesn't have to have anything in it, it just has to exist). Run the program again and you should see the following:

```
> touch input.data
> open_close_string
"./input.data" opened for reading.
"./output.data" opened for writing.
Do work here.
Closing files.
>
```

Terrific! We now have a very basic file I/O program that we can use when input and output files are known and fixed.

Before we finish this chapter, we'll present two simple ways to get filenames from the user. The first will be via inputs from within the program and the second will be by using the rather limited `argv` arguments via the command line.

Getting filenames from within the program

Copy `open_close_string.c` into `open_close_fgetstr.c` and open the following program:

```c
#include <stdio.h>
#include <stdlib.h>
#include <string.h>
#include <sys/errno.h>   // for errno

int main( void ) {
  FILE* inputFile;
  FILE* outputFile;
```

```
char inputFilename[80] = {0};
char outputFilename[80] = {0};

fprintf( stdout , "Enter name of input file: " );
fscanf( stdin , "%80s" , inputFilename );
inputFile = fopen( inputFilename , "r" );
if( NULL == inputFile ) {
fprintf( stderr, "input file: %s: %s\n", inputFilename ,
strerror( errno ) );
exit( 1 );
}

fprintf( stdout , "Enter name of output file: " );
fscanf( stdin , "%80s" , outputFilename );
outputFile = fopen( outputFilename , "w" );
if( NULL == outputFile ) {
fprintf( stderr, "input file: %s: %s\n",
outputFilename , strerror( errno ) );
   exit( 1 );
  }

 fprintf( stdout,"\"%s\" opened for reading.\n",inputFilename  );
 fprintf( stdout,"\"%s\" opened for writing.\n",outputFilename );
 fprintf( stderr , "Do work here.\n" );
 fprintf( stderr , "Closing files.\n" );
 fclose(  inputFile );
 fflush( outputFile );
 fclose( outputFile );
}
```

Notice the lines that are in bold. Only these lines have changed from the preceding program. For the input file and the output file, a string array of 80 characters is specified, an input prompt for the filename is given, and the filename is read using sscanf(). Save, compile, and run this program. If you enter input.data and output.data at the prompts, you should see the following output:

```
> cc open_close_fgetstr.c -o open_close_fgetstr -Wall -Werror -std=c11
> open_close_fgetstr
Enter name of input file: input.data
"input.data" opened for reading.
Enter name of output file: output.data
"output.data" opened for writing.
Do work here.
Closing files.
>
```

This technique is handy to use when filenames never change. However, very often, filenames will change, so we need a more flexible way to get filenames as input.

Getting filenames from the command line

Next, copy the program into open_close_argv.c and modify it to match the following program:

```c
#include <stdio.h>
#include <stdlib.h>
#include <string.h>
#include <sys/errno.h>   // for errno

void usage( char* cmd )  {
  fprintf( stderr , "usage: %s inputFileName outputFileName\n" ,
           cmd );
  exit( 0 );
}

int main( int argc, char *argv[] )  {
  FILE* inputFile  = NULL;
  FILE* outputFile = NULL;
  if( argc != 3 ) usage( argv[0] );
  if( NULL == ( inputFile = fopen( argv[1] , "r") ) )  {
    fprintf( stderr, "input file: %s: %s\n",
             argv[1], strerror(errno));
    exit( 1 );
  }
  if( NULL == ( outputFile = fopen( argv[2] , "w" ) ) )  {
    fprintf( stderr, "output file: %s: %s\n",
             argv[2], strerror(errno));
    exit( 1 );
  }

  fprintf( stderr , "%s opened for reading.\n" , argv[1] );
  fprintf( stderr , "%s opened for writing.\n" , argv[2] );
  fprintf( stderr , "Do work here.\n" );
  fprintf( stderr , "Closing files.\n" );
  fclose(  inputFile );
  fflush( outputFile );
  fclose( outputFile );
}
```

In this program, we added the usage() function. Next, we added argc and argv to the main() parameters because here, we'll get input from the command line.

Before we start to open any files, we need to make sure we have three parameters—the program name, the input filename, and the output filename. When opening each file, use the appropriate argv[] string for each one. Note that once we have opened the filenames given in argv[], we really don't need them again for the remainder of the program.

Edit, save, compile, and run this program. You should see the following output:

```
> cc open_close_argv.c -o open_close_argv -Wall -Werror -std=c11
> open_close_argv
usage: open_close_argv inputFileName outputFileName
> open_close_argv blah
usage: open_close_argv inputFileName outputFileName
> open_close_argv input.data output.data
input.data opened for reading.
output.data opened for writing.
Do work here.
Closing files.
>
```

As you can see, the first time that open_close_argv is run, no command-line arguments are given and the usage() function is called. The next time that open_close_argv is run, only one argument is given and the usage() function is again called. Only when open_close_argv is called with two arguments is usage() no longer called and we can attempt to open the named files. Note that when opening a file for input, the file *must* exist or an error will occur. However, if you open a file for writing or appending that does not exist, a new file with that name will be created. In this case, input.data already exists, so opening the file is successful.

We now have several ways to get filenames to open file descriptors. We'll see in the next chapter how to expand these simple programs to create an unsorted name file and then use them again to read that unsorted name file and write out a sorted name file.

Summary

In this chapter, we expanded our knowledge of streams to text and binary streams. We learned about the various stream properties and briefly explored file functions that manipulate text streams and binary streams. We also learned about some common file functions, including fopen(), fflush(), and flclose(). These functions were demonstrated in three different programs that obtained input and output filenames in various ways. The first way hardcoded filenames into the program. The second way gave the user a prompt for each file and read the filenames with scanf(). The last way received filenames from command-line arguments via argv.

With the knowledge we have gained from covering these topics, we are ready to start with the next chapter, where we'll begin working on these simple programs, enhancing the command-line argument process and performing useful work on the input to generate meaningful output.

23 Using File Input and File Output

In the previous chapter, we introduced many basic file concepts as well as most of the file manipulation functions. We also demonstrated a simple way to open and close files.

In this chapter, we will put that knowledge to better use by developing a program to write a sequential file and another program to read that file, sort it, and write it to a file. We will find that there are several subtleties that we will need to address; we will also be using nearly every C skill we have learned so far.

The following topics will be covered in this chapter:

- Creating a template program to process filenames given on the command line
- Creating a program to accept input from either `stdin` or a file and write output to either `stdout` or a file
- Creating a function to trim input from `fgets()`
- Creating a program to accept input from either `stdin` or a file and write the output in sorted order to `stdout` or a file

Technical requirements

As detailed in the *Technical requirements* section of `Chapter 1`, *Running Hello, World!*, continue to use the tools you have chosen.

The source code for this chapter can be found at `https://github.com/PacktPublishing/Learn-C-Programming`.

File processing

Many books have been written about the myriad data file formats that are out there. These include graphics file formats, audio file formats, video formats, and data file formats for various database files and well-known application program files, such as Microsoft Word and Microsoft Excel. Often custom file formats are closely guarded company secrets or, if not secret, are only documented in the source code that manipulates them.

Along with data file formats, there are nearly as many file processing techniques—far too many to be given even a cursory overview in a beginning C programming book. File processing techniques are generally divided into sequential-access and random-access files but this is an oversimplification. Within each of these categories, there can be many variations of how they are internally organized and subsequently processed. Furthermore, in some cases, complex computer programs may open more input and output files as they run. Often, one or more configuration files are first opened, read, and processed to determine how a program behaves. They are then closed and the program performs processing on other files depending upon the settings in the configuration file(s).

Here, we present some useful ways to open two sequential files using enhanced command-line arguments and then perform relatively simple processing on them.

Our goal in this chapter is to accept input from the console or a file, sort each line in a file, and then write out the result, either to the console or to a file. We could just create the file in a text editor and save the file; it will be more interesting to write our own program to do that. We will first start with a program to accept inputs and write outputs based on the presence or absence of the arguments given. This program will be built from a program we created in Chapter 22, *Working with Files*, open_close_argv.c, and a program we created in Chapter 19, *Exploring Formatted Input*, readString.c.

Creating a template program to process filenames given on the command line

We begin creating our data file creation program by handling command-line arguments.

In the last chapter, we created a program that expected two filenames on the command line, which were presented via argv; the input file was the first argument and the output file was the second argument. What if we wanted to permit either argument to be omitted? We could no longer rely on argument positioning; we need a way to further identify which argument is input and which argument is output.

To do that, we will revisit the built-in command-line facility `getopt()`. This facility is older and simpler than `getopt_long()`, which we demonstrated in `Chapter 20`, *Getting Input from the Command Line*. We will specify two options, `-i <input filename>` and `-o <output filename>`, neither of which will be required. `getopt()` does not have the concept of required or optional arguments so we'll have to do that processing ourselves.

`getopt()` and `getopt_long()` are declared in the header file, `unistd.h`, which is not a part of the C Standard Library. This means that if you are running Unix, macOS, or Linux, this file and function will be available to you. If you are running Windows, `unistd.h` is a part of the `CygWin` and `MinGW` compiler tools. If you are using MFC, this file might be available to you. A Windows version of `getopt()`, maintained by Microsoft, is available on GitHub at `https://github.com/iotivity/iotivity/tree/master/resource/c_common/windows`; you will see the `getopt.h` and `getopt.c` files.

Let's look at the following program:

1. Create a new file called `getoptFiles.c`. We will use this for both the data creation and the data sorting program; we'll make copies of it and modify the copies when needed later. Add the following header files:

```
#include <stdio.h>
#include <stdlib.h>
#include <string.h>
#include <unistd.h>      // for getopt
#include <sys/errno.h>   // for errno
```

We need `stdio.h` for the file I/O functions, `stdlib.h` for the `exit()` function, `string.h` for the `strerr()` function, `unistd.h` for the `getopt()` function, and `sys/errno.h` to convert any `errno` value into a human-readable string.

2. Next, add the following `usage()` function:

```
void usage( char* cmd )  {
  fprintf(stderr ,
          "usage: %s [-i inputFName] [-o outputFName]\n" , cmd );
  fprintf(stderr ,
          "        If -i inputFName is not given, stdin is used.\n"
);
  fprintf(stderr ,
          "        If -o outputFName is not given stdout is
used.\n\n" );
```

```
        exit ( EXIT_FAILURE );
    }
```

This function will be called when either wrong arguments are given to the
program or the user provides the –h command-line option. When we call this
function, something is not right or the user just wants help. Therefore, we never
return from this function; instead, we exit the program.

3. Next, add the following lines, which begin the main () function:

```
int main(int argc, char *argv[])  {
    int   ch;
    FILE* inputFile  = NULL;
    FILE* outputFile = NULL;
```

These statements declare variables we'll need in main (). Now, ch will be used by
getopt () as it processes command-line switches. File descriptors are then
declared for inputFile and outputFile.

4. We are now ready to perform command-line processing. Add the following
statements:

```
while( ( ch = getopt( argc , argv , "i:o:h" ) ) != -1 )  {
    switch (ch)  {
      case 'i':
        if( NULL == ( inputFile = fopen( optarg , "r") ) )  {
          fprintf( stderr, "input file \"%s\": %s\n",
                   optarg, strerror(errno));
          exit ( EXIT_FAILURE );
        }
        fprintf( stderr , "Using \"%s\" for input.\n" , optarg );
        break;
      case 'o':
        if( NULL == ( outputFile = fopen( optarg , "a" ) ) )  {
          fprintf( stderr, "output file \"%s\": %s\n",
                   optarg, strerror(errno));
          exit ( EXIT_FAILURE );
        }
        fprintf( stderr , "Using \"%s\" for output.\n" , optarg );
        break;
      case '?':
      case 'h':
      default:
        usage( argv[0] );
        break;
    }
}
```

In the conditional expression of the `while()`... loop, `getopt()` is called. The result of `getopt()` is assigned to `ch`. If there are no more arguments, `getopt()` returns –1 and we exit the loop normally. The arguments to `getopt()` are `argc`, `argv`, and a string of valid option letters. The `"i:o:h"` string specifies that `-i`, `-o`, and `-h` are valid character options. Note that `i` and `o` are followed by `:`, which indicates that each must be followed by another parameter after that option. If an option character is given that is not one of those specified, `getopt()` returns the `'?'` character, which we handle in the loop.

The body of the `while()`... loop is the `switch()`... statement where each `case` processes one of the options retrieved by `getopt()`. Both the `case 'i':` and `case 'o':` statements try to open the given filename parameters; if `fopen()` fails for either one, it returns `NULL` and sets `errno`, in which case we exit the program after displaying the reason for failure. Otherwise, note that we open `outputFile` for appending. This is so that we don't delete any data that may already exist in the given `outputFilename`. If the value of `ch` is `'h'` which the user entered, or if it is `'?'` because `getopt()` found an invalid option, or our `switch()`... statement encountered something it doesn't handle, `usage()` is called. At this point, we have processed all of the command-line options. Before we can do actual work, we have to see whether filenames were actually given.

5. The following statements finish the work of setting our `inputFile` and `outputFile` descriptors:

```
if( !inputFile )  {
  inputFile = stdin;
  fprintf( stderr , "Using stdin for input.\n" );
  usingInputFile = false;
}
if( !outputFile )  {
  outputFile = stdout;
  fprintf( stderr , "Using stdout for output.\n" );
  usingOutputFile = false;
}
```

Why might `inputFile` or `outputFile` be NULL? Well, just because we told `getopt()` what the valid options are, there is no facility to tell `getopt()` which ones are required or optional. So, we may have processed the command line with both options, either option, or no options at all. Here is where we handle that the case where neither the input option nor the output option was given on the command line. If `inputFile` is NULL, we set it to the `stdin` stream. Likewise, if `outputFile` is NULL, we set it to the `stdout` stream. At the end of these statements, both file descriptors will be either set to a file or set to one of the console streams, `stdin` or `stdout`. We are now ready to do some work.

6. The following statements complete `main()` and our template program:

```
fprintf( stderr , "Do work here.\n" );

fprintf( stderr , "Closing files.\n" );
fclose( inputFile );
fflush( outputFile );
fclose( outputFile );
}
```

There really is no work to do yet, so we just give a status statement. Then, we close `inputFile`, flush the `outputFile` buffer, and finally close `outputFile`.

This is a complete program. It doesn't do any useful work; we'll add that in a bit. So, save the file, compile it, and run it. We will exercise our program by giving it the −h option, just an output file, just an input file, and then both. In the last case, we'll also give an input file that does not exist. You should see the following output:

```
> cc getoptFiles.c -o getoptFiles -Wall -Werror -std=c11
> getoptFiles -h
usage: getoptFiles [-i inputFileName] [-o outputFileName]
        If -i inputFileName is not given, stdin is used.
        If -o outputFileName is not given stdout is used.

> getoptFiles -Whatever
getoptFiles: illegal option -- W
usage: getoptFiles [-i inputFileName] [-o outputFileName]
        If -i inputFileName is not given, stdin is used.
        If -o outputFileName is not given stdout is used.

> getoptFiles -o names.data
Using "names.data": for output.
Using stdin for input.
Do work here.
Closing files.
> getoptFiles -i unsorted.data
input file "unsorted.data": No such file or directory
> getoptFiles -i names.data
Using "names.data" for input.
Using stdout for output.
Do work here.
Closing files.
> getoptFiles -i names.data -o sorted.data
Using "names.data" for input.
Using "sorted.data": for output.
Do work here.
Closing files.
> []
```

First, with only the –h option, we see the usage message. Next, we give an option that is not valid to see how this looks. Then, we give just an output file; this file will be created. After that, we give just an input file that does not exist; you can see the error message fetched from `errno.h`. When we give an input file that does exist, all is well. Finally, we give both a valid input file and a valid output file.

Notice that throughout this program, rather than using `printf( ... )`, we consistently used `fprintf( stderr , ... )`. This is not merely a convention. By doing this, if needed, we could redirect the `stderr` stream to a file and thereby save anything that would otherwise go to the console.

One thing we have not considered is what happens when the user specifies the same file for input *and* output. What should happen? This program is not designed to be used in that manner nor does it perform any check to prevent the user from entering the same filename. There is any number of things we could do: prevent the user from either entering the same file or input and output or allowing the two files to be the same, for instance. In the former case, we'd have to perform a name string comparison to see whether they are the same and exit. In the latter case, we'd have to consider completely processing the input file before opening and writing the output file to prevent mayhem from occurring.

We will use this program again later as a starting point for our other programs. Since we have proven that this template program works, we can replace the `fprintf( stderr , "Do work here.\n" );` statement with program statements that do real work.

Creating a file of unsorted names

Now that we have `getoptFiles.c`, we can use it as a starting point for our next sequential file program, `createNames.c`. This program will be used to create a file of names, one name on a line, that will later become an input to the `sortNames.c` program.

In `createNames.c`, we will repeatedly read in a single name and write it out. We can test the functionality of this program by using `stdin` and `stdout` as well as reading and writing files.

However, before we can go further, we need to consider the issue of dirty input data. We can assume that a name begins with alphanumeric characters and ends with alphanumeric characters; we will assume that anything in between is part of the name, however odd it may appear. What happens if the user enters whitespace either before or after the name? Or if there is whitespace both before and after the name? Recall also that while gets() ends its input scan with <newline> and does not preserve it in the input string, fgets() also ends its input scan with <newline> but does preserve <newline>.

We will deal with these issues next.

Trimming the input string from fgets()

It would be extremely handy if the C Standard Library provided routines to trim whitespace both before and after a string. As we have seen, some of the input routines preserve whitespace, including <newline>, and some of the routines do not. Other languages provide functions such as trimLeft(), trimRight(), and trim(), that trim both the left and right sides of a string.

Thankfully, writing such a function is not too cumbersome in C. Consider the following function:

```
int trimStr( char* pStr ) {
   size_t first , last , lenIn , lenOut ;
   first = last = lenIn = lenOut = 0;
   lenIn = strlen( pString );    //
   char tmpString[ lenIn+1 ];    // Create working copy.
   strcpy( tmpStr , pString );   //
   char* pTmp = tmpStr;          // pTmp may change in Left Trim segment

     // Left Trim
     // Find 1st non-whitespace char; pStr will point to that.
   while( isspace( pTmp[ first ] ) )
     first++;
   pTmp += first;
   lenOut = strlen( pTmp );      // Get new length after Left Trim.
   if( lenOut )  {               // Check for empty string.
                                 // e.g. "    " trimmed to nothing.
       // Right Trim
       // Find 1st non-whitespace char & set NUL character there.
     last = lenOut-1;            // off-by-1 adjustment.
     while( isspace( pTmp[ last ] ) )
       last--;
     pTmp[ last+1 ] = '\0';      // Terminate trimmed string.
   }
```

```
        lenOut = strlen( pTmp );      // Length of trimmed string.
        if( lenIn != lenOut )         // Did we change anything?
          strcpy( pString , pTmp );   // Yes, copy trimmed string back.
        return lenOut;
    }
```

The `trimStr()` function takes a pointer to a string and makes a working copy of the string. Because the first character of the string could change, the function uses a pointer to the working copy. This pointer is set to the first character of the working string; it may be the same pointer as that passed in, but we can never be certain of that. In every case, the resulting string will be either, at most, the same number of characters or fewer characters; therefore, we don't have to worry about the new string running beyond the existing string array boundaries.

It first trims whitespace to the left, or beginning, of the working string, then trims whitespace to the right, or end, of the working string. When trimming from the left, there is the `while()`... loop to find the first non-whitespace. When that is found, the pointer to the beginning of the string is adjusted.

Before continuing to trim from the right, a check is done to ensure the string is not empty; it could have been a string of only whitespace, which will not be empty.

When trimming from the right, there is another `while()`... loop that begins at the highest character index and walks back toward the front of the string until it finds a non-whitespace character. When it finds one, it sets the character after it to NUL, terminating character.

It should be noted that this function alters the original string when it resets the string terminator. This is a side effect but is the intended effect of the function.

This is a handy function to use whenever you read input from the console or a file. We will use it whenever we get input using `fgets()`.

With this `trimStr()` function now available, we can proceed to the tasks of the program.

Reading names and writing names

To begin developing the `createUnsorted.c` program, first copy the `getoptFiles.c` file to the `createUnsorted.c` file. We will henceforth modify this file.

Open `createUnsorted` and, after the `const int stringMax` declaration, add the following function prototypes:

```
void   usage(   char* cmd );
int    getName( FILE* inFileDesc , char* pStr );
void   putName( char* nameStr ,    FILE* outFileDesc );
int    trimStr( char* pString );
```

In this chapter, for each program, we will follow the following general program organization:

- `#include` files
- Constant declarations
- `struct` and `enum` declarations
- Function prototypes
- `main()`
- Function definitions (these generally appear after `main()` in the same order as their prototype declarations)

This is merely a convention. In the next chapter, we will learn about a multi-file program organization that will help to naturally organize program structure.

So, after adding the preceding function prototypes, move the `usage()` function definition below the `main()` function in the file. Every other function we add will be below this function in the `createUnsorted.c` single file.

In the `main()` function, find the following statement:

```
fprintf( stderr , "Do work here.\n" );
```

Replace it with the following statements:

```
char  nameBuffer[ stringMax ];
while( getName( inputFile , nameBuffer ) ) {
  putName( nameBuffer , outputFile );
}
```

The work of this program is essentially contained in the deceptively simple-looking `while()`... loop. First, an array of 80 characters is declared. This is the buffer into which each new line of input will be read with `fgets()`, which we'll see in the `getName()` function. Then, a pointer variable is declared and points to the first character of the name buffer. Because `trimStr()` copies the newly trimmed string back to the original string, the beginning of the string does not change. Therefore, we can simply use the `nameBuffer` name without requiring an additional pointer variable.

When getName() returns 0, an empty string was entered and signals input has completed. Otherwise, getName() returns the length of a trimmed string that we need to do something with; in this case, we call the putName() function.

The first to two pieces of work that happen in this loop is the getName() function. We can think of getName() as kind of the fgets() function we wish we had all along.

After the usage() function definition, add the getName() function at the end of the program:

```
int getName( FILE* inFileDesc , char* pStr )   {
   static int numNames = 0;
          int len;

   memset( pStr , 0 , stringMax );
   if( stdin == inFileDesc )
      fprintf( stdout , "Name %d: ", numNames+1 );

   fgets( pStr , stringMax , inFileDesc );

   len = trimStr( pStr );
   if( len ) numNames++;
   return len;
}
```

The function takes a file descriptor as its first function parameter and a pointer to the string to be trimmed as its second function parameter.

We use the numNames static variable when input is coming from the console. It appears in the user prompt as a means to inform the user how many names have been entered. Next, we declare len, which will be used to determine whether we have an empty string after the buffer is trimmed.

First, memset() is called to initialize each character in nameBuffer—here, referenced in the function body as pStr—to '\0'. Then, if we are getting input from stdin, give the user a prompt for input. A prompt is unnecessary when we are reading from files. fgets() scans in the input stream for up to 79 (80-1) characters of input. At this point, there is <newline> in the buffer, which means the length of the string in the buffer will never be less than 1. We can't simply check for <newline> in the last position because 79 or more characters may have been entered and we won't have <newline>; it will still be in the input buffer. Rather than making assumptions that could later come back to bite us, we call trimStr() on nameBuffer—here, referenced in the function body as pStr. Before exiting the function, we get the new string length. If it is not 0, we increment numNames for the next call to this function, and then len is returned to the caller.

Whenever we get a non-zero length result from getName(), the work that is currently done is to output that name; this is accomplished with a call to putName(). Add the following function at the end of createUnsorted.c:

```
void putName( char* pStr , FILE* outFileDesc )  {
  fputs( pStr , outFileDesc );
  fputc( '\n' , outFileDesc );
}
```

Again recall that puts() adds <newline> to whatever string it prints. This is not so with fputs(). Just as we had to strip out <newline> with getName(), we have to put it back in the output stream with putName(). This simple function first calls fputs() using the functions input parameters and then calls fputc() to write the single character <newline> to the given output stream.

We are not quite done. Now it is time to add the trimStr() function we encountered in the preceding section to the end of the file. Once you have done that, save the file. Compile it. To see this in action, we'll run it with these command-line arguments in the following order:

1. createUnsorted
2. createUnsorted -o names.data
3. createUnsorted -onames.data
4. createUnsorted -i names.data

In the first case, stdin and stdout will be used and nothing will be saved. In the second case, every name that is entered will be appended to names.data. In the third case, more names will be appended to names.data. In the last case, names.data will be read and printed to stdout so we can what's in the file. Run the program using three or more names each time. Be sure to add whitespace before and/or after each name before hitting <enter>. Your output should look something like the following:

```
|> cc createUnsorted.c -o createUnsorted -Wall -Werror -std=c11
|> createUnsorted
Using stdin for input.
Using stdout for output.
Name 1: Tom
Tom
Name 2: Dick
Dick
Name 3: Jane
Jane
Name 4:
Closing files.
|>
|> createUnsorted -o names.data
Using "names.data": for output.
Using stdin for input.
Name 1:      Tom
Name 2: Dick
Name 3:      Jane
Name 4:
Closing files.
|>
|> createUnsorted -o names.data
Using "names.data": for output.
Using stdin for input.
Name 1: Adam
Name 2: Eve
Name 3:
Closing files.
|>
|> createUnsorted -i names.data
Using "names.data" for input.
Using stdout for output.
Tom
Dick
Jane
Adam
Eve
Closing files.
> █
```

As you can see, we entered the names Tom, Dick, and Jane, in the first case. The input strings were sent immediately to the console. In the next case, we entered
  Tom (leading whitespace), Dick   (trailing whitespace), and   Jane   (whitespace before and afterward). Running the program again with the same options, we entered Adam and Eve. In the last case, the file was input and it was written to the console, where we can see that the trimming was accomplished and that Adam and Eve were appended after the previous three names in the file.

We now have a moderately robust, yet simple, data entry program that trims input and appends it to an existing data file. There are some subtleties we still haven't considered, such as disk-full errors, end-of-file markers, and wide-character input. These are more advanced topics for a later time; nonetheless, they should not be overlooked.

Now that we have a basic file input program, we can proceed to reading names from the console or a file and sorting them to the console or a file.

Reading unsorted names and sorting them for output

In Chapter 21, *Exploring Formatted Input*, we read names into an array, sorting them as they were inserted. That works fine when the program can give feedback to the user such as when the array is full, but what if, for file inputs, we have a very large number of names? For that, we need a different data structure to read in all of the names to sort them.

Recall, in Chapter 18, *Using Dynamic Memory Allocation*, we created a linked list to contain our deck of cards, which were then randomized and dealt out to four hands. A linked list is one of many useful data structures used to dynamically store and sort large numbers of data elements. We will create another, special-purpose linked list for our list of names and add each name to the list in sorted order. This approach will be similar to what we did in Chapter 21, *Exploring Formatted Input*, but instead of using a fixed-size array, we will use an unbounded singly-linked list. Each list item will be a name. And because we will use the list in a very specific manner, we do not have to create all of the functions that a general-purpose linked list would require.

To begin the development of sortNames.c, copy the createUnsorted.c file to sortNames.c. Henceforth, we will be modifying sortNames.c. We will continue using the same general program structure with main() close to the top of the file and all other functions beneath main().

Before we start making additions to implement our linked list, let's alter the while()... loop in main() as follows:

```
char nameBuffer[ 80 ];
NameList nameList = {0};

while( getName( inputFile , nameBuffer ) )  {
  AddName( &nameList , nameBuffer );
}
PrintNames( outputFile , nameList );
DeleteNames( nameList );
```

We are declaring the `NameList` structure; this will be the starting point for the list elements that hold information about the list. The only change to the `while()`... loop is to replace `putName()` with the `AddName()` function where most of the work of sorting takes place in dynamic memory. Once all of the names have been processed, we call `PrintNames()` to write them out in sorted order. Finally, we call `DeleteNames()` to clean up all the dynamic memory of the list we no longer need after the names have been printed. As before, we explicitly close the files before exiting the program. Note that we have changed only four statements in the part of our program that does the main work of the program.

One other thing to do in `sortNames.c` is to change the following:

```
if( NULL == ( outputFile = fopen( optarg , "a" ) ) )  {
```

We change it to the following:

```
if( NULL == ( outputFile = fopen( optarg , "w" ) ) )  {
```

We are changing the open mode from `"a"` append to `"w"` write so that each time we run the program, the output file will be truncated to zero bytes rather than appending sorted results to an existing file.

This program will not compile yet because we've not declared `NameList` nor the `AddName()`, `PrintNames()`, and `DeleteNames()` functions. We may need a few other functions specifically for list management.

Using a linked list to sort names

The `sortNames()` program is still relatively simple. However, we are beginning to build segments of code that are very much unlike each other. For instance, the file handling code, which includes `getName()`, `putName()`, and `trimStr()`, is unrelated to the linked list handling code, which we will soon develop.

We could, as we have done many times before, dump all of this code in a single file, happily compile it, and run it. Or, which is a much more common practice, separate different code segments into separate files so that all of the functions in any given file have a logical relationship. For the `sortNames` program, the logical relationships are that all of the functions in one file manipulate one kind of structure, the linked list, and all of the functions in another file manipulate file I/O. Among all of the source code files, there must be one and only one `main()`. All of the files together make up a program. We will explore this in much greater depth in the next chapter, `Chapter 24`, *Working with Multi-File Programs*, but we will introduce this concept with the `sortNames` program here.

To this end, there is only more line to add to `sortNames.c`. With the other include files at the top of the file, add the following line:

```
#include "nameList.h"
```

This statement will direct the compiler to find `namelist.h` and insert it into the program input stream as if we had typed in the whole file in this location. We will next develop the `nameList.h` header file. As we shall explore in the next chapter, header files should contain nothing that allocates memory; these are primarily other `#include` statements, `typedef` statements, `struct` declarations, `enum` declarations, and function prototypes. Save `sortNames.c` and close it; we are done with it for a while.

In the file directory named `sortNames.c`, create a file named `nameList.h` and add the following to it:

```
#ifndef _NAME_LIST_H_
#define _NAME_LIST_H_

#include <stdio.h>
#include <string.h>
#include <stdbool.h>
#include <stdlib.h>

typedef char    ListData;
typedef struct _Node ListNode;

typedef struct _Node {
  ListNode*  pNext;
  ListData*  pData;
} ListNode;

typedef struct {
  ListNode*  pFirstNode;
  int        nodeCount;
} NameList;

ListNode*  CreateListNode( char* pNameToAdd );

void  AddName(      NameList* pNames , char* pNameToAdd );
void  PrintNames(   FILE* outputDesc , NameList* pNames );
void  DeleteNames(  NameList* pNames );
bool  IsEmpty(      NameList* pNames );
void  OutOfStorage( void );
#endif
```

Notice that the whole header file is wrapped—it begins and ends—with the #ifndef ... #endif preprocessor directives. These instructions are a check to see whether the _NAME_LIST_H_ symbol has not yet been encountered by the compiler. If so, define that symbol and include all of the text until #endif. If the symbol has been defined, ignore everything until #endif. This prevents multiple, possibly conflicting declarations in a program requiring many, many headers.

This header file includes other header files that we know will be needed for nameList.c. These headers may be included elsewhere; we include them here to be certain the header files we need are present—they may not be needed anywhere else.

Next, there is typedef for the custom types, ListData, ListNode, ListNode, and NameList. These are very similar to the linked list program in Chapter 19, *Exploring Formatted Output*. Lastly, the function prototypes for list manipulation functions are declared. Again, these are very similar to those we saw in Chapter 19, *Exploring Formatted Output*. Notice that some of these functions were not used in sortNames.c. You may also notice that Create<x>List was present in the program in Chapter 19, *Exploring Formatted Output*, but is absent here. The NameList structure is allocated and initialized in main() of sortNames.c so we don't really need it.

You may have also noticed that these declarations are very similar to what we have been putting at the beginning of nearly all of our programs. In fact, most of those declarations that we've been putting in our programs typically go in their own header file and are included in the file where main() is found. Again, we will explore this in greater depth in the next chapter.

We are now ready to begin defining the functions we have declared in nameList.h. Create a new file, nameList.c. The very first line in this file should be the following:

```
#include "nameList.h"
```

Note that " and " are used instead of < and >. The " and " characters tell the preprocessor to look in local directories for files instead of looking in predefined system locations for Standard Library header files.

Next, add the following function to `nameList.c`:

```c
ListNode* CreateListNode( char* pNameToAdd ) {
  ListNode* pNewNode = (ListNode*)calloc( 1 , sizeof( ListNode ) );
  if( pNewNode == NULL ) OutOfStorage();
  pNewNode->pData = (char*)calloc(1, strlen(pNameToAdd)+1 );
  if( pNewNode->pData == NULL ) OutOfStorage();
  strcpy( pNewNode->pData , pNameToAdd );
  return pNewNode;
}
```

Recall from Chapter 19, *Exploring Formatted Output,* that `calloc()` is used to allocate memory on the heap and return a pointer to it. `calloc()` is first called to allocate `ListNode` and is called again to allocate memory for the incoming string. It then copies the incoming string to the `ListNode->pData` element and returns a pointer to `ListNode`. We will later have to `free()` each of these chunks of memory allocated with `calloc()`.

Next, add the following function to `nameList.c`:

```c
void AddName( NameList* pNames , char* pNameToAdd ) {
  ListNode* pNewName = CreateListNode( pNameToAdd );
  if( IsEmpty( pNames ) ) {  // Empty list. Insert as 1st item.
    pNames->pFirstNode = pNewName;
    (pNames->nodeCount)++;
    return;
  }
  (pNames->nodeCount)++;
  ListNode* curr;
  ListNode* prev;
  curr = prev = pNames->pFirstNode;
  while( curr ) {
    // Perform string comparison here.
    if( strcmp( pNewName->pData , curr->pData ) < 0 ) {
      // Found insertion point before an existing name.
      if( curr == pNames->pFirstNode) { // New names comes before all.
        pNames->pFirstNode = pNewName;  //  Insert at front
        pNewName->pNext = curr;
      } else {                          // Insert somewhere in middle
        prev->pNext = pNewName;
        pNewName->pNext = curr;
      }
      return;
    }
    prev = curr;            // Adjust pointers for next iteration.
    curr = prev->pNext;
  }
```

```
      prev->pNext = pNewName; // New name comes after all. Insert at end.
   }
```

This is the workhorse function of `nameList.c`. It takes a `NameList` pointer and a string to add to the list and first creates a new `ListNode` class with that string. If `NameList` is empty, it adjusts the pointers and returns. Otherwise, it enters a `while` loop to find the correct position among the existing `ListNode` structures to insert the new name. The `while()`... loops must handle three possible locations—the beginning of the loop, somewhere in the middle, and, if we get out of the loop, the end of the list.

You may want to review the insertion diagrams and routines from `Chapter 19`, *Exploring Formatted Output*. Another very useful exercise is for you to create a drawing of a linked list structure and walk through each path of the function, inserting a node in the beginning, somewhere in the middle, and at the end.

Next, add the following function to `nameList.c`:

```
void PrintNames( FILE* outputDesc , NameList* pNames ) {
  ListNode* curr = pNames->pFirstNode;
  while( curr ) {
  fputs( curr->pData , outputDesc );
     fputc( '\n'          , outputDesc );
     curr = curr->pNext;
   }
}
```

This function starts at the beginning of the `NameList` structure and walks along with the list, printing out each `curr->pData` element and `<newline>`. The `curr` pointer is adjusted to the next element in the list.

To complement `CreateListNode()`, add the following function to `nameList.c`:

```
void DeleteNames( NameList* pNames )   {
   while( pNames->pFirstNode )   {
     ListNode* temp = pNames->pFirstNode;
     pNames->pFirstNode = pNames->pFirstNode->pNext;
     free( temp->pData );
     free( temp );
   }
}
```

In a similar fashion as `PrintNames()`, `DeleteNames()` starts at the beginning of the `NameList` structure and walks along the list. At each `ListNode`, it removes the node, frees the data element, and then frees the node itself. Note this is the reverse order of how `ListNode` was created.

Add the following function to `nameList.c`:

```
bool IsEmpty( NameList* pNames )  {
   return pNames->nodeCount==0;
}
```

This is a convenience function only used within functions defined in `nameList.c`. It simply returns the current `nodeCount` with the `NameList` structure.

Finally, add the following function to `nameList.c`:

```
void OutOfStorage( void )  {
   fprintf( stderr ,
           "### FATAL RUNTIME ERROR ### No Memory Available" );
   exit( EXIT_FAILURE );
}
```

This function is called if the memory is full. Granted, with today's modern memory management systems, this is unlikely. Nonetheless, it is prudent to not overlook this function.

Save `nameList.c`. We now have `sortNames.c`, `nameList.h`, and `nameList.c`. We are now ready to compile these three files into a single executable. To compile these programs, enter the following command:

```
cc sortNames.c nameList.c -o sortNames -Wall -Werror -std=c11
```

In this command line, we are telling the compiler, `cc`, to compile two source code programs—`sortNames.c` and `nameList.c`. The compiler will assume that to produce the output executable file `sortNames`, it will need the intermediate compilation results of those two source files; we don't have to name the intermediate files. Also, note that we do not need to specify `nameList.h`; that directive is given in the `#include` statement so we don't need it here.

Every other aspect of this command is the same as we've been using with all other programs.

We are now ready to experiment with `sortName.h`.

Writing names in sorted order

The only thing left now is to verify our program. We will run the program with these command-line arguments in the following order:

1. sortNames
2. sortNames -o sorted.data
3. sortNames -i names.data
4. sortNames -i names.data -o sorted data

In each test case, we will enter the names Tom, Dick, and Jane. The names.data file should be left over from when we ran createUnsorted.c earlier and contain five names. You should see the following output from the first case:

```
> cc sortNames.c nameList.c -o sortNames -Wall -Werror -std=c11
> sortNames
Using stdin for input.
Using stdout for output.
Name 1: Tom
Name 2: Dick
Name 3: Jane
Name 4:
Dick
Jane
Tom
Closing files.
>
```

You should see the following output from the second test case:

```
> sortNames -o sorted.data
Using "sorted.data": for output.
Using stdin for input.
Name 1: Tom
Name 2: Dick
Name 3: Jane
Name 4:
Closing files.
> cat sorted.data
Dick
Jane
Tom
>
```

The `names.data` file should still exist from our earlier test. Here, we use it as input and see that we've sorted those five names, as follows:

```
> sortNames -i names.data
Using "names.data" for input.
Using stdout for output.
Adam
Dick
Eve
Jane
Tom
Closing files.
>
```

In the last case, we sort `names.data` to a file and then print the file with the Unix command `cat`, as follows:

```
> sortNames -i names.data -o sorted.data
Using "names.data" for input.
Using "sorted.data": for output.
Closing files.
> cat sorted.data
Adam
Dick
Eve
Jane
Tom
> []
```

In the first case, names were entered on the console, sorted, and output to the console. In the second case, the same names were entered and written to a file. The file was displayed with the Unix `cat` command. In the third case, the `names.data` input file was read, sorted, and printed to the console. In the last case, the same input file was read, sorted, and written to another file; it was displayed with the Unix command `cat`. In each case, inputs, sorting, and outputs behaved as expected.

At this point, I hope it is clear how we've taken all of the concepts from earlier chapters to create a robust, yet simple, name or word sorting program. There are many small nuances of C Standard Library routines we have explored and compensated for by writing additional C code.

Another aspect that I hope is profoundly clear is the importance of taking a simple starting point, getting it to a working state, and then verifying the behavior of that code. Remember that each C compiler on each operating system has subtle differences. Therefore, continual testing and verification are programming habits that will serve you well throughout your programming journey.

Summary

In this chapter, we once again demonstrated the importance of developing a complex program in a stepwise manner from simpler yet operational programs. Here, we took the program from Chapter 22, *Working with Files*, and built upon it to create a template program, getoptFiles.c. We saw that getoptFiles.c can read from either stdin or a file and can write to either stdout or another file. We then built upon getoptFiles.c, which did little else than open streams, to read lines of text representing names and output those lines as they were read. In the process of doing that, we learned about the subtleties of the fgets() and fputs() functions and how to use them to our advantage by wrapping each in a more capable function of our own.

Lastly, we took the concepts of sorted names from Chapter 22, *Working with Files*, and applied them to files using dynamic memory structures to accommodate large and unknown numbers of data elements in sortNames.c. There are many concepts that were employed in sortNames.c, both large and small, from all previous chapters.

We also introduced the concept of multi-file C programs, which we will explore further in Chapter 24, *Working with Multi-File Programs*. Most of the programs you write will consist of three or more source code files and so it is imperative to understand those mechanisms.

Section 5: Building Blocks for Larger Programs

5

Most C programs consist of more than one file. In this section, we'll learn how to create and build programs with multiple files.

This section comprises the following chapters:

- Chapter 24, *Working with Multi-File Programs*
- Chapter 25, *Understanding Scope*

24
Working with Multi-File Programs

In order to solve larger problems, we often need large programs. All of the programs we have developed here have been small—under 1,000 lines of code. A reasonable size for a medium-sized program to, say, create a simple game, perform a basic but robust utility, or keep notes might consist of anywhere between 10,000 to 100,000 lines of code. A *large* program would manage a company's inventory, track sales orders and bills of materials, provide word processing or spreadsheet capabilities, or manage the resources of the computer itself—an operating system. Such programs would consist of anywhere from 100,000 lines of code to a million or more lines of code. Such programs would have teams of programmers and require hundreds of man-years of effort to create and maintain them.

As you gain experience in programming, you may find that the kinds of problems you work to solve become larger. Along with that, you will find that the size of the programs that solve those problems will commensurately become larger. These large programs are not one single large file. Rather, they are a collection of many files, compiled into a single program.

So far, we've used functions to organize operations. In this chapter, we will extend this idea to group functions into one or more program source code files. A program can then be made up of many source code files, each file having a logical grouping of functions. We can then build programs with those multiple files.

There are many benefits to splitting large programs into multiple files. Specific areas/files can be developed by different programmers or programmer teams. Maintenance of individual files is easier because they have a logical connection within a file. But the biggest benefit of using multiple files is reusability: the ability to use one or more source files in many programs.

The following topics will be covered in this chapter:

- Understanding how to group related functions into separate program files
- Understanding how to use header files versus source files
- Understanding that the preprocessor is powerful enough that we can easily hurt ourselves and others with it
- Building our multi-file program on the command line—make changes; rinse; repeat

Technical requirements

As detailed in the *Technical requirements* section of `Chapter 1`, *Running Hello, World!*, continue to use the tools you have chosen.

The source code for this chapter can be found at `https://github.com/PacktPublishing/Learn-C-Programming`.

Understanding multi-file programs

Before we get into the nitty-gritty of the differences between source files and header files, we first need to understand why we need to have multiple source files at all.

In `Chapter 23`, *Using File Input and File Output*, we saw how some of the functions in that program pertained only to opening and closing files, and some of the functions pertained only to manipulating a linked list. We used the `sortNames.c` file to define the `usage()`, `getName()`, `putName()`, `trimStr()`, and, of course, `main()` functions. Each of these functions deals with some detail of input and output. Although you could argue that `trimStr()` belongs more logically in a string-handling source code file, we use it here to clean up the string from `getName()`, so here it stays. To sort the names, we used functions declared in `nameList.h` and defined in `nameList.c`. These functions dealt only with the linked list structure. Since these functions were called from the `main()` functions, we needed their prototypes in that file; therefore, we put the structure and function declarations in a header file and included that header in both source code files.

Imagine that we have several programs that might use a linked list to sort strings. If we were careful to keep all of the structures and functions general enough for `nameList`, then we could *reuse* these functions without needing to rewrite them. In each program that needs to sort a linked list, we would need only to include the header file, `nameList.h`, and be certain that the source code file, `nameList.c`, is compiled into the final program. This serves three purposes, listed as follows:

- Functions that perform similar functions are kept together in one file. This logical grouping helps to provide order when there are hundreds, or even thousands, of functions. Related functions will be found close together, making a large, complex program more easily understood. We have already seen something like this when we have included multiple header files. For instance, all **input/output (I/O)** function prototypes can be seen in `stdio.h`, and nearly all string-handling functions are found in `string.h`.
- Any changes to those functions or structures in one file are limited primarily to just that file and not every program that uses those functions.
- By grouping related functions together, we can create *subsystems* of functions and use them to build up more complex programs with one or more subsystems.

After we explore some of the details of source files versus header files and the preprocessor, we will revisit the `carddeck.c` program, the final version from Chapter 16, *Creating and Using More Complex Structures*. That program is a single source file; we will break it up. By the time we get to do that, you should clearly understand why breaking it up is appropriate.

Using header files for declarations and source files for definitions

The two types of files we will use to group functions are header files and source code files—or, more simply, just source files. Nearly all of the programs we have created thus far have been single-file source files that have included `struct` and `enum` definitions, `typedef` keywords, function prototypes, and functions. This is not typical in C programming; we have only been doing it to keep our programs rather more condensed. It is far more typical for C programs to consist of a main source file—where the `main()` function is defined—and one or more header files and auxiliary source files. The `sortNames().c`, `nameList.h`, and `nameList.c` programs are very typical examples of a common C program.

Whenever the preprocessor sees the `#include` directive, which must be followed by a filename, it opens that file and reads it into the input stream for compilation at that location, just as if we had typed in the contents of the file ourselves. The filename must be surrounded either by < and > or by " and ". Each of these has a special meaning to the preprocessor. The angle brackets tell the preprocessor to look in predefined locations that are relative to the compiler for the given filename. The quotation marks tell the preprocessor to look in the current directory for the filename.

Creating source files

As we have already seen in our single-file programs, we can put pretty much anything and everything in a source file. We use source files primarily to define functions and we put all the rest, or almost all of the rest, in a header file to be included in the source file.

A source file can be laid out in any number of ways. We can define all functions before they are called and have the `main()` function at the very end, or we can use function prototypes at the top of the program and place our function definitions in any order, with the `main()` function typically appearing immediately after the function prototypes. However, there are perfectly good reasons to keep some things in the source file only; we will explore these reasons fully in `Chapter 25`, *Understanding Scope*.

Since we know what a source file with everything in it looks like, we will focus our attention on which things properly go into a header file and which things do not go into one.

Creating header files

Header files are used for the following reasons:

- Header files remove the clutter of function prototypes and the declaration of custom types from the source file. They are moved to a header file to be included in the source file.
- For functions that are called from a different source file, the inclusion of the header file with those function prototypes provides access to those functions. Simply including the header file then makes them available within that program.
- For custom data types that are used in other source files, the inclusion of the header file with those custom data-type declarations makes those custom types *known* within the other source files.

- Header files provide a means to organize all of the C Standard Library header files, as well as our own header files, into a single header file. An example of this would be a source file that includes, say, `stdio.h`, `stdlib.h`, and `string.h` header files, while another source file includes, say, the `stdio.h`, `math.h`, and `unistd.h` header files. Note that `stdio.h` is needed in both source files but the other standard headers are only needed in one source file. We could create a single header file—say, the `commonheaders.h`—that includes all of those headers and itself, which is then included in each of the source files. This is not always done in a program; however, when there are many source files and a wide variety of standard library headers spread all over the source files, it is a good way to centralize header-file inclusion and avoid accidentally omitting a needed header.

There are some very simple rules to follow for the contents of header files. These are driven by the fact that a given header file may be used in more than one file. Many programmers create header files for their source files without really thinking about why. A simple guideline on when to create a header file at all is shown here:

Only create a header file when it will be used in two or more files.

Or, to put it another way, see the following:

Everything in a `.h` file should be used in at least two `.c` files.

Recall that in the `sortNames` program, the `nameList.h` header file was included in both `sortNames.c` and `nameList.c`. Often, the habit of creating a header file for each source file is so commonplace that it is done without much thought. Creating such header files is similar to using { and } for the `if()`... `else`... statement blocks, even when they aren't needed; it does little harm and helps to organize your source files. I find that whenever I create the `.c` file, I automatically create the `.h` file for it as well.

So, what goes in a header file? Here are some examples:

- Function prototypes; in other words, anything that declares a function but does not define it
- Custom type definitions (`enums` and `structs`)
- Preprocessor directives such as `#define` and `#include`
- Anything that defines a type but does not allocate memory, such as `typedef` declarations and `structs` defined by `typedef` and enums

Conversely, what does *not* go into a header file? There are two main categories, as follows:

- Anything that allocates memory, such as variable declarations and constant declarations
- Function definitions

When a constant or variable is declared, memory is allocated. This occurs regardless of whether the variable is an intrinsic type or a custom type. If a variable is declared in a header file and that header file is included multiple times, the compiler will try to allocate memory each time using the same name. This results in the compiler being unable to determine which memory is being referenced by the variable identifier. This is called a **name clash**. The compiler will generate at least one error when it encounters multiple defined variables of the same identifier.

When a function is defined, the compiler remembers the address of that function, among other things. When the function is called, it then jumps to that address to execute the function. If a function is defined in a header file and that header file is included multiple times, the function will have multiple addresses for the same function and the compiler will be unable to determine which function should actually be used. This is also called a name clash. The compiler will generate at least one error when it encounters a function defined more than once.

We will later encounter a method using the preprocessor to avoid these name collisions. However, the idea of keeping variable declarations and function definitions out of header files is such a long-standing practice that to alter it is a very bad programming practice. Other programmers *expect* header files not to have memory allocation or function definitions. Once a header file exists, it is *assumed* that it can be included as many times as needed. There is no good reason at any time to alter this deeply ingrained practice.

To be clear, as we have seen, anything that could go into a header file doesn't have to; it can occur in the source file where it is used. Why we would put something in a header file or not is a topic for Chapter 25, *Understanding Scope*. For now, we will use a single header file for each C source file as a means to declutter the source file.

Revisiting the preprocessor

The preprocessor is a very powerful utility; therefore, it must be used with extremely great care. We can't eliminate it completely since it is an essential part of developing multi-file programs. In this section, we will explore how to use the preprocessor. Our goal is to find, just as Goldilocks did, the just-right amount of preprocessing to employ—not too much and not too little.

Understanding the limits and dangers of the preprocessor

The preprocessor is a simple macro processor that processes the source text of a C program before the program is read by the compiler. It is controlled via single-line preprocessor directives and transforms the original source text by interpreting macros embedded in the original source text to substitute, add, or remove text based on the given directives. The resulting preprocessed source text must then be a valid C program.

The following table provides an overview of the basic preprocessor directives:

`#include`	Insert text from another source file.
`#define`	Add a preprocessor macro definition.
`#undef`	Remove a preprocessor macro definition.
`#ifdef`	Conditionally include some text if the macro is defined.
`#ifndef`	Conditionally include some text if the macro is not defined.
`#if`	Conditionally include some text based on the value of a conditional expression.
`#else`	Conditionally include some text when the value of `#if`, `#ifdef`, `#ifndef`, or `#elif` failed.
`#elif`	Equivalent to `#else  #if` in a single directive.
`#endif`	Terminate conditional text.
`#error`	Produce a compile-time error with the designated message.
`#pragma`	Specify implementation-dependent information to the compiler.

There are a small number of other directives that have specialized use and are not covered here.

The main feature of the preprocessor is that it largely performs textual substitution. Herein lies both its power and its danger. It does textual substitution, but it doesn't understand C syntax or any syntax at all.

Knowing some dangers of the preprocessor

Because the preprocessor provides simple programming-like commands, it becomes very tempting to use it as a programming language. However, because it is merely a simple macro processor that does not understand syntax, the results of its output can be very misleading, resulting in code that compiles but behaves unpredictably.

There are circumstances where using the preprocessor in complicated ways is warranted. Those are, however, circumstances that require advanced programming techniques and rigorous verification methods that are outside the scope of this book. It is for this reason that I recommend keeping our use of the preprocessor both as simple and as useful as possible.

Using the preprocessor effectively

The following are some guidelines for using and not using the preprocessor effectively:

- If you can write a function in C, do that instead of using a preprocessor macro. You may also want to consider the use of the `inline` C declaration. `inline` provides a suggestion to the compiler to place the body of the function wherever it is called as if a textual substitution were done. This has the advantage of preserving all of the type checking, as well as eliminating the overhead of a function call. `inline` becomes useful in very high-performance programming situations.
- Use the preprocessor as a last resort for performance. Eliminating statements or function calls as a means of improving performance is known as **central processing unit** (**CPU**) cycle trimming and is highly subject to even minor variations in system configurations. Therefore, strive to pick the best, most efficient algorithm before resorting to cycle trimming.

Don't ever assume performance will be improved; actual performance must be *measured* before and after to determine any effects upon performance. Entire volumes have been written about both, to measure and to improve performance.

- Prefer `const <type> <variable> = <value>;` over `#define <name> <literal>` . In the former case, type information is preserved, whereas in the latter case, there is no type information, so we can never be certain if the macro will be used properly.
- Prefer `enum { <constantValue> = <value>, ... }` over `#define <name> <literal>`. You might want to declare an array size, say, in a structure, but the compiler won't allow you to use a `const int` value. Many consider C's array definition a deficiency of the language, and many programmers use `#define` largely for this reason. Rather than drag the preprocessor into it, you can declare an identifier in an `enum` block and give it a constant value. We will see how this works in the program at the end of this chapter.
- Control the use of included headers with simple preprocessor directives.

The last item deserves further exploration. When a header file is included in a source file, the entire contents are copied into the source file at compile time. If the header file is also included in another header file, as often happens, it will again be included in the source file. The way to prevent this is to use three preprocessor directives in the header file, as follows:

```
#ifndef _SOME_HEADER_FILE_H_
#define _SOME_HEADER_FILE_H_

// contents of header file
...
...
...

#endif
```

The first directive tests whether the _SOME_HEADER_FILE_H_ macro has already been defined. If so, this means that this particular header file would have already been processed at least once, and all of the text of the file is ignored until the last directive, #endif, which should be the last line of the header file.

Actually, the first directive tests whether the _SOME_HEADER_FILE_H_ macro has not already been defined. If it has not, the next directive defines it, and the rest of the header file text is inserted into the source file. The next time this file is encountered by the preprocessor, the macro will have been defined and this test will fail, excluding all text until the #endif directive.

This method ensures that a header file will always only be included once. To use this method effectively, the macro symbol for the header file should be unique. Typically, using the filename with all caps and underscores in the manner shown is effective and guarantees uniqueness.

Debugging with the preprocessor

So, we have seen two instances of using the preprocessor effectively: for #include files and limiting redundant processing of #include files. The last simple and effective use for the preprocessor is as a tool for debugging large and/or complex programs of multiple files.

Using the conditional directives, we can easily control what source code is inserted into the source file or excluded from the source file. Consider the following directives:

```
...
#if TEST_CODE
    // code to be inserted and executed in final program
```

```
    fprintf( stderr, "This is a test. We got here.\n" );
  #endif
  ...
```

If the `TEST_CODE` macro is defined and has a nonzero value, the statements within the `#if` and `#endif` directives will be included in the source file. For this code to be included, we can define the macro in a couple of ways. First, it can be defined in the main source file with the following code:

```
#define TEST_CODE 1
```

This statement defines the `TEST_CODE` macro to have a value of 1 (nonzero, which implies `TRUE`). If we wanted to turn off the test code but keep the macros in place, we would change the line in the preceding code snippet to the following:

```
#define TEST_CODE 0
```

This both defines `TEST_CODE` and gives it a value of 0 (zero, which implies `FALSE`), which will prevent the test statements from being inserted into the source code.

An alternate way is to define the macro on the command line for compilation, as follows:

```
cc myProgram.c -o myProgram -Wall -Werror -std=c11 -D TEST_CODE=1
```

The `-D` option defines the `TEST_CODE` macro and gives it the value of 1. Note that command-line macros are processed before directives in any file.

When I have needed to test a wide variety of features in a very complex program, I have actually used a set of macros such as the following:

```
#if defined DEBUG
  #define DEBUG_LOG 1
  #define DEBUG_LOG_ALIGN 0
  #define DEBUG_LOG_SHADOW 0
  #define DEBUG_LOG_WINDOW 0
  #define DEBUG_LOG_KEEPONTOP 1
  #define DEBUG_LOG_TIME 1
#else
  #define DEBUG_LOG 0
  #define DEBUG_LOG_ALIGN 0
  #define DEBUG_LOG_SHADOW 0
  #define DEBUG_LOG_WINDOW 0
  #define DEBUG_LOG_KEEPONTOP 1
  #define DEBUG_LOG_TIME 0
#endif
```

This set of macro definitions existed alone in a header file. I could then turn on or off a whole set of debugging macro symbols via the command line by simply adding `-D DEBUG` to the command-line options. Sprinkled throughout this program, which consisted of over 10,000 lines of code in approximately 230 files, were `#if defined DEBUG_LOG_xxx ...` `#endif` directives with a few lines of code to provide logging as the program was executing. I've found this rudimentary method, sometimes called **caveman debugging**, to be effective.

A similar mechanism can be used to insert one set of statements or another set of statements into the source file. Consider the following directives:

```
...
#if defined TEST_PROGRAM
    // code used to test parts of program
    ...
#else
    // code used for the final version of the program (non-testing)
    ..
#endif
```

When the `TEST_PROGRAM` macro is defined, the statements up to `#else` are inserted into the source file. When `TEST_PROGRAM` is not defined, the statements in the `#else` branch are inserted into the source file.

This method is handy when you need to use a set of source files for testing and need the `main()` function for testing but don't need it when the source is part of another set of source files. On the other hand, care must be exercised to prevent test code behavior from varying too widely from the final code. Therefore, this method is not applicable in all cases.

Any further discussion of debugging is beyond the scope of this book.

Sometimes, you may find that you want to explore several ways to do the same thing in C. However, after your exploration, you have two or more methods but you only need a single one. Rather than comment out the statements you don't want, you can put them all in the `#if 0 ... #endif` block. The 0 value will always be `false` and the statements between `#if` and `#endif` will be excluded at compile time from the source code file. Some of the programs in the source code repository for this book will use this method to exclude an alternate method, to perform a series of steps.

We now have four effective yet simple uses for the preprocessor, as follows:

- To include header files
- To limit redundant processing of header files
- For caveman debugging
- To exclude a set of statements with `#if 0 ... #endif` when we are experimenting with our program

We are now ready to create a multi-file program from a single-file program.

Creating a multi-file program

We will take the final version of the `carddeck.c` single-file program from Chapter 16, *Creating and Using More Complex Structures*, and reorganize it into multiple header files and source files. You may want to review the contents and organization of that file now before we begin.

We are going to create four `.c` files, each with their own `.h` file; we will create eight files in total. These files will be named as follows:

- `card.c` and `card.h` to manipulate the `Card` structure
- `hand.c` and `hand.h` to manipulate the `Hand` structure
- `deck.c` and `deck.h` to manipulate the `Deck` structure
- `dealer.c` and `dealer.h` to be the main program file; `dealer.h` when possible will be included in each of the source files

First, create a separate folder where these eight new files will exist. You may copy `carddeck.c` to this folder or you may choose to leave it in its original location. We want to copy and paste pieces of the original source file into each of our eight new files. If possible, with your editor, open `carddeck.c` in a separate window. It is from this window that you will be copying sections of `carddeck.c` and pasting them into new files. This is the approach we will be taking. An alternate approach, which we are not going to describe here, would be to copy `carddeck.c` eight times to each of those files and then pare down each of them to their new purposes.

In the end, this collection of programs will run as before and produce exactly the same output as before. This will be proof of our successful transformation.

Extracting Card structures and functions

As we extract this file, we will be going through `carddeck.c` to find the relevant bits. Take the following steps:

1. Create and open the `card.h` header file, and put in the following new lines:

    ```
    #ifndef _CARD_H_
    #define _CARD_H_

    #endif
    ```

    This is our starting point for this header file. We use the macro directives, as explained earlier, to ensure that anything in this file is only preprocessed once. The `_CARD_H_` macro is used nowhere else in the program but in this single header file. Everything else that we put in this file will be after `#define _CARD_H_` and before `#endif`.
    Next, we would normally add the necessary header files. We will save this for later when we finish the `dealer.c` and `dealer.h` files.

2. In `carddeck.c`, you now should see a number of `const int` definitions. The only ones of these that pertain to the `Card` structure are `kCardsInSuit`, `kWildCard`, and `kNotWildCard`. Rather than keep them as this type, we will use the following `enum` declaration to define them:

    ```
    enum {
      kNotWildCard = 0,
      kWildCard    = 1,
      kCardsInSuit = 13
    }
    ```

    This is done to give these identifiers actual constant values. We will need this when we declare a `hand` or `deck` structure and need to specify the array size with a constant value. The `const int` type, while it can't change after initialization, is a read-only variable, not a constant; enum values are constants.

3. Next, copy the `typedef enum { ... } Suit;` declaration, the `typedef enum {...} Face;` declaration, the `typedef struct { ... } Card;` declaration, and the three `Card` functions, `InitializeCard()`, `PrintCard()`, and `CardToString()`, from `carddeck.c` to `card.h`. This header should now look as follows:

    ```
    #ifndef _CARD_H_
    #define _CARD_H_
    ```

```
enum {
  kNotWildCard = 0,
  kWildCard    = 1,
  kCardsInSuit = 13
};

typedef enum  {
  club  = 1,  diamond,  heart,  spade
} Suit;

typedef enum  {
  one = 1,  two ,  three ,  four ,  five ,  six , seven ,
  eight  , nine ,   ten ,  jack , queen , king , ace
} Face;

typedef struct  {
  Suit suit;
  int  suitValue;
  Face face;
  int  faceValue;
  bool isWild;
} Card;

void InitializeCard( Card* pCard , Suit s , Face f , bool w );
void PrintCard(      Card* pCard );
void CardToString(   Card* pCard , char pCardStr[20] );

#endif
```

We have grouped all of the constant values (via enum), the Card structure definition, and functions that operate on a Card in a single file. Save this file.

Typically, in card.c, you would include card.h and any other standard library headers. But in this program, we are going to have a single header file that is included in all source files. We will get to that when we finish dealer.h. The first line in card.h should be #include "dealer.h".

4. To finish this extraction, open card.c and find the three functions, InitializeCard(), PrintCard(), and CardToString(), in carddeck.c and copy them into card.c. Your card.c source file should look as follows:

```
#include "dealer.h"

void InitializeCard( Card* pCard, Suit s , Face f , bool w )  {

  // function body here
```

```
    ...
    }

    void PrintCard( Card* pCard )  {

      // function body here
      ...
    }

    void CardToString( Card* pCard , char pCardStr[20] )  {

      // function body here
      ...
    }
```

The `card.c` source file has a single `#include` file and three function definitions that manipulate a card. We have omitted the statements in the function bodies of these functions for brevity. Save this file. We are now ready to move on to the `Hand` files.

Extracting Hand structures and functions

Just as we extracted the `typedef`, `enum`, and `struct` instances, along with the functions for the `Card` structure, we will do the same for `Hand` structures, as follows:

1. Create and open the `hand.h` header file and put in the following new lines:

   ```
   #ifndef _HAND_H_
   #define _HAND_H_

   #endif
   ```

   This is our starting point for this header file. Looking again through `carddeck.c`, we see that there are a couple of `const int` types related to `Hand` that we need to add as `enum` instances, as follows:

   ```
   enum {
     kCardsInHand = 5,
     kNumHands = 4
   };
   ```

2. We can next add the `typedef struct { ... } Hand;` declaration and the 4 function definitions related to the `Hand` structure: `InitializeHand()`, `AddCardToHand()`, `PrintHand()`, and `PrintAllHands()`. However, notice that a parameter to one of these functions is a `Card*` parameter, therefore the compiler will need to know about the `Card` structure when it encounters this prototype. We will need to include the `card.h` header file. After making these additions, `hand.h` should look as follows:

```
#ifndef _HANDH
#define _HANDH

#include "card.h"

enum {
  kCardsInHand = 5,
  kNumHands    = 4
};

typedef struct {
  int    cardsDealt;
  Card* hand[ kCardsInHand ];
} Hand;

void InitializeHand( Hand* pHand );
void AddCardToHand(  Hand* pHand , Card* pCard );
void PrintHand(      Hand* pHand , char* pLeadStr );
void PrintAllHands(  Hand* hands[ kNumHands ] );

#endif
```

3. `hand.h` now has the constant values needed, the structure definition for `Hand`, and the function prototypes to manipulate the `Hand` structure. Save `hand.h`.

4. Create and open `hand.c`. As with `card.c`, find the four function definitions in `carddeck.c` and copy them into `hand.c`. Add the `#include "dealer.h"` directive to `hand.c`. It should now appear as follows:

```
#include "dealer.h"

void InitializeHand( Hand* pHand )  {
  // function body here
  ...
}

void AddCardToHand( Hand* pHand , Card* pCard )  {
  // function body here
```

```
      . . .
    }

    void PrintHand( Hand* pHand , char* pLeadStr )  {
      // function body here
      . . .
    }

    void PrintAllHands(  Hand* hands[ kNumHands ] )  {
      // function body here
      . . .
    }
```

The `hand.c` source file has a single `#include` directive and four function definitions that manipulate a card. We have omitted the statements in the function bodies of these functions for brevity. Save this file. We are now ready to move on to the `Deck` files.

Extracting Deck structures and functions

Just as we extracted the `typedef`, `enum`, and `struct` instances, along with the functions for the `Card` and `Hand` structures, we will do the same for `Deck` structures. Take the following steps:

1. Create and open the `deck.h` header file and put in the following new lines:

   ```
   #ifndef _DECK_H_
   #define _DECK_H_

   #endif
   ```

   This is our starting point for this header file. Looking again through `carddeck.c`, we see that there is one `const int` related to `Hand` that we need to add as an `enum`, as follows:

   ```
   enum {
     kCardsInDeck = 52
   };
   ```

2. We can next add `typedef struct { ... } Deck;` and the four function
   definitions related to the
   `Deck` structure—`InitializeDeck()`, `ShuffleDeck()`, `DealCardFromDeck()`,
   and `PrintDeck()`. However, notice that the `Deck` structure contains
   two `Card` arrays and one function returns a `Card*`, pointer to Card structure,
   therefore the compiler will need to know about the `Card` structure when it
   encounters this structure and the function prototype. We will need to include
   the `card.h` header file. After making these additions, `deck.h` should look as
   follows:

```
#ifndef _DECK_H_
#define _DECK_H_

#include "card.h"

enum {
  kCardsInDeck = 52
};

typedef struct   {
  Card   ordered[  kCardsInDeck ];
  Card*  shuffled[ kCardsInDeck ];
  int    numDealt;
  bool   bIsShuffled;
} Deck;

void  InitializeDeck(    Deck* pDeck );
void  ShuffleDeck(       Deck* pDeck );
Card* DealCardFromDeck(  Deck* pDeck );
void  PrintDeck(         Deck* pDeck );

#endif
```

3. `deck.h` now has the constant value needed, the structure definition for `Deck`,
   and the function prototypes to manipulate the `Deck` structure. Save `deck.h`.

4. Create and open `deck.c`. As with `card.c`, find the four function definitions
   in `carddeck.c` and copy them into `deck.c`. Add the `#include`
   `"dealer.h"` directive to `deck.c`. It should now appear as follows:

```
#include "dealer.h"

void InitializeDeck(    Deck* pDeck )   {
  // function body here
  ...
}
```

```
    void ShuffleDeck(      Deck* pDeck )  {
     // function body here
      ...
    }

    Card* DealCardFromDeck( Deck* pDeck )  {
     // function body here
      ...
    }

    void PrintDeck(        Deck* pDeck )  {
     // function body here
      ...
    }
```

The `deck.c` source file has a single `#include` directive and four function definitions that manipulate a deck. We have omitted the statements in the function bodies of these functions for brevity. Save this file. We are now ready to finish the `dealer` files.

Finishing the dealer.c program

Having extracted `Card`, `Hand`, and `Deck` declarations and functions, we can now finish the program. Take the following steps:

1. Create and open the `dealer.h` header file and add the following new lines:

   ```
   #include <stdbool.h>
   #include <stdio.h>
   #include <string.h>
   #include <stdlib.h>
   #include <time.h>

   #include "card.h"
   #include "hand.h"
   #include "deck.h"
   ```

   Looking again through `carddeck.c`, we see that all that is left to be transferred to `dealer.h` are the standard library header files. We also created three header files for each of the three `.c` source files; we add them to this header file. Recall that we also included this header file in each of the three source files. Also, remember that we added `#ifndef` ... `#endif` exclusion directives around each of those header files so that they will ever only be preprocessed once. This header file contains all of the standard library headers any of the source files could need and it contains the header files for each of the three source files. Save this file.

2. Create and open `dealer.c`. The only thing left to transfer to `dealer.c` is the `main()` function. The `dealer.c` file should appear as follows:

```
#include "dealer.h"

int main( void )   {
  Deck   deck;
  Deck* pDeck = &deck;
  InitializeDeck( pDeck );
  PrintDeck(        pDeck );
  ShuffleDeck( pDeck );
  PrintDeck(    pDeck );
  Hand h1 , h2 , h3 , h4;
  Hand* hands[] = { &h1 , &h2 , &h3 , &h4 };
  for( int i = 0 ; i < kNumHands ; i++ )   {
    InitializeHand( hands[i] );
  }
  for( int i = 0 ; i < kCardsInHand ; i++ )   {
    for( int j = 0 ; j < kNumHands ; j++ )   {
      AddCardToHand( hands[j] , DealCardFromDeck( pDeck ) );
    }
  }
  PrintAllHands( hands );
  PrintDeck(        pDeck );
  return 0;
}
```

The `main()` function controls all the work of this program. It declares a `Deck` structure and calls the `Deck` functions to manipulate that deck. The `#include` file that provides the declarations for this in `deck.h` is included here within `dealer.h`. Next, four `Hand` structures are declared, and a `Hand` function is called to initialize the hands. The `#include` file that provides the declarations for this in `hand.h` is included here within `dealer.h`. Then, cards are dealt from the deck and placed into the hands. Within `main()`, there is no direct reference to a `Card`. Therefore, `card.h` is not directly needed for `dealer.c`. However, the structures and functions for `Card` are needed by both `Hand` and `Deck`. The source files for `Hand` and `Deck` need to know about `Card` structures and functions. These kinds of header file interdependencies are the primary reason they are all put into a single header that is included in each source file.

An alternative approach would have been to include in each file only the header files that are needed to compile that source file. In this approach, dealer.c would only need to include deck.h and hand.h. In deck.c, included files would be deck.h, card.h, stdio.h, stdlib.h, and time.h. In hand.c, included files would be hand.h, card.h, and stdio.h. In card.c, included files would be card.h, string.h, and stdio.h. This approach was not taken because using a single header file is both more reliable and more flexible if/when these source files are used in a larger program.

We have eight files that make up our program now. Let's see how to build it.

Building a multi-file program

In all of our single-file programs, we used the following command line to build them:

```
cc <sourcefile>.c -o <sourcefile> -Wall -Werror -std=c11
```

In the two-file program of Chapter 23, *Using File Input and File Output*, we used the following command line to build it:

```
cc <sourcefile_1>.c <sourcefile_2>.c -o <programname> ...
```

The compiler command line can take multiple source files and compile them into a single executable. In this program, we have four source files, so in order to compile this program, we need to put each source file on the command line, as follows:

```
cc card.c hand.c deck.c dealer.c -o dealer ...
```

The order of the list of source files does not matter. The compiler will use the results of the compilation of each file and build them together into a single executable named dealer.

Compile the program with the preceding command. The program should compile without errors. Run the program. You should see the following output:

```
> cc dealer.c deck.c hand.c card.c  -o dealer -Wall -Werror -std=c11
> dealer
52 cards in the deck
Deck is not shuffled
0 cards dealt into 4 hands
The ordered deck:
(  1)     2 of Spades    (14)     2 of Hearts    (27)     2 of Diamonds    (40)     2 of Clubs
(  2)     3 of Spades    (15)     3 of Hearts    (28)     3 of Diamonds    (41)     3 of Clubs
(  3)     4 of Spades    (16)     4 of Hearts    (29)     4 of Diamonds    (42)     4 of Clubs
(  4)     5 of Spades    (17)     5 of Hearts    (30)     5 of Diamonds    (43)     5 of Clubs
(  5)     6 of Spades    (18)     6 of Hearts    (31)     6 of Diamonds    (44)     6 of Clubs
(  6)     7 of Spades    (19)     7 of Hearts    (32)     7 of Diamonds    (45)     7 of Clubs
(  7)     8 of Spades    (20)     8 of Hearts    (33)     8 of Diamonds    (46)     8 of Clubs
(  8)     9 of Spades    (21)     9 of Hearts    (34)     9 of Diamonds    (47)     9 of Clubs
(  9)    10 of Spades    (22)    10 of Hearts    (35)    10 of Diamonds    (48)    10 of Clubs
( 10)  Jack of Spades    (23)  Jack of Hearts    (36)  Jack of Diamonds    (49)  Jack of Clubs
( 11) Queen of Spades    (24) Queen of Hearts    (37) Queen of Diamonds    (50) Queen of Clubs
( 12)  King of Spades    (25)  King of Hearts    (38)  King of Diamonds    (51)  King of Clubs
( 13)   Ace of Spades    (26)   Ace of Hearts    (39)   Ace of Diamonds    (52)   Ace of Clubs

52 cards in the deck
Deck is shuffled
0 cards dealt into 4 hands
The full shuffled deck:
(  1)   Ace of Clubs    (  2)     3 of Hearts    (  3)     2 of Spades    (  4)     4 of Diamonds
(  5)  Jack of Diamonds (  6)     3 of Diamonds (  7)     7 of Spades    (  8)  King of Diamonds
(  9) Queen of Hearts   ( 10)  Jack of Clubs    ( 11)     3 of Clubs    ( 12)     4 of Hearts
( 13)     6 of Diamonds ( 14)    10 of Clubs    ( 15)     2 of Clubs    ( 16)     6 of Hearts
( 17)  Jack of Spades   ( 18)     5 of Diamonds ( 19)     6 of Clubs    ( 20)    10 of Spades
( 21)  Jack of Hearts   ( 22)     8 of Diamonds ( 23)     9 of Hearts    ( 24)  King of Spades
( 25)     7 of Diamonds ( 26)   Ace of Spades   ( 27)     5 of Clubs    ( 28)     3 of Spades
( 29)     9 of Clubs    ( 30)     9 of Diamonds ( 31)     8 of Spades    ( 32)  King of Clubs
( 33)     5 of Spades    ( 34)    10 of Hearts    ( 35)  King of Hearts   ( 36)     9 of Spades
( 37) Queen of Spades   ( 38)     7 of Clubs    ( 39)   Ace of Hearts   ( 40)    10 of Diamonds
( 41)     5 of Hearts    ( 42)     2 of Diamonds ( 43)     7 of Hearts    ( 44)     8 of Clubs
( 45)     2 of Hearts    ( 46) Queen of Clubs    ( 47)     6 of Spades    ( 48)     8 of Hearts
( 49) Queen of Diamonds ( 50)   Ace of Diamonds ( 51)     4 of Spades    ( 52)     4 of Clubs
                    Hand 1:
                       Ace of Clubs
                     Jack of Diamonds
                    Queen of Hearts
                        6 of Diamonds
                     Jack of Spades
          Hand 2:
              3 of Hearts
              3 of Diamonds
           Jack of Clubs
             10 of Clubs
              5 of Diamonds          Hand 3:
                                        2 of Spades
                                        7 of Spades
                                        3 of Clubs
                                        2 of Clubs
                                        6 of Clubs
                    Hand 4:
                        4 of Diamonds
                     King of Diamonds
                        4 of Hearts
                        6 of Hearts
                       10 of Spades

52 cards in the deck
Deck is shuffled
20 cards dealt into 4 hands
The remaining shuffled deck:
( 21)  Jack of Hearts   ( 22)     8 of Diamonds ( 23)     9 of Hearts    ( 24)  King of Spades
( 25)     7 of Diamonds ( 26)   Ace of Spades   ( 27)     5 of Clubs    ( 28)     3 of Spades
( 29)     9 of Clubs    ( 30)     9 of Diamonds ( 31)     8 of Spades    ( 32)  King of Clubs
( 33)     5 of Spades    ( 34)    10 of Hearts    ( 35)  King of Hearts   ( 36)     9 of Spades
( 37) Queen of Spades   ( 38)     7 of Clubs    ( 39)   Ace of Hearts   ( 40)    10 of Diamonds
( 41)     5 of Hearts    ( 42)     2 of Diamonds ( 43)     7 of Hearts    ( 44)     8 of Clubs
( 45)     2 of Hearts    ( 46) Queen of Clubs    ( 47)     6 of Spades    ( 48)     8 of Hearts
( 49) Queen of Diamonds ( 50)   Ace of Diamonds ( 51)     4 of Spades    ( 52)     4 of Clubs
> █
```

Note that this output is exactly the same as that shown in Chapter 16, *Creating and Using More Complex Structures*.

Once you get this program working, spend some time commenting out one or more header files, and recompile to see what kind of errors you get. For instance, what happens when you comment out #include deck.h? What happens when you comment out #include hand.h? What happens when you comment out #include card.h? After each experiment, make sure you undo your experiment and verify that you can again compile the program. Once you have explored those experiments, you might also want to try the alternative approach to including headers mentioned at the end of the preceding section, *Finishing the dealer.c program*.

Summary

In this chapter, we took a single source file made up of many structures and functions that operate on them and grouped them into four source code files and four header files. We saw how we could—and should—group structures and functions that operate on them into a source file and a corresponding header file. All of the functions were related, in that they operated on the structures declared in that file's header file. These many source files were then compiled into a single program. We could then build programs with those multiple files. We also explored simple yet efficient ways to use the preprocessor without overusing it. Lastly, we saw how to build a multi-file program by specifying each .c file on the compiler command line.

This chapter is just an introduction to multi-file programs. In the next chapter, Chapter 25, *Understanding Scope,* we will expand our knowledge of multi-file programs so that we can both limit which variables and functions can only be called from within a single file, as well as expand the visibility of variables and functions.

Understanding Scope

In every program we have created thus far, functions have been available—which means callable—from everywhere else within the program. Even in the multi-file program of Chapter 24, *Working with Multi-File Programs*, every function in every file is available/callable from within every other file. This is not always appropriate, nor is it desirable. Likewise, some variables should only be accessed from within specific functions, or for use within a specific group of functions.

There are many instances where it is appropriate to limit the availability of a function or the accessibility of a variable. For instance, some functions may operate on a given structure and should only ever be called by other functions that also operate on that structure; these functions would never be called by any other functions. Similarly, we might want a value to be accessible to all functions within a program or we might want to limit its access to just a group of functions, or even a single function.

The visibility of functions and variables is known as **scope**. The scope of a variable or function depends upon several factors with a program: its *visibility*, its *extent*, and its *linkage*. In this chapter, we will explore the different kinds of scope as they apply to variables and functions.

The following topics will be covered in this chapter:

- Being able to define the three aspects of scope: visibility, extent, and linkage
- Understanding the scope of variables declared within statement blocks
- Understanding the scope of variables declared outside of statement blocks
- Understanding special cases of a variable's scope
- Demonstrating statement-block variables, function-block variables, and file/global variables
- Understanding compilation units
- Understanding file scope
- Understanding program scope

Technical requirements

As detailed in the *Technical requirements* section of `Chapter 1`, *Running Hello, World!*, continue to use the tools you have chosen.

The source code for this chapter can be found at `https://github.com/PacktPublishing/Learn-C-Programming`.

Defining scope – visibility, extent, and linkage

Often, when the *scope* of a variable or function is mentioned, it is referring only to the visibility of the variable or function. Visibility essentially determines which functions or statements can *see* the variable to either access it or modify it. If the variable is visible, it can be accessed and modified, except—as you may recall from `Chapter 4`, *Using Variables and Assignment*—when it is declared as a `const` variable, it can only be accessed but cannot be changed. As we will see, visibility is but one component of a variable's scope. The other components of scope are *extent* (or the lifetime of the variable) and *linkage* (or in which file the variable exists).

The visibility, extent, and linkage of variables and functions depend upon where they are declared and how they are defined. However, regardless of how or where they are defined, they must be defined before they can be accessed. This is true for both functions and variables.

Scope applies to both variables as well as functions. However, the considerations for each of them are slightly different. We will address the scope of variables first, and then expand those concepts to the scope of functions.

Exploring visibility

The visibility of a variable is largely determined by its location within a source file. There are a number of places a variable can appear, which determines its visibility. Some of these we have already explored. The following is a comprehensive listing of types of visibility:

- **Block/local scope**: This occurs in function blocks, conditional statement blocks, loop statement-body blocks, and unnamed blocks. These are also called **internal variables**. The visibility of variables declared in this scope is limited to the boundaries of the block where they are declared.
- **Function parameter scope**: Even though this scope occurs in function parameters, the function parameters are actually within the block scope of the function body.
- **File scope**: These are also called **external variables**. A variable declared outside any function parameter or block is visible to all other functions and blocks in that file.
- **Global scope**: When an external variable in one file is specially referenced in other files to make it visible to them. This is also called **program scope**.
- **Static scope**: When a variable has block scope with a function but whose *extent*, or lifetime, differs from automatic variables.

We have primarily been relying upon block scope for all of our programs. In some cases, we have had brief encounters with both global scope variables and static variables.

Note that internal variables exist within a block, whereas external variables exist in a source file outside of any function blocks. The block of the internal variable may be a function body, or, within a given function, it may be a loop body, a conditional expression block, or an unnamed block. We will explore examples of these later in this chapter.

However, the scope of a variable involves more than just visibility.

Exploring extent

The scope is also determined by the lifetime, or *extent*, of the variable. We explored the lifetime of variables and memory in `Chapter 17`, *Understanding Memory Allocation and Lifetime*. We revisit this topic here since it relates to the other components of scope: visibility and linkage.

The extent of a variable begins when a variable is created (memory is allocated for it) and ends when the variable is deallocated or destroyed. Within that extent, a variable is accessible and modifiable. Attempting to access or modify a variable outside of its extent will either raise a compiler error or may lead to unpredictable program behavior.

Internal variables have a somewhat limited extent, which begins within a block when the variable is declared and ends when the block ends. External variables are allocated when the program loads and exist until the program ends.

A variable's extent is also specified by a *storage class*, or how it is allocated, used, and subsequently deallocated. There are five classes of storage, as follows:

- **auto**: This is the default storage class when no other storage class is specified. When an auto variable is declared within a block, it has an internal variable extent. When an auto variable is declared outside of a block, it has an external variable extent.
- **register**: This is equivalent to auto but it provides a suggestion to the compiler to put the variable in one of the registers of the **central processing unit** (**CPU**). This is often ignored by modern compilers.
- **extern**: Specifies that the variable exists in another file; in that other file, the variable must be an external variable. Therefore, its extent is the life of the program.
- **static**: A variable declared with this class has the visibility of the block scope but the extent of an external variable—that is, the life of the program; whenever that block is re-entered, the static variable retains the value it was last assigned. static also has a special meaning for function declarations, which we will see later in this chapter.
- **typedef**: Formally, this is a storage class, but when used, a new data type is declared and no storage is actually allocated. A typedef scope is similar to a function scope, described later in this chapter.

Perhaps you can now see why memory allocation and deallocation are closely related to the extent component of the scope.

We can now turn to the last component of scope: linkage.

Exploring linkage

In a single source file program, the concept of linkage doesn't really apply since everything is contained within the single source file (even if it has its own header file). However, when we employ multiple source files in a program, a variable's scope is also determined by its *linkage*. Linkage involves declarations within a single source file—or *compilation unit*.

Understanding compilation units

A compilation unit is essentially a single source file and its header file. That source file may be a complete program or it may be just one among several or many source files that make up a final executable. Each source file is preprocessed and compiled individually in the compilation phase. The result of this is an intermediate *object file*. An object file *knows* about external functions and variables via header declarations but defers the resolution of their actual addresses until later.

When all source files have been successfully compiled into object files, the link phase is entered. In the link phase, the addresses of functions in other files or libraries are resolved and the addresses of external global variables are resolved. When all unresolved addresses have been successfully resolved (linked together), the object files are then combined into a single executable.

In the `dealer.c` program, there were four source files. Each of those four files was an individual compilation unit. At compile time, each of those source files was compiled into four separate object files. Those four object files were then linked together and combined to form a single executable.

Everything within a compilation unit is visible and accessible to everything else within that compilation unit. The linkage of functions and variables is typically limited to just that compilation unit. In order to cross linkage boundaries (source files), we must employ header files with the proper storage classes for variables (`extern`) as well as `typedef` declarations and function prototypes.

So, the linkage component of a scope involves not only the declarations within a single source file but also makes those declarations available in another compilation unit.

Putting visibility, extent, and linkage all together

We now have an idea of the components involved in a scope. Within a single file, the visibility and extent components are somewhat intertwined and take primary consideration. With multiple files, the linkage component of a scope requires more consideration.

We can think of scope starting from a very narrow range and expanding to the entire program. Block and function scope has the narrowest range. External variables and function prototypes have a wider scope, encompassing an entire file. The broadest scope occurs with the declarations from within a single file and expanded across multiple files.

Some clarification is needed regarding **global scope**. Global scope means that a function or variable is accessible in *two or more* source files. It is very often confused with **file scope**, where a function or variable is only accessible in the single file where it is declared. So, when a programmer refers to a *global variable*, they often mean an *external variable with file scope*.

The preferred way to give a function or variable global scope is to (1) define and initialize them in the originating source file with file scope, and (2) to make them accessible in any other file via linkage by the use of the `extern` declaration for that variable (`extern` is optional for functions).

Older compilers would allow any external variables with file scope to be accessible across *all* source files in a program, making them truly global variables. Linkage scope was therefore assumed across all source files in the program. This led to much misuse and name clashes of global variables. Most modern compilers no longer make such an assumption; linkage scope across file/compilation unit boundaries must now be explicit with the use of `extern`. Such `extern` variable declarations are easily done through the use of header files.

We can now focus on the specifics of the scope of variables.

Exploring variable scope

Having defined the components of a scope, we can explore what scope means for variables in their various possible locations within a program: at the block level; at the function parameter level; at the file level; and at the global- or program-level scope.

Understanding the block scope of variables

We have already seen several instances of block scope. Function bodies consist of a block beginning with { and ending with }. Complex statements such as conditional statements and looping statements also consist of one or more blocks beginning with { and ending with }. Finally, it is possible to create an unnamed block anywhere with any other block that begins with { and ends with }. C is very consistent in its treatment of blocks, regardless of where they appear.

Variables declared within a block are created, accessed, and modified within that block. They are deallocated and are no longer accessible when that block completes; the space they occupied is gone, only to be reused by something else in the program.

When you declare and initialize variables within a function, those variables are visible to all statements within that function until the function returns or the final } is encountered. Upon completion of the block, the variable's memory is no longer accessible. Each time the function is called, those variables are reallocated, reinitialized, accessed, and destroyed upon function completion. Consider the following function:

```
void func1 ( void )  {
    // declare and initialize variables.
  int    a  = 2;
  float f = 10.5;
  double d = 0.0;

    // access those variables.
  d = a * f;

  return;
} // At this point, a, f, and d no longer exist.
```

The block within which a, f, and d exist is the function body. When the function body is exited, those variables no longer exist; they have *gone out of scope*.

When you declare and initialize variables within a conditional statement block or the loop statement block of one of C's loops, that variable is created and accessed only within that block. The variable is destroyed and is no longer accessible once that block has been exited. The `for()`... loop `loop_initialization` expression is considered to be a part of the `for()`... loop `statement_body`; as such, the scope of any variable counter declared there is valid only within the `for()`... loop `statement_body`. Consider the following function:

```
#include<math.h>

void func2( void )   {
   int aValue = 5
   for ( int i = 0 ; i < 5 ; i++ )   {
      printf( "%d ^ %d = %d" , aValue , i , exp( aValue ,   i );
   }
   // At this point, i no longer exists.
   return;
}   // At this point, aValue no longer exists.
```

The `aValue` variable has scope through the function block, even in the block of the `for()`... statement. However, the `i` variable is only visible within the loop block body of the `for()`... statement. Not only is it exclusively visible with that block, but also, its extent is limited to that block.

Consider the following nested `for()`... loop:

```
int arr[kMaxRows][kMaxColumns] = { ... };
...
for( int i=0 ; i<kMaxColumns ; i++ )   {
   printf( "%d: " , i );
   for( int j=0 ; j<kMaxRows ; j++ )   {
      printf( " %d " , arr[ j ][ i ];
   }
   // j no longer exists
}
// i no longer exists
```

In the outer `for()`... loop, `i` is declared and has scope until the outer loop is exited. In the inner `for()`... loop, `j` is declared and only has a scope with this loop body. Notice that `arr[][]` is declared outside of both of these and has scope even in the innermost loop body.

Consider the following hypothetical `while()`... loop:

```
bool done = false;
int totalYes = 0;

while( !done ) {
  bool yesOrNo = ... ; // read yesOrNo value.

  if( yesOrNo==true ) {
    int countTrue = 0;
    ... // do some things with countTrue
    totalYes += countTrue;
    done = false;
  } else {
    int countFalse = 0;
    ... // do some things with countFalse
    totalYes -= countFalse;
    done = false;
  }
}
printf( "%d\n" , totalYes );
```

This code fragment does not do anything useful. We are using it, however, to demonstrate the scope of each local variable.

In this code segment, `done` and `totalYes` are declared outside of the `while` loop and have scope throughout these statements. Within the loop block, `yesOrNo` is declared and only has scope within the loop. In the `if()`... `else`... statement, each branch has a local variable declared that only has scope within that branch block. Once the `if()`... `else`... statement is exited, regardless of which branch was taken, neither `countTrue` nor `countFalse` exist; they have gone out of scope. When we finally exit the `while()`... loop, only the `done` and `totalYes` variables remain; all of the other local variables have gone out of scope.

Finally, it is possible to create an unnamed block, declare one or more variables within it, perform one or more computations with it, and end the block. The result should be assigned to a variable declared outside of that block, or else its results will be lost when the block is deallocated. Such a practice is sometimes desirable for very complex calculations with many parts.

The intermediate results do not need to be kept around and can be allocated, accessed, and deallocated as computation progresses, as in the following function:

```
int func3( void )   {
  int a = 0;
  {
    int b = 3;
    int c = 4;
    a = sqrt( (b * b) + (c * c) );
    printf( "side %d, side %d gives hypotenuse %d\n" ,
  }
  return a;
}
```

In `func3()`, an unnamed block is created that declares b and c. Their scope is only within this block; they are created when this block is entered and destroyed when it is exited. Outside of this block, a is declared, whose scope is both the unnamed block and the function block.

Understanding function parameter scope

Function parameter scope is the same as block scope. The block, in this case, is the function body. Even though the parameters seem to appear outside of the body of the function, they are actually declared and assigned inside the function body when the function is called. Consider the following function:

```
double decimalSum( double d1 , double d2 )   {
    double d3;
    d3 = d1 + d2 ;
    return d3;
}
```

The d1 and d2 function parameters are part of the function body and therefore have the block scope of the function. The d3 variable also has the block scope of the function. All of these variables go out of scope when the function returns to its caller.

Understanding file scope

To declare a variable with file scope, we can declare it anywhere in a source file but outside of any function body. Consider the following code segment from `nameSorter.c` (Chapter 21, *Exploring Formatted Input*):

```
#include <stdio.h>
#include <string.h>
#include <stdbool.h>

const int listMax   = 100;
const int stringMax =  80;

...
```

We have declared the `listMax` and `stringMax` variables as external variables outside of any function block. Instead of using those literal values in that program, we used `listMax` and `stringMax` whenever we needed those values. It has a scope that is visible throughout this file.

Now, suppose this program was part of a multi-file program. The other source files would not be able to use those variables; their scope is limited to just `nameSorter.c`. In the next section, we will see how to make these variables accessible to other files.

Understanding global scope

To make external variables in one file available to another file, we need to declare them with the `extern` storage class. Suppose `nameSorter.c` is part of a `sortem.c` program and `sortem.c` needs to access those values. This would be done with the following declaration:

```
#include <...>
#include "nameSorter.h"

extern const int listMax;
extern const int stringMax;

...
```

Note that `sortem.c` uses the same type declarations found in `nameSorter.c` but adds the `extern` keyword. The external variables are declared/allocated in `nameSorter.c`, and so have file scope in that file and external variable extent. Their linkage scope has been extended to `sortem.c` so that those variables are now visible throughout that source file. Any other file part of the `sortem.c` program that might need to use `listMax` and `stringMax` would simply need to add the same declaration as a part of its compilation unit.

This can be done in several ways: one is to add the `extern` declarations to the `.c` file. Only those files that have the `extern` declarations would be able to access those variables.

The other way is to put the `extern` declarations in a header file. To do this, we would modify `nameSorter.h`, as follows:

```
#ifndef _NAME_SORTER_H_
#define _NAME_SORTER_H_

extern const int listMax;
extern const int stringMax;

...

#endif
```

In this manner, any source file that includes `nameSorter.h` also has access to the `listMax` and `stringMax` external variables.

We can now explore the function scope.

Understanding function scope

The scoping rules for functions are considerably simpler than for variables. Function declarations are very similar to external variable declarations. As we have variables that must be declared before they can be accessed, functions must be declared or prototyped before they can be called, and—like external variables—function declarations also have a file scope. They can be called anywhere within a source file *after* they have been prototyped or defined.

We have already seen how we can define functions in such a way that prototypes are not needed. We simply define them before they are ever called. Most often, however, it is far more convenient to simply declare function prototypes at the beginning of source files. When this is done, functions can be called from anywhere within the file, and there is no need to worry about whether a function has been declared before calling it.

To make functions extend beyond their compilation unit to have a global scope, their prototypes must be included in the source file that calls them. We saw this in our very first program, `hello.c`, where the `printf()` function was prototyped in the `stdio.h` header file and called from within our `main()` function. In `Chapter 24`, *Working with Multi-File Programs*, we saw how to include our own function prototypes in a header file and include them in all of the source files.

These same rules apply to `struct` and `enum` declarations defined by `typedef`.

So, we can make functions global to all source files in a program. But can we make certain functions only apply to a given source file? The answer is: *certainly*. We do this with information hiding, through scope rules.

Understanding scope and information hiding

We have seen how to cross linkage boundaries with functions by including header files with their prototypes. If we wanted to limit a function's scope to only its compilation unit, we could do that in one of two ways.

The first way is to remove from the header file any function prototypes we do not want to cross the linkage scope. In that way, any other source file that includes the header will not have the excluded function prototype and will, therefore, be unable to call it. For example, in the `sortName.c` file from `Chapter 23`, *Using File Input and File Output*, only the `AddName()`, `PrintNames()`, and `DeleteNames()` functions were ever called from within the `main()` function. The other functions in `nameList.c` did not need to be global. Therefore, `nameList.h` only needs the following:

```
#include <stdbool.h>
#include <stdlib.h>

typedef char    ListData;

typedef struct _Node ListNode;

typedef struct _Node {
  ListNode*  pNext;
  ListData*  pData;
```

```
  } ListNode;

typedef struct {
  ListNode*   pFirstNode;
  int         nodeCount;
} NameList;

void   AddName(      NameList* pNames , char* pNameToAdd );
void   DeleteNames( NameList* pNames );
void   PrintNames(  FILE* outputDesc ,  NameList* pNames )
#endif
```

We have removed a few function prototypes. We still need the `typedef` declarations because they are needed for the compiler to make sense of the types found in the function-prototype parameters.

We then need to add those function prototypes to `namelist.c`, as follows:

```
#include "nameList.h"

NameList*   CreateNameList();
ListNode*   CreateListNode( char* pNameToAdd );
bool        IsEmpty();

void        OutOfStorage( void );

NameList* CreateNameList( void ) {
  ...
```

These four prototypes are now only within the scope of the `nameList.c` compilation unit. If for any reason we needed to call any of these functions from outside of this source file, we'd have to return them to the `namelist.h` header file.

There is, however, a more explicit way to exclude these functions from being called globally.

Using the static specifier for functions

We saw earlier how the `static` storage class keyword was used for variables. When used with function prototypes or function definitions, it takes on a different purpose. With function prototypes, the `static` keyword indicates that the function will also be defined later with the `static` specifier, as follows:

```
#include "nameList.h"

static NameList*   CreateNameList();
static ListNode*   CreateListNode( char* pNameToAdd );
static bool        IsEmpty();

static void        OutOfStorage( void );

NameList* CreateNameList( void ) {
...
```

Each of these functions needs to be defined with the `static` keyword, which is now part of its full prototype. The `static` keyword in the function definition means that the function will not be exported to the linker. In other words, the `static` keyword in both the prototype and definition prevents the function from ever being called globally from any other file; it can only be called from within the file where it is defined. This is important and useful if a program has many source files and some of the function names clash; those functions that have the same name but operate on different structures can be limited to those specific files where they are needed.

Let's demonstrate these concepts in a working program. We will create a set of trigonometry functions in a file called `trig.c`, as follows:

```
  // === trig.h
double circle_circumference( double diameter );
double circle_area( double radius );
double circle_volume( double radius );
extern const double global_Pi;
  // ===

static double square( double d );
static double cube(  double d );

const double global_Pi = 3.14159265358979323846;

double circle_circumference( double diameter )  {
  double result = diameter * global_Pi;
  return result ;
}
```

```
double circle_area( double radius )  {
  double result = global_Pi * square( radius );
  return result;
}
double circle_volume( double radius )  {
  double result = 4.0/3.0*global_Pi*cube( radius );
  return result;
}
static double square( double d )  {
  double result = d * d;
  return result;
}
static double cube( double d ) {
  double result = d * d * d;
  return result;
}
```

We have not created a header file for this program to simplify this scope demonstration. First, three function prototypes are declared; they will be defined later in this file. Next, we declare the `global_Pi` constant as an `extern`; note that there is no assignment here. We could have omitted it in this file because it is defined and initialized next; if we had created a header file, it would have been necessary.

Next, we declare two static function prototypes, `square()` and `cube()`. Declared in this manner, these functions can be called anywhere from within this source file but cannot be called from anywhere outside of this source file.

Next, the `global_Pi` external variable (with scope currently in this file) is declared and initialized. Note that here is where memory is allocated for `global_Pi` and that this declaration is in the `.c` file, and would not be in a header file. We will soon see how to make this truly global.

The remainder of this file is function definitions. Note that each function has a variable named `result` but that variable only has a local scope for each function. Each time any one of the functions is called, `result` is created, initialized, used to compute a value, and then provides the return value to the caller. Note that `global_Pi` is available to each function block. Lastly, note that `square()` and `cube()` are called by functions within this source file but because they are static, any linkage to them from outside of this source file is not possible.

Now, let's turn to the `circle.c` program, which is the main source file and needs to access variables and functions in `trig.h`. This program is shown as follows:

```
#include <stdio.h>

// === trig.h
double circle_circumference( double diameter );
double circle_area( double radius );
double circle_volume( double radius );

extern const double global_Pi;
// ===

static const double unit_circle_radius = 1.0;

void circle( double radius);

int main( void ) {
  circle( -1.0 );
  circle(  2.5 );
}
void circle( double radius )  {
  double r = 0.0;
  double d = 0.0;
  if( radius <= 0.0 ) r = unit_circle_radius;
  d = 2 * r;
  if( radius <= 0 ) printf( "Unit circle:\n" );
  else              printf( "Circle\n");
  printf( "          radius = %10.4f inches\n" , r );
  printf( "  circumference = %10.4f inches\n" , circle_circumference( d )
);
  printf( "            area = %10.4f square inches\n" , circle_area( r ) );
  printf( "          volume = %10.4f cubic inches\n" , circle_volume( r ) );
}
```

As in `trig.c`, the lines within `// === trig.h` and `// ===` would have appeared in the `trig.h` header file had we created it and applied `#include` to it. Let's pause here and examine what these four lines are enabling. First, the function prototypes are providing linkage scope so that they may be called from within this file; those function definitions exist in a different source file, `trig.c`. Next, the `extern ... global_Pi;` statement now makes access to this variable possible from within this source file. The `square()` and `cube()` static functions are not visible to this source file.

Next, a `unit-circle-radius` static variable is declared. This variable can only be accessed from within this source file.

Next, the prototype for `circle()` is declared; it will be defined after `main()`.

In `main()`, `circle()` is only called twice. Within the `circle()` function, there are three local variables: `radius` (function parameter scope), `r`, and `d` (both with local block scope). These variables are only visible from within the block scope of the function. Note that if `radius` is less than `0.0`, the external constant with the `unit_circle_radius` file scope is accessed.

In this example program, a `global_pi` constant variable was used as a global variable; this is read-only. Had we needed to change the value of this global variable, we could have done so by omitting the `const` keyword, and then given it new values from anywhere within any source file that has linkage scope to them. Likewise, the static `unit_circle_radius` external constant could be made a variable by removing the `const` keyword. However, because it is declared static, it can only be accessed from within `circle.c`, and so is not truly global.

Create and save `trig.c` and `circle.c`. Compile and run the program. You should see the following output:

```
> cc trig.c circle.c -o circle -Wall -Werror -std=c18
> circle
 pi is 3.141592653590

Unit circle:
            radius =      1.0000 inches
    circumference =      6.2832 inches
             area =      3.1416 square inches
           volume =      4.1888 cubic inches

 pi is 3.141592653590

Circle
            radius =      2.5000 inches
    circumference =     15.7080 inches
             area =     19.6350 square inches
           volume =     65.4498 cubic inches

>
```

The output of this program is important only insofar as it proves the scoping rules of functions and variables presented. In `circle.c`, try commenting out the external `global_Pi` statement and see if the program compiles and runs as before. Also, in `circle.c`, try calling `square()` or `cube()` and see if the program compiles. In `trig.c`, try accessing the `unit_circle_radius` static constant.

Summary

In the previous chapter, we created a program where every structure and every function in each source file was available to every other source file. Such accessibility is not always desirable, especially in very large programs with many source files.

In this chapter, we learned about the three components of scope: visibility, extent, and linkage. For variables, we applied those concepts to various levels of scope: block/local, function parameters, file, and global scope. We then learned how these concepts applied to the five storage classes: `auto`, `register`, `extern`, `static`, and `typedef`.

We saw how functions have simpler scoping rules than variables. We saw how header files allow functions to be global across multiple files, wherever the header is included. We then applied the `static` keyword to functions to limit their scope to just a single compilation unit.

Epilog

Congratulations! You did it!

If you have read through to the end of this book, have been diligently typing in every program, and have been performing the suggested experiments on those programs, you will have achieved a solid foundation in the fundamentals of C programming. Make some time to celebrate, even if only for a little bit or if only on your own.

Taking the next steps

Take some time to review each of the programs. You may want to pick out some that you have found to be particularly useful for future reference. You may also want to revisit those programs that you had some difficulty mastering.

You are now ready to take the next steps with developing both your C skills and your programming skills. Everything you have learned in this book is applicable to most programming languages and environments. Here are some suggestions about what might be worthwhile next steps.

More advanced C topics

Even though C is often called a simple or concise programming language, it can take years to fully master some of the more advanced features of C programming. Not every topic of C has been covered in this book. The following is a list of those features, with some explanation of each feature and why it was left out of this book:

- **Unions**: An alternate form of a structure that can take more than one form, depending upon how the union is used. Unions are particularly useful for system-level functions. In my own experience, I have never needed to create a union structure.

- **Recursion**: A method where a function calls itself repeatedly until some stop condition is met. There are some algorithms that are ideally solved with recursion. To use recursion effectively, both thorough knowledge of those algorithms and an understanding of the performance of the given system are essential.

- **Function pointers**: This feature was touched upon in the printing functions of `carddeck.c` in `Chapter 16`, *Creating and Using More Complex Structures*. A programmer could go a very long time without ever needing to use this feature.

- **The preprocessor**: As has been pointed out in `Chapter 24`, *Working with Multi-File Programs*, the preprocessor is both powerful and dangerous. To use it effectively, a broader understanding of performance is essential, as well as a high degree of debugging skill.

- **Random-access file processing**: The examples we used for file processing have been on sequential files only. C provides the mechanisms for random-access file processing. However, because most of these problems are now solved with databases that were not available 50 years ago, this type of file processing is considered less important today.

- **Error handling**: Each system has its own mechanisms for dealing with errors. We touched upon the Unix `errno` facility in `Chapter 22`, *Working with Files*. Whichever system you program for, be certain to understand and use its error-handling and reporting mechanisms in your programs.

- **Multithreading**: Various systems provide different ways to perform as if two or more parts or threads of a program are operating at the same time. This feature is both operating system-dependent and requires a thorough understanding of operating system concepts.

- **Debugging**: The debugging systems on each operating system are largely specific to each system. Many of the debugging concepts are common across all debuggers, but the details and capabilities vary widely from system to system. In this book, we have introduced and illustrated probably the most basic debugging technique that does not require a debugger: caveman debugging. To become proficient in code-level debugging requires both an in-depth knowledge of assembler language as well as a thorough understanding of operating system concepts.

As you gain more skill and understanding of programming concepts and techniques, you will be exposed at some level to each of these features. As you can see, some of them are related to C but others are more related to the specific operating system on which your programs will run.

More advanced programming topics

Programming and solving problems with computers often involve much more than just being skilled at a programming language. Now that you have some programming knowledge and skill with C, you should strive to broaden your programming knowledge in the following areas:

- **Algorithms**: Deal with how to approach solving many different kinds of problems. A linked list is one such algorithm. You should strive to gain a general understanding of a wide variety of algorithms and when to use each of them.
- **Application frameworks**: Today's operating systems are complex computing environments that offer a standard set of functionalities to every user. This functionality is provided by the operating system vendors via application frameworks. The application framework does the nitty-gritty work of these features. To provide users a feature-rich yet consistent application, the programmer must understand and use the specific application framework of a given operating system.
- **A build system**: A build system such as `make` or `cmake`, when set up properly, automates the process of building and properly rebuilding programs that consist of many source files. If/when you use an **integrated development environment (IDE)** such as Visual Studio, Xcode, Eclipse, and so on, those applications will have their own build systems integrated into them. Gaining more than a rudimentary knowledge of build systems is essential for today's programmer.
- **Graphical user interfaces** (**GUIs**): GUIs are a part of application frameworks on most operating systems today, yet GUI programming requires an additional set of knowledge and skills to program effectively.

- **Fundamental database programming**: When C was invented, nearly all data was stored in files. This is not true today, where a large percentage of data that is created and consumed on computers is housed in some kind of database. Modern database systems provide a rich set of functions with which programs can query, retrieve, and store data in the database.

- **Networking**: We now live in a completely interconnected world thanks to the **World Wide Web** (**WWW**). Every operating system provides **application programming interfaces** (**APIs**) to interact with the networking subsystems of the host operating system. And, while web servers perform most of the low-level functionality needed, application programs often need to interact with other computers via the network interface.

- **Performance**: Rudimentary performance concepts often go hand in hand with understanding algorithms. However, there are many instances where a deeper understanding of the performance of a particular program or system is required. There are specialized concepts and techniques to understand a system's performance, as well as improve various aspects of the program/system performance.

Again, as you gain more skills and understanding of programming concepts and techniques, you will be exposed at some level to each of these areas of computing. Some of them are independent of any programming language. However, some are related to the specific operating system on which your programs will run.

Picking a project for yourself

One of the most effective ways to deepen your knowledge and skills in any area of endeavor is to pick a project for yourself and then complete that project. It could be a simple project that takes `dealer.c`, for instance, and uses that to create a *Blackjack* game or other card game. Or, you might want to create a simple to-do list program using your knowledge of files and structures. It could also be an ambitious project that provides a screen to enter data that will be stored in a database on a remote server.

Regardless of the project, not only will you gain greater knowledge but you will also have learned how to acquire more knowledge to accomplish your project(s). And if you choose to make programming your vocation, you will have working programs to demonstrate your skills.

Resources

There are many books available for all levels of C programming skill. These can be found on the Stack Overflow website at `https://stackoverflow.com/questions/562303/the-definitive-c-book-guide-and-list`.

A note about Stack Overflow: I have found that most of the answers to questions available on the Stack Overflow website are often useful *starting points*; very rarely have I ever gotten a complete or totally correct answer from that site. It is useful, to be sure. Take what you find there and run the programs in your environment. Modify the solutions to your situation. But do not stop there. Most often, you will learn about something you had never considered—when that happens, keep questioning and experimenting for yourself.

On the other hand, I have also learned things from Stack Overflow that I'd never even considered before. So, it can be a rich and useful resource if approached carefully.

Another website worth exploring is comp.lang.c, *Frequently Asked Questions* (`http://c-faq.com`), where you will find common questions answered in generally useful ways.

As C has evolved, it is important to rely upon books that reflect that evolution; at a minimum, books should be based on the C99 standard, although it is becoming more common to see books that focus on C11 and even C18 standards.

It is also useful to join and participate in a local programming user group. Such groups meet at regular intervals and are often focused on a single technology. Likewise, there are many online chat and message boards focusing on a single technology. Beware, though, as they can soon enough become time sinks.

Appendix

C definition and keywords

The C specification has become quite large. You can read the full specification for each version at `http://www.iso-9899.info/wiki/The_Standard`.

C keywords

The following table provides a list of reserved keywords in C by category. These keywords cannot be redefined in your programs. Some of these have not been explained in this book:

Types	Storage Classes	Flow of Control
char	auto	break
const	extern	case
double	register	continue
enum	static	default
float	typedef	do
int		else
long		for
short		goto
signed		if
sizeof	**C11 Keyword Additions**	return
struct	_Alignas[2]	switch
union	_Alignof[2]	while
unsigned	_Atomic[2]	
void	_Generic[2]	**Miscellaneous**
_Bool[1]	_Noreturn[2]	inline[1]
_Complex[1]	_Static_assert[2]	restrict[1]
_Imaginary[1]	_Thread_local[2]	volatile

[1] Added to the C99 standard.

[2] Added to the C11 standard. Many of these keywords facilitate quite advanced functions in computer programming.

Table of operators and their precedence

The following table lists the precedence and associativity of C operators. Operators are from listed top to bottom, in descending precedence. The grouping operator, (), has the highest precedence. The sequence operator (,) has the lowest precedence. There are five classes of operators: postfix, prefix, unary, and binary:

Operators	Description	Class	Precedence	Associativity
()	Grouping	N/A	17	N/A
a[k]	Array subscripting	Postfix	16	Left to right
f(...)	Function call	Postfix	16	Left to right
.	Direct member access	Postfix	16	Left to right
->	Indirect member access	Postfix	16	Left to right
++ --	Increment and decrement	Postfix	16	Left to right
(type) {init}	Compound literal	Postfix	16	Left to right
++ --	Increment and decrement	Prefix	15	Right to left
sizeof	Size	Unary	15	Right to left
~	Bitwise NOT	Unary	15	Right to left
!	Logical NOT	Unary	15	Right to left
- +	Negative sign and positive sign	Unary	15	Right to left
&	Address of	Unary	15	Right to left
*	Indirection	Unary	15	Right to left

(*type*)	Cast	Unary	14	Right to left
* / %	Multiplicative	Binary	13	Left to right
+ −	Additive	Binary	12	Left to right
<< >>	Left shift and right shift	Binary	11	Left to right
< > <= >=	Relational	Binary	10	Left to right
== !=	Equality and inequality	Binary	9	Left to right
&	Bitwise AND	Binary	8	Left to right
^	Bitwise XOR	Binary	7	Left to right
|	Bitwise OR	Binary	6	Left to right
&&	Logical AND	Binary	5	Left to right
||	Logical OR	Binary	4	Left to right
? :	Conditional	Ternary	3	Right to left
= += −=	Assignment	Binary	2	Right to left
*= /= %=	Assignment	Binary	2	Right to left
<<= >>=	Assignment	Binary	2	Right to left
&= ^= |=	Assignment	Binary	2	Right to left
,	Sequence	Binary	1	N/A

Summary of useful GCC and Clang compiler options

The following is a list of the compiler switches already encountered with the addition of other useful switches and why you might want to use them:

Switch	Description
`-Wall`	Turns on warnings for a wide variety of possible errors.
`-Werror`	Turns all warnings into errors.
`-std=c11` `-std=c18`	Controls which C standard to use for compilation.
`-D <symbol>`	Defines the `<symbol>` macro.
`-U <symbol>`	Undefines `<symbol>`.
`-o <file>`	Directs compiled executables to the named `<file>` name instead of `a.out`.
`--help`	Displays the compiler help screen.
`--version`	Displays the compiler version.
`-O[n]` `-Os`	The optimization level, where for `[n]`, `0 = none - 3 = aggressive`. `s` tells the compiler to optimize for size; most operating systems are optimized for size only.
`-g`	Generates debugging information to be read by the debugger program when the program executes.
`-H`	Prints the name of each header file used. Each name is indented to show how deep in the `#include` stack it is.

There is a dizzying array of options switches for the GCC compiler. These can be found at the GNU website at `https://gcc.gnu.org/onlinedocs/gcc/Option-Summary.html`.

ASCII character set

We have a table of 256 ASCII characters. The table is reproduced here for convenience; it was generated from the program we created in Chapter 15, *Working with Strings*:

```
> gcc printASCIIwithControlAndEscape.c -o printASCIIwithControlAndEscape  -Wall
-Werror -std=c11
> printASCIIwithControlAndEscape
                Table of 7-Bit ASCII and
              Single-Byte UTF-8 Character Sets

| Control Characters |     Printable Characaters (except DEL)     |
|--------------------|--------------------------------------------|
| SYM Fmt Ch Dec  Hex | Ch Dec  Hex | Ch Dec  Hex | Ch  Dec  Hex |
|--------------------|-------------|-------------|--------------|
| NUL \0 ^@  0    0  |    32 0x20  | @  64 0x40 ||  `  96 0x60  |
| SOH    ^A  1   0x1 | !  33 0x21  | A  65 0x41 ||  a  97 0x61  |
| STX    ^B  2   0x2 | "  34 0x22  | B  66 0x42 ||  b  98 0x62  |
| ETX    ^C  3   0x3 | #  35 0x23  | C  67 0x43 ||  c  99 0x63  |
| EOT    ^D  4   0x4 | $  36 0x24  | D  68 0x44 ||  d 100 0x64  |
| ENQ    ^E  5   0x5 | %  37 0x25  | E  69 0x45 ||  e 101 0x65  |
| ACK    ^F  6   0x6 | &  38 0x26  | F  70 0x46 ||  f 102 0x66  |
| BEL \a ^G  7   0x7 | '  39 0x27  | G  71 0x47 ||  g 103 0x67  |
| BS  \b ^H  8   0x8 | (  40 0x28  | H  72 0x48 ||  h 104 0x68  |
| HT  \t ^I  9   0x9 | )  41 0x29  | I  73 0x49 ||  i 105 0x69  |
| LF  \n ^J 10   0xa | *  42 0x2a  | J  74 0x4a ||  j 106 0x6a  |
| VT  \v ^K 11   0xb | +  43 0x2b  | K  75 0x4b ||  k 107 0x6b  |
| FF  \f ^L 12   0xc | ,  44 0x2c  | L  76 0x4c ||  l 108 0x6c  |
| CR  \r ^M 13   0xd | -  45 0x2d  | M  77 0x4d ||  m 109 0x6d  |
| SO     ^N 14   0xe | .  46 0x2e  | N  78 0x4e ||  n 110 0x6e  |
| SI     ^O 15   0xf | /  47 0x2f  | O  79 0x4f ||  o 111 0x6f  |
| DLE    ^P 16  0x10 | 0  48 0x30  | P  80 0x50 ||  p 112 0x70  |
| DC1    ^Q 17  0x11 | 1  49 0x31  | Q  81 0x51 ||  q 113 0x71  |
| DC2    ^R 18  0x12 | 2  50 0x32  | R  82 0x52 ||  r 114 0x72  |
| DC3    ^S 19  0x13 | 3  51 0x33  | S  83 0x53 ||  s 115 0x73  |
| DC4    ^T 20  0x14 | 4  52 0x34  | T  84 0x54 ||  t 116 0x74  |
| NAK    ^U 21  0x15 | 5  53 0x35  | U  85 0x55 ||  u 117 0x75  |
| SYN    ^V 22  0x16 | 6  54 0x36  | V  86 0x56 ||  v 118 0x76  |
| ETB    ^W 23  0x17 | 7  55 0x37  | W  87 0x57 ||  w 119 0x77  |
| CAN    ^X 24  0x18 | 8  56 0x38  | X  88 0x58 ||  x 120 0x78  |
| EM     ^Y 25  0x19 | 9  57 0x39  | Y  89 0x59 ||  y 121 0x79  |
| SUB    ^Z 26  0x1a | :  58 0x3a  | Z  90 0x5a ||  z 122 0x7a  |
| ESC \e ^[ 27  0x1b | ;  59 0x3b  | [  91 0x5b ||  { 123 0x7b  |
| FS     ^\ 28  0x1c | <  60 0x3c  | \  92 0x5c ||  | 124 0x7c  |
| GS     ^] 29  0x1d | =  61 0x3d  | ]  93 0x5d ||  } 125 0x7d  |
| RS     ^^ 30  0x1e | >  62 0x3e  | ^  94 0x5e ||  ~ 126 0x7e  |
| US     ^_ 31  0x1f | ?  63 0x3f  | _  95 0x5f ||DEL 127 0x7f  |
>
```

The Better String Library (Bstrlib)

Here is the introduction to Bstrlib taken from its document file:

> *The bstring library is an attempt to provide improved string processing functionality to the C and C++ language. At the heart of the bstring library (Bstrlib for short) is the management of "bstring"s which are a significant improvement over '\0' terminated char buffers.*

The full documentation can be found at `https://raw.githubusercontent.com/websnarf/` `bstrlib/master/bstrlib.txt`. The documentation is thorough in providing motivation and seems to be complete in that it describes every function and their possible side effects, if any. If you decide to incorporate this library into your programs, I strongly suggest you read and study this document. In this brief introduction to Bstrlib, we will focus entirely on the C functions of the library, not the C++ functions.

The Bstrlib home page can be found at `http://bstring.sourceforge.net`. The source can be found at `https://github.com/websnarf/bstrlib`.

A quick introduction to Bstrlib

Bstrlib is a set of programs that is meant to completely replace the C standard library string handling functions. It provides the following groups of functions:

- Core C files (one source file and header)
- Base Unicode support, if needed (two source files and headers)
- Extra utility functions (one source file and header)
- A unit/regression test for Bstrlib (one source file)
- A set of dummy functions to abort the use of unsafe C string functions (one source file and header)

To get the core functionality of Bstrlib, a program only needs to include one header file, `bstrlib.h`, and one source file, `bstrlib.c`, for compilation, along with the other program source files.

Unlike C strings, which are arrays of `'\0'`-terminated characters, `bstring` is a structure defined as follows:

```
struct tagbstring {
   int mlen;            // lower bound of memory allocated for data.
   int slen;            // actual length of string
   unsigned char* data; // string
};
```

This structure is exposed so that its members can be accessed directly. It is far better to manipulate this structure through functions because all of the functions perform memory management so that we don't need to (apart from allocating and freeing `bstring`).

There are functions to create a `bstring` structure from a C string, allocate `bstrings` that contain C strings and free them, copy and concatenate `bstrings`, compare and test the equality of `bstrings` and C strings, search for and extract substrings within a `bstring`, find and replace string functions, and create various `bstring` conversion functions. All of these are described in the documentation, which is impressive. Bstrlib also provides functions that return lists of strings and their own `bstreams`. There is quite a lot this library offers, if you are willing to take the time to learn it.

OK, without repeating the documentation, let's take a look at some very simple examples.

A few simple examples

These examples are very, very simple and are meant to give you a feel for what using Bstrlib is like. The examples provided on the SourceForge website are quite advanced string handling examples. They are extremely useful and well worth studying.

Our first Bstrlib example will be the *Hello, world!* program, as follows:

```
#include <stdio.h>
#include "bstrlib.h"

int main( void )   {
   bstring b = bfromcstr ("Hello, World!");
   puts( (char*)b->data );
}
```

This program, `bstr_hello.c`, creates a `bstring` from a C string and then prints it using `puts()`. To compile this program, be sure that the `bstrlib.h` and `bstrlib.c` files are in the same directory as this program. Then, enter the following command:

cc bstrlib.c bstr_hello.c -o bstr_hello -Wall -Werror -std=c18

In our next example, we will split a string into multiple strings based on a delimiter and then print them. We can do this with the C standard library, but it is rather complicated to do (which is why we didn't even try it earlier). With Bstrlib, it's simple, as you can see in the following program:

```
#include <stdio.h>
#include "bstrlib.h"

int main( void ) {
   bstring b = bfromcstr( "Hello, World and my Grandma, too!" );
   puts( (char*)b->data );
```

```
    struct bstrList *blist = bsplit( b , ' ' );
    printf( "num %d\n" , blist->qty );
    for( int i=0 ; i<blist->qty ; i++ )   {
      printf( "%d: %s\n" , i , bstr2cstr( blist->entry[i] , '_' ) );\
    }
  }
}
```

This program, bstr_split.c, first creates a bstring from a C string and prints it out.
Then, it creates a bstrList variable by calling bsplit() with <space> as the delimiter in
a single line. The last three statements print each element of the list.

To compile this program, make sure the bstrlib.h and bstrlib.c files are in the same
directory as this program. Then, enter the following command:

cc bstrlib.c bstr_split.c -o bstr_split -Wall -Werror -std=c18

Recall how in Chapter 23, *Using File Input and File Output,* we needed to write a
trimStr() function to clean up input from fgets(). That function was approximately 30
lines of code. In our last example, we will compare this function to Bstrlib. We'll create a
test program that uses seven different test strings and then trim them once with our
function, renamed CTrimStr(), and a bstrlib version, named BTrimStr():

1. First, we'll set up main(), which repeatedly calls testTrim(), as follows:

```
#include <stdio.h>
#include <ctype.h>
#include <string.h>
#include "bstrlib.h"

int  CTrimStr( char* pCStr );
int  BTrimStr( bstring b );
void testTrim( int testNum , char* pString );

int main( void )   {
    testTrim( 1 , "Hello, World!\n" );
    testTrim( 2 , "Box of frogs \t \n" );
    testTrim( 3 , " \t  Bag of hammers" );
    testTrim( 4 , "\t\t  Sack of ferrets\t\t   " );
    testTrim( 5 , "   \t\n\v\t\r   " );
    testTrim( 6 , "" );
    testTrim( 7 , "Goodbye, World!" );
}
```

This declares our `testTrim()` function prototypes, the `test` function, which calls the `trim` functions and seven test cases, each consisting of a string with various forms for the trimming that is required.

2. Next, we add our `testTrim()` function, which calls both `CTrimStr()` and `BTrimStr()`, as follows:

```
void testTrim( int testNum , char* pInputString )  {
  size_t len;
  char testString[ strlen( pInputString ) + 1];
  strcpy( testString , pInputString );
  fprintf( stderr , "%1d. original: \"%s\" [len:%d]\n"    ,
            testNum, testString , (int)strlen( pInputString ) );

  strcpy( testString , pInputString );
  len = CTrimStr( testString );
  fprintf( stderr , "   CTrimStr: \"%s\" [len:%d]\n" ,
            testString , (int)len ) ;

  bstring b = bfromcstr( pInputString );
  len = BTrimStr( b );
  fprintf( stderr , "   BTrimStr: \"%s\" [len:%d]\n\n" ,
            (char*)b->data , (int)len );
}
```

This function consists of three parts. The first part copies the input string to a working string that the `trim` functions will manipulate, and then prints the original test string. The second part resets `testString`, calls `CTrimStr()`, and then prints the result. The third part creates a `bstring` from the input string, calls `BTrimStr()`, and prints the result.

3. `CTrimStr()` is reproduced here for reference, as follows:

```
int CTrimStr( char* pCStr )  {
  size_t first , last , lenIn , lenOut ;
  first = last = lenIn = lenOut = 0;
  lenIn = strlen( pCStr );   //
  char tmpStr[ lenIn+1 ];    // Create working copy.
  strcpy( tmpStr , pCStr );  //
  char* pTmp = tmpStr;             // pTmp may change in Left Trim
segment.
    // Left Trim
    // Find 1st non-whitespace char; pStr will point to that.
  while( isspace( pTmp[ first ] ) )
    first++;
  pTmp += first;
```

```
    lenOut = strlen( pTmp );       // Get new length after Left Trim.
    if( lenOut )  {                // Check for empty string.
                                   //  e.g. "    " trimmed to nothing.
      // Right Trim
      // Find 1st non-whitespace char & set NUL character there.
      last = lenOut-1;             // off-by-1 adjustment.
      while( isspace( pTmp[ last ] ) )
        last--;
      pTmp[ last+1 ] = '\0';       // Terminate trimmed string.
    }
    lenOut = strlen( pTmp );       // Length of trimmed string.
    if( lenIn != lenOut )          // Did we change anything?
      strcpy( pCStr , pTmp );      // Yes, copy trimmed string back.
    return lenOut;
}
```

This function was explained in Chapter 23, *Using File Input and File Output,* and will not be repeated here.

4. The bstring test trim function is as follows:

```
int BTrimStr( bstring b ) {
   btrimws( b );
   return b->slen;
}
```

It takes the given bstring, trims it with a call to btrimws(), and then returns the length of the new string. We really didn't need to write this function at all; we only did so to compare it to our own CTrimStr() function.

5. To compile this program, make sure the bstrlib.h and bstrlib.c files are in the same directory as this program. Then, enter the following command:

cc bstrlib.c bstr_trim.c −o bstr_split −Wall −Werror −std=c18

You can find these example source files in the source code repository.

C strings are very simple, but the C string library functions are rather complex and have a number of issues that all programmers must pay very close attention to. bstrings are a little more complicated to initialize, but the library itself provides a very rich set of string handling, string list handling, and bstream functionality.

Unicode and UTF-8

This is a very deep and broad topic. The purpose of this section is to provide a cursory introduction to the topic, as well as to provide some resources to learn much more about this topic.

A brief history

In the early days of computers, there was 7-bit ASCII, but that wasn't good enough for the everyone, so someone came up with 16-bit Unicode. This was a good start, but it has its own problems. Finally, the guys who invented C got around to inventing UTF-8, which is backward-compatible with ASCII and dovetails into UTF-16 and UTF-32, so anyone around the world can write `"Hello, World!"` in their own language using their own characters on just about any computer. An added benefit of UTF-8 is that it is easily converted into/from Unicode when needed. Unicode didn't stop there; it evolved as well. Unicode and UTF-8 are different encodings, but they are still somewhat interrelated.

Where we are today

Unicode now replaces older character encodings, such as ASCII, ISO 8859, and EUC, at all levels. Unicode enables users to handle practically any script or language used on this planet. It also supports a comprehensive set of mathematical and technical symbols to simplify scientific information exchange.

UTF-8 encoding is defined in ISO 10646-1:2000 Annex D (`https://www.cl.cam.ac.uk/ ~mgk25/ucs/ISO-10646-UTF-8.html`) and in RFC 3629 (`http://www.ietf.org/rfc/ rfc3629.txt`), as well as *Section 3.9* of the Unicode 4.0 standard. It does not have the compatibility problems of Unicode and earlier wide-character encodings. With UTF-8 encoding, Unicode can be used in a convenient and backward-compatible way in environments that were designed entirely around ASCII, such as Unix. UTF-8 is the way in which Unicode is used under Unix, Linux, macOS, and similar systems. It is clearly the way to go for using Unicode under Unix-style operating systems.

Moving from ASCII to UTF-8

There are two approaches to add UTF-8 support to any ASCII program. One is called **soft conversion** and the other is called **hard conversion**. In soft conversion, data is kept in its UTF-8 form everywhere and only very few software changes are necessary. In hard conversion, any UTF-8 data that the program reads will be converted into wide-character arrays and will be handled as such everywhere within the application. Strings will only be converted back into UTF-8 form at output time. Internally, a character remains a fixed-size memory object.

Most applications can do very well with just soft conversion. This is what makes the introduction of UTF-8 on Unix feasible at all. The C standard library headers to address wide characters and Unicode are `wchar.h`, `wctype.h`, and `uchar.h`.

A UTF-to-Unicode example

To give you an idea of what it is like to convert between Unicode and UTF-8, consider the following program:

```
#include <stdio.h>
#include <locale.h>
#include <stdlib.h>
#include <stdio.h>

int main(void)  {
  wchar_t ucs2[5] = {0};
  if( !setlocale( LC_ALL , "en_AU.UTF-8" ) )  {
    printf( "Unable to set locale to Australian English in UTF-8\n" );
    exit( 1 );
  }
  // The UTF-8 representation of string "æ°è°ƒæ*Œà¤"
  // (four Chinese characters pronounced shui3 diao4 ge1 tou2) */
  char utf8[] = "\xE6\xB0\xB4\xE8\xB0\x83\xE6\xAD\x8C\xE5\xA4\xB4" ;

  mbstowcs( ucs2 , utf8 , sizeof(ucs2) / sizeof(*ucs2) );

  printf( "  UTF-8: " );
  for( char *p = utf8 ; *p ; p++ )
    printf( "%02X ", (unsigned)(unsigned char)*p );
  printf( "\n" );
  printf( "Unicode: " );
  for( wchar_t *p = ucs2 ; *p ; p++ )
    printf( "U+%04lX ", (unsigned long) *p );
  printf( "\n" );
```

```
    }
```

The main work of this program is the call to `mbstowcs()`, which converts from UTF-8 to Unicode, which is here represented as a 16-bit `wchar_t` variable.

For further reading, refer to the following links:

- Check out `https://www.joelonsoftware.com/2003/10/08/the-absolute-minimum-every-software-developer-absolutely-positively-must-know-about-unicode-and-character-sets-no-excuses/` for a great overview by Joel Spolsky.
- `https://www.cl.cam.ac.uk/~mgk25/unicode.html` also provides a deep dive into UTF-8 and Unicode for programmers.
- Finally, go to `https://home.unicode.org` to find more resources for Unicode and UTF-8.

The C standard library

The C standard library offers quite a bit of functionality. The first thing to be aware of when using any part of this library is what's in it. The following tables provide the header filenames and descriptions of the functions prototyped in each header file.

The following table shows the library files before C99:

Filename	Description
alloca.h	Non-standard
assert.h	Contains the `assert` macro, used to assist with detecting logical errors and other types of bugs in debugging versions of a program
ctype.h	Defines a set of functions used to classify characters by their types or to convert between upper and lowercase in a way that is independent of the used character set (typically ASCII or one of its extensions, although implementations utilizing EBCDIC are also possible)
errno.h	For testing error codes reported by library functions
float.h	Defines macro constants specifying the implementation-specific properties of the floating-point library
limits.h	Defines macro constants specifying the implementation-specific properties of the integer types
locale.h	Defines localization functions
math.h	Defines common mathematical functions
setjmp.h	Declares the `setjmp` and `longjmp` macros, which are used for non-local exits

`signal.h`	Defines signal-handling functions
`stdarg.h`	For accessing a varying number of arguments passed to functions
`stddef.h`	Defines several useful types and macros
`stdio.h`	Defines core input and output functions
`stdlib.h`	Defines numeric conversion functions, pseudo-random numbers generation functions, memory allocation, and process control functions
`string.h`	Defines string-handling functions
`time.h`	Defines date- and time-handling functions
`unistd.h`	POSIX functions (may not exist on non-Unix systems)

The following table shows which files have been added to C99:

Filename	Description
`iso646.h`	Defines several macros that implement alternative ways to express several standard tokens, used for programming in ISO 646 variant character sets
`wchar.h`	Defines wide string-handling functions
`wctype.h`	Defines a set of functions used to classify wide characters by their types or to convert between upper and lowercase
`complex.h`	A set of functions for manipulating complex numbers (optional).
`fenv.h`	Defines a set of functions for controlling the floating-point environment.
`inttypes.h`	Defines exact-width integer types
`stdbool.h`	Defines a Boolean data type
`stdint.h`	Defines exact-width integer types
`tgmath.h`	Defines type-generic mathematical functions

The following table shows which files have been added to C11:

Filename	Description
`stdalign.h`	For querying and specifying the alignment of objects
`stdatomic.h`	For atomic operations on data shared between threads (optional)
`stdnoreturn.h`	For specifying non-returning functions.
`threads.h`	Defines functions for managing multiple threads, mutexes, and condition variables (optional)
`uchar.h`	Types and functions for manipulating Unicode characters

If you have been compiling programs throughout this book, these files will already exist on your system. You need to find out where they are so that you can open them with an editor and examine exactly what is in them.

Method 1

In a terminal/console with a Unix shell (such as csh, tsh, bash, and so on), do the following:

1. Create a simple program—for example, hello.c.
2. Add the header file you want to find and save it.
3. In a bash command shell, execute the following:

```
cc -H hello.c
```

Ouch! Way too much information. What you are seeing is the full #include stack of every single header file that is included in each header file. As you can see, some are included a lot of times.

You can also see that a lot of header files include other header files.

Method 2

In a terminal/console with a Unix shell (such as csh, tsh, bash, and so on), do the following:

1. Create a simple program—for example, hello.c.
2. Add the header file you want to find, and save it.
3. In a bash command shell, execute the following:

```
cc -H hello.c 2>&1 | grep '^\.\ '
```

This command, which looks like a lot of gobbledegook, is doing the following:

1. It invokes the compiler with the -H option. The list of header files is sent to stderr.
2. 2>&1 redirects stderr to stdout.
3. stdout is then redirected via a pipe (|) to grep, a regular expression parser.
4. grep is told to search the beginning of each line for <period><space>:
   - '...' is the search string.
   - ^ indicates the beginning of a line.
   - \. is a period (this is important as a dot (.) alone has special meaning in grep).

- \ is a space (this is important as a space alone has special meaning in `grep`).

2. You will now only see one or two header files without all of the `#include` stacks.

Method 3

This one is the simplest of all if you have the `locate` program on your system.

In your terminal/console, enter the following command:

```
locate <filename.h>
```

You might also get a *lot* of output from this since your system might have many versions of these header files.

Method 2 is best because it tells you exactly which header file the compiler is using.

Once you have found the function you want to know more about in one of these files, you can then use the Unix `man` command to read about it on your system. To do so, enter the following into a terminal/console:

```
man 3 <function>
```

This tells `man` to look in section 3 for the given function. Section 3 is where C functions are described.

Alternatively, you could try the following:

```
man 7 <topic>
```

Section 7 is where general topics are described. There is a lot of information there.

 If you are new to `man`, try entering `man man` and it will tell you about itself.

Other Books You May Enjoy

If you enjoyed this book, you may be interested in these other books by Packt:

Practical C Programming

B. M. Harwani

ISBN: 978-1-83864-110-8

- Discover how to use arrays, functions, and strings to make large applications
- Perform preprocessing and conditional compilation for efficient programming
- Understand how to use pointers and memory optimally
- Use general-purpose utilities and improve code performance
- Implement multitasking using threads and process synchronization
- Use low-level programming and the inline assembly language
- Understand how to use graphics for animation
- Get to grips with applying security while developing C programs

Extreme C

Kamran Amini

ISBN: 978-1-78934-362-5

- Build advanced C knowledge on strong foundations, rooted in first principles
- Understand memory structures and compilation pipeline and how they work, and how to make most out of them
- Apply object-oriented design principles to your procedural C code
- Write low-level code that's close to the hardware and squeezes maximum performance out of a computer system
- Master concurrency, multithreading, multi-processing, and integration with other languages
- Unit Testing and debugging, build systems, and inter-process communication for C programming

Leave a review - let other readers know what you think

Please share your thoughts on this book with others by leaving a review on the site that you bought it from. If you purchased the book from Amazon, please leave us an honest review on this book's Amazon page. This is vital so that other potential readers can see and use your unbiased opinion to make purchasing decisions, we can understand what our customers think about our products, and our authors can see your feedback on the title that they have worked with Packt to create. It will only take a few minutes of your time, but is valuable to other potential customers, our authors, and Packt. Thank you!

Index

F

9 781789 349917